Dynamic Physical Education Curriculum and Instruction
for Secondary School Students

Robert P. Pangrazi

Paul W. Darst

Arizona State University
Tempe, Arizona

105102

Burgess Publishing Company
Minneapolis, Minnesota

Acquisition editor: Wayne E. Schotanus
Development editor: Anne E. Heller
Assistant development editor: Charlene J. Brown
Copy editor: Betsey I. Rhame
Art director: Judy Vicars

Library of Congress Cataloging in Publication Data

Pangrazi, Robert P.
   Dynamic physical education curriculum and
instruction for secondary school students.

   Includes bibliographies and index.
   1. Physical education and training—United States—
Curricula.   2. Physical education and training—Study
and teaching (Secondary)—United States.   3. Physical
education and training—Canada—Curricula.   4. Physical
education and training—Study and teaching (Secondary)—
Canada.   I. Darst, Paul W.   II. Title.
GV365.P36   1985   613.7'0973   84-23232
ISBN 0-8087-3346-X

Burgess Publishing Company
7108 Ohms Lane
Minneapolis, MN 55435

Contents

Preface

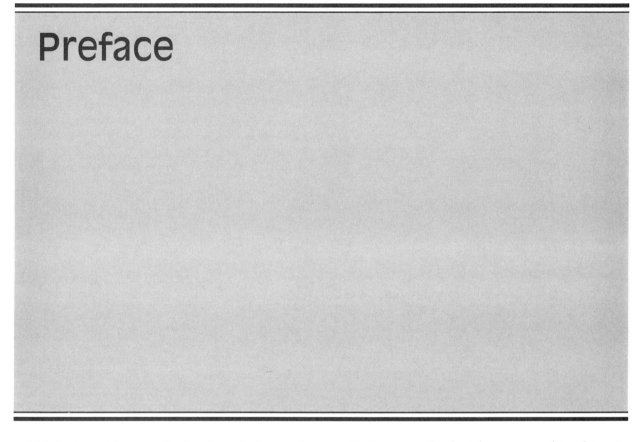

This text provides an articulated curriculum and instruction model for secondary school (grades 7–12) physical educators. The authors are keenly aware of elementary school physical education curriculum models and have developed the concepts in this text based on the premise that curriculum should be integrated and sequenced starting with kindergarten and continuing through the senior year of high school. The text should be an aid to teachers, directors of physical education programs, and students in teacher training. Both authors are teacher educators, and the format of the text originated from university and public school experiences.

The concepts and ideas have been tested and retested many times using students and teachers in public and private middle, junior, and senior high schools. The text provides practical ideas and applications for teachers. It is an applied curriculum and instruction book that offers the reader a unique combination of curriculum theory, instructional pedagogy, and practical applications.

The authors adopted a basic premise that no idea would be presented unless it had been field-tested. We have personally used all concepts, ideas, and

activities over the last four years of teaching in junior and senior high schools.

Curriculum arrangements are presented, analyzed, and discussed, along with the wave of new activities filtering into secondary programs. Included are adventure activities such as orienteering as well as Frisbee, aerobic rhythmic exercise, team handball, and jogging. Current information is provided on instructional strategies such as contingency contracting and behavior games.

The format of the book is such that the text can be used for both curriculum and methods courses. It should also serve as a resource guide for teachers in the field. Part I (Chapters 1–2) includes chapters that focus on the role of physical education in the secondary school and current practices. The authors discuss physical activity habits in the United States and Canada, program objectives, new activities, arrangement of activities, and various policies, procedures, and problems. Current laws, regulations, and trends affecting secondary programs are analyzed and evaluated.

Part II (Chapters 3–5) focuses on principles and procedures for developing a meaningful curriculum. These chapters discuss curriculum variables, ways of developing policies and procedures that deal effectively with students, and program objectives. Chapter 5 presents field-tested curriculum models for junior and senior high schools and a discussion of the advantages and disadvantages of each approach. Lastly, this section offers the theory of curriculum development and a step-by-step approach that teachers need to follow to create a meaningful curriculum.

Part III (Chapters 6–14) develops from a strong theoretical base and details practical applications for instructional policies and procedures. The topics include organization for teaching, teaching styles, motivational procedures, legal liability, and public relations. These are important areas that teachers must handle properly in the practice of their daily teaching duties.

Part III covers the many areas that teachers must comprehend if they are to be effective. Practical ideas for motivating and disciplining students are offered, with many examples of actual situations. Instructional teaching styles are discussed in terms that are meaningful and applicable for the beginning teacher. An emphasis is placed on self-evaluation to improve the quality of instruction. Since few teachers receive enough meaningful outside feedback from administrators, Chapter 10 should help teachers learn to document and analyze their teaching effectiveness.

Grading plans and approaches are offered in a way that presses each teacher to make a decision as to how a grading plan will best fit the individual situation. Pros and cons of each style are discussed so teachers can begin to develop defensible and rational grading approaches. Important topics such as liability, intramural and athletic programs, and public relations are given in-depth coverage, with a chapter devoted to each.

Section IV (Chapters 15–19) is the instructional activity program. Introductory activities, physical fitness approaches, and rainy day suggestions for indoor teaching are covered, with a discussion of theory and proper sequence and a detailed explanation of skills. This section contains materials dealing with team sports, lifetime sports, physical conditioning routines, outdoor adventure activities, rhythmics, and aquatics. The chapters include practical ideas for skill work, lead-up activities, and specific learning contracts.

A chapter on wellness is included in this section, because the authors firmly believe that wellness instruction must be integrated into the curriculum if long-range results are to occur. Activities to make wellness an integral part of the curriculum are offered along with necessary information for living a full and productive life.

The approach in this section is to give teachers activities basic to a unit plan, but each teacher still has the responsibility of developing a comprehensive plan of instruction. When Part IV is examined as a whole, the teacher will find a wide variety of contingency contracts, grading approaches, lead-up games and activities, and rainy day materials that can be used as a basis for developing personalized units of instruction.

The text provides a comprehensive theoretical and practical model for developing an articulated curriculum and effective instructional approach in grades 7–12. It is intended for teacher preparation courses in classes dealing with methods of teaching, curriculum development, and organization and administration of physical education. It should also serve as a curriculum resource manual for graduating seniors and practicing teachers.

A book of this magnitude could not be completed without the help of many people, including Anne Heller, Judy Vicars, Betsey Rhame, and other members of the Burgess staff. Two people who were instrumental in helping us field-test all the activities were Steve Fedorchek and Ken Coyle. A big thank you goes to our wives, Debbie and Charlene, for their support and patience.

PART I

PHYSICAL EDUCATION TODAY

Chapter 1

The Role of Physical Education in the Secondary School

Physical education is a sometimes misunderstood discipline in secondary schools today. Many people mistakenly equate the physical education program with the school athletic program. A large share of the public believes that a school with a good football team must inherently have a good physical education program because the physical education program helps to develop and prepare athletes for the sport program. Unfortunately, the public seldom conceptualizes that the goals of the athletic program focus primarily on developing winning teams, while the goals of physical education are directed toward meaningful educational experiences for all students. Often when teachers (who also coach) try to maintain excellence in teaching and coaching, the unilateral goal of the athletic program makes accomplishing the goals of physical education difficult.

People have varied images of the physical education environment. Some envision a rigid class in which students dress in the required uniform and exercise in straight lines under the watchful eye of a military-oriented instructor. A negative atmosphere exists in which running laps and exercise are used as punishment for not dressing or not being properly self-disciplined. Others view physical education as a subject to be avoided because of crowded classes, smelly locker rooms, and a lack of time for changing clothes. The activities include a core of traditional team sports that a teacher selected from a repertoire of activities that were developed 10 or 15 years earlier. Current and popular physical activities are missing from the program.

Many people remember physical education as a time for playing some type of game on a daily basis. Little or no organized teaching or learning occurred in the process. Teachers simply rolled out the ball and let students play a game or tournament for three to five weeks. George Leonard (1977), noted author and philosopher, describes a traditional secondary physical education class in the following manner:

Students scramble into their gym clothes and then stand at attention for dress inspection. Next, a period of group calisthenics including push-ups, jumping jacks, and sit-ups is followed by a lap around

3

the track. Students then choose up sides and move on to the traditional game of the day, i.e., flag football, basketball, softball, and volleyball. The final activity of the day is the shower and in many schools, a shower inspection to make sure that all students have participated. Coed activities and individualized instruction are unheard of in these situations. (p. 2)

This situation involves a number of problems, and it is a pity that the aforementioned scenarios have existed in our schools for years. Many adults have these situations etched in their mind. Even more unfortunate, however, is that these same scenarios still exist in schools across the country. Physical miseducation is a dragon that rears its ugly head for various reasons, and is extremely tough to slay.

On the other side of the coin, the scene is quite different in certain schools across the country. Secondary students are getting an opportunity to choose between activities such as cycling, golf (Figure 1.1), rock climbing, disc sports, and wilderness survival. A high school in California offers 45 elective choices, including sailing, scuba diving, martial arts, Frisbee, and yoga. Short two-week minicourses as well as semester-long in-depth units are offered.

Many schools are changing to a relaxed, humane atmosphere. Strict dress codes are being relaxed and students are being given a voice about what they want to wear for activity. Instructional procedures include learning stations in which students work on different tasks at different levels. Teachers move about the gymnasium, giving infor-

mation to, correcting, encouraging, and praising students.

Physical fitness activities may include aerobic dancing, rope jumping, circuit training, obstacle courses, partner resistance activities, and running an orienteering course. These activities are arranged in a systematic progression that enables all students to find personal satisfaction and success. More highly skilled students are provided with challenging activities that force them to expand their physical limits (Figure 1.2).

Clearly the two aforementioned programs have many differences. One can easily see why many people have greatly misunderstood physical education. Programs vary significantly from place to place and situation to situation. The physical activity knowledge, attitudes, and behaviors of people are strongly influenced by the type of physical education program they experience. Consequently, in developing an effective physical education program, we must start with a clear understanding of what physical education is and what it should be doing in school settings.

WHAT IS PHYSICAL EDUCATION?

Physical education is an educational process that focuses on increasing people's knowledge and affecting people's attitudes and behaviors relative to physical activities, including exercise, sports, games, dance, aquatic activities, and outdoor adventure activities. It can take place inside or outside the schools. It can be formal or informal. It

Figure 1.1. Golf instruction

Figure 1.2. Exercising using an obstacle course

can include a father teaching his son how to play golf or a boy receiving information from the coach of a youth soccer team. It can include a girl taking private gymnastics lessons or a mother explaining to her son about pacing during a 10-km run. It can be a young boy explaining the rules of football to his grandfather or a wife teaching her husband how to play racquetball. It is a group of 7th graders learning to play badminton in a junior high school. It is the passing of information, attitudes, and skills from one person to another (Figure 1.3).

The process of physical education is an important concern of our schools. Physical education instructors have a tremendous responsibility to develop and teach from a systematically organized curriculum for kindergarten through grade 12 that favorably influences all students and enhances their physical activity habits. Today's youth deserve a well-conceived and well-developed program of physical education, because it can improve their quality of life and have an impact on their way of living. This passing on of knowledge, skills, and attitudes is certainly a legitimate educational concern.

WHAT SHOULD PHYSICAL EDUCATION BE ACCOMPLISHING?

Physical educators have long purported to accomplish a wide variety of goals in the schools. Claims have been made in the areas of physical fitness, motor abilities, intellectual skills, character development, and personal social-emotional

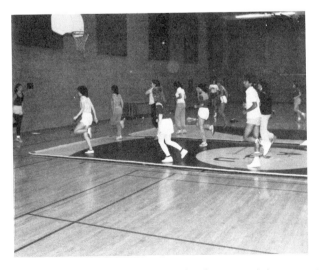

Figure 1.3. Aerobics is a popular fitness activity.

adjustment, among others. These claims have varied from time to time and place to place, depending on the trends in education and society.

In recent years, it seems as if the schools, including the physical education program, have been asked to accomplish more while resources to support programs have been cut. Various educational critics continually cite the ineffectiveness of school programs in meeting instructional goals. Perhaps people have expected the physical education program to become something that it cannot or should not be. The focus of programs should be narrowed somewhat to emphasize a lesser number of major goals.

INCORPORATING PHYSICAL ACTIVITY INTO A LIFE-STYLE

The most important goal of a secondary physical education program should be to help students incorporate some form of physical activity into their life-style. Accomplishment of this objective requires curriculum, instruction, and teachers to have a positive effect on students' knowledge, attitudes, and skill behaviors relative to physical activities. This does not mean that the secondary program should avoid other goals in different areas. It does mean that this is the most important goal and should be strongly emphasized.

The ultimate measure of a successful school physical education program is not the current level of knowledge or the physical skills of students, nor is it the number of participants on the varsity athletic teams. Certainly it is not the number of victories that the football or basketball teams accumulate. The ultimate measure of success is the number of students who incorporate physical activities such as exercise, sport, dance, and outdoor adventure activities into their life-style throughout life. As Siedentop (1980b) states:

> We teach because we hope to influence not only the present abilities of students but also their future behavior and predispositions to continue to engage in our subject matter. We are interested in the growth of the student now, but education just for now makes little sense. Most of what we hope to provide for the student is really directed toward the future of the student. We naturally want the student to learn and perform well now, to have fun now, and to enjoy the learning experience now. But, the nature of education has always been that it attempts to do things now that will have long-term effects, that is, that will affect the future behavior of the student. We are interested, in the final analysis, in

what happens to students after they finish our course; indeed, after they finish all formal education. (p. 267)

Physical educators should still be interested in passing on knowledge and developing the physical skills of students; however, a strong, organized emphasis must be placed on the affective dimension of learning. For example, students may learn the physical skills of basketball, including dribbling, passing, and rebounding. They also may learn information about traveling, offensive fouls, and strategies for attacking a zone defense. If they do not learn to enjoy or find success in playing basketball, however, the probability of their incorporating basketball into their life-style is reduced.

Impact on and showing improvement in the affective dimension of learning is not an easy task for the physical educator compared with the relative ease of showing gains in students' knowledge and physical skills areas. Because of this difficulty, many physical educators have not planned carefully for the affective area. Patt Dodds (1976, p. 109) explains: "I submit that physical educators have expended much effort on cognitive and psychomotor teaching tasks, but have only paid lip service to the affective domain."

Without proper planning and systematically arranging the learning environment, the probability of developing positive student attitudes and physically active life-styles is greatly reduced. Secondary curriculum plans and instructional strategies should be concerned with developing learning environments that help students to enjoy physical activities for a lifetime.

PHYSICAL SKILL DEVELOPMENT

Another important program goal is to help students improve their physical skills. People tend to repeat activities that they do well or find rewarding. Success is a great motivator. If students improve their volleyball bumps, Frisbee sidearm throws, or tennis serves, the chance is better that they will repeat the activity and incorporate it into their lifestyle. Skill development does not occur overnight or in a three-week unit. Students must be counseled into procedures and opportunities for developing physical skills outside the school program. Teachers need to provide a support system for students as their skills begin to improve and as the positive benefits of physical activity begin to appear. Students start to change their attitude toward

physical activity when personal skill levels are improved. They need to be aware that physical skill development is not easy and demands long, continuous effort. Too many students expect instant success. Teachers should help students to find individual levels of success, for success can be different for different people.

PHYSICAL FITNESS DEVELOPMENT

Physical educators have an important responsibility to provide students with successful encounters with exercise and physical activities that lead to improved health-related physical fitness. This includes cardiovascular efficiency, flexibility, body fat reduction, and muscular strength and endurance. Students need to experience the types of activities that result in the benefits of physical fitness on a first-hand basis. Physical educators must do much more than lecture students on the benefits of physical activity and tell them to run a lap around the track. Improving health-related physical fitness means putting students through an organized arrangement of activities that improves fitness systematically throughout the year.

Physical fitness development is similar to physical skill development in that it requires time, energy, and self-discipline. Students need to be aware of these various factors that influence fitness development. Eating habits, types of activities, heredity, and frequency of activity are just a few of the factors that students must understand. Physical education programs play an important role in helping students to develop activity habits that will benefit their physical health.

SOCIAL-EMOTIONAL SKILL DEVELOPMENT

Physical activity environments provide a number of unique opportunities for students to experience and develop social-emotional skills. Getting along with other people, being part of a team, accepting an official's judgment, losing the final game of a tournament, or changing clothes in a crowded locker room are just a few of the many experiences that may occur in a physical education class. These are important experiences for students. Physical educators have a responsibility to help guide and direct students in understanding these various social-emotional behaviors. Specific social-emotional behaviors for various types of physical activities are also important, and a trained specialist should pass these on to students.

KNOWLEDGE

A physical education program should provide students with a wide range of knowledge surrounding all of the aforementioned goals or objectives. A knowledge component is intertwined with all of the other objectives. Indeed, accomplishing any of the other objectives is impossible if students do not have a certain amount of knowledge. For example, getting students to enjoy tennis without understanding the rules, strategies, and etiquette is difficult, and most people cannot incorporate an aerobic activity into their life-style without understanding the possible health-related benefits.

As students increase their knowledge of physical activities, they should also increase their enjoyment and rate of participation. This is unfortunately not always the case. Many people understand the rules, regulations, and benefits of physical activity and yet have not incorporated any activity into their life-style. This is why physical education programs must do more than just provide students with knowledge about physical activity. Students must experience success while participating in and learning about physical activity.

HOW DO WE FULFILL THESE GOALS?

Certainly the accomplishment of all of these goals is a difficult challenge for physical educators. Given the circumstances in many schools, goals will not be fulfilled quickly or without great effort. Curricula and teaching methods have, however, been field-tested and studied with these goals in mind, and procedures are available to help maximize the effectiveness of physical education programs. The following are suggestions for curriculum and instruction that will help students to incorporate physical activity into their life-style.

CHOICE OF ACTIVITIES

Evidence indicates that 7th-grade students have started to narrow their activity interests and are beginning to specialize in specific activities (Anderson 1958). This narrowing of interests continues as students progress through high school into adulthood. The implication is that junior high school students are ready to begin making some

choices about the kinds of physical activity they want to include in their life-style. The authors do not mean that programs should be based totally on the activity interests of 7th and 8th graders. Students at this age need activity experiences and counseling in many categories of activities. As they move from 7th through 12th grade, they should gradually be given more responsibility for choosing a personal activity program.

Many secondary physical education programs have converted to elective programs in which students receive more choice (Wilson and Altieri 1978). Elective program advantages such as increased student participation, enthusiasm, and motivation, as well as increased enthusiasm and motivation of teachers who have specialized in specific activities have been documented (Klappholz 1978). Students in the 10th grade and above should have choice in all physical activities and should not be forced into activities that they are not interested in learning and that might cause them repeated failure. Students in grades 7–9 should be required to take several categories of activities such as team sports, lifetime sports, fitness activities, dance, aquatics, and adventure activities. This ensures a measure of breadth in activity experiences. If possible, they should be permitted to choose from a number of activities in each category. In the fitness area, for example, they might choose aerobic dance, weight training, or jogging. In the lifetime sport area, the choices might be tennis, golf, or bowling.

VARIETY OF ACTIVITIES

The curricula of physical education have expanded greatly in recent years. New and exciting activities such as Frisbee, aerobics, yoga, and rock climbing are being included in programs (Kaplan 1976). A broad-based program increases the possibility that all students will find an enjoyable physical activity. Physical educators should try to offer as many activities as possible in their situation. A balance among team sports, individual sports, dance, aquatics, outdoor activities (Figure 1.4), and physical conditioning activities should be a major program goal.

Off-campus facilities and community resources should be used to supplement the on-campus facilities. Golf ranges, bowling alleys, ski slopes, and field space in the nearby community can add variety to curricular offerings. Personnel from the community can also add instructional expertise in new activities.

Figure 1.4. Adventure activity (photograph courtesy of OLD TOWN Canoe Company, Old Town, Maine)

DEPTH OF ACTIVITIES

In grades 10–12, instructors should make every possible attempt to create programs that offer intermediate and advanced levels of instruction. Students at these developmental levels are ready to choose one or two activities in which they want to excel. Advanced instruction is different from a free-play recreational situation that has been common in many programs. Depth refers to *organized instruction* rather than simply increasing the amount of participation time. Physical educators must move away from the notion that physical education programs should focus only on beginning levels. Many students do not participate in intramurals, sport clubs, athletics, or outside-school programs, and therefore the physical education program should provide in-depth instruction for students. A high level of skill development usually increases a person's tendency to repeat and enjoy activity.

AFTER- AND OUTSIDE-SCHOOL ACTIVITY PROGRAMS

After-school activity programs such as sport clubs, intramurals, and interscholastic athletics can be effective environments for students to improve their skills and become more proficient. These programs also provide opportunities for young people to meet others with similar interests. A variety of important qualities can be experienced through these programs (e.g., teamwork, dedication, per-

severance, deferred rewards, and loyalty). These qualities should be nurtured in today's youth.

Outside-school activity programs include youth sport, YMCA, parks and recreation, and private sport-oriented programs. Physical educators should become involved in the leadership aspects of both the after- and outside-school programs. This should help to ensure the quality of these programs and guard against the many possible abuses. Unqualified leaders with inappropriate goals for a program can mean a disastrous experience for a group of young, immature children. These programs must be developed with the idea of fostering a love of physical activity in children (rather than promoting escape or avoidance behaviors). Physical educators should be able to help parents, other teachers, and adults to organize these programs with the proper goals in mind (Figure 1.5).

ACTIVITY COUNSELING

Students in grades 7–9 should receive formal guidance and counseling early in their secondary education experience to direct them to activities that match their interests and physical abilities. The physical educator can help students to understand their physical shortcomings and the possibilities for alleviating problems. This means data collection and the development of procedures for interpreting the data to students and parents. Obese children, for example, should be channeled into activities in which they can find success, as well as into aerobic activities that help to burn calories and aid in weight control. Students with strong upper bodies should be encouraged to try activities that require this physical feature. Students with poor cardiovascular efficiency should be introduced to aerobic activities. An assigned activity

Figure 1.5. A lacrosse club in action

counselor can help each student to make wise decisions about physical activity.

Students in grades 10–12 should be reminded of the benefits of physical activity, the types of available activities, and so forth. They also need counseling in several other areas such as behavioral self-modification techniques that can aid them in the change and maintenance of fitness habits (Hall 1978). Students should understand environmental factors and obstacles that work against their attempts to participate in physical activities. Employment parameters, marriage, children, and climate are a few factors that affect activity life-styles. Learning to keep records, set goals, and establish reinforcement procedures can help students with their activity habits.

Another important area of activity counseling deals with the changing interests and activities of people as they grow older. We have been conditioned to think that physical activity is only for the young. This attitude needs to be changed in light of the revelation that numerous benefits are derived from being active at all age levels. Fitness and play activities are important regardless of age.

ATMOSPHERE AND TEACHING BEHAVIOR

The overall atmosphere of the physical education environment has an impact on students and on their attitude toward physical activity. Students need a positive, success-oriented program rather than a negative, authoritarian situation that focuses on failure. Teachers should look carefully at all policies, procedures, dress codes, evaluation practices, and other aspects of the environment that affect students. The instructor should use an active teaching role, including demonstrating, participating, encouraging, giving feedback, and hustling. When students leave the physical education environment, they should have a good feeling about physical activity and a desire to return for more.

Research on teaching continues to provide information about ways to improve the teaching-learning process. Teacher modeling behavior can be an effective strategy for influencing specific types of student behavior (Westcott 1978). Suggestions have been made concerning ways in which physical education teachers can use modeling (Landers 1978, McKenzie 1982). Students need to see models of persons who have incorporated physical activity in their life-style. Teachers can discuss their exercise habits with students and allow students to see them participating in and enjoying physical activity. Teachers should be aware of the powerful effect their behavior has on students, and should use this to help students develop healthy activity habits.

Teacher enthusiasm is another behavior that can be quite useful in a physical education environment (Locke and Woods 1982). Evidence shows that this difficult-to-define behavior is a teaching skill that is associated with student learning (Roberts and Becker 1976). Teachers need to display their love of and excitement for physical activity and their joy in teaching.

Teacher expectations are another critical factor in developing a positive atmosphere for teaching (Brophy and Good 1974). If students are expected to be unmotivated and troublesome, then the possibility is strong that these behaviors will occur. If students are expected to learn and work hard, then the chance is better that they will. Abundant evidence shows that teachers' expectations for students will come to fruition. This is called the Pygmalion effect, or self-fulfilling prophecy (Rosenthal and Jacobson 1968).

Curriculum planners and physical education teachers need to consider and deal effectively with these aforementioned suggestions: (1) choice of activities, (2) variety of activities, (3) depth of activities, (4) after- and outside-school activities, (5) activity counseling, and (6) atmosphere and teaching behavior. These ideas can be incorporated into a program, at least to some degree, without much strain on the budget. Each situation has a number of practical factors (e.g., students, facilities, teachers) that will influence the degree to which these suggestions can be developed. A program of curriculum and instruction that focuses on these areas will have an excellent chance of helping students incorporate physical activity into their life-style.

HOW WELL IS PHYSICAL EDUCATION DOING?

If the ultimate goal of physical education programs is to influence the lifetime physical activity habits of people, then looking carefully at current activity habits seems important. It is also necessary to conjecture about the positive or negative effect that physical education has on these activity habits. Answers to the question "How well is physical education doing?" include some bad news and some good news.

BAD NEWS ABOUT ACTIVITY HABITS

There is unfortunately some bad news concerning people's physical activity habits. Consider the following:

1. The President's Council on Physical Fitness and Sports completed a national survey (1973) on adult physical fitness in late 1972. The survey found that 45% of all adults did not engage in any regular physical activity, while 55% said they were involved in regular activity. Of those who indicated that they were active, the most popular activities were walking, bowling, swimming, bicycling, and golf.

2. A study on fitness in America conducted by Harris and Associates and sponsored by the Perrier Company (1979) found that 59% of Americans 18 years and older were participating in some form of physical activity on a regular basis. The active group, however, had only 15% in a high-active category, 16% in a moderately active category, and 28% in a low-active category. This means that 69% of Americans are in either a low-activity or an inactive category. The survey indicated that the most popular activities were walking, swimming, and bowling.

   The survey also indicated that many people did not understand the type of activity needed to become fit and stay fit. For example, 35% of the public believed that bowling provides enough exertion for fitness. In addition, 57% believed that baseball provides enough activity to maintain fitness.

3. In a recent Lou Harris survey on the leisure activities of Americans, the top activities were eating, watching television, and listening to the radio. Much farther down on the list were golf, tennis, and swimming.

4. A recently published survey on fitness and lifestyle in Canada (1983) showed that only 56% of Canadians were active (3 hr per week for 9 months of the year). Thirty-one percent of the people were moderately active (less than 3 hr per week), and 11% were sedentary. The most popular activities were walking, bicycling, swimming, jogging, and gardening. The size of the active group dropped as age increased.

5. Many people still have a poor attitude toward any type of physical activity. The late educator Robert Hutchins was often quoted as saying, "Whenever I feel the urge to exercise coming on, I lie down until it passes over."

6. From 50% to 75% of the population is overweight, depending on the statistics or definition of overweight that is used.

7. Cardiovascular disease is still the leading cause of death in the United States and Canada. Every fifth man will have a heart attack by age 60. The percentage of women affected by heart disease is increasing rapidly. Studies show that approximately 50% of school-aged students have one or more of the risk factors for coronary heart disease, including obesity, poor cardiovascular fitness, high blood pressure, and high cholesterol levels. Exercise and weight control are significant factors in controlling the disease.

8. Millions of people have lower back problems that could be controlled with a stretching-flexibility program.

9. Numerous people have some type of mental health problem that might be alleviated or at least reduced through some type of physical activity. A number of leading mental health experts have prescribed running and other forms of aerobic exercise.

10. Spectators throughout the United States and Canada attend various sports events, but the number of participants is quite low.

11. Many adults lack specific knowledge about exercise, nutrition, weight control, and health-related fitness.

12. The high rates of television watching by both children and adults continue to cut into physical activity time.

13. Evidence shows that the fitness boom of the 1980s is not affecting schoolchildren, older adults, or lower income families (Kirshenbaum and Sullivan 1983). It is a movement promoted primarily by the fitness industries (e.g., health clubs, clothing and shoe industries) and is affecting only the white, upperclass college graduate, and not the poorer or nonwhite high school graduate. Some sectors of society are more active, but when the total population is considered, there are still large numbers of unfit, inactive people.

14. As people grow older, they are less likely to participate in physical activities that are demanding (Gordon et al. 1976). The primary reason appears to be sociological rather than physiological (Ostrow 1982). Many elderly adults believe that vigorous activity is hazardous to their health, and are not aware that

maintaining fitness throughout life is well documented to have many physical and mental benefits.

GOOD NEWS ABOUT ACTIVITY HABITS

Fortunately, there are also many positive indicators concerning physical activity habits in the United States and Canada.

1. The Perrier survey (Harris and Associates 1979) indicated a general trend toward more people being physically active. It showed a significant increase in running and calisthenics. The survey also pointed out that most people understand (in general terms) that physical activity does provide a number of health-related benefits, even though many do not understand the specifics about the types of activities and types of benefits. Parents are also more concerned about involving both sons and daughters in a physical activity program while they are growing up. The survey showed a tremendous increase in the number of women involved in regular physical activity.

2. The aerobic dance craze has recently attracted many men and women of all ages across the country to a regular, vigorous activity program. A plethora of books, records, and tapes are available on aerobic dance. Jane Fonda (1981) is an example of one of many people who have influenced men and women with aerobics behavior, books, tapes, and records.

3. Probably the most visible form of the current fitness renaissance is the distance-running movement. From 2-mi fun runs to 10-km races and 26-mi marathons, people are enjoying distance running. Some type of distance run is available almost every weekend in most geographic areas.

4. Another positive sign is the number of parcourse or exercise trails that have been constructed in parks and school grounds and the increased use of these facilities by adults. This Scandinavian idea has become popular across the country. A parcourse consists of a series of systematically arranged exercise stations set up around an outdoor area. The stations focus on many muscle groups and on different components of physical fitness.

5. Bicycle usage, bicycle path construction, and motocross racing tracks gradually have been increasing. More people are bicycling to and from work as well as for fitness and recreation. The American Bicycle Association expected 110,000 members to participate in bicycle motocross racing by 1983.

6. A newsletter from the President's Council on Physical Fitness and Sports (1980) reported that an A. C. Neilson Company survey showed that racquetball was the fastest growing participant sport in the nation between 1976 and 1979; the sport had increased by 283%, with 10.6 million participants.

7. The continued growth of clubs of the health-racquet-weight training type indicates positive activity habits of adults.

8. Bowling and golf are still quite popular with many people. The many facilities and leagues available are a sign of continued involvement.

9. Most communities have several leagues available for youth and adults through the YMCA or the city recreation program. The most popular activities are basketball, softball, and volleyball for adults, and football, soccer, and baseball for youngsters. Instructional opportunities are also available in yoga, weight training, backpacking, and other popular activities.

10. Most statistics on outdoor adventure-type activities indicate dramatic increases. Hiking, backpacking, rock climbing, and cross country skiing continue to grow in popularity. The number of backpackers in Yosemite National Park went from 77,000 in 1967 to 220,000 in 1972. The number of people climbing Mt. Whitney in California increased from 2000 to 20,000 in a seven-year span. Many rock climbing areas now require advance reservations to control the number of climbers. Cross country skiers numbered 2000 in 1964 and 500,000 in 1974.

11. Most communities have a private martial arts academy offering some type of Eastern movement form, including yoga and some form of the martial arts (e.g., kendo, tai-chi, karate, kung fu, or aikido).

12. The International Frisbee Association claims that more Frisbees are sold each year than footballs and basketballs combined. In some areas, Frisbee golf courses are becoming quite popular.

13. The increased popularity of books and magazine and newspaper columns featuring fitness, nutrition, and wellness is another indicator of public interest in these areas.

PHYSICAL EDUCATION CONTRIBUTIONS TO ACTIVITY HABITS

What part have physical education programs played in the good and bad news on physical activity habits in the United States? This is an interesting yet difficult question to answer, with evidence on both sides of the issue.

Brunner (1969) found that 63% of American adults interviewed believed that what they learned as students in physical education (20 years earlier) was not applicable for use as adults. The people surveyed felt that too much emphasis was placed on team sports like football, basketball, and baseball, and that more time should have been spent on activities that keep adults fit and can be done alone or with one other person (e.g., handball, tennis, swimming, or squash). Straub (1976) complains that too many programs emphasize team sports such as basketball, football, and baseball, rather than lifetime sports such as golf, tennis, and skiing. He argues that participation opportunities in the team sports are too limited and that physical education programs must change their emphasis to lifetime sports.

Many programs have emphasized the team sports-athletics model because it helps to develop the superior athlete and improve the after-school athletic team. These teams are a showcase for excellence and generate funds and community spirit. The evidence seems to indicate, however, that this type of program is not effective in developing lifetime sports participants. If lifetime participation is a major program goal, the team sports model will only contribute to the bad news about activity habits.

On the other side of the issue, the President's Council on Physical Fitness and Sports survey (1973) indicated that those who took physical education in school were more likely to exercise in later life than those who did not take physical education. In a recent survey by Lindeman et al. (1981) of Utah high school students in grades 9–12, 68% of the students indicated that physical education classes were beneficial to them. In addition, 72% of those students expressed a desire to enroll voluntarily in additional physical education classes. It would be interesting to see how many of the Utah students are still involved in regular physical activity 20 years from now.

Siedentop (1980a) has argued that the physical education curriculum is in a cultural transmission category rather than a social reconstruction category. Physical education programs have incorporated activities that follow the activity choices of society, rather than provide a leadership role in shaping activity preferences. For example, society's recent interests in wellness, wilderness sports, and the martial arts are having an effect on physical education curricula. This theory suggests that many adult activity interests and habits are formed outside school physical education programs in settings such as the private sports instruction industry. Perhaps it is time to focus physical education programs on social reconstruction. We need to develop programs that do influence students' activity habits and preferences, and these preferences should include types of activities that offer health-related benefits and a form of play.

Clearly, if physical educators want to affect lifetime physical activity habits positively, they must carefully consider the ideas and steps presented. Programs that continue to use a negative atmosphere and to focus primarily on the highly skilled athlete involved in team sports will not be successful. Teachers should be enthusiastic role models interested in all students and in a variety of lifetime activities. Curricula need to be organized so that students will be positively addicted to activities that can be enjoyed for a lifetime.

WHY BE PHYSICALLY ACTIVE FOR A LIFETIME?

HEALTH-RELATED BENEFITS

Persons who have incorporated regular physical activity into their life-style have a good chance to experience a number of health-related benefits. Depending on the type of activity, the intensity of participation, and the regularity of participation, an active person should be able to:

1. Control his or her weight
2. Improve the cardiovascular-respiratory system
3. Strengthen various muscle groups
4. Improve flexibility
5. Enjoy a variety of physical activities
6. Be more efficient and productive in work activities
7. Have a better self-image
8. Be healthier and enjoy life more

Many variables contribute to the accomplishment of these health benefits. It is not a simple situation in which increasing physical activity means increased benefits. For example, if people want to lose or gain weight, they must learn about nutrition, caloric intake, and the caloric expenditure involved in various types of physical activity. An adult who wants to minimize the risk of coronary heart disease needs to deal with a number of risk factors besides physical activity. Chapter 17 offers specific information about physical fitness and health benefits.

A FORM OF PLAY

Play has been explained as a basic innate human behavior (Huizinga 1962). It is common to all cultures and societies although it may take different forms in each culture. In our culture, common forms of play include music, art, drama, and various forms of physical activity such as sports, games, dance, and outdoor adventure activities. Some examples of play could be the following:

1. Singing in a community choir
2. Playing golf over the weekend
3. Painting pictures of landscapes while on a vacation
4. Participating in an aerobic dance class
5. Acting in a theater group
6. Playing on a church softball team
7. Jogging in a 10-km run

These activities derive their meaning from the concept of play and are referred to as the ludic arts (Siedentop 1978).

Physical activity as a form of play can be of personal and cultural significance. It is an important and basic part of our society. The ludic arts are self-justifying activities that are a part of what many people refer to as "the good life." They do not have to be defended on the basis of their contribution to other areas such as emotional control or character development. If the ludic arts do give people experiences with loyalty, teamwork, dedication, and responsibility or perseverance, then so much the better, but playing on a softball team at 60 years of age is important simply as a personal human experience. Physical educators need to understand the importance of an active play life for all people and to defend the self-justifying aspect of play activities.

PHYSICAL ACTIVITY FOR PLAY AND HEALTH BENEFITS

People need to incorporate physical activities into their life-style that are a form of play and also have health-related benefits. Some activities provide both, while others provide only one. For a physically fit individual, distance running can be both a form of play and a healthful activity, but an obese adult will not initially find much meaning in running beyond the burning of calories and the related weight loss. As one continues to lose weight, however, while increasing cardiovascular efficiency and mileage, running can develop into a form of play. The person who enjoys bowling is enjoying a form of play only and must realize that additional vigorous activities are necessary to obtain the various health benefits of exercise. Bowling alone will have little impact on physical fitness.

Sometimes an activity can have different meanings for a person at different times. A person might get up while it is still dark on four or five mornings a week and run 3 to 5 mi. The process might not be playful and the motivation might be strictly for fitness reasons such as feeling better or controlling weight. To persist in this process would probably require great self-discipline. The same person might thoroughly enjoy a weekend 10-km run without any consideration for physical fitness. Similarly, a golfer might not enjoy hitting a bucket of balls at the driving range but might find hitting balls on the golf course quite enjoyable.

Physical educators must emphasize and protect the playfulness of activities. Once an activity becomes playful to an individual, getting the person to incorporate it into his or her life-style is easy. People also need physical activities for the health-related benefits, and physical educators must not neglect this area. When the motivation is totally health related, getting people to repeat activities is much more difficult. It is best if we can help people to combine health-related activities with play. The authors do not mean that activities such as bowling and golf are less valuable personally than jogging or aerobic dance. Physical educators must help people to incorporate both types of activities into their life-style. For some individuals, one activity may serve both play and physical fitness objectives. For others, several different activities may be required to meet each objective.

Summary

Physical education is an important part of today's secondary school curriculum. It is an educational process aimed at increasing the students' knowledge about, and attitudes and behaviors toward various forms of physical activity, including exercise, sports, games, dance, aquatics, and outdoor adventure activities. All students should learn to incorporate some type of physical activity in their life-style. Physical activity is important for the health-related benefits and as a form of play.

There are positive and negative indications of the effectiveness of physical education programs. Successful programs are developing quality curriculum and instruction for all students. In these programs, students are being given a choice of activities, exposure to a wide variety of activities, more opportunities for in-depth instruction, and access to organized counseling procedures. The overall atmosphere has been changing slowly from a negative to a positive orientation. Students need to learn to enjoy physical activity and to develop positive approach tendencies.

References

Anderson, J. Growth and development today: Implications for physical education. Paper presented at the National Conference on Social Changes and Implications for Physical Education and Sports Recreation, Estes Park, Colorado, June 1958.

Brophy, J., and Good, T. *Teacher-Student Relationships*. New York: Holt, Rinehart & Winston, 1974.

Brunner, B. 1969. How will today's physical education classes be remembered in 1989? *JOPERD* 40(2): 42.

Dodds, P. 1976. Love and joy in the gymnasium. *Quest* (Summer): 109–116.

Fitness and Lifestyle in Canada. May 1983. Canada Fitness Survey, 506–294 Albert Street, Ottawa, K1P 6E6. (Report funded by Fitness Canada.)

Fonda, J. *Jane Fonda's Workout Book*. New York: Simon & Schuster, Inc., 1981.

Gordon, C., Gaitz, C. M., and Scott, J. Leisure and lives: Personal expressivity across the life span. In *Handbook of Aging and the Social Sciences*, edited by R. H. Binstock and E. Shanas. New York: Van Nostrand Reinhold Co., 1976.

Hall, D. 1978. Changing attitudes by changing behavior. *JOPERD* 49(4): 20–21.

Harris, L. & Associates. January 1979. The Perrier Study: Fitness in America.

Huizinga, J. *Homo Ludens: A Study of the Play Element in Culture*. Boston: Beacon Press, 1962.

Kaplan, J. 1976. Jim dandy gym. *Sports Illustrated* 45(20): 44–48.

Kirshenbaum, J., and Sullivan, R. 1983. Hold on there, America. *Sports Illustrated* 58(5): 60–74.

Klappholz, L. 1978. The case for selectives in physical education. *Physical Education Newsletter*, February issue.

Landers, D. 1978. How, when, and where to use demonstrations: Suggestions for the practitioner. *JOPERD* 49(1): 65–67.

Leonard, G. 1977. Why Johnny can't run and other gym class scandals. *Arizona JOHPERD* 21(1): 2–7.

Lindeman, L., Wardrop, D., and Leake, R. 1981. Utah high school physical education interests and attitudes. Utah State Office of Education, Salt Lake City, UT.

Locke, L., and Woods, S. 1982. Teacher enthusiasm. *Journal of Teaching in Physical Education* 1(3): 3–14.

McKenzie, T. 1982. Research on modeling: Implications for teacher training programs. *Journal of Teaching in Physical Education* 1(3): 23–30.

Ostrow, A. 1982. Age grading implications for physical activity participation among older adults. *Quest* 33: 112–123.

President's Council on Physical Fitness and Sports Newsletter. 1973. Special edition. Washington, DC, May issue: 1–27.

President's Council on Physical Fitness and Sports Newsletter. 1980. Washington, DC, July issue: 1.

Roberts, C., and Becker, S. 1976. Communication and teaching effectiveness. *American Educational Research Journal* 13: 181–197.

Rosenthal, R., and Jacobson, L. *Pygmalion in the Classroom*. New York: Holt, Rinehart & Winston, 1968.

Siedentop, D. 1978. Some basic talk about what's basic. *National Association of Secondary School Principals Bulletin*. May issue: 1–4.

Siedentop, D. 1980(a). Physical education curriculum: An analysis of the past. *JOPERD* 51(7): 40–41.

Siedentop, D. *Physical Education—Introductory Analysis*. 3rd ed. Dubuque, IA: Wm. C. Brown Group, 1980(b).

Straub, W. *The Lifetime Sports-Oriented Physical Education Program*. Englewood Cliffs, NJ: Prentice-Hall, 1976.

Westcott, W. Effects of teacher modeling on the subsequent behavior of students. Doctoral dissertation, The Ohio State University, 1977. In *Dissertation Abstracts International*, 1978, 38: 6605A–6606B.

Wilson, B., and Altieri, P. 1978. Complying with Title IX—Increasing participation through the elective program. *Arizona JOHPERD* 21(2): 6–7.

Chapter 2

Current Practices and Directions in Secondary Physical Education

Secondary physical education programs have come under scrutiny as changes have occurred in recent decades. Curricular offerings and arrangement procedures have undergone significant changes for various reasons. A multitude of new and different activities have been packaged and arranged. The policies, procedures, and problems have changed considerably in recent years. Many adults would be surprised at the overall atmosphere and offerings available in today's secondary physical education programs. Traditional programs limited to calisthenics and team sports such as football, basketball, and softball are slowly changing and evolving into programs with a different focus. Many programs, however, still need to be changed and updated.

POSITIVE NEW ACTIVITIES

LIFETIME SPORTS

In the last 25 years, the most significant change in secondary physical education offerings has been the inclusion of the "lifetime" or "carry-over" sports.

These sports are primarily individual or dual activities that can be used for a lifetime as opposed to team sports that are difficult to continue after the school years. A major factor in the development of the lifetime sports concept was the Lifetime Sports Education Project (LSEP) sponsored by the American Alliance for Health, Physical Education, Recreation, and Dance (AAHPERD).[1] The LSEP originally focused on bowling, archery, badminton, tennis, and golf. Instructional materials and teaching clinics were developed by the LSEP to encourage physical educators to expand their curriculum (Figure 2.1).

Lifetime sports have become tremendously popular and have been expanded to include a host of new activities such as Frisbee, racquetball, and squash. The AAHPERD estimates that 75% of the nation's secondary schools emphasize lifetime

---

1. This organization formerly was called the American Alliance for Health, Physical Education, and Recreation (AAHPER). In 1980, the name was changed to reflect a growing involvement in dance. The abbreviation AAHPERD will be used for all organization references in this text, regardless of the actual name at the time.

Figure 2.1. Playing handball, a lifetime sport

Figure 2.2. Orienteering (reprinted from *Outdoor Adventure Activities for School and Recreation Programs* by P. W. Darst and G. P. Armstrong, 1980. Minneapolis, MN: Burgess Publishing Co., p. 152)

sports in their physical education programs. The expanded offering of lifetime sports has provided many participation opportunities for students and adults not interested in the traditional team sports. Secondary physical education programs are better able to serve all students when a wide variety of lifetime sports is offered, because different students are successful with different activities. Every student should be able to find success with some kind of physical activity (e.g., some students enjoy Frisbee much more than football and basketball).

OUTDOOR ADVENTURE ACTIVITIES

Another category of activities gaining popularity in the past ten years includes the outdoor adventure or wilderness sports. Backpacking, rock climbing, orienteering, and bicycling are just a few of the many new activities in this category (Darst and Armstrong 1980). These activities are similar to the lifetime sports and are primarily individual or dual activities that can be enjoyed over a lifetime. The emphasis is on risk and excitement in using the earth's natural environments such as snow, water, mountains, ice, rivers, and wilderness areas. Exploration, travel, and adventure are important elements in these activities. To train students in outdoor adventure skills, many schools are developing on-campus facilities such as climbing walls, rope courses, and orienteering sites (Figure 2.2), as well as using nearby community environments such as ski slopes, parks, rivers, and mountains. These activities emphasize competition with oneself and the environment in contrast to competition with other people. This is an attractive feature to many students. Outdoor adventure activities can also be enjoyed with family and friends during expanded leisure hours. They give people an opportunity to get away from the city and experience the natural environment in a time of vanishing wilderness areas.

HEALTH-RELATED PHYSICAL FITNESS

A combination of the running craze, the wellness movement, and the fitness renaissance that has emerged across the nation is rekindling interest in physical fitness types of activities. Aerobic rhythmic exercise, Jazzersize, jogging, weight training (Figure 2.3), and weight control classes are extremely popular with secondary students and adults. Schools are offering numerous classes called Superstars competition, shipshape class, systematic conditioning, and aerobics, which emphasize such areas as nutrition, obesity, coronary heart disease, flexibility, and strength. The AAHPERD has developed a new health-related fitness test that focuses on cardiovascular efficiency, abdominal strength and endurance, flexibility, and body composition. Norms are available to aid students,

Figure 2.3. Weight lifting class

Figure 2.4. Playing modified lacrosse

teachers, and parents with information on the health-related parameters of physical fitness. Now is an opportune time for physical educators to develop learning experiences for students in this area.

EASTERN-INFLUENCED ACTIVITIES

Eastern philosophy has had some influence on secondary school programs. The various forms of the martial arts, including judo, karate, aikido, kendo, and tae kwan do, are popular at the college and university level and are slowly filtering into the secondary school curricula. Yoga, transcendental meditation, relaxation techniques, and self-defense classes are common in many high school and junior high school programs. These activities seem to be popular with students.

NEW TEAM SPORTS

Finally, the development of new or modified team sports is continuing in many schools. Activities such as team handball, global ball, speed-a-way, flickerball, angleball, modified lacrosse (Figure 2.4), and pillow polo are a few of the newer team sports that are popular in various areas of the country. Some of these are new activities, while others are modifications of existing sports. They add another positive dimension to programs because of the increased variety and opportunities for success with certain types of students.

The new team sport activities provide many interesting and exciting challenges for both students and instructors. In teaching almost any activity, there may be problems with safety, liability,

competent instruction, equipment, and people's comfort zones, but the advantages of offering new team sports are well worth the encountered problems. A wide variety of activities should enhance the objective of developing in all students a positive attitude toward a lifetime of physical activity.

ARRANGING AND PACKAGING ACTIVITIES

LENGTH OF ACTIVITY UNITS

The length of activity units has shortened over the past decade, especially at the junior high level. In quality programs, the six- to nine-week units are becoming obsolete. In many junior high programs, two- to three-week units are the norm. Most high schools offer three-, four-, or five-week units. These shorter units have enabled physical educators to expand the breadth of their programs and to give students an introduction to a wider variety of activities. Some people are critical of this trend because of the reduction in depth of instruction, but students will choose to develop depth in an activity after they have had a successful encounter early in their school career. The short units also reduce boredom and frustration, which are common among junior high age students. With more program breadth, educators will have a better opportunity to provide all students with some type of physical activity that they can currently enjoy and then use throughout a lifetime.

Depth in an activity is available in many high school curricula in which students can choose a semester-long unit. This specialized approach is part of an elective or optional program instead of a required program. This type of class gives students a chance to gain in-depth skill in an activity of their choice after they complete the required program. Many schools are offering semester- or year-long units focusing on popular activities such as dance, gymnastics, tennis, and physical conditioning. The approach is productive if the school can afford to make the offerings without reducing the quality of the basic required program. The junior high program should provide breadth, and the high school program should add depth and a wide variety of elective activities.

LEVELS OF INSTRUCTION

A new development in some of the larger high schools has been the offering of different levels of instruction such as beginning and intermediate classes. Some schools have even used the classifications of *beginning, team,* and *recreational.* Three-week units are being offered for beginning basketball, team basketball, and recreational basketball. The beginning class might cover dribbling, passing, pivoting, rebounding, and so forth, while the team class would cover such areas as offensive strategy, zone defenses, and techniques on beating a half court trap. The final recreational class would focus primarily on team play and tournaments. Students could take three units in a progressive, systematic procedure. An advantage of this approach is that teachers can do a better job of instruction because classes are more homogeneous in motivation. Students usually feel more comfortable in a group in which similar attitudes and abilities prevail.

ELECTIVE OR SELECTIVE CURRICULA

The elective or selective approach to physical education curricula has had an impact on schools across the nation. The terms (elective and selective) have, however, been used differently in various situations. Usually they refer to students' choosing to take an optional or elective year of physical education, or the students' choosing between several options during each activity interval of four to six weeks. Students can select either tennis, weight training, or soccer during the first three-week unit, and either racquetball, archery, or flag football during the second three weeks. Choice can occur not only during the elective year but also during the required year or years. The choice process starts in some schools as early as the 7th or 8th

grade, while in others it does not begin until the 10th grade. This type of program gives students an opportunity to choose activities in which they are genuinely interested and to avoid activities in which they have little interest. At Greenway High School in Arizona (Wilson and Altieri 1978), school officials found that some students would not elect an extra year of physical education because they wanted to avoid one or two specific activities such as swimming, gymnastics, or wrestling. Students would sacrifice an entire year of physical education to avoid certain activities. Because of this situation, curriculum planners need to implement an elective program in which students can choose from four or five activities during each four-week unit of the elective year.

Another advantage of the elective approach is that students will be more motivated when they have influenced the selection of learning activities. Fewer problems should occur in the areas of participation and discipline. More students involved in the program can also mean more teachers, equipment, and facilities. Teachers in this type of program should be able to specialize in several activities and teach repeated units in their areas of expertise. This in turn improves the instructional process because of the reduced number of teacher preparations.

Flexibility in class size is yet another advantage. Certain activities can easily accommodate more students, depending on the equipment and facilities. For example, golf and tennis might have smaller classes than soccer and flag football.

Finally, considering the above advantages, teachers should be more motivated and enthusiastic about teaching in this type of program. The elective program can thus improve the motivational level of both students and teachers. Any educational practice that can affect the teaching-learning environment should be considered when developing programs in secondary physical education. Problems do have to be worked out concerning grades, registration procedures, teaching attitudes, and class roll procedures. There are, however, several solutions available to a teaching staff that believes in the advantages of the approach. Elective programs can be an influence in a positive direction.

TITLE IX AND COEDUCATIONAL CLASSES

Title IX of the Educational Amendments Act of 1972 has had a significant impact on most secondary physical education programs. The law is based on the principle that school activities and programs are of equal value for both sexes. Students should not be denied access to participation in school activities on the basis of sex. This law has stirred up much debate and controversy. Interpretations and details are still being worked out by school districts, state departments of education, and the judicial system.

Legal ramifications have forced schools to provide equal access to physical education activities for both boys and girls (Figure 2.5). Coeducational classes have become the rule instead of the exception. Separate classes for boys and girls have been eliminated. This does not imply that boys and girls must wrestle together, share locker facilities, or have the same activity interests. It does mean that boys can participate in a dance class or girls can elect a weight training class if they have interest in these respective areas. In principle, the law also means that instruction is provided by the most qualified person regardless of sex.

The law does allow schools to group students by ability, even if the result is groups consisting of primarily one sex. The law also allows teachers to segregate sexes during the game or competitive aspect of contact sports such as wrestling, basketball, football, ice hockey, and others. Teachers must also be sure that grading standards or procedures are not having an adverse effect on one sex, because this is a specified regulation of Title IX. Standards must be equally fair to both sexes.

Title IX has created some problems for physical educators. Teachers have been forced to expand their comfort zones in dealing with students of the opposite sex. Grading procedures, safety, locker room policies, and sexuality issues are a few of the areas that teachers have had to rethink with coeducational classes. For some, these changes have been

Figure 2.5. Coeducational class

interesting, exciting, and challenging, while for others the law has brought about negative feelings for the entire situation. For the latter, Title IX has been the cause of all that is wrong with today's physical education programs.

Amidst all of the controversy, it is important to examine the objectives of the physical education program, and how the objectives of secondary physical education can be accomplished in the situation specified by Title IX. There are new problems, but there are also clear advantages to coeducational programs in the areas of social development, activity offerings, and instructional quality. Teachers should be responsible for *all* students in their classes, regardless of ability, sex, or race. Many of the complaints that arise are often nothing more than a smokescreen for laziness, ineptness, or bias.

THE HANDICAPPED STUDENT AND PUBLIC LAW 94-142

Public Law 94-142, the Education of All Handicapped Children Act, was signed in 1975 by President Ford. This law, which has affected secondary physical education, ensures that all children with handicaps receive an appropriate public education that serves their unique needs. Physical education has been specified as an important part of the handicapped child's curricula or individualized education program (IEP). The IEP is prepared jointly by the teacher, the parent, and the child, if appropriate. It contains extensive information covering the child's present status, program objectives, learning activities, and evaluation procedures.

The law has compelled physical educators to develop specialized classes and programs for many students with handicaps. Other students have been mainstreamed into the regular physical education program as part of the least restrictive environment advocated by P. L. 94-142. School districts have been required to hire qualified instructors for these programs, as well as to encourage current teachers to develop skills for providing meaningful experiences for mainstreamed children with handicaps.

A federally validated program for children with handicaps that is being implemented throughout the country is the Physical Education Opportunities Program for Exceptional Learners (PEOPEL) (Burkett et al. 1980). The program involves a one-to-one peer teaching model in which student volunteers who are nonhandicapped are paired with students who are handicapped. The volunteers are put through an extensive training program and receive physical education credit for their efforts. The program has been field-tested and offers many advantages for students, such as a high rate of feedback, individual attention, and more instruction.

The law clearly creates some problems for physical educators in planning, organizing, managing, and evaluating daily and yearly programs for the handicapped. In most situations, the teacher must establish learning environments concurrently for students with and without handicaps. People with handicaps deserve quality physical education experiences, and program offerings must continue to improve in this area.

CONCEPTUAL APPROACHES

A development that started at the college level and has slowly filtered down to the secondary school level is called the conceptual approach. An example of the conceptual approach is the *Fitness for Life* text by Corbin and Lindsey (1983). This approach has been called a lecture-laboratory method. Students spend time receiving information in a lecture situation and then try out or test the information on themselves or on peers in a laboratory setting. Emphasis is placed on information, appraisal procedures, and program planning. Students are expected to understand the "how, what, and why" of physical activity and exercise. They learn to use diagnostic tests in areas such as cardiovascular endurance, muscular strength and endurance, flexibility, body composition, and motor ability.

These programs have been field-tested in various situations. In some schools, the concepts make up the entire physical education program, while in others, the concepts may be only a portion of the requirement, such as a semester class or six-week unit. Several books are available with lesson sequences and other instructional materials such as slide-tape lectures, scripts, review questions, tests, dittos, overhead transparencies, and laboratory experiments.

The conceptual approach seems to be popular for several reasons. First, many believe that an academic approach focused on knowledge and cognitive growth instead of on physical skill is a more respectable educational endeavor. Others believe that when student knowledge is increased, attitudes and behaviors will also change, causing physical activity to be incorporated into the student's life-style. This is not a proved phenomenon. Increasing a person's knowledge does *not* ensure

a change in behavior, and students must also experience and attempt physical activity and fitness as well as understand conceptually. Concepts should be an important part of a physical education program, but there must be a balance of both knowledge concepts and physical skill development in the physical education curriculum.

INTERDISCIPLINARY COURSES

In a few secondary schools, physical education is being combined with other disciplines such as biology, geology, and geography. In these programs, students have opportunities to learn about subjects such as hunting and fishing, taxidermy, rock formations, safety, and environmental concerns. Emphasis is placed on combining physical skill development with knowledge. For example, students can learn about the flora and fauna of an area while concurrently learning camping and backpacking skills. This is the basic thesis of many outdoor education programs in which several disciplines are integrated to teach students about the outdoors.

This approach also balances the acquisition of knowledge and physical skill development, and offers some interesting challenges for students and teachers. Teachers can take advantage of geographical locations, different learning environments, and the interests of students living in these areas. The physical education teacher can team teach with teachers from other subject areas such as biology, zoology, or geography. In this way many interesting learning experiences can be developed.

INDEPENDENT STUDY OPTIONS

Independent study programs give students an opportunity to earn physical education credit for advanced study or off-campus courses that are not available in the basic curricula. Students at a high school in California can earn credit for off-campus study involving surfing, ice skating, horseback riding, bowling, golf, and other disciplines. These programs are usually available to students only after they have completed the basic requirements. Some type of monitoring and weekly check-in procedure is arranged with the student, parent, and teacher agreeing to a contract. Many of these programs also contain a fitness component, and students must show some type of maintenance or improvement in the fitness area (e.g., body composition or cardiovascular endurance).

Students keep a log of their various activities with an anecdotal record of skill work, games, scores, opponents, and evaluation procedures. Written work is usually required on rules, etiquette, current personalities, research areas, or officiating. If problems occur with students not completing their work, they are returned to the regular program or are dropped from the independent study program. Some schools have special independent study areas in the library or in a room close to the gymnasium where students can check out materials or view video tapes and loop films.

Some problems occur with students abusing the program and with monitoring procedures, equipment check-out, legal liability, financial arrangements, and evaluation procedures. The program does, however, offer some possibilities for advanced and new activity study and can add an exciting dimension to the curricula. The independent study approach may help students develop self-management skills and become self-motivated because they have selected activities that appeal to them, and they are largely responsible for what they learn from the experience.

OFF-CAMPUS COMMUNITY FACILITIES

Another positive approach involves off-campus community facilities. This approach allows schools to use community bowling alleys, golf courses, ski slopes, and skating rinks to enhance the physical education program. Many schools are bussing students to a nearby bowling alley or golf course each Friday over a three-week unit. A school in Pennsylvania takes students to a ski slope for downhill skiing lessons. Sometimes the schools provide the transportation and participation funds, while in other cases, the students pay the expenses. Funding can also be provided through car washes, candy sales, and raffles. Programs and procedures are limited only by a teacher's ingenuity and creative direction.

The nearby facilities in the community can add a valuable dimension to secondary programs. Physical educators need to broaden their areas of competency and to use the resources at their disposal. Delbert Oberteuffer, a noted physical educator, once asked a physical education teacher who taught at a school situated near a beautiful lake, "Do you teach swimming, boating and sailing here?" "No," replied the teacher, "we don't have the facilities." Finding a way to use community resources for the betterment of students is surely possible.

POLICIES AND PROCEDURES

REQUIREMENTS

Each state department of education sets requirements for physical education. Policy differences from state to state are great. Some require a number of minutes per week for each grade level, while others specify a number of days per week. Several states have no physical education requirement. Each school district usually sets requirements within the framework provided by the state department of education. This is not a new policy, but it is important for physical educators to understand that requirements are developed within this framework. Consequently, district policies can be changed significantly and still be within the state guidelines. As an example, in Arizona there is no requirement at the state level for physical education, yet most Arizona high schools have at least a one-year physical education requirement. Other Arizona schools have a two- or three-year requirement, while some offer only an elective physical education program. The state requirement will significantly affect the curriculum, the students, and the teachers.

Curriculum planners must be informed about state and local requirements. Currently, the general trend has been for states to reduce physical education time in favor of more time for mathematics, science, and English. Many people still consider physical education to be a "frills" area, and it appears that physical educators will have to continue to justify their existence in the schools.

A newer approach to requirements at the local level in the selective-elective type of curriculum involves specifying requirements by activity category, such as team sports, lifetime sports, gymnastics, aquatics, recreational activities, and dance. An example would be requiring a student to complete 12 activities in one year. The requirement might be that 3 of the activities must be team sports, 3 must be lifetime sports, and 1 each must be selected from the areas of dance, aquatics, and gymnastics. The remaining activity choices would be left to the student. This procedure involves giving students a choice within a requirement and ensures that students will receive a variety of activities as well as the opportunity to choose according to their interests. Students have some choice but not total freedom, so a more balanced curricular approach is thus assured.

TESTING AND COUNSELING PROCEDURES

Many secondary schools have set up a series of compulsory units that require students to assess their physical abilities and make decisions about physical activities in which they can find success and remediate weaknesses. An organized counseling program helps channel students into physical education activities that can enhance their strengths and alleviate weaknesses. A three-week unit for freshmen students might focus on testing a wide variety of health and motor fitness parameters. A battery of tests would be put together for these areas. The AAHPERD health-related fitness test could be administered (Figure 2.6). Students would then use this data as they entered a three-week course focused on planning a personalized physical education program. Teachers would counsel students into activities in which they could use their strengths and improve areas of weakness. For example, students with poor cardiovascular efficiency could be directed to aerobic activities such as jogging, swimming, bicycling, or aerobic dance. Students with excellent flexibility might be directed to gymnastics classes. Teachers should strongly encourage students to select activities to help them *both* develop strengths and work on weaknesses.

The testing and counseling procedures are set up in a systematic, organized fashion. A physical education advisor is assigned to each student to guide her or him through the process in an attempt to give students some information on which they can base sound decisions about their future. This type of testing and counseling program combined with the previously described elective-selective program is an effective way to fuse students' interests with their physical ability requirements. This model provides a blend of information about physical activity and gives students experiences in improving physical skills and physical fitness. Students should leave the program with approach tendencies for physical activity instead of avoidance behaviors. The details of this model will be discussed in Chapter 5.

PHYSICAL EDUCATION ATMOSPHERE

Many physical educators across the country have taken a hard look at the overall atmosphere of the physical education program. Students sometimes do all they can to avoid the subject. Activity offerings are often out-of-date. Classes are almost always overcrowded. Dress requirements cause students to rebel. Showers are required after every activity, and time allotted for showers frequently makes it impossible to get to the next class on time. Teachers may do little or no actual teaching and sometimes act like military drill instructors. Grades are often based on a negative approach, and exercise is sometimes used as punishment. With this picture in mind, we can easily see why many physical educators are advocating a change in the overall atmosphere.

Many schools have relaxed or liberalized the dress codes and grading procedures. Students at San Rafael High School in California (Kaplan 1976) stated that what they liked best about the new physical education program was not the 45 electives and numerous exotic activities, but a relaxed dress code that enabled them to wear clothes of their choice. Students referred to gym uniforms as "monkey suits" or "prison garb," and the process of dressing out as "torture." In some schools, the grading procedures have been switched to a pass-fail basis. In other situations, students are able to choose the type of grading option they prefer.

Physical educators need to look carefully at the effects of the policies and procedures that they are using in programs. If these procedures are discouraging students from a lifetime of physical activity, they should be reevaluated. If dress codes and grading procedures are chasing students away and developing avoidance behaviors, acceptable alternatives must be developed.

INSTRUCTIONAL PROCEDURES

Another encouraging direction that many secondary programs are taking involves creating a teaching-learning atmosphere that is both positive

Figure 2.6.   Health-related fitness testing

and caring. Instructional procedures are being planned carefully so students can be successful immediately. The instructor's reactions to failure are kept minimal and momentary. Teachers are learning to focus their feedback and reactions on positive student behaviors rather than always using a "correction complex" that continually reacts to what students are doing wrong. Contract approaches and individualized instruction have been used successfully to shape students' skill behaviors. Teachers are realizing that they must take an active role in the teaching-learning process by demonstrating, participating, encouraging, and hustling. Students are influenced significantly by the visible model of a person who has incorporated physical activities into his or her life-style.

Many teachers are now using positive methods to discipline, control, and motivate. Students are taught to enjoy physical education instead of learning to avoid the environment. Running and exercise are not used as a form of punishment. Students are rewarded for competitive efforts even if their team happens to lose on a given day. Teachers use students' first names and interact with all students on a daily basis. Students are given a degree of choice and fre ¹om in the learning process, and they are consequently more motivated and work harder.

To some educators, these positive directions sound like ideals that cannot be carried out in the "real world," yet all of the approaches previously discussed are occurring in schools across the country. New ideas and programs are not developed and implemented easily, but when a better program is developed and when the teaching-learning process is improved, teachers feel more optimistic and more involved in their profession.

PROBLEMS

TEACHING VERSUS COACHING

Many people have a difficult time separating the physical education program from the athletic program. The athletic program is concerned with recruiting, coaching, and administering teams that will compete against other school teams. These goals are significantly different from the goals of the secondary physical education program, yet athletics and physical education are often linked because the programs must share facilities, equipment, fields, and teachers.

In addition, a great deal of pressure often comes from the local community to produce winning teams. The pressure to develop outstanding physical education programs is not nearly as great, and the visibility of the two programs is markedly different. This creates a difficult situation for the teacher-coach. The coach may support the concept of an outstanding curriculum, but may not find enough time and energy to do both. The physical education program has to take a back seat in many situations.

This problem has no simple solutions. Many teachers want to work in both programs. The pressure to produce winners is apparent, and the individual instructor will determine the quality of the physical education program that is implemented. Many people do excellent work in both areas, but it is not an easy task.

INSTRUCTION VERSUS CONTROL AND FREE PLAY

For many years, educators were viewed favorably by administrators and peers for having identically dressed students in neat, straight lines. Many people still adhere to this point of view, and students may be completely "under control" even though little instruction and learning are taking place. In fact, students may often be learning to dislike or avoid physical activity and exercise because of the control procedures used by an instructor. Teachers sometimes become so concerned with control and discipline that they lose sight of the primary goals of physical education. If students are learning to dislike physical education because of the control techniques used, teachers need to look carefully at their procedures. A degree of control and discipline is necessary for an effective learning environment, but not a degree of control that destroys students' love of activity.

In contrast, there are many situations in which students have come to believe that secondary physical education class is a time to play a game without any instruction or a time to work on the physical skills needed for successful game participation. Students think they should have free time all the time for game participation. This attitude is a result of the policy of "rolling out the ball" espoused by many teachers. It then becomes difficult for other teachers to organize a structured learning environment when students are accustomed to the free play approach. Students also have difficulty when they have a different instructor every three weeks. Some teachers may "roll out the ball," while others attempt to organize structured lessons.

EQUIPMENT, FACILITIES, AND CLASS SIZE

A continuing problem that physical educators at all levels face is the problem of inadequate equipment and facilities. For some reason, many administrators believe that physical education classes can be larger and can manage with less equipment than an academic class. They fail to realize that it is impossible to learn to dribble a basketball without having access to a basketball on a regular basis. Students are also frustrated by standing in line and waiting for a turn to dribble the ball. Teachers have a difficult situation with 40 students on six tennis courts. Economic conditions make these problems difficult, and physical educators must strive to get a fair share of the budget. Students are not asked to learn to read and write without books, paper, and pencils. Physical education is as important as other discipline areas and should receive an equal share of the budget dollar.

LEGAL LIABILITY

Many lawsuits appearing in various aspects of society are of concern to physical educators. Teachers are not immune to liability lawsuits as evidenced by an increasing number of cases of parents and students suing teachers, administrators, and school boards. This situation is unnerving when teachers attempt new activities or new teaching techniques that involve any type of risk. Many teachers and administrators have become extremely cautious and conservative about activities that have a reputation of any danger, yet many of these activities are actually safer than activities that have traditionally been included in the curriculum. A teacher can refuse to offer new activities for fear of a lawsuit. Ultimately, students become the victims in this process, as teachers refuse to offer any units that have some degree of risk.

Teachers certainly need to acquire adequate knowledge about safety and instructional procedures before implementing a new activity. They should not be scared off solely on the basis of ignorance. Legal ramifications must be understood when developing a broad and balanced curriculum. With proper information and careful planning, the instructional risks of various activities can be minimized. If sound policies and procedures are followed on a daily basis, teachers should not worry about legal liability. An in-depth discussion of legal liability can be found in Chapter 13.

PRIVATE SPORTS INSTRUCTION

Opportunities for sports and fitness instruction in the private sector continue to grow and expand rapidly. These programs are quite effective in meeting the demands of consumers. Gymnastics clubs, soccer leagues, Pop Warner football, motocross bicycle racing, little league baseball, and racquet clubs are a few examples of programs that are available to students. Students receive in-depth instruction, practice with adequate equipment, have many competitive opportunities, and receive trophies, T-shirts, and similar rewards. Many of these situations are excellent programs and provide students with valuable experiences. They do, however, create two major problems for school-based physical education programs.

The first problem is that private instruction creates a wide range of backgrounds, experiences, and abilities among students who are participating in school physical education. Students from middle- and upper-class families may have a wealth of experience in sports such as tennis, golf, soccer, and gymnastics, while students from lower income families will probably have little experience. It is difficult with limited equipment to develop a beginning gymnastics unit that is meaningful to 8th grade students who have had five years of intensive training at a private sports academy. This same point can be illustrated by comparing students involved in a soccer league for several years with students who have never played the game. Teachers face a difficult challenge in motivating students with such diverse backgrounds.

The second problem can be more significant in terms of impact on the school program. As opportunities in the private sector increase, public support for the school physical education curricula may lessen. Some people currently believe that secondary school physical education programs can be eliminated because of the many opportunities in the private sector. "Let students learn physical activities outside the school setting so there is more time and money for academic subjects" is the viewpoint often voiced. An opposing viewpoint argues that private instruction opportunities are available only to the upper middle class and that lower socioeconomic groups will have limited opportunities. The trend toward private instruction is continuing to grow and the possibility is strong that the private sports industry may become a serious competitor of school programs. Physical educators face the challenge of developing quality programs that provide meaningful learning experiences for all students regardless of background.

Summary

Secondary physical education programs are continually evolving and changing. Lifetime sports, outdoor adventure activities, martial arts, and a renewed emphasis on physical fitness have expanded the secondary curricula. Running, aerobic dance, health-related knowledge concepts, and weight training are highly visible signs of how the fitness renaissance has affected school programs. The arrangement and packaging of activities have also changed. Shorter introductory units at the junior high school level and longer, specialized units at the high school level are common.

Title IX of the 1972 Educational Amendments Act and Public Law 94-142 have created some interesting situations concerning coeducational classes and handicapped students. Conceptual, interdisciplinary, and independent study courses have become popular in some school programs. Off-campus facilities in the neighboring communities are being used for such activities as golf, bowling, skiing, and sailing.

Some problem areas include an over-emphasis on coaching, unreasonably large classes, limited facilities, potential legal liability, and competition from the private sports industry. Educators are constantly analyzing the values and problems of secondary physical education as the profession continues to move toward excellence.

References

Burkett, L., et al. 1980. PEOPEL. *JOPERD* 51(7): 28–30.

Corbin, C., and Lindsey, R. *Fitness for Life*. 2nd ed. Glenview, IL: Scott, Foresman & Co., 1983.

Darst, P., and Armstrong,. G. *Outdoor Adventure Activities for School and Recreation Programs*. Minneapolis: Burgess Publishing Co., 1980.

Kaplan, J. 1976. Jim dandy gym. *Sports Illustrated* 45(20): 44–48.

Wilson, B., and Altieri, P. 1978. Complying with Title IX—Increasing participation through the elective program. *Arizona JOHPERD* 21(2): 6–7.

PART II

CURRICULUM DEVELOPMENT

Chapter 3

Curriculum Theory and Practical Factors

A curriculum is an overall plan for the entire physical education program. The curriculum contains the scope, structure, sequence, and arrangement of learning activities for each school year. The sequence of activities is arranged progressively throughout the year and from year to year. Each succeeding year in the curriculum should build on the program activities offered in previous years. The curriculum is intended to guide teachers in developing and conducting learning experiences that give a group of students an opportunity to acquire knowledge, attitudes, and behaviors identified as goals or objectives. It is the "what and why" of education as opposed to the "how," which is referred to as instruction. Curriculum and instruction should not be separated because they are interdependent. For example, the objectives of a curriculum are significantly affected by the instructional emphasis. A direct or command style of instruction has a different impact on students from a problem solving or guided discovery approach. The length, content, or organizing center of a unit also influences the type of instruction that will be most effective. Teachers need to be aware of how curriculum and instruction affect one another, and consequently, curriculum and instruction should be studied together.

A curriculum is usually arranged around one major or main theme. This theme is called an **organizing center.** Learning experiences or activities are arranged around the organizing center to accomplish the goals of the program. The most common organizing center for physical education curricula has been movement forms, sport, and physical activity. Commonly included are units on basketball, softball, square dancing, and jogging. Additional organizing centers used in physical education include (1) physical fitness components such as cardiovascular efficiency, strength, and control of body fat, (2) wellness knowledge and activities involving stress management, nutrition, weight control, substance abuse, personal safety, physical fitness, environmental awareness, and behavioral self-control, (3) movement themes such as propelling, catching, striking, and balancing, (4) analysis of movement elements such as force, time, space, and flow, (5) student motives such as appearance, health, and achievement, (6) disciplinary knowledge from such areas as biomechanics, motor learning, exercise physiology, and sport philosophy, and (7) social themes such as competition, cooperation, and sportsmanship. Most programs follow an eclectic philosophy that focuses on several themes from several of the areas mentioned.

The yearly and year-to-year curriculum plans should serve as tools for teachers. Curricula are organized in two planes, horizontal and vertical. The horizontal organization is the yearly plan and is concerned with arranging activities for the school year. The vertical curriculum is concerned with scope and sequence for all of the school years, kindergarten through grade 12. Both should reflect the overall philosophy of the program and be organized to accomplish desired outcomes. The curricula offer direction to both teachers and students and should be posted in the teaching area. Several specific horizontal (yearly) curriculum plans will be presented in Chapter 5.

A yearly plan avoids the pitfalls of running out of time or activities. It gives departments of physical education a singular purpose and eases the burden when equipment and facilities are shared. Instructors can agree on the units that should be taught and on the amount of time that should be consigned to each unit. Each instructor then has a curriculum with similar content, differing only in the order of presentation of units. This allows effective use of equipment and facilities that have to be shared in most secondary school settings.

Another important reason for yearly planning concerns the area of curriculum evaluation. If department members desire to evaluate their program of study, evaluation would be difficult if each teacher taught a unique curriculum. Similarly, if there is no yearly plan, determining the strengths and weaknesses of the curriculum becomes impossible. Why were physical fitness scores low? Why do students choose not to participate in the program? What activities should be added or deleted? Which activities are of high interest or low interest? These and other questions can be answered when the curriculum framework is known. In turn, parts of the curriculum can be modified and evaluated later. There is no substitute for a stable and well-planned curriculum.

This chapter will focus on curriculum views and perspectives, current curricular theories, and a number of practical factors that influence the type of curriculum that can be offered to students. Curriculum planners should carefully consider all of these areas as they begin to prepare a specific curriculum for a specific situation.

CURRICULUM PERSPECTIVES

Siedentop (1980a) has suggested that there are three different views that should be considered when planning curriculum and its impact on students. The most inclusive of these three perspectives is the sum total of all areas and aspects of the school, including the cafeteria, hallways, locker rooms, library, and bookstore. These areas, plus such policies and procedures governing the school as attendance, dress codes, disciplinary procedures, evaluation schedules, and study hall procedures, can have an impact on student learning. The overall organization and atmosphere of the school play a role in the attitudes, values, and social development of students.

A second curriculum perspective is the traditional way of viewing and studying each separate, formal course of study. This would involve the history curriculum, the mathematics curriculum, the music curriculum, or the physical education curriculum. Each academic area has a sequence of courses and specific topics or activities within each course. These courses of study are carefully planned and arranged so the stated objectives are accomplished. Curriculum study and research have focused primarily on this second perspective. Teachers in physical education and in other subject areas channel the majority of their professional efforts into this curriculum aspect.

The third and newest perspective for viewing curriculum is called the "functional" curriculum (Berliner 1979). The term refers to the actual amount of instructional lesson time during which a student is appropriately engaged in the specific subject matter. This time is called academic learning time (ALT) and is being studied extensively in physical education environments (Metzler 1981). Time spent dribbling, passing, or shooting a basketball with a low error rate is high ALT, while time spent waiting in line, changing clothes, or rotating stations is not included in ALT. Studies show that many physical education environments are characterized by low rates of ALT. Usually, no more than 15% of class time was spent engaged in ALT (Metzler 1979).

The functional curriculum and the concept of ALT are representative of a scientific approach, which uses empirically derived data to make decisions about curriculum and instruction. This approach is a sound strategy for improving the quality of physical education programs for students at all levels. It provides hope for improvement in areas that have historically been tied to untested assumptions and hypotheses.

A fourth curriculum perspective that cuts across all of the above areas has generated interest in physical education and is called the "hidden" curriculum (Bain 1975). The hidden curriculum is all of the unplanned and unrecognized values that are imparted through the educational process. Often, teachers and administrators have not looked carefully at their behavior toward students, the policies and procedures used, and the decisions that were made on funds, activities, schedules, or personnel. Because they did not look carefully at these areas, discrepancies or inconsistencies exist between what teachers say and what they actually do. Their implicit (hidden) values are not consistent with their explicit philosophy.

A good example of this situation is a teacher purporting to develop positive attitudes in students toward physical activity but then forcing students to run laps or do push-ups for lack of effort or for failure to "dress out" properly. Other teachers develop such a dreadfully negative atmosphere with grading or overly critical instructional procedures that students do everything possible to escape or avoid the environment. The hidden curriculum of the school can contribute to the development of approach or avoidance tendencies (Mager 1968). Students are learning continually to like or dislike school and the process of learning. Efforts must be made to study and develop the hidden curriculum so that it can have a positive effect on what students learn.

Physical educators usually evaluate the contributions of the specific activities in the formal course of study. They may neglect to consider carefully such aspects of the aforementioned hidden curriculum as dress codes, showering policies, grading techniques, discipline procedures, instructional strategies, or teaching behaviors. Clearly, curriculum planners need to have information about and skills in all four of the curriculum perspectives. Ignoring any of these areas will have a significant negative impact on students.

For example, a teacher who does not look carefully at the effect of an imposed dress code may have some major problems with student participation. Grading procedures will have a powerful impact on students' attitudes toward physical education. A well-developed formal curriculum plan will be ineffective if low rates of academic learning time (ALT) are prevalent in classes. The absence of coeducational activities, lifetime sports, or dance activities deprives students of a well-balanced curriculum. A teacher's emphasis on winning certainly affects students when the losing team always runs an extra lap or performs some extra duty. Physical educators must consider carefully the four perspectives as policies, procedures, yearly plans, daily plans, and other aspects of dealing with students are formulated. Specific suggestions will be made throughout this text with respect to each of these four areas.

CURRICULUM AND INSTRUCTIONAL THEORY

A theory is a set of interrelated ideas or concepts that systematically explains a given subject. **Curriculum theories** provide a basis for making decisions about objectives, content, structure, sequence, and evaluation of the curriculum plan. A curriculum theory also provides a physical education curriculum planner with ideas about alternatives available for the selection and organization of content. The curriculum theory should predict the interrelationship between content and the instructional process (Bain 1978).

An **instructional theory** is different from a curriculum theory in that it focuses on the elements or components of the teaching-learning process. It is concerned with how the instructional components affect student learning. For example, instructional theory is concerned with methods of presenting material, practice time, information feedback, management time, and student motivation. Conversely, curriculum theory is concerned with what should be taught and why, rather than with how it should be taught. From a practical standpoint, however, curriculum theory cannot be separated from instructional theory. To the real-world teacher, a curriculum without instructional procedures is useless. Similarly, organized instructional procedures are without value when a curriculum is poor. This is why teachers must study curriculum and instruction together. We need to be prepared to develop skills in both areas. Often, one of the areas is neglected.

TRADITIONAL, ACTIVITY-CENTERED, OR MOVEMENT FORMS THEORY

By far the most common curriculum theory in use today at the secondary level is the activity-centered or movement forms approach. This is a traditional approach using units of physical activity, or movement forms, as the basic organizing center. These activities not only provide the content of the theory; they also provide the structure or format. The units may vary in length from one week to one year. The specific activities are culturally important forms of physical activity. The forms are usually classified in the following areas:

1. Team sports: basketball, softball, or soccer
2. Individual or lifetime sports: gymnastics, tennis, or Frisbee
3. Dance: folk, square, modern, or country swing
4. Physical conditioning activities: jogging, weight training, or aerobics
5. Recreational games: horseshoes, shuffleboard, or table tennis
6. Outdoor adventure activities: bicycling, skiing, or orienteering
7. Aquatics: swimming, skin diving, or water sports

The curriculum is usually arranged with a balance of activities from these categories. Activities are included on the basis of a number of practical factors such as student interest, teacher interest, class size, facilities, equipment, and climate. New activities or modified forms of old activities are added to the curriculum from time to time by an enterprising teacher who has picked up ideas from a professional journal or convention. Activities in a physical education curriculum generally follow the activity preferences of society, usually with a significant time lag. The arrival of the "new" activities in physical education curricula—activities reflecting the fitness renaissance, the wellness movement, the interest in outdoor adventure activities, and the Eastern influence in the martial arts and yoga—are thus indicative of the desires of the people whom the program serves.

Instruction in these activities proceeds from introductory lessons to advanced and specialized courses. Students are grouped by grade level rather than by ability or developmental level. In most situations, students proceed through a sequence of required physical activities in a year. An effective trend is the elective (or selective) format that allows students to choose activities in which they would like to participate. This format enhances the interest, enthusiasm, and motivational level of both students and teachers.

The use of activities or movement forms in this theory is based on the idea that they contribute to the goals of general education (i.e., developing the total person socially, emotionally, intellectually, and physically). The popular "education through the physical" philosophy emphasizes the use of physical activities to develop a person in the areas of physical fitness, motor abilities, mental abilities, and social abilities. Another current philosophy places emphasis on the intrinsic value of physical activities as a form of play (Siedentop 1980b). This theory advocates movement forms for the intrinsic meaning and satisfaction they provide people. Activities do not have to be justified on the basis of external values such as fitness or social development.

CONCEPTUAL THEORY

A curriculum theory that has gained popularity in many universities, colleges, high schools, and junior high schools focuses on developing physical fitness concepts for life (Corbin 1984). This approach to fitness places an instructional emphasis on lecture, laboratory experiments, and developing exercise programs for a lifetime of activity. One particular program (Corbin and Lindsey 1983) is organized around the following questions:

1. Why is physical activity important to every person?
2. How should physical activity take place?
3. What forms of physical activity are available?

Information and activities are provided on the following topics: Cardiovascular fitness, strength, endurance, flexibility, fat control, skill-related fitness, correct ways to exercise, and how to plan an exercise program.

Another conceptual approach to curriculum focuses on the components of human wellness (see Chapter 15). Wellness is viewed by many as an important state of health that is an ongoing process throughout life. It is a preventive approach to health and expands on the fitness concepts model. Students need information and skills that pertain to human wellness. Advocates of this theory point to the numerous health problems that abound in our society. A healthy life-style for all students is the major objective of this theory.

The wellness model is more comprehensive than the fitness concepts theory. Units of instruction in the wellness theory include stress management, alcohol and drug abuse, nutrition, weight control, physical fitness, coping skills, personal safety, environmental awareness, behavioral self-control, and problem-solving skills related to these specific topics.

Both approaches focus mainly on knowledge and understanding of physical fitness and wellness. The approach is more academic than the movement forms theory. Program advocates find the emphasis on knowledge an advantage and say that it adds credibility to the program. It is important to understand that an increase in time spent on lecture and analysis means a reduction in time spent performing physical skills. Students need information, but they also need successful encounters with physical activity, and that means time allotted for performing physical skills. Determining exactly how much time should be spent on knowledge acquisition and how much on physical skill development is difficult. The bottom line is getting students to incorporate physical activity into their lifestyle.

Most schools using a conceptual approach offer a balance of movement forms and knowledge concepts. The authors recommend several units on wellness activities (including fitness) to supplement or complement the secondary physical education curriculum (see Chapter 5). The secondary school curriculum should not focus exclusively on fitness, wellness, or movement, but should have objectives in all three areas.

MOVEMENT ANALYSIS THEORY

Curriculum applications of movement analysis theories have primarily affected elementary physical education, although some junior and senior high school programs have been influenced by Rudolf Laban's (1963) movement concepts of time, space, force, and flow. Curriculum content in this theory is included to illustrate movement elements and to give students experiences with them. The movement elements serve as the basic organizing center. The units focus on such elements as force, balance, striking, motion, stability, and leverage. These movement elements or concepts can be applied to many sport skills (Seidel et al. 1980).

This curriculum theory also emphasizes terminology, knowledge, and analytical abilities. Instructional emphasis includes indirect methods called problem solving or guided discovery. For example, students spend time analyzing various levels of movement for dribbling a basketball or playing defense in basketball. In racquetball, court position and relationships with opponents might be studied in a discovery approach. Again, as with the conceptual theory, when more time is spent on knowledge and analysis, less time may be available for developing physical skills. This is an important consideration for a curriculum planner.

MOTIVE OR PURPOSE THEORY

Jewett and Mullan (1977) have developed a purpose-process curriculum framework for physical education based on students' motives or purposes for participating in physical activity. The theory focuses on three major purposes that all people share: individual development, environmental coping, and social interaction. These three major purpose concepts are made up of 22 purpose elements, including circulorespiratory efficiency, catharsis, challenge, awareness, teamwork, competition, and leadership. The content of the curriculum provides experiences related to all of the purpose elements. This framework was designed to help teachers make curricular decisions based on a theoretical model.

The Basic Stuff Series (1981) sponsored by the AAHPERD is a compilation of knowledge from the subdisciplines of physical education into a format useful for physical education teachers. A booklet is available for each of the following areas: exercise physiology, humanities, kinesiology, motor development, motor learning, and psychosocial aspects of sport. The intent of the series is to promote the inclusion of disciplinary knowledge in physical education curricula, grades K–12. Part I of the series focuses on the knowledge concepts, and Part II provides learning experiences that teachers can use for teaching the concepts.

The Basic Stuff Series is discussed in this motive theory section because the concepts section in the series is arranged around student motives or purposes for participating in physical activity. The common student motives that are identified and discussed include: achievement (doing better), health (feeling good), appearance (looking good), social interaction (getting along), and coping with the environment (surviving). These motives or purposes can serve as an organizing center for a curriculum. A curriculum could offer a balance of activities from these areas, and students could select activities that best fit their perceived motives. Some secondary schools are using the disciplinary knowledge in conjunction with student motives. The Basic Stuff Series fits nicely with this model because it offers content from the various subdisciplines for each motive (Part I) and instructional activities for three age levels around each motive (Part II).

A curriculum that is based on a motives theory would have to devote time to discussing values, motives, and knowledge concepts. Again, these discussions may divert time from physical skill development. Weighing these areas of emphasis carefully is important because only a finite amount of time is available. If one area is emphasized, then another area may have to be reduced or eliminated. Knowledge concepts are important, but if the increased emphasis reduces the time available for physical skill development, then an important program objective may be slighted. Knowing about physical activity is *not* the same as experiencing physical activities. If students are to incorporate activities into their life-style, they need opportunities to experience success and to develop competency with various physical activities.

DEVELOPMENTAL LEVEL THEORY

Another popular curriculum theory is based on the idea that different physical activities and arrangements of physical activities should comprise the curriculum for students who are at various development stages. In other words, students should be involved in a different form or arrangement of physical activity depending on their physical, social, emotional, and intellectual development. Students are ready for or capable of activities or modifications of activities at certain levels of development. Curriculum planners must understand the characteristics, interests, and abilities of the students for whom the curriculum is being developed.

Primary grade programs using this model might emphasize basic skills in managing the body (balance, body parts, laterality), locomotor skills (walk, skip, run), nonlocomotor skills (bend, twist, reach), and manipulative skills (throw, catch, kick). Upper elementary and junior high students would continue with these skills plus the addition of specific sport skills (forehand, backhand, golf swing), modified games, and dance, all of which are introduced through short units of instruction and a wide variety of lead-up activities. High school programs would focus on more specialized physical skills, sport strategies, and knowledge such as corner kill shots, half-court zone traps, and measurement of percent body fat.

Junior high programs could be concerned with student characteristics such as the wide range of skeletal age, the adolescent growth spurt, short attention spans, and low tolerance for failure. Studies (Gruelich and Pyle 1959) have shown that a five to six year variation in skeletal age may be present in one grade level. Translated, this means that 11-year-olds in the 7th grade might vary in skeletal age from 8 to 14 years. Increased skeletal age usually correlates closely with success in the skilled positions in youth sport programs (Hale 1956). This has important implications because students are usually grouped by grade level with similar chronological ages together, yet students who are less mature physically are not ready for many specific sport skills or in-depth instruction. They should be channeled into multi-activity programs with short units and an emphasis on body management and basic movement skills. Students who are physically advanced should be encouraged to seek opportunities outside of the school program (e.g., youth sports, YMCA leagues, city park and recreation programs, and private clubs).

Senior high programs could be concerned with highly developed motor abilities, the increasing physical performance differences between boys and girls, longer attention spans, and the growing desire for independence. Opportunities for student choice, in-depth instruction, and advanced skill development can be important curriculum characteristics. High school students should not be forced into required activities in which they have no interest or ability. These students have narrowed their interests to a few selected activities. Grades 10–12 are a time to develop a high level of skill or to choose a new activity for in-depth development.

PRACTICAL IMPLICATIONS

In addition to understanding curriculum theories, another important aspect of curriculum construction is the careful analysis of the many practical factors that can affect the curriculum in a positive or negative manner. The specifics of each given situation, the people, the programs, and the facilities, will determine whether the factor is positive or negative. It is important for curriculum planners to think in positive terms, because negative or restrictive thinking will only hinder the development of a quality program. Negative factors can usually be changed and turned into positive factors as the curriculum develops, but people who think in restrictive terms will find this difficult.

PERSONAL PHILOSOPHY

The curriculum developer must have a sound philosophy of physical education. Careful consideration should be given to the following questions:

1. What is physical education?
2. What are the objectives of physical education?
3. What activities should be used to accomplish these objectives?
4. How should these activities be arranged and packaged?
5. What policies and procedures should be used as guidelines?

All physical educators should think carefully about these questions and should verbalize the answers to students, faculty, administrators, school board members, and community members. An existing curriculum cannot be changed or a new one developed without an organized philosophy of physical education. Oftentimes, physical educators have not organized their opinions about the curriculum. An undeveloped philosophy can be a restrictive factor in curriculum construction.

A personal philosophy can also be a restrictive factor when the person is afraid of change and will not expand his or her "comfort zone." Physical education curricula continue to evolve and change. New activities are slowly filtering into programs. Someone who clings to a philosophy that was developed years earlier is probably creating a curriculum that is developing escape or avoidance tendencies in students.

Physical educators should continually reevaluate their philosophy of physical education, and efforts should be made to bring the curriculum in line with that philosophy. A well-thought-out philosophy that is continually evolving for sound educational reasons is certainly a positive factor in curriculum construction.

PHYSICAL EDUCATION STAFF MEMBERS

It is important for each staff member to have a well-organized philosophy of physical education. All staff members should be involved in interpreting a sound philosophy to other interested and important people. Staff members do not have to follow the same philosophy, however, but they must show respect for the ideas of peers, especially in front of other people. A positive situation exists when staff members have developed and shared philosophies with fellow staff members. Compromises must be worked out privately when differences of opinion exist. Extremely different philosophies on a staff can create a restrictive situation.

Physical activity interests and abilities of the staff are important factors in curriculum development. A well-balanced curriculum demands a wide range of activity interests and abilities on the staff (i.e., dance, aquatics, wilderness activities, team sports, physical conditioning activities, and lifetime sports). In an elective-type curriculum, staff members can specialize in several activities. A specialist can greatly improve the quality of instruction in an activity.

An important factor in hiring staff members should be their teaching competencies and how these blend with the competencies of the rest of the staff. A positive situation exists when a staff has a wide variety of activity interests and abilities. It is also positive if staff members are willing to expand their teaching abilities through in-service training and additional course work.

The number of staff members is another important consideration in curriculum construction. If a choice needs to be made between staff and equipment, an increase in staff size is desirable. An additional teacher means reduced class sizes, more activity offerings, and an increase in student-teacher contact. If physical educators believe that their subject is as important as any other curriculum area, they should defend the concept of a teacher-student ratio in physical education equal to the ratio in math, science, or English classes.

THE SCHOOL ADMINISTRATION

The support of various school administrators can have a significant impact on the physical education curriculum. It is important for physical education teachers to interpret the goals of the program to administrators. Many administrators, like the general public, have misconceptions about physical education. Communication between the staff and the administration is therefore an important positive factor. In most cases, administrators will agree with and support the philosophy of the physical education staff if they perceive it to be built on sound educational principles.

The administration can help the physical education curriculum in the following areas:

1. Number of staff members and class size

2. Hiring staff members to fill specific departmental needs

3. Construction and development of facilities and teaching areas (e.g., racquetball courts, weight room, parcourse, or swimming pool)

4. Purchase of equipment and teaching aids (e.g., golf clubs, bowling sets, loop films, or jump ropes)

5. Support for innovative ideas or new activities (e.g., pilot unit on orienteering, an off-campus cross country skiing lesson, or a team-teaching presentation of a golf unit)

6. Maintenance and upkeep of existing teaching stations (e.g., watering the fields, cleaning the gymnasium, or repairing weight machines)

7. Support for staff development with in-service workshops, professional conferences, and current literature

8. Support in providing useful and meaningful feedback to teachers on their teaching performance (e.g., collecting data on management time, productive time, active learning time, or behavior patterns)

Physical educators need to make an active effort to gain the support of the school administrators. This support can yield many positive dividends over a period of time, since administrators have the power to influence and implement various situations.

THE COMMUNITY: PEOPLE AND CLIMATE

The people in the community surrounding the school are an important factor for consideration. Physical educators should become familiar with the types of people prevalent in the community. Occupations, religions, educational levels, cultural values, and physical activity habits are just a few of the factors that can affect curriculum development. Parents have a strong influence on the activity interests and habits of their children. By secondary school age, students have acquired specific habits that the physical education department must be aware of as they develop a program. The people in a suburban, upper-class community are going to be quite different from those in an urban, inner-city community. Students from these communities will also be different because of parents and various learning experiences. Both situations have pros and cons, and physical educators need to be aware of these.

The geographic location and the climate of the area are important factors to be considered. The terrain of the mountains, deserts, or plains combined with weather conditions particular to each area have an effect on the activity interests of people. Extremely hot or cold climates markedly influence what activities can be arranged in the curriculum and at what time of the year they should be scheduled. Cross country skiing, bicycling, and outdoor swimming are examples of such activities. In addition, the climate plays a role in the way that an activity is taught. For example, outdoor jogging during midday in September in central Arizona is next to impossible because of the extreme heat. Plans and alternatives for rainy and cold climates must also be developed by curriculum planners.

The interests of people and the climate of the community can be used as positive factors in curriculum development. The initial core of activity offerings can be built around currently popular activities. There is a high probability that students will have an interest in these activities and will be motivated to participate and learn. Teachers should use these high-probability activities or events to create a positive, successful atmosphere so that students develop a backlog of success. This is helpful when the teacher then attempts low-probability events or activities that may not be initially interesting or motivating (e.g., exercising or jogging). The climate and weather can be used positively by offering interesting units that require the snow, ice, desert, or wooded areas. The nearby community may have a number of desirable teaching environments such as a bowling alley, golf course, or ski slope. Physical educators should think positively about the community and the climate.

Little can be done to change the climate, but influencing and changing the people of the community may be possible. Many citizens have misconceptions about physical education and physical activity in general. There are many ways to help educate the public and gain citizens' support. Chapter 14 discusses procedures for enhancing public relations.

FACILITIES AND EQUIPMENT

The available teaching facilities will dictate, in part, the activities that can be offered in the curriculum. Facilities include the on-campus areas as well as off-campus areas in the neighboring community. On-campus facilities are areas such as the gymnasium, wrestling room, weight room, tennis courts, field space, and hallways. Off-campus facilities might be a golf driving range, a horseback riding stable, a sailing pond, a stream for canoeing, a community swimming pool, or a hiking trail in a nearby park. Equipment includes materials such as bats, balls, tennis racquets, badminton birds, jump ropes, and records. Equipment is usually defined as the materials used on or with a teaching facility.

Teachers should look continually for ways to improve and expand existing facilities and equipment. On-campus facilities can be increased by using a foyer area for aerobic dance, adapting an old storage area for golf, or expanding a locker room into a weight room. A creative look at existing facilities may provide new teaching areas.

Off-campus facilities can open a new world of teaching environments. Many areas may be close by, within walking distance, while others require some type of transportation. The school may be able to provide a bus or special funds may be raised for transportation. Many schools are now bussing students to nearby bowling alleys, ski slopes, and hiking areas. When off-school facilities are used, school officials should be asked to look into the legal liability aspects of each situation.

Equipment can be added with departmental funds or with special funds raised by students for physical education. Some types of equipment can be made by school maintenance departments or by students as industrial arts projects. Safety factors should be checked carefully in all cases. In some units, students can bring equipment from home, such as tennis racquets, racquetballs, or bicycles. Curriculum planners need to be creative and to consider every possibility for expanding the equipment and facilities in their situation.

LAWS AND REQUIREMENTS

The laws, regulations, and requirements at the national, state, and local levels are another factor demanding consideration. Physical educators must understand these regulations in order to develop programs that comply with the laws. Educators should also remember, however, that these laws and regulations were developed by people and are subject to change. People can modify laws if the legislation is not helping programs achieve their objectives. Appropriate procedures are available to change laws and government regulations, and educators must become actively involved in the change process when change is necessary.

At the national level, Title IX of the Educational Amendments Act of 1972 and Public Law 94-142 have had a significant impact on curriculum in physical education. Specifics of these laws, as dis-

cussed in Chapter 2, are still being debated and interpreted differently by school districts, state departments of education, and the judicial system. Physical educators need to evaluate these laws carefully and then develop curricula that are in compliance.

Each state department of education has regulations and guidelines governing the physical education requirements for that particular state. The local school district then develops guidelines within the framework of the state requirements.

SCHOOL SCHEDULE

The schedule or organizational pattern of the school will have an impact on curriculum development. Schedules are of two basic types: the block or traditional schedule and the flexible schedule.

The block or traditional plan (Figure 3.1) divides the school day into five or six equal time blocks or periods. Each class, such as math, science, or physical education, meets for the same length of time on each day of the school week. The advantages of the traditional schedule are that it is easier to set up, more economical, and easier to administer. Students are in the same class at the same time each day. This provides students and administrators with a stable routine.

Flexible schedules (Figure 3.2) provide a varying length of time for classes depending on the nature of the subject matter and the type of instruction given. A biology lecture might meet three days a week for 45 min, while a laboratory for biology would meet for 1.5 hr. A flexible schedule might allow physical education students to travel to a local ski slope and meet for a 3-hr block of time one day a week. The length of each class varies daily for each subject matter area.

Schools use different types of flexible schedules, which are set up to meet the needs of the people involved. In physical education, a flexible schedule can provide time for travel off campus, the option of grouping students for different types of instruction (large or small groups), or the use of limited and specific types of equipment. Some administrators and teachers complain about the "dead spots" of time in a flexible schedule. Students may have a 15 min spot of free time between classes, which causes concern because they need a place to go and may abuse the use of the free time. Many schools have provided a "commons" area where students can gather during these free intervals.

Period	Time	Monday	Tuesday	Wednesday	Thursday	Friday
Homeroom	8:00–8:15					⟶
1	8:15–9:10	General math				⟶
2	9:15–10:10	English				⟶
3	10:15–11:10	Biology				⟶
Lunch	11:15–11:45					⟶
Study hall	11:45–12:15					⟶
4	12:15–1:10	Physical education				⟶
5	1:15–2:10	History				⟶
6	2:15–3:10	Home economics				⟶

Figure 3.1.   Block or traditional schedule

The advantages of the flexible schedule would seem to enhance the physical education curriculum. The problems created can be managed by careful planning and the joint efforts of teachers and administrators. Physical education can add off-campus activities (e.g., golf, bowling) and improve the quality of instruction with an organized flexible schedule. A traditional block schedule limits physical education to a 45–60 min daily period, including time required for changing clothes. This obviously hinders many possibilities for activities and instructional methods.

BUDGET AND FUNDING

The budget and funding procedures commonly differ from school district to school district. Usually, the physical education department head is involved with developing and submitting the budget. It is therefore important for him or her to understand the funding procedures and to carefully plan an aggressive strategy for obtaining a fair share of the school's budget. Many times administrators have misconceptions about class size and amounts of equipment that physical educators need to develop an effective program. Physical educators should seek parity with other school departments in terms of class size and equipment. Students cannot learn to read and write without materials and supplies, and they cannot learn physical skills without the necessary equipment.

The department's budget is usually focused on equipment and supplies. Funds for personnel and facilities come from a larger, total-school budget. Physical educators need to understand the overall school budget and funding procedures, because personnel, facilities, and equipment are important factors in curriculum construction. The highest budget priority should always be additional personnel before new facilities or equipment. (Priorities and procedures for ordering equipment are discussed in Chapter 6.)

In addition to the basic departmental budget, funds may be available through outside sources. Sometimes the athletic department will share equipment with the physical education department. Boundary cones, jump ropes, and basketballs, for example, can be used by both departments. With tight budgets, this is an effective way to cut costs. Various community and parent groups like the Lions or Rotary Club may help with short-term funding for special facility or equipment needs such as a weight room, racquetball courts, or tennis racquets. Some schools allow departments to have special fund-raising campaigns involving the students and faculty. Car washes, candy sales, or admission to special sports demonstrations are useful projects for generating funds.

The best programs are not necessarily the ones with the most funding, but a certain amount of funding is certainly useful in producing a high-quality curriculum. All possible options for funding should be considered, and educators must be aggressive in their search for adequate funding.

Module	Time	Monday	Tuesday	Wednesday	Thursday	Friday
1	8:00–8:15	English	Industrial arts lab	English	Biology lab	English
2	8:15–8:30	English	Industrial arts lab	English	Biology lab	English
3	8:30–8:45	English	Industrial arts lab	English	Biology lab	English
4	8:45–9:00	General math	Industrial arts lab	General math	Biology lab	General math
5	9:00–9:15	General math	Industrial arts lab	General math	Biology lab	General math
6	9:15–9:30	General math	Industrial arts lab	General math	Biology lab	General math
7	9:30–9:45	Biology lecture	Industrial arts	Biology lecture	Industrial arts	Open
8	9:45–10:00	Biology lecture	Industrial arts	Biology lecture	Industrial arts	Open
9	10:00–10:15	Biology lecture	Industrial arts	Biology lecture	Industrial arts	Open
10	10:15–10:30	History	Typing	History	Typing	History
11	10:30–10:45	History	Typing	History	Typing	History
12	10:45–11:00	History	Typing	History	Typing	History
13	11:00–11:15	Open	Typing	Open	Typing	Open
14	11:15–11:30	Lunch	Lunch	Lunch	Lunch	Lunch
15	11:30–11:45	Lunch	Lunch	Lunch	Lunch	Lunch
16	11:45–12:00	Physical education	Open	Physical education	English lab	Physical education
17	12:00–12:15	Physical education	Open	Physical education	English lab	Physical education
18	12:15–12:30	Physical education	Open	Physical education	English lab	Physical education
19	12:30–12:45	Physical education	Open	Physical education	English lab	Physical education
20	12:45–1:00	Physical education	Open	Physical education	English lab	Physical education
21	1:00–1:15	Physical education	Open	Physical education	English lab	Physical education
22	1:15–1:30	Typing lab	Open	Open	Open	Open
23	1:30–1:45	Typing lab	Open	Open	Open	Open
24	1:45–2:00	Typing lab	General math lab	Open	History lab	Physical education
25	2:00–2:15	Typing lab	General math lab	Open	History lab	Physical education
26	2:15–2:30	Typing lab	General math lab	Open	History lab	Physical education
27	2:30–2:45	Typing lab	General math lab	Open	History lab	Physical education
28	2:45–3:00	Open	General math lab	Open	History lab	Physical education
29	3:00–3:15	Open	General math lab	Open	History lab	Physical education

Figure 3.2. Flexible schedule

ATHLETICS, INTRAMURALS, AND SPORT CLUBS

Many people talk about how these three programs should be an extension of the basic physical education curriculum. The programs can serve a valuable function by offering additional opportunities for students to participate in physical activities and develop positive activity habits. All students should be able to find success in one or several of these programs. The programs give students a variety of experiences, depending on the specific situation (i.e., winning, losing, teamwork, friendship, deferred goals, perseverance, and dedication). The experience depends in part on how each program is developed and emphasized.

Physical educators should be aware that the availability, leadership, and emphasis of these three programs can have a significant positive or negative impact on the physical education curriculum. Many schools use the physical education curriculum as training for the athletic program. In many situations, athletes lift weights year round and receive physical education credit for athletic program participation. These students become highly specialized and do not have an opportunity to learn any lifetime sport skills. The educator must remember that the goals of the athletic program are usually different from the goals of the physical education program. Community pressure can be extremely powerful in influencing the athletic program. Physical educators need to take leadership roles in all three programs and make sure that proper goals are stressed and protected.

All three programs can be used to develop interest and enthusiasm for the physical education curriculum. Efforts should be made to coordinate offerings in the curriculum with offerings from athletics, intramurals, and sport clubs. A student taking a basic junior high basketball class may decide to play intramural basketball or to try out for the freshman team. A student in the school ski club may elect to take skiing in the physical education curriculum. A student playing intramural tennis may improve enough to make the varsity tennis team. Equipment and facilities can be bought, developed, and shared by all four groups. These programs can complement each other in a number of ways if a cooperative effort is made by program leaders. Physical educators should use their experience and knowledge of these programs to help develop other leaders from the school and community. With help and training, a math or science teacher can direct the intramural program or organize a sailing club for students, or a parent from the community might work with a teacher in organizing a backpacking or fishing club.

ELEMENTARY SCHOOL PHYSICAL EDUCATION

A sound secondary physical education program should be built on the foundation of the elementary school physical education curriculum. Many school districts do not have adequate communication between elementary and secondary program organizers. Each section simply "does its own thing" without regard for other grades. Secondary curriculum planners should understand the elementary school program goals, activities, and teaching procedures. The transition from elementary to secondary programs will be smoother if learning activities and teaching procedures progress with continuity.

The daily format of the junior high program can be similar to the elementary school format with an introductory activity, a fitness activity, and a lesson focus. Students can learn about continuity drills, management procedures, and sideline soccer in the elementary school and then follow through with similar activities in the junior high program. Drills and skill work for basketball at the senior high level can be built on the junior high drills and skill work. Physical fitness activities such as circuit drills, exercises to music, and squad leader exercises can be used at all three levels (elementary through secondary) with a few modifications. Similar teaching styles, methods, and behaviors are used advantageously at various times for all levels (e.g., station work, contracts, or teacher-leader activities).

A well-organized and educationally sound elementary curriculum that is linked with a similar secondary physical education curriculum is certainly a positive situation for students and teachers. Many advantages are possible in terms of time management, learning progressions, staff motivation, student motivation, equipment purchasing, and idea sharing. An articulated physical education curriculum, kindergarten through grade 12, has long been needed and can offer a number of interesting advantages.

Summary

The curriculum is the what and why of education as opposed to the how, which is instruction. The curriculum contains the scope, structure, and sequence of learning activities within each year.

Progression is provided horizontally (throughout the year) and vertically (throughout all grades).

A curriculum theory is a set of interrelated ideas that provide a basis for making decisions about objectives, content, sequence, and evaluation. The curriculum is usually arranged around one major theme or theory called an organizing center. The most common organizing center for secondary physical education is movement forms, or activity-centered theory. Units focus on team sports, lifetime sports, aquatics, dance, physical conditioning, recreational games, and outdoor adventure.

Many practical factors influence the type of curriculum that can be developed in each situation. These factors must be carefully analyzed with the attitude that restrictive practical factors can be turned into positive factors over a period of time.

References

Bain, L. 1975. The hidden curriculum in physical education. *Quest* 24: 92–101.

Bain, L. 1978. Status of curriculum theory in physical education. *JOPERD* 49(3): 25–26.

Basic Stuff Series I and II. Reston, VA: AAHPERD, 1981.

Berliner, D. Tempus educare. In *Research on Teaching,* edited by P. Peterson and H. Walberg. Berkeley, CA: McCutchan Publishing, 1979.

Corbin, C. Teaching fitness for life: A status report. Paper presented at the National AAHPERD Convention, Anaheim, CA, 1984.

Corbin, C., and Lindsey, R. *Fitness for Life.* 2nd ed. Glenview, IL: Scott, Foresman & Company, 1983.

Gruelich, W., and Pyle, S. *Radiographic Atlas of Skeletal Development of the Hand and Wrist.* 2nd ed. Stanford, CA: Stanford University Press, 1959.

Hale, C. 1956. Physiological maturity of little league baseball players. *Research Quarterly* 27(3): 276–284.

Jewett, A., and Mullan, M. *Curriculum Design: Purposes and Processes in Physical Education Teaching-Learning.* Reston, VA: AAHPERD, 1977.

Laban, R. *Modern Educational Dance.* 2nd ed., revised by L. Ullman. New York: Praeger Publishers, 1963.

Mager, R. *Developing Attitude Toward Learning.* Belmont, CA: Fearon Publishers, 1968.

Metzler, M. The measurement of academic learning time in physical education. Doctoral dissertation, The Ohio State University, 1979.

Metzler, M. An intervention strategy to increase ALT-PE(M) in archery. Paper presented at the National AAHPERD Convention, Boston, April 1981.

Seidel, B., et al. *Sports Skills. A Conceptual Approach to Meaningful Movement.* 2nd ed. Dubuque, IA: Wm. C. Brown Group, 1980.

Siedentop, D. 1980(a). Physical education curriculum: An analysis of the past. *JOPERD* 51(7): 40–41.

Siedentop, D. *Physical Education—Introductory Analysis.* 3rd ed. Dubuque, IA: Wm. C. Brown Group, 1980(b).

Chapter 4

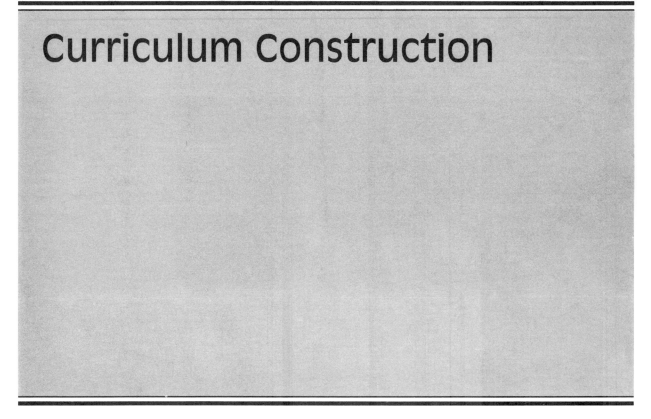

Curriculum Construction

A curriculum should be developed by following a number of basic steps in a sequential order. These basic steps should follow the analysis of current curriculum theory and the various practical factors influencing curriculum. Curriculum theory and the ideas of experts in this area can provide a solid basis for a program. Physical educators sometimes lose sight of what physical education should be in the school setting and fail to develop a strong, solid base of support for program enhancement.

DESIRES OF SOCIETY

Years ago, when people banded together and decided to set aside land and build schools, they did so because they wanted their children to acquire certain information, attitudes, and skills in a systematic manner from a trained specialist. These people had certain ambitions for their youth. Even though society has changed dramatically since that time and much new information has been discovered, people still have a number of desires that they want passed on to the next generation. Many of

these desires have direct implications for curriculum construction in physical education. The first step for curriculum planners is to analyze the desires of society.

DESIRE TO BE PHYSICALLY FIT, HEALTHY, AND ATTRACTIVE

This desire is especially important to physical educators because of the contribution that physical activity can make in these areas. That activity aids in achieving weight control, cardiovascular efficiency, flexibility, and strength is well documented. The public is aware of the humiliation and problems that individuals face throughout life if they are obese, weak, or unattractive. Physically fit people feel positive and successful and portray a positive image to others. These successes add up to a positive self-concept. In contrast, obese people often have great difficulty with simple daily activities such as dressing, sitting down, or walking. They may have a negative self-image, and often cannot participate in or enjoy many activities.

DESIRE TO PLAY

Play has been much discussed as an important behavior that permeates all cultures in a variety of forms. Sports, dance, and various types of physical activity are serious forms of play. Many other forms of play, including music, drama, and art, are also important in society. Indeed, play is as important to most people as work, and an enjoyable play life is as valuable as a productive work life. In fact, to many, play is the most important aspect of their life. It is what they would call "paradise" or "the good life." They look forward to a round of golf, a jog along a canal, or a backpacking trip in the mountains. Physical education can make a significant contribution to this universal desire to play.

DESIRE FOR KNOWLEDGE

The human race continues to search for knowledge in all areas. People are curious about the world around them. Physical education has an extensive body of knowledge that contains various subfields. These are exercise physiology, kinesiology, motor learning, history of sport, philosophy of sport, sport psychology, and sport sociology. Many opportunities and areas of physical education are available to satisfy this desire for information.

DESIRE FOR SUCCESS, APPROVAL, AND SATISFACTION

People tend to repeat those activities that provide them with some type of success. They also tend to avoid those activities in which they are not successful. Various types of success usually lead to recognition, approval, or self-satisfaction. People participate in activities in which they are successful because feelings of success lead to satisfaction and happiness. Physical activities are in this category and thus make a significant contribution to people's lives.

DESIRE FOR SOCIAL AND EMOTIONAL COMPETENCE

Most people are concerned about how other people feel about them. People want others to accept, respect, and like them. Adults want their children to develop acceptable social and emotional skills so that they can enjoy life. Schools are the major social agency in our culture. Information is imparted in the school setting regarding dating, mental health, sex education, nutrition, driver education, and many other important areas. Physical education offers unique opportunities in this social-emotional area because of the nature and arrangement of its subject matter. Competitive situations involving winning, losing, and accepting referee decisions, and coeducational activities with emphasis on movement skills provide a rich source of social and emotional experiences for youth. Physical education teachers can have a tremendous impact on students in this area.

DESIRE TO COMPETE

Most societies are competitive in nature. Indeed, competition is present in almost all aspects of our culture. People learn to compete at an early age, and many employers believe that the best competitors are the most successful workers in the business world. Adults want their children to be competitors and winners. In many youth sport leagues, children are forced at an early age to compete for league championships, trophies, and adult approval. In bicycle motocross racing, 5-year-old children in beginning, novice, and expert classes race around a track in pursuit of victories, trophies, and points that may bring them a funding sponsor so they can travel across the country to more races. Some people believe that this early competitive experience is beneficial for youngsters, but others seriously question these practices. Regardless of the stand taken, the fact is that most societies are competitive. The competitive nature of sports and physical activity requires physical educators to have a stand on competition. Physical education programs can have a strong influence on youth and their ability to compete.

DESIRE FOR RISK, ADVENTURE, AND EXCITEMENT

Perhaps because of increased urbanization, mechanization, and impersonal, fast-paced lifestyles, many people are turning to high-risk, adventurous activities for fun (Darst and Armstrong 1980). This desire might also explain why many people use drugs and alcohol for excitement and escape from reality. Physical activities such as rock climbing, skiing, white water canoeing, and backpacking are increasing in popularity and give people an opportunity to do something new, risky, and exciting. The physical education curriculum can provide many experiences to satisfy this desire.

DESIRE FOR RHYTHMIC EXPRESSION

Most people enjoy listening to and moving to rhythmic sounds. Many forms of rhythmic activity have been popular in a wide variety of cultures throughout history. Rhythms can be both enjoyable and motivational. A variety of rhythmic activities is an important part of a physical education curriculum.

DESIRE FOR CREATIVE EXPRESSION

People are looking for ways to express their autonomy and individuality. Clothes and hair styles have been especially popular as a means for people to show who or what they are to the world. The manner in which people play and use their leisure time is another opportunity for self-expression. The work world usually puts so many limits on individuality that people channel their creative and individual desires into play or leisure pursuits. Physical activities provide numerous possibilities for creative outlets structured by the rules that govern the activities. In basketball, students enjoy attempting Daryl Dawkins-type slam dunks or Larry Bird-type passes and assists. In gymnastics, the opportunity to develop a creative routine to music or to perfect new moves may be challenging. New plays and defenses are always being created in football. The challenges are unlimited, and the opportunities for creative expression appeal to students. Physical education curricula should be planned carefully to help satisfy this desire.

OBJECTIVES OF PHYSICAL EDUCATION

The objectives for an educational program should evolve from the desires of the people whom the program serves. Objectives should be formulated with the desires of both the public and the physical education professionals in mind. In other words, a program based only on the desires of the public sector may not be educationally sound. The knowledge and understanding of trained professionals must be considered.

Formulating objectives is the second step in curriculum construction. Objectives are goals to be reached by the students in a program. They provide a clear description of behaviors to be achieved. Objectives also provide focus and direction for the program. They should be written in terms of student behavior, and should focus on what skills, knowledges, and attitudes students will possess when they finish various activities and units.

Objectives can be written in general terms or in specific behavioral or performance terms. A general objective would be: The student will be physically fit, or the student will have volleyball skills. A specific behavioral or performance objective might be: The student will run 1.5 mi in 12 min, or the student will do 35 push-ups in 1 min. Overall curriculum objectives should be written in general terms, but unit plans and daily lesson plans should use specific objectives with precise behavioral definitions. The sum of all of the daily lesson objectives should equal all of the objectives for one unit. The sum of all of the unit objectives should equal the total curricular objectives. The sum of the curricular objectives from each academic area should equal the objectives of the total school curriculum.

The following are examples of general objectives that could be used as overall curriculum objectives:

1. The students will incorporate physical activity into their life-style.
2. The students will display a positive attitude toward physical activity.
3. The students will maintain an appropriate level of health-related physical fitness.
4. The students will develop their physical skill level.
5. The students will acquire knowledge about sports, games, dance, exercise, and fitness.
6. The students will develop social and emotional skills that will enable them to be responsible citizens.
7. The students will feel good about their physical self.

These are general objectives that can be used in curriculum construction. Specific behavioral or performance objectives that are useful for lesson and unit plans will be discussed in the planning and teaching strategies chapters (Chapters 7 and 9). For review of the general objectives of physical education, refer to Chapter 1.

CHARACTERISTICS AND GENERAL INTERESTS OF STUDENTS

The next step in curriculum construction is to take a close look at the developmental level, the characteristics, and the interests of students for whom the curriculum is being designed.

A cynical teacher once said, "Teaching would be a good job if it weren't for all those students." Without students, there would be no need for teachers, teaching strategies, or curriculum. Students are the most important factor to consider when developing a physical education curriculum. They are our basic resource, and teachers must keep this in mind at all times. Potential teachers should spend time with students to learn about their interests, characteristics, and abilities. This can be accomplished by reading information, by talking with students and parents, and by formally collecting data with different types of instruments.

Student characteristics are those typical or distinctive features that represent a given developmental or age level. As students grow and develop, certain characteristics appear and disappear. Within a specific age range, most of the students will exhibit similar characteristics. There will always be extreme ends of the normal curve regarding developmental levels. Students will vary in height, weight, social abilities, and in many other areas at each chronological age.

Developmental characteristics are usually examined by chronological age level. The problem with this approach is that four or five different developmental age levels may exist within a given chronological age range (i.e., the 7th grade may have students with developmental ages from 10 to 14 years). Most schools, however, group students by chronological age rather than developmental level because of administrative ease. Physical education teachers must be aware of the wide range of developmental ages that can exist at a given grade level. These developmental differences will affect physical abilities and performance in physical activities.

Student characteristics can be categorized as physical, social, emotional, and intellectual. Curriculum planners need to consider carefully all four of these areas, because physical education programs can contribute to all four areas. Some physical educators believe mistakenly that their program contributes only to the physical area, but physical activities do not occur in a learning vacuum. Students are also involved mentally, socially, and emotionally, and physical education thus makes a unique contribution to all four areas.

The developmental characteristics of students are a key factor in the design of a curriculum. Social, emotional, physical, and intellectual characteristics are important variables in determining the types of activities, the length of units, the amount of student choice, and the content to be emphasized.

The characteristics of junior high school students are different from those of senior high students, and these developmental levels need to be considered as separate entities. It is difficult to sort out characteristics by each of the four categories. In discussing first the junior high and then the senior high school students, the authors will therefore present two sections, one dealing with the physical area and the other dealing with a combination of the social, emotional, and intellectual areas.

PHYSICAL AREA—JUNIOR HIGH STUDENTS, AGES 11–14

The following physical characteristics should be considered carefully when planning curriculum for the junior high level:

1. Students go through a rapid and uneven growth spurt.
2. Girls go through this spurt about 1.5 years earlier than boys.
3. Girls are usually taller and more physically mature early in this period. Once boys experience the growth spurt, they pass girls in height and weight.
4. Awkwardness, poor coordination, low strength, and low endurance are common during rapid growth spurts.
5. Students usually need more sleep during a growth spurt.
6. An increase in appetite occurs.
7. Posture is often poor due to social pressure.
8. Ossification of the bones is usually not complete.
9. A wide range of physical maturity exists.
10. Students go through puberty and develop secondary sexual characteristics. Boys experience facial hair, pubic hair, a voice change, genital and shoulder development. Girls develop breasts, pubic hair, a widening of the hips, and an accumulation of body fat.
11. Motor abilities are developing slowly due to the increase in growth velocity.
12. The range of motor ability broadens, and the skill level differences of students become increasingly apparent.
13. Boys are stronger and may have more endurance than girls.

14. Many girls have an advantage over boys in the areas of balance and flexibility.

SOCIAL, EMOTIONAL, AND INTELLECTUAL AREAS—JUNIOR HIGH STUDENTS

Because physical education also involves other areas besides the physical, curriculum planners for the junior high level should keep in mind these characteristics of youngsters ages 11–14:

1. Students have a strong desire for independence. They believe that adults (authority figures) are old-fashioned and out-of-date. A desire to make decisions for themselves exists in most cases.
2. Students are torn between adult and peer values.
3. Moods change quickly, for this is an emotional and unpredictable period. Students may be unstable, angry, fearful, and easily upset.
4. Fighting with parents and peers is common at this age, as is competitiveness.
5. Peer groups provide the standards for behavior. The peer group represents independence because of the absence of adults. Leaders, followers, and loyalty start to evolve from group dynamics.
6. Students are interested in improving themselves, especially in the physical area. Weight training, body building, and figure control or development are of special interest.
7. Strong concerns about size and abilities are common. Grooming, clothes, and appearance become important. Students are self-conscious about their bodies.
8. Interest in the opposite sex begins in this age range. Many students try to impress the opposite sex in various ways. Girls are usually ahead of boys socially and may begin to date older boys.
9. Social activities are becoming important, and dances, movies, parties, and athletic events become social meeting places.
10. Intellectual development continues throughout this period. Students can concentrate longer, are able to understand more complex concepts, and are better able to follow directions. An interest in the "why" of physical activity occurs. Daydreaming and fantasizing are lessening for many students.
11. The variety of student activities decreases continually throughout this period and into adulthood. Students are beginning to make decisions about areas in which they want to specialize. This has strong implications for future sport and physical activity participation.
12. Students have often lived in several places and have traveled to many areas.
13. A strong interest in risk, excitement, and adventure is common.

In summary, this is a challenging and difficult period for students. They are confused by their changing physical appearance and the transition process from childhood to adulthood. Many important decisions are being made about their careers and goals for life. For physical education teachers, the situation is extremely challenging, and can be quite frustrating and demanding as well as rewarding. Physical education can play a significant role in these students' lives.

PHYSICAL AREA—SENIOR HIGH SCHOOL STUDENTS, AGES 15–18

The following are physical characteristics of senior high school students that need to be considered if the curriculum is to enhance the students' physical development:

1. Increases occur in motor abilities, coordination, strength, endurance, and speed. Boys surpass girls in these areas.
2. Boys surpass girls in height and weight. Sexual characteristics reach maturity in both boys and girls.
3. Boys continue to develop muscularly. Bone growth and the ossification process are usually complete.
4. By the end of this period, most students are physically mature. It is a good time to develop motor abilities.
5. Students continue to have large appetites.

SOCIAL, EMOTIONAL, AND INTELLECTUAL AREAS—SENIOR HIGH SCHOOL, AGES 15–18

High school students continue to change and develop in these areas. The following are characteristics common to this age group:

1. The peer group and its activities are a dominant factor in students' lives.

2. Social activities continue to be important and expand outside the home and school.

3. Dating, going steady, marriage, and careers dominate the activities and interests of this period.

4. Students are still critical of adults, teachers, and other authority figures. The conflict continues between peer and adult values.

5. Competition increases with grades, athletics, and dating.

6. Students are still very emotional, even though many have made adjustments to their new bodies and the nature of school. Senior high students are usually better adjusted and happier than the junior high school youngsters.

7. Students continue to be concerned about their appearance and abilities. They are interested in ways to improve themselves and impress the opposite sex.

8. Students are approaching their full intellectual potential. Their memory, ability to reason, ability to concentrate, and imagination are improving and developing. They have more experience and knowledge on which to base decisions.

9. Strong concerns about security, attention, and affection exist for most students. Divorce, single-parent families, multiple moves, and changing American values have had an impact on young people by the time they reach this period.

10. This group is looking for risk, excitement, and adventure. Teenagers' preoccupations with drugs and adventure activities probably stem from this desire.

11. The continued narrowing of interests and the development of specializations are important factors in physical education curriculum development. Students need an opportunity to express their independence by choosing specialized, in-depth activity classes. They should not be forced into activities in which they are not interested.

The senior high school years are important in transforming adolescents into adults. Students must face the realities of the world and make decisions about education, careers, marriage, religion, politics, and life-styles. Teachers have a valuable responsibility for imparting information, attitudes, and skills, and physical educators certainly have a challenging task.

PHYSICAL ACTIVITY INTERESTS OF STUDENTS

Historically, the physical activity interests of people have strongly influenced physical education curriculum. As the interests of people changed, programs have evolved from an early fitness-oriented model to a team sports approach and, finally, to an emphasis on individual lifetime activities. Currently popular activities, such as aerobic dance, outdoor adventure activities, distance running, and the martial arts, are slowly filtering into school physical education curricula because people are interested in these activities and the activities fulfill program objectives.

The general activity interests of society and the specific interests of students in a secondary school are important factors in curriculum construction. A curriculum formulated without concern for the interests of students will probably not accomplish its objectives or help a teacher to develop positive student attitudes. In addition to popular new activities, various communities will generate a special interest in areas such as golf, tennis, or sailing, while others may focus more on basketball, baseball, or football. The geographic location, the economic situation, and the background of the community members will all have an impact on the activity interests of students, and these activity interests are important in helping an educator decide which units to offer in the curriculum.

Program planners should continually examine student interests and the types of activities that are being offered. Too often, programs are based on the activity interests of teachers, administrators, and parents, rather than students. In particular, many teachers will not teach activities in which they are not skilled. This activity comfort zone is too narrow to accomplish program goals and results in a program based on the interests of the physical education teachers rather than on the students' interests. This is why many students develop escape or avoidance behaviors in physical education. They actually like physical activity, but they do not like the activities being taught or the way that they are being taught. Teachers need to expand their teaching repertoire of activities and methods to include students' interests.

In a selective-elective curriculum, schools have mistakenly offered activity units that educators presumed would be popular with students. In reality, the students were not interested and did not sign up. Problems with scheduling, facilities, and teaching assignments then result. For example, an inner-city school tried offering three-week units on golf, bowling, and archery in an elective curriculum. In each section, only one to five students registered for the units. The classes were cancelled and different activities offered to fill up the classes. Clearly, the students were not interested in these activities.

In another example at a high school (Wilson and Altieri 1978), a survey of seniors helped to determine that students were not returning to physical education after the required freshman year because the curriculum did not provide any choice of specific units. All of the units were required by all students if they chose to take an optional year of physical education. Many students were avoiding the entire year because they did not wish to take one or two of the three-week units. In other words, students would avoid an entire year because of one or two compulsory activities. Not all students reacted to the same activity; some were not interested in wrestling, while others disliked swimming or gymnastics. Eventually, school officials developed a program in which students had four or five activity choices. Students could then select activities that interested them. As a result of the new curriculum approach, student enrollment showed a large increase. Grades 10–12 are *not* the time to force students into activities in which they have little or no interest.

The Utah State Office of Education conducted a survey of high school students' interests in physical activity (Lindeman et al. 1981). The sample included 1834 students from 15 high schools in the Salt Lake City area. Most of the students were in the 11th and 12th grades with an equal distribution of boys and girls. One of the survey questions asked, "Which physical activities would you be most interested in taking as a physical education class?" The top ten selected activities are as follows:[1]

1. Outdoor survival—68.9%
2. Body conditioning, figure control—67.6%
3. Jogging, running—62.9%
4. Martial arts—57.3%
5. Weight training—53.8%
6. Lifesaving, water safety—47.8%
7. Racquetball—47%
8. Recreational games—46.7%

9. Tennis—46.4%
10. Cycling—45.3%

A traditional team sport did not appear until number 15 on the list. These top ten interests in the Utah survey seem to reflect society's general interests in the wellness movement, outdoor adventure activities, and the martial arts. Many physical educators, however, believe that students are interested primarily in team sports like football, basketball, and baseball. These educators may be expressing their personal interests and misrepresenting the interests of students.

DETERMINING STUDENT INTERESTS

Many schools are beginning to use an interest survey or checklist to gather data about specific student activity interests. These should be completed in the spring of the year to help determine the curricular offerings for the following fall and spring semesters. The survey should be administered to potential physical education students who will be enrolled the following year. In some cases, the survey will be given to students who will be feeding into the school the following year. For example, 6th graders should be surveyed before they enter junior high school, and next year's beginning senior high school students should be surveyed while still in junior high.

The survey should be administered every other year to all demographic groups within the schools (i.e., boys, girls, athletes, nonathletes, various racial groups, and various grade levels). As many students as possible should be surveyed to ensure valid information. Ideally, the survey can be administered in a class or homeroom period (math, science, or English) that is required for all students.

Most schools have access to data processing and computers, and a specialist is usually available to help set up programs for data analysis. A program can be designed to analyze the student population in a number of ways that are useful in constructing curriculum. For example, interests can be analyzed by age, sex, or racial group.

The interest survey should include all possible physical activities that would accomplish the objectives of physical education. It is important to avoid restrictive thinking when describing activity offerings in a survey. For example, the lack of a pool, racquetball courts, ski slopes, or various types of equipment for specific activities should not prohibit an educator from including these activities

---

1. The percentage is that portion of students who indicated that they would be interested in the activity.

on the survey. Travel to off-campus facilities in the nearby community may be possible in the future. Most communities have nearby golf driving ranges, racquet clubs, bowling alleys, pools, ski slopes, or wooded areas that could be used for the school program. Data collected from interest surveys can be used as a basis for expanding physical facilities, adding a pool, racquetball courts, tennis courts, or a weight lifting room. If student interest can be shown, administrators may be convinced that facilities and equipment, course offerings, or new teachers should be added to the physical education program.

An example of an interest survey is shown in Figure 4.1. The interest survey should be revised every other year, and new activities that evolve from the trends in society should be included in the survey. Educators must make an effort to keep current with the activity trends in the community and across the nation. Professional and popular literature will help provide information about the general trends.

Interests in the community can be determined by looking at the various recreation programs offered through the YMCA, the parks and recreation department, private clubs, community leagues, and large businesses. The number of facilities such as bowling alleys, golf courses, ski slopes, and swimming pools will provide additional information about interests in the community. The interests of community adults will have an impact on students. This is important information for the curriculum planner.

SELECTING ACTIVITIES

After considering all of the aforementioned areas, the next curriculum construction step is to gather activities that can be used to accomplish program goals. Curriculum theory, practical considerations, the desires of people, and the characteristics and interests of students are all important factors that must be analyzed carefully before selecting appropriate activities. An educational program should blend the desires of society and the objectives of the program with the developmental characteristics and interests of students.

A program planner must realize that the interests of students cannot be the sole basis for a curriculum. Boys and girls cannot make all of the decisions concerning what courses they want and what activities should be in the curriculum for they

are not trained in educational programming. This does not mean, however, that activities selected by the educator cannot be interesting or enjoyable.

For example, 8th graders going through the adolescent growth spurt should be required to take short units covering a wide variety of physical activities that provide them with success in basic movement skills like running, dribbling, and throwing. Long, in-depth units with specialized skills would probably be boring and frustrating for students at this developmental level. Conversely, an 11th grader should have an opportunity to choose a semester unit in modern dance, tennis, racquetball, or another area that is highly specialized and is in line with her or his interest. Senior high school is not the time to require students to take a unit that they have little or no desire to pursue. A 7th grade girl should be required to try a variety of health-related fitness activities, but should also be able to choose an aerobics unit from several available options. A 10th grade boy interested in body building should have the option to choose from several levels of weight training.

Activity selection should also not be based solely on the interests or teaching competencies of the teachers directing the programs. Too often, teacher interests were determined 10 to 15 years earlier, and are not the activities that are popular in our society today. This is why teachers must continually expand their activity knowledge and expertise.

The curriculum planner should try to provide a balance of activities from different categories. Common categories emphasized are team sports, lifetime sports, physical conditioning, dance activities, aquatic activities, adventure activities, and self-testing activities. Activities in various categories can overlap, depending on the definition of the category. The important point is that all students should have some experience with several activities selected from as many categories as possible in each school setting. Practical factors such as climate, facilities, and equipment will dictate the breadth of activities that a curriculum can provide. Too often, however, the curriculum is heavily tipped toward team sports because of class size, facilities, equipment, or lack of interest or ability on the part of the teacher.

An unbalanced curriculum is not appropriate for students who are interested in activity categories not offered. For example, many students will enjoy Frisbee, orienteering, modern dance, or skin diving. They may not enjoy football, basketball, wrestling, or volleyball. If the curriculum is unbalanced, then these students will not have access to

PHYSICAL ACTIVITY INTEREST SURVEY

Name _____

Grade _____ Age _____ Sex _____

Athletic team _____

Instructions: Which of the following physical activities or sports would you be most interested in taking as a course in the physical education program? Please list your top 5 choices on the line provided. Place a number 1 in front of your highest choice, a number 2 in front of your next choice, and so on until you reach choice number 5. Remember to make only 5 choices.

Aquatic Activities
_____ Lifesaving, water safety
_____ Skin and scuba diving
_____ Surfing
_____ Swimming, diving
_____ Water sports (polo, volleyball, basketball)

Individual Activities
_____ Archery
_____ Badminton
_____ Fencing
_____ Frisbee
_____ Golf
_____ Gymnastics
_____ Handball
_____ Racquetball
_____ Recreational games (bowling, horseshoes, shuffleboard, etc.)
_____ Roller-skating
_____ Skateboarding
_____ Squash
_____ Tennis
_____ Track and field

Physical Conditioning Activities
_____ Aerobic dance
_____ Body conditioning, weight control
_____ Martial arts (judo, karate, kendo, etc.)
_____ Weight training
_____ Yoga

Outdoor Adventure Activities
_____ Backpacking
_____ Canoeing, kayaking

_____ Cycling (bicycling)
_____ Fishing
_____ Horseback riding
_____ Hunting
_____ Ice skating
_____ Outdoor survival
_____ Orienteering
_____ Rock climbing
_____ Sailing
_____ Skiing (cross country)
_____ Skiing (downhill)
_____ Snow shoeing

Rhythmic Activities
_____ Ballet
_____ Country swing dance
_____ Disco
_____ Folk and square dance
_____ Jazz dance
_____ Modern dance
_____ Social dance

Team Activities
_____ Baseball
_____ Basketball
_____ Field hockey
_____ Flag football
_____ Ice hockey
_____ Lacrosse
_____ Soccer
_____ Softball
_____ Speedball-speed-a-way
_____ Team handball
_____ Volleyball
_____ Wrestling

Directions for the teacher: Remind students to select only 5 choices, using the numbers 1–5 on the lines beside the activities. When analyzing the data, it is helpful to transpose numbers 1 and 5 and numbers 2 and 4. In other words, a 1 becomes a 5 and a 5 becomes a 1. A 2 is worth 4 and a 4 worth 2. The numbers are added for each activity. The activities with the most points are the most popular and those with the least points are the least popular.

Figure 4.1. Physical activity interest survey

potentially fulfilling activities. Teachers must make every effort to offer a balanced program.

Activities should be selected and directed with the objectives of the program in mind. The skillful curriculum planner chooses activities that influence the habits of people in both the health-related and play areas. Activities cannot be justified unless they are fulfilling program goals. Initially, many students are not interested in health-related fitness activities and have to be positively directed toward those activities. They need a gentle push to engage in the activities until the reinforcing aspects of physical exercise have developed a "positively addicted" person. All students should be able to find activities for play and health-related fitness in the physical education curriculum. A social reconstruction approach (Siedentop 1980) should be followed with regard to the physical activity habits of people. Physical education programs must take a leadership role in trying to shape people's activity preferences, and teachers should select activities with this goal in mind.

ARRANGING ACTIVITIES

After selecting the activities, the next step is arranging them in a sequential order over the length of the school year, and from the first year to the second year, and so on until the students have graduated. A number of theoretical and practical factors should be considered in the arrangement of activities.

HORIZONTAL VERSUS VERTICAL

There are two major directions in curriculum development. The first is horizontal and deals with the activities that are to be taught during the school year for a specific grade level. The horizontal organization of the curriculum is most often developed by physical educators. It describes to the instructors what activities are to be taught, when they are to be taught, and how long they will be taught. Without this organizational scheme, teachers would have little direction and knowledge about how to help students achieve desired goals.

The vertical curriculum is less often tended to by curriculum planners. It delineates what activities will be taught at different grade levels. When done correctly, the vertical curriculum demands that teachers at the elementary, junior high, and senior high schools be keenly aware of what is being taught at each respective level. In physical educa-

tion, the common practice has been to teach the same activities, in much the same manner, year after year. Important concepts such as sequence, progression, and continuity are often ignored as teachers at different grade levels work independently of each other. An effective vertical curriculum has related knowledges, skills, and attitudes distributed over the 10- to 12-year school career of students. School districts with well-developed curricula demand the cooperation of all physical educators at all levels.

DEPTH VERSUS BREADTH

The length of a unit of activity usually varies from one week to one semester. The developmental level and interests of students should affect the length of a unit. The schedule of the school and the number of days per week that a class meets also affect unit length. Finally, the departmental philosophy on the concepts of *depth and breadth* in an activity will influence the length of units and the arrangement of varying levels of units.

Breadth in a curriculum refers to the offering of many short units throughout the year. A curriculum that offers 18 units that are each 2 weeks long is an example of breadth. Depth in a curriculum refers to the offering of fewer but longer units. A curriculum that offers 4 units, each of which is 9 weeks long, has depth in these activities. Depth can be added to a curriculum by offering intermediate- and advanced-level units in addition to beginning units. Examples of this will be discussed in Chapter 5. Generally, a junior high school program should provide activity breadth, and the senior high school program should focus on depth.

PROGRESSION AND CONTINUITY

Activities should be arranged from the simple to the complex. Students need to experience success quickly and then find challenges in the activities after having some success. The arrangement should also move from safe activities to activities with a controlled element of risk and danger. Proper steps, intervals, or sequences should be provided between activities so that students will be successful and will develop positive attitudes toward the activities. The curriculum planner builds on students' previous skills and knowledge. This can be done both within the year (horizontally) and between the years (vertically). For example, team handball uses skills from soccer, basketball, and volleyball, and can be included after these three units have been taught. Intermediate basketball should build on beginning basketball, and soccer in the 8th grade should build on soccer in the 7th grade.

A curriculum coordinator or department head within each school should supervise the arrangement of activities for that school. A coordinator at a higher level should supervise communication and progression of activities between the elementary and junior high and between the junior high and senior high schools.

AFTER-SCHOOL PROGRAMS

Athletics, intramurals, sport clubs, YMCA and YWCA leagues, and parks and recreation programs offer students many activity programs after school. Specific activities are usually offered at the same time each year. Interest and motivation in specific activities usually increase during the time of the year when the activities are offered. Physical educators can capitalize on this heightened interest period by coordinating the physical education sequence of activities with these various programs. For example, a track and field unit could end with the city track meet sponsored by the parks and recreation department. Soccer should be offered in the fall in conjunction with the popular YMCA soccer leagues. Basketball could be coordinated with the school intramural program, and wrestling could be offered before an AAU wrestling tournament. Coordinating all activities with all after-school programs can be difficult. These efforts will be worthwhile, however, in terms of student motivation and increasing the number of students in after-school programs.

WEATHER AND FACILITIES

The sequence of activities must be coordinated with weather conditions and the availability of equipment and facilities. Skiing, sailing, ice skating, and other outdoor activities require specific weather conditions that occur only at certain times of year. Some schools have outdoor pools available during the early fall and late spring periods. Off-campus areas may be available only during certain times of the year due to climate or public interest in the activity (e.g., golf ranges, bowling alleys, or surfing beaches). All of these factors should be checked carefully before making the final arrangement of activities.

EVALUATION AND IMPROVEMENT OF CURRICULUM

The final and ongoing step in developing an effective curriculum is evaluation. Program evaluation that focuses on the general objectives of the program is called summative evaluation. Summative evaluation provides information on how well the curriculum as a whole affects students. Differentiating between curriculum and instruction is difficult. These areas intertwine in affecting students, and a program will not improve without constant evaluation in both areas.

Evaluating curriculum involves looking at three aspects: the curriculum itself, the performance of the students, and the effectiveness of the instructor. To evaluate curriculum, summative evaluation can be completed using a variety of checklists, rating scales, and self-appraisal instruments. Students' responses can be analyzed and their performance evaluated with knowledge tests, fitness tests, performance objectives for physical skills, attitude and self-concept inventories, and free-time activity questionnaires (see Chapter 11). Instruction and teaching procedures can be evaluated using several coding instruments and devices (see Chapter 10).

Instruments for evaluating curriculum can be either formal or informal. The evaluation should serve to remind the instructor of the program goals and objectives, and should offer insight into program direction and progress. Figure 4.2 is an example of an informal evaluation instrument.

Figure 4.3 is a formal instrument that can be used to evaluate programs on a point basis. The list of items presented can be a self-evaluation tool for analyzing the program. Each item should be rated according to the scale explained at the top of the form.

Summary

Curriculum construction should follow a series of basic steps arranged in a sequential order. Physical educators should consider the desires of the public and then decide on objectives to be accomplished. Next, the curriculum planner must look closely at the characteristics, interests, and developmental levels of students whom the program serves. Specific learning activities are then developed and arranged in a progressive and sequential manner. The final step is an evaluation of the program to see if objectives are being accomplished.

CURRICULUM EVALUATION QUESTIONS

1. Are students incorporating physical activity into their life-style?
2. Are students returning to optional programs after they have completed the mandatory years?
3. Are students acquiring competency in physical skills?
4. Do students understand the concepts of developing and maintaining personal fitness for a lifetime?
5. Are students reaching a desirable level of physical fitness through participation in the program?
6. Do students possess the requisite knowledge required to participate in a wide variety of sports, games, and exercises?
7. Have students acquired social and emotional skills necessary for productive participation in school and society?
8. Does the curriculum leave students with a broad understanding of the wealth of physical activities available to them (balance)?
9. Does the curriculum allow students to leave school with a high level of competency in a few activities (depth)?
10. Does the curriculum follow a progressive sequence within the school year as well as between school years (horizontal and vertical curriculum)?

Figure 4.2. Informal curriculum evaluation questions

Figure 4.3. Formal curriculum evaluation instrument

CURRICULUM EVALUATION

0 points: Unacceptable. There is no compliance with the stated criteria.

1 point: Inadequate coverage. There is doubt about any compliance and little attention is paid to the stated criteria.

2 points: Adequate coverage. It is apparent that attention has been given to the criteria; however, there is room for improvement.

3 points: Excellent coverage. The program is exemplary in meeting the stated criteria.

Read each criterion, determine the extent to which there is compliance, then write in the appropriate scale score. If there is doubt about meeting certain criteria, list the lower of the two scores.

PHILOSOPHY AND PROGRAM IMPLEMENTATION

_____ 1. A written statement is available that describes the philosophy and principles on which the program is based.
_____ 2. Physical education is seen as an integral part of the total school curriculum and receives support similar to any other area of the school curriculum.
_____ 3. The program is constructed based on the desires of its constituency.
_____ 4. A written and updated version of a K–12 curriculum guide is available for the conduct and implementation of the program.
_____ 5. The physical education curriculum delineates horizontal and vertical structure. Teachers know what is to be taught during the school year as well as what is taught at different grade levels.
_____ 6. Activities are listed in units of instruction in proper progression and sequence.
_____ 7. Daily lesson plans are developed from the units of instruction and provide direction for instruction.

continued

Figure 4.3/*continued*

_____ 8. Physical education is regarded as an instructional program with emphasis on educating the child in contrast to providing time for tournaments or free play.

_____ 9. Students are taught the "how and why" of physical activity. Emphasis is placed on cognitive learning as well as on psychomotor learning.

_____ 10. All students take part in a regular program of physical education. Substitution of music, driver education, and athletics for physical education does not occur.

_____ 11. Programs at the junior high school level emphasize variety and exposure to a large number of activities.

_____ 12. The high school program allows students to elect the activities in which they choose to participate.

_____ 13. Students with handicaps can participate fully in the program and are offered a wide range of opportunities.

_____ 14. Students with medical problems are identified and monitored for follow-up examinations regularly.

_____ 15. A physician's written statement is the only way students are permanently excused from physical education.

_____ 16. The school has a nurse trained to treat accidents.

_____ 17. Provisions are made for dealing with students desiring to be excused from physical education classes. The plan is consistent and educationally sound.

_____ 18. The grading system used in physical education is consistent with that used in other curriculum areas.

_____ 19. There are provisions for public relations and sharing the program with parents. Demonstrations and information are shared regularly with the public.

_____ 20. The physical education faculty has a plan for professional growth that includes inservice training, professional meetings, university course-work, conferences, and independent study.

_____ 21. Instruction is regarded as a dynamic process and is analyzed through self-evaluation and by outside personnel. Evaluations take place at regular intervals.

_____ 22. Intramurals are seen as an outgrowth of the physical education program. A wide variety of activities is offered for student participation.

_____ 23. The athletic program is seen as a separate entity and not as an end result of or goal for the physical education program.

_____ 24. Teachers separate physical education instruction and athletic coaching. Physical education is taught for the student body and athletics are offered for those students who excel.

Comments:

CURRICULUM ANALYSIS

1. The physical education program provides learning experiences to help each student attain the following:

_____ a. A personalized level of physical fitness and body conditioning.

_____ b. Specialized sport skills in a wide variety of activities.

_____ c. Knowledge of rules, techniques, and strategy related to individual, dual, and team sports.

_____ d. Desirable social standards and ethical behavior.

_____ e. Knowledge and practice of safety standards for self and others.

_____ f. Competence in activities that can be used for leisure pursuits.

_____ g. Knowledge and practice of concepts leading to human wellness.

_____ 2. Activities are progressively organized and adjusted to suit the maturity and skill levels of youngsters.

_____ 3. Students are treated with dignity and encouraged to participate in all phases of the program.

_____ 4. The program offers a variety of activities that will be attractive to all students. This includes skilled and unskilled, low-fit, and handicapped students.

_____ 5. Each daily lesson has a portion (10–15 min) of time devoted to physical fitness development.

_____ 6. An up-to-date library of physical education books, filmstrips, and related materials is available for students and teachers.

_____ 7. There is an aquatic program available in the school or community so all students have the opportunity to learn to swim.

_____ 8. Indoor and outdoor teaching stations are available for instruction.

_____ 9. The yearly curriculum is written. It is reevaluated each year, and modifications are made that facilitate attainment of objectives.

_____ 10. Units of instruction vary in length depending on the maturity and skill level of students. Block plans for each unit are developed and include skill instruction on a regular basis.

_____ 11. Lead-up games are taught to students in order to isolate and develop specific skills that need to be learned.

_____ 12. Student input is welcomed. Instruments designed to monitor student interests and desires are administered on a regular basis.

_____ 13. Students are allowed to make choices about the types of activity they want to learn.

_____ 14. Units that focus on self-assessment are offered during the freshman year. Results are used to help students find the types of activities they want to participate in for a lifetime.

Comments:

FACILITIES, EQUIPMENT, AND SUPPLIES

_____ 1. Maximum use of facilities for physical education instruction is apparent.

_____ 2. Outdoor facilities meet the basic acreage standard of 5 acres plus 1 acre for each additional 100 students.

3. Outdoor facilities include the following:

_____ a. Areas where different games and activities can be conducted without interference.

_____ b. Areas for court games.

_____ c. Backstops and goals for softball, soccer, and basketball, team handball, and field hockey.

_____ d. Suitable fencing for safety and control.

_____ e. Outdoor grassy areas that are free from rock, sprinkler heads, and other hazards that might cause injury.

4. Indoor facilities meet the following standards:

_____ a. They are clean, sanitary, and free from hazards.

_____ b. They are well lighted, well ventilated, heated, cooled, and treated for proper acoustics.

_____ c. They are surfaced with a nonslip finish and include painted game area lines.

_____ 5. Periodic inspection of all facilities and equipment, both indoor and outdoor, is conducted, and a written report sent to the appropriate administrators.

_____ 6. Storage facilities are adequate for supplies and portable equipment.

_____ 7. Adequate provision is made for off-season storage of equipment, apparatus, and supplies.

continued

Figure 4.3/*continued*

_____ 8. An office is provided for the physical education instructors that has a telephone for emergencies and clear vision into the locker room areas.

_____ 9. Basic supplies are sufficient for all instructional units. This includes a piece of equipment for each student when necessary.

_____ 10. Equipment necessary to teach units properly is available. This includes tumbling mats, basketball goals, volleyball standards and nets, gymnastic equipment, and so forth.

_____ 11. Personal storage lockers are available for students.

_____ 12. Adequate room is available for students for changing into proper physical activity attire.

_____ 13. Equipment and supplies necessary for the testing and evaluation program are available.

_____ 14. Tape recorders, record players, and records are available in sufficient number for the rhythmic program.

_____ 15. An adequate yearly budget is available for equipment repair, replacement, and development of new units of instruction.

Comments:

References

Darst, P., and Armstrong, G. *Outdoor Adventure Activities for School and Recreation Programs.* Minneapolis: Burgess Publishing Co., 1980.

Lindeman, L., Wardrop, D., and Leake, R. 1981. Utah high school physical education interests and attitudes. Utah State Office of Education, Salt Lake City, UT.

Siedentop, D. 1980. Physical education curriculum: An analysis of the past. *JOPERD* 51(7): 40–41.

Wilson, B., and Altieri, P. 1978. Complying with Title IX—Increasing participation through the elective program. *Arizona JOHPERD* 21(2): 6–7.

Chapter 5

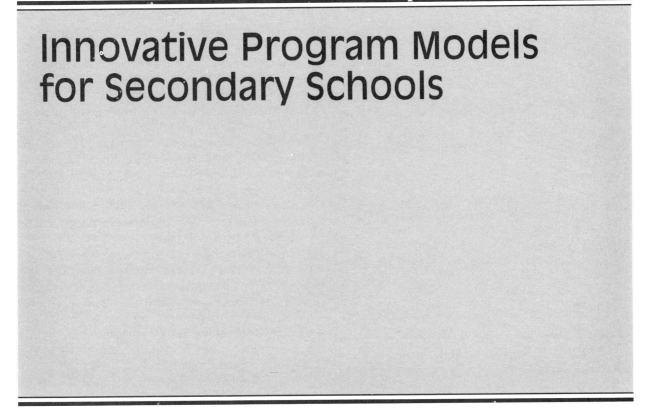

Innovative Program Models for Secondary Schools

A curriculum program model is the arrangement of learning activities over the entire year. There are numerous curriculum program models that exist in the secondary schools across the United States. Many factors affect the type of model used in each situation (see Chapter 3). Some of these factors are difficult to change in a short period of time (e.g., the state requirement for physical education; a school district requirement for physical education; the district philosophy on athletics, driver education, marching band; and the type of schedule that the school is following). Other factors and components of a curriculum model can, however, be changed in a short period of time without dramatically disrupting the school routine and schedule.

These components of a curriculum can be developed within the existing framework of a given situation. Because of the variances among states and among school districts, the degree to which these factors can be implemented will be quite different. These factors include: types of activities, the balance of activities, the required activities, the length of units, the arrangements of units, the amount of student choice, the coeducational classes, the physical fitness sequences, the monitoring sys-

tems for fitness and skill development, the reporting system to the parents, and many others.

A small school in upstate New York, a large school in eastern Pennsylvania, or a medium-sized school in central Arizona can all have a quality program within the existing framework of each situation. Certainly, some programs will have more students, more teachers, more facilities, and better equipment. Requirements, schedules, and administrative support may be quite different in each situation. Quality programs are not, however, a function of large facilities, abundant equipment, extensive physical education requirements, large numbers of teachers, or small class sizes. Quality programs are usually developed by a group of hard-working, dedicated professionals who are doing the best possible job within the existing framework. They are battling continually to improve the program and to change those aspects of the existing framework that are detrimental to the accomplishment of the program goals. Curriculum developers should work positively within the present framework and try slowly to change the existing parameters that cause difficulties.

This chapter will discuss physical education

programs in the secondary school at three levels, 7th and 8th grades, 9th grade, and grades 10–12. The chapter is arranged in this manner because of the inconsistent placement of the 9th grade in different school districts. Many schools place the 9th grade in the junior high school (grades 7–9), while others place it in the high school (grades 9–12). The discussion will focus on the curriculum that currently exists at each of these levels along with the advantages and disadvantages of the existing models. An innovative curriculum model with recommendations will be presented for each level, followed by a series of curriculum analysis questions for each level. This series of questions will help curriculum planners analyze existing program models for each specific level. The answers to the questions will provide planners with information about specific factors and components of each model. Less experienced curriculum planners are often unsure about what to analyze and which direction to follow.

JUNIOR HIGH SCHOOL MODELS— GRADES 7 AND 8

Curriculum models designed for elementary school children and for high school students are abundant and specifically designed for the respective ages of participants. Models for 7th and 8th grade students are practically nonexistent. In most cases, junior high programs are adaptations of an elementary or high school curriculum model. In many programs, virtually no consideration is given to the unique characteristics, abilities, interests, and developmental levels of students at this age. In fact, the physical education curriculum at the junior high level has generated little professional attention. Siedentop (1980a) notes:

> Also, there is a continuing under-emphasis of the middle school curriculum, a fact that we can ill afford to ignore much longer, particularly in physical education where the developmental aspects of that period seem so susceptible to well-conceived, sensitively planned programs of physical education. (p. 41)

Most of the 7th and 8th grade program models resemble existing high school models. Programs are patterned after the high school format. What will become evident is that this arrangement is not the best situation for the majority of junior high students.

SCHEDULE OF CLASSES

Most junior high schools follow a block or traditional schedule with classes meeting every day for a constant length of time (45–55 minutes). Another common schedule pattern is called a 3/2 "swing" schedule. Physical education is paired with another subject area or a study hall, and the students attend class three days per week during the first semester and two days per week during the second semester. The students attend the study hall or the other subject area class (usually health) on the opposite days. The students "flip" their schedules at the end of the first semester from Monday, Wednesday, and Friday to Tuesday and Thursday. Another common 7th and 8th grade schedule arrangement is to meet for physical education only twice a week all year long.

In a flexible schedule arrangement (see Chapter 3), classes might meet for varying lengths of time throughout the week. For example, one meeting might last for 45 min, and then two additional meetings would last for 90 min each. The flexible arrangement allows for lecture-laboratory approaches, travel time off campus, and better use of teachers and facilities.

Each of these arrangements offers some advantages and disadvantages for students, teachers, and school districts in terms of money and teaching-learning effectiveness. Programs that schedule students for daily physical education class (as compared with class held every other day) cost more money in terms of teaching personnel but can provide more opportunities for successful encounters with physical activities. Teachers have a better chance to guide and counsel students when they interact with them daily. The effectiveness of the learning environment is reduced when teachers see a new group of students every other day. With a flexible schedule more money is spent on administrative maintenance, but the program can provide unique opportunities for exploring new learning environments (e.g., travel off campus to special facilities and activities such as scuba diving, skiing, or rock climbing that require larger time blocks).

LENGTH OF ACTIVITY UNITS

There is great variance in the length of each unit in the 7th and 8th grade curriculum. Planners must remember that the number of class meetings per week is a key factor in deciding the length of a unit. A three-week unit that meets daily offers 15 sessions, while a three-week unit that meets twice a week allows only 6 sessions. Although both are three-week units, there is a large difference in what can be accomplished given each schedule.

A common model in the 7th and 8th grades consists of long units focused on seasonal athletic activities. Units are six to nine weeks and focus on the athletic sport that is in season. Students would take four to six activities in a year. The model might look similar to the following:

First 9 weeks—Flag football or soccer
Second 9 weeks—Basketball
Third 9 weeks—Wrestling
Last 9 weeks—Softball or track and field

The following is a model using six-week units:

First 6 weeks—Swimming
Second 6 weeks—Volleyball
Third 6 weeks—Basketball
Fourth 6 weeks—Gymnastics
Fifth 6 weeks—Track and field
Last 6 weeks—Softball

Another common model is to offer two units during each nine-week grading period. One unit would be five weeks and the other four weeks. In this way, students take eight units per year. Two examples of this model are as follows:

Model A

First 9 weeks	Soccer	(5 wks)
	Flag football	(4 wks)
Second 9 weeks	Tennis	(5 wks)
	Basketball	(4 wks)
Third 9 weeks	Volleyball	(5 wks)
	Tumbling	(4 wks)
Last 9 weeks	Track and field	(5 wks)
	Softball	(4 wks)

Model B

First 9 weeks	Field hockey	(5 wks)
	Speed-a-way	(4 wks)
Second 9 weeks	Volleyball	(5 wks)
	Dance	(4 wks)
Third 9 weeks	Basketball	(5 wks)
	Gymnastics	(4 wks)
Last 9 weeks	Tennis	(5 wks)
	Track and field	(4 wks)

The final model uses short two- and three-week units that offer students 12 to 18 different activities during the year. The following is an example:

Weeks	Activity
1–3	Swimming
4–6	Volleyball
7–9	Tennis
10–12	Flag football
13–15	Dance
16–18	Basketball
19–21	Badminton
22–24	Tumbling
25–27	Recreational games
28–30	Speed-a-way
31–33	Track and field
34–36	Softball

The models range from 4 units per year to 18 units per year. The students in the 4-unit model will get an in-depth experience with those four activities, while the students in the 18-unit approach will receive a shorter, broader experience with many different activities. The students involved in curriculum models between these two extremes will absorb a compromise between breadth and depth. The issue of breadth versus depth continues to be a controversy among physical educators.

Bain (1980) states that junior high units should be a minimum of 10–12 weeks with in-depth instruction available for those activities of interest to students. Benson (1982) also believes that short units (2–4 weeks) only offer students an opportunity to do poorly and provide little change in skill level. The authors (Pangrazi and Darst et al. 1982) have argued previously for short units for this age group because of the developmental characteristics of junior high students. These youngsters, who are going through puberty, a rapid growth spurt, and a period of slow motor development, need successful experiences with a wide variety of activities. Longer units can lock students into a frustrating and boring experience with repeated failure for a long period of time. Variety and novelty in a success-oriented atmosphere are important motivational keys for this age youngster. Students can find success in short units when emphasis is on exposure and on learning about one's personal strengths and weaknesses.

Many teachers at the junior high school level claim that the learning environment is more productive when units are changed often. Students and teachers are more highly motivated when a new activity begins. Too often, long units turn into a prolonged class tournament without structured skill work. Students begin to expect physical education classes to consist of long units of tournament play, and they are forced into highly competitive situations without the opportunity to develop adequate skill level. This only adds to the frustration of the less skilled students.

TYPES OF ACTIVITIES

The most common category of activity in the junior high school is athletic team sports (e.g, flag football, basketball, volleyball, wrestling, track and field, softball). Many physical educators claim that these are the most popular activities with students and that they are the most economical activities in terms of facilities and equipment.

Many programs have added lifetime sports such as tennis, badminton, bowling, and golf. These activities are claimed to have more carry-over value for later life. Other schools have added units on currently popular activities such as aerobic dance, martial arts, jogging, and outdoor adventure activities like backpacking, canoeing, and rock climbing.

Some schools have tried to develop a balance of team sports, lifetime sports, physical conditioning activities, dance activities, aquatic activities, and the new activities. Programs that offer an activity balance from these various categories have a better chance of positively affecting all students within the school. Certain students will find success with certain categories of activity, and the programs with good variety will provide more students with opportunities for success. For example, some students enjoy Frisbee, orienteering, and golf, while others prefer basketball, football, and baseball.

PHYSICAL FITNESS ACTIVITIES

Many programs open each day's lesson with a series of exercises to develop several components of physical fitness. Stretching-flexibility activities, strength development activities, and cardiovascular-respiratory-type activities usually dominate fitness routines. Too often, there is not enough variety, progression, or challenge in the activities being used. Many 7th and 8th grade fitness programs are characterized by the following: ten jumping jacks, ten toe touches, ten sit-ups, ten push-ups, and a lap around the field. Small wonder students get bored and disillusioned with physical fitness!

Programs that are offering students a wide variety of physical fitness activities and routines in a progressive and challenging manner will have a better chance of successfully influencing students. The junior high school age is an important time for people to have successful encounters with physical fitness activities. The learning sequences for this segment of the curriculum must be organized and set up for each year. Educators simply cannot justify the "three exercises and a lap" approach as a means to a lifetime of physical fitness.

One final word: These are the years in which students decide to "turn on" or "turn off" to physical activity. Just as there is no one way to live one's life, so there is no one way to achieve physical fitness that is meaningful for everyone. Emphasis should be placed on helping youngsters understand the different ways of maintaining fitness by exposing them to a wide variety of fitness development activities. Exposure alone, however, is not enough. They must develop knowledge and understanding of what works for them and why it works.

REQUIREMENTS AND CHOICE

Most junior high school physical education departments require that students take all of the activities that have been organized for the school year. Students usually do not have any choice about what activities they will learn. This arrangement is probably still the most common format regarding requirements.

A new trend, which started at the high school level and has filtered down to some junior high programs, allows students the opportunity to choose the activities they want to take in physical education. The students are given a choice of several different activities for each unit. Classes may be open to both boys and girls, depending on their interests. In this model, male and female teachers work together and decide who is the better qualified to teach a specific activity. Each teacher can then develop two or three specialties and repeat teaching those specialties to different students, rather than having to teach every different activity to the same students.

This same model has been used with all of the boys grouped together and all of the girls grouped together in a separate curriculum. The boys would choose between several "boys' activities" and the girls would select from different "girls' activities." A problem with this approach is the narrowing of options. There are not as many choices as there would be if boys and girls chose from the same activities. For example, with two male teachers and two female teachers, the joint-curriculum model would provide four choices for all students, while the segregated model would provide only two choices for the boys and two choices for the girls. Another problem with the segregated model is that students may be denied access to certain activities because of sex stereotyping (e.g., boys not offered dance or gymnastics, or girls not offered weight training or flag football).

An example of an alternating four- to five-week unit of a coeducational curriculum with choices for students follows:

First Semester

First 9 weeks:
1. Volleyball, yoga, or soccer (4 wks)
2. Flag football, archery, or tennis (5 wks)

Second 9 weeks:
3. Gymnastics, volleyball, or badminton (4 wks)
4. Basketball, team handball, or field hockey (5 wks)

Second Semester

Third 9 weeks:
1. Aerobics, speed-a-way, or basketball (4 wks)
2. Wrestling, orienteering, or volleyball (5 wks)

Last 9 weeks:
3. Softball, track and field, or badminton (4 wks)
4. Swimming, Frisbee games, or yoga (5 wks)

Students can make four choices at the beginning of each semester. This model has been used coeducationally with boys and girls being able to select any activity except a contact sport such as wrestling or flag football. If more than three teachers are available, then the students can make more choices.

The choice concept can be used with any length unit and any type of organizational schedule, and with either coeducational or segregated classes. This curriculum model offers the following advantages:

1. More student motivation and enthusiasm and a desire to take more physical education because of a higher interest level
2. Less problems with dressing, participation, and discipline
3. Better use of teaching expertise and the development of specialists

4. Improved instruction over a period of time
5. Increased teacher motivation and enthusiasm

A curriculum model that increases the motivation level of both students and teachers needs to be given consideration by those who develop programs.

Another variation of this model that some schools are using involves several requirements by activity category to ensure that a measure of breadth is provided. For example, students are required to take a certain number of team sports, lifetime sports, conditioning activities, dance units, aquatics, or recreational activities during the 7th and 8th grades. This concept is referred to as a **choice within a requirement.** Depending on the number of units offered, each student is required to take a specified number of activities from each category. If the program offers 24 three-week units over a two-year period, the requirements might include:

1 unit of wellness concepts
2 units of aquatics
2 units of dance
4 units of physical conditioning
6 units of lifetime sports
6 units of team sports
3 units of elective activities

24 units total

COEDUCATIONAL CLASSES

The issue of coeducational classes continues to be a point of controversy. Some junior high schools have all physical education classes assigned with 50% boys and 50% girls. Other schools conduct a few coeducational units such as square dance, volleyball, or track and field, but offer the majority of units segregated by sex. Still other programs allow students to choose classes based on interest, so the class composition has no fixed gender percentage. In some schools, boys and girls are never taught together during physical education and are completely segregated. This is an unfortunate, illegal, and unacceptable situation, yet physical educators continue to take stands on both sides of the issue. A great deal has been written on the subject (Melograno 1979, Blaufarb 1978a,b) and many coeducational programs have been highly successful with boys and girls learning together.

Chapter 2 presents the issues and problems associated with Title IX and coeducational classes in physical education. The authors' experiences in this area have led to positive feelings about coeducational classes. Program objectives can be accomplished in a coeducational format. Students in grades K–6 are usually integrated in physical education classes, and there is reason to believe that they should be able to move into a coeducational format in the junior and senior high school programs.

Certainly, there are problems to be solved, such as dressing, showering, grading, puberty, comfort zones of teachers, attitudes, interest development, learning about individual differences, increasing activity choices, and improving instructional quality. Sensitive teachers working together can develop an exciting and challenging program for boys and girls. Wrestling or other contact sports are not advocated, but a balanced program that is based on the characteristics and interests of students can be effectively implemented. The complaints that many people espouse can be solved by teachers who have a strong desire to actually make the program work.

ADAPTED PHYSICAL EDUCATION FOR SPECIAL STUDENTS

Special students are identified as those having problems to such a degree that the handicap interferes with their learning. Examples are mental retardation, visual impairment, hearing impairment, speech impairment, orthopedic impairment, learning disability, serious emotional disturbance, and neurological impairment (e.g., epilepsy, palsy, or other nervous disability).

Public Law 94-142 specifies that each handicapped student must receive special attention so that his or her educational needs are met. Any approach that treats the handicapped person as a cripple dehumanizes the individual. The thrust of an adapted physical education program should focus on the potentialities of the person with a handicap, on what she or he can do rather than what the person cannot do. Many special students have physical deficiencies for which a quality physical education program can offer direct assistance. In the case of the severely and profoundly mentally retarded, much of the educational program is physically oriented and can be enhanced by a physical education program.

The law further specifies that each handicapped student is to be educated in the least restrictive environment possible. This means that the schools must provide a range of services, from placement in regular classes with nonhandicapped peers (mainstreaming) to more restrictive environments. Some educators have reacted to P.L. 94-142 with global or categorical mainstreaming, which is not the intent of the law. The key is a formal determination of which educational setting most benefits a particular handicapped student. This means prudent placement in an educational environment that is as normal as possible (normalization) while still assuring with reasonable certainty that the student will achieve success in that placement. The placement may indeed be mainstreaming, but there are other possibilities as follows:

1. **Full Mainstreaming.** Handicapped students function as full-time members of a regular school routine. They go to all classes with nonhandicapped students and participate in physical education within the limitations of their handicap.
2. **Mainstreaming for Physical Education Only.** Handicapped students are not members of academic classes, but participate in physical education with nonhandicapped students.
3. **Partial Mainstreaming.** Students take part in selected physical education experiences but do not attend classes on a full-time basis, because they can be successful in only some of the offerings. Their developmental needs are usually met in special classes.
4. **Special Developmental Classes.** Handicapped students are in segregated, special education classes.
5. **Reverse Mainstreaming.** Nonhandicapped students are brought into a special physical education class to promote intergroup peer relationships. The PEOPEL program, as described in Chapter 2, is an example of this approach.

Segregation can be maintained only if it is in the best interests of the student. The thrust of segregated programs should be toward establishing a level of skill and social efficiency such that the special student can eventually be transferred to a less restrictive environment.

SUGGESTED PROGRAM MODEL— GRADES 7 AND 8

The 7th and 8th grade curriculum should be designed for the specific characteristics, abilities, and interests of this age student. Junior high school students need to experience success, variety, and challenge. Because most of them have a broad range of interests, the curriculum should offer opportunities to explore many different activities. Counseling procedures should be built into the program to guide students toward activities in which they can find success. Common problems include peer pressure, the emotional conflicts surrounding development of secondary sexual characteristics, a rapid growth spurt, awkwardness, poor motor skills, frustration, and boredom. Curriculum content and instructional strategies should deal with these problems.

Students should receive physical education on a daily basis or at least on a time basis equivalent to all other subject areas. The teacher-student ratio should be consistent with academic class ratios. Physical education is as important as math, science, and English, and the physical education schedule should be consistent with and analogous to other areas of the total school curriculum.

The daily lesson plan format for both 7th and 8th grades should include an introductory or warm-up activity (3–5 min), a physical fitness routine (10–15 min), and a lesson focus and game activity (25–30 min). (See Chapter 7 for details of the lesson plan format.) This format should be consistent and an outgrowth of the K–6 curriculum. A consistent instructional format within each class provides teachers and students with a measure of stability.

Introductory Activities

The introductory activity occupies 3 to 5 min of the total lesson format. The purpose of this portion of the lesson is to prepare students physiologically for strenuous activity. An allied purpose is to psychologically ready students for activity. Students usually take a few minutes to become emotionally involved in activity after a day of sitting in classes. The introductory activity requires minimal organization and demands large muscle movement. It may be an integral part of the fitness routine or can be a separate entity. In either case, the introductory activity should raise the heart rate, warm up the body, and stretch the muscles in anticipation of the fitness development activity. Teachers should change the introductory activity each week to add variety to the warm-up procedure. The 7th and 8th grade students can perform the same introductory activity. Table 5.1 shows a recommended yearly sequence (36 weeks). An in-depth discussion of introductory activities is found in Chapter 16.

Table 5.1. Introductory Activities for Grades 7 and 8

Week	Activity
1	Orientation and simple games
2	Basic movements (e.g., start, stop, pivot)
3	Walk, trot, and sprint
4	Partner over and under
5	Run, stop, and pivot
6	Move, change direction, and pose on signal
7	European running
8	Flash drill
9	Marking and tag games
10	Quickness drills
11	Throwing and catching
12	Hula-Hoop movements
13	European running variations
14	File running drill
15	Manipulative skills
16	Follow-the-leader
17	Group over and under
18	New leader warm-up
19	Jumping and hopping skills
20	Walk, trot, and sprint
21	Leaping Lena
22	Rooster drill
23	Bend, stretch, and shake
24	Marking and tag games
25	Group agility drills
26	Shuffle drills
27	Running techniques
28	Partner movements
29	Fartlek running
30	Follow-the-leader
31	Throwing and catching on the move
32	Move, change direction, and pose on signal
33	Partner over and under
34	Seat rolls
35	Weave drills
36	Rubber band

Fitness Development Activities

The fitness development activity uses 10 to 15 min of the lesson, and its primary purpose is the development of physical fitness. Fitness routines should offer total fitness development to students. In other words, an attempt should be made to develop and enhance major components of fitness, especially flexibility, muscular strength and endurance, body composition, and cardiovascular endurance. The activities should be demanding, progressive in nature, and of a type that students may choose to perform after graduation. Students must experience a wide variety of fitness routines so they can learn to select methods acceptable to them for a lifetime. They should leave school with the understanding that there are many ways to develop and maintain physical fitness, and the responsibility for doing so lies with them.

Students in grades 7 and 8 should stay with the same routine for four weeks in order to show a gain in fitness development. Success in the fitness area helps motivate students and serves as a basis for future motor skill development. Students need to learn that success can be achieved in the fitness area through continued effort. The new AAHPERD Health Related Physical Fitness Test can be used to monitor student progress in the fitness area, and a fitness report should be sent to parents at least once a year. Fitness testing does not take a great deal of time. Students can self-test themselves, and enter their raw scores in a microcomputer. A printout reveals graphically the student's fitness profile. This entire self-testing process maintains the purpose of teaching students skills that they can use for a lifetime.

Fitness routines recommended for 7th and 8th graders are shown in Table 5.2. The discussion and examples of these routines are found in Chapter 17.

Lesson Focus and Game

The lesson focus and game should last 25 to 30 min, depending on the length of the period. This is the instructional part of the lesson with major emphasis on skill development, cognitive learning, and enhancement of the affective domain. This phase of the lesson contains skills to be taught, drills, and lead-up activities necessary for skill practice, all of which culminate in games and tournaments. The length of the activity units in the lesson focus should be short, in the range of two to three weeks if the classes meet daily. Three-week units should be a combination of two activities such as flag football and Frisbee. The combination-type unit allows a daily alternation of the two activities.

Students should have some choice as to which units they take. They should, however, be required to take at least one unit from each of the following categories: team sports, lifetime activities, physical conditioning activities, dance, and aquatics. Teachers need to decide which activities fit the various categories. The category requirement ensures a measure of activity breadth for each student. Students should also be required to take one short unit on self-testing procedures and wellness concepts (see Chapter 15). This unit should include formal guidance and counseling relevant to current and lifetime fitness. Each student will thus have five required categories and one specific required unit. The remaining units are chosen by each student in any category. Students may repeat units or take higher level units after their requirements have been completed.

The specific activity units that are offered should be determined jointly by a student-interest survey and the opinions of the physical education staff. Activity units must be used to accomplish program goals and should be changed from year to year depending on the interests of students and the

Table 5.2. Physical Fitness Routines		
Weeks	Grade 7	Grade 8
1–4	Teacher-leader activities	Teacher-leader activities
5–8	Stretching and running techniques	Stretching and running techniques
9–12	Four corner course	Weight training stations
13–16	Exercises to music	Exercises to music
17–20	Obstacle course and isometrics	Grass drills and partner resistance
21–24	Squad leader exercises	Squad leader exercises
25–28	Astronaut drills	Circuit training
29–32	Continuity drills	Rhythmic aerobic activity
33–36	Parachute activities	Parachute activities

opinions of teachers. The program should provide a balance of activities from the aforementioned required categories.

A school with four physical education teachers might offer the curriculum model shown in Table 5.3. During the first unit of each semester, students would make their eight choices based on the required categories and their personal interests. At that time, students would be reminded to select activities based on their interests and the curriculum requirements, rather than making activity choices because a certain teacher is favored or friends are in the class. The composition of the class should be determined by interest and requirements rather than by gender of students. The only exceptions are contact activities such as wrestling, basketball, soccer, or flag football. These classes can be designated "boys" or "girls," or an alternative might be to allow both boys and girls in the same class and then separate them for competitive situations. With this alternative, however, a problem with numbers of students may arise in some activities such as soccer or flag football.

Previous learning is considered in the arrangement of units in the horizontal or yearly curriculum. Activities that use skills similar to those acquired in more common activities can be placed later in the year (e.g., team handball, speed-a-way, and floor hockey can build on basketball, volleyball, and soccer).

Within the vertical curriculum, the 7th grade program should build on the K–6 program in terms of skills, cognitive learning, class arrangement, and so forth. The 8th grade curriculum should then build on the 7th grade. Increased knowledge, more in-depth strategies, and higher level skills are the focus of the 8th grade program. Because of scheduling problems, some schools must put 7th and 8th grade students in the same class. This is acceptable but difficult because of the extremely wide range of developmental levels in these two grades. Teachers must be aware of developmental differences and provide a variety of learning activities for different levels within each unit (see Chapter 9).

Physical skill development within the units

Table 5.3.   Junior High Curriculum Model for a Four-Person Department

Weeks	Lesson Focus or Unit Choice
	First Semester (Weeks 1–18)
1–2	Self-testing and wellness concepts (required)
3–4	Swimming, volleyball, flag football, or Frisbee games
5–6	Swimming, tennis, badminton, or soccer
7–8	Weight training and wrestling (boys), basketball (girls), lacrosse, or tennis
9–10	Badminton, gymnastics, soccer, or Frisbee games
11–12	Basketball (boys), aerobic dance, lacrosse, or field hockey
13–14	Recreational games and orienteering, basketball (girls), team handball, and wrestling (boys)
15–16	Basketball (boys), aerobic dance, speed-a-way, or field hockey
17–18	Flag football, jogging, yoga, or team handball
	Second Semester (Weeks 19–36)
19–20	Coeducational dance—folk, square, and country (4 sections, required).
21–22	Recreational games and orienteering, speed-a-way, yoga, or jogging
23–24	Physical conditioning, volleyball, Frisbee games, or soccer
25–26	Gymnastics, badminton, tennis, or field hockey
27–28	Track and field, softball, physical conditioning, or volleyball
29–30	Modern dance, self-defense and juggling, jogging, or lacrosse
31–32	Track and field, softball, Super Stars and new games, or team handball
33–34	Swimming, modern dance, recreational games, or flag football
35–36	Swimming, yoga, speed-a-way, or recreational games

should be monitored with a series of performance objectives for each unit (see Chapters 8 and 9 plus the activity chapters). These objectives can be part of the motivation and evaluation schemes. Knowledge tests can be administered every six or nine weeks, depending on the school's grading periods.

Options Within the Model

A junior high school that is different from the previous example in terms of philosophy, requirements, schedule, number of teachers, student interests, climate conditions, teaching facilities, or available equipment could still implement this curriculum model and use the main concepts by modifying the different curriculum components to fit the existing framework. These are the basic options that might be implemented:

Option 1. Students could be assigned to one teacher and could take a required unit from that teacher for every other unit. With two-week units, this ensures that students will have at least nine units with the same teacher. A choice of activities would occur every other unit. Students would have nine required units and nine units with a choice of activity and teacher. This provides a balance of required and choice units. Students get to know one teacher well and have choices in the alternate units. The required units should be coeducational, and the choice units should be based on student interest.

Option 2. This option has students assigned to the same teacher all year in a coeducational setting. For every unit or every other unit, the teacher allows students to vote on several activity choices. A majority class vote determines which activity is to be taught. Some of the units could be required and some elective. Students would get to know one teacher very well and have a balance of chosen and required units. One problem with this option is possible difficulty among the teachers in scheduling equipment and facilities. Another drawback is that teachers must prepare for many activities. For example, three different classes may all choose basketball for the same unit, and the facility may accommodate only two basketball classes. In addition, if two-week units are used, a teacher has to prepare for and teach 18 different activities.

Option 3. This model has a set curriculum with no student choice and the same teacher. Problems with facilities are eliminated because the sequence of activities can be coordinated before the year starts. Teachers have to teach a variety of activities and are not able to specialize in specific activities. Stu-

dents do not have any choice of activities. Teachers get to know their students well.

The different models all provide a number of advantages and disadvantages depending on the situation and the teachers involved. All factors should be analyzed carefully as to what is best for students and teachers, and compromises must be made in order to develop a quality program.

CURRICULUM ANALYSIS QUESTIONS FOR GRADES 7 AND 8

The existing curriculum model needs to be thoroughly analyzed before improvements can begin to take place. The following curriculum analysis questions are offered for evaluating an existing program.

1. What is the physical education requirement?
2. What type of schedule exists? (Meetings per week and minutes per meeting)
3. What is the length of the activity units? (Breadth versus depth)
4. What types of activities are offered? (Variety)
5. Is there a balance of activity categories? (e.g., team sports, lifetime sports, aquatics, dance)
6. Is there an attempt to include currently popular activities?
7. Do students have any choice of activities?
8. Are coeducational classes available?
9. What types of fitness activities are offered?
10. Is there a variety of fitness activities included?
11. Are the fitness activities arranged sequentially throughout the year? (Progression)
12. Is there a monitoring system for fitness, physical skills, and knowledge?
13. Is there a system for reporting to parents on physical education specifically?
14. Is there a difference between the 7th and 8th grade programs? (Vertical curriculum organization)
15. Do activities within the year build on previous learning? (Horizontal curriculum organization)

CURRICULUM MODELS FOR GRADE 9

The 9th grade year is the last required unit of physical education in many schools. Physical education is often an optional or elective unit in grades 10–12. It is consequently especially important for 9th graders to leave this final required year with positive approach tendencies toward physical activity. Students should leave the program with a desire to return for additional physical education units and a desire to pursue a lifetime of physical activity.

Ninth graders are usually in a transition state from junior high to senior high school. Some districts put the 9th graders with the 7th and 8th graders, while other districts place them with the 10th, 11th, and 12th grade students. Both arrangements have advantages and disadvantages, and decisions are usually based on such factors as class size, building space, and projected district growth.

The 9th grade curriculum model often takes on the model of the other grades with which the students are placed. The requirements, schedule pattern, length of units, types of activities, amounts of choice, class composition, adapted program, and other factors are frequently the same as those discussed in the junior high school section. The major difference is that the length of the 9th grade units tends to be longer than most 7th and 8th grade units. Some schools allow 9th graders to take longer, specialized units (nine weeks or one semester) in subject areas such as dance, gymnastics, or weight training that are usually offered in a senior high school. Different levels of units may also be available for some 9th graders (e.g., beginning, intermediate, and advanced basketball).

SUGGESTED PROGRAM MODEL FOR GRADE 9

The grade 9 curriculum model for physical education needs to be especially attractive to students, because this may be their last required year of physical education. Making a curriculum attractive does not mean compromising educational objectives. Programs must be designed with specific, valuable objectives in mind, and students should not be allowed to make all curricular decisions in any situation.

A program can be made both attractive and educationally sound by incorporating a number of factors. First, students should have some activity choices for each unit. At this grade level, they need continued opportunities to explore different activities in which they may have an interest. Second, the program should incorporate organized self-testing, personal counseling, and a wellness orientation to give students additional information for making decisions about physical activity and their life-style. Third, the choices of activity should include a wide variety of different categories of physical activity, especially new and popular units such as the martial arts, aerobics, outdoor adventure activities, and jogging. Fourth, the program

must offer more depth in certain activities so students can develop a higher skill level. This means having different unit levels such as beginning, intermediate, and advanced, or at least an opportunity to repeat favorite units. Finally, efforts should be made to develop a positive learning environment so students will learn to like learning and will have a desire to return to additional learning environments.

Classes should meet daily and units can be increased to three weeks in length. Students are still required to take units in the following categories:

   1 unit of Wellness concepts
   1 unit of Team sports
   1 unit of Lifetime sports
   1 unit of Dance
   1 unit of Aquatics
   1 unit of Physical conditioning
   6 units of electives

This requirement ensures a small measure of breadth, and the electives can be used for depth in an activity or for additional breadth, depending on the interests of the student. Ninth graders should be able to repeat a class or take an intermediate-level class as part of their electives. Because students at this age have started to narrow their activity interests, they should be able to start specializing in favorite activities. Their developmental level will allow them to improve quicker than the 7th or 8th graders in the motor skills area. Students who take two units of the same activity should demonstrate visible improvement in skill development.

A short introductory or warm-up activity (3–5 min) is useful to prepare students for the physical fitness segment. These activities should be attractive and challenging. Low organization and large muscle activities should dominate this segment. An example is the popular "high five" activity in which football or basketball teammates slap their hands together with arms overhead after performing some feat of excellence. Ninth graders can be challenged to hit "high fives" after a 90-, 180-, or 360-degree turn to the left or right. This is a good way to prepare students for vigorous fitness activities.

The introductory activity should be changed at least every week. The yearly sequence suggested for grades 7 and 8 can be built on with the many additional examples offered in Chapter 16. For added interest, modified or new warm-up activities can be created, depending on the seasonal time of the year, the type of fitness activity that follows (strength, endurance, flexibility), the type of lesson focus activity that follows (basketball, golf, tennis), or the currently popular television or movie shows (Superstars, *Jaws*, *E.T.*).

A vigorous and demanding physical fitness routine (10–15 min) should follow the introductory segment. A different routine every two weeks gives students a final chance to explore many different fitness activities. Emphasis should be placed on imparting knowledge to students so they understand which activities affect various parameters of fitness. Students need to be taught and encouraged to make decisions relative to physical fitness and their personal fitness routines. They should self-test twice during the year with the AAHPERD Health Related Physical Fitness Test. The results can be reported and interpreted for students and parents. A specific reporting system should be developed (see Chapter 11), and supplementary information provided so that parents and students understand the components of health-related fitness and how to develop and maintain fitness.

The two-week routines in Table 5.4 are suggested for a 9th grade curriculum. Instructors should explain carefully and demonstrate progression and overload principles to students.

Results of a student interest survey combined with the opinions of teachers can be used to determine the activity units offered during the lesson focus segment (25–30 min). The curriculum should be extended into the community to use nearby facilities such as bowling alleys, golf ranges, and ski slopes. Community resources can become an important part of the program both in terms of facilities and instructional personnel. Schools must begin working in concert with the evolving private sports industry.

Physical skills can be monitored with performance objectives for each unit. Educators can use a textbook such as Dougherty's (1983) *Physical Education and Sport for the Secondary School Student* to enhance the knowledge component of a curriculum. Students should take a written test every nine weeks after completing three units. Reading assignments, written work, and outside class projects should be given on a regular basis.

Instructors must take care to build the curriculum horizontally throughout the year, as well as building vertically on the 8th grade program. Increased skill level and more knowledge should be offered for those activities included in previous years.

The sequence of activity units in Table 5.5 is

Table 5.4. Two-Week Routines for a 9th Grade Curriculum

Weeks	Physical Fitness Routines
1– 2	Teacher-leader activities
3– 4	Stretching-flexibility routines
5– 6	Running techniques, drills, and procedures
7– 8	Exercises to music
9–10	Weight training stations
11–12	Four corner courses
13–14	Continuity drills
15–16	Obstacle course and isometrics
17–18	File and interval running
19–20	Squad leader activities
21–22	Circuit training
23–24	Grass drills and partner resistance
25–26	Parachute fitness activities
27–28	Fartlek and random running
29–30	Astronaut drills
31–32	Rope-jumping activities
33–34	Student choice
35–36	Student choice

Table 5.5. Activity Units for a 9th Grade Curriculum With Six Teachers

Weeks	Activity Unit Offerings
1–3	Wellness concepts and fitness testing (6 sections)
4–6	Swimming I and II (2 sections) Flag football Badminton Dance I Recreational games
7–9	Swimming I and II (2 sections) Flag football Volleyball Dance I Physical conditioning and weight training
10–12	Dance II Frisbee games Speed-a-way Basketball Team handball Flag football
13–15	Dance II Tennis I Field hockey

continued

Table 5.5/*continued*

Weeks	Activity Unit Offerings
	Basketball
	Wrestling
	Recreational games
16–18	Aerobics and weight training (2 sections)
	Dance III
	Tennis I
	Badminton
	Lacrosse
19–21	Soccer (2 sections)
	Dance I
	Tennis II
	Volleyball
	Team handball
22–24	Gymnastics
	Basketball II (2 sections)
	Physical conditioning and weight training
	Orienteering and new games
	Field hockey
25–27	Gymnastics
	Basketball II
	Frisbee games
	Lacrosse
	Speed-a-way
	Tennis I
28–30	Dance II
	Volleyball II
	Recreational games
	Wrestling II
	Softball (2 sections)
31–33	Coed dance and fitness self-testing (6 sections)
34–36	Swimming I and II (2 sections)
	Recreational games (2 sections)
	Superstars competition (2 sections)

suggested for a 9th grade curriculum with six teachers and appropriate facilities.

The curriculum options discussed in the 7th and 8th grade section are also possible for the 9th grade model. Two different options discussed in that section could be implemented in the grade 9 structure.

CURRICULUM ANALYSIS QUESTIONS FOR GRADE 9

Curriculum planners should analyze the existing program carefully by answering the following questions. The questions can also help student teachers to analyze an existing program.

1. What is the physical education requirement?
2. How often and how long do the classes meet each week?
3. How long are the units?
4. Do students have choice in selecting units?
5. Is there a variety and balance of units?
6. Is there opportunity for depth of instruction?
7. Is there an organized physical fitness component with variety and progression?
8. Is there an organized monitoring system for skills, fitness, and knowledge?
9. Is there a specific system for reporting to parents?
10. Are there any reading or written assignments?
11. How does the program build in vertical and horizontal components?
12. Are there any formal guidance and counseling aspects to the curriculum?
13. How are students prepared to make meaningful choices about physical activity for a lifetime?
14. How is the curriculum extended into the community?
15. On what basis are new activities added to the curriculum?

SENIOR HIGH SCHOOL MODELS— GRADES 10, 11, AND 12

Senior high school physical education programs vary greatly from state to state and from the large urban schools with 10 to 15 physical education teachers to the small rural schools with 1 or 2 teachers. State requirements are different and some school districts allow a number of substitutions for physical education (e.g., marching band, choral music, health education, and athletics). The local school district and its faculty have the ultimate responsibility for developing the program within the state guidelines. Some districts have a four-year requirement, while others do not have any requirements. In other situations, a district may have a three-year requirement but may allow four different substitutions such as cheerleading, athletics, orchestra, or pom poms to fulfill the requirement. Yet another district may have a two-year requirement with a schedule allowing only two class meetings per week.

The large comprehensive high school may have swimming pools, racquetball courts, a dance studio, and multiple weight rooms; the small school may have only an outdoor field and a single gymnasium. Nearby community facilities also vary considerably in each situation. The climate conditions are another major factor. Schools in central Arizona, for example, can use tennis and racquetball courts year-round, but a school in northeast Ohio must keep students indoors for most of the winter.

All of these factors have a dramatic effect on the physical education program. Even when requirements, facilities, and weather conditions are similar, a significant difference may exist in the schedule, the length of units, the types of activities, the amount of choice, and the class composition.

The variety of models discussed in the grades 7, 8, and 9 sections are also in effect at various high schools across the United States. There are daily schedules, flexible schedules, and 3/2 swing schedules. Some schools have short units, others have four- to five-week units, and still others offer specialized year-long units of modern dance, weight training, or gymnastics. Most programs are still dominated by team sports and lifetime sports; however, many have added aerobics, martial arts, yoga, bicycling, and other new activities. Some high schools give students a choice of activities while others have a set, required sequence. Coeducational classes are the rule in many schools, but others give high school students a choice of a coeducational or a segregated class. In some high schools, students have a choice of activities, and the consequent class composition is determined by interest rather than gender. Adapted classes for special students can follow one of the formats discussed in the 7th and 8th grade section.

SUGGESTED PROGRAM MODEL FOR GRADES 10, 11, AND 12

At this grade level, students are narrowing their range of interests to fewer and fewer specialized areas. This is the case with physical education activities as well. Students are capable and should be able to choose the specific activities they want to pursue. According to Siedentop (1980b):

> Beyond the multi-activity program, students should gradually take over more and more responsibility for electing their own program of physical education. By the 10th grade, the program should be fully elective. Adolescence is no time to force students into certain activity settings as opposed to others. It is a time for growing independence, and physical education should reflect that developmental need, providing structure and guidance in an elective program. (p. 280)

Bain (1980) believes that the high school is a transition from required, supervised participation to voluntary, self-directed participation. She believes that secondary programs should emphasize intramurals and sport, exercise, and dance clubs. Students could enroll in a club rather than a physical education class.

The program should be fully elective, with daily schedules that meet for nine weeks. All classes, except contact sports, should be open to both male or female students. Nine-week units allow for in-depth instruction and a high level of skill competency. High school students have the ability to persist at tasks for a longer period and can benefit from longer units of instruction. After nine weeks of instruction, students should have a sufficient level of skill and knowledge so that the reinforcing aspects of the activity will motivate them to continue outside the school environment. The curriculum should emphasize activities that can be enjoyed for a lifetime (e.g., tennis, racquetball, bicycling, and rock climbing).

Students switch lesson focus activities only after nine weeks of instruction and practice. They can repeat a lesson focus unit, or they can take four different units in one year. Facilities, student interest, and faculty expertise will determine which activities are taught each nine weeks. Community facilities should be used as much as possible within such existing parameters as funds, travel arrangements, and legal liability. The community facilities might include rock climbing areas, parks for orienteering, ski slopes, rivers for canoeing or kayaking, bowling alleys, nautilus equipment, or riding stables. A general physical activities handbook such as Seaton et al. (1983) or Dougherty (1983) should be used to supplement instructional activities found in each unit in this text.

The physical fitness portion of the lesson (10–15 min) should also be elective in nature. Each available teacher coordinates a physical fitness activity at a different teaching station. Specific activities might include stretching, weight lifting, jogging, running intervals, exercising to music, rope jumping, bicycling, and various combinations. Students can attend their preferences on certain days of the week and then switch to different activities on alternate days. After the fitness portion of the lesson, students move to their selected lesson focus with their main teacher. This allows students to select the type and variety of fitness activity they desire.

A high school that has eight teachers available per period and appropriate facilities could offer the following physical fitness stations:

1. Slow long distance running
2. Interval training (running)

3. Continuity drills
4. Weight training
5. Aerobic dancing
6. Exercises to music
7. Stretching and flexibility activities
8. Obstacle course and isometrics

If facilities are limited and certain fitness activities are extremely popular (e.g., weight training, aerobic dancing), then a rotation schedule will have to be worked out and posted in the locker room, or more sections will have to be added at the expense of less popular routines. A rotation plan might allow students whose last names start with the letters A–M to participate on Monday and Wednesday, while those with names beginning with N–Z participate on Tuesday and Thursday. In this situation, teachers would also have to solve potential problems with attendance procedures for students who might ride a special bus to a ski slope or walk to a bowling alley. There might be times when these students would have to miss the fitness portion of the lesson due to the nature of their selected lesson focus. At least once or twice each year, all students should be involved in self-testing using the AAHPERD Health Related Physical Fitness Test to monitor their personal fitness status.

Table 5.6 shows the lesson focus units that could be offered in this same school with eight available teachers.

These classes would be switched from year to year, depending on how classes were attended. Student interest surveys can help determine what units students will select. Teachers can become specialists in specific activities such as racquet sports, outdoor-type activities, or weight training and conditioning, and can thus improve the quality and level of instruction that students receive.

This curriculum format should help school programs compete with the growing private sports instruction industry for community dollars. A public relations program can communicate this information to the general public. The physical education profession can no longer afford to offer programs that show little or no concern for student preference.

Many options in this model can be developed to fit the facilities, equipment, schedule, and philosophy of a particular high school. A school with six-week grading periods may want to have six-week rather than nine-week units. A school with a 3/2 swing schedule may desire units that are longer than nine weeks. Students located in certain geographic locations may be especially interested in units on surfing, ice hockey, fishing, canoeing, or

Table 5.6. Activity Units for a High School Curriculum With Eight Teachers	
Weeks	**Elective Class Offerings**
1–9	Golf and bowling combination Tennis Wellness concepts Orienteering and Frisbee Modern dance Weight training Swimming and diving Volleyball
10–18	Racquetball Tennis Basketball Gymnastics Modern dance Weight training Camping and backpacking Rock climbing
19–27	Golf Bowling Bicycling Badminton Modern dance Weight training Conditioning Yoga
28–36	Soccer Water sports Racquetball Orienteering and Frisbee Modern dance Weight training Sailing and canoeing Volleyball

lacrosse. Certain communities have strong interests in specific activities such as golf, sailing, or horseback riding, and community facilities can then be an integral part of the school program. All of these factors need to be considered and incorporated in each specific situation.

CURRICULUM ANALYSIS QUESTIONS FOR GRADES 10, 11, AND 12

Planners of a senior high physical education curriculum should pose the following questions about their program:

1. What is the physical education requirement?
2. What type of schedule exists?
3. How long are the units?

4. Do the students have any choice of units?
5. How many units are required?
6. Is variety, balance, and depth of units offered?
7. Is the fitness component organized with variety, progression, and overload principles in mind?
8. What type of monitoring system exists for physical skills, physical fitness, and knowledge?
9. Are there any self-testing procedures for students?
10. Are there any formal guidance and counseling procedures?
11. Are there any reading or written assignments for students?
12. Is the curriculum organized to consider both horizontal and vertical components?
13. How is the curriculum extended into the community?
14. Are community facilities or personnel used in the curriculum?
15. What information is used to add activities to and delete activities from the program?

ARTICULATING THE PROGRAM: KINDERGARTEN THROUGH GRADE 12

More often than not, physical education curricula are developed in parts. There is usually a curriculum model for the elementary school level, one for the junior high school and another for the senior high school. Each model is written and organized independently of the others. A district-wide plan that considers factors such as state requirements, facilities, scheduling, and equipment is seldom developed. In many cases, elementary physical education specialists do not know junior and senior high school physical education teachers, let alone have an understanding of the curriculum at each level. Teachers often "do their own thing" without concern for or knowledge of what is done at other levels. This leads to a fragmented program that shows little connection between levels. Time, energy, and learning activities may be wasted, duplicated, or omitted in a curriculum that is not vertically articulated.

The model for grades 7–12 presented in this chapter builds vertically on the K–6 elementary model developed by Dauer and Pangrazi (1983). It follows basically the same daily lesson plan format, and uses arrangements of learning activities appropriate for the developmental level of students involved at a specific grade level. The entire

Table 5.7. Kindergarten–12 Curriculum Components

	K	1	2	3	4	5	6	7	8	9	10	11	12
						Grades							
Required units	–	–	–	–	–	–	–	Elective units					
Variety and exploration	–	–	–	–Specialized units									
Balance and breadth	–	–	–	–	–	–	–	–	Depth				
Physical fitness	–	–	–	–	–	–	–	Physical fitness					
Required and varied	–	–	–	–	–	Choice							
Wellness concepts	–	–	–	–	–	Wellness concepts							
Required	–	–	–	–	–	–	–	–	–	Choice			

K–12 model emphasizes individual success, physical fitness, exploration, guidance and counseling, self-testing, monitoring, physical skill development, requisite knowledge, wellness concepts, choice within requirement, and preparation for a lifetime of physical activity. Students are given requirements, choices, and activities as shown in Table 5.7.

Summary

This chapter provides school districts with a sound, progressively arranged physical education curriculum that has been field-tested by the authors in many school districts. Options have been used depending on the specific factors involved. The model is built on educational theory and research, as well as on practical factors influencing teaching-learning environments. It gives students many successful encounters with physical activity, so they will leave the physical education program with approach tendencies for learning in general and for physical activities in particular. Teachers develop expertise in specialized areas, which improves their motivational level and the quality of instruction. These are some of the advantages of a curriculum that has been developed through diaglogue with and the expertise of teachers and experts in physical education.

References

Bain, L. 1980. Socialization into the role of participant: Physical education's ultimate goal. *JOPERD* 51(7): 48–50.

Benson, J. 1982. An alternative direction for middle school physical education. *The Physical Educator* 39(2): 75–77.

Blaufarb, M. *Complying with Title IX of the Educational Amendments of 1972 in Physical Education and High School Sports Programs.* Reston, VA: AAHPERD Publications, 1978(a).

Blaufarb, M. *Title IX Sex-Integrated Programs That Work.* Reston, VA: AAHPERD Publications, 1978(b).

Dauer, V. P., and Pangrazi, R. P. *Dynamic Physical Education for Elementary School Children.* 7th ed. Minneapolis: Burgess Publishing Co., 1983.

Dougherty, N., ed. *Physical Education and Sport for the Secondary School Student.* Reston, VA: AAHPERD Publications, 1983.

Melograno, V. *Designing Curriculum and Learning: A Physical Coeducational Approach.* Dubuque, IA: Kendall/Hunt Publishing, 1979.

Pangrazi, R., et al. 1982. The needed link: A physical curriculum designed exclusively for junior high students. *The Physical Educator* 39(2): 71–74.

Seaton, D. C., et al. *Physical Education Handbook.* 7th ed. Englewood Cliffs, NJ: Prentice-Hall, Inc., 1983.

Siedentop, D. 1980(a). Physical education curriculum: An analysis of the past. *JOPERD* 51(7): 40–41.

Siedentop, D. *Physical Education—Introductory Analysis.* 3rd ed. Dubuque, IA: Wm. C. Brown Group, 1980(b).

PART III

DEVELOPING A QUALITY INSTRUCTIONAL PROGRAM

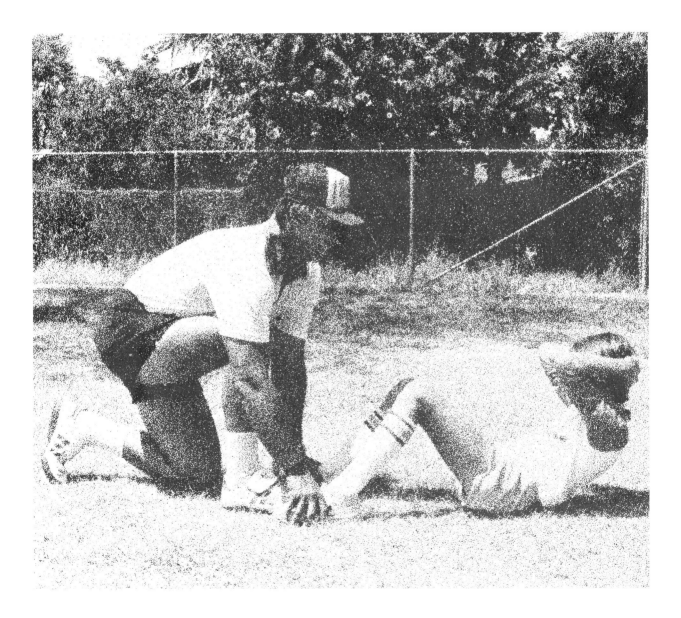

Chapter 6

Implementing the Curriculum Effectively

Policies, Procedures, and Equipment

The development and implementation of a high-quality physical education program require that a number of policies and procedures be determined, communicated, and applied consistently to all students. Effective physical education programs have a well-developed set of written guidelines that are presented to the students on the first day of school and are reinforced continually throughout the year. Policies and procedures should be evaluated constantly to determine if they are actually contributing to program objectives. An excellent curriculum will not be effective without a well-developed set of policies and procedures and an ongoing revision process.

These guidelines should be written in a handbook or booklet and be available for all students, parents, and administrators. Teachers should discuss the information with students and require that students discuss the information with their parents. Some type of form indicating that parents have read the guidelines should be signed and returned to the physical education teacher (Figure 6.1). Many students and parents have misconceptions about the nature of physical education, and clarifying all aspects of the program as soon as possible is therefore important.

The physical education handbook should cover the following areas: (1) philosophy of the program, (2) curriculum objectives, (3) program scope and graduation requirements, (4) uniform and dressing requirements, (5) showers and towels, (6) locks and lockers, (7) attendance and participation, (8) excuses and makeup procedures, (9) equipment, and (10) grading procedures. The handbook should be brief, clear, and succinct, and completed in 5 to 10 pages. A cover letter (Figure 6.1) should be enclosed and include a return slip for the physical education teacher. Parents and students must be encouraged to question any aspect of the program that they find unclear or disagreeable.

PHILOSOPHY AND OBJECTIVES

Communicating the department's views and objectives for the program is especially important. (Refer to Chapter 1 for a general discussion of physical education and program objectives.) Many

---

OVATION HIGH SCHOOL PHYSICAL EDUCATION DEPARTMENT
OVATION, AZ

Dear Parents:

This booklet contains the policies and procedures of the physical education department. We would like you to read carefully and discuss the program regulations with your son or daughter. These policies and procedures are important for making the learning environment a pleasant experience for all students.

We desire to have all students leave physical education classes with a positive attitude and the urge to be physically active throughout their lifetime. If you have any questions about the curriculum or the policies and procedures of the department, please call me at 925-4724.

Please sign the slip at the bottom of the sheet and have your youth return it to school.

Thank you.

Sincerely,

_____

Physical Education Teacher

- -

We have read the booklet and understand the policies and procedures.

_____   _____
Parent   Student

_____
Date

Figure 6.1.   Letter to parents regarding policies and procedures

people have varying views of physical education (e.g., strictly as a physical training program or a training ground for the athletic program), and many adults have little information about the new approaches to physical education. A short one-page discussion dealing with philosophy and objectives can be a sound beginning for parental and student understanding of the nature and importance of the program.

PROGRAM SCOPE AND GRADUATION REQUIREMENTS

Parents and students need to understand how physical education fits into the graduation requirements of the school. Many schools in each state will have varying amounts of physical education as a graduation requirement. In some districts, physical education credit is awarded for partici-

pation in athletics, cheerleading squads, marching band, ROTC, and driver education classes. These substitutions are a controversial topic that has been argued for years. Many physical educators have strong feelings on both sides of the issue as to what should be included in the scope of the physical education program.

The best way to answer the question of which activities should be awarded physical education credit is to examine the objectives of the program. If an activity fulfills the program objectives, then credit should be awarded for participation in that activity. If the activity does not fulfill the objectives, then physical education credit should not be awarded. Athletics, marching band, ROTC, and driver education are all important and valuable experiences for students but, in most cases, they do not fulfill the total objectives of physical education. If a school board wants to award credit for participation in these activities, administrators should designate the credit appropriately, rather than labeling it physical education.

It is easy to understand why some people argue the physical benefits of the marching band or the skills developed while playing on a basketball team. These are, however, only a small portion of the objectives of a quality physical education program. Students need to experience success with a variety of lifetime sports and fitness activities, and to receive knowledge about health, exercise, and nutrition. This information is imparted to students and their parents through the physical education program. The program handbook is a starting point for developing parent and student awareness.

Another important aspect of the program scope relates to coeducational classes. Many parents will have had little or no experience with sexually integrated physical education classes, and convincing them of the benefits of coeducational classes may be difficult. Parents and students need time to slowly expand their comfort zones regarding this issue. The departmental handbook can begin "socializing" people to the idea of sexually integrated classes.

UNIFORMS AND DRESS REQUIREMENTS

Students should be strongly encouraged to change into active wear for physical education classes. The importance of comfort, safety, and hygiene must be emphasized. Many schools still require a specific uniform and enforce strict dress codes. Uniforms and dress codes can create many problems and continue to be a source of controversy. Students will often avoid physical education environments simply because of a dress code requirement, yet these same students will admit that they enjoy physical activities and would take a class if no dress code existed. The benefits of having all students dressed alike does not seem worth developing escape and avoidance behaviors in students.

Controversy over uniforms and dress codes should not develop into a critical issue. If the school favors a dress code, a student committee can be formed each year to select a new uniform. Clothing companies will provide several available options with school colors, emblems, or mascots. Students can then decide which uniform they desire, or they can be given the option of buying a different type of uniform. Several choices should be available. Adolescence is not a time to force students to wear the same clothes. It is, rather, a time of growing independence, and allowing students to select their

physical education attire will not be detrimental to the accomplishment of program objectives (Figure 6.2).

In addition, each physical activity class is different and may require some type of specialized clothing that is appropriate for the activity. Rock climbing or horseback riding classes may require the wearing of long pants for safety. Aerobics, yoga, and the martial arts also necessitate specialized clothing for freedom of movement. Students certainly need warm attire in outdoor, cold-weather environments.

Another problem is the legality of an imposed dress code. Some state laws stipulate that if a school requires a specific dress code, the school must purchase uniforms for those students unable to do so. Dress codes can also create problems for students with a specific religious belief disallowing the wearing of gymnasium attire. Still other students may have physical deformities or embarrassing conditions that they wish to keep covered. For example, a student who has a severe case of acne on his back may not want to go swimming without a shirt and expose his upper body.

These problems underline why a flexible policy on uniforms and dress requirements is desirable. The perceived advantages of having a strict dress code—developing discipline, school spirit, and cooperation; enhancing the identification of teams; reducing discrimination against poorer or wealthier students; and reducing unit cost of attire because of large orders—are all on shaky grounds and do not appear to be worth the problems generated. Teachers and students should both influence the

Figure 6.2.   Participating in a variety of uniforms

decisions on dress requirements, and teachers should have the flexibility to make decisions that facilitate the learning process of each individual in each situation.

The department should have a policy regarding students who, because of financial problems, cannot afford a uniform or a change of clothes. Often, a special fund can be made available through candy or bake sales. The parent-teacher association may be able to provide funds through one of its projects. Sometimes used or unclaimed clothes can be cleaned and worn by students who cannot afford to buy a uniform.

A recommended policy on the laundering of gymnasium clothes should be presented to students. Some schools require students to bring in clean clothes every Monday for the physical education teacher to inspect. The authors believe that this area should be one of personal choice, as with the laundering of regular street clothes. Depending on how often a class meets, teachers should encourage students to launder their gym clothes once or twice a week. If hygiene problems occur, students and eventually parents should be contacted. Getting students to develop personal management skills early in the physical education setting is important.

Junior high school students can be quite careless in keeping track of personal belongings. Students who wear similar uniforms must identify them with some type of permanent ink or name tag because of the numerous opportunities for mix-ups, losses, or pilferage.

Teachers need to be good models of appropriate attire for physical activities. An active teaching role is certainly enhanced by appropriate dress, and students are strongly influenced by the behavior of their teachers. It is difficult to defend teaching in blue jeans when students are not allowed to participate in similar attire. Educators must be careful to analyze personal policies and behavior. Many times, teachers fail to realize the inconsistencies they have developed in the learning environment. This is part of the hidden curriculum that was discussed in Chapter 3.

ATTENDANCE, PARTICIPATION, AND EXCUSES

Teachers should work continually at making the learning environment a positive experience for students. If students enjoy the experience, there are fewer problems with attendance and participation. The overall curriculum and the instructional procedures will have more of an effect on students than the policies and procedures dealing with attendance and participation. Many teachers spend so much time and energy on developing and enforcing these latter policies and procedures that they lose sight of the importance of curriculum and instruction. Students will be more enthusiastic about physical education if a quality curriculum and an effective instructional program exist.

Nevertheless, teachers do need to develop policies for attendance, participation, and excuses from class. A positive approach system in which students can earn various reinforcers (e.g., points, activity time, privileges) for attending and participating is an effective strategy. Too often, teachers use a negative or "chop" system by which students lose points or privileges or receive lower grades for inappropriate behavior. This approach creates a negative environment, while the positive approach has the opposite effect. Students can be awarded one point per day for attendance, one point for dressing, and points for participating, rather than subtracting or cutting points for not attending and participating. This award system allows students to earn points in a positive environment. Attendance and participation behaviors provide a certain measure of success on a daily basis, rather than producing the avoidance or escape tendencies that arise from the repeated loss or "chop" of points. The positive system approaches problems in a different manner in order to develop a healthy atmosphere.

All medical excuses and notes from parents should be presented to the school nurse at the beginning of the school day rather than during class time. Teachers should spend class time on instruction rather than analyzing excuses. In addition, the nurse is more qualified than the physical educator to make decisions about medical problems requiring special attention. The nurse should make the final decision on participation and should communicate with the physical education teacher both verbally and in writing. A form can be developed to facilitate this communication (Figure 6.3). Teachers must be aware of student differences. Some students will want to return to the activities too soon, while others may not want to return even when appropriate.

If students cannot participate for three consecutive days, they should be recommended to a physician. A physician's report (Figure 6.4) should then

---

SCHOOL NURSE EXCUSE FORM

Student _____   Date _____

Please excuse the above named student from physical education class for the following day(s):

_____

The reason the student is excused is: _____

_____

_____

_____

_____

...e of form ...between ... physical ...hat credit ...o people ...ons.

...h as being ...r cramps ...is. Some ...ms while ...owledge- ...alities of ...students the same is usually misdirected.

Religious beliefs relative to participating on various holidays or holy days often result in students' asking to be excused. This should be handled individually with each student and through the school administration. If any confusion arises about excuses due to minor illness or religious beliefs, then students should be allowed to see the school nurse for illnesses and a guidance counselor or administrator about preferences and beliefs.

Teachers need to remember that students are people who have bad days, headaches, cramps, family problems, and other type of concerns that will affect their daily performance. Sometimes students need a little extra encouragement to participate, and at other times they may need a day off. Effective teachers take the time and make the effort to get to know their students so they have some basis for judging individual situations. In contrast, some teachers believe that students are "cheating" on them if the student does not want to participate on a given day. Initially, students should be given the benefit of a doubt, because they may indeed have a problem. If the same student continues to have participation problems, the teacher will have to contact the parents or apply some alternative procedures.

A policy for tardiness should also be developed. A precise starting time for each class must be followed consistently. Students need to know exactly what time the class begins, and excessive tardiness may have to be built into the makeup policies and procedures for grades.

PHYSICIAN'S REPORT

Date _____

Dear Dr. _____

   The following student, _____ , has requested that he/she be excused from physical education activities. We would like your help in designing a program that is appropriate for this student's physical condition. Our program offers a wide variety of physical activities. Please complete the following information to enable us to develop a personalized program.

   Thank you for your time.

Sincerely,

_____

Physical Education Department Head

- -

1. Type of illness, injury, or handicap _____

   _____

2. Restrictions _____

3. Activities to be avoided _____

4. Duration of restriction _____

5. Other important information _____

   _____

6. Physician name _____

   Address _____ Phone _____

7. Signature _____ Date _____

Please send form to: Person _____

                     School _____

                     Address _____

Figure 6.4. Physician's report

CLASS MAKEUP POLICIES AND PROCEDURES

All students should be given an opportunity to make up missed classes because of excused absences. Every attempt should be made to focus the makeup work on the activities that were missed.

Attending another physical education class or an extra class on the same activities is a useful idea. Possibilities for makeup work can focus on knowledge activities, performance activities, or spectator activities. Depending on the objectives of the lessons missed, some activities will be more valuable than others. The following are examples that could be used in each area.

MAKEUP WORK—KNOWLEDGE ACTIVITIES

The following alternatives might be offered to students who missed a knowledge activity. Students would be instructed to complete one of the following assignments and turn it in to the instructor:

1. Read an article in the sports section of the newspaper and write a one-page analysis (form provided).
2. Read an article in any sports magazine and write a one-page analysis (form provided).
3. Read a short biographical sketch about a noted sports figure and write a one-page analysis (form provided).
4. List and define 15 terms from any of the following activities: basketball, field hockey, flag football, lacrosse, orienteering, physical conditioning, recreational games, running techniques, soccer, swimming, team handball, and volleyball.
5. List and explain ten rules from any sport.
6. Diagram the playing area of any of the activities listed in no. 4.
7. Read a book related to a sport and write a one-page analysis (form provided).
8. Student choice (with teacher approval).

The form reproduced in Figure 6.5 can be used for student reports on these knowledge activities.

MAKEUP WORK—PERFORMANCE ACTIVITIES

Students who have missed performance activities might be told to participate in any of the following activities and to write a one-page analysis (form provided):

1. Run a mile for time.
2. Run a parcourse.
3. Ride a bike for 30 min.
4. Attend an aerobics class.
5. Lift weights for 30 min.
6. Play 18 holes of disc golf.
7. Play one set of tennis.
8. Play two games of racquetball.
9. Play 18 holes of regular golf.
10. Engage in a workout at a health spa.
11. Student choice (approved by instructor).

The form in Figure 6.6 can be used for reports in the performance area.

MAKEUP WORK—SPECTATOR ACTIVITIES

Tell students to observe one of the following events and write a one-page analysis (form provided). These events can take place at the junior or senior high school, community college, college, or professional level. Any of the following event activities is acceptable: football, soccer, cross country running, tennis, volleyball, basketball,

---

ARTICLE REPORT

Name _____

Date _____

Publication _____

Author _____

Major idea of article:

Your opinion of the material:

What are the benefits of this material to you?

Parent or guardian signature _____

Figure 6.5. Knowledge analysis sheet

PERFORMANCE ANALYSIS

Name _____

Activity _____

Date _____

Explain the activity you participated in.

Explain the physical benefits of this activity.

What were your score, time repetitions, and so forth?

Parent or guardian signature _____

Figure 6.6. Performance analysis sheet

softball, baseball, wrestling, track and field, swimming, and student choice (approved by instructor). Figure 6.7 is a form that can be used for reporting on spectator activities.

SHOWERS AND TOWELS

Students should be encouraged to shower after all vigorous activity sessions. Teachers must spend some time discussing hygiene and why showering is necessary. Students need to understand the importance of developing lifetime health habits.

Showering, like the uniform issue, should not evolve into a polarizing conflict. Many physical educators have developed avoidance behaviors in students because of inflexible or poorly managed showering policies. For example, one teacher required students to shower after every class including golf, archery, riflery, and discussion sessions. Showering is surely not necessary after every physical education class. Other teachers have given students only 5 to 7 min to shower and change clothes. This is not enough time for students to fix their hair and clothes and prepare to return to the classroom. Students' caring about their appearance is an important aspect of personal development. Physical education teachers who overlook this fact often alienate students.

Teachers need to analyze carefully the nature of each lesson and the allotted time schedule. Swimming, for example, requires more preparation time at the end of class, and an archery activity does not necessitate showering. Showering policies should be flexible so teachers can make the appropriate time adjustments in lessons. Many students are uncomfortable showering in front of peers due to menstruation, underdeveloped bodies, acne problems, deformities, or various other problems. Private showers can help alleviate this concern. Teachers need to be sensitive to the fact that poorly planned and poorly administered showering and dressing procedures can turn students off to physical activity for a lifetime.

When students are resistant to taking showers, teachers need to search for the underlying reason. Possibly an adjustment of times allotted can remedy the problem, and if the activities are not vigorous, showering may not be necessary for all students.

Students should have a say in matters of personal health and cleanliness. If teachers make all of the decisions for students, little is learned about making decisions in later life. If students complain about peers who possess strong body odor, the matter should be discussed with the student and, possibly, with his or her parents. Some type of motivational system can be devised if necessary to encourage students to shower (see "Behavior Games" in Chapter 8). Awarding points, activity time, or free time can be used to motivate showering behaviors. Teachers should try to avoid incorporating showering and dressing behaviors in the grading system, but it may be necessary in certain situations.

Figure 6.7. Spectator analysis sheet

Students need to be reminded of the hazards in showering facilities. The shower room can be a dangerous area, and horseplay cannot be tolerated. Care must be taken when walking to and from the area, and absolutely no glass containers for food, drink, shampoo, or soap are allowed.

A policy on towels should also be determined. The simplest procedure is to have students bring towels from home along with their activity clothing. Students are then responsible for changing towels and uniforms on a regular basis. Names can be marked on the towels to minimize loss.

Some districts provide students with towels for physical education class. The towels can be purchased by the school and laundered on a regular basis in school facilities. This arrangement helps reduce mildew and odor problems created by students leaving wet towels in their lockers, and students are also motivated to shower because there are clean, dry towels available. The school must, however, purchase towels and laundering equipment, and hire someone to oversee the process. The towels need to be checked out and in each day, and a security system developed. This approach thus creates a number of additional management problems for teachers.

Still other schools use a towel service company that provides freshly laundered towels on a daily basis. This approach is usually more expensive but easier to manage.

Funding for a towel service can come from the school's general budget, a student fee, a booster club project, or a physical education department project such as selling candy, painter hats, or car washes. Each school district has fund-raising and budget procedures that need to be followed. The physical education staff needs to weigh carefully the advantages and disadvantages of each towel supply procedure before making a decision. It is also possible to try several methods before deciding on a specific procedure.

LOCKS, LOCKERS, AND THE LOCKER ROOM

Locker room procedures must be carefully organized to increase the efficiency of students moving to and from classes. Students need to know which doors to use at various times and for various activities. Classes will be coming and going all day, so the development of efficient traffic flow patterns to and from the locker room is a necessity.

Various types of locks and lockers are available. Most schools assign students a combination lock and a small wire basket or metal locker in which to keep their activity clothes. A longer, larger locker is usually available for street clothes during each activity period. The longer lockers commonly alternate with the shorter lockers throughout the locker room. This helps to spread students around and to use the entire area. The older students should be assigned the upper locker rows to ensure that students can reach higher rows. The school usually provides the combination lock, and the teacher keeps a master list of combinations in his or her office. Students may be allowed to bring their own locks, but this can create problems for teacher access in emergency situations. Teachers must also keep a master list of which student occupies which locker. This can be done with a student locker assignment sheet (Figure 6.8). Problems such as forgotten combinations or misplaced locks can be readily solved when the teacher has a master list of combinations and the locker assignment sheet.

Supervision procedures for the locker room must be arranged to ensure safety and theft prevention. The room should be locked during class time to prevent thefts. Teachers should walk through the locker room regularly to check for unlocked lockers and clothes and towels that are left out by accident. This routine will also reduce the loss due to theft. In some situations, teacher aides can be hired to supervise the locker room, distribute towels, and help maintain the management policies.

EQUIPMENT

Proper types of equipment in adequate amounts are a must for implementing a high-quality program. Students cannot learn various physical skills without the proper equipment. Physical education departments need basketballs, tennis racquets, and Frisbees, just as math and reading departments need books, paper, and pencils. Students cannot learn to play tennis without a racquet, some tennis balls,

STUDENT LOCKER ASSIGNMENTS

Teacher _____

Class period _____

Locker Number	Student's Name (Alphabetical Order)	Lock Number	Combination

Figure 6.8. Locker assignment sheet

and the opportunity to practice on courts. In many instances, physical education departments are asked to get along without proper amounts of equipment. A class of 35 students needs more than five basketballs, six volleyballs, or ten tennis racquets. Many administrators have to be shown that physical education is much more than one or two games of a specific activity. Students cannot learn to read without books, and they cannot learn physical skills without the proper equipment and adequate practice time.

PURCHASE

Funds from the general school budget should be used to purchase equipment for the physical education program, and the physical education budget and student-teacher ratio should be equal to those of other academic areas of the school. The physical education budget must be separate from the athletic budget. Some pieces of equipment can be shared, but a definite distinction should be made between the two budgets.

Equipment priorities should be determined by student interest surveys and the number of students who will be able to use the equipment. Certain activities are offered more frequently than others, and equipment for these should be a higher priority. Certain types of equipment may receive lower priority because students are able to bring their own from home. This is a policy that must be determined by the department.

Equipment should be ordered from local dealers if at all possible. They are an important part of the community and will usually provide fast and efficient service for the local schools. In addition, they usually support the schools and will provide the best possible prices on equipment. Regional or nationwide companies may be able to provide reasonable prices on some equipment. Service, however, is often slower, and an order may not be filled for one to six months. Check with other teachers and schools on the reputation and reliability of specific companies before placing a large order. State and regional physical education conventions are attended by the equipment dealers in each area. This is a good opportunity to meet the dealers and discuss prices and new equipment.

The quality and price of equipment should be studied carefully before making a purchase. Check with other schools to see what experiences they have had with specific equipment. The cheapest price is not always the best deal. Durability and longevity are especially important. Equipment dealers may not know how well certain equipment will hold up over a period of time. This is why talking with people who are currently using the equipment is important.

The concept or progression in buying equipment is usually quite useful in negotiating with budget committees or school boards when a large amount of capital is necessary for equipment. If several thousand dollars is needed to add equipment for a new activity, it may be possible to implement the activity in three phases over three years. The activity could be started with $800 to $1000 for the first year, and more equipment could be added gradually over the next few years. A budget committee is usually more receptive to this approach.

A show of student interest and student willingness to bring in personal equipment for particular activities is also an effective strategy for gaining administrative support for an activity. Offering a cycling unit with each student bringing in a bicycle to use in the class, or offering a golf class in which students use their own clubs are effective means of generating student and administrative interest in new activities.

Another source of equipment is to have it constructed by the physical education staff, the maintenance department, or the industrial arts classes. Starting blocks, relay batons, soccer goals, team handball goals, and jump ropes are examples of equipment that can be constructed. Care must be taken to ensure that all safety specifications have been met. There are several books and articles that describe how to make homemade equipment (Dauer and Pangrazi 1983, Corbin and Corbin 1983).

Physical education equipment can also be purchased jointly with other schools, city parks and recreation departments, and the athletic department. Many districts, for example, jointly purchase free weights and weight machines for the use of athletes, physical education classes, and adult community education programs. Joint purchases are an excellent way to share costs and involve the entire community. This method can be used for purchasing tennis, racquetball, badminton, volleyball, softball, basketball, and aerobic dance equipment.

STORAGE, DISTRIBUTION, AND MAINTENANCE

An accurate equipment inventory should be completed at the beginning and the end of each school year. Records should be kept from year to year to determine the needs of the department and to facilitate the purchasing process. Documenting the type and amount of equipment lost each year will also provide information for improving the security and distribution procedures.

A storage area (Figure 6.9) that is easily accessible to both male and female teachers is desirable. It is also important for the storage area to be in close proximity to the teaching stations (i.e., the gym, fields, and courts). It is inconvenient to pick up and return equipment to an area that is too great a distance from the station. The storage area should contain labeled shelves, bins, and containers for all pieces of equipment. Every piece should have a designated space. All teachers, student leaders, and students who have access to the area need to cooperate fully in keeping the area clean and orderly. It is easy to become quite disorganized when many different people are sharing equipment.

Teachers need adequate methods for transporting equipment to and from the teaching areas. Various types of ball bags, shopping-type carts, and portable ball carts are available. These will reduce the amount of class management time expended on equipment transport. Students can be given responsibilities for the movement of equipment if they are trained properly.

A system should be developed for using equipment that is not designated on the yearly master curriculum. A sign-up and check-out list should be posted in the storage area along with the yearly sequence of activities. The department head or equipment coordinator should then be notified if any changes are made in the schedule with regard to equipment. This will prevent problems with teachers not having the equipment necessary for their classes. Equipment should not be loaned to outside groups without following the designated procedures. If equipment is shared or loaned to other groups, it must be marked or identified with some regulation code to prevent losses or mix-ups with equipment from other sources.

Procedures should also be developed for repairing and maintaining equipment. Decisions on which equipment to repair and who will repair it must be made. If the repair work is minor and can be completed at school, then who will do the work and where will it be done? If equipment must be sent out for repair, then where will it be sent and how will it be sent?

These decisions are all part of the ongoing process of implementing a quality physical education curriculum. Equipment is part of a program's lifeblood. Without adequate equipment, the effectiveness of the teaching-learning environ-

Figure 6.9. Storage area

ment is greatly reduced, because students without equipment will become bored, unmotivated, and troublesome for the teacher. How can students learn to dribble, pass, and shoot a basketball when they must stand in line and take turns sharing a ball with five or six other students? The goal of a program should be to provide every student with a piece of equipment. The productive learning time can thus be greatly enhanced.

GRADING PROCEDURES

The grading procedures are an important part of the policies and procedures described in the department handbook, and should be determined and discussed with students during the first week of classes. Parents should also be made fully aware of this area. Evaluation and grading recommendations are discussed in detail in Chapter 11.

Summary

The policies, procedures, and equipment are important aspects of implementing a high-quality program. Department members must come to agreement on many issues, and all of these issues should be in keeping with the program's objectives. The resultant policies should then be presented to students, parents, and administrators. A certain amount of freedom and flexibility must be built into the implementation process. For example, teachers should be allowed to make decisions that are best for certain students in certain situations. Upholding the policies and procedures should not become more important than the well being of teachers and students. An adequate amount of equipment is crucial to an effective program. Many alternatives for acquiring equipment should be explored.

References

Dauer, V.P., and Pangrazi, R. P. *Dynamic Physical Education for Elementary School Children*. 7th ed. Minneapolis: Burgess Publishing Co., 1983.

Corbin, D. and Corbin, C. 1983. Homemade play equipment. *JOPERD* 54(6): 35–38.

Chapter 7

Planning and Organizing for Instruction

A distinction was made earlier in the text between curriculum and instruction. Curriculum is the what and why of education, and instruction is the how. Curriculum and instruction are interdependent in that a quality curriculum is not effective without quality instruction and vice versa. The result of a well-developed curriculum and clear instructional procedures is a systematic presentation of activities, knowledges, and attitudes. The curriculum gives direction and guidance to instructional procedures. To assure quality instruction, teachers should carefully plan daily presentations using the accepted curriculum. The focus of this chapter is to examine the essential components of instruction and how to plan for those components.

PLANNING FOR QUALITY INSTRUCTION

The importance of planning a lesson cannot be overemphasized. Instructors at the junior and senior high school level have, at times, been criticized for their lack of planning. A cycle of not planning sometimes begins when student teachers observe master teachers doing little, if any, planning. The emphasis placed on developing meaningful lesson and unit plans in professional preparation courses seems unnecessary when a master teacher appears successful without the aid of thoughtful planning. The beginning teacher is unable, however, to meaningfully judge the effectiveness of the master teacher because of a lack of perspective and experience. The master teacher also may have taught the material for many years and may have evolved a method of presentation through trial and error. In any case, teachers must understand that it is possible to present a lesson without planning, but the quality of the lesson can, in almost all cases, be improved through research, preparation, and a well-sequenced plan.

A strong case for planning can be made if a teacher desires to be creative and develop the ability to interact well with students. Teachers, regardless of their experience and ability, have many elements to remember while teaching. When presenting a lesson, many situations occur that are impossible to predict. For example, dealing with discipline problems; the need to modify the lesson spontaneously; relating to students by name; offering praise, feedback, and reinforcement; and developing an awareness of teaching behavior patterns are difficult to predetermine. If the content of the lesson is planned, written, and readily available, the teacher does not have to concentrate solely on the content of the lesson and can place greater emphasis on other, equally important phases of teaching.

Lesson planning is somewhat unique to each teacher. The competency of the individual in various activities will determine to some extent the depth of the lesson-planning effort. More research and reading will have to be done for a unit activity in which the teacher has little experience. If the teacher is unfamiliar with a unit and still refuses to plan, the quality of instruction will be poor. Too often the scope of a curriculum is limited by the competencies of teachers who are unwilling to prepare and learn new skills and knowledges.

The purpose of planning a lesson is to increase the effectiveness of the instructor. Lesson plans should be designed for specific situations. Regardless of the content of the lesson, the general points below should be considered when developing a plan:

1. Learning physical skills demands practice and repetition. Each lesson should be organized to maximize the amount of meaningful participation and to minimize the amount of teacher verbalization and off-task student behavior.

2. Practice combined with instruction and meaningful feedback assures skill development. Instructional sequences and procedures to increase the amount of feedback can be written into the lesson plan. Key points to be learned may require regular and specific feedback to ensure that correct learning patterns occur.

3. Lesson plans should consider the ability level of the students. A range of activities should be built into each lesson plan so students can progress at varying rates, depending on their level of skill. The activities should be written in proper progression to enhance the rate of learning.

4. Equipment needed should be written into the lesson plan. This prevents the problem of being in the middle of a lesson only to find that needed equipment was not gathered. The initial placement of equipment and how it is to be distributed and put away are tasks that should be planned before teaching.

5. Time needed for management activities can be minimized by prior planning. The plan should list whether students are to be in small groups or partnered, the type of formation required, and how these procedures will be carried out.

6. Outcomes of the lesson should be listed. The direction of the lesson is assured when both instructor and students know where they are going. The outcomes can be written in brief form but should state clearly to students what they are expected to learn.

7. Since lesson plans are highly personal, they can be written in code. All information need not be written out in longhand. For example, effective teachers often write their lesson plan on 3-by-5-in. cards, which can be carried easily and used with a minimum of distraction. The important point is that the card contents reflect the instructor's thought and planning that have occurred before the actual teaching session.

8. Estimated time should be allotted to various activities in the lesson. For example, the amount of time for roll call, warm-up activity, fitness development, and activities in the lesson focus should be estimated. The time schedule need not be strictly adhered to, but it should be followed closely enough so that all planned activities are taught.

9. Planning should be seen as an important phase of teaching. Few teachers instruct for more than four to five hours per day. If an eight-hour day is expected of other workers, instructors should expect that part of their remaining working time will be used for planning. Consider a comparison with coaching. All highly successful coaches spend a great deal of time planning, observing films, and constructing game plans. The game may not last more than an hour or two, but many hours of planning took place before the contest. Teachers of physical education should recognize the need to spend some time each day planning for four to five hours of daily teaching. The results of a well-planned lesson are rewarding to both students and teacher.

10. Planning should build in success for students. Enough challenge to motivate and enough variety to maintain a level of interest should be written into the plan. A balance of safety and challenge is required in the school setting.

UNIT PLANNING

Units of instruction offer a meaningful method for organizing activities. Without units, teachers would have difficulty offering scope and sequence for various instructional activities throughout the year. Units are usually two-, three-, or four-week sequences of instruction dealing with the same activity or concept. Units can, however, be five weeks or longer, depending on the type of curriculum developed.

Instruction units are developed from the curriculum theory and the organizing center that is used in a specific curriculum. Most units focus on physical activity or movement forms such as team sports, lifetime sports, dance, or physical conditioning. On the other hand, some units have been developed to emphasize a concept or idea such as cardiovascular efficiency, body composition, flexibility, or strength. Other people have organized instructional units on students' motives or purposes such as achievement, appearance, and coping skills. Still others have planned units on analyzing movements with regard to time, space, force, and flow. Many different organizing centers have been used for unit construction (see Chapter 3).

When unit plans are developed, using a wide variety of sources is preferable to being restricted to one textbook. The unit can reflect a range of activities gathered from different experts in the particular activity field. Another advantage of the unit plan is that it gives teachers a broad perception of the direction in which instruction should proceed. This prevents fragmentation. An instructor with a coherent unit plan does not simply teach from day-to-day in the hope that everything will somehow fit together in the end.

ELEMENTS OF A UNIT PLAN

There are many different ways to write and organize units of instruction. Most plans contain the following elements, even though they may be titled differently or listed in a different order. Regardless of the organization method, the plan elements should contain the following information.

Objectives of the Unit

The objectives state what the students are expected to know on completion of the unit, and students should be made aware of what they are expected to learn. Objectives may be written in the three learning domains. For example, what cognitive understandings should students have and are they to be tested in this area? What are the social and emotional concepts students should develop through participation in this unit? Finally, what skills, techniques, and game strategies should be learned on completion of the unit? Objectives must be written before organizing the activities and experiences, because the objectives will determine what is to be included in the unit.

Skills and Activities

This section is the instructional core of the unit and is organized according to unit objectives. Specific skills to be developed, drills to facilitate skill development, lead-up games to be taught, and culminating experiences are listed in this section. Scope and sequence are also developed in this section, which helps to assure a meaningful presentation. When activities are listed in proper sequence, instructionally sound and legally safe lessons are more easily written. The learning experiences may be listed as desirable student outcomes to assure simple translation by student and teacher.

Instructional Procedures

This plan area determines how the activities will be presented to assure the maximum amount of learning. Points to be included are instructional techniques, observations on the efficient use of equipment, necessary safety procedures, and teaching formations.

Equipment, Facilities, and Instructional Devices

Equipment needed and facilities to be used are delineated in this section. Instructional devices such as loop films, charts, pictures, and books should be included. Other possibilities might be to attend a game between skilled teams, or to invite speakers and outstanding athletes to the class setting.

Listing equipment and facilities allows the teacher to quickly see what is available and whether other teachers are using it for a unit being taught concurrently. If facilities or equipment need to be modified, for example, lowering goals or deflating balls, this should be listed also.

Culminating Activities

This section identifies how the unit might be concluded. A tournament between selected teams, an intraschool contest, or a school demonstration playday might result. In any case, the unit should finish with an activity that is enjoyable to students and leaves them with a positive feeling toward the unit of instruction.

Evaluation

The final plan section outlines how student progress is to be monitored. Monitoring can be carried out by the instructor, or students can be given guidelines for self-evaluation. Written tests might be administered to evaluate the knowledge gleaned through the instructional process. Skill tests could be used to assess the level of performance and skill development. An attitude inventory might be administered to judge the impact of the unit on the affective area of learning.

Another phase of evaluation is to ask students to comment on the unit and its method of presentation. Student evaluations can offer direction for modifying the unit and making it more effective in the future.

Suggested Weekly (Block Plan) Schedule

The purpose of a block plan is to distribute the activities in the unit into weekly segments. This gives the teacher a rough sense of timing and an indication of what should be taught and when. A block plan can help alleviate the problems of trying to implement a unit only to find that not enough time remains to teach the desired activities or that not enough activities were planned for the designated time frame. The weekly schedule need not be written in detail. It does ease the burden of writing lesson plans because the material to be taught has been identified. Daily lesson plans can then be developed easily from the block plan.

Figure 7.1 is an example of a three-week block plan for a unit on racquetball. A three-week block plan is included with many of the activities in Chapter 19.

Bibliography and Resources

The bibliography contains materials for both students and teacher. Students are given a list of materials that they can peruse if they desire more information. Materials should be identified as to where they can be found by students. Teachers should have a separate list and collection of resources that they use for instruction. For example, pamphlets on nutrition or physical fitness, available films, bulletin board materials, and textbooks might be parts of the resource section.

The following outline offers a skeleton structure for designing detailed unit plans.

I. Title and grade level
II. Analysis and description of setting
   A. Previous experiences and exposure to activity
   B. Limiting factors: class size, class organization, mixed grades, facilities and equipment, period of day class meets
   C. Rationale for including the activity
III. Objectives
   A. General unit objectives
   B. Specific behavioral objectives
      1. Psychomotor (physical performance) skills
      2. Knowledges, rules, and strategies
      3. Attitudes and values
IV. Organization
   A. Time (length of unit)
   B. Space available
   C. Equipment and supplies
   D. Basic grouping of students
   E. Number of groups
V. Content
   A. Introduction of the activity
   B. Rules
   C. Skills, diagram all drills
   D. Activities and lead-up games
   E. Skill tests
   F. Written tests
   G. Block plan for entire unit
   H. Grading scheme
VI. References and resources

DAILY LESSON PLAN FORMAT

The suggested daily lesson plan has three major components (see Chapter 5): the introductory or warm-up activity, the fitness development activity, and the lesson focus (Pangrazi and Dauer 1983). Each of these areas contains four columns of information: lesson content, instructional procedures, desired student outcomes, and notes and refer-

Introduction	Review	Review	Review	Review
What is racquetball?	Grip, forehand, backhand	Serves, rules	Forehand, backhand	Backwall shots
Grips—ready position	Equipment	**Teach**	**Teach**	**Teach**
Forehand stroke	**Teach**	Backwall shots	Court position	Ceiling shots
Backhand stroke	Serves—Drive, Z	Hinders	Kill shots	Passing shots
Contract procedures	Lob	**Activities**	**Activities**	**Activities**
Practice bounce and hit	**Activities**	Backwall practice	Performance objectives	Ceiling games
Rule of the day	Serves—practice	Serve practice	or short game	One, two, or three shots
	Bounce and hit	Rule of the day	Rule of the day	
	Rule of the day			
Review	**Teach**	**Review**	**Review**	**Review**
Problem rules	Cutthroat	Problem areas	Rules	Kill shots
Serve strategy	Doubles	**Activities**	**Activities**	**Activities**
Court coverage	**Activities**	Performance objectives	Performance objectives	Rotation work up
Activities	Performance objectives	Five and out	Regular game	
Accuracy drills	Eight ball rally	Ceiling games	Cutthroat or doubles	
Drive serve	Rotation work up			
Lob serve				
Backhand				
Backhand games				
One or two shots				
Activities	**Review**	Written exam	**Activities**	Final performance
Performance objectives	Rules, strategy	**Activities**	Performance objectives	objectives work
Backhand games	Shots, serves	Performance objectives	Tournament games	Review course objectives
Regular game	**Activities**	Tournament games	Cutthroat or doubles	Final games
Tournament	Performance objectives			
	Tournament games			Return exam

Figure 7.1. Racquetball block plan

ences. Figure 7.2 shows a sample lesson plan. A discussion of each of the parts of the sample lesson plan follows.

LESSON CONTENT

The first column in the lesson plan identifies the skills to be taught and the activities to be used. These are listed in correct progression, thus assuring that instruction will occur in line with the developmental capabilities of students. Progression in lessons assures that activities will be presented in a safe manner and that students will have a successful experience. The skills and related activities need not be written out in detail. The key point is that the instructor can quickly comprehend the activities when teaching. If more detail is needed, the notes and references column directs the teacher to a proper source.

ORGANIZATION AND TEACHING HINTS

This column contains a list of instructional procedures that should be followed when presenting the activities. For example, how the equipment is organized, what formations are to be used, key points of instruction to be shared with students, and what type of specific feedback should be offered are all covered here. This column becomes more meaningful as the teacher develops experience. Newly discovered instructional procedures can be recorded and maintained for the next time the lesson is taught.

EXPECTED STUDENT OUTCOMES

The purpose of this part of the lesson plan is to delineate what students are expected to experience, learn, and perform. Specific physical skills should be listed. Various facts about physical fitness and sport participation, as well as expected values and attitudes that the class should discuss, are all detailed in this section. With careful planning of expected student outcomes, teachers can offer a wide variety of experiences throughout the school year to help students develop in all domains—the psychomotor, cognitive, and affective.

NOTES AND REFERENCES

This column is for recording the sources of information used in the lesson plan. Since the instructor may desire more information on a subject, various references should be listed. Notes about the effectiveness of the lesson, how it could be improved, and activities to add or delete can also be written in this section.

ANALYZING THE LESSON PLAN

There are different approaches to writing lesson plans, but regardless of the style used, the plan should include the necessary elements for assuring effective instruction. The following questions can help teachers analyze a lesson plan to assure that it is both comprehensive and effective.

Have you included the following?

1. Title, length of lesson, and facility
2. A list of equipment, supplies, and instructional devices
3. Objectives of the lesson
4. References for further information

Does the instructional process do the following?

1. Provide for continuity with previous lessons
2. Review past material through lead-up activities
3. Communicate to students why the material is important for them to learn
4. Build motivational techniques into the presentation
5. Provide for students with varying interests and abilities
6. Include the special student

Does the lesson plan cover the following points?

1. Provide for warm-up, offer students a physical fitness activity, and include an instructional component
2. Outline new material clearly and with enough depth
3. Progress from simple to complex skill development
4. Progress from known activities to the unknown
5. Include notations for demonstrations and use of instructional devices
6. Include key questions and points that should be covered
7. Combine physical education activities with other academic areas when possible

Does the lesson plan meet the following criteria?

1. Readable and easily used by others
2. Usable during the actual instructional process

Figure 7.2. Softball lesson plan (modified from *Lesson Plans for Dynamic Physical Education for Elementary School Children,* 3rd ed. by R. P. Pangrazi and V. P. Dauer, 1983. Minneapolis: Burgess Publishing Co., pp. 271–274)

SOFTBALL

Supplies and equipment needed:
Station 1: 2 batting tees, 4 balls, 2 bats
Station 2: 1 ball for each 2 students (can use fleece balls)
Station 3: 4 bases (home plates), 4 balls
Station 4: 2 balls, 2 bats
28-ft parachute and 10–12 long jump ropes

Movement Experience—Content	Organization and Teaching Hints	Expected Student Objectives and Outcomes	Notes and References
Introductory Activity (2–3 min) **Long Rope Routine** Form a loose column and hold a long jump rope in the right hand. 1st signal: Run in a column with one student leading the way. 2nd signal: Shift the rope overhead from right hands to left hands without stopping. 3rd signal: Two inside students let go of rope, outside students begin turning the rope for the two who have released. They continue jumping the rope until the next signal. 4th signal: The outside students move to the inside positions and vice versa. Sequence is then repeated.	Group students by fours. The sequence should be smooth with little hesitation. Students can think of other activities to perform with the rope on the second signal. Option: Have students carry two long ropes and work on Double Dutch on the third and fourth signals.	PM.[a]—Student will be able to jump the long rope 10 times consecutively without a miss. Cog.[b]—Student will be able to develop one new idea to be used by the group on second signal.	(Description of long rope routine.)
Fitness Development Activity (7–8 min) **Parachute Exercises** 1. Toe toucher 2. Curl-ups 3. Dorsal lifts 4. V-sit	The parachute is a good tool for teaching group coordination. Encourage students to work together and to do activities simultaneously.	PM.—Students will be able to perform the exercises together. Aff.[c]—Many approaches and activities can be used to develop fitness. Discuss the need for variety in developing fit-	(Description of parachute exercises.)

5. Backward pulls
6. Side pulls
7. Hip walk and scooter
8. Elevator
9. Run in place—hitting knees on edge of chute

Have students use different grips such as cross-arm grip and overhand, underhand, and mixed grips.

ness programs. This is a good time to discuss the reasons for teaching a broad range of activities.

Lesson Focus (15–20 min)

A. Softball (Multiple Activity Station Teaching)

First day: Take entire class from station to station, explaining procedures at each, then set up one practice station activity (no rotation on first day).

Second day: Rotate through remainder of stations, which began first day (3 rotations). This completes one full circuit.

Squad formation.

Have signs at each station giving direction and skill hints. This completes a full rotation schedule.

Captain gathers equipment in designated spot before changing to next station.

Aff.—Willingness to cooperate at each station is crucial to success of lesson. Discuss and emphasize importance of cooperation among peers.

(Description of softball activities.)

STATION 1

Batting
1. Weight on both feet
2. Bat pointed over right shoulder
3. Trademark up on swing
4. Elbows up and away from body
5. Begin with hip roll and short step
6. Swing level
7. Follow through
8. Eyes on ball

Batting From Tee
1. Stand back (3 ft) from tee, so when stepping forward, ball is hit in front.
2. Show three types of grips.

Divide squad, with one batter, one catcher (next batter), and one or more fielders.

Points to avoid:
1. Lifting front foot high off the ground
2. Stepping back with rear foot
3. Dropping rear shoulder
4. Chopping down on ball (golfing)
5. Dropping elbows

PM.—Student will be able to meet the ball squarely on the tee.

Cog.—Student will know different points in good batting.

Cog.—Strenuous exercise causes blood pressure to rise because the heart beats faster and more blood is trying to get through the vessels. Why do some people have high blood pressure even at rest?

(Description of batting.)

aPM. = Psychomotor
bCog. = Cognitive
cAff. = Affective

continued

Figure 7.2/*continued*

Movement Experience—Content	Organization and Teaching Hints	Expected Student Objectives and Outcomes	Notes and References
STATION 2 **Throwing and Catching** 1. Show grips. 2. How to catch: Stress "give," eyes on ball.	One ball for each two players. Partners stand about 10 yd apart.	PM.—Students will be able to increase their catching potentials and increase their accuracy in throwing (3 styles).	(Description of throwing and catching.)
Practice Throwing 1. Overhand 2. Side arm 3. Underhand toss	Suggest spacing to conform to skill. Use "soft" softballs.	Cog.—Students will be able to define and recognize good points of throwing and catching.	
STATION 3 **Pitching** 1. Rules: a. Face batter, both feet on rubber, and ball held in front with both hands. One step is allowed, and ball must be delivered on that step. b. Ball must be pitched underhanded. c. No motion or fake toward the plate can be made without delivering the ball. d. No quick return is permitted, nor can the ball be rolled or bounced toward batter. e. Practice both regular pitch and windmill.	Divide squad into two groups. Each has a catcher, pitcher, and "batter," who just stands in position. A home plate and pitching rubber are helpful. Stress legal preliminary position before taking one hand off the ball to pitch.	PM.—Students will be able to pitch in accordance with the rules. Cog.—Students will know rules governing pitching. PM.—Students will be able to pitch 50% of balls in strike zone. Cog.—Softball is not an effective sport for exercising the cardiovascular system. Most of the time is spent sitting or standing with little, if any, aerobic activity.	
STATION 4 **Throwing or Batting Fly Balls** 1. Begin with high throwing from the "batter." 2. Have fielders return the ball with a one-bounce throw to "batter." 3. Show form for high and low catch. Show sure stop for outfielders.	Divide squad into two groups.	PM.—Student will begin to handle (catch) easy fly balls with confidence. PM.—Fielders will improve in estimating flight of ball and getting under it in time.	(Description of throwing or batting fly balls.)

3. Designed for evaluation of the curriculum effectiveness

In any case, formats used by teachers should cover the areas listed above. This will ensure that the lesson plan format is easily read, augments the instructional process, and provides for students of different abilities.

PLANNING FOR THE ESSENTIAL ELEMENTS OF INSTRUCTION

The essential elements of instruction can be divided into these general categories: communication skills, instructional devices, management skills, and student motivation and discipline. It is important for teachers to plan carefully for these categories because of their impact on students. Unlike many of the variables in the teaching environment over which teachers have little control (e.g., number of students in a class, types of students, equipment available, or the schedule of the school), these essential areas can be greatly controlled by the teacher. Many teachers, however, do not plan as carefully as they should in these areas, or they have developed a narrow comfort zone with regard to options in these areas. Most of the planning in the four categories is usually not written into the unit or daily lesson plan. This type of planning is an ongoing process that takes place all of the time, that is, during college preparation experiences, in student teaching and in-service seminars, and while thinking a lesson through mentally. For example, many teachers are constantly thinking about and planning better ways to communicate information, to set up a drill for skill work, to motivate students to work harder, or to shorten time taken for calling roll. We do not mean that these points should not or cannot be written into lesson plans. We stress, rather, the importance of teachers having planned thoroughly in these areas.

COMMUNICATION SKILLS

The teaching-learning process involves the exchange of information between teachers and students. Communication must occur both ways: teachers with students and students with teachers. Communication behaviors can take many different forms. Some different types of communication are a lecture on the strategy of a zone defense in basketball, directions for moving the class to four different stations for skill work, information feedback on a student's skill attempts, questions about the rules of a game, praise for lining up quickly at the end of class, or a smile for a well-executed lay-up. Communication forms can involve a number of sensory modes including the visual, verbal, and tactile. Visual cues involve demonstrations, loop films, and pictures. The teacher's gestures, facial expressions, or thumbs-up signs are a nonverbal type of visual communication. Indeed, some experts suggest that much of what students learn is picked up through nonverbal means (Galloway 1971). Verbal communication involves lectures, discussions, directions, and all other spoken words. Tactile communication encompasses physical contact such as manually manipulating a student's arms or legs for swimming instruction, or physically restricting a student's arm position in archery.

Effective teachers have developed efficient communication skills. Information is communicated in a minimum of time. If a teacher talks too long, students will lose valuable practice time. Teachers who talk too long may also exceed the attention span of students. Teachers should make sure that their information is clearly expressed in terms that are within the vocabulary range of the students. A variety of sensory modes should be used, because different students process information in different ways. Verbal information should be presented slowly enough so that students are able to comprehend, and the complexity of the information should be appropriate to the language development level of the students.

Teachers should also encourage students to communicate with each other during physical education classes. Students can provide peers with important information for developing skills. Student communication can also be verbal, visual, or tactile.

Lectures and Demonstrations

In order to learn motor skills, students need a model to imitate and information on two or three key points. An instructional lecture should be planned carefully around a specific objective. The lecture should be limited to several key points and should last only a few minutes or less. Teachers must be sure that the vocabulary used is appropriate and clear. Too much information or unclear information is a waste of class time.

A short demonstration of a skill combined with a verbal explanation is an effective procedure. Both the demonstration and the explanation should be brief and clear. Complex, extensive information is not useful to most students. If the teacher is not a good model of the skill, then other alternatives should be found (i.e., a highly skilled student, another teacher, a loop film, or photographs from a book). Teachers who instruct in a wide variety of activity areas will probably have to find some alternatives for skill demonstrations. They must, however, constantly attempt to improve their physical skills so they can be a good model for students. Teachers should also set an example as persons who have incorporated physical activity into their life-styles. This will help in conveying to students an enthusiasm for physical activity.

Questions and Feedback

Questions are an important communication form in the teaching-learning process. Teachers should use questions to evaluate the effectiveness of their lectures, demonstrations, or other types of instructional materials, including reading sheets, books, and pamphlets. They should also encourage students to ask questions, because questions foster the communication process. The use of questions in a lesson must be planned carefully with an objective in mind. There are different categories of questions for specific goals (Siedentop 1983). Recall questions focus on memory. Convergent and divergent questions require an analysis and a conclusion in a specific direction, such as problem-solving or guided-discovery styles. Value questions give students an opportunity to present an opinion that is neither right nor wrong.

Information feedback is what students receive after they have completed a skill attempt. Feedback on the results of many skill attempts is obvious as, for example, in the case of golf shots, basketball shots, or baseball swings. It is inherent in the specific activity, and students know immediately the results of the skill attempt. Feedback on the form or topography of many skill behaviors is, however, difficult to attain. Teachers play an important role in developing learning environments that provide students with useful information feedback on how well they are performing a skill.

Feedback is usually communicated by the teacher to the student immediately after a skill attempt has been made. Teachers need to plan carefully for information feedback in classes. Most physical education instructors rely heavily on corrective feedback, and the observation has been made that many physical educators have a correction complex. Corrective statements are not inappropriate

if the learning environment has a balance of positive and corrective feedback. Many educators believe that an educational environment should have a 3:1 or 4:1 ratio of positive feedback to corrective feedback. The higher ratio of positive feedback certainly enhances the overall positive atmosphere of the class.

Planning for feedback should include thinking about the specific student skill behaviors that a teacher is trying to foster. The feedback should be prescriptive in nature so that it helps to eradicate errors the teacher has diagnosed. Many different ways can be used to tell students that they are performing at an acceptable level. Feedback statements can be general, specific, verbal, or nonverbal. Including a student's first name with the feedback is a meaningful way to make students realize that the teacher is aware of them and is sincere about their skill development. The following are some examples of different types of feedback:

Corrective or Prescriptive

Get the shot put angle up to 42 degrees.
Bend your knees more and uncoil.
Adjust your grip by spreading your fingers.
Accelerate through the ball.
Keep your wrists stiff and start the action with your shoulders.
Transfer your weight as you contact the ball.

Positive General

Good job.
Way to go.
Nice defense.
All right, Jim.
Very nice hustle.
Interesting question, Mike.
OK, class.

Positive Specific

Good angle of release.
Perfect timing on the outlet pass.
Way to hit the soft spot in the 1-3-1 zone.
Great job looking off the undercoverage.
That's the way to vary your serves. It keeps them off balance.
Mike, good job keeping your head down.

Nonverbal Positive or Corrective

Winking or smiling
Thumbs up or down
Pat on the back

Clapping the hands
Facial gestures
Making a V sign
Shaking the fist

Teachers should plan a variety of feedback, including statements that use first names and give specific positive information, and some nonverbal messages. Variety is necessary to avoid satiation and redundancy. Feedback should be directed at key points of the specific skill, and the terminology should be appropriate to the student's age and developmental level. Teachers should attempt to interact with every student every day. Common feedback to small groups or to the entire class concerning similar errors or positive behaviors can be a useful strategy for affecting more students.

INSTRUCTIONAL DEVICES

Instructional devices include a variety of materials, equipment, or people—any of which supplement, clarify or improve certain instructional procedures. These devices can be used to present information, stimulate different senses, provide information feedback, restrict movements, control practice time, or aid in evaluation and motivation. The devices may be simple, such as targets taped on the wall or boundary cones to dribble around in basketball (Figure 7.3), or they may be more sophisticated, such as loop films, movies, video tape recorders, or ball machines for tennis. Student leaders can also be useful in a number of ways as instructional aides.

It is the teacher's role to carefully plan instructional devices that will enhance the teaching-learning process. Because most public school envi-

ronments have a large student-to-teacher ratio, teachers do not have enough time for each student. Instructional devices help the teacher impart more information and improve the motivational aspects of the class. A number of challenging and success-oriented activities can be developed using instructional devices. The following are examples:

1. In basketball, targets can be taped on a wall for various types of passes. A stopwatch can be used to time students dribbling through a course of boundary cones. Pictures, diagrams, and handout sheets can provide students with graphic information on various skills and rules.

2. In volleyball, Hula-Hoops, jump ropes, or tape on the floor can be used as targets for setting, bumping (Figure 7.4), or serving. A rope can be extended across the top of the net to help students hit serves above or beneath the rope to ensure height, accuracy, or velocity. Loop films are available to provide an excellent model for the various volleyball skills.

3. In tennis, empty ball cans are excellent targets for working on serves. A tennis ball suspended on a small rope that can be adjusted up or down on a basketball hoop will force students to get the "feel" of extending the arm for serves and overhead shots. A list of performance objectives (Chapter 19) for partners can control practice time and provide structure for a tennis class.

4. In track and field, a student leader might help run a station on low hurdles by timing heats and providing corrective feedback. A string between two chairs can be used in the long jump

Figure 7.3. Instructional devices

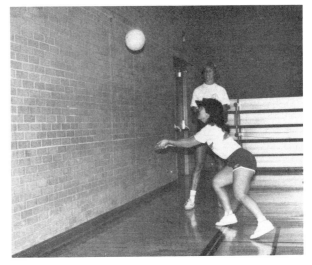

Figure 7.4. Volleyball bump against the wall

to help students to attain more height. Laminated posterboard diagrams of the release angle of the shot put combined with a discussion can give students important information before practice time begins (Figure 7.5).

5. In badminton, targets can be used to mark sections of the court. Shuttlecocks are suspended on a rope, similar to the tennis ball example, for practicing overhand shots. A rope suspended on high jump standards will force students to get the proper height on clear shots. Loop films can serve as another learning station. Performance objectives tied to specific reinforcing events will motivate students to work on specific skills.

6. In flag football, a punting station can use the goal post for height and accuracy, boundary cones for placement accuracy, and a stopwatch for hang time. A swinging tire or a Hula-Hoop suspended from a tree or goal post can be used for passing accuracy and boundary cones for passing distance. Blackboards, magnetic boards, and overhead projectors are all useful for diagraming plays and defensive strategy. Student leaders can supervise each station, record the completion of various skills, and help provide corrective feedback for each student.

A creative teacher uses instructional devices in many different ways. These devices certainly do not replace the teacher, but they do help supplement the teaching-learning environment. Effective teachers are continually trying to add devices that motivate students, provide more feedback, or increase practice attempts. Teachers with a limited budget can still create instructional devices with such basic components as a roll of tape, several ropes, string, and Hula-Hoops. An extensive budget does not always produce the best learning environments. A hardworking, ingenious teacher can develop effective instructional aids. Students seem to enjoy the challenge and success related to practicing with various types of instructional devices. Variety and novelty thus enhance the teaching-learning situation.

MANAGEMENT SKILLS

Effective teachers are efficient managers of students. Teachers should strive to help students develop the ability to manage themselves. Management policies need to be planned carefully for every aspect of the learning environment. The term **management time** refers to the class time when no instruction or practice is taking place. The following are examples of management time activities:

1. Students dressing for class
2. Teachers taking class roll
3. Teachers explaining and directing the rotation format for skill work
4. Students rotating from station to station
5. Students picking up equipment and moving to a practice area
6. Students forming a circle or an open formation for exercises
7. Students returning equipment and returning to the locker room

Management time usually has two phases involving both the teacher and students. The first is called "teacher talk time" on management. This includes the time it takes a teacher to explain the management procedures and give students the proper discriminative cues for action. An example would be when the teacher tells each of the four squads to move to a designated spot and begin practicing. This talk time would take a certain amount of time. The second phase of management time refers to the students' response latency, or the time it takes students to respond and begin the appropriate activity. An example would be the time elapsed while students pick up equipment and before they begin practicing their skills. Total management time is a combination of teacher talk time on management and the students' response latency.

Management time is directly related to instruction time, because excessive management time

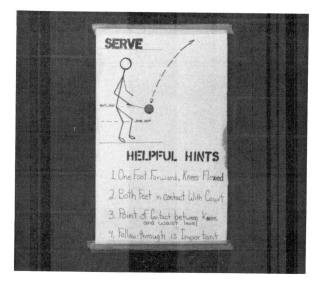

Figure 7.5. A poster of skills

reduces the time available for instruction and practice. Totally eliminating management time is impossible, but it is certainly possible through proper planning to keep management time to a minimum. Both teacher talk time and student response latency can be carefully planned.

Teacher Talk Time on Management

This is a communication skill that should take a minimum amount of time and be clear to students. Students must know where they are going and what they are supposed to be doing. Teachers should plan exactly what they are going to say to the students. Directions must be given slowly and succinctly, using a limited amount of information. The language should be appropriate to the students' age level. In certain situations, directions can be enhanced with a diagram or a graphic display of the organizational scheme. The diagram might be posted in the locker room and also could be used concurrently with the explanation. The old adage that a picture is worth a thousand words is appropriate in many situations.

Student Response Latency

Many variables affect the students' rate and speed of response. The nature of the activity, the students' motivational level and feelings about the teacher, the time of day, and the weather are a few examples. The teacher is able to control only some of these variables, while others are fixed. A positive, success-oriented atmosphere helps to improve the students' response time. Positive teacher reactions focused on appropriate student managerial behaviors are effective. Examples of such reactions include:

1. Way to go class, everyone dressed and ready in 4 minutes.
2. Jim, great hustle back to your squad.
3. Thank you for getting quiet so quickly.
4. Look at squad one line up quickly.
5. Mary, excellent listening today, much better.
6. Way to stop on the whistle, nice work.

Another effective strategy is setting goals for management time (Darst and Pangrazi 1981) and publicly posting the results. Reinforcing contingencies can be tied to the accomplishment of these goals (Siedentop et al. 1974). Activities like playing games, free time, novelty activities, or going in from class early are effective rewards for respon-

sible management behaviors. Behavior games (Chapter 8) can also be used to improve special management problems (Hamilton 1974).

Additional Management Strategies— Rules, Roll Call, and Squads

Teachers need to identify and post specific rules governing management aspects of the class. Dressing time, class starting time, roll call procedures, signals for attention, equipment pickup and return, and class ending time are examples of aspects of a class that needs guidelines. Consistency with these management rules and with the policies and procedures discussed in Chapter 6 will help teachers have an easier time with management throughout the year. Teachers should work to develop students who will follow rules and manage themselves independently of the teacher. A teacher who models self-management skills will certainly have a positive impact on students' managerial behaviors. For example, teachers who are dressed and ready for class on time each day can expect the same from students. On the other hand, teachers who are often late in starting class or who wear blue jeans periodically can hardly expect students to be punctual or appropriately dressed. Teachers communicate their enthusiasm for physical activity with appropriate management behaviors.

An effective method for taking roll each day helps reduce management time. One useful approach is to use squads and squad leaders. Each squad leader reports any absentees to the teacher orally or by filling out an attendance sheet. Another approach is to paint numbers on the floor and assign students to a number (Figure 7.6). The teacher or student leader glances quickly through the numbers and records the absentees. Some teachers post a sign-in sheet for attendance, which students quickly

Figure 7.6. Students standing on numbers

initial. Yet another approach is to check attendance while students are beginning the first class activity. The important point is that teachers should choose a method that saves time and fosters self-management qualities in students.

Squad formations can be a consistent procedure for starting and finishing each class period (Figure 7.7). They are often an effective means for arranging students for various class functions. Squads may meet at a designated spot in the gymnasium, at the pool, or on the playing field. Boundary cones are useful markers for assembling squads. Teachers should assign the squads and the squad leaders, and post the assignments in the locker rooms. Squads should be comparable in number of students and in physical size and ability levels of students. Squad leaders can be changed every three weeks, and the entire squad composition should be changed every nine weeks.

Squad leaders should have specific opportunities to lead. The position carries extra responsibilities such as leading fitness activities, helping with equipment, taking attendance, setting up station work, or organizing team strategies. All students should get the chance to be a squad leader at sometime throughout the year.

An even number of squads is effective in most cases. This enables the teacher to organize two, four, or six teams for games very quickly. Teachers can help develop a certain *esprit de corps* within each squad by letting students select a squad name and by rewarding squads for good management behaviors. The best organized squads might be allowed to select equipment first, receive extra play time, or participate in novelty-type activities. Teachers should reward good management behavior.

STUDENT MOTIVATION AND DISCIPLINE

Student motivation and discipline go hand in hand in an educational environment. If students are highly motivated to learn physical skills, then few discipline problems will exist. Multiple factors determine the motivational level of students. Family, friends, past educational experiences, past activity experiences, and other factors affect student motivation in physical education. Many teachers feel that the biggest problem they face on a daily basis is student apathy and a lack of motivation. Planning for this essential element in the teaching-learning process is critical. Teachers who believe that students should appear at the gymnasium door with an established desire to learn about physical activity will have a number of motivational problems to solve. The instructor has a responsibility to develop positive approach tendencies in students toward physical activity. This should be an important objective of all physical education teachers. Chapter 8 will focus on student motivation and discipline techniques.

Figure 7.7. Squad formation (reprinted from *Dynamic Physical Education for Elementary School Children,* 7th ed., by V. P. Dauer and R. P. Pangrazi, 1983. Minneapolis: Burgess Publishing Co., p. 52)

Summary

Planning is the first step in developing a quality instructional program. Unit plans and daily lesson plans are necessary for executing and improving instruction in secondary physical education. Planning is unique to each teacher, but there are common essential elements of instruction that must be carefully thought out. Communication skills, instructional devices, management procedures, motivational techniques, and disciplinary procedures require specific planning. Teachers who fail to plan are usually planning to fail.

References

Darst, P., and Pangrazi, R. 1981. Analysis of starting and stopping management activity for elementary physical education teachers. *Arizona JOHPERD* 25(1): 14–17.

Galloway, C. 1971. Teaching is more than words. *Quest* 15: 67–71.

Hamilton, K. The application of a competency-based model to physical education student teaching in high school. Doctoral dissertation, The Ohio State University, 1974.

Pangrazi, R., and Dauer, V. *Lesson Plans for Dynamic Physical Education*. 3rd ed. Minneapolis: Burgess Publishing Co., 1983.

Siedentop, D. *Developing Teaching Skills in Physical Education*. 2nd ed. Palo Alto, CA: Mayfield Publishing Co., 1983.

Siedentop, D., Rife, F., and Boehm, J. Modifying the managerial effectiveness of student teachers in physical education. Unpublished paper, The Ohio State University, 1974.

Chapter 8

Student Motivation and Discipline

Motivation and discipline are critical aspects of the teaching process and are discussed in the same chapter because the two areas are closely related. The terms and techniques used when dealing with these areas are similar. Students who are motivated are usually well disciplined and vice versa. Strategies and techniques used to motivate students are also used for discipline, or developing appropriate behaviors for educational environments. These terms are intertwined and cannot be separated easily. It is difficult to discriminate between a motivated student and a disciplined student.

The authors believe strongly that motivation and discipline are crucial to a high-quality instructional program. Teachers should plan carefully to develop these elements through a positive and preventive approach with classes. For too long, many physical educators have motivated and disciplined students with a negative approach using various punishment strategies such as extra running or exercises, grades being lowered or chopped, or high rates of verbal abuse and ridicule. The atmosphere has been characterized as rigid, mili-

tary-oriented, and negative. Physical education classes should be warm, positive, and success-oriented. Teachers need to work hard to make their classes a place where students want to participate and learn new skills and information. This is essential for a high-quality instructional program.

MOTIVATION

Motivation is a complex phenomenon that is debated constantly and means different things to different people. In a broad sense of the term, experts talk about each person's motivation being influenced by external and internal forces. Sage (1977) defined motivation as a combination of internal mechanisms and external stimuli that arouse and direct behavior. Examples of external stimuli that affect students' behavior are parents, brothers, sisters, peers, teachers, grades, awards, trophies, ribbons, and past experiences with school and with physical activity. Internal forces or mechanisms that affect students are not as easily observed and defined but include, for example, feelings of success or accomplishment, such as self-satisfaction, self-knowledge, or self-confidence.

Motivation is a process that leads students into learning experiences and keeps them persisting at these experiences until they find some type of success. Rushall and Siedentop (1972) define motivation as the act of working toward some type of reinforcement. Reinforcers are consequences for behaving in a certain manner. These consequences can be internal, external, positive, or negative. Students are continually receiving certain reinforcers or consequences during the school day. Grades, praise from teachers, scolds from an assistant principal, a feeling of accomplishment, a pat on the back from a friend, or a certificate of merit from a teacher are all examples of reinforcers. These consequences help to control student behavior. Depending on a student's background, certain reinforcers will be more effective than others. Motivation is determined by consequences; it gets students started and keeps them progressing toward educational objectives.

Students arrive at physical education class with many different motivational levels due to many different types of internal and external influences. Some students will be highly motivated while others will have little interest in physical activities. Many teachers admit that the largest problem they face each day is trying to keep students motivated to learn. Students who are highly motivated certainly have an advantage over those who are less motivated. Teachers know that highly motivated students can learn many complex skills without extensive instruction. The learning process without instruction is not as efficient as learning with quality instruction, but when students are motivated, progress will still occur because motivation is a key element in the process.

Inexperienced teachers who believe that all students will come to class highly motivated to learn have a "romantic" view of youth. Motivational techniques must be planned carefully and incorporated into each day's lesson. This is a major portion of a teacher's responsibility. Creating highly motivated students is an important objective of the physical education program. An effective learning environment should produce students who use class time wisely and leave school highly motivated to incorporate physical activity into their life-style.

In many cases, teachers need to use a variety of "external" motivational methods that will develop a positive, success-oriented gymnasium atmosphere. This approach should help all students develop internal feelings of success with physical activity, and these internal feelings will in turn help students maintain their positive motivational level for a longer period of time—perhaps for a lifetime. In other words, if students are not motivated, teachers should use external motivational methods to develop students' internal motivational levels. This may encourage students to persist in a physical activity after they leave the school environment and the direct influence of the teacher. Special care should be taken to keep a negative approach and punishment procedures to a minimum. These procedures may work effectively in the short term, but they often produce several side effects that are detrimental to accomplishment of the overall goals of physical education. Students will behave appropriately in class as long as the teacher is present and applying the negative consequences. Many students, however, may be learning to dislike physical activity, teachers, schools, and the learning process in general. Once they leave the environment, they will avoid all contact with physical activity. This is a situation that should not occur. Students should leave classes with a desire to continue with physical activity. The final goal of physical education with regard to motivation is to develop self-motivated students in the area of physical activity.

VARIOUS METHODS OF MOTIVATION

QUALITY CURRICULUM

Motivation is an excellent example of how curriculum and instruction must be intertwined to produce an effective teaching-learning environment. Both curriculum and instruction are important factors influencing student motivation. For example, if the curriculum is poorly developed and arranged, it will be difficult to motivate students with instructional techniques. The same is true if a poor instructional system accompanies a high-quality curriculum. Teachers must strengthen both areas in order to motivate students.

A curriculum that provides students with a choice of activities will enhance the motivational level, because students can select an activity in which they are interested. A wide variety of different activity offerings from various categories such as team sports, lifetime sports, aquatics, physical conditioning, recreational games, dance, and adventure sports will provide opportunities for all students to be successful. Depth in a curriculum gives the higher skilled students an opportunity to be challenged and will enhance their skill level. The length of activity units also affects the motivational level of students. In general, 7th and 8th graders need shorter units, and 11th and 12th graders can handle longer, specialized units. All of these aspects of the curriculum are an important starting point for enhancing the motivational level of students. Teachers must start with the curriculum.

POLICIES AND PROCEDURES

The policies and procedures for curriculum and instruction are also intertwined and will have an important impact on student motivation. Dress codes, dress requirements, showering time, attendance procedures, class makeup policies, grading schemes, and other factors will all contribute to motivation. All of these areas can be planned with a positive or a negative orientation. Too many teachers still use a negative approach because it works quickly and is thus reinforcing for the user. Unfortunately, this approach sends out negative messages to students about teachers, physical activity, and schools in general.

Grades may be the most common way in which teachers attempt to motivate students. Grades are quite effective in many cases, because students have learned that grades are an important indicator of achievement. Some teachers do not realize, however, that grades are not important to many students, especially in certain socioeconomic groups. Teachers who rely primarily on grades to motivate students will be unsuccessful in many situations. The authors contend that teachers need a well-developed repertoire of motivational techniques in order to have an impact on all students. We believe that a total reliance on grades is ineffective.

LEARNING ACTIVITIES

Drills, skill work, modified games, and lead-up activities all have a strong influence on students' attitudes and motivational level. These learning activities need to be arranged so that all students can find success and challenge in the physical education environment. Success and challenge can be built into the activities by offering a progressive arrangement of experiences from simple to complex with small steps along the way. Students should be able to progress at their own speed through the activities. As they build a backlog of success, learning activities should become more challenging.

An effective example of this instructional approach is the use of **performance** or **behavioral**

objectives in a learning station arrangement. A performance objective is a statement of what students should be able to perform. Examples are as follows:

1. The student will complete 15 push-ups in 30 sec.
2. The student will run a mile in 8 min.
3. The student will hit 10 consecutive volleyball forearm passes up in the air at least 10 ft high.
4. The student will dribble the basketball through a set of 5 cones in 25 sec.
5. The student will punt the football 3 consecutive times within the boundaries at least 25 yd.

The performance objective should contain (1) the behavior to be performed, (2) the conditions or setting, and (3) the acceptable criterion level of performance. The following examples identify the three parts of a well-written performance objective:

HANDBALL EXAMPLE

Conditions	Behavior	Criterion
Standing 6 ft from the back wall in the middle of the court	bounce the handball against the back wall and hit the ball	3 of 4 shots below a red line

Standing 6 ft from the back wall in the middle of the court, the student will bounce the handball against the back wall and hit 3 of 4 shots below a red line drawn 3 ft above the floor of the court (right hand).

VOLLEYBALL EXAMPLE

Conditions	Behavior	Criterion
Standing 5 ft from the bleachers	hit forearm passes against the bleachers	10 consecutive at a height of at least 10 ft

Standing 5 ft from the bleachers, the student will hit 10 consecutive forearm passes against the bleachers at a height of at least 10 ft.

The key point is that students must be able to understand what they are expected to do in the activity. The specificity of the objective depends on the level of the learner. Students who are given clear-cut goals and a system for monitoring their own skill development will be more motivated to learn.

A **learning station** is a designated area in the gymnasium, on the soccer field, or in any appropriate area where students can practice specific learning activities such as performance objectives, viewing loop films, taking a rules test, or working with a partner. An effective instructional approach for soccer that combines performance objectives and learning stations might be organized as follows:

Dribbling Tasks

1. Dribble the soccer ball a distance of 20 yd 3 consecutive times, making each kick no more than 5 yd (1 point).
2. Dribble the soccer ball through an obstacle course of 6 pylons over a distance of 30 yd in 25 sec or less (1 point).
3. With a partner, pass the soccer ball back and forth 5 times while in a running motion for a distance of 50 yd 2 consecutive times (1 point).

Trapping Tasks

4. When the ball is rolled to you by a partner from 10 yd away, trap it 4 of 5 times, using the instep method with the right and then the left foot (1 point).
5. Same as no. 4 using the sole of the foot (1 point).
6. With a partner tossing the ball, trap 4 of 5 shots using the chest method (1 point).

Kicking Tasks

7. Kick the ball to a partner, who is standing 10 yd away, 5 consecutive times with the right and left inside of the foot push pass (1 point).
8. Same as no. 7 using the instep kick. Loft the ball to your partner (1 point).
9. Kick 4 of 5 shots that enter the goal in the air from a distance of 20 yd (1 point).

Heading and Throw-in Tasks

10. Head 3 consecutive balls in the air at a height of at least 10 ft (1 point).
11. Head 6 consecutive balls back and forth with a partner (1 point).
12. Make 4 of 5 throw-ins from out-of-bounds into a Hula-Hoop placed 15 yd away (1 point).

The soccer field practice area could be arranged as in Figure 8.1 with four learning stations, and the performance objectives could be written on a card at each station. Students could spend 3–5 min working on the objectives at each station and then rotate on to the next station. The objectives are arranged so that students can experience success quickly and frequently with the first few objectives

and then be challenged with the later objectives. Objectives can be changed daily or repeated, depending on the progression of the class. Points earned through completion of the performance objectives can also help motivate many students. The points can be tied to other reinforcing activities.

In another example, this format is used to teach volleyball. These performance objectives have been tested on secondary students in several different settings.

Forearm Pass (Bump)

1. Bump 12 consecutive forearm passes against the bleachers at a height of at least 10 ft (1 point).
2. Bump 12 consecutive forearm passes into the air at a height of at least 10 ft (height of a basket rim) (1 point).
3. Bump 10 consecutive forearm passes over the net with the instructor or a classmate (1 point).

Overhead Set Pass

4. Hit 15 consecutive set passes against the bleachers at a height of at least 10 ft (1 point).
5. Hit 15 consecutive set passes into the air at a height of at least 10 ft (1 point).
6. Hit 12 consecutive set passes over the net with the instructor or a classmate (1 point).

Serves

7. Hit 3 consecutive underhand serves into the right half of the court (1 point).
8. Hit 3 consecutive underhand serves into the left half of the court (1 point).
9. Hit 3 consecutive overhand serves into the right half of the court (1 point).
10. Hit 3 of 4 underhand serves into the left half of the court (1 point).

A gymnasium can be set up with volleyball stations similar to Figure 8.2.

The performance objectives and learning stations described in this text have been field-tested extensively and can be used in many ways as part of the instructional and motivational strategy. Samples are given in Chapter 19. (See also the section on contracts in Chapter 9.) The advantages of using this approach are the following: (1) Students know exactly what is expected of them, (2) parents, administrators, and supervisors know what teachers expect of students, (3) a method is present for grouping students (e.g., teams, squads, learning

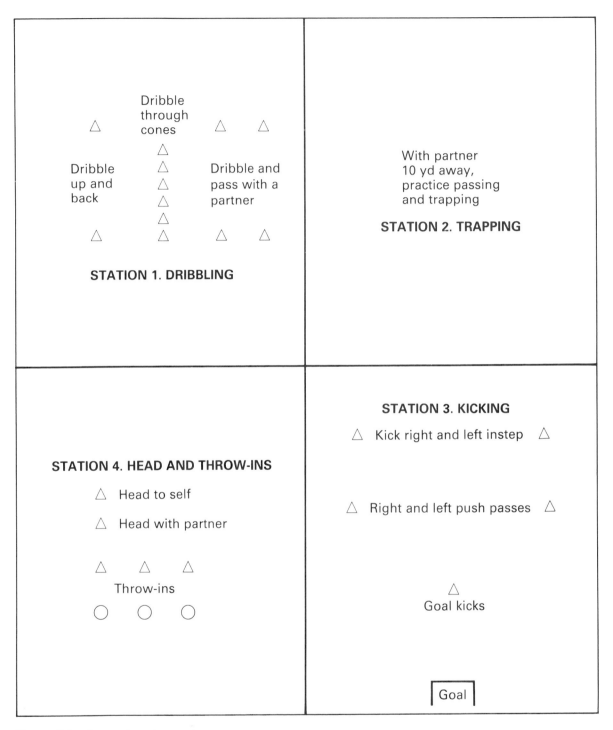

Figure 8.1. Soccer learning stations

groups), (4) a method for giving grades is part of the instruction contract, (5) objectives can be used as a motivational device for entering a game, tournament, or other enjoyable activity, (6) they allow for a degree of individual pacing, and (7) they help to control the students' practice time, which frees the teacher to become a better agent of feedback.

All drills, skill work, and games should be analyzed carefully for motivational value. Activities that are too difficult will lead to frustrating, unproductive experiences, while activities that are too easy will result in boring, unchallenging environments. Regulation games should not be played by students who are not capable in terms of strength,

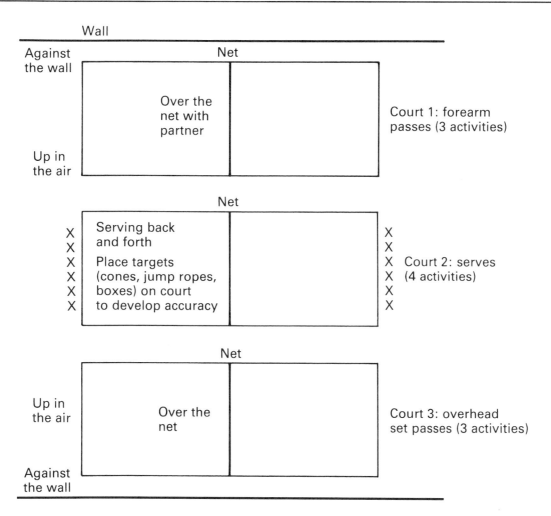

Figure 8.2. Volleyball stations

endurance, or skill level. There are many modified, lead-up-type games that can be used with students at various ability levels. These modified games can also add variety for students, so they do not become satiated with one activity (see Chapter 19 for learning activities).

Another important factor relevant to learning activities is that of active versus inactive learning. Anderson (1978) found that students in physical education classes spend large amounts of time waiting, relocating, and listening passively to instruction, sometimes as much as two-thirds of the class time. Time actually spent engaged in activity learning was about 27% of the total class time. It appears that Anderson's data are probably applicable to many physical education environments. Many teachers do not plan carefully, have poor organizational skills, or lack adequate amounts of equipment. A class in which students spend most of the time getting organized, relocating, lis-

tening to a lecture, or waiting for a turn with a piece of equipment cannot be motivating. Evidence is mounting from the research on academic learning time (McLeish 1981) that classes in which students do not have opportunities to practice are ineffective in producing student learning and positive attitudes. Teachers must therefore plan carefully for active learning by organizing adequate amounts of equipment and by limiting the time spent on unproductive activities.

Learning activities can also be planned according to the Premack principle (1964). This principle is sometimes referred to as Grandma's law, or "Eat your spinach, then you may have dessert." The principle uses activities that students enjoy to motivate them to participate in activities that they do not currently enjoy. Teachers can arrange the environment so that students must spend a certain amount of time completing a certain number of attempts at a less popular activity before they can gain access to a favorite activity. For example, 7th grade students might have to complete the following nine performance objectives for basketball before they would be allowed to participate in a 3-on-3 class tournament.

Dribbling

1. Bounce (dribble) the ball 15 times consecutively with the preferred hand with control (1 point).
2. Walk forward 25 ft while dribbling the ball with the preferred hand with control (1 point).
3. Run forward 50 ft while dribbling the ball with the preferred hand with control (1 point).

Passing (With a Partner)

4. Make 8 of 10 chest passes to a partner standing 10 ft away (1 point).
5. Make 8 of 10 bounce passes to a partner standing 15 ft away (1 point).
6. Make 6 of 10 overhead passes to a partner 15 ft away (1 point).

Shooting

7. Make 7 of 10 lay-ups from the preferred side (1 point).
8. Make 5 of 8 set shots from inside the key (1 point).
9. Make 4 of 8 set shots from the perimeter of the key (1 point).

In this situation, the nine performance objectives are the unfavorable activities, and the 3-on-3 tournament is the favorable activity.

Another example would be to allow students to participate in basketball for 10 min after they have completed the fitness activities such as running or exercising. It is best for teachers to select reinforcing activities that are within the realm of physical education. In some situations, however, when student motivation and interest are very low, teachers may have to use reinforcements outside the physical education area. These might include free time, playing cards, watching television, talking with peers, or playing pool. Such rewards are harder to defend educationally, but they may be necessary in extreme situations.

Access to novelty activities, competitive games, and class tournaments are usually effective reinforcing activities. Frisbee games such as golf, baseball, Guts, and Ultimate have been especially effective. Teachers need to analyze carefully the likes and dislikes of their students in order to plan learning activities that motivate. The final goal of using the Premack principle is to get students to enjoy some type of physical activity.

The instructional devices discussed in Chapter 7 that communicate information to students about their skill attempts are also good motivational devices and enhance learning activities. Targets on the wall or floor, ball machines, stopwatches, and obstacle courses are a few examples. All provide students with a challenge, more practice attempts, feedback, and success with physical activity. With these elements in the teaching-learning process, most students are more motivated. Such devices add variety and novelty to learning activities and help to keep students involved in a task. Effective teaching requires planning for a variety of instructional devices to motivate students each day.

COMMUNICATION SKILLS

The communication techniques that a teacher uses will have an impact on student motivation. Teachers who take a positive approach to communication with students and establish a warm, caring environment seem to be more effective (Medley 1977). A positive approach to student motivation is recommended because of the long-range effects on both students and teachers. Both teaching and learning are simply more enjoyable experiences when students and instructors can look forward to participating in a positive environment, and at the end of the day, when people leave school, they will feel better about learning, teaching, and the overall school atmosphere. The positive approach seems to enhance the overall motivation of both teachers and students over a longer period of time.

Teachers should focus their interactions with students on behaviors that are deemed appropriate (e.g., listening, hustling, following directions, performing well, cooperating, and dressing properly). They must plan to catch students behaving appropriately, rather than trying to catch them behaving inappropriately. Before each class, teachers should decide which student behaviors they are going to emphasize with positive interactions. Praise and positive information feedback can be given frequently while students are doing what they are supposed to be doing. In addition to praise and other positive verbal behaviors, teachers can also use nonverbal behaviors such as clapping hands, a fist in the air, an OK sign with the hand, a wink, a pat on the back, a nod of the head, smiling, or the thumbs-up sign.

A positive, caring teacher also communicates feelings about physical activity by modeling appropriate behaviors. Participating in various sports and games, bicycling to and from school, running in a 10-km race over the weekend, being enthusiastic about class games, hustling, smiling, and laughing during class will show students a genuine love and concern for physical activity. If students experience a highly motivated teacher both in and out of class, they are more likely to emulate the teacher's behaviors.

Teachers should use students' first names on a regular basis to give students the feeling that the teacher really knows and cares about each person in the class. Cheffers and Mancini (1978) found that most physical education teachers emit few behaviors relative to the acceptance of students' feelings or ideas. It is easy to see why many students develop escape and avoidance behaviors from these environments. Listening to students' ideas, feelings, and concerns enhances the learning environment. Teachers should attempt to interact positively with every student at least once a day.

DISCIPLINE

Discipline can be viewed in the same manner as motivation. It is a behavior control process that leads students to behaviors that are deemed appropriate in the teaching-learning situation. The process can take either a negative or a positive approach. Unfortunately, many teachers and administrators equate discipline with a negative approach and the extensive use of punishment. In fact, many teachers are evaluated each year primarily on their ability to discipline (or punish) and keep students in line, rather than on the learning that takes place in their classes. Educational research shows no evidence that students disciplined by a negative approach learn more than students disciplined by a positive approach.

Discipline and motivation are intertwined in the teaching process and should be developed through a positive and preventive approach. Students who are highly motivated will also be highly disciplined. Teachers who are effective, positive motivators will have few problems with inappropriate student behaviors. Because these two areas are interdependent, all of the motivational techniques mentioned previously will help to develop highly disciplined students. Other behavior management techniques can also be used to discipline students.

TECHNIQUES OF DISCIPLINE

CLARIFYING BEHAVIORS AND CONSEQUENCES

Ultimately, teachers must make the decisions about appropriate and inappropriate student behavior in their physical education classes. Sometimes students, parents, and administrators are also involved in the process of deciding what is appropriate and what is not appropriate. Appropriate behaviors are usually defined as those behaviors that contribute positively to the learning environment. In contrast, inappropriate behaviors detract from learning. These behaviors can be related either to physical skill development or to the development of social-emotional skills.

Appropriate behaviors usually include attending class, being on time for class, following directions, participating, cooperating with peers and teachers, and showing emotional control. Inappropriate, disruptive-type behaviors that detract from the learning environment include tardiness, profanity, obscene actions, defiance of authority, talking out of turn, and interfering with the rights of others. Certain schools and teachers will permit and accept a broader range of behaviors, while others might not permit the same behavior in a similar situation. A part of maturation is the student's learning to discriminate between teachers regarding the behaviors deemed appropriate in their classes.

All teachers have some notion of what they believe is appropriate and inappropriate behavior in their class. Many times, however, they do not write down the appropriate behaviors and do not effectively communicate these notions to students. An important step in behavior control is to decide exactly which behaviors are important and which behaviors are unacceptable. These can then be listed, passed out, and discussed with students at the beginning of the year. The list could also be posted in the locker room and in the gymnasium, and parents and administrators could be made aware of the various behaviors. Everyone would thus have a basic understanding of what the teacher considers appropriate and inappropriate. This will start the process of students learning appropriate behaviors.

Teachers also need to develop a number of strategies concerning the consequences for both appropriate and inappropriate behavior. Students and parents should understand the consequences involved and how they will be applied in various situations. An example of consequences for inappropriate behavior might include the following progression:

Step 1: An informal, private conference between the teacher and student focusing on the behavioral aberration. An agreement should be reached regarding the consequences of future behavior.

Step 2: A telephone call to the parents to discuss the problem and possibilities for a solution.

Step 3: A conference with the teacher, parent, student, and principal or counselor to discuss the problem and develop a plan for changing the behavior. A written copy of the plan should be distributed to all people involved in the situation.

Step 4: Severe disciplinary actions

    a. Loss of privileges: These could include access to the library, cafeteria, clubs, athletics, or dances. Parents should be notified in writing about the procedures used.

    b. In-school suspension: A school can have a designated area and a supervisor for in-school suspension. Strict rules and guidelines for school work, privileges, and procedures must be set for this program.

    c. Short- and long-term suspensions: The school principal should have the power to suspend a student from school for 3 to 10 days, depending on the severity of the behavior and the student's behavioral history. Strict policies and procedures should be arranged and followed carefully. An appeal process must be available to students. Parents must be notified in writing as to the steps that have been followed.

    d. Expulsion: This is the final step that may be used in extremely severe instances. The principal usually initiates the action with a letter to the student and parents. An official action from the Board of Education may be required to expel a student. Due process and appeal procedures must be used and made available to the student.

Many secondary schools have some type of disciplinary referral form (Figure 8.3). This form is used to keep an accurate record of behavioral problems, and is a part of the communication process between students, teachers, parents, administrators, and counselors. The referral form can be an effective tool for controlling student behavior in certain situations. A problem is that the approach is time-consuming, and some teachers may be unwilling to use it.

TEACHERS' REACTIONS

Teachers' reactions to appropriate and inappropriate behavior are an effective procedure for increasing and decreasing specific behaviors. Verbal reactions can be positive in the form of praise, or negative in the form of scolds. The available evidence shows that many teachers consistently use high rates of negative reactions and relatively low rates of positive reactions (Boehm 1974, Hamilton 1974, Darst 1976). A case was presented previously for the possible negative side-effects of an environment based on coercion and punishment. Teachers need to focus positive reactions on appropriate student behaviors. This is an effective preventive disciplinary strategy that enhances a positive and productive environment. Indeed, the evidence suggests that students learn more and feel better about learning in a positive environment.

Initially, teachers should emit many positive reactions that give specific and immediate information when students are behaving appropriately. Examples include:

1. Thanks for getting dressed and ready to participate so quickly.
2. Squad three is listening well.
3. John, way to follow directions.
4. Good hustle between stations.
5. Sally and Sarah are working hard today.

Too often, teachers focus scolds on 1 or 2 students in the class, while 29 or 30 other students are receiving little teacher attention for behaving appropriately. Teachers should avoid repeating too many general positive statements like good job, good work, good hustle, way to go, good going, and nice work, because students can become satiated with general statements and the positive statements will then lose their effectiveness. Teachers should also make sure that the intensity of their statements is commensurate with the behavior of the student. Students who are not behaving appropriately should not receive positive reactions from the teacher in an unqualified manner.

Figure 8.3. Disciplinary referral form

UNIFIED PUBLIC SCHOOLS

School _____

Phone _____

DISCIPLINARY REFERRAL:	Student's Name	Sex	Grade-Class	Date

1. The purpose of this report is to inform you of a disciplinary incident involving your son/ daughter.	Date of Incident	Time	Teacher's Signature

2. You are urged both to appreciate the action taken by the teacher and to cooperate with the corrective action initiated.

Parent's Name

Address

REASON FOR REFERRAL:

☐ Annoying to classmates   ☐ Rudeness, disrespect   ☐ Excessive talking

☐ Disturbing class   ☐ Profanity   ☐ Restless, inattentive

☐ Insubordination, disobedience ☐ Fighting   ☐ Ditching

☐ Smoking   ☐ Threatening, harassing others ☐ Truancy

☐ Other (State the problem) _____

_____

_____

_____

ACTION TAKEN PRIOR TO REFERRAL:

☐ Held conference with student ☐ Telephoned parent   ☐ Sent previous report home

☐ Consulted counselor   ☐ Held conference with parent ☐ _____

Do you desire to participate in a conference with Pupil _____ Parent _____ Guidance _____

Case referred to _____ Administration _____ Counselor for further action

Initial conference was held by _____

continued

Figure 8.3/*continued*

PRESENT DISPOSITION:

☐ Student regrets incident, cooperative

☐ Recurring incidents will be reported

☐ Student placed on probation

☐ Student placed on closed classes, which requires a Parent-Administrator conference

☐ Student suspended

☐ _____

_____

☐ Parent is requested to call the school representative indicated _____

_____

_____

Additional Comments: _____

_____

_____

Logged

1 ☐ 2 ☐ 3 ☐
4 ☐ 5 ☐ 6 ☐

COPIES: 1. Parent 2. Office 3. Admin. 4. Admin. 5. Counselor 6. Teacher

---

Scolds and other negative teacher reactions are necessary and useful from time to time in decreasing inappropriate behavior. Scolds should be delivered infrequently and with a certain amount of severity. Teachers should attempt to remain unemotional and to focus on the student's inappropriate behavior. Students must understand that the scold is not focused on them as a person but on their inappropriate behavior, and they must also understand exactly what the appropriate behavior is in the given situation. The appropriate behavior is usually obvious to students, but they may need to be reminded of the rules.

Another useful teacher reaction is called *extinction*. This term refers to the technique of ignoring certain inappropriate behaviors that are not seriously disruptive to the learning environment. Many times, student behavior is maintained by the attention of the teacher and the peer group. For example, a student will misbehave, and the teacher will publicly scold the behavior. The friends of the student will laugh at the situation. Peer laughter is reinforcing to the student, and the behavior will occur again. If the behavior is not seriously distracting, then ignoring the behavior coupled with a positive reaction to an appropriate behavior occurring at a later time may be more effective in this situation. The teacher might also explain to the class that they, too, should ignore the student's inappropriate behavior. In this way, the student loses the attention of both teacher and peers.

Teacher reactions play a powerful role in controlling student behavior and establishing an effective, positive learning environment. Careful plans should be made regarding the use of these reactions. Teachers must think about the specific student behaviors that they will praise, scold, and ignore. A list of specific student behaviors and the accompanying teacher reactions should be developed by each teacher. An instructor's list might look like this:

Praise	Scold	Ignore
Listening	Fighting	Talking out
Following directions	Pushing	Raising a hand
Hustling	Disrupting others	Snapping fingers
Being on time	Cursing	Showing off
Proper dress	Obscene gestures	Constantly asking questions

Various situations may require still other, different reactions. Teachers should strive, however, to be consistent in their reactions, so students will know what to expect and will learn to behave accordingly.

TIME-OUT PROCEDURES

Time out is a strategy whereby the teacher removes the student from a positive or enjoyable situation (Martin and Pear 1983). It is similar to the penalty box in an ice hockey game. If a student is behaving inappropriately, then the teacher can publicly or privately ask the student to go to the time-out area. The area should be far enough away from the class to avoid the ridicule of peers, but close enough to be within the supervision of the teacher. The area can be specifically designated in the gymnasium, or it can be an area in an outside field such as under a tree, on a bench, or in a baseball dugout.

A designated time allotment should be assigned for a specific infraction, similar to hockey penalties. In other words, the penalty should fit the crime. It is important to remember that the time-out procedure should be used only for severe behavior problems. If the procedure is used for many minor problems, it may become reinforcing for students to go to the penalty box, and the teacher may end up with too many students in the time-out area.

Another problem with this approach is that certain students may not enjoy the physical activities of the day and will act inappropriately simply to get time out. This is why teachers must get to know all of the students in their classes and use different behavioral strategies with different students. A student who finds class activities unrewarding may be opting to stay in the time-out area.

BEHAVIOR CONTRACTS

A **behavior contract** is a written statement specifying certain student behaviors that must occur in order to earn certain rewards or privileges. The contract is usually signed by the student and the teacher involved, and is drawn up after a private conference to decide on the appropriate behaviors and rewards. Letting the student make some decisions dealing with the contract is often useful.

The behavior contract may be a successful strategy for students with severe behavior problems. Every attempt should be made to use rewards that occur naturally in physical education class (e.g., Frisbee play, jump rope games, aerobics. basketball). In some cases, however, different types of rewards may have to be used. For example, a student who is interested only in rock music and motorcycles could be allowed to spend some time reading, writing about, or discussing one of these topics. As behavior improves and the student's attitude becomes more positive, the rewards should be switched to physical education activities. The contract is gradually phased out over a period of time as students gain control of their behavior and can participate in normal class environments.

Contracts can be written for a small group of students or for an entire class with similar problems, but teachers must be careful about setting up a reward system for too many students. The system can become too complex or time-consuming to supervise properly. The contract is best used with a limited number of students in several problem situations. Examples of behavior contracts are given in Figures 8.4 and 8.5. The contract in Figure 8.4 can be used with an individual, a small group, or an entire class of students.

BEHAVIOR GAMES

Behavior games are an effective strategy for quickly changing student behaviors in the areas of management, motivation, or discipline. If a teacher is having severe disruptive problems in any of these areas, a well-conceived behavior game may turn the situation around in a short period of time. These games can be packaged for a group of students to compete against each other or against an established criterion level. The goal of the game is to use group contingencies to develop behaviors that enhance the learning environment and eliminate behaviors that detract from the environment.

Various forms of behavior games have been used successfully by physical educators and athletic coaches (Darst and Whitehead 1975, McKenzie and Rushall 1973, Paese 1982). Behavior games have proved effective in dealing with these types of inappropriate behaviors: nonattendance, tardiness, nondressing, cursing, talking out, low practice rates, and high rates of management time. The following is an example of a behavior game that was used successfully with 7th graders in an effort to improve management behaviors:

1. The class is divided into four squads. Each squad has a designated color for identification. Four boundary cones with appropriate colors are set up as a starting area.
2. The rules of the game are as follows:
   a. Each squad member has to be dressed and in the proper place at a designated starting time. Reward: 2 points

January 12, 1984

I, a. Student, agree to the following rules:

1. Dress properly each day.
2. Be on time for class each day.
3. Do not disturb other students during Physical education class.

If all three rules are followed in a day, I will earn 10 minutes of basketball time for myself and a friend after school on Fridays anytime from 3:00 to 3:50.

Anne Student, student

B. Pangrazi, teacher

Figure 8.4.   Individual behavior contract

b. Each squad member has to move from one activity to another activity within the specified time (10, 20, or 30 sec) and begin the appropriate behavior. Reward: 1 point for each instance

c. Each point earned is rewarded with 1 min of free activity time on Friday. Free activity time includes basketball, Frisbee, jump ropes, and flag football, or any other activity popular with students.

d. The squad with the most points for the week earns a bonus of 5 points.

3. The teacher explains the allotted time for each management episode (10, 20, or 30 sec) and gives a "go" signal. At the end of the allowed time, the teacher gives a "stop" signal and awards points for appropriate behavior.

4. Squads that are successful are praised by the teacher, and the points are recorded on a small card. The unsuccessful squads are not hassled or criticized, just reminded that they did not earn a point.

5. On Fridays, the appropriate squads are awarded the special free-time activities, while the others continue work on the regularly scheduled class activities.

6. The game is slowly phased out as students begin to manage themselves better.

The results of the game were as follows:

1. The use of group contingencies and free-time activities reduced the overall class management time.

2. The free-time activities were within the physical education curriculum objectives and served as a break from regular activities.

3. The free-time activities gave the teacher an opportunity to interact with students on a personal level.

```
                          BEHAVIOR CONTRACT
    I.Class Preparation                Points
       A. Attendance                    1
       B. On time                       1
       C. Properly dressed              1

   II.Social Behavior
       A. Showering                     1
       B. Lack of inappropriate         5
          behaviors
          Cursing                    9 points per day
          Fighting                  (36 points per week)
          Disruption

   During Friday's class, points may be exchanged for time in aerobics,
   weight training, Frisbee, or basketball.

   I agree to these conditions.


   _____
      Student


   _____
      Teacher
```

Figure 8.5. Group behavior contract

4. The students enjoyed the competition and the success they experienced when they emitted appropriate behaviors.
5. They also enjoyed the free time with novelty activities.
6. The positive approach of the game seemed to improve the overall teaching-learning atmosphere. The students were more attentive and cooperative.
7. The teachers felt that more time was available for instruction because of the reduction in management time.

Another important point to remember in structuring behavior games is that all students or squads should be able to "win" the game. Games do not have to have a winner and a loser. All participants in a behavior game should be able to win. Teachers must also be aware that sometimes one or two students may find it reinforcing to cause their team to lose the behavior game. They will try to break every rule to force their team to lose consistently. In these cases, the teacher should hold a special team discussion and possibly a team vote to eliminate those students from the team and from the game. The disruptive students could be sent to a time-out area or channeled into some special, alternative activity. They might even be asked to sit out from an entire day's activities. Again, caution is urged in exercising this option, because a time out may be exactly what these students had in mind as a final goal.

Another effective behavior game can be used to help students persist at learning activities in a station-type approach. Many times teachers will set up four or five learning stations for activities such as basketball, volleyball, soccer, or football. Performance objectives or learning tasks are posted at each station for the students to practice. Some of the students, however, are not motivated and do not use their time productively until the teacher rotates to the station where they are working. The teacher then prods the group, hassles a few students, and praises a few others. The overall environment is not very productive, and the teacher gets tired of hassling unmotivated students. A possible solution to this situation is the following game:

1. Divide the class into four or five squads. Let the students pick a name for their squad.
2. Set up the learning stations with the activities to be practiced. An equal number of squads and learning stations is necessary.
3. Program a cassette tape with popular music. The tape should have short gaps of silence for the duration.
4. Tell students that if everyone in their squad is properly engaged in practicing the appropriate tasks, a point will be awarded to their squad at each gap in the music. If one or more persons are not engaged, then no point will be awarded.
5. The points can be exchanged for minutes of free time for reinforcing motor activities such as Frisbee or jump ropes. Fridays could be designated for reward time.
6. The music should be changed regularly, and the interval between gaps should be changed and slowly stretched until the gaps are eliminated. The music then serves as a discriminative cue for future practice time.

Many teachers have found that students enjoy exercising and practicing skills while listening to music. The music seems to enhance the motivational level of the environment. Students can be allowed to bring in their own music as a special reward for productive behavior. Teachers should be sure that the music is not offensive to others because of sexual, ethnic, or religious connotations.

A final use of the behavior game can be as a challenge or change of pace and an enjoyable learning activity. The teacher may not have serious behavior problems in the class but may simply want to add an enjoyable learning activity. An example of this is the "burnout" game. It can be used in the following manner:

1. Fridays can be designated as "burnout" day. The last 5–10 min of the period can be used for the game.
2. In order to qualify for the "burnout" award, a student must have attended, been on time, dressed properly, and worked diligently all week.
3. On a rainy or nonparticipation day, each student submits a piece of paper with a written explanation of a "burnout" challenge-type activity that she or he would enjoy. Examples

might include a stork-stand on one foot, one-arm push-ups, pull-ups, hanging on a rope for time, doing a headstand, or juggling without dropping an object. Students should be encouraged to select activities in which they excel. These challenge suggestions can be kept in a jar or hat for future choices.

4. A "burnout" award is made up and hung on a locker, pasted on a bulletin board, announced over the morning news, or put in any similar, visible medium. A photograph of the "burnout" winner might be posted each week in the hall of fame.
5. On Friday, the teacher and the entire class try the burnout challenge to determine a winner. The winner might also receive several privileges like selecting the next activity from the jar or hat. The activity could be selected on Monday, and students might then practice during the week.
6. Teachers must make sure that the winner "qualified" for the award with the appropriate behaviors during the week.
7. Teachers can make the game enjoyable and something that students look forward to each week.

Summary

Motivation, management, and discipline mean different things to different people. These areas are intertwined and are influenced by both curriculum and instruction. Many factors affect these areas for secondary students. Parents, siblings, peers, past teachers, past learning experiences, as well as current learning activities, teacher behavior, and various behavioral management strategies have an impact on motivation, management, and discipline.

Effective teachers have found that a positive approach to these areas works better than a negative approach. A preventive approach is positive and reduces the need for punishment, coercion, and similar negative procedures. If teachers do their jobs using a positive approach, students are more likely to become active, cooperative participants, because physical education class will be an enjoyable place to learn new skills. Teachers with a positive attitude usually feel better about their profession and are more motivated to continue improving the teaching process.

References

Anderson, W. 1978. Introduction. In *What's Going on in the Gym. Motor Skills: Theory into Practice*, edited by W. Anderson and G. Barrette, Monograph 1.

Boehm, J. The effects of competency-based teaching programs on junior high school physical education student teachers and their pupils. Doctoral dissertation, The Ohio State University, 1974.

Cheffers, J., and Mancini, V. 1978. Teacher-student interaction. In *What's Going on in the Gym. Motor Skills: Theory into Practice*, edited by W. Anderson and G. Barrette, Monograph 1.

Darst, P. 1976. The effects of a competency-based intervention on student teaching and pupil behavior. *Research Quarterly* 47(3): 336–345.

Darst, P., and Whitehead, S. 1975. Developing a contingency management system for controlling student behavior. *Pennsylvania JOPER* 46(3): 11–12.

Hamilton, K. The application of a competency-based model to physical education student teaching in high school. Doctoral dissertation, The Ohio State University, 1974.

Martin, G., and Pear, J. *Behavior Modification—What It Is and How to Do It*. Englewood Cliffs, NJ: Prentice-Hall, Inc., 1983.

McKenzie, T., and Rushall, B. Effects of various reinforcing contingencies on improving performance in a competitive swimming environment. Unpublished paper, Dalhousie University, 1973.

McLeish, J. Effective teaching in physical education. Victoria, B.C.: Department of Education, University of Victoria, 1981, mimeo.

Medley, D. *Teacher Competence and Teacher Effectiveness*. Washington, DC: American Association for Colleges of Teacher Education, 1977.

Paese, P. 1982. Effects of interdependent group contingencies in a secondary physical education setting. *Journal of Teaching in Physical Education* 2(1): 29–37.

Premack, D., et al. 1964. Reinforcement of drinking by running: Effect of fixed ration and reinforcement time. *Journal of the Experimental Analysis of Behavior* 5: 91–96.

Rushall, B., and Siedentop, D. *The Development and Control of Behavior in Sport and Physical Education*. Philadelphia: Lea and Febiger, 1972.

Sage, G. *Introduction to Motor-Behavior: A Neuropsychological Approach*. Reading, MA: Addison-Wesley Publishing Co., 1977.

Chapter 9

Instructional Strategies

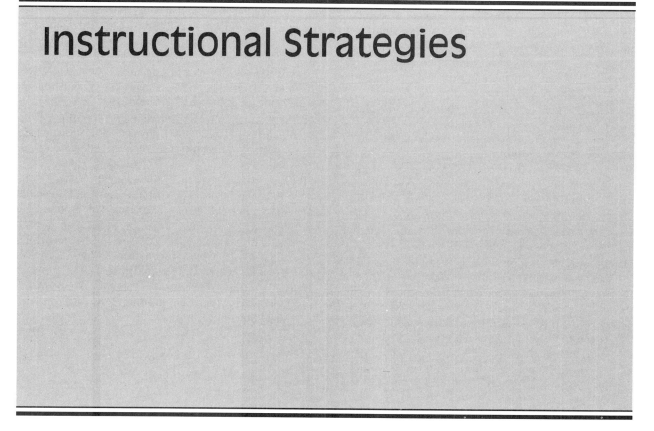

The physical education literature is full of instructional strategies, styles, methods, and approaches (Mosston 1981, Singer and Dick 1980, Zakrajsek and Carnes 1981). Different people have presented, labeled, and categorized these strategies in many ways. Many of the terms overlap and can be quite confusing to the beginning teacher. Generally, an **instructional strategy** is an overall scheme for organizing all aspects and elements in the educational environment. The scheme provides direction for the specific involvement and role of the teacher and students in the process. The elements of the process are described, and a prediction is made about how the elements will affect student behavior.

The instructional strategy should provide a direction for (1) presenting students with information, (2) organizing students for practice, (3) providing feedback to students on how they are doing, (4) keeping students engaged in appropriate behavior, and (5) monitoring students' progress toward goals or objectives. Instructional strategies should be analyzed in terms of the teacher's planning and setup of the environment, the teacher's

behavior during the lesson, the student's behavior during the lesson, and student outcome variables. Teacher planning and setup includes any evidence of preplanning such as lesson plans, organizational arrangements, or instructional devices. The teacher's behavior includes instructions, questions, management cues, feedback, and demonstrating. Student behavior during the lesson includes activity time, waiting, receiving information, management time, and so forth. Student outcome variables include physical fitness levels, physical skills, knowledge, social-emotional behaviors, and attitudes toward physical activity. Analysis and evaluation strategies for these areas are discussed in Chapters 10 and 11.

In secondary physical education, there is no best universal instructional strategy. Even though most educators will speak to the merits of their favorite approach, no evidence suggests that any one strategy is more effective than another in all situations. Frymier and Galloway (1974) have concluded that there is no one best way of doing anything in education. Too many variables must be considered before an appropriate strategy can be selected for a specific situation. These variables include (1) the objectives of the lesson such as physical skills, knowledge, and social behaviors, (2) the nature of the activities involved such as tennis, volleyball, swimming, or fencing, (3) the nature of students, including individual characteristics, interests, developmental level, motivation, and background, (4) the total number of students in the class, (5) the equipment and facilities available, such as tennis racquets and courts, and (6) the abilities, skills and comfort zone of the teacher.

Secondary teachers should develop a repertoire of instructional strategies that can be used with different objectives, students, activities, facilities, and equipment. Teachers who have a variety of approaches can use different combinations in many ways. These combinations can be a motivational device for both students and teachers. Variety is the spice of life and this holds true for the use of instructional strategies.

Teachers need to make a conscious effort to maintain their professional interest and enthusiasm. Too often, they become comfortable with a teaching position and with one favorite instructional strategy. They may begin to lose their enthusiasm because of large classes, inferior working conditions, low salaries, or problems with poorly motivated students. Complaints are constantly heard from teachers about boredom, lack of new challenges, and burnout. Perhaps the use of a different instructional strategy in an appropriate setting could improve the environment for both students and teachers. A new teaching strategy is certainly not a panacea for all of the ills of the educational system, and strategies should not be selected without considering all of the appropriate variables. Certain strategies do, however, offer certain advantages in certain situations. A teacher who has developed a high-quality instructional program should consider different approaches.

This chapter will present instructional strategies for secondary physical education teachers. The strategies have been field-tested in many different secondary environments, and various combinations of strategies have been used with different activities. Teachers can use several different combinations in one day's lesson or in a unit plan; they do not have to adopt just one strategy at a time. In fact, many teachers are comfortable and effective using several strategies in one lesson. Examples will be discussed with each strategy that follows.

Mounting evidence from teacher effectiveness research (Medley 1977, McLeish 1981, Siedentop 1983) indicates that, regardless of the teacher's

instructional strategy, an educational environment will be more effective if it has the following characteristics:

1. *Students are engaged in appropriate learning activities for a large percentage of class time.* Effective teachers use class time wisely. Little time is wasted on noncontent activities such as taking attendance, dressing, lunch tickets, or yearbook photos. Teachers should plan carefully and insist on appropriate learning activities that deal with the subject matter.

2. *The learning atmosphere is success-oriented, with a positive, caring climate.* The evidence clearly shows that teachers who develop a positive and supportive atmosphere are more effective in terms of student learning. The old idea of creating a harsh, negative climate has proved not to be the best way to foster learning and positive attitudes toward physical activity.

3. *Students receive clear objectives and high rates of information feedback from the teacher and the environment.* Students need to know what they are going to be held accountable for in the physical education class. Class activities should be arranged so students spend large amounts of time on the required objectives. Positive and corrective feedback should be available from the teacher. The environment should be set up so students can receive feedback on learning attempts even when the teacher is not available. Peers and instructional devices can be used to provide feedback.

4. *Student progress is monitored regularly.* Students must be expected to make progress on the class objectives, and records need to be kept relative to the various objectives. If progress is not monitored regularly, then students cannot be held accountable and the environment will not be as effective.

5. *Low rates of management time and smooth transitions from one activity to another characterize the environment.* Effective teachers are effective managers of students. Students are moved from one learning activity to another smoothly and without wasting time. Time-saving procedures are planned and implemented efficiently. Students spend little time waiting during class transitions.

6. *Students spend a limited amount of time waiting in line or in other unproductive behaviors.* Effective environments are characterized by high rates of time engaged in the subject matter. In

physical education, this means high rates of time spent practicing, drilling, and playing. Physical education should be activity-oriented, and students should spend their class time doing the activity.

7. *Teachers are organized and have high expectations for student achievement.* Learning activities should be structured so students will be challenged. The activities must not be too easy or too difficult. Students need both success and a challenge with learning activities. Teachers must expect students to learn and must hold them accountable for their progress.

8. *Teachers are enthusiastic about what they are doing and are actively involved in the instructional process.* Students need to see an enthusiastic model—someone who has incorporated physical activity into his or her life-style. Active involvement means active supervision, enthusiasm, and high interaction rates with students.

Teachers should keep these key points in mind as they select, plan, and implement various instruction strategies. All of these environmental characteristics can be present when using different strategies.

COMMAND (DIRECT) INSTRUCTION

This instructional strategy is the most commonly used approach in secondary physical education today. It is characterized by a teacher being the central figure and presenting the same information to all students at the same time with the same method. Students then practice the same activity at the same level for the same length of time. The teacher makes all decisions regarding objectives, content, instruction, practice time, and evaluation procedures. The student's basic responsibility is to follow the directions of the teacher.

A common scenario for the strategy would begin with an explanation and demonstration of the skills to be developed. The students are then organized into partners, small groups, or squads for practice. The teacher gives a signal for practice to commence on the specific skill and then moves around the area—correcting errors, praising, scolding, encouraging, and so forth. The teacher gives a signal to stop, and the students gather around the teacher for a few final evaluative comments before dismissal for the period. The teacher serves as the major demonstrator, lecturer, motivator, organizer, disciplinarian, director, and error corrector. Students have few opportunities to make decisions in this strategy. They learn instead to depend on the teacher to perform all of these functions.

A specific example of a command-style lesson on basketball for 7th graders would follow this sequence: The teacher gives a lecture and demonstration on dribbling. She points out that students should use their fingertips, lower their center of gravity, watch the defenders, and become proficient with both hands. The students are then organized in four lines with eight to ten students in each line. A practice drill is explained and demonstrated. On the teacher's signal, the first student in each line dribbles the ball up to midcourt with the right hand and back with the left hand. The remaining students are waiting patiently in line for their turn. The teacher corrects a few students who are dribbling too high, praises a few for proper form, scolds a few students for horsing around in line, and reminds a few to change hands when they turn around to come back. After a period of time, the teacher gives a stopping signal and makes a few general comments on how well or how poorly the class is performing. She then moves on to another dribbling drill or possibly another basketball skill such as passing, shooting, or rebounding.

Students can certainly learn with this instructional strategy, and it does offer a tightly controlled class environment that is safe for students. Unfortunately, in this situation the students are spending large amounts of class time passively watching or listening to a lecture-demonstration and waiting in line for a turn. Students will consequently be spending low rates of time engaged in physical activity and will probably become bored and frustrated during the time waiting in line. This lesson could be improved by having more practice lines, more basketballs, more active students, and less unproductive waiting time. Instead of four lines, there could be eight or ten lines of dribblers.

Another common problem with this approach is that teachers basically have to teach to the "norm" of the class. Higher skilled and lower skilled students are hindered because the learning activities are either too easy and not challenging, or too hard and cause repeated failure. In this strategy, teachers often do not provide enough options for the various ability levels. If a wide range of basketball abilities exists in the class, then the teacher should change to a different strategy in which several options can be offered (e.g., four different dribbling drills ranging from standing in place and dribbling to dribbling through a set of cones in 20 sec). The range of students' abilities is an important factor in selecting an appropriate instructional strategy.

The command style of teaching has had a poor reputation in physical education circles for several years because it appeared at the end of Mosston's continuum of teaching styles (1981) and showed only a limited amount of cognitive student involvement. Mosston's popular model of teaching physical education proposes seven styles of teaching that move from a teacher-centered approach at one extreme to a student-centered approach at the other. As students move along the approach spectrum, there is more emphasis on cognitive involvement in a student-centered approach. Cognitive involvement is a noble goal for physical education, but it is certainly not the only goal. In fact, one form of the command style labeled "direct instruction" (Rosenshine 1979) has recently been found to be quite successful in terms of student achievement and positive student feelings about themselves and the school. This pattern of teaching has been researched mainly in elementary classroom situations, but the direct instruction model does appear to have merit in secondary physical education settings because of the positive student outcomes from the strategy.

Command instruction, like any other type of instruction, can be effective or ineffective depending on how it is used and administered. It can be an effective strategy for teaching physical skills, and is an especially important approach when activities present an inherent hazard or danger with students who are immature. Activities such as fencing, riflery, and rock climbing should be tightly organized and supervised with a teacher-directed format (Figure 9.1). Students should have little freedom until they understand the hazards and show that they can be careful.

Overall, the command style can be an effective strategy for physical education instruction. The following points should be adhered to throughout the lessons:

1. Instructions and demonstrations should be brief, clear, and to the point. Many teachers talk too long and add too much detail for students to comprehend. Students need to get into the activity as quickly as possible.
2. Practice should be organized so that as many students as possible are kept active within the limits of the situation (i.e., equipment, facilities, and hazards).
3. The specific learning activities should fit the

Figure 9.1. Hazardous activity (reprinted from *Outdoor Adventure Activities for School and Recreation Programs* by P.W. Darst and G.P. Armstrong, 1980. Minneapolis: Burgess Publishing Co., p. 86)

abilities of the "average" students in the class. Activities that are too difficult will create frustration, and activities that are too easy will become boring. Teachers should encourage higher skilled students with challenges that are possible within the parameters of the situation.
4. Management time should be minimal, and smooth transitions should take place from one activity to the next.
5. The environment should be positive, caring, and success-oriented, rather than negative and authoritarian.

Beginning teachers with new students, large classes, or situations that have had high rates of inappropriate student behavior should start with a highly structured command or direct instructional approach proach. Students can then be gradually conditioned over a period of time toward a strategy that gives them more choices and flexibility.

TASK INSTRUCTION

The task style of teaching (Figure 9.2) focuses on specific learning tasks or performances. The teacher selects the tasks and the arrangement of the tasks for the students to practice. The tasks are usually set up in several learning areas or stations. The students rotate through each learning station and work on the assigned tasks. They have more freedom in this instructional strategy than in the command approach, because they can work through the tasks at the station at their own speed and at a

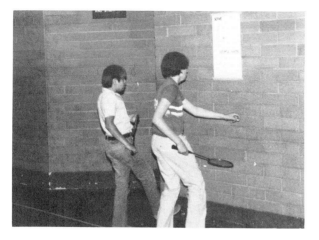

Figure 9.2. Students practicing a task

personal level of proficiency. At each station, the students may have one task or several tasks that they can practice. They start and stop working on the tasks without specific teacher directions. For example, the students may be given 5 min to work at each station that has four or five tasks. The teacher displays a rotation cue or signal after the 5 min is over.

This instructional style allows the teacher to move off center stage and away from being the central figure in the instructional process. The teacher can then become a better agent of feedback by visiting the various learning stations and by interacting with students who need help on the tasks. The teacher does not have to spend as much time directing and managing the entire group. This approach does require more preparation time in planning and setting up tasks. Adequate facilities, equipment, and instructional devices are necessary to keep students productive and working on the appropriate tasks.

These general guidelines should be considered when selecting, writing, and presenting tasks for secondary physical education classes:

1. Select tasks that cover all of the basic skills that make up the activity.
2. Select tasks that will provide students with success and challenge. The tasks should be within the appropriate ability range of the students. Remember that the highest skilled student should be challenged and the lowest skilled student should be successful.
3. Avoid tasks that are dangerous and could cause a student to receive an injury.
4. For the station approach, the task cards can be taped on the wall, to boundary cones, or placed on the ground or floor if students can avoid stepping on them. Another alternative is to give students a copy of the tasks on a sheet of paper to take with them to each station. The task sheets can be stored at school in a locker and can be taken home to use for practice after school.
5. For 7th and 8th graders, the tasks should be written simply with a key word or phrase that the students will understand. For 9th–12th graders, the tasks can be written the same way, or if students are more sophisticated, tasks could be written as performance objectives with the behavior, conditions, and criterion level identified (see Chapter 8 for soccer and volleyball performance objectives and the activity chapters for examples).
6. Task descriptions should always use the appropriate vocabulary of the age group involved. The tasks explain what the student is to do and how the student is to do it (see the examples in Figure 9.3). Teachers must make sure that students understand the tasks and are able to practice when the teacher is not present.
7. Tasks should be presented verbally with a brief demonstration. Students should be given enough information to get started, not an in-depth lecture that takes excessive time.
8. Tasks should incorporate a combination of instructional devices that add feedback, variety, and a challenge to the environment. Examples of such devices include targets, cones, hoops, ropes, and stopwatches.

Figure 9.3 shows a list of basketball tasks with descriptions of what to do and how to perform each task. Task lists can be printed on one or two cards at each station.

The task style of instruction can be used with a variety of grouping patterns for students. Students may work alone, with a partner, or with a small group. The partner or reciprocal grouping pattern (Mosston 1981) can be useful with large classes, limited amounts of equipment, or with certain skills in which the partner can time, count, record, or analyze the skill work. For example, one student can dribble through a set of cones while the partner is timing and recording. In another example with a group of three students, one student might bump a volleyball against the wall, another could analyze her form with a checklist, and the third student could count and record. Many students enjoy the social aspect of being able to work on the tasks with a partner or friend.

BASKETBALL UNIT

Dribbling Tasks (What to do)
1. Standing—right and left hand—25 times
2. Half speed—right and left hand—baseline to midcourt
3. Full speed—right and left hand—baseline to midcourt
4. Around the cones—25 sec

Dribbling Cues (How to do)
1. Finger tips
2. Lower center of gravity
3. Opposite hand in front
4. Eyes on opponents

Ball Handling (What to do)
1. Around head—left and right—5 times each
2. Around waist—left and right—5 times each
3. Around each leg—left and right—5 times each
4. Figure 8 around legs—10 times
5. Hand switch between legs—10 times
6. Bounce between legs and switch—10 times

Jump Shots (What to do)
1. 3 ft away—right angle, center, left angle
2. 9 ft away—right angle, center, left angle
3. 15 ft away—right angle, center, left angle
4. 20 ft away—right angle, center, left angle

Jump Shot Cues (How to do)
1. Straight-up jump
2. Wrist position
3. Elbow position
4. Slight backspin on ball
5. Follow through

Passing Skills (What to do)
Strike the target from 8 ft, 10 ft, 12 ft, 15 ft

1. Chest—10 times
2. Bounce—10 times
3. Overhead—10 times
4. One hand overhead (baseball)—10 times

Passing Cues (How to do)
1. Use your peripheral vision—do not telegraph.
2. Step toward target.
3. Transfer your weight to the front foot.
4. Aim for the numbers.

Figure 9.3.   Basketball tasks

Some teachers are not as comfortable with the task style because there appears to be less order and control than with the command strategy. With proper planning, organization, and supervision, however, teachers can effectively order and control the environment in task style teaching. In many situations, teachers are not comfortable with this approach simply because they lack experience. They tend to teach in the same way that they were taught, and the command style is thus perpetuated because it is so often used.

Teachers and students need time to expand their comfort zones in experimenting with the task style. The approach can be effective in motivating students because of the variety and levels of learning tasks. Students may take some time to adjust to the increased freedom, flexibility, and opportunities to make decisions, but this gives them an opportunity to develop self-management skills, because the teacher is not making every decision. Task teach-ing offers interesting challenges for both teachers and students.

CONTRACT (INDIVIDUALIZED) INSTRUCTION

Contract instruction is a more sophisticated form of task instruction. In the contract approach, a specific external reward system is attached to the accomplishment of the tasks, and this arrangement increases the motivational level of the students. The students work on the tasks because they want to earn the rewards that are tied to the tasks. Students are usually given several options concerning the tasks that can be completed. The tasks are arranged progressively so they increase in difficulty. Students can select the tasks that they are especially interested in completing. The teacher and the students agree formally on what tasks the students will complete and what rewards will be earned. The contract approach is considered to be a form of individualized instruction, because the teacher and the student can adjust objectives, learning activities, content, instruction, and evaluation in order to meet the characteristics and interests of the student.

Rewards in the contract system are usually tied to the grading scheme. Points are awarded for completing certain tasks, and the accumulation of more points means a higher grade. In situations in which grades are not an effective reward, task completion can be tied to participation in a game activity. For example, students might be required to complete ten basketball tasks before they could enter a 3-on-3 class tournament. In other situations, when students are not motivated by grades or by the game activity, they might be allowed to exchange points for a variety of predetermined reward activities such as exercising to music, jumping rope to music, playing Frisbee golf, playing dodge ball, and reading a sports article. These rewards can be novelty activities or other activities that are not generally available to students. Contracts that use a variety of rewards have a better chance of motivating the majority of students in the class.

Contract instructional systems have been used successfully with many activities, including badminton, volleyball, soccer, tennis, racquetball, skin diving, and gymnastics (Darst 1976, Darst and Darst 1978, Claxton 1981, Darst and Model 1983). The approach has been used with upper elementary, junior high, senior high, and college-aged students. Junior and senior high students will work well in a contract system if they are gradually given opportunities to make decisions and control their practice behaviors. This type of instruction is especially effective with physical activities that require the development of individual skills (e.g., bumps, sets, forehands, backhands).

GUIDELINES FOR DEVELOPING CONTRACTS

Rushall and Siedentop (1972) have suggested the following guidelines for developing contingency contracts in physical education:

1. Define the specific tasks or behaviors in observable, measurable terms (e.g., volleyball bumps, badminton clears, tennis serves, and soccer kicks, rather than vague, hypothetical terms such as positive attitudes, physical fitness, or self-concept).
2. Specify clearly the final performance for the end

of the unit. Knowing the specific final goal will increase student motivation. Final goals such as bump 10 consecutive shots, serve 3 or 4 into a target area, or kick a goal in 3 of 4 shots will also serve as a competitive challenge for students.

3. Develop a monitoring and measurement system. This enables students to see daily improvement and to set goals that progress toward the final, terminal objective. In addition to teacher assessment, peer assessment and self-assessment should be used in the monitoring system. This will aid in developing self-control.
4. Rewards should be given only for successful completion of the target performance. This can be speed, strength, endurance, accuracy, or a combination. For example, volleyball serves require a combination of speed and accuracy. An objective must therefore be set up that measures both parameters. Students could hit serves between the net and a rope strung 10 ft higher than the net. The serves must land inbounds and 10 ft or less from the backline. This would ensure both speed and accuracy. Many other physical skills, such as dribbling in soccer, pitching in baseball, or dribbling in basketball, require similar combinations.
5. The relationship between the performance and the reward should be clear to students.
6. The relationship between the performance and the reward should be fair for all students involved in the contract. The reward should be commensurate with a reasonable amount of effort and with the performance. It would be ineffective and unfair to demand too high a level of performance in too short a time for a small reward.
7. Performances should be arranged in a progressive sequence so students can experience success quickly and frequently. As students build a backlog of success, the tasks should then become more difficult and challenging.

Figure 9.4 is a volleyball contract that uses grades as rewards. Such a contract is appropriate for upper-level high school students. The core objectives are required, and the students can choose from the optional objectives.

Figure 9.5 is a flag football contract that has been used with 7th and 8th graders. It follows the same format as the volleyball contract with points tied to a grading scheme, and core and optional performance objectives.

Figure 9.4. Volleyball contract

VOLLEYBALL

Core Objectives

Forearm Pass (Bump)
1. Bump 12 consecutive forearm passes against the wall at a height of at least 10 ft **(1 point)**.
2. Bump 12 consecutive forearm passes into the air at a height of at least 10 ft **(1 point)**.
3. Bump 10 consecutive forearm passes over the net with the instructor or a classmate **(1 point)**.

Overhead Set Pass
4. Hit 15 consecutive set passes against wall at a height of at least 10 ft **(1 point)**.
5. Hit 15 consecutive set passes into the air at a height of at least 10 ft **(1 point)**.
6. Hit 12 consecutive set passes over the net with the instructor or a classmate **(1 point)**.

Serves
7. Hit 3 consecutive underhand serves into the right half of the court **(1 point)**.
8. Hit 3 of 4 underhand serves into the left half of the court **(1 point)**.
9. Hit 3 consecutive overhand serves inbounds **(1 point)**.

Attendance and Participation
10. Be dressed and ready to participate at 8:00 A.M. **(⅓ point daily, 5 points for 15-day unit)**.
11. Participate in 15 games **(1 point)**.
12. Score 90% or better on a rules, strategies, and techniques test (2 attempts only) **(5 points)**.

Optional Objectives
1. Standing 2 ft from the backline, bump 3 of 5 forearm passes into an 8-ft circle surrounding the setter's position. The height must be at least 10 ft, and the ball must be thrown by the instructor or a classmate **(1 point)**.
2. Bump 3 of 5 forearm passes over the net at a height of at least 12 ft that land inbounds and not more than 8 ft from the backline **(1 point)**.
3. Standing in the setter's position (CF), hit 3 consecutive overhead sets at least 10 ft high that land in a 5-ft circle where the spiker would be located. The ball will be thrown by the instructor or a classmate **(1 point)**.
4. Hit 3 of 5 overhead passes over the net at least 12 ft high that land inbounds and not more than 8 ft from the backline **(1 point)**.
5. Standing in the setter's position (CF), hit 3 of 5 back sets at least 10 ft high that land in a 5-ft circle where the spiker would be located. The ball will be thrown by the instructor or a classmate **(1 point)**.
6. Volley 12 consecutive times over the net with the instructor or a classmate by alternating forearm passes and overhead passes **(1 point)**.
7. Alternate forearm passes and overhead passes in the air at a height of 10 ft or more for 12 consecutive times **(1 point)**.
8. Spike 3 of 4 sets inbounds from an on-hand position (3-step approach, jump, extended arm, hand contact) **(1 point)**.
9. Spike 3 of 5 sets inbounds from an off-hand position **(1 point)**.
10. Recover 3 consecutive balls from the net. Recoveries must be playable (8 ft high in the playing area) **(1 point)**.
11. Hit 3 consecutive overhand serves into the right half of the court **(1 point)**.
12. Hit 3 of 4 overhand serves into the left half of the court **(1 point)**.
13. Hit 3 of 5 overhand serves under a rope 15 ft high that land in the back half of the court **(1 point)**.
14. Officiate at least 3 games, using proper calls and signals **(1 point)**.
15. Coach a team for the class tournament. Plan strategy, substitution, and scheduling **(1 point)**.

continued

Figure 9.4/*continued*

> 16. Devise and carry out a research project that deals with volleyball. Check with the instructor for ideas **(1 point)**.
>
> Grade Structure: C = 20 points
>   B = 28 points
>   A = 34 points

In many sections of Chapter 19, a list of performance objectives is provided for the teacher's use. These can be arranged as part of a contract, or they can be used for motivation, instruction, and grading. The objectives will have to be modified according to the particular situation. They may be too difficult for certain students and too easy for others. The important point is that all students should be able to find success and challenge with some of the objectives. Modification of the objectives requires some experimenting by the teacher.

The performance objectives that are listed focus primarily on physical skills rather than on cognitive activities. Certain teachers may want a specific combination of cognitive and physical skills to be built into the contract. The contract provides the framework on which to hang the type of objective that a teacher wants to stress in a certain situation. For example, a contract could provide a balance of objectives related to attendance, participation, physical skills, and cognitive activities. The contract approach allows teachers to be flexible in the choice of objectives, and allows students flexibility in the selection of certain objectives and levels of performance (see "Contract Grading" in Chapter 11).

APPLYING AND ADMINISTERING CONTRACT INSTRUCTION

The teacher needs to explain the entire format so that students understand the objectives, rewards, learning activities, grading procedures, and other responsibilities. Contracts should be available to students so they can explain them to their parents, work on the objectives at home in their free time, or keep records of their performances at school. Students need to understand how involvement in this strategy is different from other strategies. Some students will take longer to adapt and become comfortable with this instruction format.

Teachers should explain and demonstrate the performance objectives to the students in the learning areas where they will be practicing. The various instructional devices and targets should also be introduced. Students need a brief explanation and demonstration to get them started on the objectives. The gymnasium or playing field should be arranged with learning areas for specific objectives, such as the dribbling area, passing area, shooting area, or ball-handling area. The objectives can be posted at each learning station, or students can carry a copy of the objectives with them.

A rotational scheme and grouping pattern can be organized, depending on the maturity and motivational level of students. One arrangement is to have students in equal-sized groups at each learning station and to rotate groups after a fixed period of time. Students spend 3–5 min at each station and then rotate to the next station. Another alternative is to allow students the freedom of rotating to a learning area whenever they are ready for specific objectives. The grouping patterns of practicing individually, with a partner, or with a small group can be used according to facilities, equipment, objectives, and student choice. Teachers need to consider the amount of freedom, flexibility, and choice that students can handle and still be productive in their practice time. It is best to start with small amounts of freedom and gradually expand the choice options and program flexibility as students get used to the system. If students are given too much freedom too quickly, the results can be counterproductive.

The completion of the performance objectives can be monitored by the teacher, student peers, student leaders from another class, or some combination of all three of the aforementioned. If the class size is small and the number of objectives is small, the teacher may be able to do all of the monitoring. Otherwise, a combination of procedures is recommended. Teachers need to involve students, peers, and student leaders in the process. Students' involvement in the monitoring should enhance their understanding of the objectives, and will also give students an additional responsibility in the instructional environment. The system involves students cognitively in the process while they wait their turn to use specific equipment.

Figure 9.5. Flag football contract

FLAG FOOTBALL

Core Objectives

Passing Tasks

1. Throw 10 passes to the chest area of a partner standing 10 yd away **(1 point)**.
2. Throw 3 of 4 consecutive passes beyond a target distance of 20 yd **(1 point)**.
3. Throwing 5 passes, knock over 3 targets from a distance of 10 yd **(1 point)**.
4. Throw 4 of 6 passes through a tire from a distance of 10 yd **(1 point)**.

Centering Tasks

5. With a partner 5 yd away, execute 10 over-the-head snaps to the chest area, using correct holding, proper rotation, and follow-through techniques **(1 point)**.
6. Facing the opposite direction from a partner 5 yd away, execute a proper center stance with feet well spread and toes pointed straight ahead, knees bent, and two hands on the ball. Snap the ball back through the legs for 10 consecutive times **(1 point)**.
7. Same as no. 6 but move back 10 yd **(1 point)**.
8. Center snap 4 of 6 times through a tire a distance of 5 yd away **(1 point)**.

Punting Tasks

9. With a partner centering the ball, from a distance of 10 yd away punt the football using proper technique to another set of partners 15 yd away 3 consecutive times **(1 point)**.
10. Same as no. 9 but at a distance of 20 yd **(1 point)**.
11. Punt the ball 3 consecutive times within the boundary lines of the field and beyond a distance of 20 yd **(1 point)**.
12. Punt the ball 3 consecutive times for a hang time of 2.5 sec or better (use stopwatch) **(1 point)**.

Catching Tasks

13. With a partner run a "quick" pass pattern and catch the ball 2 of 3 times (5–7-yd pattern) **(1 point)**.
14. With a partner run a 10–15-yd "down and in" pass pattern and catch the ball 2 of 3 times **(1 point)**.
15. With a partner run a 10–15-yd "down and out" pass pattern and catch the ball 2 of 3 times **(1 point)**.
16. With a partner run a 5–7-yd "hook" pattern and catch the ball 2 of 3 times **(1 point)**.

Attendance and Participation

1. Be ready to participate in football activities 5 min after the last bell rings each day (⅕ **point daily = 1 point weekly)**.
2. Use proper locker room behavior (will be discussed or posted) at all times (⅕ **point daily = 1 point weekly)**.
3. Score at least 90% on a written test (2 attempts only) **(5 points)**.

Optional Objectives

1. Attend two football games (flag or regular) during the grading period **(1 point)**.
2. Throw 3 of 4 passes through a tire from a distance of 10 yd **(2 points)**.
3. Throw 3 of 4 passes through a tire from a distance of 15 yd **(3 points)**.
4. Throw 3 of 4 passes through a moving tire from a distance of 10 yd **(3 points)**.
5. Throw 3 of 4 passes through a moving tire from a distance of 15 yd **(4 points)**.
6. Catch 2 passes in a game **(2 points)**.
7. Intercept a pass in a game **(2 points)**.
8. Write a one-page report on a fiction or nonfiction book related to the topic of football **(3 points)**.

---

continued

Figure 9.5/*continued*

9. Diagram a football field with all the dimensions and markings, and turn in your diagram to the instructor **(3 points)**.
10. Write up a list of at least 15 football terms with definitions, and turn in to the instructor a neat, finalized copy **(3 points)**.
11. Officiate at least 1 flag-football game during the class time, using correct calls and signals **(1 point)**.

Grade Structure: C = 22 points
 B = 27 points
 A = 32 points

Teachers or student leaders can use a performance chart to monitor objectives at each learning station, or they can carry a master list from station to station (Figure 9.6). This will depend on the number of objectives to be completed at each station.

Another approach is to develop a performance sheet for each student that combines teacher and peer monitoring (Figure 9.7). This allows peers to monitor some objectives and the teacher to monitor the more difficult objectives. Another system would allow students to privately monitor themselves on the performance objectives (Figure 9.8). Students could then work alone on the objectives. Teachers should experiment with several monitoring approaches depending on the activity, the number of objectives, the students' abilities, the size of the class, and the equipment and facilities. Because of the various advantages of each approach, teachers should decide on the best one for their situation. For example, if teachers try to do all of the monitoring, they will spend large amounts of time checking off objectives and may

PERFORMANCE CHART

Station 3					Parallel Bars										
Name	1	2	3	4	5	6	7	8	9	10	11	12	13	14	15

Figure 9.6. Performance chart for gymnastics

PERFORMANCE OBJECTIVES: BEGINNING HANDBALL

Name _____

Instructor Checked	Class Member Checked	
		1. Stand approximately 6 ft from the back wall and in the center of the court. Bounce the ball against the side wall and hit 3 of 4 shots below the white line with preferred hand.
		2. Same as no. 1 but 3 of 5 with the nonpreferred hand.
		3. Hit 3 of 5 power serves that land within 2 ft of the side wall and are otherwise legal.
		4. Hit 3 of 4 lob serves within approximately 3 ft of the side wall that do not bounce out from the back wall more than 8 ft.
		5. Stand approximately 6 ft from the back wall, bounce the ball against the back wall, and hit 3 of 4 shots below the white line on the front wall with the preferred hand.
		6. Same as no. 5 but 3 of 5 with the nonpreferred hand.
		7. Hit 3 of 4 diagonal or "Z" serves that hit the front, side, floor, opposite side, in that order. (The ball may hit, but need not hit the back wall for the serve to be effective.)
		8. Hit 3 of 4 Scotch serves or "Scotch toss" serves that hit the front, side, floor, back, side, in that order. This is similar to the "Z" serve in execution, except that the ball hits the back wall after bouncing on the floor.
		9. Return 3 of 4 serves hit to you by the instructor. (One of each of the following will be used: power, lob, diagonal, and Scotch.)
		10. Execute 3 of 4 attempts at "3-hit drill." (Instructor will explain in detail.)
		11. Execute 3 of 4 attempts at "4-hit drill." (Instructor will explain.)
		12. Hit 3 of 5 ceiling shots with preferred hand. The ball will be thrown or hit by instructor and must be returned to the ceiling, front wall, and floor, in that order.

Note: Entry into ladder tournament is contingent on completion of any 8 of the 12 objectives. To receive a grade of A for the class, you must exhibit proficiency in all 12 objectives.

Objectives 1–8 may be checked by a class member, however, the instructor may spot-check any objectives at his or her discretion.

Objectives 9–12 will be checked by instructor. Performance objectives may be tested in courts 1 and 4.

Figure 9.7. Performance objectives—Handball

SKIN DIVING CONTRACT—NUMBER 1

Use of FACE MASK

Mark the date that each performance objective is met.

_____ 1. Adjust face mask strap to your head size.

_____ 2. Apply saliva to face mask—rub all around face plate, <u>do not rinse</u> (fog preventive).

_____ 3. Vertical tilt: Fill mask with water and hold to face without strap. In chest-deep water, go under in vertical position and by tilting head backward, away from chest, push against upper edge of mask and exhale gently. Completely clear mask 3 of 5 attempts.

_____ 4. Horizontal roll: Fill mask with water and hold to face without strap. While in a horizontal position, roll onto left shoulder, push gently with right hand against side of mask, and exhale gently. Completely clear mask 3 of 5 attempts.

_____ 5. Repeat no. 3 with strap around back of head.

_____ 6. Repeat no. 4 with strap around back of head.

_____ 7. In 6 ft of water, submerge to bottom of pool by pinching nostrils and gently exhaling into mask until you feel your ears equalize. Successfully equalize pressure in 4 of 5 attempts.

_____ 8. In 9 ft of water repeat no. 7.

_____ 9. Repeat no. 3 in deep water.

_____ 10. Repeat no. 4 in deep water.

_____ 11. Throw mask into shallow water, submerge, and put mask on. Complete vertical tilt clear in one breath, 4 of 5 attempts.

_____ 12. Throw mask into shallow water, submerge, and put mask on. Complete horizontal roll clear in one breath, 4 of 5 attempts.

_____ 13. Same as no. 11 in 6 ft of water.

_____ 14. Same as no. 11 in 9 ft of water.

_____ 15. Same as no. 12 in 6 ft of water.

_____ 16. Same as no. 12 in 9 ft of water.

Figure 9.8. Skin diving contract

become frustrated because not much time is left for other teaching activities. If student leaders are involved, then it takes teacher time to train them properly. A problem with peer evaluation is that students are sometimes too lenient with the criterion levels of performances. A similar problem can occur with self-assessment. The teacher needs to spot-check any student monitoring procedure.

In some secondary schools, teachers have used contracts as part of an individualized, independent study approach with a learning laboratory-resource center (Cottman 1976). Students can select the level of an activity that they want to pursue. Learning packets with objectives, study guides, learning activities, and assessment procedures are available for a wide variety of activities. Students can work independently on objectives, view loop films, read books, and prepare for an assessment procedure. Assessment usually progresses from self, to peers, and finally to the teacher. This approach requires teachers to develop many kinds of learning materials, and procedures also need to be developed for supervising the distribution and return of those materials. Assessment procedures can sometimes become too time-consuming, and must then be reevaluated. Another major problem is getting students to develop the self-control to use time productively without direct teacher supervision.

Overall, contract instruction can offer the following advantages in secondary physical education programs, depending on how the instruction is planned, arranged, and monitored:

1. Students, parents, and administrators know exactly what is expected and accomplished by students.
2. The reward system enhances the motivational level of students.
3. Students at most competency levels are able to find success and challenge with objectives.
4. Students can progress through the objectives at their own rate.
5. Students have some choice of learning activities and the sequence of learning activities.
6. Students have some choice concerning the grouping arrangement of skill practice (e.g., alone, with a partner, or with a small group).
7. Students have to accept a certain amount of responsibility.
8. The contract form emphasizes student performance.
9. The contract format frees the teacher to give individual attention and become a better agent of feedback.
10. The contract format can provide students with large amounts of time spent engaged in the subject matter.

Problems that may need to be solved when using the contract approach include the following:

1. The performance objectives are time-consuming to write and require constant revision.
2. A monitoring system needs to be developed that does not take up too much class time.
3. Instructional devices are necessary to provide variety and feedback. These increase the setup and take-down time of each class for the teacher.
4. Many teachers and students will need time to get used to the contract format. Both students and teachers are often more comfortable initially with the familiar teacher-centered approach. Changing to a contract format will require some time for adjustment.

INQUIRY INSTRUCTION

The inquiry model of instruction is process-oriented, rather than product-oriented. The experience that students go through during the process is considered more important than the final product, or solution. Students experience learning situations in which they have to inquire, speculate, reflect, analyze, and discover. They must be cognitively active in this type of instruction. The teacher guides and directs students, rather than commanding or telling. The students must discover the solutions, because the teacher never gives the answers or solutions.

The teacher is responsible for stimulating the students' curiosity about the subject matter. This interest and curiosity will then enhance student involvement with the subject. The teacher uses a combination of questions, problems, examples, and learning activities to lead students toward one or more final solutions. The steps involved must follow a sequence and be arranged logically so that students can move from one step to the next after a certain amount of thinking. The steps should not be too small or too large, because students will then become either bored or frustrated. The instruction environment is one of open communication. Students are comfortable experimenting and inquiring without fear of failure.

Some physical educators believe that inquiry methods of instruction should have a more prominent place in educational methodology (Schueler 1979). Students do need opportunities to inquire, solve problems, and discover, instead of experiencing only those approaches that heavily emphasize listening, absorbing, and complying. Arguments have been made to expand the focus of physical education methodology to include the inquiry style. Proponents of this style believe that it enhances students' ability to think, helps students be more creative, and gives students a better understanding of the subject matter and more enjoyment during the learning process, enhances students' self-concept, and helps develop life-long learning patterns. Some educators argue that students who do not experience inquiry methods are dormant, unchallenged, and unused. These are broad and dramatic claims that are not well documented, but they should be considered by physical educators.

Critics of the inquiry method point out the following problems with the approach: too much time spent on one subject or topic, a focus on trivial or nonessential learning, most motor skills have one best solution that should be quickly explained, secondary students already know the answers, and, lastly, the instruction is difficult to plan because each class has a wide range of student knowledge and ability.

These methods do appear to offer some advantages when learning about certain physical education activities and issues. The methods can and should be used in those situations to give teachers yet another teaching tool in their repertoire of skills.

GUIDED DISCOVERY

The inquiry method in physical education is generally characterized by two approaches called *guided discovery* and *problem solving* (Mosston 1981). The teacher using the guided discovery style leads students through a series of experiences in the hope that they will discover the one planned solution. The teacher has a best, specific answer that she or he wants students to discover. Brief learning activities can guide students to discover the following:

1. Court coverage in tennis, badminton, racquetball, and handball
2. Angles of release for distance throwing with the shot put, discus, football, and softball
3. How to hit the baseball or softball to various fields by altering the batting stance and foot pattern
4. Ready position for basketball, baseball, football, and tennis
5. Need for a variety of passes in soccer, basketball, team handball, and other sports

Students can be put through these activities with several options, and then a brief discussion can take place privately or in a group to see if students have discovered the proper solution. This approach can be a small portion of the lesson that is completed quickly.

PROBLEM SOLVING

The problem-solving method involves a divergent approach, rather than converging on one solution. The students are put through a series of experiences and are helped to devise as many acceptable solutions to the problem as possible. The teacher encourages students to be creative and to come up with unique solutions. Students must analyze the pros and cons of each solution. This style can be useful in discussions and assignments dealing with values, social issues, wellness concepts, and controversial topics related to sport and physical education. Honesty in sports, cooperation with teammates, competition for young children, violence in sport, amateur versus professional sports, athletes taking drugs to improve performance, arguing with officials, women participating in sports, and masculine and feminine roles are examples of topics that could be researched, explored, discussed, or debated in a physical education class.

Wellness is a meaningful curriculum area that lends itself to the problem-solving approach. Many different approaches and methods can be used for maintaining an optimum fitness level. Students can learn to solve their personal fitness problems with physical activity programs that are personalized to meet their needs. Problem-solving approaches are also useful in resolving the issues of proper diet and weight control. Stress reduction, alcohol and drug abuse, and tobacco use are areas that can be dealt with effectively using problem-solving techniques.

The teacher is responsible for creating an open environment in which students can explore all aspects of these controversial topics. Books, articles, movies, interviews, questions, and discussions are possibilities for accumulating and sharing information. Students should be encouraged to gather information and to weigh carefully all alternatives before making a decision. The teacher has to remember that his or her opinion should not carry more weight or emphasis than student opinion. A strategy for starting the problem solving is called a "trigger story." The following are examples:

> You and your partner are involved in a tightly contested golf match with another twosome. Your partner hits his drive into the woods. While you are getting ready for your second shot, you turn and see your partner kick his ball out of the woods into an area where there is a clear shot to the green. His kick was not visible to either of your opponents. What would you do in this situation?

> You are playing a Pop Warner football team. During the game, you make an aggressive, yet legal tackle on your opponent's best running back. The running back receives a leg injury as a result and has to be carried off the field. Your teammates cheer and praise you for injuring the star player. Your coach also praises you when you come off the field. What should you do?

> At a bicycle motocross race, you hear the father of a five-year-old criticizing his daughter for losing

the championship race. The daughter is crying. You hear the father say to the mother: "She has to learn to compete. That's what life's all about." How do you react?

You are coaching a 9th grade girls volleyball team. The game is close and everyone is excited. The mother of a member of your team is being obnoxious. She yells mean things at players on both teams, at the coaches, and at the officials. During a time out, the referee comes over and says, "Can't you do something about her?" What would you do?

Your team is warming up when the referee walks in. Everybody recognizes him. He refereed your last game that you lost because he called a foul every time you moved. A member of your team loudly says, "Not him again!" What would you say?

Right after the fourth game of the season, which your team just lost by four points, you are walking out of the locker room when you hear a parent say to a player on your team—"Boy, did you embarrass me tonight. You were terrible!" How would you react in this situation?

A problem-solving approach can be a useful teaching method in some physical skill areas, particularly when skills can be performed or developed in more than one way. Teachers can allow students to experiment briefly with these skills to determine which approach would be most effective for them. Some examples are the batting stance in baseball, golf grips and swing, putting grip and stroke, starts for sprints, high jumping technique, training methods for distance running, and designing and attacking defenses and offenses in team sport activities. Students could work on these skills in small groups and then report the findings to the class. The teacher can control the discussion and lead students to several acceptable solutions. In some cases, all solutions may not be acceptable, because they may be dangerous, illegal, or ineffective in certain situations.

The inquiry instruction model offers an interesting alternative for secondary school physical educators, and should be used at certain times with certain activities.

Summary

Instructional strategies provide an overall direction for the participants in the educational environment. A secondary physical education teacher should develop a teaching comfort zone that includes command, task, contract, guided discovery, and problem-solving instructional strategies. Each strategy has advantages that can be useful with certain students, with certain activities, and with certain conditions. There is no one best strategy for all situations, and no matter what strategy is selected, teachers should develop a positive, success-oriented environment in which students spend a large percentage of their time engaged in productive learning experiences. Management time should be minimal, and transitions should occur smoothly. Students' performances should be monitored and learning activities sequenced in a progression. All of these goals can be accomplished with a variety of instructional strategies.

References

Claxton, D. A tennis contract for college students. Unpublished paper, Department of Physical Education, Grand Canyon College, 1981.

Cottman, G. *A Guide to Contract Teaching in Physical Education.* Westover, MD: Georganna S. Cottman, 1976.

Darst, P. 1976. Volleyball contracting—An effective tool for learning. *Arizona JOHPERD* 20(1): 14–16.

Darst, P., and Darst, C. 1978. Individualizing skin diving teaching and learning. *Foil* Fall Issue: 22–27.

Darst, P., and Model, R. 1983. Racquetball contracting—A way to structure your learning environment. *JOPERD* 54(7): 65–67.

Frymier, J. D., and Galloway, C. M. 1974. Individualized learning in a school for tomorrow. *Theory Into Practice* 13(2): 65–70.

McLeish, J. Effective teaching in physical education. Victoria, B.C.: Department of Education, University of Victoria, 1981, mimeo.

Medley, D. Teacher Competence and Teacher Effectiveness. Washington, DC: American Association for Colleges of Teacher Education, 1977.

Mosston, M. *Teaching Physical Education.* 2nd ed. Columbus, OH: Charles E. Merrill Publishing Co., 1981.

Rosenshine, B. Content, time and direct instruction. In *Research on Teaching: Concepts, Findings, and Implications,* edited by P. Peterson and H. Walberg. Berkeley, CA: McCutchan Publishers, 1979.

Rushall, B., and Siedentop, D. *The Development and Control of Behavior in Sport and Physical Education.* Philadelphia: Lea & Febiger, 1972.

Schueler, A. 1979. The inquiry model in physical education. *The Physical Educator* 36(2): 89–92.

Siedentop, D. *Developing Teaching Skills in Physical Education*. 2nd ed. Palo Alto, CA: Mayfield Publishing Co., 1983.

Singer, R., and Dick, W. *Teaching Physical Education—A Systems Approach*. 2nd ed. Boston: Houghton Mifflin Company, 1980.

Zakrajsek, D., and Carnes, L. *Learning Experiences—An Approach to Teaching Physical Education*. Dubuque, IA: Wm. C. Brown Group, 1981.

Chapter 10

Evaluating the Instructional Process

A difficult task in the educational setting is to find an instructional evaluation scheme that is readily accepted by teachers. Most teachers acknowledge the importance of evaluation if improvement is to occur, but they then become concerned about who will do the evaluation, what will be done, and when. Another particular concern of physical educators is that they may be evaluated by principals who do not understand instruction in the gymnasium. In many cases, procedures and instruments used in the classroom setting are ineffective or meaningless in the gymnasium, because the primary focus of the physical education lesson is skill development through movement.

Another problem occurs when an outside evaluator sits in on an instructional session. Teachers act differently when they are being observed, and thus the results of the evaluation may not be indicative of the actual daily performance of the instructor. Teachers may not have faith in the expertise of the evaluator, and may resent being evaluated by someone they do not respect. The wide range of problems inherent in being evaluated by others indicates the need for a system of self-evaluation whereby teachers can gather data on their teaching and interpret that data at their leisure. Changes can then be made when the teacher sees the need, rather than making changes because an outside evaluator enforced modifications.

The focus of this chapter is self-evaluation. Emphasis is placed on learning to identify areas that need to be modified and improved, and then developing systematic methods for gathering meaningful data in those areas. It is important that the data be as measurable and objective as possible in order to paint a clear and concise picture. For too long, teaching has been evaluated and changed using opinions and hunches of experts who make subjective observations. Seldom do teachers learn how to gather data that shows them that they are improving, regressing, or standing pat. Without data, analyzing the direction and success of teaching is difficult.

THE NEED FOR SYSTEMATIC OBSERVATION

Instruction has most often been evaluated using inexact and insensitive methods such as intuition, checklists, rating scales, and observation. Over the years, these methods have proved to be relatively ineffective in improving the quality of instruction. The use of an evaluator's intuition relies on the expertise of a supervisor, who observes the instructor and then recommends changes and reinforces specific practices. Supervisors who have the same exact background as the teacher are, unfortunately, hard to find and are often unable to follow up on their evaluations. Improvement is difficult to identify because the evaluation offers little or no quantification. It is thus quite possible that the supervisor will forget what the quality of the first lesson was compared with the present teaching episode. In this situation, evaluating whether or not improvement has taken place is next to impossible.

Checklists and rating scales are often used as evaluation tools and give the appearance of an objective, quantified method (Figures 10.1, 10.2, 10.3). The ratings are unfortunately quite unreliable, and become more so when the number of choice points is increased. The scales and checklists are open to a wide spread of interpretation depending on who is performing the evaluation. Most of the evaluation done using checklists and rating scales is subject to the impressions and opinions of the evaluator rather than resulting from objective data.

This points out the need for a systematic method of observing teachers that quantifies the teaching processes. In its purest form, the data gathered is reliable and can then be used for research methods. Siedentop (1983) is a recognized leader in developing systematic methods for teacher evaluation and research. His techniques have led to a great deal of educational research in the area of pedagogy. The focus of this chapter is the use of methods that are systematic in nature and feasible for self-evaluation. Methods advocated here emphasize using systematic observation for self-improvement. If the reader chooses to conduct research projects, the Siedentop text *Developing Teaching Skills in Physical Education* (1983) should be used as a primary resource. Another useful text for developing research techniques is *Systematic Observation Instrumentation for Physical Education* by Darst et al. (1983). The authors strongly subscribe to the methods advocated in these texts, and in this chapter will show how these methods can easily be applied and implemented in the typical school setting by physical education teachers.

METHODS FOR SYSTEMATICALLY OBSERVING INSTRUCTION

Instruction can be systematically observed using a variety of methods to gather information. The use of these instruments is simply and easily done. The major problem arises in defining the area to be evaluated and then deciding which decisions about the data should be made. The important point is that definitions should be written and then followed consistently if the data are to be meaningful. The methods require little more than pencil, paper, tape recorder, and stopwatch. A video tape recorder can add another dimension, but is not a necessity.

EVENT RECORDING

In simplest terms, this involves recording the number of times a predefined event occurs during a specified time period. Event recording identifies the frequency with which certain behavior occurs. It provides the quantity of events, not the quality. For example, the event recording might be defined as the number of times the teacher interacts with students, or the number of times a positive statement is made. A teacher might tally the number of practice attempts students receive after a skill has been introduced, or the number of times the class is asked to stop and come to attention. Event recording results are usually divided by the number of minutes in the evaluation session to give an event rate per minute. This enables the teacher to compare lessons that involve different content or teaching styles.

To minimize the amount of time needed for analysis, a sampling technique can be used. For example, if the lesson is 30 min long, four bouts of recording, each lasting 2 min at evenly distributed points in the lesson, would reduce the burden of recording and would still yield representative results. Any observable behavior of teachers, students, or between teachers and students can be recorded when the behavior has been clearly defined.

Student _____ Activity _____ Grade _____						
	5	4	3	2	1	Comments
1. Use of language						
2. Quality of voice						
3. Personal appearance						
4. Class management						
5. Presentation and teaching techniques						
6. Professional poise						
7. Enthusiasm, interest						
8. Adaptability, foresight						
9. Adequate activity						
10. Knowledge of subject						
11. Appropriate use of student help						
12. Demonstration (if any)						
13. Progression (if applicable)						
14. General organization						

General evaluation
    5–Superior
    4–Above average
    3–Average
    2–Below average
    1–Poor

Evaluating Teacher

_____

Date _____

Figure 10.1. Example of a rating scale

DURATION RECORDING

Whereas event recording offers insight into the frequency of certain behavior, duration recording reveals the length of time that the behavior takes in terms of minutes and seconds. Time is the measure used in this type of recording. As with event recording, duration recording does not have to be done for an entire lesson. Representative sampling techniques can be used so that three or four bouts of observation, 3 min per bout, can be used to generalize about the entire session.

These data are usually converted to percentages so comparisons can be made from lesson to lesson.

NAME: _____
       (Last)   (First)   (Middle)

SUBJECT OR
GRADE LEVEL: _____

Type (X) in space that indicates your appraisal of the student teacher:	Superior	Above Average	Average	Below Average	Unsatis-factory	Not Known		Superior	Above Average	Average	Below Average	Unsatis-factory	Not Known
Appearance							Innovativeness						
Mental alertness							Communication skills						
Poise and personality							Lesson planning ability						
Enthusiasm							Rapport with students						
Health and energy							Classroom control skills						
Emotional stability							Student motivation skills						
Tact and judgment							Teaching skills						
Desire to improve							Provides for individuals						
Dependability							Understands students						
Professional attitude							Knowledge of subject						
Cooperation							Potential as a teacher						

ADDITIONAL COMMENTS:

(Give this completed and signed form to the student teacher)

Name _____ (Supervising Teacher) _____ Date _____

Name _____ (College Supervisor) _____ Date _____

Figure 10.2. Example of a rating scale

EVALUATION FORM

Activity _____   Date _____

Student Teacher _____ Elementary _____ Secondary _____

College Supervisor _____ Cooperating Teacher _____

This evaluation of student teaching serves as a tangible basis for discussion among the cooperating teacher, the college supervisor, and the student. The following symbols will be used: Plus (+) indicates a positive feature of the student teacher's work; minus (−) indicates a need for improvement.

TEACHING COMPETENCIES

☐ Appearance	☐ Planning and organization
☐ Use of language	☐ Execution of lesson-teaching technique
☐ Voice	☐ Knowledge of subject
☐ Enthusiasm	☐ Demonstration of skills
☐ Poise	☐ Appropriate progression
☐ Creativeness	☐ Provisions for individual differences
	☐ Class management-control
	☐ Adaptability, foresight
	☐ Appropriate choice of activity

COMMENTS:

Figure 10.3. Example of a checklist

This is done by dividing the entire observation time into the amount of time devoted to the specific observed behavior. For example, if 20 min of observation took place and if the student was observed to be in activity for 10 of the 20 min, the percentage would be 50%. This would be expressed as "50% of the total time was spent in activity." This approach is recommended for identifying the duration of certain behaviors, such as practice, managerial, or instructional behaviors.

INTERVAL RECORDING

Interval recording is used to record behavior patterns for short time intervals. In interval recording, the intervals should be 6 to 12 sec in length, with one interval for observing and the other for recording. If a teacher used 6-sec intervals during

a 1-min session, five intervals would be for observing and five for recording the results. According to Siedentop (1983), it is important to have at least 90 data points (observe-record = 1 point) to establish the validity of the technique. It would be possible to generate 100 data points in 20 min using 6-sec intervals.

The data generated from this technique are usually converted to a percentage of the data points in which the behavior occurred. If, for example, the behavior occurred in 40 of 100 data points, the figure would be 40%. The percentages are then compared from lesson to lesson. A simple way to keep track of intervals is to wear a recorder headset that "beeps" every 6 sec. The observer can alternate observing and recording with each signal. This technique is reliable, particularly when the intervals are short, and can be used to record the amount of instructional time, managerial time, academic learning time, and other types of observable behavior.

PLACHECK SAMPLING

Placheck (Planned Activity Check) recording is similar to interval recording in that behavior is observed at different intervals, but this technique is used to observe group behavior. At regular intervals during a lesson, the observer scans the group for 10 sec. The scan should begin at the left side of the instructional area and move to the right side, taking note of which students are not on task. The observer makes only one observation per student, and does not go back or change the decision, even if the student changes behavior during the 10-sec interval.

The technique is used to identify student effort, productive activity, and participation. It is usually best to record the less frequently occurring behavior to ease the burden of counting. For example, if the teacher is interested in identifying the percentage of students involved in the assigned activity, recording the number of students *not* participating might be easier. The intervals should last for 10 sec and should be spaced randomly throughout the lesson. There should be eight to ten observation intervals. Again, signals to observe can be recorded on a tape recorder at random intervals to cue the observer. This technique will yield information concerning the behavior of the group.

SYSTEMATIC OBSERVATION FOR SELF-IMPROVEMENT

Each teacher has different strengths and weaknesses and different concerns for improvement. The approach used for systematic observation directed at self-improvement may vary greatly from teacher to teacher. Instructors need to decide which variables they want to evaluate, and then determine the best possible way to record and monitor the data.

Evaluating one area at a time is usually best at the start. Trying to record more than one variable at a time may frustrate and confuse. It may also confound the picture by making it difficult for the teacher to decide how to change the teaching behavior in question.

After the teacher decides which behavior needs to be changed, a plan for meaningfully evaluating the area must be developed. This means identify-

ing the behavior that affects the desired educational outcome, and deciding which method of observation is most appropriate. At that point, a coding form must be developed to facilitate recording the data.

Coding sheets should be specific to each situation and suited to the teacher. Areas on the sheet should provide for recording the teacher, the date, the focus and content of the lesson, the grade level and competency of the students, the duration of the lesson, and a short description of the evaluation procedure. The sheets should be consistent for each type of behavior so the instructor can compare progress throughout the year.

Deciding what behavior will be recorded depends on the instructor's situation. For example, can the data be gathered by students who are not participating? Can another teacher easily gather the data? Can the data be gathered from an audio tape or is a video tape necessary? Is the instructor willing to let others gather the information, or does the teacher believe that it is important to keep the data confidential? These and other questions will determine what areas the teacher is able to evaluate. The authors find that in most cases the teacher is least threatened by self-evaluation techniques and is more willing to change when change is not required by outside authorities. Another advantage of self-evaluation is that teaching behavior is least changed when outside observers are not present. Self-evaluation techniques thus reveal the actual patterns exhibited in day-to-day teaching.

Many areas that can be evaluated are discussed later in this chapter along with coding forms. The reader should remember that these are only examples, which can be easily modified to meet the specific needs of the instructor. The important point is that teachers make self-evaluation an ongoing and integral part of the teaching process. Teachers should think continually about ways to improve. Teachers never stay the same; they either improve or slack off.

IMPROVING THE QUALITY OF INSTRUCTION

Quality instruction results when an effective teacher implements a well-planned lesson. Many successful teachers have learned how to do this over a period of years through the inefficient method of trial and error. Sheer experience does not, unfortunately, guarantee that one will grow into an outstanding teacher. Witness the fact that there are many experienced yet mediocre teachers. The key to improving teaching ability is experience coupled with meaningful feedback about the teacher's performance.

Teachers often have difficulty finding someone capable of offering evaluative feedback. Principals and curriculum supervisors may be too busy to evaluate teaching regularly, or they may not possess the skills necessary for systematically observing teaching behavior. This only accentuates the importance of learning to self-evaluate one's teaching as the primary avenue for improvement. Without regular and measurable means of evaluation, improving the quality of teaching becomes next to impossible. Teachers have long been told to talk less, move more, praise more, learn more names, and increase student practice time—primarily without documented methods of measurement. This section shows the many phases of teacher behavior that are observable and therefore measurable. The data can be gathered by the teacher, by teaching peers, or by selected students.

The authors' evaluation emphasis is on the do-it-yourself approach. Feedback that is gained in the privacy of one's office is easier to digest and less threatening. Teachers may set personal goals and chart their performance without others knowing. When teachers choose to evaluate their teaching procedures, they are usually willing to change. This attitude is often in contrast to the teacher's resistant attitude when principals or department heads impose external evaluation. Instructors often do not see a need for such evaluation, doubt the validity of the process, and thus refuse to change.

PRACTICE TIME (TIME ON TASK)

For students to learn physical skills, they must be involved in meaningful physical activity. Physical education programs deal with a finite amount of scheduled time per week. **Practice time,** or time on task, has also been identified by some as ALT-PE (Metzler 1979). This is an acronym for Academic Learning Time-Physical Education, and is defined as activity in which students are practicing skills in a setting that enables them to experience accomplishment. Instructors need to gather data about the amount of time students are involved in productive, on-task activity. In one well-regarded school district, the authors found that the average amount of activity time per 50-min period was only 9 to 12 min. One might certainly question whether much learning could take place in this program.

To evaluate practice time, duration recording is most effective. A student or fellow teacher can observe a lesson and time the intervals when students are involved in practicing skills. The chart in Figure 10.4 is an example of the results of a duration recording for practice time.

The teacher's goal should be to increase the amount of time that students spend on skill practice. A teacher might therefore choose to increase the amount of practice time by using more equipment, selecting only drills that require a minimum of standing in line, or streamlining the amount of verbal instruction.

How to Do It

1. Design a form for collecting the data (Figure 10.5).
2. Have a nonparticipating student or colleague identify students who will be used for the evaluation. These are the students the evaluator will observe to see when they are involved in practice and for how long.
3. Turn on the stopwatch when the students are engaged in practice activity, and record the interval of practice.

| Teacher: | Debbie Massoney | |
| School: | Jason Junior High | |
Parts of the lesson	Practicing	Inactive, off task, listening
Introductory activity	2.5 min	1.0 min
Fitness development	11.5 min	2.5 min
Lesson focus	15.0 min	7.5 min
Total	29.0 min	11.0 min

Figure 10.4. Results of a duration recording for practice time

PRACTICE TIME

Teacher _Eugene Petersen_   Observer _P. W. Darst_

Class _2nd period_ Grade _8_ Date and time _11/15/83 — 9:15_

Lesson focus _Basketball_ Comments _week two_

Starting time _9:25_ End time _10:00_ Length of lesson _35 min_

35	10	2:04	25	29	1:39	17	55	34
43	1:55	1:01	33	10	10	18	1:17	4:50
24	39	31	34					

Total practice time _20 min 13 sec_

Percent of class time devoted to practice _57.8 %_

Number of episodes _22_ Average length of episodes _55.1 sec_

Figure 10.5. Duration recording of practice time

4. Total the amount of time for student practice (in minutes) and divide it by the length of the lesson. This will compute the percent of practice time in a given lesson.

INSTRUCTIONAL TIME

An educational process requires that teachers instruct. The throw-out-the-ball approach is nothing more than leisure time activity in a school setting. Instructors should be aware of the amount of instruction they offer students. **Instructional time** refers to initial demonstrations, cues, and explanations to get students started on an activity. This time deals directly with physical education content. (See Chapter 7 for elements of instruction.)

It is important to find a meaningful balance between instruction and practice. An observer can tally the number of instructional episodes and the length of each episode occurring in a daily class. At a later time, the average length of instruction can then be evaluated, as well as the proportion of the lesson that was used for instruction. Instructional episodes should generally be short and frequent, with an attempt made to limit episodes to 45 sec or less.

How to Do It

1. Design a form for duration recording.
2. Have a colleague or a nonparticipating student turn on the stopwatch every time the teacher begins an instructional episode and stop the watch when instruction stops. Record the episode on the form, clear the watch, and be ready to time the next instructional episode. An alter-

native method would be to record the lesson using an audio tape recorder, and then rerun the tape at the end of the day and time the instructional episodes. Be sure to establish a criterion for identifying the difference between instructional and management episodes. (For a description of management episodes, see pages 102-103.)

3. Total the amount of time spent on instruction.

4. Convert the amount of time to the percentage of lesson time devoted to instruction by dividing the length of the lesson into the time spent on instruction. The average length of an instruction episode can be determined by dividing the total instructional time by the number of instructional episodes. Figure 10.6 is an example of a form that might be used.

CLASS MANAGEMENT EPISODES

Effective teachers are efficient managers of students. **Management time** is usually that time when no instruction or practice is taking place. Management occurs when students are moved into various formations, when equipment is gathered or put away, and when directions are given about these areas. It also includes taking roll, keeping records, recording fitness scores, and changing clothes (see Chapter 7 for a description of management skills). Figure 10.7 is an example of a form that can be used to evaluate the amount of management time. This form involves duration recording using a stopwatch.

Understanding the amount of time being used for class management, and the length and number of episodes, can be meaningful to teachers. The

---

INSTRUCTIONAL TIME

Teacher _Charlene Darst_   Observer _B. Pangrazi_

Class _1st period_ Grade _10_ Date and time _3/22/83 — 9:05_

Lesson focus _Golf_   Comments _1st class meeting of unit_

Starting time _9:15_ End time _10:00_ Length of lesson _45 min_

15	10	8	35	17	1:03	31	9	8
14	21	10	21	43	7	3:19	25	

Total instructional time _8 min 56 sec_

Percent of class time devoted to instruction _19 %_

Number of episodes _17_ Average length of episode _31.5 sec_

Figure 10.6.   Duration recording of instructional time

number of episodes and the length of each can be recorded by an observer. These data are useful for analyzing how much lesson time is devoted to the area of management. A high percentage of management time can serve notice to instructors of an inefficient organizational scheme or of students' slow response to explanations.

How to Do It

1. Design a form that gathers the data desired (Figure 10.7).
2. Record the lesson with an audio tape recorder. Time the length of each management episode, and record each episode in a box on the form.

3. Total the amount of management time and divide it by the length of the period to compute the percent of management time during the lesson.
4. Total the number of episodes and divide this number into the amount of time devoted to management to find the average length of a management episode.

RESPONSE LATENCY

Response latency is the amount of time it takes a class to respond when commands or signals are given. Response latency may occur when instructions are given to begin practicing an activity or to stop an activity. An observer can thus evaluate the

---

MANAGEMENT TIME

Teacher ___Don Hicks___ Observer ___Connie Pangrazi___

Class ___5th period___ Grade ___7___ Date and time ___11/7/83 — 2:05___

Lesson focus ___Frisbee___ Comments _____

Starting time ___2:13___ End time ___2:50___ Length of lesson ___37 min___

55	10	21	1:15	19	18	55	33	16
43								

Total management time ___5 min 45 sec___

Percent of class time devoted to management ___15%___

Number of episodes ___10___ Average length of episodes ___34.5 sec___

Figure 10.7. Duration recording of management time

amount of time that elapses from the moment a command is given to start or stop an activity to the moment when the students actually begin or stop. The amount of time that elapses is the response latency and is wasted time. An accompanying criterion needs to be set for the percentage of students who are expected to be on task. It is not unreasonable to expect 100% of the students to respond to the command. If less than 100% of the class is expected to respond, a gradual loss of class control may occur. The average amount of response latency can be calculated, so the instructor can then set a goal for improving student behavior. A certain amount of response latency should be expected. Few groups of students stop or start immediately, and most instructors have a strong feeling about the amount of latency that they are willing to tolerate. After more than a 5-sec response latency, teachers usually become uneasy and expect the class to stop or start.

How to Do It

1. Develop a form on which to gather the data (e.g., Figure 10.8).
2. Have a nonparticipating student or colleague time the response latency each time the class is asked to stop (start). The clock should run from the time the command to stop is given until the next command is given, or until the class is involved in productive behavior. For example, the teacher gives the command to stop the activity and return to squads (watch is started). The students stop the game and slowly return to squads. The teacher waits until all students are sitting quietly before giving the next direction (watch is stopped). Remember that starting and stopping response latency are two separate behaviors and should be recorded separately.
3. Identify the number of response latency episodes and divide this number into the total amount of time logged for response latency to calculate the average response latency.

STUDENT PERFORMANCE

Some classes will have a greater percentage of students performing at optimum levels than others. Reasons for this will vary. A class may be poorly motivated, have difficulty understanding instructions, or be out of control. In any case, instructors should evaluate the percentage of students who are performing in a desired manner. This can be accomplished by using the **placheck** (Planned Activity Check) observation technique (Siedentop 1983). The placheck can be used to identify a range of behavior. The instructor must determine the area of evaluation. Examples of areas that could be evaluated are students performing the stipulated activity, productive behavior, effort, and interest in the activity. Once the baseline data are gathered, teachers can begin to increase the percentage of students involved in the desired observable behavior.

How to Do It

1. Design a form for recording the desired data. Figure 10.9 is an example of a form that can be used for placheck observation. The example can be used to identify three different areas of student performance.
2. Place eight to ten audio signals (whistle) at random intervals on a tape recorder to signal when a placheck should be conducted.
3. Scan the area in a specified and consistent direction from left to right every time the tape-recorded signal sounds. The class is scanned for 7 to 10 sec while the number of students who are not engaged in the desired behavior is recorded.
4. Convert the data to a percentage by dividing the total number of students into the average number of unproductive students and multiplying the result by 100. Eight to ten plachecks spaced randomly throughout a class period will yield valid information about the conduct of the class.

INSTRUCTIONAL FEEDBACK

The type of feedback that teachers offer to students will strongly influence the instructional presentation. It is possible for instructors to analyze their interaction patterns and to set meaningful goals for improvement. Both students and teachers often assume that teaching is an art and that one is born with the necessary qualities. To work on developing useful patterns of communication is therefore unnecessary. Nothing could be further from the truth. Developing successful communication skills is an uncomfortable process that all teachers must accept if they want to be effective. Few teachers enter the profession with the ability to communicate with warmth and clarity. The process of changing communication behaviors will create discomfort and concern but will ultimately

RESPONSE LATENCY

Teacher _Paul Darst_   Observer _Reid Wilcox_

Class _5th period_   Grade _9_   Date and time _2/5/83 — 12:45_

Lesson focus _Team Handball_ Comments _____

Starting time _12:50_ End time _1:33_ Length of lesson _43 min_

Starting Response Latency

3	12	17	5	5	11	18	9	7
11	3	5	6	14				

Stopping Response Latency

12	13	8	18	5	5	14	12	11
3	10	19	18	17				

Total amount of starting response latency _2 min 6 sec_

Percent of class time devoted to response latency _4 %_

Number of episodes _14_ Average length of episode _9 sec_

Total amount of stopping response latency _2 min 45 sec_

Percent of class time devoted to stopping response latency _6 %_

Number of episodes _14_ Average length of episode _11.8 sec_

Figure 10.8. Response latency

STUDENT PERFORMANCE

Teacher _Bob Pangrazi_____ Observer _Norma Pike_____

Class _2nd period_____ Grade ___12___ Date and time _1/26/83 — 9:20_____

Lesson focus _Weight Lifting_____ Comments _____

Starting time _9:28___ End time _10:12_____ Length of lesson _44 min_____

Active/inactive

On task/off task

5	4	12	7	8	5
9	2	1	8		

Effort/noneffort

Number of Plachecks ___10_____

Total number of students in class ___33_____

Average number of students not on desired behavior ___6.1_____

Percentage of students not on desired behavior ___18%_____

Figure 10.9. Placheck observation of student performance

pay rewarding dividends. Evaluation in the following areas can offer feedback for creating useful change.

Praise and Criticism

When students are involved in activity, teachers give a lot of feedback dealing with student performance. This feedback can be positive and constructive, or negative and critical in nature. It is easy to ask a student or peer to record or tally the occurrences of praise and criticism. The occurrences can be tallied and evaluated at the end of the day. The teacher should calculate the number of instances and the ratio of positive to negative comments. Using these data, the instructor can then begin to set goals for increasing the number of comments per minute and modifying the ratio of positive to negative comments. A not unusual expectation is that a teacher should average one to two comments per minute with a positive to negative ratio of 4:1.

General Versus Specific

Feedback given to students can be specific or general in nature. Comments like "Good job," "Way to go," and "Cut that out" are general in nature. General feedback can be either negative or positive; it does not specify the behavior being reinforced. In contrast, specific feedback could identify the student by name, mention the actual behavior being reinforced, and might be accompanied by a valuing statement. An example would be, "Michelle, that's the way to keep your head tucked! I really like that forward roll!"

To evaluate this instructional area, teachers can tally the number of general and specific feedback instances. Since both types of feedback can be negative or positive in nature, this also can be counted. The use of first names is important in personalizing the feedback and directing feedback to the right individual. The number of times that first names are used could be totaled. Increasing the number of valuing statements can also be monitored. The totals in all of the categories should be divided by the length of the lesson (in minutes) to render a rate per minute. Figure 10.10 is an example of a form that can be used to tally the feedback behaviors described in this section.

Positive feedback should be specific whenever possible so that students know exactly what it was they did well. An instructor might say, "Your throw to second base was exactly where it should have been!" This type of feedback creates a positive feeling in a class and thus is important. Sometimes, however, teachers use this type of feedback to such an extent that it becomes a habitual form of communication (i.e., "good job, nice serve"). These comments do not identify the specific desirable behavior and may be ignored by students. It is also possible that an undesirable behavior may be reinforced when feedback is general.

Corrective Instructional Feedback

Effective teachers are usually excellent at coaching students to higher levels of performance. This involves giving performers meaningful corrective feedback. Corrective feedback focuses on improving the performance of the participant. Teachers should try to ignore poor performances if students are already aware of them.

Corrective instructional feedback is specific whenever possible, so performers know what it is they must correct. An example of corrective instructional feedback might be, "Your throw to second base was too far to the left of the base! Try to throw the ball directly over the base." This type of feedback tells the student what was incorrect about the skill attempt and how the skill should be performed.

Nonverbal Feedback

Much performance feedback can be given nonverbally. This is certainly meaningful to students and may be equal to or more effective than verbal forms of communication. Examples of nonverbal feedback that could occur after a desired performance are a pat on the back, a wink, a smile, a nod of the head, the thumbs up sign, and clapping the hands. Nonverbal feedback can also be negative: a frown, shaking the head in disapproval, walking away from a student, or laughing at a poor performance.

It is possible to tally the number of positive and negative nonverbal behaviors exhibited by a teacher. Either a student or another instructor can do the tallying. Students are often better at evaluating the instructor in this domain, because they are keenly aware of what each of the instructor's mannerisms means.

How to Do It

1. Design a form to collect the data. Figure 10.10 is an example of a form that can be used.
2. Audio tape a lesson for playback and evaluation at a later time.
3. Record the data desired to be analyzed. It is usually best to take one category at a time when beginning. For example, analyze the use of first names during the first playback, and then play the tape again to evaluate corrective feedback.
4. Convert the data to a form that can be generalized from lesson to lesson (i.e., rate per minute, rate per lesson, or ratio of positive to negative interactions).

STUDENT CONTACT AND TEACHER MOVEMENT

When instructors are involved in the teaching process, they are in constant contact with students. Contact means that they are moving among and offering personalized feedback to the youngsters. The number of times an instructor becomes personally involved with a student can be counted.

TEACHER BEHAVIOR EVENT RECORDING

Teacher _Joe Waters_   Observer _Gary Krahenbuhl_

Class _1st period_ Grade _11_ Date and time _10/21/83 — 8:45_

Lesson focus _Lacrosse_   Comments _____

Starting time _8:56_ End time _9:41_ Length of lesson _45 min_

		3	6	9	12	15	Minutes 18	21	24	27	30	Event Total
General instructional feedback	+	II	III	I		I	TH			III	I	16
	−	I			II	I		III		I	I	9
Specific instructional feedback	+	I					I		III	I		6
	−			II					II			4
Corrective instructional feedback		II	I		III	I	II			I	I	11
First names		IIII	I	I	THJ	II	III			II		18
Nonverbal feedback	+	I				II	II	I		II	I	9
	−			I							I	2

Ratio + to −: general instructional feedback _+ 1.77_

Ratio + to −: specific instructional feedback _+ 1.5_

Ratio + to −: nonverbal feedback _+ 4.5_

Ratio + to −: all instructional feedback (verbal and nonverbal) _+ 2.06_

Figure 10.10. Teacher behavior event recording of instructional feedback

This type of feedback differs from total class interaction and demands that the instructor have keen insight into each student's behavior and particular concerns.

Allied to this area is teacher movement. Instructors often have a particular area in the gymnasium from which they feel comfortable teaching. Before instruction can begin, the teacher moves back to this area. The teacher's movement pattern causes students to drift to different areas, depending on their feeling about the activity or the instructor. Students who like the instructor will move closer, whereas students who dislike the teacher or are uneasy about the activity may move as far away as possible. This results in a configuration in which the good performers are always near the instructor and the students who may be somewhat deviant in performance are farther away and thus more difficult to observe.

These problems can be avoided if the instructor moves throughout the teaching area. Teacher movement can be evaluated by dividing the area into quadrants and tallying the number of times the instructor moves from section to section. A tally is made only if the teacher speaks to a student or to the class as a whole. Do not make a tally when the teacher merely passes through a quadrant. The amount of time spent in each quadrant can also be evaluated. The teacher should spend approximately the same amount of time in each area. When students cannot predict where the teacher will be next, they have a greater tendency to remain on task.

The most accurate recording is of the amount of time a teacher stays in a quadrant. The length of time can be recorded on the form in relationship to where the teacher stands. At the end of the lesson, the amount of time a teacher has spent in each quadrant can then be analyzed. Another technique is to code the type of teacher behavior that occurs each time the instructor moves into a new quadrant. For example, an "M" might signify management activity, an "I" instructional activity, and a "P" practice time. This tally would reveal the amount of time the instructor spent in each area and also where the teacher moves to conduct different types of class activities.

How to Do It

1. Develop a coding form similar to the one in Figure 10.11.
2. Ask a nonparticipating student or a colleague to record the desired data on teacher movement. Another alternative that is better is to video tape the lesson and evaluate it at a later time.
3. Evaluate the data by calculating the number of moves per lesson and the number of moves during instruction, management, and practice.

Summary

Quality teaching results when curriculum is well planned and sequenced. Activities should be planned on a daily basis to assure continuity of instruction. Teachers can evaluate their own teaching behavior and set goals for improvement and change. The result is an instructor who is confident, well organized, and acutely aware of the teaching process.

References

Darst, P. W., Mancini, V. H., and Zakrajsek, D. B. *Systematic Observation Instrumentation for Physical Education.* West Point, NY: Leisure Press, 1983.

Metzler, M. The measurement of academic learning time in physical education. Doctoral dissertation, The Ohio State University, 1979.

Siedentop, D. *Developing Teaching Skills in Physical Education.* 2nd ed. Palo Alto, CA: Mayfield Publishing Co., 1983.

TEACHER MOVEMENT

Teacher _Danny Marcello_   Observer _Ellen Colleary_

Class _5th period_   Grade _9_   Date and time _3/17/83 — 1:05_

Lesson focus _Volleyball_   Comments _____

Starting time _1:15_   End time _2:01_   Length of lesson _46 min_

Total number of moves _28_

Number of moves (I) _8_   (M) _8_   (P) _12_

Average number of moves per min _.6_

Figure 10.11 Teacher movement recording

Chapter 11

Student Evaluation and Grading

Teachers find the need for evaluation to be two-fold. The first concern is to evaluate students in order to give them an indication of what and how well they are learning. The second area of concern is evaluation of the program and its objectives. This is most commonly done by evaluating students, looking at group statistics, and then determining whether objectives such as fitness and skill development have been accomplished. Regardless of how evaluation is managed, the emphasis on accountability has continued to place more importance on this area. No longer are school boards willing to support a program that does not document its impact on students. Similarly, students are much less willing to accept a grade in physical education if it is not grounded on principles similar to those in academic areas.

It is sometimes difficult to determine why evaluation takes place. For example, when fitness testing is conducted, is it for the purpose of assigning grades to students, reporting their personal progress, or evaluating the fitness component of the program? Evaluation of students can in fact serve many different purposes, all of which are impor-tant. This means that the instructor should consider carefully what results are desired before undertaking various types of evaluation. Since evaluation results can be used for more than one purpose, no attempt is made here to separate grading and program evaluation. The instructor's task is to determine how the results will be applied.

EVALUATION—DIFFERENT VIEWPOINTS

When one asks how evaluation of students should be done, clearly there are many different ideas as to what is best. This section examines the different approaches, offers insight into each, and leaves readers with the responsibility of selecting the approach that works best for their needs.

EDUCATIONAL OBJECTIVES VERSUS ADMINISTRATIVE TASKS

Most physical educators generally agree that physical education should help students achieve in four areas: skill development, physical fitness, personal values, and cognitive development. Some grading systems attempt to assign weight to each of the areas when compiling a grade. Regardless of the amount of emphasis given to each area, the final grade is reached by accomplishment in each of the areas. This contrasts with grading of administrative tasks through which students earn a part or all of their grade by showering, attendance, participation, promptness, and wearing the proper uniform. Using this approach means that students can earn a grade that has little to do with accomplishment and progress toward the objectives of physical education.

A problem occurs when students receive a grade that is earned in a manner completely different from the rest of the school curriculum areas. For example, if a student misses some classes in math, forgets to bring a pencil, and is tardy, teachers may be concerned and ask parents and a school administrator to help rectify the problem. The teacher would seldom think of flunking the student, however, if all tests were passed with an A grade. In other words, the student has earned a grade based on the accomplishment of educational goals. The reverse situation is important to examine. If a student fails all examinations in math, a grade of F in the course would undoubtedly be the result, even if the student had attended every day, was never tardy, and carried out other administrative tasks demanded by the teacher. If grades in other curriculur areas of the school are earned through accomplishment of educational objectives, it is probably wise to follow suit in the physical education area.

Administrative tasks are usually enforced through school or district-wide regulations. For example, most districts have ways of dealing with excessive absences or tardiness. The teacher need not further penalize a student through a grade reduction. Sometimes students are graded on participation, which is similar to receiving a grade just because one is physically present in class. On the other hand, students should be able to choose not to participate in class only when they are excused by the administration or by the school nurse (i.e., for sickness or injury). Participation alone should not be used as a factor in assigning grades. Rather, all students should be expected to participate unless excused by administrative edict.

If a student does not attend class, it is certainly defensible to ask the student to repeat the class. This is usually done by assigning a failing grade. In most academic areas, instructors would also act in this manner, and thus excessive absences are a criterion that is acceptable in any academic area. The point here is that the grading system in physical education should be in line with the grading system in the rest of the subject matter areas. When physical educators choose to grade otherwise, the grade soon becomes meaningless to other teachers and students. In some school districts, the physical education grade is no longer calculated in the overall grade point average or does not figure in graduation requirements. When this occurs, it becomes easy to say that physical education should no longer be required of all students since the grade is actually meaningless. The bottom line is to grade in a manner that is compatible with other subject matter areas.

PROCESS VERSUS PRODUCT

Another area of concern when evaluating is whether the process or the product of education is more important. Those who emphasize the process of education defend the importance of ensuring that students leave school with warm and positive feelings toward physical education. They state their beliefs in the following manner: "I am not concerned about how many skills my students learn, I just want them to walk out of my class with positive vibrations about physical education." The assumption is that students who feel positive about physical education will be willing to participate physically throughout their lifetime. These teachers assign grades based on how hard a student tries (effort), and are willing to give a higher grade to a less skilled performer who tries hard than to a skilled performer who exhibits low effort.

The people who reside in the product camp focus only on student accomplishment and see effort as something that is laudable, but not a part of the grade. They often state their philosophy as follows: "I don't really care whether students like me or physical education. What is ultimately important is their performance. After all, the students who are best in math earn the highest grades, so why should it be any different in physical education?" This usually means that the teacher will give the highest grade to the best performer, regardless of other factors. It also means that some students, no matter how hard they try, will never receive an above-average grade.

This is a difficult problem to resolve among professionals and is always debated emotionally. One point is that students should learn how society works from the grading system. People are not rewarded in life based on how hard they try, but rather, on their performance. For example, if real estate agents try hard but never sell a house, they will not make any money. The payoff is for selling houses, not for trying hard to sell houses.

Another problem lies in the area of developing competency in various physical skills. Research shows (AAHPERD 1954) that 78% of all hobby interests are established before the age of 12. Interests are established based on competency in different areas. A relatively low percentage of adults select new hobbies in areas in which they feel incompetent. If this is the case, then school physical education programs are going to have to graduate students whose sport competencies allow them to feel comfortable in public view. This is a strong point in favor of developing a grading system that focuses on skill development and performance.

The best solution is to develop a grading system that rewards performance and to present the program in a positive manner. Much is to be said for developing a positive attitude in one's students toward activity, and attitude development usually depends in large part on how the teacher presents the material rather than on the grade received. Instructors should help students to understand that they perform differently from each other in math or science and receive a respectively higher or lower grade. Physical education is similar to academic subject areas in that those who perform best will be entitled to the highest grade. The bottom line is that society rewards performance rather than effort, and the grading system should be a prelude to adjusting to societal demands.

RELATIVE IMPROVEMENT

Many physical educators believe that effort, or "just doing the best that you can," is the most important factor in assigning grades. In an attempt to reward effort, they then base student grades on the amount a student improves. This usually involves pretesting and posttesting in order to determine the amount of progress made throughout the grading period. This approach contrasts sharply with basing the grade on absolute performance, and may mean that the best performer in the class does not receive the highest grade because of lack of improvement.

Grading on improvement is time-consuming and requires that the same test be given at the beginning and end of the semester or unit. The test may or may not be a valid reflection of what should be learned in the class, and may not be sensitive enough to reflect improvement made by both poor

and outstanding performers. Testing at the beginning of a unit can also be discouraging and demoralizing if a student performs poorly in front of peers. It can also be hazardous in some activities, such as gymnastics or archery, which require intensive instruction to prevent accident or injury.

Another problem that becomes apparent is the issue of performing for a grade. Students learn quickly that if they perform too well on the pretest, they will be penalized at posttest time. It is thus important to perform at a low level in order to demonstrate a higher degree of improvement on the posttest. A related problem lies in the fact that improvement is sometimes easier at lower levels of skill than at high levels of performance. Most teachers are aware of the rapid improvement beginners make before reaching a learning plateau. A skilled performer may be at a level where improvement is difficult to measure. In this case, the skilled performer receives a lower grade than the poor performer.

Finally, grading on improvement is not compatible with society or with other subject areas in the school setting. Society does not pay people for improvement, but rather for performance. Teachers in other academic areas do not give a higher grade to the student who has improved the most, regardless of where he or she started. The bottom line is that grading on improvement is difficult and time-consuming, and results in a system that may at times reward lack of effort and low ability.

GRADING ON POTENTIAL

Some teachers choose to grade on potential rather than on the present state of performance. In other words, the student's grade may be boosted by the teacher because the student is believed to be a good athlete who can really do all of the skills. This policy is unfortunately a double-edged sword and results in a situation in which students may be penalized for not having ability or for lacking potential.

The approach depends on the feelings of the teacher about the student in question. It is based on intangibles, and may result in a grade being assigned because the student is "just like her brothers." When grades are based on the teacher's subjective beliefs rather than on criteria that can be measured and evaluated, the grades become difficult to defend. The bottom line is that a grading system should be based on tangible data that can be recorded from observable behavior and performance.

NEGATIVE VERSUS POSITIVE SYSTEMS

In an attempt to make the grading system defensible and concrete, many teachers have started using point systems. In most point systems, both performance objectives and administrative factors are listed as grade components. A student may be able to earn a grade through performance, attitude, and knowledge. Unfortunately, point systems can become a negative influence when handled incorrectly. For example, some teachers give all students 100 points at the start of the semester and then "chip off" points for various unsatisfactory levels of performance. A student may lose points for not trying, not performing, or not knowing answers on a test. Students soon realize that energy should be spent on avoiding any behavior that loses points.

This contrasts with a system that rewards positive behavior. When the student performs well, points are assigned and the student can earn the grade desired through self-direction. In a negative system, the teacher makes all the judgments about points lost and receives in turn the negative feelings of the student. When positive behavior is rewarded, students feel as if the teacher cares about their welfare and growth.

Sometimes when a negative system is used, the teacher begins to focus on what students cannot do, rather than on what they can do. Energy is spent on "policing" students and threatening to take away points if they do not behave. Most students do not respond well to this approach, since a loss of points does not require an immediate change in behavior and a redirection. Note also that the loss of points will result in a reduction of the final grade, a consequence that may be six to nine weeks away. Few students will respond positively to grade leverage of this type. In fact, the only students who usually care about their grades are those performing well in the first place. Threatening to lower the grade of a student who does not like physical education or school in general only further alienates the student and is based on a system of negative reinforcement that is usually ineffective. The bottom line is that the grading system should be a positive situation, which encourages students to perform.

PASS-FAIL VERSUS LETTER GRADES

Another approach to grading concerns the issue of whether letter grades should be assigned to students or whether the course should be offered on a pass-fail basis. Pass-fail has become more common today because of the push to avoid having physical education grades count in the academic grade point average. This approach prevents students from receiving a low grade in physical education while earning As in subject matter areas. Problems are unfortunately inherent in this approach.

When a pass-fail grading system is used, it offers no method for rewarding the outstanding performer. The student who earns a grade of C or D receives the same final grade as the top performer in the class. This approach thus reinforces making a minimal effort to accomplish goals, because differing levels of performance are not rewarded. The pass-fail system also does little to show students that they have improved. For example, if a student is performing at the C level and then earns a B by the end of the next quarter, the *pass* grade reflects no change in performance. Grading systems should reward improved standards of performance.

Some teachers endorse pass-fail grading because it eases the burden of evaluation. They no longer have to worry about bookkeeping chores, because the grade is only grossly indicative of student progress. Recording anything more than the minimum performance required for passing the class becomes meaningless. Some teachers therefore support this grading system because of ease of implementation.

When the grading system in physical education differs from those in other subject matter areas, defending the program in the school setting becomes difficult. If physical education does not require grading integrity, the subject probably should not be counted in the grade point average. The problem lies in the final outcome. If the physical education department chooses to operate in a manner unrelated to the rest of the school system, it then becomes vulnerable to nonsupport and abandonment. The bottom line is that physical education should be considered an integral part of the school system and should be graded in a manner consistent with other subject matter areas.

METHODS OF GRADING

There are many approaches to grading in junior and senior high schools. Realistically, none of the schemes solves all problems or results in an ideal reporting system. Methods of grading are chosen because of the school philosophy, the teacher philosophy, and the desires of parents. For example, if parents are unhappy with the grading system, they will complain to the school administration. If these dissatisfactions are expressed regularly and by a relatively large number of parents, the superintendent may take the matter under advisement. This results in a scrutiny of the overall program, the objectives of the program, the philosophy of the teachers, and the feelings of students. An instructor cannot, therefore, take a teaching position and begin a grading program without first considering the school district policies and the desires of fellow teachers.

All grading systems have strengths and weaknesses. These need to be weighed in terms of how closely the system meets the needs of students and the concerns of parents, as well as the goals of the teachers. A number of evaluation approaches will be offered in this section, and some may be better suited than others to the reader's situation. Remember, however, that all of these approaches have worked at one time or another because of various school parameters.

SUBJECTIVE OBSERVATION SYSTEMS

Many teachers have used observation systems at different times. Much evaluation takes place by observing students and making a subjective judgment about their performance. One of the drawbacks of the observation system is that it is not extremely reliable; two different teachers may differ dramatically in their assessment of the same student. On the other hand, observation can be done with a minimum of effort, requires little time, and gives students immediate feedback.

The observation system can be improved by using a check sheet or scorecard (Figure 11.1). This means that criteria are listed and can be ranked on a scale of points. Even though using the check sheet will increase the reliability of the data, the overall approach is still basically subjective.

A score sheet like the one in Figure 11.1 can be used to evaluate what a teacher may believe is student attitude. This type of score sheet can also be used to evaluate skill development. For example,

---

ATTITUDE CHECK SHEET

Assign 0 to 5 points during each observation with 5 being the highest score. A number of observations should be made during the semester in order to reveal consistency and improvement.

Student _____ Date _____ Lesson Focus _____

1. Tries all activities	0	1	2	3	4	5
2. Is on time	0	1	2	3	4	5
3. Consistently gives a maximum effort	0	1	2	3	4	5
4. Shows concern for others	0	1	2	3	4	5
5. Listens to and applies criticism	0	1	2	3	4	5
6. Shows enthusiasm	0	1	2	3	4	5
7. Participates with all students	0	1	2	3	4	5
8. Shares ideas with teacher and class	0	1	2	3	4	5
9. Demonstrates leadership	0	1	2	3	4	5
10. Volunteers to help others	0	1	2	3	4	5

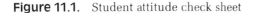

Figure 11.1.   Student attitude check sheet

teachers select the types of skills they believe a student should learn in a basketball unit. While the unit is underway, the teacher observes individual students and assigns a score. Grades can then be awarded on the basis of various areas evaluated, with students who accumulate the most points receiving the highest grade.

PERSONAL INTERVIEWS

The interview system can be used to monitor students. In this approach, the teacher sits down with individual students and questions their knowledge, as well as monitoring their skill levels. The strength of the approach lies in the relationship that the teacher develops with students. The personal interview can make students feel wanted and cared for, since few students have the opportunity to share with an instructor how much they have learned in a class. The weaknesses of the approach are in the areas of time and objectivity. For example, a teacher who comes in contact with a large number of students would find it impossible to sit down and talk individually with each one. The approach is also highly subjective and may result in a grade being assigned on the quality of the interview rather than on the knowledge and performance of the student. The interview system can be made somewhat more objective if checklists of questions and skill evaluations are developed and followed with each student.

Even if this approach cannot be used on a broad scale, interviewing can be a useful tool for evaluating the effectiveness of the program and the instruction. Teachers can select key students to interview to see how well they are learning, how they feel about the instructional approach, and what they might like added to the program. Seldom do teachers sit down and discuss the wants and concerns of students. This approach can enhance an important phase of instruction.

SELF-EVALUATION

If one of the important phases of evaluation is to teach students how to assess their performances, then a self-evaluation scheme can be a useful component of a grading system. Some teachers believe that grading students destroys the students' respect for the teacher, and undermines the students' feeling that the teacher is concerned about them.

The most common approach is to teach students to set goals and the strategies for reaching the goals,

and then to teach them the methods of evaluating their performance. When student self-evaluation is used, the instructional approach is closely related to evaluation technique. The reason for this lies in the amount of time required to teach students to set meaningful goals and strategies and to apply evaluation techniques. In most cases, teachers who use this approach also evaluate the students. The final grade is then a composite of student and teacher evaluation.

Another variation of the self-evaluation approach is to allow the class to develop goals that they want to achieve. The class decides democratically what they wish to accomplish, and the teacher then decides how best to accomplish the goals. At the end of the instructional session, both students and teacher evaluate the progress made and the final grade.

Some teachers like to add a third phase to the evaluation process by having students evaluate students. This results in a three-pronged evaluation scheme: teacher, student, and self-evaluation. One of the strongest reasons given for using this approach is that it makes students feel more involved in the educational process. Students are more likely to believe that the grading system is fair when it manifests itself through teacher, peer, and self-evaluation.

For these systems to function smoothly and effectively, goals and objectives must be written in outline form. Students need a checklist of activities couched in behavioral terms. This helps to rule out personality conflicts and maintains skill accomplishment as the primary focus. Teachers will sometimes find a large discrepancy between their assigned grades and the students. This may reveal a personality conflict between student and teacher. A useful idea for checking the reliability of the grades is to calculate the correlation between the three sets of scores. The three groups are usually closely related if adequate guidelines were developed for conducting the evaluations.

CONTRACT GRADING

Contract grading is a student-paced approach to grading that allows students to progress at differing rates. All students can achieve well using this approach, because emphasis is placed on mastery rather than time. For example, gifted students may progress faster than less skilled students. The less skilled can, however, practice at home, receive extra help, and ultimately end up at the same level of accomplishment.

Contract grading specifies the performance and

criteria that a student has to accomplish to earn a specific grade. The performance objectives are written in approximate order of difficulty with both the quantity and quality of the performance spelled out. It then becomes easy for students to assess their performance and to determine what is necessary to earn their desired grade.

The strengths of this approach are that it eliminates a lot of subjective evaluation, and also reduces student concern about grades, since students follow their own progress and are keenly aware of how well they are doing. Another plus is that students can choose different methods of learning necessary skills. Each of the objectives is graded as *no credit* or *pass*. A student is either capable of accomplishing the performance objective or must continue to practice, without penalty, until it is learned. Some teachers do not allow students to proceed to a new objective until the previous one has been passed. In theory, this seems to be a sound approach since each objective is supposed to be based on skills learned prior to the present objective. In practice, however, the approach is usually unwise. Experience has shown that students who cannot perform objectives will be able to easily accomplish others that follow later in the sequence. This occurs because it is impossible to determine exactly how an individual learner will progress, and because an exact science of sequencing skill development is presently unavailable.

A difficulty in using contract grading is writing performance objectives that are not too easy or too difficult to accomplish. For example, if students cannot accomplish the objectives, they will become discouraged and view the process as unfair. On the other hand, if the objectives are too easy, students will not be challenged to learn new skills and may become bored. Initially, the units have to be written based on the experience of the teacher and then modified from year to year in an attempt to find the correct level of difficulty.

Another problem that may occur is that of evaluation and determining which students have mastered the objectives. For example, if a teacher has a class size of 30 or more students, evaluation can become a full-time task. If instructors are determined to be the sole evaluator, they will have little time to instruct. A compromise is usually a reasonable solution. Students can evaluate themselves or have a peer evaluate them for the duration of the unit, then two or three days at the end of the unit can be designated for instructor evaluation. Since all of the skills cannot be evaluated by the teacher in this amount of time, randomly selected

performance objectives can be tested in order to check the reliability of the peer and self-evaluation process.

Figure 11.2 is an example of performance objectives that can be used for a three-week unit on lacrosse. Twenty points are possible. A checklist (Figure 11.3), with the objectives listed across the top of the paper and student names down the side, can be used to record student accomplishment as they pass the various objectives.

For the sake of discussion, students could then earn their grades by accumulating points. Assume that three 3-week units are taught during a quarter grading period. A total of 60 points would be possible (20 per unit), and the following scale could be used to assign grades:

A = 55 or more points
B = 50–54 points
C = 45–49 points
D = 40–44 points

When students know exactly what they must accomplish in a class and how their grade is determined, they bear more of the responsibility for learning. This can result in an increase in motivation.

GLOBAL GRADING

For want of a better title, global grading is defined as assigning points or percentages for the different domains of learning. As discussed previously, this is a common approach that has been used often and is criticized frequently. The approach attempts to assign a grade to categories such as attitude, physical skill development, physical fitness, and knowledge. The areas are weighted, depending on the desires of the individual teacher. Table 11.1 summarizes a global grading plan.

It becomes apparent that teachers using this system are making many subjective judgments. The weakness of the approach lies in the fact that a student with high skill may receive a failing grade, whereas a low-skilled student can receive an above-average grade. With this approach, students have difficulty determining how they are being graded and when they are making progress. Since the teacher makes many subjective judgments about attitude and skill application, it is possible for students to feel that the situation is out of their control.

Some teachers view the opportunity to reward students for effort and participation as a strength of this approach. As discussed earlier, many teach-

LACROSSE

Core Objectives (1 point each)

1. With a crosse, throw an overhand shot 4 of 8 times through a target from a distance of 10 yd.
2. Throw an underhand shot 4 of 8 times through a target from a distance of 10 yd.
3. Throw a sidearm shot 4 of 8 times through a target from a distance of 10 yd.
4. Using any throw technique mentioned above, throw the ball through a target 3 of 5 times from a distance of 10 yd.
5. With a partner, catch the ball with an overhand catch 3 of 5 times from a distance of 10–15 yd.
6. Catch the ball with an underhand catch 3 of 5 times from a distance of 10–15 yd.
7. Catch the ball with the backhand catch and reverse pivot 3 of 5 times from a distance of 10 yd.
8. With a partner rolling the ball from a distance of 10 yd, use the side retrieve technique 5 of 10 times.
9. Using the cover retrieve technique, scoop a "dead" ball up 5 of 10 times.
10. Defend 4 of 8 shots taken by a partner from a distance of 10 yd.

Optional Objectives (2 points each)

1. With a partner passing the ball from a distance of 20 yd, use a running side retrieve technique 5 of 10 times.
2. Using the cover retrieve technique, scoop up a "dead" ball 5 of 10 times.
3. With a crosse, throw an overhand shot 4 of 5 times through a target from a distance of 15 yd.
4. Throw an underhand shot 4 of 5 times through a target from a distance of 15 yd.
5. Score 1 of 3 shots past a goalie from a distance of 10–15 yd.

Figure 11.2.   Lacrosse contract

Name	Core Objectives										Optional Objectives				
	1	2	3	4	5	6	7	8	9	10	1	2	3	4	5

PERFORMANCE OBJECTIVE MONITORING FORM

Figure 11.3.   Performance objective monitoring form

Table 11.1 Global Grading Plan

Area	% of Grade	Evaluative Process

Attitude
  Attendance
  Punctuality
  Proper dress
  Participation
	20%	Attendance records and teacher observation

Physical skill
  Proper form
  Application
  Consistency
  Effort
	30%	Performance objectives and teacher observation

Physical fitness
  CV endurance
  Leg strength
  Arm-shoulder
    strength
  Trunk strength
  Flexibility
  Body fat
	30%	Fitness testing

Knowledge
  Tests
  Work search
  Crossword puzzles
	20%	Written tests, crossword puzzles, and word searches

ers believe that attending and trying are reason enough to earn a grade.

The grading system is thus a reflection of the instructor's philosophy and must be chosen carefully. Teachers should not allow the students' fear of a grade reduction to be the reason for including attitude and administrative elements in the grading scheme. The instructor has the responsibility of motivating students to perform administrative tasks and to participate. It is a questionable practice, at best, to assume that students will perform because of the threat of receiving a lowered grade, which will not be reported in some cases for nine weeks.

EVALUATING THE COMPONENTS OF PHYSICAL EDUCATION

The method of grading to be used influences the choice of areas to be evaluated. For example, if fitness is regarded as an important component of physical education, then the teacher is likely to choose to evaluate this area. The evaluation will serve to demonstrate the students' progress and to indicate whether the program is accomplishing fitness goals as desired. Evaluation is an important phase of the instructional process. Teachers must be watchful,

however, of the amount of time spent on this area. It is easy to use four to six weeks of the school year for evaluation if one does not identify what is absolutely necessary as opposed to somewhat esoteric evaluation. Little learning takes place during testing, and it can be an uncomfortable and unproductive time for students.

WELLNESS EVALUATION

A wellness evaluation should be undertaken on a yearly basis to identify and assess factors that, left untreated, could result in later health problems. Oftentimes, the data are gathered at different places in the school setting by such personnel as school nurses and physical education teachers. The information should be collated and made available to teachers, students, and parents. The wellness profile should also be included in the student's permanent folder, and results should be interpreted to students and sent home to parents. The wellness profile is not intended to diagnose disease, but rather to offer basic measurements of health status. If results of the measurements give cause for concern, parents can make the decision to visit the family physician.

The wellness profile (Figure 11.4) should consist of two parts. The first is a listing of the data

Figure 11.4. Wellness profile (much of this material has been adapted from a program developed by Dr. Thomas Crow, Clovis Public Schools, Clovis, CA 93612)

WELLNESS PROFILE

It is important to understand your personal health. As an ongoing component of the physical education program, you recently participated in the health screening. Listed below are the results and corresponding percentile scores for a person in your age group. An explanation of the items included in this screening is listed below.

HEALTH COMPONENT	SCORE	PERCENTILE SCORE
Skinfold	_____ % body fat	_____
Sit and reach test	_____ centimeters	_____
Sit-ups (one minute)	_____ repetitions	_____
Aerobic field test (run-walk one mile)	_____ minutes: seconds	_____
Height	_____ inches	_____
Weight	_____ pounds	_____
Blood pressure Systolic	_____ mm Hg	_____
Diastolic	_____ mm Hg	_____

Dental and oral inspection _____

The profile is not meant to diagnose disease, but to indicate basic measurements of health. If you are concerned or uncertain, please take this form to your doctor or clinic. Please feel free to contact the school nurse if you have any questions.

EXPLANATION OF WELLNESS PROFILE ITEMS

Skinfold: This measurement relates to the amount of fat a person carries. People who have too much fat are more likely to have problems such as diabetes (excessive sugar in the blood) and high blood pressure.

Sit and reach: The sit and reach test measures flexibility of the lower back and hamstring (back of thigh) muscle group. A lack of flexibility often contributes to low back pain.

Sit-ups: Sit-ups measure the strength and endurance of the abdominal muscle group. Strength in this area is important for proper posture and to prevent low back pain.

Aerobic field test: The aerobic field test consists of running or walking a mile in the least amount of time possible. This test is the best single indicator of cardiorespiratory endurance, which is important in preventing heart disease.

Height and weight: These are general measurements of a child's growth. It is important that children's growth be observed regularly to assure that the body is developing normally.

Blood pressure: Blood pressure is recorded using two values. The top number (systolic) represents the pressure in the arteries when the heart is pumping blood. The

continued

Figure 11.4 / *continued*

	bottom number (diastolic) is the pressure in the arteries when the heart is at rest. High blood pressure increases the risk of heart disease.
Dental and oral inspection:	An inspection of the gums and teeth is conducted to visualize noticeable inflammation, sores, and cavities.

Interpreting the results:

Results are in two categories. The first is the raw score, which is your actual performance. The second score is the percentile score and allows you to compare yourself with others of similar age. For example, if you scored in the 60th percentile, it means that your performance was higher than 60% of the students tested. It also means that 40% of the evaluated students scored higher than you. By examining the listed percentile scores, you can get a general indication of your health status in comparison with other students your age.

gathered, and the second a description of what each item measures and why it is important to sound health. If a battery of professionals is brought together, the profile information can be gathered quickly. With the help of school nurses, physical education instructors, and clerical aides, it is usually possible to gather all the data in one period, with the exception of the distance run. Data other than those in Figure 11.4 can also be included in the wellness profile (e.g., visual screening, auditory screening, posture checks, and immunization and medical examinations).

PHYSICAL FITNESS EVALUATION

A wide battery of physical fitness tests is available. There is much to be said, however, for using a standardized test that is administered to a large number of students. For example, the AAHPERD Health Related Physical Fitness Test (AAHPERD 1980) has been used on many students. Norms have been developed, and this allows students to compare their performance with that of thousands of other students. It is difficult to evaluate how fit a student is if the test items are not checked for reliability and validity. The items are measuring something, but it may not be physical fitness. Many states have developed physical fitness tests. Teachers may find using the state test more meaningful in order to compare their students with others in the state.

An efficient system using the AAHPERD Health Related Physical Fitness Test has been developed by Hastad at Northern Illinois University (1983). For a minimal fee, teachers can purchase optical scan sheets and the data processing. Students record their performance on the sheets (Figure 11.5), and the sheets are then sent in for processing. The results are returned with the following comparisons: (1) how the student ranked nationally, (2) how the student ranked statewide, and (3) how the student performed compared with others in the school. The approach is quite useful for analyzing the effectiveness of the physical fitness program since it offers a great deal of data analysis with minimum teacher effort.

The AAHPERD Health Related Physical Fitness Test consists of four items. It requires a minimum of equipment and can be administered in a short period of time. The items and the reason for their inclusion in the test are as follows:

1. **Distance Runs.** Four options are given, depending on the age of the students and the feasibility of the test. The options are the 1-mi run, the 1.5-mi run, the 9-min run for distance, and the 12-min run for distance. The longer distance and time are usually chosen for students 13 years and older. The reason for including the distance runs is to assess cardiorespiratory function. The distances and times included in the test appear to be the most valid indicator of cardiorespiratory fitness that can be administered easily in the school setting.

2. **Sum of Skinfold Fat.** This test is administered easily and measures the amount of fatness by totaling skinfolds taken in the triceps and subscapular areas (see Figure 2.6). Skin calipers are necessary and can be purchased at a reasonable cost (approximately $20.00). The purpose of the skinfold test is to give a more accurate indication of body composition than one gets from checking ideal weight charts.

3. **Modified Sit-ups.** The test is constructed to see how many sit-ups can be completed in 60 sec. Hands are folded across the chest and placed on the shoulders; the feet are held by a partner, and the performer curls up to the sitting posi-

Figure 11.6. Modified sit-up

Figure 11.5. Optical scan score sheet (reprinted by permission of James Marett, Department of Physical Education, Northern Illinois University, De Kalb, IL)

Figure 11.7. Sit and reach

tion (Figure 11.6). The purpose of the test is to evaluate abdominal muscular strength and endurance. A reason for much adult back pain is said to be lack of abdominal strength and lack of lower back flexibility. This item and the next give students an indication of their fitness level in this important area.

4. **Sit and Reach** (Figure 11.7). The sit and reach test measures the flexibility of the low back and posterior thighs. A sit and reach box is required and can be constructed easily out of plywood. Dimensions and instructions are given in the AAHPERD test manual. The test consists of sitting with the feet against the box, placing the hands on top of the box, and reaching forward as far as possible. Scores are recorded in centimeters.

Norms for students age 5–17 are listed for each item in the test manual, as well as exercises and

activities for improving fitness in each of the areas. Figures 11.8 and 11.9 are examples of record-keeping procedures for the AAHPERD Health Related Physical Fitness Test.

SPORT SKILL EVALUATION

The majority of time in physical education is spent on skill-oriented activities. Most physical educators believe that students should be held accountable for skill development, but instructors seldom monitor students' progress. It is possible to evaluate both general motor development and sport skill development, but because the general motor development may not predict success in sports, monitoring performance in the sport skill area is usually best.

The sport skill tests can be used to evaluate the effectiveness of instruction in physical education classes. Achievement can be measured objectively

CUMULATIVE FITNESS RECORD

NAME _____

GRADE	5				6				7				8			
DATE	TEST 1 ___19___ MO.		TEST 2 ___19___ MO		TEST 1 ___19___ MO		TEST 2 ___19___ MO.		TEST 1 ___19___ MO		TEST 2 ___19___ MO.		TEST 1 ___19___ MO.		TEST 2 ___19___ MO.	
AGE (to last year)																
HEIGHT (inches)																
WEIGHT (pounds)																
COMPONENT	RAW SCORE	PERCEN-TILE	RAW SCORE	PERCEN-TILE	RAW SCORE	PERCEN-TILE	RAW SCORE	PERCEN-TILE	RAW SCORE	PERCEN-TILE	RAW SCORE	PERCEN-TILE	RAW SCORE	PERCEN-TILE	RAW SCORE	PERCEN-TILE
DISTANCE RUN																
SKINFOLDS																
SIT-UPS																
SIT-AND-REACH																

Figure 11.8.   Cumulative fitness record of the AAHPERD Health Related Physical Fitness Test (reprinted by permission of the American Alliance for Health, Physical Education, Recreation and Dance, 1900 Association Drive, Reston, VA 22091)

and the results used for assigning grades to students. Skill tests contain activities that are important to effective functioning in sports and are thus applicable to skill practice and development. They can help students objectively chart improvement in skill development over a long period of time. Lastly, the skill tests can function as a diagnostic tool for analyzing weak points of performance and can help the instructor in creating individual skill development assignments.

Many sport skill tests have been designed by experts in physical education. Tests have been developed for baseball, basketball, football, golf, gymnastics, handball and racquetball, soccer, swimming, tennis, and volleyball. This list is not inclusive, as tests for other sports can be found. A useful source of standardized tests is the text by Johnson and Nelson (1979). The following is an example of a standardized test for evaluating performance in handball.

Cornish Handball Test

The test consists of five test items: the 30-sec volley, the frontwall placement, the backwall placement, the service placement, and the power test. When the tests were analyzed for validity, however, the power test and the 30-sec volley alone predicted handball performance almost as effectively as all five items together. To conserve time, it is therefore recommended that only the two items be used.

Equipment.   Several handballs are required. The service line is the only marking necessary for the volley test. For the power test, a line is drawn on the front wall at a height of 6 ft. Lines are also drawn on the floor as follows: the first line is 18 ft from the front wall; the second line is 5 ft behind the first; the third, fourth, and fifth lines are each 5.75 ft apart. These lines form six scoring zones. The area from the front wall to the first line scores

PERSONAL DATA

	Trial 1	Trial 2
Age (to last year)	_____	_____
Height (in inches)	_____	_____
Weight (in pounds)	_____	_____

	Trial 1		Trial 2	
	Date _____		Date _____	
	Score	Percentile*	Score	Percentile*
Distance Run	_____	_____	_____	_____
Skinfolds				
Triceps	_____	_____	_____	_____
Subscapular	_____	_____	_____	_____
Sum of Two	_____	_____	_____	_____
Sit-ups	_____	_____	_____	_____
Sit-and-reach	_____	_____	_____	_____

*See tables in AAHPERD Health Related Physical Fitness Test Manual, Chapter 2

PERSONAL PROFILE

Figure 11.9.   Record-keeping forms of the AAHPERD Health Related Physical Fitness Test (reprinted by permission of the American Alliance for Health, Physical Education, Recreation and Dance, 1900 Association Drive, Reston, VA 22091)

one point, as does the first of the five zones behind. The second, third, fourth, and fifth zones score two, three, four, and five points, respectively. A stopwatch is needed for the volley test.

Power Test Directions.   The subject stands in the service zone and throws the ball against the front wall. Subject lets the ball hit the floor on the rebound before striking it. The subject then hits the ball as hard as possible, making sure that it strikes the front wall below the 6-ft line. Subjects must throw the ball against the wall before each power stroke. Five trials are given with each hand. A retrial is allowed for an attempt in which the subject steps into the front court or fails to hit the wall below the 6-ft line. **Scoring:** The value of the scoring zone in which each trial first touches the floor is recorded. The subject's score is the total points for the ten trials.

Thirty-Sec Volley.   The subject stands behind the service line, drops the ball, and begins volleying it against the front wall for 30 sec. The subject should hit all strokes from behind the service line. If the ball does not return past this line, the subject is allowed to step into the front court to hit the ball, but must then get back behind the line for the succeeding stroke. If the subject misses the ball, the instructor hands over another ball, and volleying continues. **Scoring:** The score is the total number of times the ball hits the front wall in 30 sec.

The instructor should bear in mind that tests evaluate components of a sport only and can never completely evaluate actual performance under competitive pressure. Skill tests can also become so complex that the teacher may find them unacceptable in the instructional setting. Some tests require a large number of trained personnel for administration, which may not be feasible. Regardless of these restrictions, however, an instructor should arrange to conduct some skill evaluations. It is important that students begin to know that they are being held responsible for learning specific skills.

Constructing a Skill Test

If the teacher finds that the available tests are not satisfactory, developing one's own test that is feasible and valid may be possible. (In this case, the test would measure what it purports to measure, namely, ability in the specific sport.) Designing a test is a demanding process and requires quite some time. The following are steps that should be adhered to should the teacher choose to develop a skill test.

1. The sport must be analyzed to determine which skills appear to be necessary for successful performance. The test writer must be able to isolate the skill in order for it to be used as the basis for a test.
2. Standard procedures to be used when testing must be written and followed carefully during trial testing. This ensures that the test will be administered in the same manner each time it is used.
3. The test should be administered to a selected group of students. Include in the trial group some outstanding performers as well as some less skilled students. The purpose of the trial testing is to see if the test is capable of predicting who the better performers are.
4. If the test appears to be somewhat predictive of the best through the poorest performers, then it can be said to be *valid*. To check the validity,

rate all of the performers in the trial group and compare the completed group rating with the results found using the test. This comparison would involve computing a correlation coefficient for validity.

5. A tournament could then be conducted to see if the test accurately predicts performance in the game situation. The best performers in the tournament should score higher than the less skilled performers on both the test and in the tournament situation.
6. To check the reliability of the test, one group should be retested to see if the results are similar to the first test period. If results are similar, then the test can be said to be **reliable** and give similar results in a test-retest setting.

The procedure is time-consuming, but this approach ensures that the test will be valid and reliable, and gives the teacher some certainty that the test is measuring the desired outcome. When possible, finding a test that someone else has developed and implementing it in the school setting is easier.

KNOWLEDGE EVALUATION

Knowledge tests can be given to assess the students' understanding of the rules, strategy, and history of a sport or activity (Figure 11.10). The tests should be developed according to the ages of the students involved at the different grade levels. Test questions can be multiple choice, true-false, completion, or essay. To minimize the amount of time necessary to complete the test, it is generally best to avoid essay questions. This will also reduce the amount of time needed for grading the tests. Figure 11.11 is an example of a test that might be admin-

Figure 11.10.   Taking a knowledge test

Figure 11.11. Knowledge test

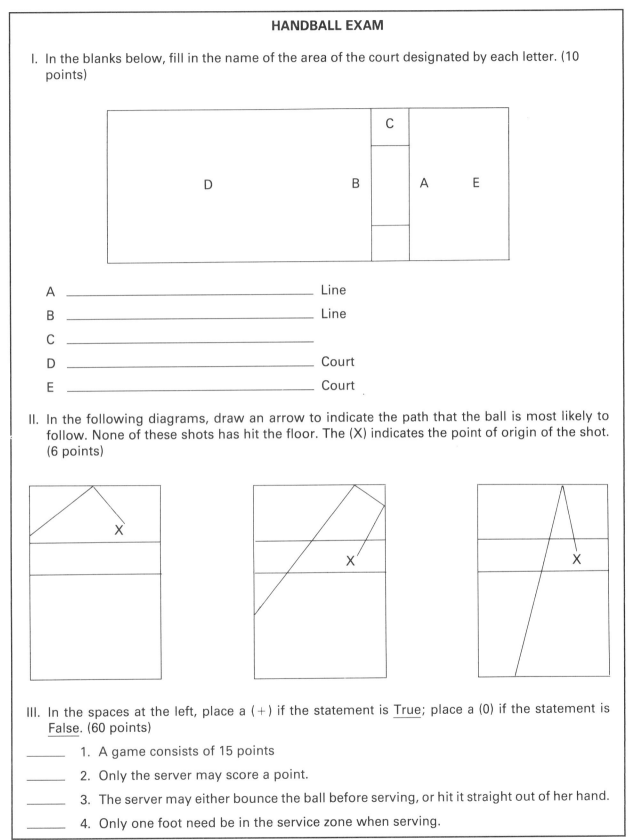

HANDBALL EXAM

I. In the blanks below, fill in the name of the area of the court designated by each letter. (10 points)

A _____ Line

B _____ Line

C _____

D _____ Court

E _____ Court

II. In the following diagrams, draw an arrow to indicate the path that the ball is most likely to follow. None of these shots has hit the floor. The (X) indicates the point of origin of the shot. (6 points)

III. In the spaces at the left, place a (+) if the statement is <u>True</u>; place a (0) if the statement is <u>False</u>. (60 points)

_____ 1. A game consists of 15 points

_____ 2. Only the server may score a point.

_____ 3. The server may either bounce the ball before serving, or hit it straight out of her hand.

_____ 4. Only one foot need be in the service zone when serving.

continued

Figure 11.11/*continued*

_____ 5. In doubles, the partner with the better left hand usually plays the left side.

_____ 6. The choice for the right to serve is decided by the toss of a coin, and the side winning the toss starts the first and third games.

_____ 7. If a player swings and misses on the serve, he is given only one more chance.

_____ 8. A legal serve must bounce in the back court on a fly or after touching one side wall.

_____ 9. In doubles, only one person serves in the first and second service. After that, both players on each team serve.

_____ 10. A player is out if he is hit with his own shot on the fly, but it is a hinder if his own shot hits him on one bounce.

_____ 11. It is common courtesy to alternate serves to each court, but in tournament play there is no such rule.

_____ 12. The more walls that a shot hits, the deader the rebound will be.

_____ 13. When playing a "lane shot," it is usually best to hit the ball underhand.

_____ 14. It is good to use the side wall when using the "lob serve."

_____ 15. The "kill shot" should be attempted when the ball is chest high.

_____ 16. The most advantageous court position is just behind the short line.

_____ 17. It is often wise to let a waist-high shot bounce off the back wall so that it can be returned from a lower height.

_____ 18. In doubles, a player may call a hinder when she is obstructed from hitting the ball by her partner.

_____ 19. In doubles, the server's partner must lean against the side wall until the ball passes the service line.

_____ 20. The ball should be contacted at the junction between the fingers and the palm.

IV. In the spaces at the left, place the letter of the answer that best completes the statement. (24 points)

_____ 1. Which of the following is <u>not</u> a serve?
   A. Scotch toss serve
   B. Ceiling serve
   C. Power serve
   D. Z serve

_____ 2. All of the following concerning body position for hitting the "kill shot" are correct <u>except</u>:
   A. Bend the knees and waist.
   B. Weight transfer is from the front foot to the rear foot.
   C. Contact should be at shin level or lower.
   D. The forearm should be parallel to the floor.

_____ 3. All of the following are "shorts" <u>except</u>:
   A. Hitting the side wall and then the front wall.
   B. Hitting the front wall and then having the ball bounce in front of the short line.
   C. Hitting the front wall and then the two side walls.
   D. Hitting the front wall and then the ceiling.

4. All of the following statements concerning receiving the serve are true <u>except</u>:
   A. The receiver must be behind the short line while the ball is being served.
   B. The receiver may return the service on either the volley or the first bounce.
   C. A short may be returned if so desired.
   D. The receiver does not have the option of returning the service on a foot fault.

5. How many bounces are permitted on the serve?
   A. 2
   B. 3
   C. 4
   D. unlimited amount

istered to junior high school students at the completion of a unit on handball.

Sometimes an acceptable alternative is to give students a crossword puzzle or a word search in place of a written test. (See units on archery, badminton, and bowling in Chapter 19 for examples of puzzles and word search.) Teachers can check students' knowledge using both of these approaches, and the students seem to enjoy the activities more than a conventional test.

Summary

The primary goal in grading students is to enhance the educational process. Students should grow from the situation, and teachers should know that they have an effective means of objective evaluation. Evaluation results can also be used to check the effectiveness of the teaching-instructional program as well as the progress of the students. The focus of a well-designed grading system is to report the progress of students in a manner that can be comprehended easily by students and parents. The grading system chosen will, to a large degree, determine the philosophy of the physical education program. Teachers therefore need to make a consistent effort to consider how effectively their grading program is reaching their desired aims and objectives.

References

AAHPERD. *Children in Focus*. Reston, VA: AAHPERD, 1954.

AAHPERD Health Related Physical Fitness Manual. Reston, VA: AAHPERD, 1980.

Hastad, D. N., Marett, J. R., and Plowman, S. A. *Evaluation of the Health Related Physical Fitness Status of Youth in the State of Illinois*. De Kalb, IL: Northern Illinois University Press, 1983.

Johnson, B. L., and Nelson, J. K. *Practical Measurements for Evaluation in Physical Education*. Minneapolis: Burgess Publishing Co., 1979.

Chapter 12

Intramurals, Sport Clubs, and Athletics

Intramural sport programs are often a low-priority item in today's junior and senior high schools. In a study (Maas 1978) of programs in Ohio and Iowa, approximately two-thirds of the schools did not sponsor an organized intramural program. Common reasons given for not having an intramural program were always allied to the athletic program. In most school districts, the athletic program is the number one priority after-school activity, and therefore gets the facilities, the money, and the qualified personnel. In contrast with the athletic program, a well-developed intramural program can serve the needs of a large number of students, while offering activity and recreation in a school-sanctioned setting.

A study in Michigan (Seefeldt 1976) revealed that as many as 80% of students who participate in athletics in elementary school drop out or are eliminated during the secondary school years. This would not be an alarming figure, considering that athletic programs are for the elite, if there were other avenues for students to enjoy sports. One of the best and most economical programs is the intramural program. If, however, the school district does not hire proper personnel to administer the program, it soon degenerates into a second-rate program that fails to attract participants. The ensuing discussion offers direction for developing a quality intramural program that is based on student interest and conducted through student input and energy.

INTRAMURALS

WHAT, WHO, AND WHY OF INTRAMURAL PROGRAMS

What is an **intramural program**? It is organized activity for students that is an extension of the physical education program. Student attendance and participation are voluntary, and the program is limited to the boundaries of a specific school. The intramural program can be a laboratory for using the skills and knowledges gained in the physical education program. In terms of supervisory personnel, equipment, and facilities, the intramural program should be funded by the school district.

In some cases, fees are required if the activity involves private facilities such as bowling, skating, and horseback riding.

When a broad variety of activities is offered in the intramural program (Figure 12.1), physical education teachers can delegate more class time to instruction, because the opportunity to play the sport can occur in the intramural setting. The intramural program can also be a social meeting ground for students. Youngsters have the opportunity to participate in an activity that they may enjoy and use throughout a lifetime.

Who participates in an intramural program? Hopefully, every student in the school setting. The program should offer something of interest to all students and should also provide appropriate competitive experiences for students of all sizes, shapes, and skill levels. All students should have ample opportunity to find success and enjoyment in the setting, regardless of their physical stature or ability level.

Why have an intramural program? An intramural program offers students an opportunity to develop interest and competence in a wide range of recreational activities. The program also gives students an opportunity to develop and maintain a reasonable level of fitness. Evidence has shown that if people do not develop competence and confidence during their school years in their ability to participate in recreational activities, they seldom participate in later life. In the intramural program, students learn to compete against each other and to cooperate with each other in an environment that has little at stake in terms of winning and losing. The program can be a setting for developing friendships that last a lifetime.

The intramural program can also be a place to learn leadership and followership skills. Students learn to compromise and assert themselves. Through these programs, students, parents, and teachers often become closer friends. Finally, the program offers students a place to spend some of their out-of-school time in a supervised setting (Figure 12.2), rather than walking the streets with nothing to do. Few programs for youth offer so many benefits at such a low cost to society.

RECREATION VERSUS COMPETITION

Since a successful intramural program should attract all types of students, the question arises as to whether competition or recreation should be featured. If competition is the overriding concern, then tournaments that identify champions and reinforce winners are featured. Competition emphasizes practicing as much as possible, only playing participants who are the best, and avoiding mistakes as much as possible.

If recreation is featured, emphasis is placed on participation and playing all teams an equal number of times. Tournament and league standings are avoided or not posted, and students play each game as an entity in itself. Rewarding recreation emphasizes attendance and participation, and all students are expected to play the same amount. Awards and trophies are not offered, but in some cases, certificates of participation are given.

Which direction should the intramural program take? As usual, there is no easy answer, but there are some points to be considered. Since many of the students may have been cut from an athletic program, they may still have the desire to compete. On the other hand, many of the participants may not have participated on an athletic team after the elementary school years, and they may simply desire a positive experience. In a survey by Fagan (1979), 581 students in a public high school were asked if they would like to have a competitive program, a

Figure 12.1. Intramural racquetball

Figure 12.2. Intramural lacrosse

recreation-oriented program, or a mixture of both. The results indicated that 9% preferred a competition-oriented program, 9% wanted a recreation program only, and 82% desired a combination of recreation and competition. This is not surprising, since one of the elements of a game is the opportunity to match skill and wits with an opponent in a competitive setting. The survey result also points out that students want to have an opportunity to relax, play, and communicate with peers. The best programs probably offer students a balance of competition and recreation in an activity setting geared to meet student needs.

ACTIVITIES

The types and varieties of activities offered to students are at the heart of the intramural program. There should be activities to meet the desires of *all* students. In some cases, the intramural program has been an outgrowth of the athletic program rather than of the physical education program and has been directed by athletic coaches. The result is probably a program that is conducted in a manner similar to the athletic program. In most cases, this type of program is doomed to fail. The scope of intramural activities should be unlimited and dictated by students. If students are expected to participate in the program in their free time, it is going to have to cater to their desires and wants. Never should the intramural program be regarded as "minor" league for athletes who might make the varsity team at a later date.

A student survey is a good idea to see in what areas student interests lie and to establish the magnitude of those interests. Copies of the survey can be given to homeroom teachers to be returned when they are completed. Compilation of results should then be posted, so students can clearly see that the activities offered are a result of their expressed interests. The survey also serves as a strong tool when bargaining with the administration for program facilities and equipment. When principals understand that many students desire certain activities, the physical educator then has some leverage to gain program support. Figure 12.3 is a sample of the type of survey that could be administered. The survey will also serve to indicate to students the number and variety of activities that can be offered.

After the survey has been administered and compiled, information about the activities most desired, times when the program will be offered, and possible experts to help with instruction are identified. A program in line with student interests is much easier to develop if a diagnostic instrument similar to the one in Figure 12.3 is administered.

LEADERSHIP

Leadership of an intramural program is a joint obligation. The school district should fund personnel to supervise the program and to minimize liability programs. Students, on the other hand, also have a responsibility to organize committees and to implement a successful program. They should develop the policies, rules, and procedures that guide the program.

A most effective way of ensuring student input and energy in implementing the intramural program is to develop an intramural council. The council can consist of 6 to 10 students and should be balanced by sex and grade level. This body makes the final decisions about the wide-ranging aspects of the program. Committees that report to the council should be developed and maintained with productive students. Some of the following committees might be organized to serve the intramural council:

Activity Development. The activity development committee is responsible for selecting intramural activities as well as facilities, equipment, and personnel necessary for implementation.

Rules and Regulations. The rules and regulations committee develops guidelines for administering the program. This committee is also the enforcement body when rule infractions occur.

Scheduling and Statistics. The scheduling and statistics committee schedules games and contests, maintains school intramural records and league standings, and oversees other related matters.

Referees. The officiating committee recruits referees, trains them, and interprets and makes rulings dealing with protests.

Public Relations. The public relations committee develops all materials for promoting the program; seeks funding from private organizations; and sponsors car washes, raffles, and other money-making activities.

Safety. The safety committee develops an approved list of procedures for first aid and emergency situations, and provides a trained student capable of providing first aid care who agrees to be present at activities.

The formation of the student intramural council should not supersede the need for qualified adult personnel, and the school district should be will-

Figure 12.3. Sample high school intramural survey

HUMERUS HIGH SCHOOL INTRAMURAL SURVEY

Student name _____ Class standing _____

1. Would you participate in the intramural program if activities were offered that interest you?
   Yes _____ No _____ If no, why not?

2. What do you like most about the present intramural program?

3. What do you like least about the present intramural program?

4. If you choose not to participate, would you be willing to help out in the program in other roles? Check those ways in which you could offer your aid. Officiating _____ Publicity _____ Secretarial _____ Scorekeeping _____ Other (identify) _____

5. It is possible to develop a program that emphasizes competition, recreation, or a combination of both. Which would you desire? Competition _____ Recreation _____ Both _____

6. What days and what time of the day would be best for your participation?

Day	Time
Monday _____	_____
Tuesday _____	_____
Wednesday _____	_____
Thursday _____	_____
Friday _____	_____
Saturday _____	_____

7. Should awards be given to winning participants? Yes _____ No _____ Please justify your answer.

8. Please list any other points that would make the program better suit your needs.

9. The following is a list of activities that might be offered. Please circle 5 that you would most like offered in the intramural program. If an activity that you want is not offered, please write it in the blank at the end of the form.

Archery	Checkers	Flickerball	Lacrosse
Badminton	Chess	Floor hockey	Lawn bowling
Bait and fly casting	Cooperative games	Frisbee golf	Marbles
Basketball	Croquet	Golf	New games
One on one	Cross country	Driving	Orienteering
Two on two	Darts	Putting	Paddle tennis
Other	Decathlon	Gymnastics	Relays
Free throw shooting	Deck tennis	Handball	Riflery
Billiards	Fencing	Horseshoes	Roller hockey
Bowling	Field hockey	Ice hockey	Roller skating
Box hockey	Figure skating	Judo	Shuffleboard
Cards	Flag football	Kite flying	Skiing

continued

Figure 12.3 / *continued*

Soccer	Speed-a-way	Tetherball	Volley tennis
Softball	Steeplechase	Track and field	Water basketball
Fast pitch	Swimming	Tumbling	Water polo
Slow pitch	Table tennis	Volleyball	Weight lifting
One pitch	Tennis	Two player	Wrestling

Others _____

10. Do you know of any experts who could teach and help organize any of the activities designated above? If so, please describe how they can be contacted.

ing to hire adequate help. Without district funding, there is usually little administrative commitment to the program, and a lack of administrative commitment leads ultimately to program failure.

Motivating Students to Participate

There are many methods for promoting intramural programs and encouraging participation. Regardless of the method used, to have the program work, students must see the benefits of participating. The program must exude a spirit and be an "in thing" to do. Some of the following suggestions have been used with success in varying situations and can be modified to meet the needs of a particular school.

Intramural Bulletin Board. Bulletin boards, located throughout the school, display schedules, standings, and future activities. Pictures of champions can also be posted and labeled.

Patches. Winners are awarded arm patches with a school designation, the year, and activity. Some successful programs have awarded patches for participating in a certain number of activities regardless of winning or losing.

T-Shirts. This is similar to the awarding of patches, except that T-shirts are given to winners or participants. The school can hold a T-shirt day on which teachers and participants wear their shirts to school.

Point Total Chart. Points are given for winning first, second, third, or fourth place in an activity, or points can be awarded simply for participation in an activity. The points may be awarded to homeroom teams or on an individual basis. The point total chart keeps a running tally throughout the year.

Trophies. Trophies are awarded to home-

rooms based on point totals at the end of the school year. An excellent idea is to award an "outstanding participant trophy" to those who earned the most participant points.

Newspaper Reports. These articles are written by students and are placed in the school or local newspaper. They motivate best when they explicitly name a number of students.

Field Trips. Field trips are awarded to all participants at the end of the activity. For instance, at the end of the basketball tournament, all participants might attend a college or professional game together.

Extramural Competition. A playday activity can be organized between one or more schools that have similar activities. The participants meet at one school on a Saturday and compete against each other. These students would be a group of nonathletes, and the playday provides an opportunity for them to compete in a setting similar to athletic competition.

Two schools of thought are involved when promoting intramural programs. One awards notoriety and trophies to winners, while the other offers awards and equal publicity to all participants. A case can be made for both approaches. A final consideration might lie in the fact that winners receive a great deal of reinforcement, but others of lesser accomplishment may need additional positive strokes, which makes equal publicity for all students important in the implementation of a successful program.

FACILITIES AND EQUIPMENT

Without proper facilities and equipment, an intramural program has little chance for success. A major concern is the conflict between athletics and intramurals. A large amount of time and money has been poured into athletic programs, and athletics can be expected to take first priority in terms of facility use. At best, the programs should compromise on the use of facilities at opportune times, such as the final game of the intramural tournament.

Another way to work through the facility problem is to schedule program activities out of season. For example, intramural basketball programs could be scheduled in the fall or spring, and this would alleviate the conflict. Another possibility is to schedule intramural activities during low-demand times; before school, over noon hour, and later in the evening might find facilities available. Community facilities such as churches, the YMCA or YWCA, and city park and recreation areas can be used at times to increase the number of participants who can be accommodated. Scheduling becomes paramount in assuring that facilities will be available. The scheduling committee should work with the athletic director and staging director to avoid as many conflicts as possible.

Equipment should be provided mainly by the district. Some successful programs have been funded by student activities such as car washes or raffles, but in general, when the district chooses not to give funding, the program is held in low esteem. If the program involves private facilities (e.g., bowling alleys, golf courses, or skating rinks), club members will usually receive reduced rates.

Having an equipment committee that determines how and when money will be spent on equipment is a good idea. The committee also becomes responsible for maintaining and repairing equipment. The school should provide a storage area for intramural equipment that is used solely by intramurals. It usually does not work well to use physical education program equipment for the intramural program. When equipment is lost or damaged, hard feelings result and program support is lost.

OFFICIALS

Critical to the success of any athletic endeavor is the quality of the officiating. The intramural program should be officiated by students. It is unrealistic to think that teachers will be willing to work ball games. A sound approach is to develop an officiating committee that has the responsibility of acquiring and training officials. Many students who do not play competitively are willing to officiate and enjoy being an integral part of an event.

Students should be recruited as soon as possible, so they can acquire experience from older stu-

dent officials and work confidently with experienced officials. They should be trained in rules and game mechanics prior to a tournament and should be allowed to practice with as little pressure as possible. The word of the officials is absolute. If a disagreement arises, it is filed and resolved through proper protest channels.

Scheduling officials and being sure that they make their assignments is crucial. Turner (1978) proposes an excellent plan that is easy to implement. Figure 12.4 is a chart showing who is assigned to officiate. The initials to the left of the typed name indicate that the individual has read and accepted the assignment. Blank lines are provided for the names of people who are willing to officiate, if needed. If an official has accepted an assignment, but then cannot carry it out, he or she must contact the first person who has signed up for that day. When a replacement has been found, the person who cannot make the appointment notifies the intramural office.

Officials can be given points for the number of games they work; they can also be awarded patches, T-shirts, and trophies for their accomplishments in a fashion similar to participants. Without some recognition, students have little motivation for carrying out the thankless obligations of officiating.

EQUATING COMPETITION

All participants should know that they have an opportunity to succeed in the intramural setting. Students seldom continue to participate if they foresee a constant diet of losing or other negative experiences. Grouping by ability has both advantages and disadvantages. It can be awkward to have skilled and unskilled players together when the activity demands a great deal of progression and skill performance. In those cases, having similarly skilled students play together and compete against teams of similar ability is probably the better arrangement. On the other hand, placing less skilled athletes with skilled athletes may improve the performance level of the unskilled students and enhance their confidence. It also provides opportunities for skilled persons to aid the less skilled.

When grouping for teams is done, the following methods are suggested. Homerooms can compete against homerooms. This is the most heterogeneous method of grouping. Students of varying skill levels will then play on the same team. If students have been randomly assigned to homerooms, this may be a feasible method to use for grouping, since all homerooms should be approximately equal in

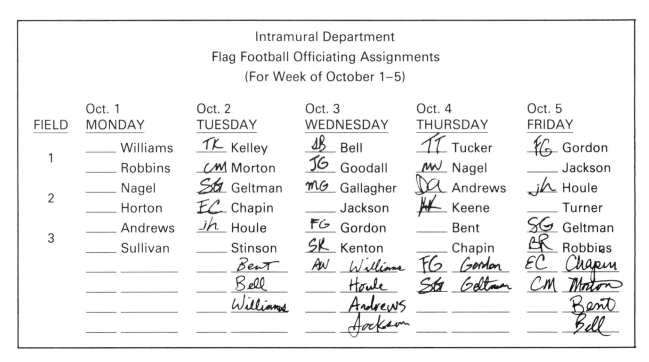

Figure 12.4. Chart of officials' assignments (reprinted with permission from The JOURNAL of Physical Education, Recreation, and Dance, February, 1978, p. 42. The JOURNAL is a publication of the American Alliance for Health, Physical Education, Recreation and Dance, 1900 Association Drive, Reston, VA 22091)

ability. Another method is to use divisions of competition. Depending on the activity, students can be grouped by ability, size, or age. Homerooms could sponsor two or more teams of different ability that would play in different leagues. The advantage of homeroom sponsorship lies in the camaraderie developed among students and the possibility of enhancing the classroom relationships. Probably the best solution is to equalize the competition regardless of homeroom assignments or other segregating factors. Choosing teams that are somewhat equal can be done in the following ways:

1. Leaders are elected by the students. The leaders then choose teams in a private session held away from the rest of the participants.
2. Students are arranged by height or weight. The names of students within a certain range are put in one box, and a different range of heights in yet another box. Teams are then selected by drawing the names of an equal number of students of similar size for each team.

Whatever method is used to form teams, the supervisor should be sensitive to maintaining a balance of competition and preventing embarrass-

ing situations. Teams should never be selected in such a fashion that the poorest player is chosen last. The intramural experience should be positive and all students should look forward to the experience. If the program is to succeed, participants are needed, and should be treated as important and meaningful people.

TOURNAMENTS

A variety of tournaments can be organized to carry out the intramural program. The type will depend on the number of entries, the number of sessions or how many days the tournament will continue, the facilities and equipment available, and the number of officials, scorers, and other helpers on hand. The following types of tournaments are used often with success.

Round Robin Tournament

The round robin tournament is a good choice when adequate time is available for play. In this type of tournament, every team or individual plays every other team or individual once. Final standings are based on win-loss percentages. To determine the amount of time the tournament will take to complete, the following formula can be used:

$$\frac{TI\,(TI - 1)}{2}$$

where TI = number of teams or individuals. For example, if there are five teams in a softball unit, 5(5 − 1) ÷ 2 = 10 games to be scheduled.

To arrange a tournament for an odd number of teams, each team should be assigned a number (number the teams down the right column and up the left column). All numbers rotate, and the last number each time draws a bye. An example using seven teams follows:

Round 1	Round 2
7	6
6−1	5−7
5−2	4−1
4−3	3−2

Round 3	Round 4
5	4
4−6	3−5
3−7	2−6
2−1	1−7

Round 5	Round 6
3	2
2−4	1−3
1−5	7−4
7−6	6−5

Round 7
1
7−2
6−3
5−4

To arrange a tournament for an even number of teams, the plan is similar, except that the position of team number 1 remains stationary and the other teams revolve around it until the combinations are completed. An example of an eight-team tournament follows.

Round 1	Round 2
1−2	1−8
8−3	7−2
7−4	6−3
6−5	5−4

Round 3	Round 4
1−7	1−6
6−8	5−7
5−2	4−8
4−3	3−2

Round 5	Round 6
1−5	1−4
4−6	3−5
3−7	2−6
2−8	8−7

Round 7
1−3
2−4
8−5
7−6

Ladder Tournament

A ladder format can be used for an ongoing tournament that is administered by a teacher or informally by students. Competition occurs by challenge and is supervised minimally. Various arrangements are possible, but participants usually challenge only those opponents who are two steps above a participant's present ranking. If the challenger wins, she or he changes places with the loser. The teacher can establish an initial ranking, or positions can be drawn out of a hat. Figure 12.5 shows an example of a ladder.

Figure 12.5. Ladder tournament chart (reprinted from *Dynamic Physical Education for Elementary School Children*, 7th ed. by V. P. Dauer and R. P. Pangrazi, 1980. Minneapolis: Burgess Publishing Co., p. 446)

Pyramid Tournament

A pyramid tournament is similar to a ladder tournament, but more challenge and variety are possible because there is a wider choice of opponents (Figure 12.6). In the pyramid tournament, players may challenge any opponent one level above their present ranking. In another variation, players must challenge someone at their level and beat that person before they can challenge a person at a higher level.

Elimination Tournament

The disadvantage of the elimination tournament is that the poorer teams are eliminated first and do not get to play as many games as the more proficient teams. The skilled thus get better, and the less skilled sit out without the opportunity to improve. The advantage of the elimination tournament is that it can be completed in a shorter amount of time than, for example, the round robin tournament. Double-elimination tournaments are somewhat better than single elimination, because two losses are required before a team is relegated to the sidelines. Remember that students come to intramurals to play rather than to sit on the side and watch others play. Figure 12.7 is an example of a simple single-elimination tournament with six teams.

SPORT CLUBS

Sport clubs are filled with students who are bonded by their common interest in some sport or activity. The concept originated in Europe and has become more common in the United States, due in large part to the inability of school districts to fund a wide variety of activities. The clubs are for students, are run by students, and are often funded by the students. They offer young people the chance to organize a club that meets the specific needs of a group and the opportunity to socialize with friends.

Sport clubs are sometimes administered by guidelines set by the intramural director in a school district. The clubs can be an outgrowth of either the intramural or athletic program. The types of sport clubs to be developed are usually dictated by students. The following steps are typical of a system for developing a sport club network in the school setting.

Figure 12.7. Elimination tournament chart (reprinted from *Dynamic Physical Education for Elementary School Children*, 7th ed. by V. P. Dauer and R. P. Pangrazi, 1983. Minneapolis: Burgess Publishing Co., p. 447)

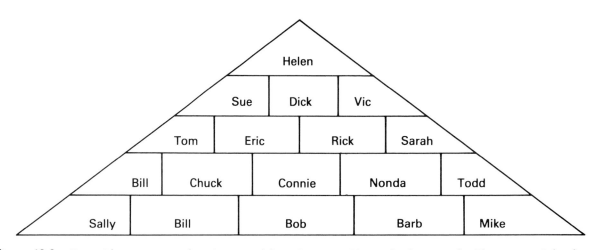

Figure 12.6. Pyramid tournament chart (reprinted from *Dynamic Physical Education for Elementary School Children*, 7th ed. by V. P. Dauer and R. P. Pangrazi, 1983. Minneapolis: Burgess Publishing Co., p. 447)

Determine the Interests of Students. This step is similar to the one discussed earlier in the intramurals section. The survey instrument (Figure 12.3, page 177) can be used to determine student interests and concerns for sport clubs as well. It is usually best to develop one or two clubs first to demonstrate the effectiveness of this approach to the district administrators.

Meet With Interested Students. Before the meeting with students, it is important to find a faculty member or some other person who would serve as the club's advisor. The advisor should have a keen interest in the area and at least a minimal amount of expertise. For example, it would be foolish to appoint a teacher as an advisor to the backpacking club if he had never backpacked. During the first meeting, the dues necessary for conducting club activities should be discussed. If the cost is prohibitive, many students may choose not to participate. Students should also discuss the joys and dangers of participating in the activity. School guidelines for clubs can be discussed so students understand clearly the parameters involved.

Develop a Constitution. After the initial meeting, students who are still interested will meet again to develop a constitution. This document should delineate membership requirements, the function and selection of officers, and meeting dates. An outline form can be used to aid in the development of similar club constitutions.

Establish Rules and Regulations. Clubs need to determine the scope of their organization and the requirements of club members for retaining an active membership. If competition with other clubs is involved, travel funding and housing requirements should be explicitly outlined. The need for adult chaperones and drivers, and the need for a waiver of responsibility signed by parents should be a part of the rules network. The basic premise of the rules is to eliminate misunderstandings and to encourage a safe, liability-free club setting.

Seek Funding, Facilities, and Equipment. With the help of the advisor, students should determine what facilities and equipment are available and when they can be scheduled. Seeking outside funding from private organizations and service clubs is also an important consideration. In some cases, school time may be given for clubs to conduct meeting and planning sessions. Applicable facilities such as bowling alleys or swimming pools need to be contacted to see if 1 or 2 hr per week can be reserved for club activities.

Conduct a Periodic Evaluation. The clubs should be evaluated on a regular basis to see if interest is waning, whether the needs of students are being met, and whether the manner of club conduct needs to be modified. Sometimes when clubs are developed based on the interests of students, that interest can decrease to such an extent that the club should be discontinued. New student interests also develop that should result in new club formations. A periodic evaluation may result in a new club advisor, better ways to facilitate club goals, or an attempt to stimulate renewed interest in the club.

IMPLEMENTING A CLUB SPORT

The following areas should be considered when developing a club sport. They are considerations that school district personnel need to be aware of if a successful program is to be implemented.

Liability

Students who participate in the club should have liability insurance. Depending on the activity, the regular school insurance may cover the student during participation. On the other hand, if the activity is exceptionally risky (e.g., skiing, rugby), supplementary insurance may be needed. Parents must certify that the student is covered by their insurance policy if students choose not to purchase insurance offered by the district's carrier.

A signed parental responsibility waiver form is necessary for participation in club activities. Even though the waiver form does not waive the student's right to sue and seek redress, a signed form communicates to the school district that the parents approve and are aware of their student's participation in the program.

Instructors and advisors to the program must be competent to administer the activity. If the school district advisor lacks proper training, experts outside the school should be secured. These may be parents or interested community volunteers. In most cases, the responsibility for supplying a safe environment falls on the school district.

Procedures for handling injuries are important and may involve having a physician on call. Written procedures should be available and understood by all club members in case an accident occurs. For example, what steps will be taken if someone is injured on a backpacking trip? Accidents do happen, and there is much less trouble if proper emergency procedures have been planned for such an occurrence.

Budget

It would be ideal if the school district funded sport clubs. In some cases, student fees are assessed at the start of the school year and distributed on an equal basis to all clubs. This provides a financial foundation, but almost all clubs require additional funding. The most common methods used are cake sales, car washes, rummage sales, sales of old and outdated equipment, candy sales, and donations.

When travel and lodging are necessary, students are usually expected to absorb the cost. School districts will often provide a bus if the activity is scheduled when buses are available. Travel by private car is the least acceptable method of transport due to the possibility of an accident and subsequent liability problems.

Many clubs have an equipment bank in which equipment is stored for use year after year. The club thus develops an adequate source of equipment over a period of years. Used equipment from local colleges and high school athletic programs can sometimes be secured to augment the equipment bank.

Coaching

Qualified coaches and other school-affiliated advisors are usually involved in administration of the athletic and intramural programs. This means that club advisors and coaches may have to be selected from the community. Some type of screening should be undertaken by the school district to see that the advisors are properly qualified. The club programs will have to be conducted at a time when these people are available, for many potential advisors are employed during the school day. If the activity is recreational in nature, then interested parents may carry out the supervisory responsibilities. All adults involved should be approved by the school district and required to sign a form agreeing to abide by district policies.

Facilities

Facilities usually have to be scheduled at low-use times. Sport clubs are often last in line for facilities, after the athletic and intramural programs. Facilities need to be found in the community if the clubs involve sports that are offered interscholastically. For example, city parks have softball fields that can be used. Some school districts choose not to approve clubs dealing with sports that are offered at the intramural and interscholastic level. The philosophy behind this ruling is that club sports should offer opportunities that are not available through other avenues. If that is the case, then most sport club programs will be conducted in private facilities such as bowling alleys, swimming pools, ski areas, skating rinks, riflery and archery ranges, and racquetball clubs.

Achievement Clubs

Many of the activities suggested in the intramurals section for motivating students can also be used with club sport activities. In addition, some clubs can be formed for which students are eligible only after they have met predetermined standards of achievement. Examples might be a push-up club, jogging club, bike-riding club (Figure 12.8), distance swimming club, and a weight lifting club. In each case, students can join the club and be a part of the group only after they have met the minimum standards.

INTERSCHOLASTIC ATHLETICS

The interscholastic athletic program usually stands at the top of the pyramid in terms of attention, time, and money focused on the program. Sports in the school setting should contribute to the educational purposes of the institution. There are many arguments as to whether the athletic program is a negative or positive influence on students. In this chapter, the authors will not attempt

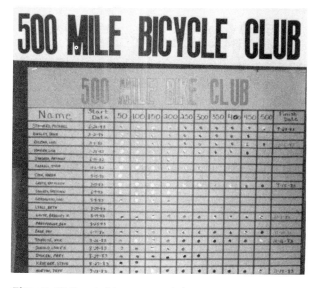

Figure 12.8. Achievement club poster

to pass judgment on the athletic program, but rather to examine both sides of the issue, identify guidelines for a quality program, and suggest various screening methods for teachers who choose to coach. Athletics should not be considered either inherently good or bad. How the athletic program is conducted makes it a positive or negative experience for participants. It is entirely possible to create a positive experience for students through a competitive sports program, but the program should not be the "tail that wags the dog."

VALUES OF AN ATHLETIC PROGRAM

A strong athletic program can develop a sense of belonging among the participants. Students like to see what they can accomplish by themselves and with the help of peers. Team sports teach them that goals can be reached only if teammates are willing to cooperate. It becomes quickly apparent that cooperation precedes competition. Conducting a competitive game is impossible when teammates do not cooperate and follow the established rules.

Athletics often teach students that the journey is more important than the destination. The work done to reach a goal is the essence of an athletic experience, and students learn that after the victory, continued hard work is still necessary. This lesson may carry over to adult life and help the participant continue to succeed.

Athletics give students something to talk about and something to do. Many of the problems of youth arise because of boredom and little to do when the school day is over. Athletics give status to participants and make them feel that they are important to others. The program also allows students to share their positive accomplishments with others and to learn to appreciate the accomplishments of friends.

The athletic program serves as a laboratory for gifted students. It can offer students a chance to perfect their skills to a high level with the aid of a knowledgable coach. Students who are athletically gifted are appreciated and rewarded for their accomplishments. Society offers few opportunities to practice with proper facilities and to receive coaching at little or no cost. The athletic program also brings a community of people together for a common cause. Parents and business people begin to develop pride in their community and find a common ground for communication. The athletic team can be a unifying factor that brings people of all backgrounds together.

Participation in athletics can teach students how to maintain a level of physical fitness and to care for their body. They learn about the need for self-discipline when one desires to reach a goal. The importance of sacrifice, following training rules, and practicing regularly become an attitudinal set of participants. Sportsmanship and self-control must be practiced if students are to find success. Rules and regulations become an integral part of sport participation and illustrate to students the importance of following predetermined rules. Students also learn that they are penalized when rules are broken, and those unwilling to cooperate are seldom welcome to participate. Finally, the athletic program can show students how highly regarded and important excellence is to people. Athletics should try to embody excellence and the Olympic ideal. Students set goals and make sacrifices in an attempt to achieve excellence without any guarantee or assurance of success.

Athletics can motivate students to stay in school. Studies have shown that the dropout rate among athletes is less than among nonparticipating students. The athletic program can be the incentive that offers students an important reason for continuing their schooling.

DETRIMENTAL EFFECTS OF AN ATHLETIC PROGRAM

The athletic program mobilizes large amounts of time, energy, and money to aid a relatively small number of participants. This sometimes leads to neglect of the less-skilled performer. In contrast, an athlete who receives special attention can develop the attitude that athletes are better than others and are eligible for personal favors and special attention. This can lead to a situation whereby student athletes develop a value set that is detrimental when their playing days are over.

Participation in athletic programs often interrupts the educational environment. Athletes leave school to go on trips, or receive released time to practice. The athlete may begin to believe that it is more important to be a successful athlete than a competent student.

Another possible effect of the athletic program is a loss of personal identity. Athletes are told when to eat, when to practice, when they can have free time, and when to study. They may soon begin to wonder if they can make any important decisions for themselves and whether they have the right to live their own lives.

Increased aggression and violence are sometimes the result of an athletic program. The intense rivalry between schools can encourage groups of students to perform violent and destructive acts. One theory of aggression states that it is a learned behavior and that athletics strongly encourage aggressive acts. Whether or not the theory is correct is less important than making sure that students are coached to do their best without hurting or maiming others. If athletes are encouraged to "kill the bum," it is quite possible that aggressive tendencies may be stimulated.

The pressures of coaching are apparent to all who have filled a head coaching position in a major sport. This pressure is often unjust and can lead to unacceptable coaching behavior. Athletic coaching is a good example of holding an individual accountable for the end result (winning) regardless of how that individual reaches the goal. When this occurs, students often suffer from the coach's lack of concern and caring about personal problems and injuries. Until an equal emphasis is placed on the process of coaching as well as on the product, the athletic setting will be less than a positive and developmental experience.

At times, parents and community members can become so deeply involved in the athletic program that they apply pressure on students to win at all costs. Student athletes begin to feel that if they do not win, they will not be accepted as an integral part of the community. The athletic program then becomes an incessant effort on the part of students to achieve the adults' goals. In these situations, the adults have forgotten that the athletic program was developed for students in an effort to contribute to the youngsters' personal growth. When the program becomes instead an adult program with adult goals, students cannot separate what is important from what is not.

Another concern for athletes is injury. All participants assume the risk of injury through involvement. If the desire to win exceeds the desire to provide a safe environment, then some students may be ordered to play with an injury or may receive injuries due to lack of proper care and treatment. Concern for the health of participants is paramount to any other program goal.

DEVELOPING A QUALITY ATHLETIC PROGRAM

Depending on how it is organized and presented, an athletic program can be a positive or negative experience for students. The following guidelines, if attended to, should help to ensure meaningful experiences for participants. All districts will have to interpret the guidelines based on their specific situation, but it is difficult to imagine that a worthwhile program will result if the guidelines are deviated from to a large degree.

1. The athletic program should be voluntary in nature. All students who choose to participate should have an opportunity to compete. All athletes should have the opportunity to play if they have practiced and disciplined themselves. Cutting players from a squad is an accepted practice, but there should be another arena in which those players can compete. This may mean a junior varsity, C squad, or strong intramural or sport club program. If athletics is regarded as an educational experience, all students have the right to receive that experience.

2. The program should be based on the maturation level of participants. This is particularly important at the junior high school level, because these students exhibit a wide range of development. Grouping by age, ability, or size may be necessary if the program is to be meaningful.

3. The athletic program should be an after-school program. The practice of giving a period of school time for practice is discriminatory and runs counter to the established rule that an academic education is the school's top priority. Along the same lines, excusing athletes from physical education is also difficult to justify. If the program is educational, then all students, regardless of background, should be able to benefit from it.

4. The athletic program should offer a broad spectrum of activities for participants; the fewer activities offered, the fewer participants. The program should also be balanced in offering activities to all groups—skilled and unskilled, boys and girls, and handicapped.

5. Organization of the athletic program should meet the needs of students. The concerns of the spectators should be met only after the program has been developed. Many sports are being dropped because they are not drawing large numbers of spectators and are therefore not making money. If this unfortunate trend continues, football and basketball could conceivably represent the total athletic program.

6. The program should require that all participants be certified medically healthy by a phy-

sician. The program should be evaluated regularly in terms of safety practices to ensure that proper procedures are being conducted.

7. Procedures to be followed should an accident occur must be written, posted, and sent to parents. Most districts ask that parents sign a waiver of responsibility form before a student can participate. This is an opportune time to explain the safety and first-aid procedures being followed. Insurance for all participants is a must.

8. As idealistic as it may sound to many coaches, the program should emphasize enjoyment and participation over winning at all costs. Skill development and a positive experience are a heritage that students can take with them after graduation. One might well question what has been gained if students win most of their games but lose the desire to participate in sports once they leave school.

9. Physical conditioning should be an important phase of the program. Preconditioning is essential to the safety and welfare of players, and should precede intense, early-season practice sessions.

10. Facilities should be shared by all facets of the athletic, intramural, and sport club programs. It is understandable that athletics expect to take first priority, but someone needs to direct the situation so that all programs are given acceptable use of the facilities and equipment.

11. Awards, trophies, and other incentives used to identify outstanding achievement should be minimized. This is not to avoid rewarding excellence, but to encourage proper discretion. If awards are given in excess, they become meaningless.

12. The athletic program should be constantly evaluated. In some cases, the program is seldom scrutinized until an infraction occurs. Periodic evaluations by the athletic director, principal, and coaching staff can aid in preventing possible problems. Evaluation should also serve the purpose of improving offerings for both boys and girls, upgrading scheduling efficiency, and showing the need for in-service training.

The Athletic Council

To help assure that a quality athletic program is maintained, many school districts are developing an athletic council. The council is generally a district-wide body and is made up of the superintendent (or a representative), principals, the athletic director for the district, coaches from each of the schools, and student representatives from each school. All schools, sports, and sexes should be equally represented.

The athletic council can help plan and evaluate the total district program and can help deal with problems such as finance, facilities, and personnel. The council can promote the athletic program and serve as a screening body when outside parties choose to become involved with the program. This body may also be responsible for evaluating coaches and hearing grievances. Sometimes, for example, parents have a concern but are hesitant to approach the coach involved. The council could hear such cases confidentially without revealing the plaintiff's identity.

The council can work to enhance the image of the coaching community. It can be a place where coaches work together to achieve the highest ideals and to reach common goals. In summary, the council should be a valuable asset for coaches, administrators, and athletes.

SECURING QUALIFIED COACHES

Qualified coaches are the cornerstone of a sound athletic program. The majority of coaches are highly motivated and dedicated professionals. In most cases, they have to be motivated by their enjoyment of sport rather than by the financial remuneration, for coaching is one of the lowest paid professions. An athletic director recently calculated that assistant coaches were receiving about 50¢ per hour. The majority of coaches enter the profession because they were successful athletes and found positive experiences in the athletic program. Being an outstanding athlete seldom guarantees success in coaching, however. Coaches need to have a wide range of abilities. The following attributes are representative of the characteristics of successful coaches:

Strong Character.   The coach should be a model for athletes to emulate. How the coach relates to others, the individual's physical appearance, honesty, integrity, and other personal qualities often teach students more about athletics than the actual participation experience. Many administrators find cause for concern when coaches swear, drink, or smoke excessively, and most students cannot deal with the double standard of a coach who advocates team fitness but does not practice fitness, who tells them to be respectful but yells when a mistake is made, who preaches honesty but shows them how to foul without being caught. Many athletes remember their coach much longer than they remember the actual playing experience.

Knowledge of Growth and Development Patterns. The coach must have a strong background in motor development and motor learning. Understanding the physical limits of athletes is as important as understanding their capabilities under pressure. The coach should also have some knowledge of psychology and the emotional development of secondary-level students. Knowing when to reinforce, when to scold, and when to praise are key components of a successful coaching career.

Knowledge of the Activity. Coaches should know the fundamentals of the sport that they are coaching and the best ways to present and teach the basic skills. A good coach understands strategy and is adept at knowing when to use various types of game plans. The coach must be an excellent teacher, and in many cases, the best coaches are also regarded as the best teachers. Concurrent with a knowledge of the sport is the ability to plan carefully. Both teaching and coaching demand a high degree of planning to succeed. Effective coaches always attempt to account for every minute of practice time so that idle or wasted time is minimized.

Coaching Certification

The need for certification in the coaching profession is great. The belief is still widely held that anyone can coach—regardless of background or training. Unfortunately, almost anyone can find the opportunity to coach due to the lack of certification requirements and standards.

In a recent survey, Noble and Sigle (1980) found that 34 states allowed nonteachers to coach on a regular or emergency basis. Twenty states had no minimum requirements other than age, and only 8 states required a teaching certificate.

Training is necessary in many important areas if coaches are to function in ways that are productive and enhancing to athletes. The AAHPERD Task Force on Certification of High School Coaches identified the following areas as essential in the training of coaches: (1) medical aspects of coaching, (2) sociological and psychological aspects of coaching, (3) theory and techniques of coaching, (4) kinesiological foundations of coaching, and (5) physiological foundations of coaching. Coaching is an impressive responsibility, and regardless of certification, coaches should make an attempt to seek the best possible training.

The Teaching-Coaching Conflict

A personal conflict often occurs when teachers choose to coach. Particularly in physical education, a teacher who is required to coach long hours has a difficult task. Many physical education instructors are not hired for their expertise in teaching, but rather for their ability to coach more than one sport. This policy can result in a situation in which teaching takes second place to coaching, and most of the teacher's planning and energy are dedicated to the coaching assignment.

Teachers who also coach often end up working 10 to 12 hr a day. The pay is low, but the rewards can be great. Coaching ability is scrutinized regularly in terms of the winning and losing record, and teachers may become caught up in the pressure of trying to be a winning coach for fear of losing their position. In this situation, it takes a strong and gifted person to place equal emphasis on teaching and coaching. Physical educators should not lose sight of the fact that about 90% of their salary comes from teaching and the remaining 10% from coaching. Many more students are affected by the outstanding teacher than by the effective coach. The ability to perform well in both roles is a difficult challenge, particularly when the majority of contingencies apply to the coaching role.

Summary

Intramurals, sport clubs, and athletics should be included in every school district program. Each area serves to offer unique benefits to students so that everyone ultimately has the opportunity to participate in a sporting event. The programs should present an equal opportunity to all students and should be so organized that the educational experience is easily available.

References

Fagan, K. Intramural survey, Arcadia High School. Unpublished report, 1979.

Maas, G. M. 1978. Promoting high school intramurals. JOPERD 49(2): 40–41.

Noble, L., and Sigle, G. 1980. Minimum requirements for interscholastic coaches. JOPERD 51(9): 32–33.

Seefeldt, V. Joint legislative study on youth sports programs: Agency sponsored sports phase I. State of Michigan, November 1976.

Turner, M. 1978. Scheduling student officials. JOPERD 49(2): 42.

Chapter 13

Liability and Safety

The nature of physical education is such that it is a high-risk activity. Teachers entering the profession of physical education assume that there will be more opportunity for accidents than in other academic areas. Over 50% of all accidents in the school setting occur in physical education. Facilities and equipment such as swimming pools, gymnastics apparatus, diving boards, and playground equipment can all be sources of injury. Activities in the curriculum also offer ample opportunity for accidents and personal injury. Football, wrestling, archery, gymnastics, pole vaulting, high jumping, and weight lifting have a record of higher accident rates than other activities. These statistics are not presented to alarm teachers, but to increase awareness of the situation. The teacher's responsibility lies in the creation of a safe environment for students, one in which risk and the opportunity for injury are minimized.

All students have a right to freedom from injury caused by others or due to participation in a program. Courts have ruled that teachers owe their students a *duty of care* to protect them from harm. Teachers must offer a standard of care that any rea-

sonable and prudent professional with similar training would apply under the given circumstances. A teacher is required to exercise the teaching skill, discretion, and knowledge that members of the profession in good standing normally possess in similar situations. Lawsuits usually occur when citizens believe that this standard of care did not exist.

Liability is a responsibility to perform a duty to a particular group. It is an obligation to do a particular thing that is required by law and enforced by court action. Teachers are bound by contract to perform their duties in a reasonable and prudent manner. Liability is always a legal matter. It must be proved in a court of law that negligence occurred before one can be held liable.

TORT LIABILITY

Tort liability is a lawsuit for breach of duty. It is concerned with the teacher-student relationship and is a legal wrong that results in direct or indirect injury to another individual or to property. The following is the legal definition of a *tort* as stated in *Black's Law Dictionary* (1968):

> A private or civil wrong or injury, other than breach of contract, for which the court will provide a remedy in the form of an action for damages. Three elements of every tort action are: existence of legal duty from defendant to plaintiff, breach of duty, and damage as proximate result.

In tort liability, the court can give a monetary reward for damages that occurred. The court can also give a monetary reward for punitive damages if a flagrant breach of duty can be established. The court usually rewards the offended individual because of the negligence of the instructor or of some other responsible individual.

NEGLIGENCE AND LIABILITY

Liability is usually concerned with a breach of duty through **negligence**. Lawyers examine the situation that gave rise to the injury to establish if liability can be determined. Four major points must be established to determine if the teacher was negligent.

Duty. The first point to examine is that of duty owed to the participants. Did the school or teacher owe students a duty of care that implies conforming to certain standards of conduct? When examining duty or breach of duty, the courts always look at reasonable care, which is exemplified by the actions of a member of the profession in good standing. In other words, to determine a reasonable standard, the court uses the conduct of other teachers as a standard for comparison.

Breach of Duty. The teacher commits a breach of duty by failing to conform to the required duty. After a required duty is established, it must be proved that the teacher did not carry out this duty. Two situations can result: (1) the teacher did something that was not supposed to have been done (e.g., put boxing gloves on students to solve their differences), or (2) the teacher did not do something that should have been done (e.g., failed to teach an activity using proper progressions).

Injury. An injury must occur if liability is to be established. If no injury or harm occurs, there is no liability. It must also be proved that the injured party is entitled to damages as compensation for financial loss or physical discomfort.

Proximate Cause. The failure of the teacher to conform to the required standard must be the cause of the resulting injury. The teacher's breach of duty must be proved to have caused the injury. Proving a breach of duty is not enough; it must be shown simultaneously that the injury was a direct result of the teacher's failure to provide a reasonable standard of care.

FORESEEABILITY

A key to the issue of negligence is foreseeability. The courts expect that a trained professional should be able to foresee potentially harmful situations. Was it possible for the teacher to predict and anticipate the danger of the harmful act or situation and to take appropriate measures to prevent it from occurring? If the injured party can prove that the teacher was able to foresee the danger involved in an activity or situation (even in part), the teacher will be found negligent, that is, failing to act in a reasonable and prudent manner.

This points out the need to examine all activities, equipment, and facilities for possible hazards and sources of accidents. For example, a common game played in the school setting is bombardment or dodge ball. During the game, a student is hit in the eye by a ball and loses her vision. Was this a foreseeable accident that could have been prevented? Were the balls being used capable of inflicting severe injury? Were students made aware of rules that might have prevented this injury? Were the abilities of the students fairly equal, or were some students capable of throwing with such velocity that injury was predictable? These types of questions would be considered in court in an attempt to prove that the teacher should have been able to predict an overly dangerous situation.

TYPES OF NEGLIGENCE

Negligence is defined by the courts as conduct that falls below a standard of care that is established to protect others from unreasonable risk of harm. The types of negligence are categorized as follows:

Malfeasance. This occurs when the teacher does something improper. The act would be ruled unlawful and wrongful and without legal basis. This type of negligence is illustrated by the following incident: A male student misbehaved on numerous occasions. In desperation, the teacher gave the student a choice of punishment—a severe paddling in front of the class or running many laps around the field. The student chose the former and suffered physical and emotional damage. Even though the teacher gave the student a choice whereby he could have avoided the paddling, the teacher is still liable for any harm caused.

Misfeasance. This type of negligence occurs when the teacher follows the proper procedures but does not perform according to the required standard of conduct. Misfeasance is based on an action that was not up to a required standard. It is usually the subpar performance of an act that might otherwise have been lawfully done. An example would be a teacher's offering to spot a student during a gymnastics routine and then not doing it properly. If the student is injured due to a faulty spot, the teacher can be held liable.

Nonfeasance. If a teacher fails to perform an act or to perform a duty or procedure, negligence can be proven. Nonfeasance is based on lack of action and failure to perform a duty. It is usually an act of omission. The teacher knows the proper procedures, but fails to follow them. Teachers can thus be negligent if they act or fail to act. In contrast to the previous example, the teacher guilty of nonfeasance would know that it is necessary to spot certain gymnastics routines, but would fail to do so.

The courts have expected teachers to behave with more skill and insight than parents (Strickland et al. 1976). Understanding and performing proper procedures and duties in a manner befitting members of the profession is thus essential, for teachers are expected to have a high standard of professional training.

Contributory Negligence. The legal situation is different when the injured student is partially or wholly at fault. Students are expected to exercise sensible care and to follow directions or regulations to protect themselves from injury. This responsibility is always directly related to the maturity, ability, and experience of the student. Improper behavior by the injured party as cause of the accident is contributory negligence, since the injured party contributed to the resulting harm. To illustrate contributory negligence, assume that the teacher has explained the shot put and all of the safety rules. As students begin to practice, one of them runs through a restricted area that is well marked and is hit by a shot. There is a strong possibility that this student will be held liable for his actions.

Comparative or Shared Negligence. Under the doctrine of comparative negligence, the injured party can recover damages only if found to be less negligent than the defendant (the teacher). Where statutes apply, the amount of recovery is generally reduced in proportion to the injured party's participation in the activity leading to the injury.

COMMON DEFENSES AGAINST NEGLIGENCE

It should be clear at this point that negligence must be proved in a court of law. Undoubtedly teachers are often negligent in performing their duties, but the injured party does not always take the case to court. When the teacher is sued, some of the following stands may be taken in an attempt to show that the teacher was not the primary cause of the accident.

Contributory Negligence. As described above, this defense attempts to convince the court that the injured party acted in a manner that was abnormal. In other words, the injured individual did not act in a manner typical of students of similar age and maturity. The defense would attempt to demonstrate that the activity or equipment in question had been used for years with no record of accident. A case would be made for the teacher's manner of presentation, that students were taught to act in a safe manner, and that the injured student acted outside the parameters of safe conduct. A key point in this defense is whether the activity was suitable for the age and maturity level of the participants.

Act of God. The defense in this situation is to put the cause of injury on forces beyond the control of the teacher or school. The case is made that it was impossible to predict that an unsafe condition would occur and that through an act of God, the injury occurred. Typical acts would be a violent gust of wind that blew over a volleyball standard, a cloudburst of rain that made a surface slick, or a flash of lightning that struck someone on the playing field. Even the act of God defense, however, is used only in cases in which the injury might not have occurred had reasonable and prudent action been taken.

Proximate Cause. This defense attempts to prove that the accident was not caused by the negligence of the teacher. To prove negligence, a close relationship must exist between the breach of duty by the teacher and the injury. Proximate cause is a common defense in cases dealing with proper supervision. The student is participating in an activity supervised by the teacher. When the teacher leaves the playing area to get a cup of coffee, the student is injured. The defense will try to show that the accident would have occurred regardless of whether the teacher observed it directly or not.

Assumption of Risk. Clearly, physical education is a high-risk activity when compared with most other curriculum areas. According to this final defense, the participant assumes the risk of an activity when choosing to be part of that activity. The assumption of risk defense is seldom used by physical education teachers, because students are not often allowed to choose to participate or not participate. An elective program that allows students to select desired units of instruction might be more defensible on these grounds than a totally required program. Athletic and sport club participation is by choice, and players do assume a greater risk in activities such as football or gymnastics.

AREAS OF RESPONSIBILITY

Teachers need to be keenly aware of areas in which they may be found negligent in fulfilling their responsibilities. These areas most often lead to lawsuits when teachers fail to conduct themselves in a reasonable, prudent, and careful manner.

SUPERVISION

Teachers have a responsibility to supervise students in all school settings and are accountable for this duty. The two types of supervision are general and specific. General **supervision** refers to always being physically present in the gymnasium or field. It also means that the teacher will be immediately available to any student who needs assistance or aid. A common general supervision situation occurs when a student is injured. The teacher must sometimes take the student to the nurse while leaving the rest of the class unattended. If an accident occurs while the class is unattended, the teacher is usually found negligent. Either another student must attend the injured party, or another teacher must be secured to attend the class.

When conducting general supervision duties, the teacher must be able to see all participants. A plan of rotation (written, if necessary) should provide for contact with all students. Discipline in the supervised area is a necessity. If the court finds that the injury occurred because of lack of student control, the teacher may be held liable.

Specific supervision requires the instructor to be with a certain group of students. An example would be the need to spot students who are per-

forming difficult gymnastics activities. If certain pieces of apparatus require special care and proper use, the teacher should have rules and regulations posted near the apparatus.

The following guidelines will help ensure that proper supervision occurs:

1. Never leave a class unsupervised, regardless of the situation. The teacher may have to answer a telephone call, go to the bathroom, secure more equipment, or discipline a student privately. Before doing any of these, another qualified supervisor must be secured. A class should never be split and sent to different areas if both areas cannot be supervised simultaneously.

2. Be aware of any possible dangers in the area. If the playing field has sprinkler heads that could cause injury, they should be marked with cones. If broken glass or other debris is on the field, the area should be marked off and avoided. It is the responsibility of the supervisor to be aware of these situations and to keep students from them.

3. Have safety rules posted in the area. Students should be made aware of the posted rules, and receive instruction and interpretation of the rules when necessary. If rules are modified, they should be rewritten in proper form. There is no substitute for documentation when defending one's policies and approaches.

4. Arrange and teach your class so that all students are always in view. This probably means supervising from the perimeter of the area. A teacher who is at the center of an area with her or his back to some students cannot supervise properly.

5. Do not leave equipment and apparatus unsupervised at any time if it is accessible to other students in the area. An example would be leaving equipment on the playing field between classes. If other students in the area have easy access to the equipment, they may use it in an unsafe manner, and the teacher will be found liable if an injury occurs.

6. Do not consent to supervise activities in which you are unqualified to anticipate possible hazards. If you are assigned to supervise such an activity, send a written memo to the department head or principal stating your lack of insight and qualification for such supervision.

7. The number of supervisors should be determined by the type of activity, the size of the area, and the number and age of the students.

INSTRUCTION

The major area of concern related to instruction is whether the student received adequate instruction before or during participation. Adequate instruction means a statement of how to perform the activity correctly, a statement of necessary safety precautions, and a statement of proper equipment and apparatus use. If instructions are given, they must be correct, understandable, and include proper technique, or the instructor can be held liable. The risk involved in an activity must also be communicated to the learner.

The age and maturity level of the student plays an important role in the selection of activities. Younger students require more care, instructions that are easy to comprehend, and clear restrictions in the name of safety. Students often have a lack of fear and caution concerning some activities, and the teacher must be aware of this in discussing safety factors. Youngsters have little fear and a great deal of faith in the instructor. This places a greater responsibility on the teacher to give adequate instruction.

Careful planning is a necessity. Written curriculum guides and lesson plans offer a well-prepared approach that is subject to examination by other teachers and administrators. Lesson plans should be developed that include proper sequencing and skill progression. Teachers are on defensible grounds if they can show that the progression of activities was based on presentations made by experts and was followed carefully during the teaching act. District and state guidelines enforcing instructional sequences and restricted activities should be closely checked.

Proper instruction demands that students not be forced to participate. If youngsters are required to perform an activity against their will, the teacher may be open to a lawsuit. In a lawsuit dealing with stunts and tumbling (Appenzeller 1970), a student claimed that she was not given adequate instruction in how to perform a stunt called "roll over two." The teacher was held liable because the student claimed that she was forced to try the stunt before adequate instruction was offered. Gymnastics and tumbling are areas in which lawsuits are prevalent due to a lack of adequate instruction. In addition to oral instruction, it is useful to post the proper sequence of skills and lead-up activities to assure proper presentation. Teachers need to tread the line carefully between helpful encouragement and forcing students to try new activities.

Since the use of punishment is a part of the instructional process for many teachers, the consequences should be examined carefully before implementation. Certainly physical punishment that brings about permanent or long-lasting damage is indefensible. The punishment used must be in line with the physical maturity and health of the student involved. The practice of having students perform laps when they misbehave may have gone unchallenged for years, but what if an asthmatic student or a student with a congenital heart disease is asked to run and suffers an attack? What if the student is running unsupervised and is injured by a fall or suffers from heat prostration? It would be difficult to defend such a punishment practice. The authors would also add that it is difficult to defend making students perform physical activity for misbehavior under any circumstances. In any case, if a child is injured while performing a physical punishment, the teacher is usually liable and is held responsible for the injury.

The primary point to remember about instruction is that the teacher has a duty to protect others against unreasonable physical or mental harm, and a duty to avoid any acts or omissions that might produce such harm. The teacher is educated, experienced, and skilled in the area, and should be able to predict situations that might be harmful.

The following points can help the teacher in planning for meaningful and safe instruction:

1. Sequence all activities in a unit of instruction and develop a written lesson plan. Most problems occur when snap judgments are made under the pressure and strain of the teaching situation.

2. Eliminate high-risk activities. If in doubt, discuss the activities with other experienced teachers and administrators.

3. Never force students to do an activity. The activities used in the curriculum must be within the developmental limits of the students. Since the range of maturity and development within a given class may be wide, some activities may be beyond the ability levels of various students.

4. If the students' grade is based on the number of activities in which they try to participate, some students may feel forced to try all activities. Teachers should tell students clearly that the choice to participate belongs to them. When they are afraid of getting hurt, they can elect not to do an activity.

5. Include in the written lesson plan the necessary safety equipment. The lesson plan should state clearly how the equipment is to be arranged, the placement of mats, and where the instructor will carry out supervision.

6. Activities should be selected for the curriculum based on the contribution they will make to the growth and development of the students. Including activities "for the fun of it" or "because students liked it" are not considered valid reasons in a court of law. The activities included should be based on the constructs of the curriculum and the consensus of experts.

7. If a student states that he or she is injured, or brings a note from parents stating that the student is not to participate in physical activity, the teacher must honor the request. These excuses are almost always given at the start of the period when the teacher is busy with many other duties (e.g., getting equipment ready, taking roll, and opening lockers). It is impossible to make a thoughtful judgment at this time. The school nurse is qualified to make these judgments when they relate to health and should be consulted about such matters. If a student continues to bring in excuses over a long period of time, the teacher can have a conference with the parents to rectify the situation.

8. Make sure the activities included in the instructional process are in line with the available equipment and facilities. An example would be the amount of space available. If a soccer lead-up activity is brought indoors because of inclement weather, it may no longer be a safe, appropriate activity.

9. If spotting is required for the safe completion of activities, it must always be done by the instructor or by trained students in the class. Teaching students how to spot is as important as teaching them physical skills. Safe conduct must be taught.

10. Have a written emergency care plan posted in the gymnasium. This plan should be approved by health care professionals and should be followed to the letter when an injury occurs.

EQUIPMENT AND FACILITIES

The equipment and facilities used in the physical education program must allow safe participation in all activities. The choice of apparatus and equipment should be based on the growth and developmental levels of the students. For example, letting elementary school children use a horizontal ladder that was designed for high school students may result in a fall that causes injury. Hazards found on playing fields need to be repaired and eliminated. The legal concept of an "attractive nuisance" should be understood. This implies that some piece of equipment or apparatus, usually left unsupervised, was so attractive to children that they could not be expected to avoid it. When an injury occurs, even though students may have been using the apparatus incorrectly, teachers and the school are often held liable, because the attractive nuisance should have been removed from the area when unsupervised.

A written checklist of equipment and apparatus should be developed and an inspection made on a regular basis. The date of inspection should be recorded to show that it was done at regular intervals. If corrective action is needed, the principal or appropriate administrator should be notified *in writing*. Telling them verbally is not enough, for this approach offers little protection for the teacher. If a potentially dangerous situation exists, rules or warnings should be posted so students are aware of the risk before participating.

Proper installation of equipment is critical. Climbing equipment and other equipment that must be anchored should be installed by a reputable firm that guarantees their work. When examining an apparatus, it is important to inspect the installation at the same time.

Maintenance of facilities is also important. Grass should be kept short and the grounds inspected for debris. Holes in the ground should be filled and loose gravel removed. Proper types of finish that prevent excessive slipping should be used on indoor floors. Shower rooms should have a roughened floor finish applied to prevent falls when the floors are wet.

The facilities should be used in a safe manner. Oftentimes sidelines and end lines of playing fields for football, soccer, or field hockey are placed too close to walls, curbings, or fences. Even though the size of the playing area may be reduced, the boundaries should be moved to allow adequate room for deceleration. In the gymnasium, students should not be asked to run to a line that is close to the wall. Another common hazard is baskets positioned too close to the playing area. The poles that support the baskets must be padded.

The proper use of equipment and apparatus is important. Regardless of the state of equipment repair, if it is misused, it may result in an injury. Students must be instructed in the proper use of equipment and apparatus before it is issued. All safety instruction should be included in the written lesson plan to ensure that all points are covered.

ATHLETIC PARTICIPATION

When students are involved in extracurricular activity, teachers or coaches are still responsible for the safe conduct of activities. A common area giving rise to lawsuits involves students who are mismatched either on the basis of size or ability. Just because the competitors are the same sex and chose to participate in the same activity does not absolve the instructor from liability if an injury occurs. The question the court examines is whether the teacher tried to match students according to height, weight, and ability. The courts are more sensitive about mismatching in the physical education setting than in an athletic contest, but mismatching is a factor that should be considered in any situation.

Participants in extracurricular activities should be required to sign a responsibility waiver form. The form should explain the risks involved in voluntary participation and discuss briefly the types of injuries that have occurred in the past during practice and competition. Supervisors should remember that waiver slips do not waive the rights of participants, and that teachers and coaches can still be found liable if injuries occur. The waiver forms do communicate clearly the risk involved, however, and may provide a strong assumption of risk defense.

Participants should be required to have a medical examination before participating. Examination records should be kept in the files and identified prominently in cases of any physical restriction or limitation. Students should not be allowed to participate unless they purchase medical insurance, and evidence of coverage should be kept in the folders of athletic participants.

Preseason conditioning should be undertaken in a systematic and progressive fashion. Starting the season with a mile run for time makes little sense if students have not been preconditioned. Coaches should be aware of guidelines dealing with heat and humidity. For example, in Arizona, guidelines are to avoid strenuous activity when the temperature exceeds 85° F and the humidity exceeds 40% (Stone 1977). When these conditions occur, running is curtailed to 10 min and active games to 30 min. Drinking water should always be available and given to students on demand.

Whenever students are transported, teachers are responsible for their safety both en route and during the activity. Licensed drivers and school-approved vehicles should always be used, and travel plans should include official approval from the appropriate school administrator. If a group of students transport each other in their own cars, the instructor has a responsibility to assure the safety of the vehicles. The cars should not be overloaded, and the instructor must lead the caravan and maintain proper speed. The group should go and return together. One special note: if the driver receives expenses for the trip, the possibility of being held liable for injury increases dramatically. Many insurance policies do not cover drivers who receive compensation for transporting students. If a teacher is transporting students and receiving reimbursement, a special insurance rider that provides liability coverage for the situation should be purchased.

SAFETY

The major thrust of safety should be to prevent situations that cause accidents. It is estimated that over 70% of the injuries associated with sports and with physical activity in general could be prevented through the use of proper safety procedures. On the other hand, accidents do occur, and proper emergency procedures should be established to cope with any situation. A comprehensive study of injuries in sport and related activities was conducted by the Consumer Product Safety Commission (1975). This study involved a network of computers in 119 hospital emergency rooms that channeled injury data to a central point. The sports and activities that produced the most injuries were, in order, football, touch football, baseball, basketball, gymnastics, and skiing. The facility that produced the most disabling injuries was the swimming pool.

Learning to recognize potential high-risk situations is probably the most important factor in preventing accidents. Teachers must have a clear understanding of the hazards and potential dangers of an activity before they can establish controls. One cannot assume that participants are aware of the danger and risk involved in various activities. Students must be told of the danger and risk before participation begins.

GUIDELINES FOR SAFETY

1. In-service sessions in safety should be administered by the most experienced and knowledgeable teachers. Department heads may be responsible for the training, or outside experts can be asked to undertake the responsibility. Giving in-district credit to participating teachers is a strong indication of a district's desire to nurture proper safety techniques.

2. Medical records should be reviewed at the start of each school year. Students who are atypical or handicapped should be noted and identified within each class listing. It is important to identify these individuals before the first instructional day. If necessary, the teacher or school nurse can call the doctor of a handicapped or activity-restricted student to inquire further about the situation and any special needs.

3. At the beginning of the semester, teachers should conduct a safety orientation. This should include a review of potentially dangerous situations, shower-room and class conduct, and rules for proper use of equipment and apparatus. Teachers must urge students to report any condition that might cause an accident.

4. Safety rules for specific units of instruction should be discussed at the onset of each unit. Rules should be posted and brought to the attention of students regularly. Posters and bulletin boards can promote safety in an enjoyable and stimulating manner.

5. If students are going to act as instructional aides, they should be trained. It is important that aides understand the techniques of spotting and offering proper instruction if they are going to be part of the educational process.

6. If equipment is faulty, it should be removed completely from the area until it is repaired. Along the same lines, equipment should not be modified or used for anything other than its original purpose.

7. An inventory of equipment and apparatus should include a safety checklist. At the end of the school year, equipment in need of repair should be sent to the proper agents. If the repair cost is greater than 40% of the replacement cost, discarding the equipment or apparatus is usually advisable.

8. Equipment should be purchased on the basis of quality and safety as well as potential use. Many lawsuits occur because of unsafe equipment and apparatus. The liability for such equipment may rest with the manufacturer, but it will have to be so proved. This means that the teacher should state, in writing, the exact specifications of the desired equipment. The substitution of a lower priced item may result in the purchase of less safe equipment. If the teacher has specified the proper equipment, however, the possibility of the teacher's being held liable for an injury will be reduced.

9. Whenever an injury occurs, it should be reported and filed. The injury report should be filed by type of injury (e.g., all ankle sprains in one folder, all broken arms in another). The report should list the activity during which the injury occurred and the conditions surrounding the injury. At regular intervals, the reports should be analyzed. The analysis may show that injuries are occurring regularly in a specific activity or on a certain piece of equipment. This process can provide direction for creating a safer environment or for defending the safety record of a sport, activity, or piece of equipment.

SAFETY COMMITTEE

A safety committee can meet at regular intervals to establish safety policies, to rule on requests to allow high-risk activities, and to analyze serious injuries that have occurred in the school district. This committee should develop safety rules that apply districtwide to all teachers. It may determine that certain activities involve too great a risk for the return in student benefit. Acceptable criteria for sport equipment and apparatus may also be established by the committee.

The safety committee should include one or more high-level administrators, physical education teachers, health officers (school nurse), parents, and students. A point to remember is that school administrators are usually indicted also when lawsuits do occur, because they are held responsible for program content and curriculum. Their representation on the safety committee is therefore important. In addition, students may be aware of possible hazards, and parents may voice concerns often overlooked by teachers.

Safety should be publicized throughout the school on a regular basis, and a mechanism should exist that allows students, parents, and teachers to voice concerns about unsafe conditions.

ASSESSING THE HEALTH STATUS OF STUDENTS

Periodic health examinations do not uncover every health problem related to participation in physical activity. Some conditions may appear only after exercise. In other instances, the condition may have developed after an examination and may have an important bearing on the health status of the student.

The task of screening children who respond poorly to exercise is not difficult; it involves identifying certain observable conditions that are indications of an abnormality. The Committee on Exercise and Fitness of the American Medical Association lists these observable signs, which may accompany or follow exercise and may be indications for referral to a physician. In any case, if the teacher identifies some of these symptoms, the school nurse should be notified and asked to examine the student. Teachers should never attempt to make medical decisions, regardless of their experience and expertise.

Excessive Breathlessness. Some breathlessness is normal with exercise, but if it persists long after exertion, it is cause for medical referral.

Pale or Clammy Skin. Pale or clammy skin or cold sweating following or during exercise is not a normal reaction to physical activity within the usual temperature ranges of the gymnasium or playing field.

Unusual Fatigue. Excessive fatigue, as evidenced by unusual lack of endurance or early failure to maintain moderate activity, suggests the need for medical referral. Attributing such reactions to lack of effort is unwise until possible organic causes have been ruled out.

Persistent Shakiness. Unusual weakness or shakiness that continues for more than 10 min following vigorous exercise is cause for concern.

Muscle Twitching or Tetany. Muscular contractions such as twitching or tetany, whether localized or generalized, sometimes occur as an unusual reaction to exercise, and are cause for referral.

In addition, such medical symptoms as headaches, dizziness, fainting, broken sleep at night, digestive upset, pain not associated with injury, undue pounding of the heart or irregular heartbeat, disorientation, or personality change are contraindications of normal functioning. The committee cautions that an occasional episode need not alarm the instructor, but recurring or persisting patterns of any of these symptoms, particularly when related to activity, indicate the need for medical review.

PLANNING FOR EMERGENCY CARE

Establishing procedures for emergency care and for notification of parents in case of injury are of utmost importance in providing a high standard of care for students. In order to plan properly for emergency care, all physical education teachers should have first aid training. First aid is the immediate and temporary care given in an emergency before the physician arrives. Its purpose is to save life, prevent aggravation of injuries, and alleviate severe suffering. If there is evidence of life-threatening bleeding or if the victim is unconscious or has stopped breathing, the teacher must administer first aid. When already injured persons may be further injured if they are *not* moved, then moving them is permissible. As a general rule, however, an injured party should not be moved unless absolutely necessary. If there is any indication of back or neck injury, the head must be immobilized and should not be moved without the use of a spine board. Remember the purpose of first aid—to save life. The emergency care plan should consist of the following steps:

1. Administration of first aid to the injured student is the number one priority. Treat only life-threatening injuries. If a school nurse is available, she or he should be called immediately to the scene of the accident. Emergency care procedures should indicate whether the student can be moved and in what fashion. It is critical that the individual applying first aid avoid aggravating the injury.

2. Unless the injury is so severe that the student must be taken directly to the hospital emergency care unit, the parents should be notified. Each student's file should list home and emergency telephone numbers where parents can be reached. If possible, the school should have an arrangement with a local emergency facility, so a paramedic unit can be called immediately to the scene of a serious accident.

3. In most cases, the student can be released to a parent or a designated representative. Policies for transportation of injured students should be established and documented.

4. A student accident report should be completed promptly, while the details of the accident are clear. Figure 13.1 is an example of an accident report form that covers the necessary details. The teacher and principal should both retain copies and send additional copies to the administrative office.

Figure 13.1. Sample student accident report form (reprinted from *Dynamic Physical Education for Elementary School Children*, 7th ed. by V. P. Dauer and R. P. Pangrazi, 1983. Minneapolis: Burgess Publishing Co., p. 46)

STUDENT ACCIDENT REPORT

_____ **SCHOOL**

In all cases, this form should be filed through the school nurse and signed by the principal of the school. The original will be forwarded to the superintendent's office, where it will be initialed and sent to the head nurse. The second copy will be retained by the principal or the nurse. The third copy should be given to the physical education teacher if accident is related.

Name of Injured _____ Address _____

Phone _____ Grade _____ Home Room _____ Age _____

Parents of Injured _____

Place of Accident _____ Date of Accident _____

Hour _____ A.M. P.M. Date Reported _____ By Whom _____

Parent Contact Attempted at _____ A.M. P.M. Parent Contacted at _____ A.M. P.M.

DESCRIBE ACCIDENT, GIVING SPECIFIC LOCATION AND CONDITION OF PREMISES _____

_____

NATURE OF INJURY _____
(Describe in detail)

CARE GIVEN OR ACTION TAKEN BY NURSE OR OTHERS _____

_____

REASON INJURED PERSON WAS ON PREMISES _____
(Activity at time—i.e., lunch, physical education, etc.)

STAFF MEMBER RESPONSIBLE FOR STUDENT SUPERVISION AT TIME OF ACCIDENT _____

IS STUDENT COVERED BY SCHOOL-SPONSORED ACCIDENT INSURANCE? ____ YES ____ NO

MEDICAL CARE RECOMMENDED ____ YES ____ NO

WHERE TAKEN AFTER ACCIDENT _____
(Specify home, physician, or hospital, giving name and address)

BY WHOM _____ AT WHAT TIME _____ A.M. P.M.

FOLLOW-UP BY NURSE TO BE SENT TO CENTRAL HEALTH OFFICE.

REMEDIATIVE MEASURES TAKEN _____
(Attach individual remarks if necessary)

School _____ Principal _____

Date _____ Nurse _____

On the back of this sheet, list all persons familiar with the circumstances of the accident, giving name, address, telephone number, age, and location with respect to the accident.

PERSONAL PROTECTION: MINIMIZING THE EFFECTS OF A LAWSUIT

In spite of proper care, injuries do occur and lawsuits may be initiated. Two courses of action are necessary to counteract the effects of a suit.

Liability Insurance. Teachers may be protected by school district liability insurance. Usually, however, teachers must purchase a policy. Most policies provide for legal services to contest a suit and will pay indemnity up to the limits of the policy ($300,000.00 liability coverage is common). Most policies give the insurance company the right to settle out of court. If this occurs, some may infer that the teacher was guilty, even though the circumstances might indicate otherwise. Settling out of court is usually done by insurance companies to save money, instead of spending a lot on legal fees to try to win the case in court.

Record Keeping. The second necessary course of action is to keep good records of accidents. Many lawsuits occur months and even years after the accident, when everyone's memory of the situation is fuzzy. Accident reports should be filled out immediately after an injury. The teacher should take care to provide no evidence, oral or written, that others could use in a court of law. Nor should the teacher attempt to make a diagnosis or to put down the supposed cause of the accident in the report.

If newspaper reporters probe for details, the teacher should avoid describing the accident beyond the basic facts. When discussing the accident with administrators, only the facts recorded on the accident report should be discussed. Remember that school records can be subpoenaed in court proceedings. The point here is not to dissemble, but to be cautious and avoid any self-incrimination.

A SAFETY AND LIABILITY CHECKLIST

The following checklist can be used to monitor the physical education environment. Any situations that deviate from safe and sound legal practices should be rectified immediately.

Supervision and Instruction

1. Are teachers adequately trained in all of the activities that they are teaching?
2. Do all teachers have evidence of a necessary level of first aid training?
3. When supervising, do personnel have access to a written plan of areas to be observed and responsibilities to be performed?
4. Have students been warned of potential dangers and risks, and advised of rules and the reasons for rules?
5. Are safety rules posted near the areas of increased risk?
6. Are lesson plans written? Do they include provisions for proper instruction, sequence of activities, and safety? Are all activities taught listed in the district curriculum guide?
7. When a new activity is introduced, are safety precautions and instructions for correct performance of skills communicated to the class?
8. Are the activities taught in the program based on sound curriculum principles? Could the activities and units of instruction be defended on the basis of their educational contributions?
9. Do the methods of instruction recognize the individual differences of students and are the necessary steps taken to meet the needs of all students, regardless of sex, ability, or disability?
10. Are substitute teachers given clear and comprehensive lesson plans so they can maintain the scope and sequence of instruction?
11. Is the grading plan based on actual performance and objective data, rather than on arbitrary and capricious standards?
12. Is appropriate dress required for students? This does not imply uniforms, only dress that ensures the safety of the student.
13. When necessary for safety, are students grouped according to ability level, size, or age?
14. Is the class left unsupervised for teacher visits to the office, lounge, or bathroom? Is one teacher asked to supervise two or more classes at the same time?

15. If students are used as teacher aides or to spot others, are they given proper instruction and training?

Equipment and Facilities

1. Is all equipment inspected on a regular basis, and are the inspection results recorded on a form and sent to proper administrators?
2. Are "attractive nuisances" eliminated from the gymnasium and playing field?
3. Are specific safety rules posted on facilities and near equipment?
4. Are the following inspected periodically?
   Bleachers
   Playing field for glass, rocks, and metal objects
   Fasteners holding equipment such as climbing ropes, horizontal bars, or baskets
   Goals, such as football, soccer, and field hockey, to be sure they are fastened securely
   Padded areas such as goal supports
5. Are mats placed under apparatus whenever a fall is possible?
6. Are playing fields arranged so participants will not run into each other or be hit by a ball from another game?
7. Is all protective equipment (e.g., football pads, headgear, and so forth) inspected regularly and discarded when substandard?
8. Is a log maintained recording the occurrence of an inspection, the equipment in need of repair, and when the repairs were made?
9. Are skinned areas raked and maintained on a daily basis, so the surface provides safe playing conditions?
10. Are landing pits filled and maintained properly?

Emergency Care

1. Is there a written procedure for emergency care?
2. Is a person properly trained in first aid available immediately following an accident?
3. Are emergency telephone numbers readily accessible?
4. Are telephone numbers of parents available?
5. Is an up-to-date first aid kit available? Is ice immediately available?
6. Are health folders maintained that list restrictions, allergies, and health problems of students?

7. Are health folders reviewed by instructors on a regular basis?
8. Are students participating in extracurricular activities required to have insurance? Is the policy number recorded?
9. Is there a plan for treating injuries that involves the local fire department paramedics?
10. Are accident reports filed and analyzed on a regular basis?

Summary

Liability is a teacher's responsibility to perform a duty to a particular group. This obligation means that teachers must develop a safe environment for students while they are participating in organized activities. Liability is always a legal matter, and it must be proved in a court of law that negligence has occurred. There are many types of negligence. Basically, negligence means that a reasonable standard of care was not met, and that the teacher therefore failed to protect students from an unreasonable risk of harm.

Many guidelines can be followed to reduce the possibility of a lawsuit. Careful planning and well-organized instruction make the teacher less vulnerable to a suit. Equipment and facilities should be regularly checked, repaired, or replaced to prevent accidents. Safety involves foreseeing possible dangerous situations and preventing accidents before they occur. A safety committee can be helpful in sharing the burden of establishing well-designed guidelines.

References

Appenzeller, H. *From the Gym to the Jury.* Charlottesville, VA: The Michie Company, 1970.

Black's Law Dictionary. 4th ed. St. Paul: West Publishing Co., 1968.

Stone, W. J. 1977. Running and running tests for Arizona school children. *Arizona JOHPERD* 21: 15–17.

Strickland, R., Phillip, J. F., and Phillips, W. R. *Avoiding Teacher Malpractice.* New York: Hawthorn Books, Inc., 1976.

U.S. Consumer Product Safety Commission. *Hazard Analysis of Injuries Relating to Playground Equipment.* Washington, DC, 1975.

Chapter 14

Public Relations

Public relations activities are vital to the future of the physical education profession. The public's current tremendous interest in physical fitness, health, wellness, and nutrition offers the profession unique opportunities. The increasing concern for preventive medicine and the emphasis on maintaining wellness make today a time of opportunity and unequaled growth for the physical education profession. Nothing is more important than the health and vitality of an individual. Unfortunately, most people do not associate physical education with learning how to make the most of one's health. In the past, the emphasis in physical education was on participation in team sports. Little information was presented on why and how certain activities could be healthful.

Physical educators have been hesitant to advertise and promote their programs. For many years, it was considered unprofessional to advertise and tell others about the merits of using the services of doctors, lawyers, or teachers. Today, however, all professional fields are using promotion. Witness the advertisements on television and in newspapers for various hospitals, doctors, and lawyers.

Even churches are erecting billboards in an attempt to increase the size of their congregation, but seldom does one see an advertisement promoting physical education as a profession.

For years, people have associated physical education with athletics. When physical education teachers tell the public in what area they teach, many will ask which sport they coach. No one can question the exposure athletics receive through parental support and the media. The critical point is that few parents and community members understand that physical education emphasizes educating for a lifetime of involvement in activity.

When the public does not understand the educational value of a profession, they find it easy to do without. For example, driver training is taught in most schools, and statistics have shown that such training reduces the number of accidents and deaths. A lower insurance rate is therefore given to those who have participated in driver education. If the public looks to physical education and sees little payoff in terms of life-style and the quality of life, then many become advocates of making the program elective or doing away with it altogether. When money is in short supply, which areas are scrutinized first? Physical education is usually at the head of the line. Why? Because the public has decided that it is of little value. This is the bottom line of public relations. A program must offer something of lifetime value to participants, and the public must come to understand that. Nothing sells physical education like a sound physical education program.

Another point of concern is trying to reach the public. Teachers often do an adequate job of reaching parents and telling them about the program, but a large number of people who pay taxes and help support education never receive any information about the schools. It is not enough to reach the parents. Colleagues, people without children in school, and other students should receive attention and concern. This large group of people will not bother to support physical education programs if physical education professionals have not kept them informed.

GUIDELINES FOR PUBLIC RELATIONS

The public relations program should be based on a myriad of factors, for many factors are certainly involved in developing a strong program of publicity and exposure. The following points should be considered:

1. Explain to students why they are in physical education. If you are attempting to influence their lives, they have a right to know why you are asking them to do various activities. In most cases, understanding why one is doing something is more important than actually performing an activity.

2. Encourage students to explain to their parents why they are experiencing various activities and learning episodes. An effective public relations agent is an excited student telling Mom and Dad all about a unit in physical education.

3. Share your program with colleagues and administrators. It is important that they understand innovations and the new activities being presented. Many times, physical educators need the support of colleagues in order to reach goals, and administrators are seldom informed about physical education programs. What do they tell complaining parents, and how do they defend a program if they are not even aware of the program?

4. Inform the community media of newsworthy happenings. For example, when a new unit of instruction is being presented, send a note to the television, radio, and newspaper organizations. Over a period of time, they have a need for material and may make contact. Maintaining an ongoing program of news releases is important. Large public relations firms often send out news releases with the expectation that not many will be used. They operate on the law of averages, that sooner or later the media will have need of some of the material.

5. Find the friends of physical education. Many people who are not associated with the profession are strong advocates. They can speak forcefully for physical education in the schools without having a vested interest. Develop a physical education booster group that is invited to visit the program on a regular basis. They need to know what is going on if they are expected to share the program with others. Another way to communicate with the group is through a "friends of physical education" newsletter that describes the various aspects of the program. Remember that the athletic program has used booster groups to strong advantage for years. There is no reason why the physical education program cannot be as successful.

6. How one acts and communicates with others has a great impact on the profession. Some teachers become disenchanted with teaching and start to communicate these feelings to students, parents, and the public. Teachers are walking billboards for their chosen profession. Students respect teachers who are enthusiastic and positive about the work they perform. Examining carefully why one chose to enter the teaching profession and explaining those reasons to others is important.

7. Communicate to others how the program influences the lives of participants. Parents and students have a right to know the benefits of a sound physical education program. Send home with the students brochures or newsletters that explain the impact of physical education on youth, and tell parents how they can help their children become more proficient in physical activity. Figure 14.1 is an example of a short booklet that communicates the what, why, and how of physical fitness to parents in simple terms.

Figure 14.1.   Physical fitness booklet (modified from a booklet by Clayre Petray, Assistant Professor, Long Beach State University)

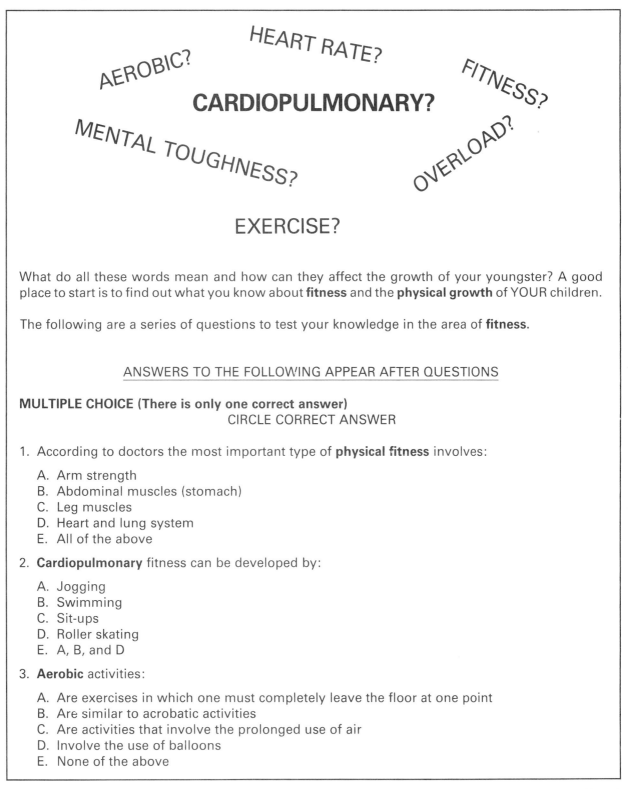

AEROBIC?

HEART RATE?

FITNESS?

CARDIOPULMONARY?

MENTAL TOUGHNESS?

OVERLOAD?

EXERCISE?

What do all these words mean and how can they affect the growth of your youngster? A good place to start is to find out what you know about **fitness** and the **physical growth** of YOUR children.

The following are a series of questions to test your knowledge in the area of **fitness**.

ANSWERS TO THE FOLLOWING APPEAR AFTER QUESTIONS

MULTIPLE CHOICE (There is only one correct answer)
CIRCLE CORRECT ANSWER

1. According to doctors the most important type of **physical fitness** involves:

   A. Arm strength
   B. Abdominal muscles (stomach)
   C. Leg muscles
   D. Heart and lung system
   E. All of the above

2. **Cardiopulmonary** fitness can be developed by:

   A. Jogging
   B. Swimming
   C. Sit-ups
   D. Roller skating
   E. A, B, and D

3. **Aerobic** activities:

   A. Are exercises in which one must completely leave the floor at one point
   B. Are similar to acrobatic activities
   C. Are activities that involve the prolonged use of air
   D. Involve the use of balloons
   E. None of the above

continued

Figure 14.1 /*continued*

TRUE-FALSE (The statement must be **entirely true** to circle T)

T F 4. Children don't need regular daily activity like adults do because they can become physically fit during recess periods at school.

T F 5. Parents do not have to worry about heart disease and their child.

T F 6. One advantage of a student's being overweight is that he or she will become more respected because of his or her size.

T F 7. A physically fit person has better digestion than one who is not.

T F 8. There is no need for concern if a child under 5 years is fat.

T F 9. Studies show that by ages 8–12, children decide what physical activities they will pursue during their free time in later life.

T F 10. Youngsters have smaller bodies and hearts than adults. They should therefore **not** be **encouraged** to push themselves past the point of being tired.

T F 11. Youngsters should be encouraged to "clean their plates" at each meal to ensure proper diet and nutrition.

T F 12. To become physically fit, students must exercise for 30 min continuously 5 days per week.

T F 13. To get in shape, it is necessary to join a health spa so that you have access to a variety of equipment.

T F 14. Although exercise makes you stronger, it also makes you more tired.

T F 15. When you begin breathing hard while exercising, this shows that you are pushing yourself hard enough to strengthen your heart muscle.

T F 16. One of the best ways to ensure that your youngster will become physically fit is to enroll her or him in competitive sports such as baseball or tackle football.

T F 17. Although a person's heart rate increases while she or he is exercising, the result is a decrease in her or his resting heart rate.

T F 18. The best way for an overweight student to lose weight is to increase his or her amount of daily activity.

T F 19. Exercise in most cases will not increase appetite.

ANSWERS!!!!!

1. **D**—HEART AND LUNG SYSTEM.
   Strengthening the heart and lung system (known as **cardiopulmonary fitness**) can prevent the onset of heart disease, the killer of almost 1,000,000 people each year.

2. **E**—A, B, and D (JOGGING, SWIMMING, AND ROLLER SKATING).
   Cardiopulmonary fitness involves the development of the heart (cardio) and lungs (pulmonary). The heart and lung system can be strengthened by activities that involve **continuous** movement of the whole body. Sit-ups build the stomach, but do not strengthen the heart muscle.

3. **C**—ARE ACTIVITIES THAT INVOLVE THE USE OF AIR.
   Aerobic activities are those in which air is utilized, and through which the heart and lungs

become more efficient (**cardiopulmonary fitness**). Aerobic activities can increase the size of, as well as strengthen, both the heart and blood vessels.

4. **False.** Although youngsters have the opportunity to be active at recess, studies show that they stop at the first sign of tiring. To increase the level of cardiopulmonary fitness, activity must be nonstop for 15–30 min.

5. **False.** Signs of heart disease have been found in children as young as 2 years.

6. **False.** Overweight students cannot move as quickly in game situations and therefore are usually chosen last as team members. Peer pressure and ridicule are great among children.

7. **True.**

8. **False.** The widely held belief that "baby fat" disappears is a **myth.** "Baby fat" most often turns into "adult fat."

9. **True.** If children are competent at using their body in a variety of movements at an early age, they will be more likely to continue to use their body throughout their life. A person's activity level is also established early. **Active** young people tend to be **active** older people: **activity** is the best means to prevent obesity.

10. **False.** The heart of young children, barring any medical complications, is stronger and proportionately larger than at any other time in life. Youngsters need to learn to be **mentally tough** so that they can push themselves past the first signs of tiring.

11. **False.** Eating habits, like activity levels, are established early. The nutritional value of a meal is determined more by the composition of the foods than by the amount.

12. **True.** Once the desired level of physical fitness is attained, 3 days per week will maintain the desired level.

13. **False.** Health spas do offer a variety of equipment, but very little of it is designed to work the **heart** for an adequate time period. For exercise to benefit the **heart,** it must be done continuously for 15–30 min. Aerobic activities such as bike riding, swimming, roller skating, and jogging can be used effectively to develop **cardiopulmonary fitness.**

14. **False.** People who are physically fit are more energetic, sleep better, and seem to enjoy life more.

15. **False.** To strengthen the heart muscle and thus develop cardiopulmonary fitness, exercise must be strenuous enough to elevate the heart rate to approximately 150 beats per min. The pulse can be taken from the wrist (with index finger), during or immediately following exercise. By counting the number of beats for 10 sec and multiplying by 6, the heart beats per minute during exercise can be determined. The pulse must be taken **immediately** upon completion of the exercise.

16. **False.** Bone growth occurs at an uneven rate until approximately age 12. A contact sport such as tackle football can cause permanent bone injuries. Baseball requires excessive throwing, which sometimes impairs bone growth in young children. Neither of these sports involves 15–30 min of continuous activity for any of the players.

17. **True.** The resting heart beat of the average person is between 70 and 80 beats per min. Through strenuous exercise, cardiopulmonary fitness is increased, and the heart muscle and blood vessels are thus strengthened and enlarged. The heart then works more efficiently, that is, moving the same amount of blood in fewer beats. A person who increases his or her cardiopulmonary fitness may lower the resting heart rate by as much as 10 beats per min.

continued

Figure 14.1/*continued*

18. **True**. Research studies have shown that increasing a person's amount of daily activity is the most successful approach to weight loss. For example, consider the fact that there are **3500 calories in 1 lb**. For a person to lose 1 lb, he or she must burn 3500 calories. Jogging or walking burns approximately 100 calories per mi. If a person takes no more than 15 min and jogs or walks 1 mi per day, without any change in diet, he or she will lose an average of **1 lb per month**. Diet, when combined with exercise, can speed up the process of weight loss.

19. **True**. Unless a person is in an extensive training program (the equivalent of running 10 mi per day or more), regular exercise will not, in most cases, increase his or her appetite.

PHYSICAL FITNESS: WHAT IS IT?

Physical fitness is a term that people of all ages should know. There are a great variety of interpretations of the meaning of this widely used term. In this booklet, the term **physical fitness** refers to the level of efficiency of the **heart and lung system,** that is, **cardiopulmonary fitness.**

The body has many important muscles, all of which need to be used or exercised regularly. The **heart and lung system,** however, is considered by most physicians to be the key to the prevention of heart disease, the number one killer in America today. Through the right type of exercise, the chances of contracting heart disease can be lessened. The heart is a muscle and reacts to exercise as do the muscles in other parts of the body. Continuous vigorous exercise has the effect of strengthening the heart muscle and can result in an increase in the size of the heart. Besides increasing the **size and strength** of the heart muscle, continuous vigorous exercise also increases the **size and number** of blood vessels in the heart and lung area. Blood is thus pumped more efficiently as the level of **cardiopulmonary fitness** increases. These important effects of vigorous exercise on the heart and lung system decrease the chance that heart disease will occur.

Your **cardiopulmonary fitness** level affects how you look and how you feel. A person who has a high level of fitness performs her or his daily work without getting overtired. When a full day's work is done, the physically fit person has energy left over for leisure time activities: a walk to the park, a bike ride, a game of ball, or a refreshing jog around the block.

As stated previously in the question and answer portion of this booklet, habits and attitudes are established at an early age. It is therefore essential that young children be taught the meaning and implications of **physical or cardiopulmonary fitness.** Such simple experiences as putting the hand on the heart muscle after vigorous activity, to "feel the heart pumping blood fast," begins to increase their awareness of this important muscle.

NOW THAT I KNOW WHAT

CARDIOPULMONARY FITNESS IS:

How Do I

Help My Son or Daughter

Become More Fit?

The **heart** is a muscle and thus can be increased in **size and strength** through exercise, **but what kind of exercises build the heart?**

1. For an exercise or activity to benefit the heart, **it must be continuous.** Activities such as jogging, walking, swimming, roller skating, or bike riding should be continued for a minimum of 5 min. Any type of aerobic activity that can be performed continuously for 5 min can be beneficial.

2. Not only must an activity be **continuous,** but it must be **vigorous. How vigorous?** Activity must be vigorous enough to increase the heart rate to 150 beats per min. To find out if your child is involved in adequate vigorous activity, take her or his pulse **immediately** following exercise. By placing your index finger on the front of the neck, you can find the pulse (from the carotid artery). Count the number of beats for **10** sec and multiply by **6** to find the number of heart beats in 1 min during exercise. If there is any delay (even 15–30 sec) in taking the pulse following exercise, it will **not** be an accurate count.

HELPFUL HINTS

There are many ways in which parents and family members can help youngsters to get added activity time throughout the week. One of the best ways to increase the amount of time that children spend in activity is to join them in the activity. Daily brisk walks or jogs to the park are great.

Bicycle riding is another fun activity that promotes fitness. Swimming as well as roller skating are terrific ways for students to have fun and keep fit. Another way is to take a soccer ball or large rubber ball to the park and run and kick it around for a half hour or so.

Other fitness ideas that you might try are kite flying, jumping rope, jogging in place, or dancing to a record. Take a few minutes to find out what students are doing actively and then see if you can increase the amount of time they spend at the activity. With a little enthusiasm and a little extra time put aside each day, your son or daughter can be on the road to cardiopulmonary fitness.

The **"fitness experience"** maintains health, keeps a person in good shape, helps prevent heart attack, and builds muscles.

8. Become actively involved in professional organizations such as the state, local, and national associations of health, physical education, recreation, and dance. Professionals sometimes forget the old adage, "United we stand, divided we fall." A professional organization is for teachers and gives them a chance to pursue and establish professional goals. Physical education has suffered from teachers deciding to get along without paying dues to an organization. Certainly one can get along without an organization, but who listens to one lonely voice? Physical educators who are only interested in coaching have unfortunately sometimes weakened these organizations by their lack of interest. They become so involved in coaching that they believe there is not enough time to participate. Some of the most dynamic and respected teachers are also coaches; these people would add a great deal to a professional organization.

The best known professional organization for physical education is the American Alliance for Health, Physical Education, Recreation, and Dance (AAHPERD). Its membership consists of teachers and professors from all levels and professional backgrounds throughout the United States. Each state has a state AAHPERD organization that is related to the national organization. Both organizations have political advocacy groups that work for bettering the standing of the physical education profession.

9. Reach out to experts in other physical activity areas. For example, there are many capable people in specialized areas, such as yoga, fencing, martial arts, and gymnastics, who could conduct special workshops or help stu-

dents begin a unit. They can add new and exciting curriculum activities that might not be strong competency areas for the physical educator. When these people are used, all prosper. Students receive sound instruction, and teachers make strong friends and advocates for their program.

10. Teach and emphasize lifetime skills and activities. When students and parents see that the skills they learn will be used throughout their lives, they are more likely to become strong advocates of a program. Few people participate in team sports after age 25, yet most want to participate in some type of activity. If competency in lifetime sport skills is not developed, few people will have the desire to participate in later life. Those who can look back and give credit to physical education will become forceful believers and backers of physical education programs in the schools.

11. Expressing appreciation to those who have participated and supported the program is important. Students often choose to cooperate and participate in a program. Giving them credit for their support is important. Administrators make a quality program possible through their support for equipment, facilities, scheduling, and the like. They need to be appreciated on a regular basis. When a demonstration program is sponsored, be sure to thank parents for their support. Working with students becomes difficult if parents are telling them that the program or the teachers are poor. Cooperative students usually have supportive parents. Thank them.

WHAT DOES THE PUBLIC NEED TO KNOW?

An important step in designing the public relations program is to determine what information should be shared with the public. It is a procedure similar to planning a lesson or drawing up a game plan in that it gives direction and goals to the public relations program. Information can then be released to the public in a meaningful progression and through different media. Some of the following points are useful in sharing the philosophy and workings of the physical education program with the public. They are areas that are sure to stimulate interest in the program.

1. Discuss the impact of the program on the physical growth and development of students. This area should be promoted extensively because exercise has so many beneficial effects that contribute to the wellness of an individual. Parents and the public should hear about the effect of regular aerobic exercise on the cardiovascular system, the impact of weight lifting on the development of the skeletal system, and how different types of conditioning programs improve various fitness attributes.

2. Emphasize the importance of physical education and of regular activity in developing a strong, positive self-concept (Pangrazi 1982). Physical fitness and the performance of motor skills affect how one feels personally. This can lead to renewed confidence in one's self.

3. Explain how the program is organized to help all students improve and develop, not just skilled athletes. The majority of students are not skilled athletes but the program must meet their needs. Parents are concerned about whether the program is designed to aid their child.

4. Share the rationale, aims, and objectives of the program with the public. When most people are asked about the goals of a physical education program, few understand that the program is different from an interscholastic athletic program. This misunderstanding is due, in large part, to a lack of communication about the program.

5. The public should know that a sound physical education program provides an opportunity for all students to participate and compete. Explain that the program is allied with intramurals and sport clubs and that students are helped to find a place, become involved, and interact with others.

6. The need to offer students organized leisure-time activities should be shared with others. Physical education is the only area in the school setting in which students are offered a chance to be physically active.

7. Reinforce the importance of health as a top priority. People seldom take time to maintain their health status. Physical education teaches students how to maintain wellness for a lifetime. When one's health is lost, working, playing, and sharing with others is difficult. Nothing is more important than good health. Sell this fact.

ESTABLISHING AN ADVISORY COUNCIL

A public relations advisory council can be most helpful in disseminating information about the program. The advisory council should consist of people such as a school board member, an administrator, teachers, interested parents, community media personnel, students, and any other key members of the community. The purpose of the committee is to determine how the program can be promoted, what program components should be shared, and how the information can be broadcast to the public. The committee is not involved in curriculum development, but rather in analyzing the program and determining how it can be promoted.

The council should be charged with developing a working policy for bringing information to the public. This usually consists of the following steps:

1. Survey a representative sample of the public to see what they know and do not know about the program. This prevents the sharing of information that is common knowledge. The survey can be a simple tool that is designed by the council to diagnose areas they deem important.

2. Develop a public relations policy to begin to disseminate information to the public in areas about which they know little.

3. Determine how the facts should be presented to make them catchy, interesting, and informative.

4. Perform a cost analysis to see what needs to be acquired in terms of supplies, equipment, and related materials in order for the council to function.

5. Assign tasks such as fund-raising, writing copy, and disseminating information to different members of the council.

The council should search out people who are friends of physical education. The council composition should be balanced with people who have different abilities. For example, some people may have media contacts, other council members may know people who are willing to be benefactors, and still others may possess expertise in writing copy.

IMPLEMENTING THE PUBLIC RELATIONS PROGRAM

The public relations program can be implemented in different ways. All methods should help the public better understand the operation of a program. Regardless of the method used, selling an inferior program is impossible. People will refuse to endorse and accept a program that does not ben-

efit its participants. One must thus begin with a quality program, for nothing sells like quality. When students tell parents about their accomplishments in the program, public relations benefits are being accrued. Strong planning, excellent teaching, and concern for students are the cornerstones of a physical education program that will be well accepted.

PERSONAL CONDUCT

A large share of the public still imagines physical educators as being slightly obese, carrying a bat in one hand, wearing a whistle around the neck, and being outfitted in baggy sweat pants. This stereotype yells at people to hustle, seldom exercises, and is often in poor physical condition. The point here is that the teacher's dress and actions will be scrutinized by the public and will continue to be a point of reference long after the image has changed. Teachers must model the behavior they desire in others. They must stay fit, exercise regularly, and use up-to-date methods of dealing with people. A physical education teacher who behaves in a professional manner does more to sell physical education than all the public relations ploys possible.

THE SCHOOL SETTING

Developing a meaningful relationship with students is important. Students must understand why various activities are being taught and how they benefit from participation. Remember that students who dislike the program communicate their dislike to parents, and parents often know little about the program other than what their youngsters tell them. If most of the messages are negative, parents will share negative comments with other parents. Students ultimately grow up to become school board members, teachers, and administrators. If their experience was negative, they may be unwilling as adults to support physical education.

Teachers in other areas need to know about the program. In too many cases, the physical educator stays in the gymnasium and seldom mingles with other teachers. This can create an atmosphere of animosity, particularly when physical educators are coaches and choose to miss faculty meetings and related social functions. Behaving in a manner consistent with the rest of the faculty members is politic.

Some physical educators have had excellent success with a faculty fitness program. They offer a program one day a week for faculty members.

During this time, they demonstrate various skills and activities that can be performed during the week. Another related program is a faculty recreation program. Faculty members can gather after school or in the evening to participate in volleyball, badminton, basketball, and other desired activities. Administrators can be invited to participate too, which offers personal contact in an informal setting.

Another activity that develops goodwill toward the physical education program is a school playday. Students participate together in an activity that is lighthearted and enjoyable. Teachers also become involved and participate with students in this recreational setting. An example of a playday would be sponsoring "loony" contests such as the water balloon throw, the trike ride, three-legged race, pie-eating contest, pit-spitting contest, and any other novel activities. The emphasis is on friendly competition and participation.

Announcements can be placed regularly in the school newspaper. Tell the school about upcoming units, about registering for the playday, when special speakers are scheduled, and about happenings in the intramural program. The school newspaper can be a source of strong public relations with students. Along the same lines, the school district newsletter that is sent to parents should be used to communicate about the program. For instance, the grading system could be explained, or the results of fitness testing.

COMMUNICATING WITH PARENTS

The more parents understand about the educational nature of the program, the more willing they may become to support it. Since many parents do not distinguish between an athletic program and a physical education program, the public relations thrust must be to help clarify the differences.

Parents can be involved actively as program participants or passively as spectators. A parents' night can be scheduled when different activities are taught by instructors to both students and their parents. This gives parents a first-hand experience with the instructional nature of the program. If parents are not asked to participate, a wide variety of student demonstrations can be planned to show the broad spectrum of skills that are taught. In either case, demonstrations should illustrate the features and organization of the program.

The physical education booster group can be used to help interpret the program to parents. Discussions and panel representations at parent-teacher organizations can be conducted, and interpretive booklets distributed. Slides of program highlights might be shown to enhance the presentation. The use of outside experts is also effective in dealing with controversial issues. Parents should be given the opportunity to ask questions and resolve points of concern.

Another way to involve parents is to use them as teacher's aides. They can help with fitness testing projects and thus begin to understand how students function in the physical education setting. Projects should also be scheduled on Saturdays or evenings so parents working outside the home can be involved.

Brochures and handouts explaining the program can be sent home with students. Parents should be encouraged to follow up and help their students practice skills at home. Surprisingly, few parents receive calls from teachers at the junior and senior high school level unless something is wrong. Parents should also be called when their son or daughter has accomplished something positive and has performed well. Parents will begin to support a program when they hear positive messages about their youngster.

A source of public relations with parents that sometimes goes unheeded is grade reporting. The wellness profile (see Chapter 15) is an excellent tool for communicating the status of the student's health to parents. The profile can forewarn parents of possible health problems that should be examined by a physician. Computer programs are now available so students can enter their fitness test results in the computer. The data are analyzed and the computer prints out a personalized report for the student. Along this same line, some districts now use these data to maintain files that follow students from kindergarten through high school. Comparative data that describe a youngster's growth and development can be sent to parents at regular intervals. When parents understand that the school is helping to maintain the wellness of their youngster, positive feelings result.

PRACTICAL IDEAS
FOR PUBLIC RELATIONS PROMOTIONS

The following ideas are possibilities for increasing the exposure of the physical education program. All of these suggestions can be modified and are offered simply to initiate ideas.

BULLETIN BOARDS, DISPLAYS, AND POSTERS

In the school setting, visual displays serve to advertise and promote the program. They show the rest of the faculty that physical educators are active and proud of accomplishments. The art specialist will sometimes help to develop posters that require special artistic ability, and students with artistic skills are often willing to work on the media products. The following are some suggestions:

1. A schedule bulletin board shows what will be done in the program three to four weeks in advance. On it are listed special events, activities to be taught, and testing days.
2. A special announcement board can be used to post special events such as intramural games, interscholastic games, guest speakers, and the showing of films.
3. Visual displays at opportune times can reach a wide variety and large number of people. Examples of such times are open houses, just before school closes for the summer, prior to Christmas vacation or spring holidays, and before school opens in the fall. At these times, parents are visiting the school and forming their opinions of the program.

Hints for Making Effective Bulletin Boards

First, select a bulletin board that is located where the largest number of people will view it. A bulletin board in the main hall of the school will remind students who are not involved in physical education of important and exciting happenings in the program. The bulletin board should attract and hold the attention of observers. The message should be immediately apparent to viewers and should stimulate interest. Do not put too much detail on the bulletin board.

Print or write in large letters. Visibility from 20 to 25 ft is a good guideline. To attract attention, use catchy titles such as Quiz, Mystery Pictures, or Unusual Facts, or use humor. The bulletin board should give specific dates and times, who to contact, and the names of program directors. Clippings and photographs are always of interest to students. Bright-colored paper, colored yarn, cutout letters, and three-dimensional designs are also effective in catching the eye of the observer.

Bulletin boards and posters should be changed often (at least every four to six weeks). If they go unchanged, they go unobserved after a while. Make sure that student accomplishments are displayed on the bulletin boards from time to time. In summary, make sure the bulletin boards list the five Ws: who, what, why, when, and where.

PARENT INVOLVEMENT

Invite parents to a physical education awards assembly or banquet. This is a good time to present physical fitness achievement awards. Another award that can be issued is the improvement award. This award would be within reach of all students and could be based on percent improvement. For example, if activities are listed on a contract basis, students could be pretested to see which skills they performed at passing standards. Criteria could then be set, such as "Increase the number of skills you know by 25%." Awards would be given to those students meeting the criteria. Figure 14.2 is a letter that could be sent to parents of students who earn the award.

COMMUNITY RELATIONS

Community organizations are interested in school instruction, and it is important that information about physical education be included in the programs and meetings of these organizations. Examples of such community organizations are coordinating councils, service clubs, youth clubs, and parent-teacher groups. These groups are always looking for speakers at their luncheon meetings. The program chair should be contacted and given an explanation of the type of physical education curriculum offered. A short description of the program can then be forwarded, along with a form such as the one in Figure 14.3. After all arrangements have been made, it is most important to deliver a well-planned and well-executed program. The program should focus on the learning accomplished through the current physical education curriculum.

WRITING TO NEWSPAPERS

The local newspaper can be the physical education program's best friend. The types of skills performed in the program are visual and will create an impact in the newspaper. Local newspapers are often looking for articles that will fill in pages and stimulate interest. The following are guidelines to help make the news release more acceptable to the news editor.

Type all articles double-spaced on white paper with wide margins. Some room should also be left

Figure 14.2. Letter to parents announcing award

Dursthill Junior High School
850 Fairview Avenue
Picante, AZ

Dear Dad and Mom,

It may surprise you to learn that I have won an achievement award. This award will be given to me during the awards banquet (assembly) on Friday, November 21, at 7:00 P.M. I hope you will be able to attend, as this historic occasion deserves your presence.

The cost for the banquet is $4.00 per person. This is a small amount to spend on such a fine daughter.

Come on, Dad and Mom! Jog out of the house and contribute to character development.

Your daughter,

at the top of the page for editing purposes. Be sure to include a name and telephone number so the editor can easily reach the contributor if a question arises. Keep paragraphs to five or fewer typewritten lines, one to three sentences per paragraph, and 10 to 20 words per sentence.

Report facts, and if you are unsure about any facts, verify the information. Begin the article with a lead sentence or paragraph that gives the who, what, why, when, where, and how of the story. Place the single most important point of the article in the lead paragraph, and arrange the rest of the facts in descending order of importance. Make the last few paragraphs short so they can be cut without affecting the story significantly. Try always to make the story emphasize the educational value of the physical education program.

When possible, include photographs with the news release. The pictures should be close-ups that show faces and emotion. Photographs should also be action-oriented and illustrate phases of the program. Type captions and attach them to the photos. Indicate who is to receive credit for the photo (e.g., "photograph by . . .").

PHYSICAL EDUCATION PUBLIC INFORMATION (PEPI)

The Physical Education Public Information project is a continuing project of the AAHPERD. The project identifies coordinators in every state who are responsible for interpreting the profession through the media. The focus of PEPI is to tell the public about the positive benefits of physical education. The organization has attempted to communicate such benefits as the contribution of physical activity to academic achievement, the effectiveness of regular exercise as low-cost health insurance, and the importance of developing skills that will last a lifetime. PEPI regularly sends advertisements to coordinators for the purpose of having them inserted in journals, brochures, and newspapers.

DEMONSTRATION PROGRAMS

Demonstration programs can attract a large number of parents. The activities should illustrate the attainment of the program objectives and also

PHYSICAL EDUCATION PROGRAM REQUEST

1. Name of organization _____

2. Location _____
           Place   Address   Room

3. Time: _____ From _____ To _____
         Day   Date   Time of Program

4. Topic preferred _____

5. Type or program desired (speaker, films, etc.) _____

6. Questions and answers, if desired: Yes ___ No ___ (Please check)

7. Background or interests of group _____

8. Chairperson introducing _____

9. Estimated size of audience (circle): 1–15, 16–20, 50–100, over 100

10. If film is involved: Can room be darkened? _____

    Is screen available? _____ Size and type of screen _____

    Type of projector _____ Microphone available _____

    Other facilities _____

11. Other factors, requests, suggestions _____

    _____

    _____

    _____

    Name of person making request _____

    Position in organization _____

    Address _____

    Telephone _____

Please telephone in request and follow up by forwarding this form to:

Name _____

Address _____

Phone _____

Figure 14.3. Request form for a physical education program be typical of the type of experiences that occur regularly. If rehearsal is going to take place, it should only be to keep the program moving smoothly. A demonstration program need not offer perfect performances. In fact, the spontaneous and natural appearance of a program will usually stimulate more response and appreciation from parents.

As many students as possible should be included in the program. Parents will usually not attend if their youngster is not included. Specialty numbers can be integrated in the program to show off outstanding performances. A printed program that includes all of the names of participants is desirable and makes all of the students feel important. If possible, ask someone unrelated to the program, such as the principal, to open the demonstration and welcome parents. The program should be fast-moving and take 45 to 60 min to complete. Parents are interested primarily in seeing their youngster perform and will not sit for much longer than 1 hr.

It is usually wise not to include competitive contests that cause some to be declared losers. Focus instead on educational performances that show skill development. Since all students can perform physical fitness activities, including this type of activity in the program is meaningful.

Summary

Public relations are important if teachers are to expect parents and the community to support the physical education program. No school curriculum area can stand by itself. Teachers must become intimately involved in improving the image of physical education instructors and in preparing instructional and promotional material. How teachers dress, talk, and interact creates an image of the typical physical education teacher. Public relations demands hard work and a concern for the future of the profession.

Reference

Pangrazi, R. P. 1982. Physical education, self-concept, and achievement. *JOPERD* 53(9): 16–18.

PART IV

THE INSTRUCTIONAL COMPONENT:
Activities and Information
for Implementing the Curriculum

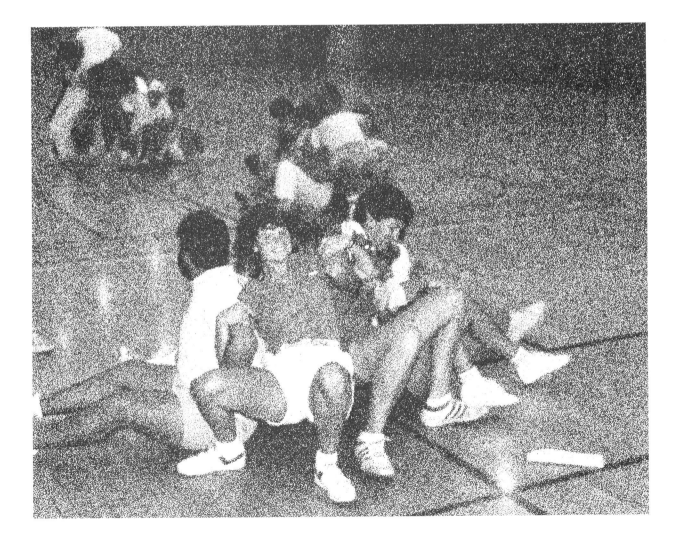

Chapter 15

Wellness for a Lifetime:

Activities for Instruction

The need for teaching students how to maintain personal wellness for a lifetime becomes apparent when one examines the skyrocketing costs of minimal health care. Health insurance policies cost 5% to 10% of an individual's gross income. A short stay in the hospital may incur a bill for thousands of dollars, yet in spite of runaway costs, Americans continue to pay and put little or no effort into maintaining a healthy life-style.

Human wellness is a state of health that allows an individual to participate in life to its fullest. Having the energy and enthusiasm to undertake activities of all types after a full day's work is characteristic of people who are well. An individual who is well is not only free of sickness or other malady, but is happy, vibrant, and able to solve personal problems.

Teaching students how to achieve a lasting state of wellness lends credibility to the physical education profession. For many years, physical educators were seen solely as teachers of physical skills who had little concern for the knowledge and comprehension involved in physical performance. The

various personalities and unique needs of the student participants were often ignored by teachers who appeared to be concerned only about the product. (Learn the skill or else!) The age-old argument of product versus process can be moderated by teaching the process of developing physical wellness, for wellness is a process. There are no trophies or other extrinsic rewards for achieving it. Wellness is personal. When it is achieved, the individual is directly rewarded by an enhanced lifestyle. Teachers can no longer ignore the importance of teaching students the what, why, and how of maintaining a healthy profile. Maintaining wellness must be viewed as a primary objective of secondary school physical education.

Why teach wellness in the physical education setting? Teachers are often skeptical about teaching material other than physical skill activities, yet the ability to develop and maintain personal wellness will remain with an individual for a lifetime. This is one of the few gifts teachers can offer to students that can be used throughout a life-span. Achieving wellness is unique and personal. What is useful to one person may be superfluous to another. Teachers must therefore teach students how to search for wellness and then maintain it once found.

At present, the credibility of the physical education profession is strained. Teachers often offer students skills and activities that they will never use again. For example, students may spend 9 weeks each year from junior high school through the sophomore year of high school involved in football. This is equivalent to 36 weeks of football, or one school year spent learning how to play football. The possibility is strong that few of these individuals will play football after graduation from high school. Few, if any, people play football after age 25, yet one year of physical education was spent playing and learning a sport that becomes literally useless in maintaining a healthy life-style in adulthood. Small wonder that many adults believe that they learned little in physical education to help them after graduation. The authors are not belittling football or asking for elimination of the sport. The point is that physical education programs have often shown an inadequate concern for teaching students the skills that are useful after they leave school.

Teaching students how to maintain a state of wellness makes activity purposeful. Students begin to understand why certain activities and games are selected in place of others. Selection of activities for a lifetime of physical involvement can only occur after students have been exposed to a wide range of instructional units. A systematic approach to curriculum development is critical in assuring that students know the many alternatives and pathways to personal fitness and health.

INTEGRATING WELLNESS INSTRUCTION INTO THE PROGRAM

Paramount to all instruction dealing with wellness is an emphasis on self-responsibility for maintaining a healthy life-style. Regardless of what students are taught, if an emphasis is not placed on teaching students how to make personal decisions, little will have been gained. Teachers need to remember that most students will do what is asked of them when they are in the school setting. The critical point is teaching students the problem-solving skills that will enable them to make meaningful decisions throughout life, when teachers are no longer present.

At the secondary school level, teachers should take a multifaceted approach to developing units of instruction dealing with wellness. The first step is to ensure that students understand how the body functions. This involves understanding the anatomy of the body, the physiological functioning of the body during exercise, and the mechanical principles involved in movement. It is beyond the scope of this text to list all the information that students should digest and comprehend. An outline and an instructional unit in each of these areas will be offered. References are listed at the end of the chapter for instruction in greater depth.

Students may receive instruction about the systems of the body in health education classes. In most cases, however, material covered in those classes does not deal with exercise and the impact it has on the body. Learning about how the body reacts and adapts to exercise is of utmost importance, and students probably will not receive this information anywhere else in the school environment.

The second step in presenting units of instruction dealing with wellness is to delineate which concepts students need to understand. This provides direction for both teacher and students. The concepts should give students a general idea of what is important and what areas must be understood to achieve proper functioning. The concepts should help the instructor organize the material to be presented. Students should be given an outline that they can follow. The concepts, when taken as a whole, offer a framework to help students make personal decisions about health maintenance. This approach is in contrast with giving students a set of objectives that must be learned and that leave little room for student input and inquiry.

The third step in organizing units of instruction in this area is to present mini-laboratory experiences that apply the concepts and bring them to life. These learning activities can be used to add substance to the instructional concepts. The laboratory experiences are simple, yet illustrate clearly how the body functions in different settings. Many of these experiences can be done in 5 to 10 min by a whole class. They are excellent rainy day activities, or students can do them as homework. Students should be encouraged to develop a notebook of activities and lab experiences that they can use for a lifetime.

The authors have offered varying curriculum models for grades 7–12 in Chapter 5. Each model contains a unit of instruction on wellness and self-testing. This approach should be analyzed carefully and considered when developing a comprehensive physical education curriculum. It is strongly recommended that instruction be offered at each grade level in this important area. The instruction should be clearly devoted to developing wellness for a lifetime, and should receive instructional emphasis on a par with other units in the physical education curriculum.

INSTRUCTIONAL STRATEGIES FOR TEACHING WELLNESS

Physical education plays a large role in enhancing the fitness and skill levels of students in order to allow them opportunities for developing an active life-style. A program goal should be helping young people to make responsible decisions about wellness and its impact on their lives. Throughout life, people are faced with many decisions that may have a positive or negative impact on their level of wellness. The ability to make responsible choices depends on a wide range of factors: understanding one's feelings and personal values, the ability to cope with stress and with problems in general, the impact of various factors on health, and practice in using decision-making skills.

DEVELOPING AWARENESS AND DECISION-MAKING SKILLS

The focus should be on helping students to view themselves as total beings. Stability occurs when all parts fit together in a smooth and consistent fashion. When a problem occurs, the balance of physiology, thinking, and function is disrupted. Individuals must then use their knowledge, coping ability, and decision-making skills to restore the equilibrium associated with personal stability. Teachers can try to help students understand their feelings, values, and attitudes, and the impact that all of these have on coping and decision-making ability. Each of these areas will be discussed in turn.

SELF-CONCEPT

Self-concept is defined as the total perception an individual has of self. Self-concept is enhanced when the individual has a strong, positive feeling of belonging and a sense of worth. These attitudes can be fostered by providing activities that focus on various themes including

1. A person recognizes that there are many individuals, yet each of us is unique.
2. A person feels loved and can love.
3. A person is able to recognize and cope with feelings and emotions.
4. A person can function in a group, yet also be comfortable alone.
5. A person likes to and is able to do many things.
6. A person is able to relate successfully to others.

A person who has a healthy self-image will be better able to make a decision in the presence of peer pressure. Individuals who feel positive about themselves are less influenced by peer pressure than persons with a poor self-concept.

Through the process of education, each student should be made to feel important and worthwhile. Youngsters will realize that they are not perfect and that change is desirable. The identification of personal strengths and weaknesses can offer direction for self-growth and for understanding personal limitations. When dealing with areas of self-concept and personal worth, students should be comfortable in expressing feelings. They should feel free to ask questions without fear of ridicule or embarrassment. Discussions should be positive and criticism constructive. As students develop more positive feelings about themselves, their ability to make responsible decisions will improve. They will be prepared to make decisions in their own best interests and in the best interests of their fellow human beings.

COPING SKILLS

Coping is the ability to deal with problems successfully. Learning to cope with life's problems is dependent on and interrelated with knowledge of self, decision-making skills, and the ability to relate to others. Specific skills that deal with coping include the following:

1. Admit that a problem exists and face it. It is impossible to cope with a problem if the problem is not recognized.
2. Define the problem and who owns it. Individuals must identify what needs to be coped with and decide if the problem is theirs or belongs to others.
3. List alternative solutions to the problem. A basic step in decision making, problem solving, and coping is to identify what alternatives are open to a person in a given situation.
4. Predict consequences for oneself and others. After the alternatives are identified, weigh the

potential consequences of each, and then rank them in order of preference.

5. Identify and consult sources of help. All sources should be considered. In order to do this, teachers should introduce students to some of the resources available and explain how to locate helpful sources.

6. Experiment with a solution and evaluate the results. If the decision did not produce satisfactory results, another alternative can often be tried. Evaluation of results also allows people to keep track of their ability to come up with satisfying solutions.

DECISION-MAKING SKILLS

Youngsters are faced with many situations about which decisions must be made. Making decisions is something everyone does every day, often without thinking. Because it is a common process, it receives little attention until a person is faced with an important decision that has long-term consequences.

Although the schools attempt to help students learn how to make personally satisfying decisions, a major portion of a teacher's time involves developing information or supplying it to students. Obtaining information, although extremely important, is only one segment of the decision-making process. A question that should be asked is "If you are going to provide information to others, what do you want them to do with that information?" Students should be given the opportunities to put information to use.

Decision making is defined as a process in which a person selects from two or more possible choices. A decision does not occur unless there is more than one course of action, alternative, or possibility to consider. If a choice exists, the process of deciding may then be used. Decision making enables the individual to reason through life situations, to solve problems, and, to some extent, to direct behavior.

Often there are no "right" answers or outcomes of the decision-making process. The decision is instead judged on the effective use of a process that results in satisfying consequences. This distinguishes decision making from problem solving. Problem solving usually identifies one best or correct solution for everyone involved.

When making decisions, it is important for students to consider each of the following steps:

1. **Gather Information.** If meaningful choices are going to be made, gathering all the available information is important. Information should be gathered from as many sources as possible. Students generally consider information valid when they see that it comes from many different sources and that they are allowed to view both sides of an issue. Teachers too often present students with information that supports only one point of view.

2. **Consider the Available Choices.** The next step is to consider all the available choices. This is an important step if students are to realize that they have many different possibilities from which to choose and that their choices will influence the direction of their life. It does not make sense to consider possibilities that students have no chance of selecting. Many choices have been made for students in the school setting, and they sometimes come to believe that others will make all the decisions for them and that they, in turn, bear no responsibility for their successes or failures.

3. **Analyze the Consequences of the Choices.** When the various choices are delineated, students must consider the consequences that accompany each choice. If the consequences are ignored, an unwise choice may be made that is detrimental to one's health. Making wise decisions about wellness demands that students be made aware of consequences. They should understand some of the reasons why people may choose to smoke or drink, even though the consequences are negative. The most important role of the teacher is helping students understand positive and negative consequences without moralizing or telling students how to think.

4. **Make a Decision and Implement It.** When all of the information has been gathered, students must make a decision and implement it in their life-style. The decisions will be personal to each student and need not be revealed to others.

Skillful decision makers have greater control over their lives because they can reduce the amount of uncertainty surrounding their choices and limit the degree to which chance or their peers determine their future.

Two individuals may face a similar decision, but because each person is different and places differing values on the outcomes, each decision will be unique. Learning decision-making skills increases the possibility that each person will achieve what he or she most values.

Decisions also have limits. Each decision is necessarily limited by what a person is capable of doing, by what a person is willing to do, and by the environment in which the decision is being made. Important to the development of these skills is the environment in which they are practiced. A nonjudgmental atmosphere is most productive. Since there is no "right" answer, the person making a decision should be free to select from any of the available choices and be willing to accept the probable consequences and results.

LEADING DISCUSSION SESSIONS

The success of discussions depends on how effectively the teacher is able to establish and maintain the integrity and structure of the lesson and the students' psychological freedom. Integrity and structure mean that all students are dealing with the same issue in a thoughtful and responsible way. Psychological freedom means that individual students participate to the degree that is most comfortable for them, (1) commenting or refraining from commenting when they choose to do so, (2) responding to directed questions or choosing to pass for the time being, (3) agreeing or disagreeing with what others in the group have said, or (4) deciding what data they need, if any, and asking for that data. This demands certain teacher behavior to establish a meaningful environment. A brief description of necessary teaching behaviors follows.

STRUCTURING

The purpose of structuring is to create a climate that is conducive to open communication by all parties. This is accomplished by outlining expectations and role relationships for both teacher and student. Structuring includes any of the following:

1. Establish the lesson climate at the beginning of the lesson by providing an explanation of what the student and teacher will be doing and how they will work together.
2. Maintain the established lesson structure by not allowing students to be pressured to respond or to be put down for their ideas.
3. Add to or modify the lesson structure estab-

lished at the beginning of the lesson. For example, this may involve changing to small-group sessions, rather than a total class discussion.

FOCUS SETTING

The purpose of focus setting is to establish an explicit and common topic or issue for discussion. Since this teaching behavior is used in different circumstances, the behavior can be formulated in different ways:

1. The teacher can present a topic, usually in the form of a question, to the group for their discussion.
2. The teacher can use focus setting to restate the original question at some point during the lesson or to shift to a new discussion topic because students have indicated that they have finished discussing the original question.
3. The teacher can use focus setting to bring the discussion back to the topic when a student unknowingly shifts to a new topic.
4. The teacher can use focus setting to label a discussion question presented by a student as a new topic and to allow discussion of that topic in place of a previous one.

CLARIFYING

The purpose in using a **clarifying** teaching behavior is to invite a student to help the teacher better understand the substance or content of the student's comment. Whenever possible, the clarifying teaching behavior should give the student some indication of what it is that the teacher does not understand. In addition, the behavior should be formulated in a way that puts the burden on the teacher for not being able to understand, rather than implying that the student was unclear or inadequate in any way. Clarifying is used only when the teacher does not understand. The teacher does not assume the responsibility of clarifying for the students.

ACKNOWLEDGING

The purpose in using an **acknowledging** teaching behavior is to let a student who is talking to the teacher know that the teacher understands what has been said and that the student has made a contribution to the discussion. Unlike most other teaching behaviors, this one can be implemented through nonverbal as well as verbal means.

How an acknowledging teaching behavior is worded and when it is and is not used must be considered carefully. This behavior is intended to be a nonjudgmental way of saying, "I understand." To use acknowledging only when the teacher understands and agrees, but to do something else when the teacher understands and disagrees, is a serious misinterpretation of the purpose and function of this teaching behavior.

TEACHER SILENCE

The purpose of teacher silence is to communicate to students through nonverbal means that they are responsible for initiating and perpetuating the discussion. Teacher silence is used only in response to student silence. It protects the students' rights and responsibility to make their own decisions about the topic being discussed. In one sense, this teaching behavior is a nonbehavior.

UNDERSTANDING THE MAJOR SYSTEMS OF THE BODY

A basic understanding of how the body functions is important if students are to learn how to maintain a healthy organism. The three major systems discussed here are the skeletal, muscular, and cardiorespiratory system. A brief discussion of each is provided with concepts and suggested learning activities offered to enhance student understanding.

THE SKELETAL SYSTEM

The skeletal system is the framework of the body. The bones act as a system of levers and are linked together at various points called joints. The joints are held together by ligaments, which are tough and unable to stretch. In a joint injury when the bones are moved beyond the normal limits, it is the ligaments that are most often injured.

Joints that are freely movable are called synovial joints. Synovial fluid is secreted to lubricate the joint and reduce friction. A thin layer of cartilage also reduces friction at the ends of the bones. A disk, or meniscus, forms a pad between many of the weight-bearing joints for the purpose of absorbing shock. When the cartilage is damaged, the joint becomes less able to move easily, and arthritis often occurs.

Muscular activity increases the stress placed on bones. The bones respond to this added stress by increasing in diameter, becoming more dense (and more resistant to breakage), and by reorganizing their internal structure, which offers more bone strength (Rarick 1973). The bones act as a mineral reserve for the body and can become deformed as a result of dietary deficiency. The bones also can change shape due to stress applied to them on a regular basis. This may give athletes, whose skeletal systems are conditioned, a mechanical advantage in performing certain skills. The skeletal system is not a static system, but changes and adapts in response to the demands placed on it.

The bones are connected to make three different types of levers, with the joint acting as the fulcrum (Figure 15.1). The muscles apply force to the joints, while the body weight or an external object provides the resistance. The levers are classified as first-, second-, or third-class levers. Examples of third-class lever actions are the movement of the biceps muscle to flex the forearm at the elbow joint, the sideways movement of the upper arm at the shoulder joint by the deltoid muscle, and the flexion of the lower leg at the knee joint by the hamstring muscles. A second-class lever occurs where the gastrocnemius muscle raises the weight of the body onto the toes. The forearm is an example of a first-class lever when it is being extended at the elbow joint (fulcrum) by the triceps muscle.

Basic Concepts

1. The skeletal system consists of 206 bones and determines the external appearance of the body. This network of bones is somewhat malleable and can be reshaped, made denser, and stronger.

2. Joints are where two or more bones are fastened together by ligaments to allow movement that is restricted by the range of motion. The range of motion at various joints can be increased by regularly performing flexibility exercises. The most flexible people have the greatest range of motion at a combination of joints.

3. Bones are held together by ligaments and muscle tissue. The stronger the muscles become, the stronger the ligaments and tendons become in response. This makes a stronger joint, which is more resistant to injury.

4. Attractive posture occurs when the bones are in good alignment. Alignment depends on the muscular system to hold the bones in correct position. Poor posture occurs when the muscles

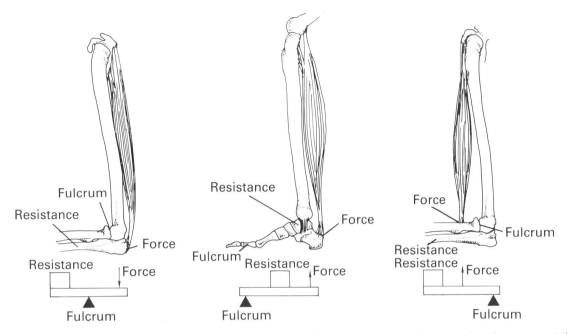

Figure 15.1. Types of levers in human joints (reprinted from *Dynamic Physical Education for Elementary School Children*, 7th ed. by V. P. Dauer and R. P. Pangrazi, 1983. Minneapolis: Burgess Publishing Co., p. 97)

are weak and increased stress is placed on the joints.

5. The bones meet at joints to establish levers. Movement occurs when muscles apply force (by contraction only) to the bones.

6. The attachment of the muscle to the bone determines the mechanical advantage that can be gained at the joint. Generally, those muscles that attach farther from the joint can generate more force. There is, however, a trade-off. When the attachment is farther from the joint, the amount of speed that can be generated is less, and vice versa.

7. The human body has three types of lever arrangement. These are classified by the fulcrum, force, and resistance. The majority of levers in the body are third-class levers, in which the point of force (produced by the muscles) lies between the fulcrum (joint) and the point of resistance (the weight of the object to be moved).

Suggested Learning Activities

1. Identify and locate the bones of major significance in movement. (Approximately 167 bones are capable of moving.) Some that can be assigned are:
   a. Arm-shoulder girdle—radius, ulna, humerus, scapula, and clavicle

   b. Back-pelvis—spinal column, pelvis, coccyx
   c. Thigh-leg—femur, tibia, fibula, patella
   d. Chest—sternum, ribs

2. Identify the type of movement possible at selected joints. Various terms should be used to identify the movements (e.g., extension, flexion, adduction, abduction, pronation, supination, plantar flexion, and so forth).

3. Diagram and list the types of levers found in the body. Illustrate the force, fulcrum, and resistance points. Identify muscle attachments and the impact of such in terms of generating force or speed in movement.

4. Obtain animal bones and analyze the various parts of the bone. Identify the bone marrow, growth plates, epiphyses, ligaments, tendons, muscle origins and attachments, and cartilage.

5. Study outdated X-ray films of children to see the different rates of ossification. Note differences in bone shape and structure between individuals.

THE MUSCULAR SYSTEM (Figure 15.2)

Muscles apply force to the bones to create movement, and always create movement through contraction. When one set of muscles contracts, the other set relaxes. Muscles are always paired. The muscle (or group of muscles) that relaxes while

Figure 15.2.   The muscular system

another set contracts is called the *antagonistic* muscle. The muscles located on the anterior side of the body are flexors and reduce the angle of a joint while the body is standing. Muscles on the posterior side of the body produce extension and a return from flexion.

People are born with two types of muscle fiber. These are commonly referred to as slow twitch and fast twitch fibers. Slow twitch fibers respond efficiently to aerobic activity, while fast twitch fibers are suited to highly demanding anaerobic activity. This explains, in part, why people perform physical activities at varying levels. People are born with a set ratio of fast and slow twitch fibers. Those with a higher ratio of slow twitch fibers are better able to perform in endurance activities; those with a greater percentage of fast twitch fibers might excel in activities of high intensity and short duration.

Strength gains are made when muscles are overloaded, and overload occurs when people do more work than they performed previously. This means that more weight must be lifted on a regular basis if gains are to occur. Exercises should overload as many muscle groups as possible in order to ensure total body development. Both the flexors and extensors should receive equal amounts of overload exercise so a proper balance between the two muscle groups is maintained. Muscular strength appears to be an important factor in performing motor skills.

Muscular exercises should apply resistance through the full range of motion in order to maintain maximum flexibility. It is recommended that strenuous exercise such as weight lifting be done on an every-other-day basis so the muscles have an opportunity to heal and regenerate. Maintaining muscular strength throughout life is important. If exercises are not done to maintain strength, atrophy will occur rapidly. It has been shown that the average American will gain 1 lb of additional weight per year after age 25. This can result in 30 lb of excess weight by age 55. During the same period, the bone and muscle mass decreases by approximately 0.5 lb per year, which results in a total gain of 45 lb of fat (Wilmore 1977).

Basic Concepts

1. Muscles contract and apply force by pulling only. They never push. When movement in the opposite direction is desired, the antagonistic muscles must contract.

2. A reduction in joint angle is called flexion; an increase in the joint angle is extension. Generally, the flexor muscles are on the anterior side of the body, and the extensors are on the posterior side.

3. Exercises should focus on developing the flexors and extensors equally if proper posture and joint integrity are to be maintained.

4. Muscles can be attached directly to the bone. A tendon, such as the Achilles, can also be the source of attachment. The origin of the muscle is the fixed portion of the muscle; the insertion is the moving part of the muscle.

5. Progression involving gradual overloading of the muscles is necessary to increase muscular strength and endurance. Males find that regular exercise can cause an increase in the girth of a muscle. Females rarely attain similar results from strenuous exercise. This is because the male hormone testosterone is responsible for the increase in muscle size and is present in greater quantity in males.

6. Different types of training are necessary for developing muscular strength and muscular endurance. Larger amounts of weight and fewer repetitions will cause a greater increase in strength; less weight and more repetitions will enhance muscular endurance.

7. There are different types of muscular contractions: isometric (without movement), isotonic (with movement), and eccentric (movement that lengthens the muscle from a contracted state). The contraction most commonly used for developing strength and endurance is the isotonic.

8. Static stretching can increase flexibility. Flexibility (the range of motion at a joint) increases due to a lengthening of connective tissue that surrounds the muscle fibers.

9. Muscle soreness occurs when the work load is applied too intensely. The soreness probably results from muscle tissue damage. Static stretching will alleviate the pain somewhat and will help prepare the body for continued activity.

10. The principle of specificity is important in developing muscular strength. Only those muscles that are exercised will develop. If the goal is stronger leg muscles, they must be exercised. There is no carry-over from other muscle groups (i.e., strengthening the arms will not cause an increase in leg strength).

Suggested Learning Activities

1. Identify major muscle groups and their functions at the joints. Discuss the origins and insertions of the muscles.

2. Study muscles from animals under a microscope. Show stained biopsies of human muscle fiber that reveal fast and slow twitch muscle fibers.

3. Perform some skill-related activities that might reveal which individuals appear to be endowed with more fast twitch than slow twitch fibers. Examples might be the standing long jump, vertical jump, and an endurance activity such as the mile run.

4. Develop a personal strength profile for students. Measure the strength of various muscle groups using a dynamometer and set goals for well-rounded strength development.

5. Perform an action research project. As an example, pretest students for strength and divide them into two equal groups. Have one group train for 12 weeks using muscular endurance techniques while the other trains for 12 weeks using muscular strength techniques. Retest and compare the results of the two groups after training.

6. Identify various sports and games, and determine what type of training will achieve maximum results.

7. Discuss certain exercises that should be avoided, such as straight-leg sit-ups and deep-knee bends.

8. Have students identify why backache occurs in over 70% of Americans. Prescribe a program of exercise that could remedy the majority of these back problems.

THE CARDIORESPIRATORY SYSTEM

The cardiorespiratory system consists of the heart (Figure 15.3), lungs, arteries, capillaries, and veins.

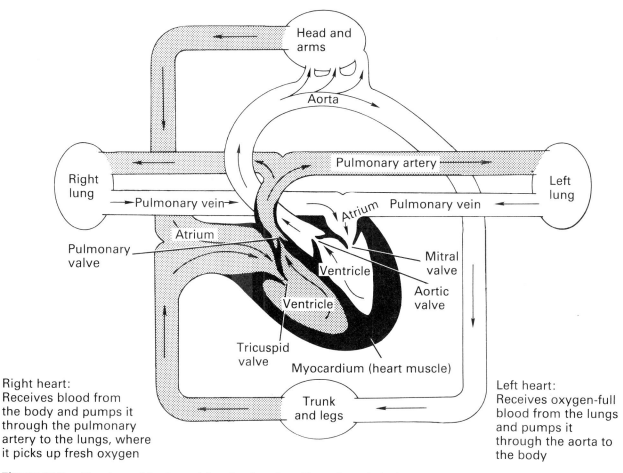

Figure 15.3. Structure of the heart (after the American Heart Association)

The heart is a muscle that pumps blood throughout the circulatory system—arteries, capillaries, and veins. The coronary arteries bring the heart a rich supply of blood. Heart disease occurs when fatty deposits block or seriously impede the flow of blood to the heart.

The heart has two chambers and is, in effect, divided in half with each side providing different functions. The left side of the heart pumps blood carrying nutrients and oxygen to the body through the arteries to the capillaries, where the nutrients and oxygen are exchanged for waste products and carbon dioxide. The waste-carrying blood is returned through the veins to the right side of the heart, from which the blood is routed through the lungs to discharge the carbon dioxide and pick up oxygen. This oxygen-renewed blood returns to the left side of the heart to complete the circuit.

Each time the heart beats, it pumps blood through both chambers. The beat is called the pulse; its impact travels through the body. Pulse is measured in number of beats per minute. A pulse rate of 75 means that the heart is beating 75 times each minute. The cardiac output is determined by the pulse rate and the stroke volume, which is the amount of blood discharged by each beat.

The pulse is measured by placing the two middle fingers of the right hand on the thumb side of the subject's wrist while the subject is seated. Taking the pulse at the wrist is usually preferable to using the carotid artery, because pressure on the carotid can decrease blood flow to the brain.

The respiratory system includes the entryways (nose and mouth), the trachea (or windpipe), the primary bronchi, and the lungs. Figure 15.4 shows components of the respiratory system.

Breathing consists of inhaling and exhaling air. Air contains 21% oxygen, which is necessary for life. Inspiration is assisted by muscular contraction, and expiration is accomplished by a relaxing of the muscles. Inspiration occurs when the intercostal muscles and the diaphragm contract. This increases the size of the chest cavity, and expansion of the lungs causes air to flow in as a result of reduced air pressure. When the muscles are relaxed, the size of the chest cavity is reduced, the pressure is increased, and air flows from the lungs.

The primary function of the lungs is to provide oxygen to the cells on demand. The amount of oxygen needed will vary depending on activity level. When an individual exercises strenuously, the rate of respiration increases in order to bring more oxygen to tissues. If the amount of oxygen carried to the cells is adequate to maintain the level of activ-

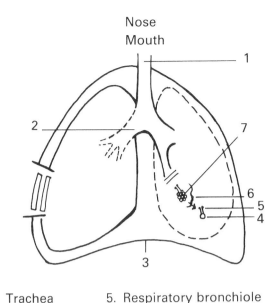

1. Trachea
2. Bronchus
3. Diaphragm
4. Alveolus
5. Respiratory bronchiole
6. Alveolar sacs
7. Terminal bronchiole

Figure 15.4.   The respiratory system (modified from *Fitness: A Lifetime Commitment*, 2nd ed. by D. K. Miller and T. E. Allen, 1982. Minneapolis: Burgess Publishing Co., p. 157)

ity, the activity is termed aerobic, or endurance exercise. Examples are walking, jogging, and bicycling for distance. If, because of high-intensity activity, the body is not capable of bringing enough oxygen to the cells, the body will continue to operate for a short time without oxygen. This results in an oxygen debt, which must be repaid at a later time. In this case, the activity is termed anaerobic exercise.

The respiratory rate will return to normal after exercise. The recovery rate will be faster if the oxygen debt built up during exercise was a small one. An individual has recovered from the exertion of exercise when blood pressure, heart rate, and ventilation rate have returned to preexercise levels.

Basic Concepts

1. The heart is a muscular organ that must be exercised like other muscles to maintain maximum efficiency. The most effective heart exercise is activity of low intensity and long duration, which is aerobic in nature.

2. Pulse rate varies among individuals. It does slow down at rest, however, as a result of aerobic training. Resting pulse rate is sometimes used as an indicator of the state of training.

3. Cardiorespiratory training appears to decrease the susceptibility of individuals to heart disease. The younger one begins maintaining fitness, the better the opportunity to retard the onset of cardiovascular disease.

4. Aerobic endurance activities (jogging, brisk walking, bicycling) appear to change the chemistry of the blood and lower the cholesterol level. There are two types of lipoproteins, high density (HDL) and low density (LDL), and exercise appears to increase the ratio of HDL to LDL. This is important, since HDL seems to prevent harmful plaque from building up in the arteries.

5. Hypokinetic diseases are somewhat influenced by sex, heredity, race, and age. Many of these diseases can be prevented, however, by controlling factors such as smoking, obesity, inactivity, improper diet, and high blood pressure.

6. The heart rate must reach the training state if cardiorespiratory benefits are to be realized. (See the learning activities for calculating the training state on pages 260–261.

7. The heart grows stronger and larger when the body is subjected to lengthy bouts of aerobic activity (30 min or more). A larger and stronger heart results in a greater stroke volume per beat.

8. When concerned about weight control, maintaining as much muscle mass as possible is important. Severe dieting often results not only in a loss of fat cells, but in a loss of muscle tissue as well. Since muscle tissue burns twice as many calories as fat tissue, it is important in weight control as well as for cosmetic and performance reasons.

9. The vital capacity of the lungs can be increased through regular aerobic exercise. This makes the oxygen exchange system more efficient.

Suggested Learning Activities

1. Discuss the acronym DANGER in regard to cardiovascular disease.

   D on't smoke
   A void foods high in fat and cholesterol
   N ow control high blood pressure and diabetes
   G et medical examinations at least every other year
   E xercise moderately each day
   R educe and lose weight if carrying excess fat

2. Compare resting pulse rates among students. Look for differences between sexes, ages, and states of training. Try taking the resting pulse rate in different positions.

3. Examine the impact that exercise has on heart rate. Record the resting heart rate. Have each person run in place for 1 min. Take the pulse rate immediately and record it. Continue taking the pulse rate at 2-min intervals three to five times to demonstrate recovery rate. Discuss individual differences in maximum heart rate and recovery heart rate.

4. Teach students how to take blood pressure. Exercise for 1 min as described above and monitor the effect that exercise has on blood pressure.

5. Demonstrate the effects on the cardiovascular system of carrying excess weight. Identify two students who weigh the same, are of the same sex, are in similar training states, and who do not carry excess weight. Monitor their resting heart rate before starting. Ask one person to perform the upcoming task while carrying two 10-lb weights. Set two markers 20 yd apart, and have both students run back and forth between the cones ten times. Immediately after they finish, monitor their heart rate and recovery rate as described above. Discuss the fact that excessive body fat is merely dead weight that must be moved, and note how the excess weight decreases physical performance.

6. Compare heart rates after 2–3-min bouts of different types of exercise. Experiment with walking, jogging, sprinting, rope-jumping, bicycling, and calisthenics. Discuss the differences.

7. Calculate the heart rate zone that should be maintained to achieve the training effect and to ensure that the individual is not under- or over-exercising. To do this, first determine the estimated maximum heart rate by taking 220 minus the student's age, then multiply the difference by 60% and 80%. An example for a student who is 15 follows:

$$220 - 15 = 205$$
$$60\% \text{ of } 205 = 123$$
$$80\% \text{ of } 205 = 164$$

The heart rate training zone for this student would be a heartbeat (or pulse rate) between 123 and 164. Have the class try different modes of exercise and see if they raise their heart rate into the training zone.

8. Identify resting respiratory rates. Have students try different types of exercise and compare the effects each has on the respiratory rate.

ROADBLOCKS TO WELLNESS

The following areas are important for students to understand. Wellness involves knowing what activities to avoid as well as what to do. Teaching about these activities should not be done by preaching and telling students what they should or should not do. Emphasis should be placed instead on showing students the pros and cons of various practices and the consequences of making certain decisions. The ultimate decision and responsibility rest with the student, not the teacher.

The major areas to be discussed in this section are stress, nutrition and weight control, substance abuse, and personal safety. All are areas in which behavior can be modified to enhance the quality of life. Students will make decisions in these areas that may dramatically affect how they live and, sometimes, whether they will live. They should become well versed in the knowledge that concerns each area.

STRESS

Stress is the body's reaction to certain situations in life. Everyone is under some stress. Stress, by itself, is probably not harmful, but how one handles stress is critical in determining the impact it will have on one's life. It is important for teachers to remember that students may be under a great deal of stress. Often, students are seen as carefree and without worries. Quite the opposite is usually the case. Students live under the stress of other's expectations, peer pressure, sexual mores, and the necessity of becoming an independent being. If teachers view students as being subject to stress, they can begin to deal with them in ways that alleviate possible stressors and allow for stress release. In this way, teachers can have an impact on the students' self-concept and how they view the world.

Psychologically, stress may take the form of excitement, fear, or anger. Physical changes also accompany psychological stress. For example, heart rate increases, blood pressure rises, ventilation rate increases, perspiration increases, body temperature may rise, and the pupils may dilate. This response to stress once aided human beings in survival and is labeled the "fight or flight" syndrome. When a situation arises that may cause one harm, the body's endocrine system prepares it to fight or flee the situation. People often speak of the "adrenaline flowing" when they are scared or worried about upcoming situations.

Unfortunately, our society and schools offer few opportunities to relieve tension through activity, and few individuals find the motivation to do so. The resulting tension and stress that build up cause individuals to expend a great deal of energy in unproductive ways. People often feel fatigued when they are unable to release stress. Many nervous habits, such as constant movement while sitting, playing with an item in the hands, and various facial twitches, are the body's attempts to relieve tension.

The ultimate question when dealing with stress might be: "What does it matter if I'm under stress? All people are." It matters because excessive stress has many detrimental effects on the body. It increases the risk of heart disease and can lead to insomnia and hypertension. Indigestion is common in stressed individuals, as is constipation. Many backaches and general body aches originate through stress. Doctors are diagnosing more and more "psychosomatic" diseases that have no physical prognosis and appear to be caused by stress. Another serious problem associated with unrelieved stress is the tendency of individuals to try to cope by using substances such as alcohol, tobacco, and drugs.

Individuals who exhibit Type A behavior (Friedman and Rosenman 1974) are much more likely to suffer from the ill effects of stress. Type A behavior is characterized by some of the following patterns:

1. Moving everywhere rapidly, even when it is unnecessary to do so
2. Feeling bored and impatient with classes and how things are being done by others
3. Trying to do two or more things simultaneously (This is referred to as *polyphasic* thought or action.)
4. Having to always feel busy and feeling uneasy when time is taken to do nothing or to do something relaxing
5. Needing to do everything faster and more efficiently than everyone else
6. Exhibiting many strong gestures such as clenching the fists, banging a hand on the table, or dramatically waving the arms

Students need to learn to identify Type A behavior and to understand various methods of modifying it to achieve more productive patterns.

Learning to cope with stressful situations is important. The first step involves developing an awareness of what types of situations cause stress. Sharing situations with others often releases the tension and allows students to feel that they are "normal" and are maturing properly. In the physical education setting, emphasis should be placed on the role that activity can play in stress reduction. Involvement in enjoyable and success-oriented physical activities can decrease tension. This involvement has a side-effect, because the required concentration will provide a diversion from worries and stressors. Note, however, that if the activity is not enjoyable and if the student consistently fails to find success, the level of stress may actually increase.

Some experts believe that exercise applies stress to the body in a systematic fashion and thus prepares the individual to deal with other stressful situations. One goal of teachers should be to provide a variety of activities and to help students select activities that will be productive and meaningful ways of relieving tension.

Another beneficial strategy is to teach various relaxation techniques that help relieve general body stress. These are discussed in a later section in this chapter.

Basic Concepts

1. Stress affects all individuals to varying degrees. Some stress is necessary to stimulate performance and increase motivation.

2. The amount of stress one is able to cope with depends on how it is perceived. Positive self-concepts help people accept threatening situations in a less stressful manner.

3. When people have difficulty dealing with stress through productive methods, such as exercise, relaxation activities, and talking with friends, they often attempt to relieve stress through unhealthy and potentially dangerous means, such as alcohol, tobacco, and drugs.

4. Stress causes changes in perceptible bodily functions. An awareness of these changes is necessary if students are to recognize when they are under stress and need to cope with its effects.

5. Stress appears to increase susceptibility to many diseases and causes psychosomatic illnesses.

6. Exercise is an excellent way to relieve stress and tension when the activity is perceived as enjoyable and success-oriented.

7. Stress is a critical risk factor that influences the onset of heart disease. Type A behavior is accompanied by an increased risk of heart disease.

8. There are different ways of relieving stress, among them are exercise, expressing feelings to friends, developing problem-solving skills, and performing accepted relaxation techniques.

Suggested Learning Activities

1. Hold an isometric contraction at the elbow joint. With the other hand, feel the contraction in the biceps and triceps. Repeat the activity with other muscle groups. Discuss how stress causes generalized body tension that can result in tensed muscles and an increase in general body fatigue. Learning to recognize muscle tension is a desired outcome of this discussion.

2. Discuss the concept of "choking" under pressure. How does this relate to athletic performance? What happens when stress is greater than the individual's ability to cope with it. Discuss how some stress increases performance, while too much decreases the athlete's ability to perform.

3. Discuss the importance of perception in stressful situations. How is stress perceived? Should students face up and admit it when they are worried or scared? Is it better to be "tough" and not tell anyone how they feel? Is it better to keep emotions inside or to share feelings with others?

4. Discuss the importance of finding activities in which students believe they are successful. How are positive self-concepts developed? Why are some people able to cope with failure and losing better than others?

5. Discuss situations in physical activity settings that give rise to increased stress, such as failing in front of others, not being selected for a team, being ridiculed for a poor performance, or losing a game that was personally important. How could these situations be handled differently?

6. Discuss the parameters of Type A behavior patterns. How can they be modified through activity and changes in behavior? Why do people develop Type A behavior? Are Type A behavior patterns productive?

7. Identify physical activities that seem to relieve tension and stress. Discuss the relationship between involvement in activity and the reduction of stress.

8. Identify and discuss unproductive attempts to relieve stress such as drinking, smoking, and drug abuse. Why are these methods chosen

rather than exercise, discussions, or relaxation activities?

9. Discuss the many effects of stress on bodily health. Give students a stress inventory to see how much stress they are under, and discuss ways of reducing this pressure.

10. Teach relaxation techniques such as deep breathing, progressive muscle relaxation, and personal meditation. Emphasize the importance of taking time for these activities on a daily basis. Just as brushing the teeth is necessary for healthy dentition, relaxation is necessary for a healthy body and mind.

NUTRITION AND WEIGHT CONTROL

Proper nutrition is necessary if students are to expect a high level of physical performance from their body. An important area of concern deals with the balance between caloric intake and expenditure in order to maintain proper weight control. Students should understand the reasons and methods for maintaining an optimum level of body weight. The impact of empty calories through excessive ingestion of junk foods should be discussed and understood. The importance of a balanced diet to help the body grow and develop needs to be explained and comprehended. Teachers should also point out that the role of exercise in weight control and muscle development is as important as a balanced diet.

Students should understand the elements of a balanced diet. The body needs fats, carbohydrates, proteins, minerals, and vitamins. A balanced diet draws from each of the four basic food groups: (1) milk and milk products, (2) meat, fish, and poultry with nuts and legumes as supplements, (3) fruits and vegetables, and (4) breads and cereals. The usual recommendation is that carbohydrates make up a little more than 50% of the daily diet, with fats contributing 30% and proteins about 12%. The impact of various vitamins and minerals on body functions should be understood as well as which foods are sources of the specific nutrients (Figure 15.5).

Moderation in the consumption of foods high in cholesterol and fat should be practiced. Some cholesterol and fat are necessary for proper body function. When too much fat is ingested, however, cholesterol and triglyceride levels in the blood plasma increase. This increase is probably detrimental to the body, for many studies have shown a relationship between high cholesterol and triglyceride levels and coronary heart disease. To travel

Figure 15.5. Guide to good eating (courtesy National Dairy Council)

in the bloodstream, fats must combine with water-soluble protein molecules called lipoproteins, which have an important effect on cholesterol and triglyceride levels. Some of these compound molecules are of a type called high-density lipoproteins (HDL), which are associated with a decreased risk of cardiovascular disease. Because polyunsaturated fats appear to increase HDL levels, the general recommendation is that some polyunsaturates be included in the diet. Students should know which foods are high in saturated and unsaturated fats, and should be encouraged to have their cholesterol levels monitored by a physician.

Depending on the criteria used, anywhere from 30% to 50% of students are overweight, meaning that their body weight is over the accepted limits for their age, sex, and body build. It is important for students to begin to develop an awareness of the caloric content of foods as well as the nutritional value. They can then begin to count calories and practice consistency in the amount of calories they ingest. Coupled with this awareness should be some comprehension of the number of calories expended through various types of physical activity (Table 15.1). Students need to understand that when caloric intake exceeds caloric expenditure, obesity is the long-term result. A well-documented and common cause of obesity is inactivity. Most experts believe that obese students do not eat more than normal weight students; rather, they exercise less.

Obesity is a roadblock to wellness. Life insurance companies view overweight people as poor risks because of their shorter life expectancy. Excessive body fat makes the heart work harder, increases the chance of having high blood pressure, and lowers the possibility of recovery from a heart attack. Even more detrimental to students is the psychological impact that obesity has on self-concept development. Students of normal weight find it much easier to perform physical tasks, because strength in relationship to body weight is a critical performance factor. Overweight students are often punished more severely than normal weight students for the same type of deviancy and may receive lower grades for similar quality work.

Basic Concepts

1. Diet should be balanced and contain foods from each of the four basic groups. This ensures that the body will receive essential nutrients.

TABLE 15.1. Caloric Expenditure

Activity	Calories per Hour
Moderate activity	**200–350**
Bicycling (5½ mph)	210
Walking (2½ mph)	210
Gardening	220
Canoeing (2½ mph)	230
Golf	250
Lawn mowing (power mower)	250
Lawn mowing (hand mower)	270
Bowling	270
Fencing	300
Rowboating (2½ mph)	300
Swimming (¼ mph)	300
Walking (3¾ mph)	300
Badminton	350
Horseback riding (trotting)	350
Square dancing	350
Volleyball	350
Roller skating	350
Vigorous activity	**Over 350**
Table tennis	360
Ice skating (10 mph)	400
Tennis	420
Water skiing	480
Hill climbing (100 ft/hr)	490
Skiing (10 mph)	600
Squash and handball	600
Cycling (13 mph)	660
Scull rowing (race)	840
Running (10 mph)	900

Source: Adapted from material from the President's Council on Physical Fitness and Sports, Washington, DC.

2. Caloric expenditure (body functions plus exercise) and intake (eating) must be balanced to maintain a healthy weight. A weight-reducing program should include a reduction in caloric intake and an increase in daily exercise.

3. Activities vary in the energy they require. Individual needs must be considered in the selection of activities to promote weight control and physical fitness maintenance.

4. Junk foods add little if any nutritional value to the diet and are usually high in calories. Foods such as sugar, margarine and butter, oils, and alcohol are high in calories but make no contribution in terms of nutrition.

5. Excessive weight makes performing physical

tasks difficult. This results in less success and in less motivation to be active, thus increasing the tendency toward obesity.

6. Obesity increases the risk of heart disease and other related diseases such as diabetes.

7. A majority of obesity cases are caused by inactivity, or lack of sufficient activity. The majority of overweight students do not consume more calories than normal weight students; they are simply less active.

8. Vitamins are not nutrients, but are catalysts that facilitate metabolic processes. Certain vitamin deficiencies can produce various diseases.

9. Various foods are excellent sources of specific nutrients. Students should be able to identify which foods to ingest to provide a balance of the needed nutrients, vitamins, and minerals.

Suggested Learning Concepts

1. Post a list of activities and their energy demands on the bulletin board. Discuss the need for selecting activities that will burn enough calories to balance caloric intake.

2. Maintain a food diary. Record all the foods eaten daily and the amount of calories in each. Compare the amount of calories ingested with the amount of calories expended.

3. Maintain a nutritious-food diary. Record all the foods eaten daily and categorize each by food group. Determine the percentage of carbohydrates, proteins, and fats in relation to all the food ingested during each day.

4. Develop a desirable and practical balanced diet that can be followed for one week. Arrange with parents to facilitate the diet within their budget restrictions.

5. Calculate the Recommended Daily Allowance (RDA) for various nutrients. Compare a daily intake with the recommendations for various minerals and vitamins.

6. Bring various foods to class that have labels offering nutrition information. Determine which foods are good buys for desired nutrients.

7. Develop an activity diary. For one week, record all activity over and above maintenance activities. Calculate the number of calories burned per day.

8. Discuss and analyze the ways in which society rewards physically fit individuals. Contrast these with the ways in which obese people are discriminated against in various situations.

SUBSTANCE ABUSE

Substance abuse is defined as the harmful use of alcohol, tobacco, or drugs. It is common in today's schools as students seek different ways to explore an expanding world. If students are expected to make wise and meaningful decisions in this area, they need to have an understanding of the impact of various substances on their physical and psychological being. Facts, both pro and con, should be presented in a nonjudgmental environment, without moralizing and preaching. It is difficult for students to make personal decisions if most of the information they receive is from peers or moralizing adults.

Alcohol, tobacco, and drugs deter wellness and are usually detrimental to total health. The use and misuse of these substances should be discussed objectively with students, because much of the information they receive is from biased sources, such as parents, peers, and various media formats. The physical education teacher can promote unbiased discussions and fact-seeking sessions that relate to wellness. Many times, the physical educator is the only person oriented to wellness promotion. As mentioned earlier, however, if the instructor feels strongly that an issue has only one acceptable point of view, then discussions should be avoided. Telling students only the reasons why *not* to do something can result in a strong polarization in the opposite direction.

Alcohol has both short-term and long-term effects. Short-term effects vary as a result of the depressant effect that alcohol has on the central nervous system. Some people become relaxed, others become aggressive, and some become active in differing degrees. Ultimately, a lack of coordination and confusion occur if a great deal of alcohol is ingested.

The long-term effects of alcohol abuse may be liver damage, heart disease, and malnutrition. The greatest concern surrounding long-term drinking is the possibility of alcoholism. Most agree that alcoholism has the following components: (1) loss of control of alcohol intake, (2) presence of functional or structural damage (physical and psychological), and (3) dependence on alcohol to maintain an acceptable level of functioning.

Students usually drink for any of the following reasons: (1) curiosity, (2) desire to celebrate with parents, (3) peer pressure, (4) to be like adults and appear more mature, (5) to rebel against the adult world, or (6) because their models or admired adults drink. Students are often ambivalent about alcohol. They know its detrimental effects, and yet they see many of their friends and models using it. The problem is a difficult one, and an understanding of both moderate use and abstinence is needed. An understanding of how to cope with peer pressure to drink alcohol is also needed, and is discussed in the next section on basic concepts.

Tobacco use is common among junior and senior high students. Smoking increases significantly the possibility of heart attacks, strokes, and cancer. Chronic bronchitis and emphysema are diseases prevalent among smokers. A recent study revealed that the average life-span of long-term smokers is seven years shorter than that of nonsmokers.

Students need to understand the impact of smoking on a healthy body. Along with this knowledge, they should examine why so many people choose to smoke. Today, the fastest growing segment of the smoking population is young girls and women. Students will make the final decision for their individual behavior, but before they do so, they need to understand thoroughly the ramifications of smoking.

The use of marijuana and of hard-core drugs should also be discussed. Outside agencies are often most helpful in discussing substance abuse in an objective manner with students. The use of steroids, pep pills, and pain relievers in athletics should also be debated. In each case, the intent should be to enhance students' awareness so they know the alternatives and consequences. Substance abuse is contrary to the whole concept of physical wellness. Physical educators need to accept the challenge of increasing student understanding and knowledge in these areas.

Basic Concepts

1. The earlier one begins to smoke, the greater the risk to functional health.
2. People smoke for psychological reasons.
3. Young people may choose substance abuse out of curiosity, for status reasons, and from peer pressure.
4. Choosing a life-style different from the majority of one's friends takes a great deal of courage.
5. Decisions about substance abuse are poor decisions if they are based on a dearth of knowledge. Wise and purposeful decisions can be made only when all of the alternatives and consequences are understood.

6. Substance abuse is often an attempt to cope with stress-related problems. Exercise and relaxation are much more productive and are healthy methods of coping.
7. The use of alcohol, tobacco, and drugs always carries the risk of addiction. When people are addicted, they are no longer in charge of their life-style. All people, to some degree, are subject to addiction; no one is immune.
8. Spending time and effort on developing personal competencies is more productive than substance abuse. Personal competency in many areas reduces the need to "be like everyone else" and contributes to a positive self-concept.
9. The use of harmful substances frequently reduces the pleasure one can receive from experiencing the world. Physical performance is often reduced through substance abuse.
10. A person can drink and smoke and still excel at athletics, but maximum performance levels may be reduced and the ultimate effect on the athlete will be harmful. Students see many professional athletes who smoke and drink. They need to be aware that this happens, but they should understand that the choice is undesirable from a wellness standpoint.

Suggested Learning Activities

1. Identify and discuss the reasons why people choose or choose not to become involved in substance abuse.
2. Discuss the importance of making personal decisions based on what is best for you. Why do we follow others and allow them to influence our decisions, even when those decisions are not in our best interest?
3. Develop a bulletin board that illustrates the many ways used by the tobacco, alcohol, and drug industries to try to get young people to buy their products. Reserve a spot for advertisements (if any can be found) that admonish and encourage students to abstain or moderate the use of various substances.
4. Students often see professional and college athletes smoking and drinking on television while hearing from teachers and coaches that these habits impair performance. Discuss why these athletes can perform at a high level even though they may drink or smoke.
5. Students often choose to be part of a peer group

at any cost. Discuss how our society often respects and honors individuals who have the courage to go their own way. Examples might be Columbus, Helen Keller, Braille, and so forth.

6. Identify and discuss the ways in which people in our society choose to relieve and dissipate stress. Discuss productive releases of tension such as recreation, hobbies, and sports.

7. Bring in speakers who are knowledgeable about the effects and uses of alcohol, tobacco, and drugs. If necessary, bring in a pair of speakers who might debate both sides of an issue.

8. Develop visual aids that identify the various effects that alcohol, tobacco, and drugs have on the body.

SAFETY AND FIRST AID

Safety and first aid have often been part of the physical education program because more accidents occur in physical education than in any other area of the school curriculum. Safety is an attitude and a concern for one's welfare and health. An accident is an unplanned event or act that may result in injury or death. Oftentimes, accidents occur in situations in which they could have been prevented. The following are the most common causes of accidents: (1) lack of knowledge and understanding of risks, (2) lack of skill and competence to perform tasks safely, such as riding a bike or driving a car, (3) false sense of security that leads people to think that accidents happen only to others, (4) fatigue or illness that affect physical and mental performance, (5) drugs and alcohol, and (6) strong emotional states (e.g., anger, fear, or worry) that cause people to do things they might not otherwise do.

Traffic accidents are one area in which many deaths could be prevented. Wearing seat belts reduces the risk of dying by 50%. Drinking alcohol while driving increases the risk of an accident 20 times as compared to a nondrinking driver. Another factor that has reduced the number of traffic deaths is the 55 mph speed limit. Since students are going to drive, driver education and an awareness of the possibility of serious injury should be a part of the wellness program.

Bicycles are another source of numerous accidents. Automobile drivers have difficulty seeing bicycles, and the resulting accidents are often serious. Students need to learn bicycle safety. The physical education setting is often the only place

in which this training occurs. Classes in bicycling for safety and fitness are usually well received by junior and senior high school students.

Swimming-related accidents are the second leading cause of accidental death among young adults. More than 50% of all drownings occur when people unexpectedly find themselves in the water. Another major cause of death from drowning is alcohol ingestion. Swimming and drinking do not mix well. Physical education programs should encourage all students to learn to swim and to learn water safety rules at sometime during their school career.

Physical education and sports are sources of injury in the school setting. Proper safety procedures should be taught, as well as first aid techniques. Students should know how to stop bleeding, treat shock, and administer mouth-to-mouth respiration and cardiopulmonary resuscitation (CPR). Many physical education programs now include a unit of instruction dealing with these topics that is required for all students. It is estimated that 100,000 to 200,000 lives could be saved by bystanders if they knew CPR.

Basic Concepts

1. Accidents are unplanned events or acts that may result in injury or death. The majority of accidents could be avoided if people were adequately prepared and understood the necessary competencies and risks involved.

2. Wearing seat belts and not drinking alcohol while driving will dramatically decrease the risk of death by automobile accident.

3. Bicycles are often not seen by car drivers. Bicycling safety classes can help lower the number of bicycle accidents.

4. Swimming-related accidents are the second leading cause of accidental death among young people. Drownproofing programs and learning to avoid alcohol when around the water will dramatically decrease the risk of death by drowning.

5. Many thousands of lives could be saved if all people knew how to perform CPR.

6. All students should know how to stop bleeding, and how to administer mouth-to-mouth respiration and CPR.

7. Basic first aid procedures to prevent further injury to victims are competencies that all students should possess.

Suggested Learning Activities

1. Discuss the causes of different types of accidents and how many accidents could be avoided.
2. Identify the types of accidents that happen to different age groups and why this appears to be the case.
3. Identify the role of alcohol and drugs in causing accidents. Why are these substances used in recreational settings?
4. Develop a bulletin board that illustrates how to care for shock victims. Practice the steps in a mock procedure.
5. Have an "accident day" when various types of accidents are staged that demand such treatments as stopping bleeding, mouth-to-mouth respiration, and CPR.
6. Outline the steps to follow in case of a home fire. Discuss how many fires could be prevented.
7. Conduct a bicycle safety fair. Have students design bulletin boards and displays that explain and emphasize bicycle safety.

ENHANCING STUDENT WELLNESS

It is apparent from the previous safety discussion that the wellness of students can be seriously impaired when safety issues are dealt with incorrectly. On the other hand, proper nutrition, avoiding substance abuse, and practicing proper safety when bicycling or riding in a car can enhance the wellness of participants. The purpose of this section is to help students further advance their wellness status through positive action, rather than by simply avoiding various foods, substances, and situations. This section takes a three-pronged approach: (1) physical fitness and activity, (2) stress reduction, and (3) self-evaluation. None of the areas will be covered in its entirety since there are many in-depth sources. A highly recommended source for helping students develop lifetime fitness is the text by Corbin and Lindsey (1983).

PHYSICAL FITNESS AND ACTIVITY

There are two types of physical fitness that are generally identified (Corbin and Lindsey 1983). The first is skill-related physical fitness and the other is health-related fitness. Skill-related fitness contains many elements that deal with sport performance, among them are balance, coordination, reaction time, agility, power, and speed. Skill-related fitness has less impact on the wellness of an individual and will not be further discussed in this section.

Health-related fitness is directly related to the wellness of individuals and is generally defined as consisting of cardiovascular fitness, strength, muscular endurance, flexibility, and body fatness. Each of these items is defined briefly as follows:

Cardiovascular fitness is the most important phase of fitness for wellness. Cardiovascular fitness is a complex concept, but, simply put, involves efficient functioning of the heart, blood, and blood vessels in order to supply oxygen to the body during aerobic activity.

Strength refers to the ability of a muscle or muscle group to exert force. Without strength, a low standard of performance can be expected, because muscles will fatigue before an individual can perform well.

Muscular endurance refers to the ability of a muscle or muscle group to exert effort over a period of time. Endurance utilizes strength and postpones fatigue so the effort can be expended for an extended period of time. Cardiovascular fitness also plays a key role in how long people can perform an activity.

Flexibility is a person's range of movement at the joints. It allows freedom of movement and ready adjustment of the body for various movements.

Body fatness refers to the percentage of body weight that is fat. People who are physically fit generally have a lower percentage of body fat than those who are unfit. For males in secondary school, 11% to 15% fat is a reasonable range, while 20% to 25% is acceptable for females (Corbin and Lindsey 1983).

It is important to help students develop a health-related fitness plan that they can use to monitor themselves throughout a lifetime. The basic steps for such a plan are as follows:

1. Identify present areas of fitness and weakness by **pretesting.** Many tests can be used to evaluate the five components of health-related fitness.
2. Identify the present activities that the students are performing by having them fill out a survey, which lists a wide variety of activities. A chart can be posted that shows the components of health-related fitness enhanced by each activity. A good source for surveys and lists of activity benefits is *Fitness for Life* by Corbin and Lindsey (1983).
3. Select some activities that will build the health-related fitness components that each student needs, as identified in step 1. Each student will

begin to have a personalized plan that is meaningful only to him or her.

4. Plan a week-long activity program that contains activities that are enjoyable and help alleviate weaknesses in various component areas. Evaluate the week-long program and develop a month-long program in order to provide longer range goals. In the program, delineate the frequency of exercise, the intensity, and the amount of time to be spent exercising.

STRESS REDUCTION

Many methods are recommended for learning to cope with stress. Only the most popular and acceptable in the school setting are covered here. An excellent text devoted entirely to this topic is *Human Stress: Its Nature and Control* (Allen 1983).

In an earlier section, exercise was discussed as an excellent method of controlling stress. It appears to allow negative feelings to dissipate and positive feelings to replace them. The relaxed feeling that occurs after an exercise bout is championed by many as the best part of activity.

Many deep-breathing exercises are available. The relaxation response advocated by Benson (1975) is supposed to replicate the effects of transcendental meditation (TM). Individuals sit comfortably and quietly and breath deeply through the nose. The word "one" is said each time the person exhales. Twenty-min bouts, once or twice a day, are recommended.

Another popular method is progressive relaxation as developed by Jacobson (1968). In this technique, a muscle or muscle group is first tensed and then relaxed slowly and smoothly. All the major parts of the body are in turn relaxed as one works down from the head to the toes.

Regardless of the activity choice selected for relaxation, students should be taught the importance of taking time to relax. People are often told that they are wasting time if they are not busy scurrying here and there. It can be an important learning situation to take 4 or 5 min at the end of a class to sit down and relax. This communicates to students that relaxation is indeed important since the instructor allows time for the activity.

SELF-EVALUATION AND BEHAVIOR SELF-CONTROL

Self-Evaluation

The final step in maintaining wellness is being able to evaluate one's self on a regular basis. Individuals ultimately answer to themselves, and thus students need not share the results of their evaluations. Many surveys can help people evaluate their level of wellness. Figure 15.6 shows one of the most effective and comprehensive developed by Travis (Olsen et al. 1983). Even though not all the items are applicable to all people at all times, this inventory will give students an idea of the types of issues that enter into human wellness.

Many other inventories, such as drinking and smoking scales, are available from various governmental agencies. Students can begin to see the extent of a problem and whether they have a problem or are improving.

Finally, students should be taught to evaluate their own levels of physical fitness. Each of the health-related fitness items can be evaluated easily. If students are not given time in the physical education program to evaluate their own fitness levels, they will probably not take the time for evaluation once they leave school. One of the best techniques is to give each student a self-testing card that has room for recording four or five different testing episodes. Allow students to self-test themselves with a friend and record their performance. Instructors can file the cards and return them when it is time for another testing period. This system allows students to monitor their physical fitness gains or losses.

Behavior Self-Control

Students should be taught how to improve their self-control by altering their behavior. Attitudes can be changed by changing behavior patterns. Behavior self-control is a systematic approach to solving problems. It involves keeping records of behavior in order to understand the positive and negative variables that influence behavior. The following steps can be taught effectively to students to help them learn to manipulate their behavior.

1. **Maintain Behavior Records.** Students can learn to monitor their exercise patterns and record the performances on personal charts. They can then begin to observe their patterns of exercise, the duration of the exercise, and the intensity of effort. Such observation becomes self-reinforcing when, for example, students see clearly that they are exercising only two days per week and showing little gain, or when they observe rapid improvement after exercising five days per week for several weeks. Another advantage of recording one's behavior is that the routine act

Figure 15.6. Wellness inventory (used with permission, copyright 1975, 1981, John W. Travis, M.D., Wellness Associates, Box 5433, Mill Valley, CA 94942. Abridged from the Wellness Index in the Wellness Workbook, Ryan and Travis, Ten Speed Press, 1981)

THE WELLNESS INVENTORY

The Wellness Inventory was developed by John W. Travis, M.D., M.P.H., as a way for people to evaluate their total well-being. It assumes a holistic approach to health, insisting that well-being, or wellness, requires attention to the whole person, in a perspective that includes physical, mental, and social dimensions.

Wellness is not simply the absence of illness, and many different levels are possible. While traditional medicine concentrates on curing or alleviating disease, the wellness approach directs people beyond the point of a mere lack of illness and encourages them to improve their positive well-being in a variety of ways.

As Dr. Travis explains in his *Wellness Inventory* (Mill Valley, Calif.: Wellness Resource Center, 1977):

Many people lack physical symptoms but are bored, depressed, tense, anxious, or generally unhappy with their lives. These emotional states often lead to physical disease through the lowering of the body's resistance. The same feelings can also lead to abuse of the body through smoking, drinking, and overeating. These behaviors are usually substitutes for other more basic human needs such as recognition from others, a stimulating environment, caring and affection from friends, and growth towards higher levels of self-awareness.

Wellness is not a static state. It results when a person begins to see himself as a growing, changing person. High-level wellness means giving good care to your physical self, using your mind constructively, expressing your emotions effectively, being creatively involved with those around you, being concerned about your physical and psychological environment, and becoming aware of other levels of consciousness.

The self-assessment exercise that follows will help give you an idea of where you stand on the wellness scale. It will also help you reflect on some of the life-style choices that have an impact both on the prevention of illness and on the promotion of total well-being, or wellness.

INSTRUCTIONS   **Put a check mark in the box following each statement that is true for you. Total up the number of marks for each section and transfer the results to the Interpretation section at the end of the test. An asterisk following a statement indicates that there is an explanatory footnote for that statement at the end of the items.**

A. Productivity, Relaxation, Sleep

1. I usually enjoy my work. ☐

2. I seldom feel tired and rundown (except after strenuous work).* ☐

3. I fall asleep easily at bedtime. ☐

4. I usually get a full night's sleep. ☐

5. If awakened, it is usually easy for me to go to sleep again. ☐

6. I rarely bite or pick at my nails. ☐

7. Rather than worrying, I can temporarily shelve my problems and enjoy myself at times when I can do nothing about solving them immediately. ☐

8. I feel financially secure. ☐

9. I am content with my sexual life. ☐

10. I meditate in some way for 15 or 20 minutes at least once a day.* ☐

Total _____

B. Personal Care and Home Safety

11. I take steps to protect my living space from fire and safety hazards (such as unsafe wiring or volatile chemicals improperly stored). ☐

12. I have a dry chemical fire extinguisher in my kitchen and at least one other extinguisher elsewhere in my living quarters. (In a small apartment, a kitchen extinguisher alone is adequate.)* ☐

13. I regularly use dental floss and a soft toothbrush.* ☐

14. I smoke less than one pack of cigarettes or equivalent cigars or pipes *per week.* ☐

15. I don't smoke at all. (If this statement is true, mark item above true as well.) ☐

16. I keep an up-to-date record of my immunizations. ☐

17. I have fewer than three colds per year.* ☐

18. I minimize my exposure to sprays, chemical fumes, or exhaust gases.* ☐

19. I avoid extremely noisy areas (or wear protective earplugs).* ☐

20. I am aware of changes in my physical or mental state and seek professional advice about any that seem unusual. ☐

WOMEN

21. I check my breasts for unusual lumps once a month. ☐

22. I have a Pap test annually. ☐

MEN

23. If uncircumcised, I am aware of the special need for regular cleansing under my foreskin. ☐

24. If I am over 45, I have my prostate checked annually. ☐

Total _____

C. Nutritional Awareness

25. I eat at least one uncooked fruit or vegetable each day.* ☐

26. I have fewer than three alcoholic drinks (including beer) per week. ☐

27. I rarely take medications, including prescription drugs. ☐

28. I drink fewer than five soft drinks a week.* ☐

29. I avoid eating refined foods or foods with sugar added. ☐

30. I add little salt to my food.* ☐

31. I read the labels for the ingredients of the foods I buy. ☐

32. I add unprocessed bran to my diet to provide roughage.* ☐

33. I drink fewer than three cups of coffee or tea (except herbal teas) a day.* ☐

34. I have a good appetite and maintain a weight within 15 percent of my ideal weight. ☐

Total _____

D. Environmental Awareness

35. I use public transportation or car pools when possible. ☐

36. I turn off unneeded lights or appliances. ☐

37. I recycle papers, cans, glass, clothing, books, and organic waste (mark true if you do at least three of these). ☐

continued

Figure 15.6/*continued*

38. I set my thermostat at 68°F or lower in winter. ☐

39. I use air conditioning only when necessary and keep the thermostat at 76°F or higher. ☐

40. I am conscientious about wasted energy and materials. ☐

41. I use nonpolluting cleaning agents. ☐

42. My car gets at least 18 miles per gallon. (If you don't own a car, check this statement as true.) ☐

43. I have storm windows and adequate insulation in attic and walls. (If you don't own your home or live in a mild climate, check this statement as true.) ☐

44. I have a humidifier for use in winter. (If you don't have central heating, check this statement as true.)* ☐

Total _____

E. Physical Activity

45. I climb stairs rather than ride elevators. ☐

46. My daily activities include at least moderate physical effort (such as rearing young children, gardening, scrubbing floors, or other work that involves being on my feet). ☐

47. My daily activities include vigorous physical effort (such as heavy construction work, farming, moving heavy objects by hand). ☐

48. I run at least 1 mile twice a week (or equivalent aerobic exercise).* ☐

49. I run at least 1 mile four times a week or equivalent. (If this statement is true, mark the item above true as well.)* ☐

50. I regularly walk or ride a bike for exercise. ☐

51. I participate in a strenuous sport at least once a week. ☐

52. I participate in a strenuous sport more than once a week. (If this statement is true, mark the item above true as well.) ☐

53. I do yoga or some form of stretching-limbering exercise for 15 to 20 minutes at least twice per week.* ☐

54. I do yoga or some form of stretching exercise for 15 or 20 minutes at least four times per week. (If this statement is true, mark the item above true as well.)* ☐

Total _____

F. Expression of Emotions and Feelings

55. I am frequently happy. ☐

56. I think it is O.K. to feel angry, afraid, joyful, or sad.* ☐

57. I do not deny my anger, fear, joy, or sadness, but instead find constructive ways to express these feelings most of the time.* ☐

58. I am able to say no to people without feeling guilty. ☐

59. It is easy for me to laugh. ☐

60. I like getting compliments and recognition from other people. ☐

61. I feel O.K. about crying, and allow myself to do so.* ☐

62. I listen to and think about constructive criticism, rather than reacting defensively. ☐

63. I would seek help from friends or professional counselors if needed. ☐

64. It is easy for me to give other people sincere compliments and recognition. ☐

Total _____

G. Community Involvement

65. I keep informed of local, national, and world events. ☐

66. I vote regularly. ☐

67. I take interest in community, national, and world events and work to support issues and people of my choice. (If this statement is true, mark both items above true as well.) ☐

68. When I am able, I contribute time or money to worthy causes. ☐

69. I make an attempt to know my neighbors and be on good terms with them. ☐

70. If I saw a crime being committed, I would call the police. ☐

71. If I saw a broken bottle lying in the road or on the sidewalk, I would remove it. ☐

72. When driving, I am considerate of pedestrians and other drivers. ☐

73. If I saw a car with faulty lights, leaking gasoline, or another dangerous condition, I would attempt to inform the driver. ☐

74. I am a member of one or more community organizations. ☐

Total _____

H. Creativity, Self-Expression

75. I enjoy expressing myself through art, dance, music, drama, sports, etc. ☐

76. I enjoy spending some time without planned or structured activities.* ☐

77. I usually meet several people a month whom I would like to get to know better. ☐

78. I enjoy touching other people.* ☐

79. I enjoy being touched by other people.* ☐

80. I have at least five close friends. ☐

81. At times I like to be alone. ☐

82. I like myself and look forward to the future. ☐

83. I look forward to living to be at least 75.* ☐

84. I find it easy to express concern, love, and warmth to those I care about. ☐

Total _____

I. Automobile Safety

If you don't own an automobile and ride less than 1,000 miles per year in one, enter 7 points as a total for this section and skip the individual items. (If you ride more than 1,000 miles per year but don't own a car, answer as many items as you can and show this copy to the car's owner.)

85. I never drink when I am going to be driving. ☐

86. I wear a lap safety belt at least 90 percent of the time that I ride in a car. ☐

87. I wear a shoulder/lap belt at least 90 percent of the time that I ride in a car. (If this statement is true, mark the item above true as well.)* ☐

88. I stay within 5 miles per hour of the speed limit. ☐

continued

Figure 15.6 / *continued*

89. My car has head restraints on the front seats, and I keep them adjusted high enough to protect myself and passengers from whiplash injuries.* ☐

90. I frequently inspect my automobile tires, lights, etc., and have my car serviced regularly. ☐

91. I have disk brakes on my car.* ☐

92. I drive on belted radial tires.* ☐

93. I carry emergency flares or reflectors as well as a fire extinguisher in my car. ☐

94. I stop on yellow when a traffic light is changing. ☐

95. For every 10 miles per hour of speed, I maintain a car length's distance from the car ahead of me. ☐

Total _____

J. Parenting

If you don't have any responsibility for young children, enter 7 as a total for this section and skip the individual items. (If some of the items are not applicable because your children are no longer young, answer as you would if they were youngsters again.)

96. When riding in a car, I make certain that any child weighing under 50 pounds is secured in an approved safety harness similar to those sold by the major auto manufacturers.* ☐

97. When riding in a car, I make certain that any child weighing over 50 pounds is wearing an adult seat belt or shoulder harness.* ☐

98. When leaving a child, I make certain that the person in charge has the telephone numbers of my pediatrician or a hospital for emergency use. ☐

99. I don't let my children ride escalators in bare feet or tennis shoes.* ☐

100. I do not store cleaning products under the sink or in unlocked cabinets where a child could reach them. ☐

101. I have a lock on the medicine cabinet or other places where medicines are stored. ☐

102. I prepare my own baby food with a food grinder—and thus do not buy commercial baby foods.* ☐

103. I have sought information on parenting and raising children. ☐

104. I frequently touch or hold my children. ☐

105. I respect my child as an evolving, growing being. ☐

Total _____

Footnotes

These footnotes provide an opportunity to reflect on the significance of some practices that contribute to the achievement of total well-being, or wellness. The number or numbers before each footnote refer to the corresponding statement in the wellness test you have just completed.

2 Fatigue without apparent cause is not normal and usually indicates illness, stress, or denial of emotional expression.

10 Meditation greatly enhances one's sense of well-being.

12 Many injuries and much damage can be prevented by putting out fires when they first start. Dry chemical fire extinguishers are necessary for oil, grease, and electrical fires.

13 Regular flossing and using a good soft toothbrush with rounded-tip bristles prevent the premature loss of teeth. Be sure to learn the proper techniques from a dental hygienist or dentist.

17 If you have more than three colds a year, you may not be getting enough rest, eating a good diet, or meeting other energy needs properly.

18 All such toxins have a harmful effect on the liver and other tissues over long periods of time.

19 Very loud noises that leave your ears ringing can cause permanent hearing loss, which accumulates and is usually not noticeable until one reaches 40 or 50. Small cushioned earplugs (not the type designed for swimmers), wax earplugs, and acoustic earmuffs (which look like stereo headphones without wires) can often be purchased in sporting goods stores.

25 Fresh fruits and vegetables provide vitamins, minerals, trace nutrients, and roughage that are often lacking in modern diets.

28 Soft drinks are high in refined sugar, which provides only "empty" calories, and they usually replace foods having more nutritional value. Artificially sweetened soft drinks consumed in excess may have long-range consequences as yet not known. (Both types of soft drinks contain caffeine or other stimulants.)

30 Salting foods during cooking draws many vitamins out of the food and into the water, which is usually discarded. Use of heavily salted foods at the table may cause a strain on the kidneys and contribute to high blood pressure.

32 Wheat bran, usually removed in the commercial milling of wheat, is the single best source of dietary fiber available. The use of approximately two tablespoons per day (individual needs vary) may substantially reduce the risk of colon cancer, diverticulosis, heart disease, and other conditions related to refined food diets.

33 Coffee and tea (other than herbal teas) contain stimulants that, if abused, do not allow one's body to function normally.

44 Humidified heated air allows one to set the thermostat several degrees lower and still feel as warm as without humidification. It also helps prevent many respiratory ailments. Houseplants will require less watering, and be happier too.

48, 49 Vigorous aerobic exercise (such as running) must keep the heart rate at 150 beats per minute for 12 to 20 minutes to produce the "training effect." Less vigorous aerobic exercise (lower heart rate) must be maintained for much longer periods to produce the same benefit. The "training effect" is necessary to prepare the heart for meeting extra strain.

53, 54 Such exercise prevents stiffness of joints and musculoskeletal degeneration. It also promotes a greater feeling of well-being.

56 Basic emotions, if repressed, often cause anxiety, depression, irrational behavior, or physical disease. People can learn to feel and express their emotions, with a resulting improvement in their well-being. Some people, however, exaggerate emotions to control and manipulate others; this can be detrimental to well-being.

57 Learning ways to express these emotions constructively (so that all parties concerned feel better) leads to more satisfying relationships and problem solving.

61 Crying over a loss or sad event is an important discharge of emotional energy. It is, however, sometimes used as a manipulative tool or as a substitute expression of anger. Many males in particular have been erroneously taught that it is not O.K. to cry.

76 Spending time spontaneously without relying on an external structure can be self-renewing throughout adult life.

78, 79 Physical touch is important for the maintenance of life for young children and remains important throughout adult life.

83 With proper self-care, most individuals can reach this age in good health.

87 Shoulder/lap belts are much safer than lap belts alone. (Shoulder belts should never be worn without a lap belt.)

continued

Figure 15.6 /*continued*

89 Whiplash injuries can be prevented by properly adjusted head restraints. These are required, in the United States, on the front seats of all autos made since 1968, but are often not raised high enough to protect passengers and driver.

91 Disk brakes provide considerably better braking power than conventional drum brakes.

92 For most cars, radial tires maintain firmer contact with the road and improve braking and handling better than bias-ply tires. They also have less rolling friction and give better gas mileage.

96, 97 Over 1,000 young children a year are killed in motor vehicle accidents in the United States. Many deaths could be prevented by keeping the child from flying about in a car crash. Most car seats do not provide enough protection—since government standards are low. Check consumer magazines for up-to-date information. Never use an adult seat belt for a child weighing under 50 pounds.

99 The bare feet of young children are often injured at the end of escalators. Wearing tennis shoes is equally dangerous, because the sturdy long laces get pulled into the mechanism and the thin canvas walls offer little protection.

102 Commercial baby foods contain high amounts of sugar, salt, modified starches, and preservatives which may adversely affect a baby's future eating habits and health. Federal legislation has been introduced to help correct this problem. Portable food grinders and blenders can be used to prepare for an infant the same food as eaten by the rest of the family. Individual servings can be packaged and frozen for future meals.

Interpretation. Add the subtotals for each section to find your total wellness score.

A. ☐ **Productivity, Relaxation, Sleep**

B. ☐ **Personal Care and Home Safety**

C. ☐ **Nutritional Awareness**

D. ☐ **Environmental Awareness**

E. ☐ **Physical Activity**

F. ☐ **Expression of Emotions and Feelings**

G. ☐ **Community Involvement**

H. ☐ **Creativity, Self-Expression**

I. ☐ **Automobile Safety**

J. ☐ **Parenting**

Total _____

Although the inventory cannot, by any means, offer a precise measurement of a person's wellness or health status, average scores tend to range from about 65 to 75 points.

of recording reminds the performer that the behavior must be done. This routine reinforcement causes the behavior performance to improve.

2. **Develop a Priority Schedule.** If students want to exercise regularly, they must schedule the activity and make it a high-priority item. In other words, exercise must be done before other less important tasks are performed. Scheduling the activity for a certain number of days at a specified time is most effective.

3. **Analyze Restrictive Factors.** Even after behavior has been analyzed and priorities are set, students may find that desired behavior patterns are not being followed. The reasons for this must then be analyzed and other changes effected to increase the probability of carrying out the behavior. For example, the time of exercise may

have to be changed, or the length of the bout. Exercising for two shorter periods per day, instead of one long period, might be the answer. Exercising with a friend or changing the mode of exercise would be other possible solutions.

4. **Establish Rewards.** To continue the activity over a long period of time, it can be helpful to establish personal contingencies that are available after performing the desired behavior. For example, students might relax and watch television immediately after exercise, or take a long, hot shower. Regardless of the reward, it must be meaningful and worthwhile to the individual. Verbalizing internally after each exercise routine is also effective as a contingency. One might say to oneself, "I feel better and look stronger after every bout of exercise." In any case, if students can identify something positive that occurs because of or after the exercise bout, they will have a tendency to continue on the path of wellness.

References

Allen, R. J. *Human Stress: Its Nature and Control.* Minneapolis: Burgess Publishing Co., 1983.

Benson, H. *The Relaxation Response.* New York: William Morrow & Co., Inc., 1975.

Corbin, C., and Lindsey, R. *Fitness for Life. 2nd ed.* Glenview, IL: Scott, Foresman & Co., 1983.

Friedman, M., and Rosenman, R. H. *Type A Behavior and Your Heart.* New York: Alfred A. Knopf, Inc., 1974.

Jacobson, E. *Progressive Relaxation.* 2nd ed. Chicago: University of Chicago Press, 1968.

Olsen, L. K., et al. *Health Today.* New York: Macmillan, Inc., 1983.

Rarick, G. L., ed. *Physical Activity, Human Growth and Development.* New York: Academic Press, 1973.

Wilmore, J. H. *Athletic Training and Physical Fitness.* Boston: Allyn and Bacon, Inc., 1977.

Chapter 16

Introductory Activities

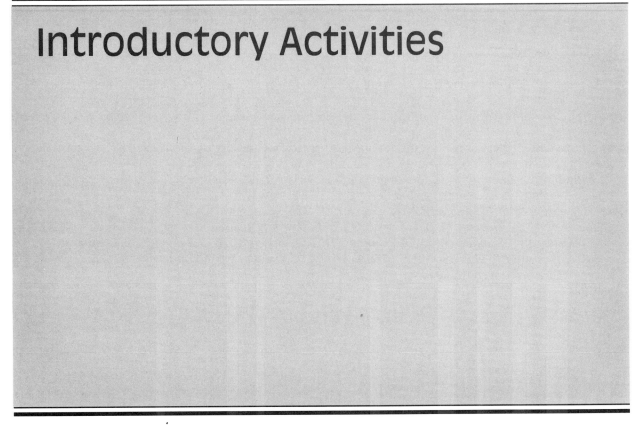

Introductory activities are used during the first part of the lesson to prepare students for ensuing participation. The activities are characterized by a minimal need for instruction and a maximum amount of movement. A difficult part of instruction is starting a lesson. The task is eased when instructors can begin with activity and little verbal interaction. Most students desire immediate activity when they arrive for class. The introductory activities can meet this need.

Introductory activities are vigorous in nature and revolve around large muscle activity. An objective of introductory activities is to develop a high level of skill in movements basic to sport and leisure pursuits. Students should understand how the activities can be applied to their personal activity interests.

Involvement in introductory activities helps prepare students for strenuous activity. They serve as a psychological and physiological warm-up for the fitness portion of the lesson. During the introductory activity, teachers can work on reaction drills in which students freeze in response to a predetermined signal. This helps refocus class management skills and reinforces the need for stopping on signal.

Introductory activities should be selected with the interests and developmental levels of the students in mind. Junior high school students, because of their rapid growth spurt, need activities that emphasize body control, coordination, and agility. Senior high school students need to understand how introductory activities will affect sport and dance performance and the activities in which they have developed competency and interest.

Vocabulary and jargon appropriate to the maturity level of the students should be used when introducing activities. Effective teachers possess some acting skills when presenting introductory activities. Capitalize on popular movies and television series, and on famous people and news items. Examples might be Larry Bird, Doctor J, *Jaws*, *E.T.*, *Superstars* competition, Jane Fonda, and Richard Simmons. This adds enthusiasm and motivation to the learning environment.

To minimize unproductive time, students should be used as leaders. They need opportunities to lead and to learn not to always depend on teachers to make all decisions. Inform the class of the goal and the desired accomplishment. Students can perform signals that are necessary for some of the day's lesson activities.

Students should learn to develop introductory activities suited to their needs. As long as the activities are vigorous and emphasize large muscle movement, they can be used in this part of the lesson. It is also entirely possible that the introductory activity may place demands on the cardiovascular system and can be used for this purpose after the fitness portion of the lesson as well. As usual, a large variety of introductory activities should be taught and presented. This will show students that there are many acceptable methods for preparing for activity.

AGILITY ACTIVITIES

Seat Roll

Students are on all fours with head up, looking at the instructor. When the teacher gives a left- or right-hand signal, students respond quickly by rolling in that direction on their seat. Seat rolls can be alternated with running in place or with rope jumping to increase the challenge.

Arkansas Flip

Begin in the same position as the seat roll. Students flip over to the left or right, without touching their seats to the floor, so they are in a crab position (half flip). The flip should be a quick, continuous movement. Students can wait for the next signal in the crab position or, if the teacher designates, can continue over to all fours position with the head up (full flip).

Quarter Eagle

Students are in a ready position with the head up, arms flexed in front of the body, knees slightly bent, feet straight ahead and shoulder width apart. The instructor gives a hand signal left or right. The class responds by making a quarter turn in that direction and returning to the starting position as quickly as possible.

A variation involves having participants move on a verbal signal such as "go." The students then make a quarter turn to the left or right, and wait for the next signal. They continue to make quarter turns on each signal.

Wave Drill (Figure 16.1)

Students are in ready position. They shuffle (without a crossover step) left, right, backward, or forward on signal. A useful variation is to place an obstacle (boundary cone) for students to shuffle over.

Variation 1. Same as original except use a crossover step.

Variation 2. Same as original except that students are on all fours.

Variation 3. Students stand between two cones or bags—stuttering the feet (rapid running in place). On a hand signal to the left or right, the performer steps over the obstacle in the corresponding direction and moves the feet in place while waiting for the next signal.

Variation 4. Same as above except that students move left or right with both feet together (ski hop). Emphasis is on watching the signal and moving quickly.

Log Roll (Three-Person Roll)

Students are in groups of three and on all fours. The instructor gives a signal left or right. The middle person rolls in that direction, while the person on that side rolls up and over the top of the middle person. The drill continues with each person rolling several times. The objective is to roll straight, get up quickly, and not touch anybody while rolling over them.

Square Drill

The class forms several 10-yd squares with boundary cones. Students stand in the middle of each side of the square and face the center. On

Figure 16.1. Wave drill

signal, they shuffle around the square to the left or right, depending on the signal of the teacher. A student can be in the center of the square to give a direction signal.

Lateral Shuffle

Place two cones about 5 yd apart. A student stands in the middle and shuffles quickly back and forth between the cones, touching the cone each time. Students try to touch as many cones as possible in 15 sec. Set up enough pairs of cones so all students can participate simultaneously.

Rooster Hop Drill (Figure 16.2)

Students hop 10 yd on one leg in the following sequence: (1) left hand touching the right toe, which is on the ground, (2) right hand touching the left toe on the ground, (3) right hand touching the right toe on the ground, and (4) left hand touching the left toe on the ground. Students can be challenged to develop different combinations and tasks.

Weave Drill (Figure 16.3)

This is similar to the wave drill, except that students shuffle in and out of a series of obstacles such as cones, blocking dummies, or boards. A shuffling step is used rather than a crossover step.

Running Weave Drill (Figure 16.4)

This is similar to the weave drill, but students run through the maze with a regular running stride. A stopwatch can challenge students to improve their time, and the maze can be arranged in many different ways. Let students set up the maze and

Figure 16.2. Rooster hop drill

Figure 16.3. Weave drill

Figure 16.4. Running weave drill

time each other. A variation could be done using the carioca step.

Leaping Lena With a Forward Roll

Students stand in a ready position stuttering the feet quickly. On the first command, students leap forward as far as possible and begin moving the feet again. Two more leaps are repeated and then a forward roll is performed. Students return to the end of the line when finished.

Burpee-Flip Drill

This can be done in small groups or in unison with the entire class. The teacher calls out the number, and students yell the number while performing the movement. The sequence is as follows:

1. Standing position
2. Bend the knees, hands on the floor or ground

3. Legs kick back into an all-fours position, head up
4. Half flip right to a crab position
5. Half flip right to an all-fours position

This drill can also be done with a left flip or with two flips, one left and one right, and so forth. Let students try this drill with a small group. Challenge them to stay together and to continue enlarging the group. Participants must call the numbers for their group.

Another variation is to put a push-up in before the flip. Step 4 would be the down motion and step 5 would be the up motion. Caution must be used to ensure that students are far enough apart in case one student flips the wrong way.

All Fours Circle (Figure 16.5)

Students lie on their stomachs with heads close together and legs extended outward like the spokes of a wheel. One person starts by placing the hands in the center and moving around the circle over the other students without touching anyone. The last person who is passed is the next participant. The drill can be done with 4 to 12 people.

Coffee Grinder Square (Figure 16.6)

Students start at one corner of the square, run to the next corner, and perform a coffee grinder on the right arm (arm extended on the ground, supporting the body weight, while the feet walk 360 degrees around the arm). At the next corner, they put their left arm down and do another coffee grinder. This continues through the four corners.

Figure 16.6. Coffee grinder square

The square should be made with something flat, such as beanbags or bases. Students should move in the same direction around the square.

Flash Drill (Figure 16.7)

Students stand in a ready position facing the teacher. The teacher exclaims "feet," and students stutter the feet quickly. The teacher then "flashes" the following hand signals:

1. Hands up: Students jump up and return to stuttering feet.
2. Hands down: Students move to the floor and return to stuttering feet.
3. Hands right: Students shuffle right.
4. Hands left: Students shuffle left.
5. Hands make a circle: Students do a forward roll and get up stuttering.

Figure 16.5. All fours circle

Figure 16.7. Flash drill

SPORT MOVEMENT CHALLENGES

The following activities can be done with sport movements such as sliding, leaping, running, and jumping. The locomotor movement is then combined with a challenging activity that is used in sport such as a pivot, stop, or change of direction.

Move and Change Direction

Students run in any direction, and change direction on signal. The change in direction can be specified or student selected. If specified, the commands might be to reverse, right angle, 45 degrees, or left turn. The change in direction should be made quickly in pivotlike fashion.

Move and Change Speed or Level

Students move throughout the area. On signal, they are challenged to move close to the floor or as elongated as possible. They can be challenged to touch the floor or give a "high five" while moving. Combinations of changing the level as well as changing the speed of the movement can be developed.

Move and Change the Type of Locomotion

Students move using a specified locomotor movement. On signal, they change to another type of movement. Challenges can be given to do the movements forward, backward, sideways, or diagonally.

Move and Quickly Stop

Students move throughout the area and quickly stop under control. Emphasis should be placed on stopping using proper technique. Students should lower the center of gravity, widen the base of support, and place one foot in front of the other to absorb the force.

Move and Perform Athletic Movement

Students move and stop on signal. They then perform an athletic skill move, such as a basketball jump shot, leaping football pass catch, volleyball spike, or soccer kick. Students should place emphasis on correct form and timing. A variation of the activity is for students to move with a partner and throw a pass on signal, punt a ball, or shoot a basket. The partner catches the ball or rebounds the shot.

Move, Stop, and Pivot

Students move under control throughout the area. On signal, they stop, pivot, and resume moving. Emphasis should be placed on making a sharp pivot and a rapid acceleration. The skill is similar to running a pass pattern in football.

Move and Perform a Fitness Task

The class moves throughout the area. When a signal is given, students perform a predesignated fitness task. Examples of tasks are push-ups, sit-ups, squat thrusts, and crab kicks. The fitness tasks can be written on a card and flashed to the class to signal the next challenge.

Move and Perform a Stretch

The class is challenged to run throughout the area. On signal, they stop and perform a designated stretching activity. (See Chapter 17 for a comprehensive list of stretching exercises.) A list of stretches that covers all body parts can be posted, and students can perform a different stretch after each signal.

INDIVIDUAL ACTIVITIES

Number Challenges

Students are challenged to move and perform to a set of three to four numbers. For example, the given set of numbers might be 25, 10, 30. The first number would signify some type of locomotor movement, the second number a set of stretching exercises, and the last an activity with equipment. Implemented, this challenge might be 25 running steps, 10 repetitions of a stretching activity, and 30 rope-jumping turns.

Four Corners

A square is marked using four boundary cones. Students spread out around the perimeter of the square. On signal, they move in the same direction around the square. As they pass a corner, they change the locomotor movement they are doing. Other challenges would be to move on all fours, in crab position, or using a frog jump.

Gauntlet Run

Students line up at one end of a football field or area of similar size. Challenges are placed every 10 yd. Examples of challenges might be to jump over benches, crawl through hoops, run through tires, long-jump a certain distance, hop backwards, high-jump over a bar, do a forward roll, or perform an animal walk. Students can begin at different challenges so the activity does not become a race. Emphasis should be placed on warming up and achieving quality movement.

Rubber Band

Students begin from a central point with the instructor. On signal, the students move away from the instructor using a designated movement such as a jump, run, hop, slide, carioca, or walk. On the second signal, students sprint back to the instructor's position where the activity originated. The cycle is repeated with different movements. As a variation, students can perform one or two stretching activities when they return to the teacher.

Rope Jumping

Each student has a jump rope. On the first signal, they begin jumping rope. On the second signal, they drop the rope and perform a stretching activity. A third signal can be used to designate performing a light, easy run. Emphasis should be placed on preparing students for fitness activity rather than offering a severe work load.

Milk Carton Kicking

Half-gallon paper milk cartons filled with newspaper, or gallon-size plastic milk containers can be used for this introductory activity. Each student has a carton and dribbles or kicks it throughout the area. Students can also work with a partner and dribble the container back and forth. The carton is a medium for encouraging movement. All kicking and dribbling should be done on the move.

Ball Activities

Each student has a ball and dribbles it throughout the area while moving. On signal, students stop and move the ball behind the back, around each leg, and overhead. Emphasis is on learning to handle the ball as well as on moving. A variation is to drop one ball on signal and play catch with a partner until the signal to resume dribbling is given.

Beanbag Touch and Go

Different colored beanbags are spread throughout the area. On signal, students run to a beanbag, touch it, and resume running. To increase the challenge, the color of the beanbag can be specified and the touch must be made with a designated body part. An example might be, "Touch 6 yellow beanbags with your left hip." Students can also move to a beanbag, perform a pivot, and resume running.

Vanishing Beanbags

Enough beanbags to allow one for each student are spread throughout the area. Students move around the area until a signal is given. On the signal, they find a beanbag and sit on it. The instructor then signals for the class to move again, and one or more beanbags are removed during this interval. Now when students are signaled to find a beanbag, some will be left without one. A challenge is offered to not be left out more than five times. Locomotor movements and different body parts can be specified to add challenge and variety.

Rolling Hoops

Each student has a Hula-Hoop and rolls it alongside while running. On signal, the hoops are dropped, and students are challenged to move in and out of 15 hoops. The number and color of hoops to move in and out of can be specified, as well as the type of activity to perform. When the task is completed, the student picks up the hoop and resumes rolling it.

Animal Walks

Two parallel lines marked with boundary cones are placed 10 to 20 yd apart. Half of the class lines up on one line and the other half on the opposite line. On signal, students animal-walk from one line to the other. Examples of walks that can be done are the dog walk, seal walk, crab walk, rabbit jumps, bear walk, and walrus walk.

PARTNER AND SMALL GROUP ACTIVITIES

Marking

This is an excellent activity for learning to elude an opponent and also for learning to stay defensively near someone. Partners are selected, and one elects to chase the other. On the first signal, the challenge is to stay as close as possible to the partner who is attempting to get away. When a second signal is given, both partners must immediately freeze. If the chaser can reach out and "mark" the partner, the chaser scores a point. Roles are reversed each time a signal is given.

Pentabridge Hustle (Figure 16.8)

Students form groups of five. They spread out as far as possible in the playing area and form individual bridges that another person can move under. On signal, the first person in the group of five moves under the other four bridging students and runs ahead and forms a bridge. The next person in sequence moves under the four bridges. This becomes a continuous movement activity. Activity success depends on making sure that students form bridges that are quite a distance apart so enough running occurs to ensure warm-up.

Over, Under, and Around (Figure 16.9)

Students find a partner. One person gets in position on all fours while the other stands alongside, ready to begin the movement challenge. The challenge is given to move over, go under, and run around the partner a certain number of times. For

Figure 16.9.   Over, under, and around

example, move over your partner 5 times, go under 8 times, and run around 13 times. When the task is completed, partners change positions and the challenge is repeated. To increase motivation, the challenge can be made to move over, under, and around different students. For a more difficult challenge, the persons on all fours can move slowly throughout the area.

New Leader

Students work in small groups. The task is to continuously move in a productive fashion that will warm up the group. One person begins as the leader. When a signal is given, a new leader steps up and leads the next activity.

Pyramid Power (Figure 16.10)

Students move throughout the area. On signal, they find a partner and build a simple pyramid or partner stand. Examples are the hip-shoulder stand, double-crab stand, double-dog stand, and shoulder stand. Students should be cautioned to select a partner of similar size and to stand on the proper points of support.

Leapfrog

Students work in groups of four or five. All students in the group move into the leapfrog base position with the exception of the last person in line. On signal, the last person leapfrogs over the others and moves into a base position. The next person now leapfrogs over the others, and the activity becomes one of continuous movement. Activity success depends on maintaining a large distance between each of the leapfrog bases.

Figure 16.8.   Pentabridge hustle

Figure 16.10. Examples of pyramid power

Tag Games

A wide variety of tag games can be used to motivate students to move. They are excellent for teaching students to elude and chase each other. Examples of tag games are

1. **Balance Tag.** To be safe, balance in a stipulated position.
2. **Push-up Tag.** Assume the push-up or other designated position to avoid being tagged.
3. **Snowball Tag.** Two people begin by being *it*. When they tag someone, they hold hands. As a number of people are tagged, the chain of people becomes long, and only those at the end of the chain are eligible to tag.
4. **Frozen Tag.** When tagged, the person must freeze with the feet in straddle position. To be able to resume play, three people must move under and through a frozen person's legs.
5. **Spider Tag.** Everyone has a partner and stands back to back with the partner with the elbows hooked. A pair of people are *it* and chase the other pairs. If a pair is tagged (or becomes unhooked), they are *it*.
6. **Triangle Plus One Tag.** Three students hold hands to form a triangle. One person in the triangle is the leader. The fourth person outside the triangle tries to tag the leader. The triangle moves around to avoid getting the leader tagged. Leader and tagger are changed often.

Follow-the-Leader

Students are grouped by pairs. On signal, the leader performs all types of movements to elude his or her partner. Zigzags, rolls, 360-degree turns, and jumps are encouraged. Partners switch after 30 sec. The same drill can be done with one leader and two or more followers.

Hoops on the Ground

Students run around the area in which hoops are spread. When the teacher calls a number, students must get that number of students inside one hoop in 5 sec or less.

Mirror Drill in Place (Figure 16.11)

Each student faces a partner. One person is the leader and makes a quick movement with the hands, head, legs, or body. The partner tries to be a mirror and perform the exact movement. The leader must pause briefly between movements. Leader and partner exchange places after 30 sec.

Formation Rhythmic Running

The class begins in circular formation. Students move to a drumbeat or other steady beat. They attempt to run rhythmically to the beat, lifting the knees and maintaining a formation or line with even spacing between students. Challenges can be added, such as clapping hands on the first beat, stamping the feet on the third beat, and thrusting a hand into the air on the fourth beat of a four-count rhythm.

As students become experienced at maintaining the formation and rhythm of the activity, they can be led into different formations such as a rectangle, square, triangle, or line. Students can also "wind up" and "unwind" the line, and can learn to cross in front of each other to "break a line."

Figure 16.11.   Mirror drill

Chapter 17

Physical Fitness

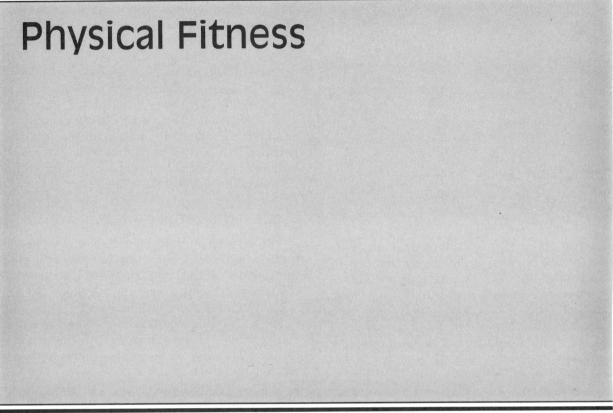

All students have the right to develop a meaningful level of physical fitness. Physical education programs that do not make time for fitness development indirectly teach students that fitness is not important for a healthy life-style. At the secondary school level, students should have the opportunity to experience and select fitness routines that are useful and motivating to them personally. Physical fitness activity should be offered as a positive contribution to total wellness. It should be something that benefits those who participate, and not something to be used as punishment when a student misbehaves.

PHYSICAL FITNESS AND WELLNESS

Secondary school students need to know the payoffs of developing a high level of fitness. It is important that they understand the impact that fitness can have on their state of wellness. If a need for fitness is not demonstrated to students, teachers cannot expect them to choose to stay physically fit when their school days are over. The following points highlight the importance of wellness and the role played by physical activity in a healthy life-style.

HEART DISEASE

Heart disease afflicts 500,000 to 2 million people, depending on the statistics one examines. It is a killer of young people as well as adults. Many think of it as a geriatric disease, yet symptoms have been found in as many as 70% of American youth. In an Iowa study (Glass 1973), 5000 youngsters between ages 6 and 18 were examined over a two-year period. Seventy percent had one or more positive risk factors, such as high cholesterol levels, high blood pressure, or obesity.

On examining the development of arteriosclerosis in humans, Dr. Kenneth Rose (1973) wrote: "The first signs appear around age two and the disease process is reversible until the age of nineteen. At nineteen, the process of the disease appears to be irreversible, and from then on, it inexorably progresses until it becomes clinically manifest, usually in the forties."

Students need to be aware of the heart disease risk factors and how they can modify each of them. The primary risk factors are high blood pressure, cigarette smoking, and high cholesterol levels. Secondary risk factors are less strongly associated with heart disease, but are still important. These are obesity, lack of exercise, stress, and heredity. As an example of how risk factors increase the possibility of heart attack, consider that if one smokes and has high blood pressure and high cholesterol levels, the risk of heart attack is increased fivefold.

CHOLESTEROL LEVELS

Exercise, or lack of it, is linked to cholesterol levels. Regular aerobic exercise appears to reduce cholesterol levels. How cholesterol travels in the blood may be more important than the serum cholesterol level. High-density lipoproteins (HDL) appear to cleanse the body of cholesterol in contrast with low-density lipoproteins (LDL), which carry cholesterol to be deposited at the cellular level. The critical point in terms of cardiovascular disease is the ratio of HDL to LDL. Exercise appears to increase the ratio of HDL to LDL and to increase lean body weight (Gilliam et al. 1978).

STRESS

Exercise appears to reduce stress levels. The tranquilizer effect of exercise has been compared with the effect of the common tranquilizer meprobamate (deVries and Adams 1972). Five treatments were given and studied using 36 anxious patients. One treatment was the tranquilizer, another was a placebo, the third was walking at a heart rate of 100 for 15 min, the fourth was 15 min of walking at a heart rate of 120, and the fifth was a controlled comparison with resting. The results showed that 15 min of walking caused a 20% to 25% reduction in muscular activity, which in turn reduced anxiety. The tranquilizer had no impact on the subjects.

Even though this study was done with elderly subjects, it bears out the point that even moderate exercise can bring about a reduction in anxiety and stress levels. One problem most teenagers must deal with is stress. They are constantly under pressure and are expected to perform well in relation to peers. Since exercise is a stressor, it can prepare the body to cope and resist other types of stress in life (Miller and Allen 1982). The impact that stress has on an individual's state of health may thus be reduced through exercise.

SMOKING

Smoking one pack of cigarettes per day increases the risk of heart disease threefold. It is difficult, if not impossible, to justify the use of tobacco. Secondary school students, however, have many motivations for smoking, and a blatant "Don't do it!" serves little purpose. Perhaps the most effective strategy is to conduct valuing sessions in which students analyze both sides of the issue. The emphasis is on making a personal decision based on each individual's unique parameters. Materials dealing with smoking and related hazards are available from the Department of Health and Human Services, Rockville, MD 20852.

BONE STRUCTURE AND FLEXIBILITY

Exercise affects skeletal development. Vigorous activity causes increased stress on the bones, which results in an increase in bone diameter and improved internal structure. Osteoporosis, or loss of bony tissue through demineralization, is the result of inactivity. This condition causes bones to be more susceptible to breaking. Exercise can reverse the process and develop bones that are highly mineralized and resistant to fracture.

Flexibility and joint mobility can be maintained through exercise, because exercise increases the elasticity of the muscles, tendons, and ligaments. Flexibility results in fewer injuries, better posture, and improved sport performance.

MUSCULATURE

Exercise causes an increase in strength, and strength is an important factor in learning motor skills (Rarick and Dobbins 1975). Strength is also important in reducing sport injuries to joints. For these reasons, weight lifting is used in athletic training regardless of the activity.

A loss of strength is often associated with increasing age. In fact, loss of strength is usually a result of inactivity instead of physiological changes. In a study (Petrofsky and Lind 1975) examining grip strength in 100 men who worked in a machine shop, no change in grip strength was found from age 22 to 62. Regular exercise is thus essential to maintain an adequate level of strength throughout life.

OBESITY

Excess weight is found in over 30% of all schoolchildren. Obesity is a factor that decreases the motor performance of students. This occurs because of the reduction in strength to body weight ratio. In many teenagers, obesity is unfortunately due to a decrease in muscular activity. As weight increases, the impulse for physical exertion decreases. As students become more obese, the cycle becomes uncontrollable, so that many overweight youngsters see no point in trying to control their weight.

Lack of activity appears to be a critical factor in cases of obesity. This heart disease risk factor not only affects the health status of individuals, but takes a psychological toll as well. In diet comparisons of obese and normal weight students, no substantial difference in caloric consumption was found. In a study of high school girls (Johnson et al. 1956), obese female students were found to eat less than normal weight girls, but they also exercised two-thirds less (in total time). Movies taken of normal and overweight youngsters (Corbin and Fletcher 1968) demonstrated a wide difference in activity levels of the two groups, but their diets were similar.

Obesity is measured by the percent body fat an individual carries. Body fat can be measured easily using skin calipers, and this measurement can be converted to give an estimate of the percent of body fat an individual carries in relation to total body weight. If an individual carries more than 20% fat, the person is carrying excess fat.

Exercise can have a strong impact on weight reduction. The two ways of reducing body fat are through exercise and diet. Diet is more often chosen because it seems less difficult. Permanent weight losses seldom occur through diet manipulation, however. The best answer for most individuals is usually a combination of moderate dieting and increased activity.

A close look at dieting reveals the relative effectiveness of the process. It is necessary to burn approximately 3500 calories to lose 1 lb of fat. A person fasting completely would still lose only 1 lb per day. Most people can easily maintain their weight on 2000 to 2800 calories per day, which reveals the difficulty of weight control by diet alone. Most of the rapid weight losses boasted by different diets are due to the loss of body fluids, not body fat. In fact, during the first two or three weeks of crash dieting, 60% to 70% of the weight lost is lean body tissue that includes body fluids (Wilmore 1980). The loss of lean body tissue is undesirable because of the loss of body strength and the effect on physical appearance.

What is the maximum amount of weight that can be lost using a starvation diet? If a female who normally consumed 2000 calories to maintain body weight went on a starvation diet, one might estimate that she would lose about 0.6 lb of fat per day. When food intake is reduced to starvation levels (Wilmore 1980), however, the body reduces its energy needs by 25% to 30%. The amount of calories burned per day is therefore reduced to 1400 to 1500, and the amount of fat lost is only about 0.4 lb per day. Under these severe restrictions, the dieter would be able to lose about 3 lb per week, at most.

Examine the impact of exercise on weight loss. Approximately 3500 calories must be burned to lose 1 lb. Depending on the size of the individual, approximately 120 calories can be burned per mile of movement. If 1 mi of running or pace walking were done everyday, 840 calories would be burned per week. At the end of a month of exercise, 3600 calories would be expended. If the individual's caloric intake were maintained, a pound of weight would still be lost. At the end of a year, 12 lb of weight would be lost. Exercise is a slower way to lose weight, but it carries many health-related benefits and the weight loss is often permanent. Remember that weight is gained slowly over a period of days, weeks, and years. Individuals should not expect to lose it in a period of one or two weeks.

LONGEVITY

If one wants to live longer, consider the results of a study done using 7000 subjects in California (Nelson 1979). Seven health habits were examined: (1) eating regularly and not snacking between meals, (2) eating breakfast, (3) getting eight hours of sleep, (4) maintaining normal weight, (5) not smoking, (6) not drinking or drinking in moderation, and (7) exercising regularly. Men who observed all seven of the healthy living practices were shown to live an average of 11 years longer than men observing only one or none of the habits. Women who observed the practices lived an average of seven years longer than those who did not. Men who participated in active sports had the lowest mortality rate.

The relationship of exercise to human wellness is becoming increasingly clear. The responsibility for good health resides with the individual to foresee and prevent health dysfunctions. Students need to relate exercise and activity with a healthy body in much the same way that they have learned to associate brushing the teeth with dental health.

A LIFETIME OF FITNESS ACTIVITY

Students often leave school with little insight into fitness and how it can be a part of one's daily life-style. The following points give students a framework for developing an approach to lifetime fitness. The points are general in nature and should help most students feel that they are capable of maintaining physical fitness.

1. Perform activity you enjoy. If it is going to be a part of your life-style, it should be enjoyable and rewarding.

2. Do not overdo it. When exercising, stop if fatigue sets in. Make the exercise pleasant—take along your dog, pick some flowers, talk to friends. Tie the routine to something enjoyable. If the experience is overly painful, most individuals will discontinue it. Rewards must occur in one form or another, such as improved appearance, weight control, or feeling less stressed.

3. Make it personal. Many adults choose fitness activities that can be done individually. Jogging, walking, and calisthenics are possible choices.

4. Make it a top priority in life. Nothing should be a higher priority than one's personal health. Without health, it is impossible to work, play, and fulfill other responsibilities.

5. Make exercise an important part of the daily routine. Exercise must be as important as work, health habits, and leisure-time activities. If it does not get equal billing, it does not get done when time is short. Allow 30 min a day for exercise.

6. Exercise at any time during the day. The only exceptions are the 1 to 2 hr after a meal, and when the weather is too hot and humid.

7. If you like to monitor personal improvement, do so, but do not get drawn into a competitive situation that reduces spontaneity and enjoyment of the activity.

8. There is some evidence (Glasser 1976) that if the following activity conditions are met, exercise will become positively addicting and a necessary part of one's life.
   a. The activity must be noncompetitive; the person chooses and wants to do it.
   b. It does not require a great deal of mental effort.
   c. The activity can be done alone, without a partner or teammates.
   d. The participant believes in the value of the exercise for improving health and general welfare.
   e. The participant believes that the activity will become easier and more meaningful if they persist. To become addicting, the activity must be done for at least six months.
   f. The activity is accomplished in such a manner that the participant is not self-critical.

COMPONENTS OF PHYSICAL FITNESS

Many components of physical fitness have been identified, such as strength, power, cardiorespiratory endurance, agility, flexibility, and speed. This discussion is concerned primarily with those components that are health-related. They are flexibility, muscular strength and endurance, body composition, and cardiovascular endurance. These components are measured by the AAHPERD Health Related Fitness Test (1980) and are important in maintaining wellness.

FLEXIBILITY

Flexibility is the range of movement through which a joint or sequence of joints can move. Inactive individuals tend to lose joint flexibility, for physical activity retains the range of movement. Through stretching activities, the length of muscles, tendons, and ligaments is increased. The ligaments and tendons are more likely to retain their elasticity if used often.

Flexibility is important to fitness, and a lack of flexibility creates many problems. Individuals who are flexible are less subject to injury in sports, possess sound posture, and may have less lower back pain. Many physical activities also demand a wide range of motion to generate maximum force.

Two types of stretching activities have been used to develop flexibility. Ballistic stretching (strong bouncing movements) was until recently the more common, but has come under scrutiny of late since it may initiate the stretch reflex. This reflex is an involuntary response to a stimulus (stretch) and causes the muscle to contract. The reflex may thus cause muscle soreness or strain and may not develop an increased range of motion.

Static, controlled stretching, without bounce, is more effective because it does not induce the stretch reflex. This activity type involves gradually increasing the stretch to the point of discomfort, backing off from the discomfort to a point at which the stretch can be held comfortably, and then maintaining the stretch for an extended time. Static stretching is safer and less likely to cause injury than ballistic stretching. It can be used to reduce muscle soreness or to prepare for strenuous activity. The length of time to hold the stretch can begin at 10 to 15 sec and be gradually increased to 30 to 45 sec.

MUSCULAR STRENGTH AND ENDURANCE

Strength is the ability of muscles to exert maximum force. It is an important component in learning motor skills. Most activities in which students are involved do not build strength in the areas where it is most needed—the arm-shoulder girdle and the abdominal region.

Muscular endurance is the ability to exert force over an extended period of time. Endurance postpones the onset of fatigue so that activity can be performed for long periods. Most sport activities demand that muscular skills, such as throwing, kicking, and striking, be performed many times without fatigue.

When muscular strength is a desired outcome of training, maximum work loads must be lifted or moved with minimal repetitions. There is great diversity in training methods among strength coaches. Three sets of 3 to 6 repetitions with high resistance is, however, commonly accepted as a way to develop strength in a specific muscle group. Strength development is accompanied by muscle hypertrophy, an increase in the number of muscle fibers recruited, and an increase in oxygen-use capacity.

To develop muscular endurance, a low-resistance, high-repetition work load is suggested. Anywhere from 10 to 20 repetitions for three sets is suggested per muscle group to develop endurance. For most athletes, a balance of strength and endurance is probably most useful.

As a rule, muscle strength and endurance workouts should be conducted three days per week. A workout followed by a day of rest is desirable. Some athletes use a six day per week program in which they exercise the upper body and lower body on alternate days. Regardless of the regimen, the rest day is probably as important as the workout day to achieve beneficial results.

Isotonics, Isometrics, and Isokinetics

The majority of exercises used for routines and weight lifting involve **isotonic contractions**. These are contractions of a muscle through its full range of motion. Walking, jogging, calisthenics, and bicycling are examples of activities that stimulate isotonic contractions.

Isometric contractions are those that occur without movement. The contraction is made against an immovable object, and muscles do not shorten as they do in isotonic contractions. Isometric exercise is a somewhat controversial method for developing strength, but it does appear to be effective. To achieve results, contractions should be an all-out effort and held for 8 to 12 sec. A shortcoming of isometrics is that they build strength only at the angle of contraction. They should therefore be implemented at various joint angles in an attempt to develop strength throughout the complete range of motion.

Isokinetic contractions are a type of isotonic contraction that demands the use of special machines. **Isokinetic contractions** are maximal contractions throughout the complete range of motion. Isokinetic devices mechanically control the work load so the resistance and rate of movement are maintained regardless of the mechanical advantage that occurs as the contraction nears completion. Isokinetic exercise appears to be more effective than isotonic or isometric exercise (Miller and Allen 1982), but the requirement of special equipment probably makes this type of exercise impractical in the school setting.

BODY COMPOSITION

Body composition, or the proportion of body fat to lean body mass, is now regarded as an integral part of health-related fitness. As discussed earlier, the percentage of body fat is calculated by applying formulas to a measurement of the thickness of selected skinfolds.

Physical fitness is difficult to envision when an individual is extremely obese. The understanding of caloric intake and expenditure is important to maintaining wellness, for it is possible to eat enough to gain weight regardless of the amount of exercise performed. Since the wellness status of individuals is dependent on body composition, students must learn the concepts and consequences in this area.

CARDIOVASCULAR ENDURANCE

This element plays a key role in living a healthy life-style and may be the most important element of fitness. **Cardiovascular endurance** is the ability of the heart, the blood vessels, and the respiratory system to use oxygen over an extended period of time.

To develop cardiovascular endurance, activity must be aerobic in nature. **Aerobic exercise** demands the constant supply and use of oxygen. Activities that are continuous and rhythmic in nature require that a continuous supply of oxygen be delivered to the muscle cells. The amount of oxygen that the body can use while engaged in continuous, rhythmic activity for a given period of time is called **maximal oxygen uptake** and is the best indicator of cardiovascular endurance. Activities that stimulate development in this area are paced walking, jogging, biking, rope jumping, aerobic dance, swimming, and continuous sports such as basketball or handball.

In contrast to aerobic activity is **anaerobic exercise,** or activity that is so intense that the body cannot supply oxygen at the cellular level. The cells can therefore continue the activity for a short time only. Examples of anaerobic activity are sprinting, running up stairs, or an all-out effort in any sport.

DEVELOPING PHYSICAL FITNESS

The following points deal with enhancing the level of fitness in students. Students should leave a physical education program keenly aware of these basic principles and able to apply them to a personal fitness program.

OVERLOAD

To increase one's present level of physical fitness, the body must be overloaded beyond the normal activity level. To ensure that systematic overloading occurs, students should be able to prescribe their own work loads. Frequency, duration, and intensity are the variables involved in arranging the amount of exercise necessary. These variables are interrelated, so changing one may require a change in another.

Frequency is the number of exercise sessions an individual performs per week. Three to five workouts are necessary for benefits to accrue. In cardiovascular endurance exercise, a strenuous and demanding workout is usually followed the next day by a mild exercise bout. As mentioned earlier, strength training demands a day of complete rest between workouts. To maintain an acceptable level of fitness, a minimum of three workouts per week is usually required.

Duration is the length of each exercise bout. For developing cardiovascular endurance, the minimum amount of aerobic exercise should be 20 to 30 min. The intensity of the exercise will have an impact on the duration of the fitness session. For most individuals, monitoring the duration of the activity instead of the intensity is best. An example would be the jogger who is torn between monitoring the amount of time spent jogging versus timing the speed (intensity) at which the distance can be run.

To measure **intensity** in aerobic activity, the heart rate should be monitored. A productive intensity requires that the heart rate reach the training state, which is 60% to 80% of the maximum rate possible. Duration and intensity can also be monitored in strength development. Most strength-inducing activities are of high intensity and therefore require an increase in duration through an increased number of sets, or repetitions.

Progression is important to maintain motivation and reduce the chance of injury. Work loads should be increased gradually by increasing the intensity and duration of exercise. Teachers can sometimes be overly enthusiastic about developing fitness in a short amount of time. Remember that achieving fitness is an ongoing process that needs to occur throughout a lifetime. The important point is to stimulate and then maintain the students' desire to exercise. A reasonable progression during the school year will help ensure that this occurs.

TRAINING HEART RATE

Heart rate can be used to determine the intensity of exercise. It gives an indication of whether the work load should be increased or decreased. To monitor heart rate, palpate at the wrist or carotid artery. When palpating the pulse at the wrist, place the index and middle finger near the joint on the thumb side (Figure 17.1). If the pulse is to be found at the carotid artery, first find the Adam's apple, then slide the index and middle finger to either side. Apply only slight pressure at either site to allow blood flow to continue.

To count the heart rate, begin the count within 5 sec after stopping exercise. The count should start at zero, be taken for 10 sec, and multiplied by 6 to give the heart rate per min. The heart rate should decrease to less than 120 beats per min after

Figure 17.1. Taking the pulse at the wrist (reprinted from *Dynamic Physical Education for Elementary School Children*, 7th ed. by V. P. Dauer and R. P. Pangrazi, 1983. Minneapolis: Burgess Publishing Co., p. 101)

exercise has been terminated for 5 min. This is called the **recovery heart rate** and gives a rough indication of fitness level.

For exercise to enhance the level of cardiovascular endurance, the heart rate must be elevated to the training state. Using the following formula, the heartbeat range that should be maintained during exercise can be calculated.

1. Determine the estimated maximum heart rate by taking 220 minus the individual's age.
2. Multiply the difference by 60% and 80%.

The two results give the range of heart rates per minute that should be maintained while exercising. For example, assume that a student is age 16. Subtract 16 from 220, which equals 204. Multiply 204 by 60% and 80%. According to these results, a heart rate between 122 and 163 beats per min should be maintained during exercise to reach the training state.

Once the training heart rate has been determined, the exercise routine can be undertaken. At the conclusion of the workout, monitor the heart rate. If it is above the beats per minute allowed by the formula, reduce the intensity of the workout. On the other hand, if the heart rate is too low, increase the intensity of the aerobic exercise.

WARMING UP AND COOLING DOWN

Warm-up activities should be conducted before an intense workout. Secondary school students probably have a lesser need for warm-up routines than older adults since they have little cardiovascular degeneration. It is important, however, that students learn that warming up and cooling down are necessary phases of exercising.

Warm-up activities should cause a gradual increase in the heart rate and body temperature. They should consist of flexibility exercises that stretch all the major muscle groups. Light-paced jogging can also prepare the heart muscle for the oncoming workout.

After the workout, cooling down should be accomplished by walking for a few minutes. This can help prevent soreness the next day by massaging the waste products of exercise into the circulatory system. When a person stops exercising, the heart continues for a time to pump blood to the muscles at a vigorous rate. If no cooling down activity is done, there is little action to send the blood back to the heart, and it will pool in the veins. This pooling may cause light-headedness, which can be prevented by proper cooling down. The walking might be followed with stretching exercises to undo the tightening of muscle groups that occurs from strenuous activity.

SPECIFICITY OF EXERCISE

Physical conditioning should match the demands that a sport or activity makes on an individual. **Specificity** infers that all skills and activities are unique and require training that is geared specifically to each. The implication of specificity is that if only a certain part or component of the body is exercised, only that part develops. A consideration of specificity emphasizes the importance of a balanced approach to fitness. For example, if one chooses only to jog for fitness, the cardiovascular system will be developed. Flexibility, however, will decrease in the lower back and hamstrings, and abdominal strength will decrease. Muscular power, as revealed by the vertical jump, will decrease also. The need for a balanced approach to fitness by including flexibility, strength development, and cardiovascular endurance activity in an exercise regimen thus becomes apparent.

EXERCISES FOR DEVELOPING PHYSICAL FITNESS

Exercises in this section are divided into four groups. The first group consists of warm-up and flexibility activities. The following groups of exercises primarily develop muscular strength and endurance in these areas: upper body, midsection, and lower body. When exercise routines are planned, they should contain a balance of activities from all groups. The following instructional procedures (and exercises to avoid) should be considered carefully when developing exercise routines.

INSTRUCTIONAL PROCEDURES

1. When a new exercise is introduced, it should be demonstrated, broken into components, and its value explained. It should be practiced at a slower-than-normal pace and then speeded up. Proper form should be emphasized.

2. Work load depends on the number of repetitions or duration of effort. The instructor should start at a minimal work load and gradually increase the amount. Lesson plans should reflect the desired work load so it is a matter of record.

3. When isometric or partner-resistance exercises are used, students should be taught to make a maximum effort for 8 to 12 sec. Students must learn to monitor the duration of their efforts and perform the activities in sets.

4. At times, allow students to set their own limits for exercises. For example, they can be given a "challenge week" during which they set the work load that they would like to accomplish. This can be the start of self-direction and personalizing fitness development.

5. In the early stages of learning rhythmic exercises, a means for starting the activities should be developed. For example, "one, two, ready, begin" could be used to start activities, and "one, two, and halt" to stop them. This helps emphasize for students the parts of an exercise.

6. Proper form is important when performing exercises. For instance, in exercises in which the arms are held in front of the body or overhead, the abdominal wall needs to be contracted to maintain proper positioning of the pelvis. The feet should be pointed reasonably straight ahead, the chest should be up, and the head and shoulders in good postural alignment.

7. Exercises in this section are not enough to develop cardiovascular endurance. Additional aerobic activity is necessary to enhance this important component of fitness. Furthermore, the aerobic activity should be varied. Too often, such activity consists of everybody running a lap. This practice is not only boring, but does little to meet the personal needs of all students. Exercise substitutes for running might be inter-

val training, rope jumping, obstacle courses, grass drills, astronaut drills, brisk walking, rhythmic aerobic exercise, and parachute movements.

AVOIDING HARMFUL PRACTICES AND EXERCISES

The following points should be considered when offering fitness instruction:

1. When developing abdominal strength, the sit-up with the knees bent should be used instead of the straight-leg sit-up. When the legs are bent at the knee, the abdominal muscles are isolated from the psoas muscle group. This concentrates development on the abdominals rather than on the lower back area, and avoids development of an excessive lower back curve. Sit-ups should be performed with a smooth curling movement with the chin tucked. This prevents the bouncing and jerking motion often observed.

2. When stretching exercises are performed, a smooth, constant pressure should be applied. Students should stretch to the point of discomfort, then back off slightly and hold the position. Bouncing to further the range of motion should be avoided, and in fact actually decreases the level of flexibility. Stretching exercises must be done in a controlled, slow, and sustained manner.

3. If forward flexion is done from a sitting position in an effort to touch the toes, the bend should be from the hips, and not the waist.

4. Straight-leg raises from a supine position should be avoided because they may strain the lower back. This problem can be alleviated by placing the hands under the small of the back.

5. Deep-knee bends (full squats) should be avoided, for they may damage the knee joints. Note that deep-knee bends have little developmental value as an exercise. It is much more beneficial to flex the knee joint to 90 degrees and then extend the joint.

6. In stretching exercises performed from a standing position, the knees should not be hyperextended. The knee joint should be relaxed rather than locked. In all stretching activities, participants must judge their own range of motion. Expecting all students to be able to touch their toes is an unrealistic goal, particularly in the early stages of exercising.

7. Caution must be used in placing stress on the neck. Examples of activities in which caution

should be used are the inverted bicycle, wrestler's bridge, and the sit-up performed with the hands behind the head. Most of these activities can be avoided, or work loads can be carefully adjusted to the capacity of the student.

FLEXIBILITY AND WARM-UP EXERCISES

The exercises in this section increase the range of motion at various joints. They also prepare the body for more strenuous activity, which may follow. In the beginning, the stretching positions should be held for approximately 10 sec. As flexibility increases, the stretches can be held for up to 30 sec.

Lower Leg Stretches

Lower Leg Stretch (Figure 17.2).   Stand facing a wall with the feet about shoulder width apart. Place the palms of the hands on the wall at eye level. Walk away from the wall, keeping the body straight, until the stretch is felt in the lower portion of the calf. The feet should remain flat on the floor during the stretch.

Achilles Tendon Stretch.   Stand facing a wall with the forearms on it. Place the forehead on the back of the hands. Back 2 to 3 ft away from the wall, bend, and move one leg closer to the wall. Flex the bent leg with the foot on the floor until the stretch is felt in the Achilles tendon area. The feet should remain flat on the floor as the leg clos-est to the wall is flexed. Repeat, flexing the other leg.

Balance Beam Stretch (Figure 17.3).   Place one foot in front of the other, about 3 ft apart. The feet should be in line as though one were walking a balance beam. Bend the forward leg at the knee, lean forward, and keep the rear foot flat on the floor. Repeat with the opposite leg forward. The calf of the rear leg should be stretched.

Upper Leg Stretches

Bear Hug.   Stand with one leg forward and the other to the rear. Bend the forward knee as much as possible while keeping the rear foot flat on the floor. Repeat the exercise with the other foot forward. **Variation:** Different muscles can be stretched by turning the hips slightly in either direction. To increase the stretching motion, look over the shoulder and toward the rear foot.

Leg Pick-up.   Sit on the floor with the legs spread. Reach forward and grab the outside of the ankle with one hand and the outside of the knee with the other. Pick the leg up and pull the ankle toward the chin. The back of the upper leg should be stretched. Repeat the stretch, lifting the other leg.

Side Leg Stretch (Figure 17.4).   Lie on the floor on the left side. Reach down with the right hand and grab the ankle. Pull the ankle and upper leg toward the rear of the body. Pull the ankle as near to the buttocks as possible and hold, stretching the front of the thigh. Repeat with the other side of the body.

Figure 17.2.   Lower leg stretch

Figure 17.3.   Balance beam stretch

Figure 17.4. Side leg stretch

Hurdler's Stretch.   Sit on the floor with one leg forward and one to the rear as though moving over a hurdle. The forward leg should be straight, and the rear leg bent and tucked in toward the buttocks. Lean gradually forward, bending at the hips and tucking the head. This stretches the back of the thigh. Next, lean backward, away from the forward leg, to stretch the top of the thigh. Repeat, reversing leg positions.

Groin Stretch.   Sit on the floor with the legs spread as far apart and kept as straight as possible. Slowly lean forward from the hips and reach with the hands. Do not bend at the neck and shoulders, because that puts pressure on the lower back. Stretch and hold in three positions: left, right, and directly ahead.

Lower Back Stretches

Back Bender.   Stand with the feet about shoulder width apart. Bend the knees slightly and gradually bend the lower back starting at the hips. Relax the arms and neck and let the upper body hang. If more stretch is desired, gradually straighten the legs.

Ankle Hold.   From a standing position with the knees bent, reach down and hold both ankles with the hands. Gradually straighten the legs, applying stretch to the lower back.

Sitting Toe Touch.   Sit on the floor with the legs straight and together. Reach forward and grab the lower legs. Gradually walk the hands down the legs toward the ankles; continue to walk the hands down and touch the toes. Remember to bend from the hips, not the upper back.

Feet Together Stretch.   Sit with the knees bent and the soles of the feet touching. Reach forward with the hands and grasp the toes. Gently pull on the toes and bend forward from the hips, applying

stretch to the inside of the legs and lower back. To increase the stretching effect, place the elbows on or near the knees and press them toward the floor.

Cross-Legged Stretch.   Sit on the floor with the legs crossed and tucked toward the buttocks. Lean forward with the elbows in front of the knees. To stretch the sides of the lower back, lean forward to the left and then the right.

Body Twist (Figure 17.5).   Sit on the floor with the right leg straight. Lift the left leg over the right leg and place it on the floor outside the right knee. Move the right elbow outside the upper left thigh and use it to maintain pressure on the leg. Lean back and support the upper body with the left hand. Rotate the upper body toward the left hand and arm. Reverse the position and stretch the other side of the body.

Table Stretch.   Stand facing a table, chair, or similar platform. Place one leg on the table while maintaining the weight on the other leg. Lean forward from the hips to apply stretch to the hamstrings and lower back. Repeat with the other leg on the table. **Variation:** Stand with the side of the body facing the table. Place one leg on the table and bend toward the table to stretch the inside of the leg. Repeat with the other side of the body facing the table.

Back Stretches

Back Roller Stretch.   Curl up by holding the lower legs with the arms. Tuck the head gently on the knees. Tip backward and then roll back and forth gently. The rolling action should be slow and should stretch the length of the back. **Variation:** Perform the same stretch but cross the legs and tuck them close to the buttocks.

Figure 17.5. Body twist

Straight-Leg Roller. In a sitting position, roll backward and allow the legs to move overhead. Support the hips with the hands to control the stretch. The legs can be straightened and moved to different positions to vary the intensity and location of the stretch.

Squat Stretch (Figure 17.6). Begin in a standing position with the legs shoulder width apart and the feet pointed outward. Gradually move to a squatting position, keeping the feet flat on the floor if possible. If balance is a problem, the stretch can be done while leaning against a wall.

Side of the Body Stretches

Wall Stretch. Stand with one side toward the wall. Lean toward the wall and support the body with the hand. Walk away until the feet are 2 to 3 ft from the wall. While supporting the weight in the leaning position, bend the body toward the wall, stretching the side. Reverse and stretch the other side.

Elbow Grab Stretch. In a standing position with the feet spread, raise the hands above the head. Grab the elbows with the hands. Lean to the side and pull the elbow in that direction. Reverse and pull to the opposite side.

Standing Hip Bend (Figure 17.7). Stand with one hand on the hip and the other arm overhead. Bend to the side with the hand resting on the hip. The arm overhead should point and move in the direction of the stretch with a slight bend at the elbow. Reverse and stretch the opposite side.

Sitting Side Stretch. Sit on the floor with the

Figure 17.7. Standing hip bend

legs spread as far apart as possible. Lift the arms overhead and reach toward one foot. Reverse and stretch in the opposite direction. Try to maintain an erect upper body.

Arm and Shoulder Girdle Stretches

Arm and Shoulder Stretch. Standing, extend the arms and place the palms of the hands together. Move the arms upward and overhead. Lift the arms as high as possible over the head.

Elbow Puller. Bend the right arm and place it behind the head. Reach to the right elbow with the left hand. Pull the elbow to the left to stretch the triceps and the top of the shoulders. Reverse the positions of the arms and repeat.

Elbow Pusher. Place the right arm over the left shoulder. Push the right elbow toward the body with the left hand and hold. Repeat in the opposite direction.

Wishbone Stretch (Figure 17.8). Move the arms behind the back and clasp hands. Keep the arms straight and raise the hands toward the ceiling to stretch the shoulder girdle. **Variation:** Stand near a wall (back toward the wall) and place the hands on it. Gently bend at the knees and lower the body while keeping the hands at the same level.

Exercises for Upper Body Development

Push-ups (Figure 17.9). The basic push-up is done from the front leaning rest position. Only the hands and toes are on the floor, and the body is

Figure 17.6. Squat stretch

Figure 17.8. Wishbone stretch

Figure 17.9. Push-up

kept as straight as possible. The exercise is a two-count movement, as the body is lowered by bending only at the elbows and then returned to the starting position.

As the body is lowered, only the chest touches the floor before the return to starting position. The push-up should be done with controlled movement. The arms can be adjusted together or apart, depending on the desired muscles to be exercised. As the arms are moved closer together, greater demands are placed on the triceps. Spreading the arms beyond shoulder width increases the work load on the muscles across the chest (pectorals). **Variation:** If it is difficult to perform a full push-up, the half (knee) push-up is excellent. Movement is the same as the push-up, but the body is supported by the hands and knees.

Inclined Wall Push-ups (Figure 17.10). This exercise can be done with either the feet or the hands on the wall. The hands version is easier and should precede the push-up with feet on the wall. In the hands version, the hands are placed on the wall while the feet walk as far from the wall as possible. The farther the performer's feet move from the wall, the more inclined and difficult the push-up will be.

When the student is able to do the inclined push-up with the hands on the wall, the feet-on-the-wall version can be attempted. This exercise is similar to doing a push-up in the handstand position and demands a great deal of strength. As the hands are walked closer to the wall, the incline becomes less, and a greater demand is placed on the shoulder girdle muscles of the performer.

Reclining Partner Pull-ups (Figure 17.11). Students find a partner of similar strength. One partner assumes a supine position on the floor while the other stands in a straddle position at chest level. Partners use a wrist-lock grip with both hands. The standing partner stands erect while the partner in supine position attempts to do a reclining pull-up. The upward pull is done completely by the person in supine position bending at the elbows. The standing person's task is to remain rigid and erect.

It is helpful for the person in supine position to start this exercise with the feet against a wall. This will prevent the person from sliding and will keep the focus of the activity on upper body development.

Rocking Chair. The exerciser moves to prone position on the floor. With the arms out to the sides of the body, the back is arched in an attempt to

Figure 17.10. Inclined wall push-up

Figure 17.11.   Reclining partner pull-up

Figure 17.12.   Rowing

raise the upper body off the floor. While the upper body is elevated, different activities and arm positions can be attempted. For example, arm circling, waving, clapping hands, or placing the hands behind the head can add challenge to this upper back and shoulder development activity. **Variation:** The lower body can be elevated instead of the upper. Various movements can then be done with the legs. In either exercise, a partner may be required to hold the half of the body not being moved.

   Crab Walk.   This activity can be modified in several ways to develop trunk and upper body strength. The crab position is an inverted walk on all fours. The stomach faces the ceiling with the weight supported on the hands and feet. Crab-walking can be done in all directions and should be performed with the trunk as straight as possible. **Variations:** The crab kick can be executed from this position by alternating forward kicks of the left and right leg. The double crab kick is done by kicking both feet forward and then backward simultaneously.

Midsection Exercises

   Rowing (Figure 17.12).   This exercise starts with the student in supine position with the arms above the head. It is a controlled two-count exercise. On the first count, the arms are moved toward the feet as the person moves to a sitting position; the knees are pulled simultaneously to the chest. On the second count, the person returns to starting position.

   Modified Sit-up (Figure 17.13).   Starting position is on the back with the knees flexed, feet on

Figure 17.13.   Modified sit-up

the floor, and the heels 12 to 18 in. from the buttocks. Arms are crossed on the chest with the hands on opposite shoulders. The student curls to a sitting position while keeping the arms touching the chest. The first count of the sit-up is completed when the elbows touch the thighs. The student then returns to the down position with the mid-back making contact with the testing surface.

   V-seat.   Starting position consists of the student's sitting on the floor. Arms are held parallel to the floor at shoulder height in front of the body. The exercise is performed by leaning slightly back, lifting the legs from the floor, and touching the feet with the fingertips. The body should form a "V". The V-seat can be repeated a set number of times or can be held for a set period of time.

Partial Curl-up. Begin the exercise in supine position with knees bent and feet flat on the floor. Arms should be folded across the chest. The exercise is performed by smoothly tucking the chin and curling the shoulders forward and off the floor. The lower back should remain on the floor throughout. Complete the activity by lowering the shoulders to the floor. The head should not touch the floor since the chin is tucked into the chest.

Alternate Knee Touch (Figure 17.14). Use the same starting position as described for the partial curl-up, but place the hands behind the head. The exercise is done by contracting the abdominal muscles and lifting both the legs and shoulders off the floor. Hold this position and alternately touch the right elbow to the left knee and vice versa before returning to the starting position.

Upper Body Twist (Figure 17.15). Lie flat on the back with arms folded across the chest. Keep

Figure 17.14. Alternate knee touch

Figure 17.15. Upper body twist

the buttocks on the floor while lifting the right shoulder and touching the right elbow to the floor near the right hip. Alternate from side to side. Hold the position for 3 to 5 sec on each contraction.

Hip Walk. Begin in sitting position with the legs straight and together. Keep the abdominal muscles contracted while moving the buttocks forward by alternately "walking" the hips. Practice moving backward as well as forward.

Lower Body Exercises

Squat Jumps. Begin in squatting position with one foot slightly ahead of the other. Assume part of the weight with the hands in front of the body. Jump as high as possible and return to the squatting position. Taking some of the body weight with the hands is important to avoid stressing the knee joints.

Treadmill. Begin on all fours with one foot forward and one behind. Rapidly alternate foot positions while taking the weight of the body on the arms. The movement of the feet can be varied by moving both feet forward and back simultaneously or by moving the feet apart and together.

Jumping Jacks. Begin in standing position with the arms at the sides and feet together. Simultaneously lift the arms overhead and spread the legs on the first count. On the second count, return arms and legs to the starting position. **Variations:** Feet and arm movements can be varied. The arms can be moved in front of the body, behind the body, and in different patterns. The legs can be split forward and backward, crossed in front of each other, and swung to the front of the body.

Running in Place. Running in place is most beneficial when the upper leg is lifted parallel to the floor. The thighs can touch the hands held slightly above the parallel line to encourage the high lift.

Side Leg Flex (Figure 17.16). Assume a position on the side of the body on the floor. Rest the head in the right hand and place the left hand along the side of the body. On the first count, lift the left leg and arm and point them toward the ceiling. Return to the starting position on the second count. Rotate to the other side of the body after performing the desired number of repetitions. **Variation:** The double side leg flex is an exercise that demands more effort. Both legs are lifted simultaneously as far off the floor as possible.

Front Leg Kick. From standing position, alternately kick each leg forward and as high as possible. This exercise should be done rhythmically

Figure 17.16. Side leg flex

so that all movement occurs on the toes. When the leg is kicked upward, the arm on the same side should be moved forward in an attempt to touch the toe of the lifted leg.

ACTIVITIES AND ROUTINES FOR DEVELOPING FITNESS

The following are methods of organizing exercises and aerobic activities to develop total body fitness. All of the routines should enhance muscular strength and endurance, as well as cardiovascular endurance.

TEACHER AND STUDENT LEADER EXERCISE ROUTINES

During the first part of the school year, teachers should lead and teach all exercises to ensure that they are learned correctly. It is also important that teachers stay involved in fitness activities throughout the year to demonstrate to students their willingness to do the activities that they are asking students to perform. In some cases, teachers have asked students to exercise and maintain fitness while they chose not to do either. Pushing others to be fit is intolerable if the teacher does not make a similar personal commitment.

When a wide repertoire of exercises has been learned, students can begin to lead the exercise routines. Leading not only means starting and stopping the exercises, but includes designing well-balanced routines that offer total body development. Students can be guided as to the desirable number of repetitions and how to count exercises as they are being performed. In any case, students

should not be forced to lead the exercises; leading should be a personal choice.

More than one student leader can be used at one time. For example, if four leaders are selected, they can be thinking of the exercises to choose when it is their turn. Leaders can be placed on four sides of the class (Figure 17.17), with the class rotating one-quarter turn to face a new leader after each exercise. If a leader cannot think of an appropriate exercise, the class can be asked to volunteer one. In any case, emphasis should be placed on learning to weave together a set of exercises that offers total body development. Continuous movement activity should also be added to the exercise routines to assure cardiovascular endurance development.

SQUAD LEADER EXERCISES

Squad leader exercises offer students the opportunity to develop fitness routines without teacher intervention. Squad leaders take their squad to a designated area and put the squad through a fitness routine. It is helpful if a blank exercise card is given to each squad leader a few days before the student will lead. The leader can develop a routine and write down the exercises and repetitions or duration of each.

Squad leaders can also assign members of the group to lead or to offer certain activities. A number of exercises can be specified to develop a particular area of the body. For example, ask leaders to develop a routine that has two exercises for the arm-shoulder girdle area, two for the abdominal region, one for the legs, three for flexibility, and 2 min of continuous movement. The responsibility for planning a fitness routine that is balanced and developmental should shift gradually from the teacher to the students.

```
                          O
                   Leader number 3

                   X   X   X   X
                   X   X   X   X
        O          X   X   X   X          O
  Leader number 2  X   X   X   X  Leader number 4
                   X   X   X   X
                   X   X   X   X
                   X   X   X   X

                          O
                   Leader number 1
```

Figure 17.17. Student led exercises

EXERCISES TO MUSIC

Without question, music increases the motivational level of students during exercise. While there are many commercial exercise-to-music records on the market, they all suffer from one major problem. They seldom meet the specific work-load requirements of different groups of students, and they cannot provide the necessary systematic overload. Teachers therefore need to develop their own homemade exercise-to-music tapes that can be tailored to meet the needs of a specific class or grade.

Homemade exercise tapes can be developed using a record player and a tape recorder. Music that is currently popular can be combined with exercises that students have already learned. Some care should be taken to avoid music that might affront some members of the community. Either the teacher or a group of students can make the tapes. When students do the taping, they have control over the selection, sequence, and number of exercises and repetitions. The routines can be adapted to particular needs and characteristics of the group. Procedures for starting and stopping exercises can be incorporated easily in the taping.

CONTINUOUS MOVEMENT ACTIVITIES

Jogging

Jogging is running at a slow pace. It is faster than walking, but slower than sprinting. Jogging is an excellent conditioner for the cardiovascular system and can be done by virtually all students. It does not require specialized equipment or a high level of specialized skill.

Any one of three approaches can be used to develop a jogging program. The first is the jog-walk approach, which emphasizes the amount of time that one is involved in continuous movement. Students determine how far they can jog before they need to slow down and walk. Walking is continued until the exerciser is again ready to jog. The goal is to decrease the length and time of the walking episodes and to increase the jogging.

A second approach to increasing endurance through jogging is to set up definite and measured intervals. An example would be setting up cones to mark jogging intervals of 110 yd and walking intervals of 55 yd. As the fitness level increases, the length of the jogging interval is increased and the walking interval decreased.

Finally, the work load can be increased by increasing either the duration of the jog or the pace of the jogging. The goal is either to maintain a constant pace and to increase the distance run, or to run the same distance at an increased pace. Increasing the speed is usually the less desirable alternative, because the intensity of the exercise may discourage students.

Jogging is performed in an erect body position with a minimal amount of lean. Excessive lean is less efficient and demands a greater amount of energy. The elbows should be bent and the arms carried in a relaxed manner. Most joggers strike the ground with a flat foot. This allows the force of impact to be absorbed over a larger surface area, which seems to be more desirable. Some joggers land on the heel and then rotate to the toe. In either case, trying to change a jogger's foot action is often ineffective.

Jogging should be a noncompetitive activity. Students should be encouraged to look for self-improvement instead of comparing their performance with others. An enjoyable technique is to ask students to jog with a partner who has similar ability. They should be encouraged to talk and visit while they jog. Point out that if they find it difficult to talk while jogging, they are probably running too fast.

Endurance and continuous activity should be rewarded. Teachers sometimes have a tendency to ask students to run a certain distance and then they reward those students who complete the distance first. This is discouraging to the majority of the joggers. Students should be permitted to run in any direction they desire until a certain amount of time has elapsed. This prevents the situation in which a few gifted runners finish first and have to sit and wait for the rest of the class to complete a given distance.

A general rule of thumb for beginning a jogging program is to ask students to walk and jog continuously for 5 min. Increase the amount of time 1 min per week up to 15 min. Individuals can increase the total amount of time while they also try to reduce the amount of walking.

Ideas for an instructional unit on jogging can be found in Chapter 19.

Walking

Walking is an activity that all people can do. The disadvantage of walking compared with jogging is that it must be done for a longer period of time to receive similar cardiovascular benefits. Walking has the advantages, however, of not requiring any special equipment and of having a low injury rate. Walking, probably more than any other activity, will be done by students when they reach adulthood.

Rope Jumping

Rope jumping is a demanding activity that requires little equipment. For some participants it can be a valuable approach to cardiovascular fitness. The energy demands of rope jumping are similar to jogging. Rope jumping can be performed for a specified amount of time or for a specified number of jumps.

A variety of activities can be done with a jump rope to help avoid the monotony and excessive fatigue of continuous jumping. The rope can be turned at fast or slow speeds while different foot steps are performed. If rope jumping is used for the fitness portion of the lesson, it should be alternated with stretching activities to give students an opportunity to recover from aerobic demands.

See Chapter 19 for ideas on developing a unit of instruction on rope jumping.

Four Corners

A large rectangle is formed using four cones as markers. Students move continually around the perimeter of the rectangle. At each corner, a different movement is performed. Examples of activity alternatives that can be performed on the long sides of the rectangle are jogging, skipping, sliding, jumping, and hopping. On the short sides of the rectangle, movements on all fours (e.g., bear walk, crab walk, seal crawl) can be performed. Another interesting variation is to use tumbling activities, or use tires and challenge students to go over, around, and through them. The need for continuous movement should be emphasized, and the rectangle should be large enough to provide a challenging work load for the cardiovascular system.

INTERVAL TRAINING

Interval training involves carefully controlling the work and rest intervals of the participant. Intervals of work (exercise) and rest can be measured in distance, repetitions, or time. Interval training is done by monitoring the heart rate. The student first needs to get the heart rate up to 120 to 140 beats per min by warming up. Strenuous activity is then performed to push the heart rate into the 170 to 180 beats-per-min range. At this

point, the runner begins the rest interval (usually walking) until the heart rate returns to 120 to 140 beats per min. Theoretically, the amount of time it takes for the heart rate to return to 120 to 140 beats per min should not exceed 90 sec. The major advantage of interval training is that endurance can be increased markedly in a short period of time.

Interval training can be used with various locomotor movements. For example, the following work and rest activities can be alternated. Intervals can be measured in either distance or time.

Work Activities	Rest Activities
Brisk walking	Slow walking
Jogging	Walking
Sprinting	Jogging
Rope jumping	Walking
Jumping in place	Walking

RHYTHMIC AEROBIC EXERCISE

At present, this type of activity is extremely popular throughout the U.S. Aerobic dance is the basis for many variations of rhythmic exercise now implemented. These routines develop a high level of cardiorespiratory fitness, as well as strength and flexibility. Popular music is used to increase the activity enjoyment.

Rhythmic aerobic exercise consists of a mixture of fundamental movements—dance steps, swinging movements, and stretching exercises. Routines are developed to pieces of music that have a definite and obvious beat.

The activities and routines should ease the burden of learning. If the movement patterns are too difficult, students become self-conscious and discouraged. Use the following points as guidelines when teaching new aerobic exercise routines.

1. Use movements that are organized in units of 4, 8, or 16 counts. When phrases in the music are repeated, it may be desirable to repeat the same or previous steps.
2. Alternate the strenuousness of the activities. This allows interval training to be built into the routines. Stretching movements can be alternated with demanding locomotor movements.
3. Routines motivate more students when they appear not to be dance activities. The challenge is to develop demanding routines that will increase the endurance level of all participants.

All students should be comfortable performing the routines.

4. Follow-the-leader activities work well with students after they have developed a repertoire of movements. Each student can be responsible for leading one activity.

5. Energetic and positive teachers strongly influence the success of the presentations. Students need to see teachers enjoying fitness activities.

Basic Steps

The basic steps and movements can be used to develop a wide variety of routines. The majority are performed to four counts, although this can be varied, depending on the skill level of the students.

Running and Walking Steps

1. **Directional Runs.** The directional runs can be done forward, backward, diagonally, sideways, or turning.

2. **Rhythmic Runs.** These runs integrate a specific movement (e.g., knee lift, clap, jump, jump-turn) on the fourth beat.

3. **Runs With Stunts.** The run is performed while lifting the knees, kicking up the heels, or slapping the thighs or heels. Runs can also be done with the legs extended, such as the goose step.

4. **Runs With the Arms in Various Positions.** The arms can be on the head, straight up or down, or on the hips.

Movements on the Floor

1. **Sit-ups or Curl-ups.** These can be used in many ways. For example, use four counts: (1) up to the knees, (2) touch the floor, (3) back to the knees, and (4) return to the floor. A V-seat can be held for two counts and rested for two counts.

2. **Side Leg Raises.** These leg raises can be done with a straight leg on the side, or with bent knees on the back extending the lower leg.

3. **Alternate Leg Raises.** The exercise is performed in supine position with one leg raised to meet the opposite hand. Repeat using the opposite leg or both legs.

4. **Push-ups.** The exercise can be done in two- or four-count movements. A four count would be: (1) halfway down, (2) touch chest to floor, (3) halfway up, and (4) arms fully extended.

5. **Crab Kicks and Treadmill.** Both exercises can be performed to four-count movements.

Standing Movements

1. **Lunge Variations (Figure 17.18).** To perform a lunge, step forward onto the right foot while bending at the knees and extending arms into the air (counts 1 and 2). Return to starting position by bringing the right foot back and pulling arms into a jogging position (counts 3 and 4). The exercise can be varied by changing the direction of the move, or the depth and speed of the lunge.

2. **Side Bends.** Begin with the feet apart. Reach overhead while bending to the side. This movement is usually done to four beats: (1) bend, (2) and (3) hold, and (4) return.

3. **Reaches.** Alternate reaching upward with the right and left arms. Reaches can be done sideways also and are usually two-count movements.

4. **Arm and Shoulder Circles.** Make arm circles with one or both arms. Vary the size and speed of the circles. Shoulder shrugs can be done in similar fashion.

Jumping Jacks Variations

1. **Arms Alternately Extended.** Jump with the arms alternately extended upward and pulled into the chest.

2. **Side Jumping Jacks.** Use regular arm action while the feet are kept together for jumping forward, backward, and sideways.

3. **Variations With Feet.** Try forward stride alternating, forward and side stride alternating, kicks

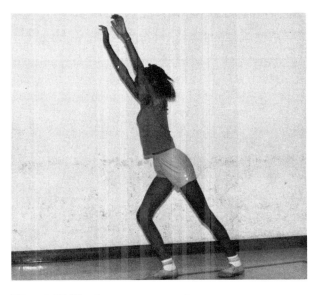

Figure 17.18. Lunge movement

or knee lifts, crossing the feet, and a heel-toe step.

Bounce Steps

1. **Bounce and Clap.** The step is similar to the slow-time jump rope step. Clap on every other bounce.
2. **Bounce, Turn, and Clap.** Turn a quarter- or half-turn with each jump.
3. **Three Bounces and Clap.** Bounce three times and then clap and bounce on the fourth beat. Turns can be performed using the four counts.
4. **Bounce and Rock Side to Side.** Transfer weight from side to side, and forward and backward. Add clapping or arm swinging.
5. **Bounce With Body Twist.** Hold the arms at shoulder level and twist the lower body back and forth on each bounce.
6. **Bounce With Floor Patterns.** Bounce and make different floor patterns such as a box, diagonal, or triangle.
7. **Bounce With Kick Variations.** Perform different kick variations such as knee lift, kick, knee lift, and kick; double kicks, knee lift, and slap knees; kick and clap under the knees. Combine the kicks with two or four count turns.

Activities With Manipulative Equipment

1. **Jump Ropes.** Using the jump rope, perform basic steps such as forward, backward, slow, and fast time. Jump on one foot, cross arms, and jump while jogging. Swing the rope from side to side with the handles in one hand and jump over it.
2. **Beanbags.** Toss and catch while performing various locomotor movements. Challenge students using different tosses.
3. **Hoops.** Rhythmically swing the hoop around different body parts. Perform different locomotor movements around and over hoops.
4. **Balls.** Bounce, toss, dribble, and add locomotor movements while performing tasks.

Sample Routine

1. March, moving arms in large circles (8 counts).
2. Hold side lunge position and circle right arm (8 counts). Reverse circling with left arm (8 counts).
3. Bounce forward twice, slapping thighs; then bounce backward twice, thrusting arms in the air. Repeat four times (16 counts).
4. Bounce and clap turn. Perform a quarter-turn

on every second bounce. Repeat four times clockwise (8 counts) and four times counter-clockwise (8 counts).
5. Repeat numbers 3 and 4.
6. Grapevine step with clap on fourth beat. Repeat to the left. Repeat sequence four times (32 counts).
7. Jumping-jack variation extending arms up and out (8 counts). Repeat four times (32 counts).
8. Bounce and twist (8 counts).
9. Side jumping jacks, two-count version. Repeat eight times (16 counts).
10. Bounce, bounce, bounce, clap—four-count movement. Repeat four times (16 counts).
11. Rhythmic running with clap on fourth beat. While running, move to a circle formation (16 counts).
12. Bounce and twist (8 counts).
13. Side leg raises (2 counts). Perform four on each leg (16 counts).
14. Rhythmic running with a clap on every fourth beat (16 counts).

RESISTANCE TRAINING

Strength development through resistance training is used by coaches of most sports. Physical education programs should instruct students in the use of weights and weight machines for proper development with an emphasis on safety. Using resistance training as an instructional unit is often difficult due to a lack of equipment and facilities.

When designing resistance training routines, all major body parts should be developed. This prevents the excessive development of specific body parts, which may lead to postural or joint problems. Exercises should be performed through the full range of motion. If training is being done for a specific sport, it may be important to analyze the sport and develop exercises that replicate the range of motion used in sport participation.

Resistance exercises should be performed at a speed similar to the movements performed in various physical activities. If a student is involved in an activity requiring speed, then the exercises should be performed at a similar speed. Similarly, if a student is involved in activities demanding high levels of endurance, then exercises should be designed to increase this attribute. If the sport or activity demands strength, the training program can be geared to develop muscular strength. In each case, the student should understand the program differences and how to develop a personal program.

Safety

Students should know and practice necessary safety precautions. The following points should be clear to all students and should be reinforced on a regular basis. The instructor is wise to post safety rules as a further reminder and to avoid the consequences of possible lawsuits.

1. Perform warm-up exercises before intense lifting. These may be a set of calisthenics or a set of resistance exercises at a lower level.
2. Correct form is necessary to prevent injury as well as to develop strength. When a heavy weight is lifted from the floor, the lift should be done with bent knees, straight back, and head up.
3. Spotters are absolutely necessary when near-maximum weight is being lifted. Exercises such as the bench press, squats, and declined presses should always have two students present to spot.
4. Weights should be checked by the instructor before each period and by students each time they use them. Collars should be tightly fastened, cables checked, and bolts on machines periodically tightened.
5. Wide leather practice belts should be used when heavy lifting is performed. This prevents injury to the lower back and abdominal wall.
6. All exercises should be explained in class before implementation. This means that proper form, points of safety, and necessary spotting are discussed before students participate.

Repetitions and Sets

There is wide variation in the proper number of repetitions and sets that need to be performed to achieve optimum results. Repetitions are the number of times a participant performs an exercise to make a set. Each set, in turn, consists of a specified number of repetitions of the same exercise. Identifying the proper number of repetitions or sets that should be done is difficult. Literally dozens of experts have researched this area and have failed to reach agreement. For the physical education setting, a middle-of-the-road approach is probably best taken. This means that three sets of ten repetitions should be performed for each exercise.

Strength or Endurance?

Muscular strength and endurance are developed using different methods. If maximum strength is desired, the exercise program should emphasize heavy resistance and fewer repetitions. If endurance is the desired outcome, the program should emphasize a high number of repetitions with less resistance. Some strength and endurance will be developed regardless of the type of program, but major gains will be in the direction of the selected emphasis.

Frequency and Rest Intervals

Frequency is usually discussed as the number of workouts per week. The most common pattern suggested is to lift every other day, three days per week. The day-long rest between workouts allows the muscle tissue to recover and waste products to dissipate. Some participants alternate by exercising the upper body and the lower body on different days. This results in a six-day program while retaining the day of rest between workouts.

The rest interval between repetitions and sets can be timed carefully to increase the intensity of the workout. By organizing the exercises in a circuit in which different muscle groups are stressed, the amount of time needed for a total workout can be reduced. In other words, recovery time is not needed between sets if the next exercise places demands on a different group of muscles.

Planning a Unit

Chapter 19 contains several ideas and activities for a unit on resistance training that can be modified or augmented to meet the needs of the instructor, the students, and the physical education program.

CIRCUIT TRAINING

Exercise stations are organized into a circuit for the sake of fitness development. Each of the stations should contribute, in part, to the total fitness of the participant. The components of fitness—flexibility, muscular strength and endurance, and cardiovascular endurance—should be represented in the circuit.

Developing a Circuit

1. If the circuit is to be used as a group activity, it should contain activities that all class members are capable of performing.
2. The stations should be organized in such a fashion that different muscle groups or fitness com-

ponents are exercised. In other words, consecutive stations should not place demands on the same area of the body.

3. Students should know how to perform all of the activities correctly. Proper form is important. Instruction can be done verbally or descriptive posters can be placed at each station.

4. Students should be evenly distributed among the stations at the beginning of the exercise bout. A rotation plan ensures that students move to the correct station.

5. Dosage can be measured in time or repetitions. Students can move on their own to the next station if they have completed the required number of repetitions. If a time criterion is used, the class moves as a whole when students have exercised for a specified amount of time.

6. To increase the demands on the cardiovascular system, one or two of the stations can include rope jumping or running in place. Another alternative is to have students run around the circuit a certain number of times before moving to the next station.

7. The circuit should generally contain no fewer than ten stations. The result of participation in the circuit is a total body workout.

Timing and Dosage

If the work load at each station is based on time, dosage can be carefully controlled. A signal to start exercising, stop exercising, and to rotate to the next station is given. This allows precise timing of intervals. When beginning circuit training, 30 sec per station is a reasonable expectation. The amount of rest between stations can also be monitored to increase or decrease the work load. An effective way of timing the circuit is to use a tape recording of popular music that students enjoy with signals to stop and start activities interspersed at proper intervals. The music is motivational, and the intervals are precisely timed.

Another approach is to rotate when a specific work load has been performed at a station. Students rotate when they have completed the task. Different work loads at the same station can be offered as a way of making the circuit meet the specific needs of students. For example, work loads could be labeled bronze, silver, and gold. The bronze workout would require the lowest number of repetitions or duration, whereas the gold would be the most demanding. Students would then exercise at their level of capability. Signs can be posted stating the number of repetitions required for each level.

Figure 17.19 is an example of a circuit that might be developed for junior high school students.

ASTRONAUT DRILLS

Astronaut drills are continuous movement activities that combine various exercises with walking and jogging. Students move randomly throughout the area or follow each other in a circle formation. The drills begin with brisk walking. On signal, the teacher or selected students lead the class in exercises or stunt activities. If a movement is not developed immediately, the class runs in place.

Combinations of the following activities can be arranged to develop a demanding routine:

Nine-Station Course

1	2	3	4
Rope jumping	Push-ups	Agility run	Arm circles
8	7	6	5
Windmill	Treadmill	Crab walk	Rowing
	9 Hula-Hooping (or any relaxing "fun" activity)		

Supplies and equipment: Jump ropes, mats for knee push-ups (if used), hoops (if used)
Time needed: 8 min—based on 45-sec activity limit, 10 sec to move between stations

Figure 17.19.   Circuit training stations (reprinted from *Dynamic Physical Education for Elementary School Children*, 7th ed. by V. P. Dauer and R. P. Pangrazi, 1983. Minneapolis: Burgess Publishing Co., p. 175)

1. Various locomotor movements such as hopping, running, jumping, leaping, skipping, and running on the toes
2. Moving throughout the area on all fours in the crab position, and using various animal walks such as the seal walk, dog walk, and rabbit walk
3. Performing exercises, such as arm circles, body twists, and trunk and upper-body stretches, while moving around the area
4. Performing stationary exercises, such as push-ups, sit-ups, and jumping jacks, to stress development of the upper body and abdominal wall

Students move throughout the area and perform as many exercises as possible. They can also develop individual routines in which the amounts of time allotted for movement activity and stationary activity are carefully controlled.

The following is an example of an astronaut drill that might be implemented. Note that the duration of the movements can be timed or the repetitions counted. These mechanics can be determined by the students or the instructor. In either case, the drill enables overload and progression to be built into the routine.

1. Walk throughout the area.
2. Run and leap.
3. Stop, perform push-ups.
4. Walk and do arm circles.
5. Crab-walk.
6. Stop, find a friend, and perform partner resistance exercises.
7. Hop for a period of time on each foot.
8. Walk on all fours.
9. Run, with the knees lifted as high as possible.
10. Stop, perform treadmill.
11. Repeat the above steps.

CONTINUITY EXERCISES

The continuity exercises can be done in open squad formation or in scatter formation. Since each student has a jump rope, students must have plenty of room to avoid hitting each other. Performers alternate between rope jumping and two-count exercises. Rope jumping is done for timed episodes and should be performed fast-time. Music with the proper rhythm can be used to help maintain the cadence. At the signal to stop rope jumping, students quickly drop the rope and move into position for the exercise. Selected exercises should be performed in a down position and be two-count

in nature. A leader says "Ready" and the students respond "One-two," while performing the exercise. For each repetition, students wait until the command "Ready" is given.

The following is an example of a routine:

First signal: Begin rope jumping.

Second signal: Stop jumping, drop ropes, and move to the push-up position. On each command of "Ready," do one push-up to a two-count cadence.

Third signal: Resume rope jumping.

Fourth signal: Drop ropes and move into supine position on the floor with the arms overhead, preparatory to doing the rowing exercise. On the command "Ready," perform the exercise to the two-count cadence.

Fifth signal: Resume rope jumping.

Sixth signal: Drop the ropes, and move into crab position. Prepare to do the double crab kick. On the signal "Ready," both feet are extended forward and back in a two-count movement.

Seventh signal: Resume rope jumping.

Eighth signal: Move into position for the side leg flex exercise. On the command "Ready," lift the upper leg and return it to starting position for a two-count movement.

Ninth signal: Resume rope jumping.

Tenth signal: Move into position for the reclining partner pull-up. On signal, pull the body up on count one, and return to the floor on count two. Switch positions with partner after the proper number of repetitions has been performed.

The number of repetitions and the duration of the rope-jumping episodes should be determined by the fitness levels of the students. More exercises can be added to the routine above. Instructors can use a tape recorder to signal the start and finish of the rope-jumping episodes.

Continuity exercises are an example of interval training. The rope jumping stresses the cardiovascular system, while the exercises develop strength and allow the performer to recover.

GRASS DRILLS
WITH PARTNER RESISTANCE EXERCISES

Grass drills require performers to move alternately from a rapid running-in-place position to a down position on the grass or floor. The activities are strenuous and are performed in quick succession at top speed. Work load progression is developed by increasing the duration of the bouts. Since grass drills are quite demanding, they should be alternated with partner resistance exercises. This type of interval training allows participants to rest the cardiovascular system while developing strength in the partner resistance exercises.

Grass Drills

Basic grass drills involve moving rapidly from one of three basic positions to another on the commands "Go," "Front," and "Back." "Go" tells students to run in place at a rapid pace on the toes, raising the knees, and pumping the arms. "Front" signals students to drop quickly to the floor in prone position with the hands in push-up position. The head should point toward the center of the circle or the front of the room. When "Back" is stated, students move into a supine position with the arms alongside the body and palms down. The head-to-leg position is opposite that of the "Front" position.

Grass drills can be done in two ways:

1. **Continuous Motion.** In this style, when "Front" or "Back" commands are given, the student moves to the corresponding position and *immediately* returns to the "Go" phase without the command being issued.
2. **Interrupted Motion.** Using this style, the performer stays in position until the "Go" command is given. This allows a number of variations to be built into the drills. For example, push-ups, sit-ups, crab-kicks, and various movements on all fours can be executed prior to issuing the "Go" command.

Partner Resistance Exercises

Partner resistance exercises are enjoyable for students because they offer variable work loads and a chance to work with a partner. Partners must be matched in size and strength so they can challenge each other. The exercises should be performed throughout the full range of motion at each joint and should take 8 to 12 sec each to complete. The partner providing the resistance gives the "Begin" command and counts the duration of the exercise. Three sets of each exercise are done by each partner as partners do the exercise and resistance role.

The following are examples of exercises that can be performed. Students should be challenged to invent their own partner resistance exercises, with emphasis placed on developing a set of exercises that strengthens all body parts.

Arm Curl-ups.   The exerciser keeps the upper arms against the sides of the body, bends the elbows,

and turns palms up. The partner puts fists in the exerciser's palms. The exerciser then attempts to curl the forearms upward to the shoulders. To develop the opposite set of muscles, push down in the opposite direction, starting with palms at shoulder level.

Forearm Flex.   The exerciser places the hands, palms down, on the partner's shoulders. The exerciser attempts to push the partner into the floor. The partner may slowly lower the body to allow the exerciser to move through the full range of motion. Try the exercise with the palms up.

Fist Pull-apart.   The exerciser places the fists together in front of the body at shoulder level. The exerciser attempts to pull the hands apart while partner forces them together with pressure on the elbows. Reverse this exercise and begin with the fists apart. Partner tries to push them together by grasping the wrists.

Butterfly (Figure 17.20).   The exerciser holds the arms straight, forming a right angle with the side of the body. The partner attempts to hold the arms down, while the exerciser lifts with straight arms to the sides. Try the activity with the arms above the head; move them down to the sides against partner's effort to hold them up.

Camelback.   The exerciser is on all fours with the head up. The partner sits or pushes on the exerciser's back while the exerciser attempts to hump the back like a camel.

Back Builder.   The exerciser spreads the legs and bends forward at the waist with the head up. The partner faces the exerciser, and clasps the hands together behind the exerciser's neck. The exerciser

Figure 17.20. Butterfly

then attempts to stand upright while the partner pulls downward.

Swan Diver (Figure 17.21).   The exerciser lies in the prone position with arms out at the sides and tries to arch the back while the partner applies pressure to the lower and upper back area.

Scissors.   The exerciser lies on one side while partner straddles the exerciser and holds the upper leg down. The exerciser attempts to raise the top leg. Reverse sides and perform the exercise with the other leg.

Bear Trap.   Perform as in the Scissors, but spread the legs first and attempt to move them together while partner holds them apart.

Knee Bender.   The exerciser lies in prone position with legs straight, arms ahead on the floor. The partner places the hands on the back of exerciser's ankle. The exerciser attempts to flex the knee while the partner applies pressure. Reverse legs. Try this exercise in the opposite direction with the knee joint at a 90-degree angle.

Resistance Push-up.   The exerciser is in push-up position with arms bent so that the body is half-way up from the floor. The partner straddles or stands alongside the exerciser's head and puts pressure on the top of the shoulders by pushing down. The amount of pressure to apply takes judgment by the partner in order to prevent the exerciser from collapsing.

ISOMETRIC EXERCISES

Isometric exercises are done without movement. They are performed solely for the purpose of developing strength. The amount of time needed to exercise the major muscle groups in this way is minimal. A complete isometric exercise can usu-ally be done in 5 min or less. These exercises do not require equipment, do not cause a high level of fatigue, and can be performed easily in a small space or office.

The disadvantage of isometric exercise is that it appears to raise the blood pressure of the individual. This may be a problem for someone who has heart disease. Other disadvantages are that isometric exercise does not benefit cardiovascular endurance and only builds strength at the joint angle at which the exercise is performed. Finally, many individuals receive little feedback from their isometric performance in terms of perspiration, increased muscle size, or healthy fatigue. They therefore see little point in continuing the activity.

To achieve results, the contractions must be maximal in nature. They should be held for 8 to 12 sec, and should be performed at various joint angles to develop strength throughout the total range of motion. An isometric routine should be performed a minimum of three days a week and should contain 10 to 15 exercises. The following is a sample routine that might be used to develop overall body strength. All of the exercises should be held at maximum contraction for 8 to 12 sec.

Handhold.   The exerciser makes a fist of one hand and holds it with the other hand. The hand holding the fist attempts to squeeze the fist as hard as possible.

Pull and Push Hands.   The exerciser locks both hands together and attempts to pull them apart. To push, the palms are placed together and pressure is applied.

Neck Developer.   To develop muscles in the back of the neck, the hands are clasped and placed behind the head. The head attempts to move backward while the hands pull forward. For the front of the neck, place the palms on the forehead and push backward while the head pushes forward. This exercise can be modified by placing a hand on the side of the head and applying force.

Arm Curl.   Hold the forearm at waist level in front of the body. Place the palm of the other hand into the hand of the flexed arm. Attempt to curl the flexed arm upward while applying downward pressure with the other hand. Switch hand positions.

Knee Hold.   Sitting on the floor, spread the knees approximately 12 in. apart. Put the hands on the inside of the knees and apply outward pressure, while simultaneously applying inward pressure with the knees. Switch the hand position to the outside of the knees and reverse the force application.

Figure 17.21.   Swan diver

Knee Lift.   Sit on the floor with one leg extended and the other flexed. Place the palms of the hands on top of the flexed knee. Lift the knee upward while applying downward pressure to the knee. Switch to the other knee.

Body Tightener.   In a standing position, contract and hold the following muscle groups: shoulders forward, shoulders back, shoulders upward, abdominals toward the spine, lower back muscles, lower leg muscles by standing on tiptoe, lift toes as high as possible, and turn the upper body as far as possible and hold, then reverse the direction of body twist.

Ankle Hold.   Sitting on the floor, cross the legs at the ankles. Lift the lower leg while applying downward pressure with the leg on top. Reverse the positions.

Leg Squeeze.   Sit on the floor with the knees bent and near the chest. Reach around the legs with both arms and clasp hands. Attempt to pull the lower legs toward the seat while applying outward pressure with the legs.

Many isometric exercises can be developed with a partner or using jump ropes or cut inner tubes to make large rubber bands. The partner resistance exercises described earlier can be performed as isometric exercises.

OBSTACLE COURSES

Obstacle courses, or parcourses, are popular throughout the U.S. Different stations are developed and the participants move from station to station as they cover the course. The type of movement done between stations can also place demands on the participants' body systems.

Courses can be run for time, or repetitions can be increased to ensure balanced fitness development. Courses should be developed to exercise all parts of the body. A variety of activities, such as stretching, vaulting, agility runs, climbing, hanging and chinning, and crawling, can be included to place demands on all aspects of fitness. Figure 17.22 represents an indoor obstacle course that might be constructed for students.

PARACHUTE EXERCISES

The parachute can be used to develop fitness activities that are exciting and challenging. Through these activities, students work together to enhance their fitness level. They should be encouraged to develop unique, new group activities. The following are examples of exercises that use the parachute.

Toe Toucher.   Sit with the feet extended under the parachute and hold the chute taut with a two-hand grip, drawing it to the chin. Bend forward and touch the grip to the toes. Return the chute to the stretched position.

Curl-up.   Extend the body under the parachute in curl-up position, so the chute comes up to the chin when held taut. Do curl-ups, returning each time to the stretched position. Encourage students to work together and snap the chute tight each time they recline.

Dorsal Lift.   In prone position, lie with the head toward the chute. Grasp the chute with the arms extended overhead. On signal, raise the chute off the floor while simultaneously raising the head and chest. Encourage students to lift the chute high enough so they can "see a friend" across the way.

Sitting Leg Lift.   In a sitting position with the legs under the chute, lift the legs on signal while holding the chute taut, and lift the chute off the floor. Hold the position for 6 to 10 sec. Try to keep the legs straight. As a variation, start in a supine position with the legs under the chute and do a V-seat.

Sitting Pulls.   Sit with the back to the parachute. Grasp the chute and raise it overhead. On signal, try to pull the chute down to the knees. Other variations are done facing the chute and raising it above the head, lowering it to eye level, and to waist level. Emphasis should be placed on using the arms and shoulder girdle to apply force, rather than leaning.

All Fours Pulls.   Get on the floor in a crab-, bear-, or seal-walk position. Grasp the chute with one hand. On signal, pull and hold the contraction for 6 to 10 sec. Repeat using the other hand and different positions.

Isometric Exercises.   A wide variety of isometric exercises can be done using the parachute. Various body parts can be exercised by applying pressure to the chute. The exercises should be held for 6 to 10 sec. Encourage students to develop new isometric techniques.

Rhythmic Aerobic Activity.   The parachute is excellent for stimulating aerobic activity. For example, students can do various locomotor movements while holding onto the chute. A sample routine with the chute follows:

1. Sixteen skips clockwise
2. Sixteen skips counterclockwise
3. Sixteen jumps to the center of the parachute
4. Sixteen hops backward and tighten the chute
5. Eight-count parachute lift overhead

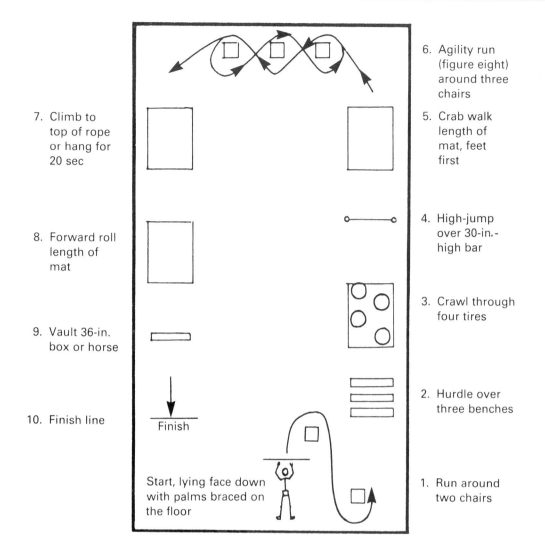

Figure 17.22. Obstacle course (reprinted from *Dynamic Physical Education for Elementary School Children*, 7th ed. by V. P. Dauer and R. P. Pangrazi, 1983. Minneapolis: Burgess Publishing Co., p. 178)

6. Eight-count lower parachute to toes
7. Four-count parachute lift overhead
8. Four-count lower parachute to toes
9. Repeat steps 5 through 8
10. Thirty-two running steps clockwise with the chute held overhead
11. Thirty-two running steps backward with the chute held at waist level
12. Perform a 16-count dome
13. Repeat steps 10 through 12
14. Finish with a parachute lift and release the chute

RUNNING ACTIVITIES AND DRILLS

A number of running drills and activities can be used to improve running techniques, agility, and fitness levels, depending on how they are administered. These are useful activities for the fitness portion of the lesson.

Form Running

This drill works well on a football field using the yard lines as markers. A squad of students lines up on the boundary line at the goal line, 10-yard line, 20-yard line, 30-yard line, and so forth. The teacher stands on the hash mark closest to the students, on about the 25-yard line. On signal, the first student in each line runs across the field on the respective yard line. The teacher continues to give a starting signal for each wave of students until all of the students are on the opposite boundary line. The teacher then moves to the opposite hash mark and starts the students running back across the field. Each time the students run across the field, they should be told to concentrate on one aspect of their running form. The following aspects can be emphasized:

1. Keep the head still—no lateral or turning movements. Eyes should be focused straight ahead. Keep the chin down.
2. Hands should be relaxed, thumb on the first pad of the index finger. Put hands in the front pocket as they move backward.
3. Elbows should be bent approximately 90 degrees, and the arms should move straight forward and back with no lateral movement across the chest. Arms gently brush the sides of the body.
4. Feet should be aligned straight ahead. Knees drive straight ahead rather than upward. High knee action can be used as another variation, although it is not necessary for good running form. The heel of the foot should come close to the buttocks.
5. The foot, knee, and hip should be in line. The body tilts forward about 5 degrees from the feet, not from the hips.
6. The length of the stride is usually shorter for longer runs (i.e., a longer stride for sprinting and a shorter stride for distance running).

It is useful to give students only one aspect of running form to concentrate on during each trip across the field. They can then emphasize and overlearn each point. Beginning slowly and increasing the speed gradually works best. Start the drill at half-speed, then proceed to three-quarter speed, and finally, full speed.

This same drill format can also be used with other running activities.

1. **Backwards Running.** Stay on the line. Roll the shoulders forward and keep them forward while running. Emphasize the arm movement forward and back. Pull that arm through with each step.
2. **Crossover Step Backward.** The teacher stands on the boundary line and the first wave of students moves 5 yd out on their respective yard lines facing the teacher. The teacher gives a left- or right-hand signal. The students start backward with a crossover step. When the teacher changes the direction signal, students rotate their hips and crossover step on the opposite side. Students must keep their eyes on the teacher

and concentrate on rotating their hips and staying on the line.
3. **Crossover Step Forward.** As students run forward, they concentrate on stepping across the line with each step. It is important to start slowly and to increase the speed gradually.
4. **Carioca.** Students stand sideways on the line with their arms held out, parallel to the ground. On a signal, the students move sideways down the line by using a crossover step in front and a return step, a crossover step in back, and finally another step. This process is repeated for the length of the field. Students should make sure that they lead with both the right and left shoulder.
5. **Shuffle Sideways.** Students stand sideways on the line in a ready position (i.e., feet shoulder width, knees bent, head up, arms flexed in front of the body). On signal, students shuffle down the line without a crossover step. Students should also lead with both the left and right sides. A variation can have students spread out down the line and face the teacher, who is standing in front of the entire group. The teacher gives a left- or right-hand signal to start the group moving.

All of the form running drills can also be done without lines if necessary. Boundary cones can be used to mark the beginning and end of each running section. Another variation is to place cones at one third and two thirds of the distance and ask students to vary their speed in each third of the distance. For example, students could jog the first third, sprint the second, and ease to three-quarter speed during the last third. Another variation is to change the type of running during each third. The following combinations might be used:

1. Jog, shuffle right, and shuffle left
2. Carioca, shuffle, and sprint
3. Backward run, crossover left, and crossover right
4. Form run, crossover front, and form run
5. Carioca left, carioca right, and sprint

File Running

Divide the class into two or three groups according to cardiovascular fitness level: high, medium, and low. Each group lines up single file and begins to jog around a given distance, such as a quarter-mile track, a field, or a set of boundary cones. Students should keep a 2 or 3-yd distance between

between each person. The last person in line sprints past the file and becomes the leader. When the new leader is in place, the new last person begins to sprint past the file. This procedure continues for a given distance or a given number of minutes. The high fitness group will cover more distance in a given time.

Walk-Jog-Sprint

This is a continuous movement activity in which the teacher controls the speed of movement with a whistle signal. Three whistles mean *sprint*, two mean *jog*, and one signals *walk*. The students start by walking around a given area (track, field, or boundary cone). The teacher then alternates the periods of jogging, sprinting, and walking for a number of minutes or for a given distance. It is important to progressively build up the time or distance.

Pace Work

Students need to practice running at an even pace for a given distance, such as a 6-, 8-, or 10-min mile. Pacing can be practiced by running shorter segments of the distance at the correct speed. Figures 17.23 and 17.24 show the required time for covering certain distances in order to maintain correct pacing. It is easiest to use a marked track, but a workable track can be developed through placement of boundary cones. Using a rectangle is helpful for ease of measurement. Students are divided into groups and challenged to run distances at a given time. For example, the fast group might work on a 6-min-mile pace: 110 yd in 22.5 sec, 220 yd in 45 sec, and 440 yd in 90 sec. The medium group could work on an 8-min pace, and the slow group could focus on a 10-min-mile pace. It is interesting to have students calculate a world

record pace for a given distance and then try to run a small segment of that distance at the record pace. For instance, have them run 50 yd at a 4-min-mile pace, or 440 yd at a 2.5-hr marathon pace.

Another strategy for teaching students about pace is to set up a square, 50 yd on a side. Place a cone at every corner and in the middle of each side. Put an equal number of students at each cone. Calculate the 25-yd time for various speeds (e.g., a 6-, 8-, or 10-min mile. Have students try to run at a given speed, and blow a whistle each time they should have completed a 25-yd run. The students

Times for 40- and 100-Yard Dashes

To run 1 mi in:	You would have to run the 40-yard dash 44 times, with each dash run in:	Or run the 100-yard dash 17.6 times, with each dash run in:
3.48 min (world record time)	5.18 sec	12.95 sec
5:00 min	6.81 sec	17.04 sec
6:00 min	8.18 sec	20.45 sec
7:00 min	9.55 sec	23.87 sec
8:00 min	10.90 sec	27.25 sec
10:00 min	13.62 sec	34.08 sec

Figure 17.23. Pace chart—1 (reprinted from *Dynamic Physical Education for Elementary School Children*, 7th ed. by V. P. Dauer and R. P. Pangrazi, 1983. Minneapolis: Burgess Publishing Co., p. 531)

Interval	To run 1 mi (1760 yd) in:								
	4:00	*5:00*	*6:00*	*7:00*	*8:00*	*9:00*	*10:00*	*11:00*	*12:00*
¾ (1320 yd)	3:00	3:45	4:30	5:15	6:00	6:45	7:30	8:15	9:00
½ (880 yd)	2:00	2:30	3:00	3:30	4:00	4:30	5:00	5:30	6:00
¼ (440 yd)	1:00	1:15	1:30	1:45	2:00	2:15	2:30	2:45	3:00
⅛ (220 yd)	:30	:37½	:45	:52½	1:00	1:07½	1:15	1:22½	1:30
¹⁄₁₆ (110 yd)	:15	:18¾	:22½	:26¼	:30	:33¾	:37½	:41¼	:45

Figure 17.24. Pace chart for a one-mile run—2

should be at a cone each time the whistle sounds. They can tell if they are going too fast or too slow.

Random Running

Random running is a simple and effective way to improve cardiovascular fitness (Pangrazi and Wilcox 1979). The emphasis is on long, slow, distance (LSD) running. Students are allowed to run randomly throughout the area at a pace that is comfortable for them. They are encouraged to find a partner and to talk while jogging.

Students who need to walk because of their subpar level of fitness can do so without experiencing the stigma of finishing last during a run. The distance each student runs is not charted. Effort is acknowledged, rather than speed or distance-running ability. Emphasis is placed on being active, involved, and moving during the entire episode, rather than on seeing how far one can run or jog.

Students can begin with a 10-min random running episode three times per week. The duration of the run can be increased 1 min per week until a maximum 20-min episode is achieved. This allows the majority of students to increase their work load in a gradual and palatable manner.

Fartlek

Fartlek is a form of training that was developed in Sweden in the 1930s and 1940s. The training is aerobic in nature and entails hard, but untimed, long distance efforts over topographic challenges. The hilly terrain is run at varied tempos. (The term *fartlek* translates to "speed play.")

Fartlek is usually done on soft surfaces. A typical workout for an athlete in training might be as follows:

1. Five to 10 min of easy jogging
2. Steady, intense speed for 1–2 km
3. Five min of rapid walking
4. Easy running broken by 50–60 m of accelerated runs that cause moderate fatigue
5. Easy running with 2–5 intermittent swift strides every 100 m to moderate fatigue
6. Full uphill effort for 150–200 m
7. One min of fast-paced running on level ground
8. Five to 10 m of easy running.

The above workout illustrates the variation involved in fartlek. Students can be given a workout that might last 10 to 20 min and encompasses the many different tempos and geographic features described. The run challenges can be written on cards, and students select runs of varying difficulty (e.g., easy, moderate, difficult, strenuous).

References

AAHPERD. *Lifetime Health Related Physical Fitness Test Manual*. Reston, VA: AAHPERD, 1980.

Corbin, C. B., and Fletcher, P. 1968. Diet and activity patterns of obese and non-obese elementary school children. *Research Quarterly* 39(4): 922–928.

deVries, H. A., and Adams, G. M. 1972. Electromyographic comparison of single doses of exercise and meprobamate as to effects on muscular relaxation. *American Journal of Physical Medicine* 51: 130–141.

Gilliam, T. B., et al. 1978. Blood lipids and fatness in children age 7–13. *Canadian Journal of Applied Sport Science* 3: 65–69.

Glass, W. 1973. Coronary heart disease sessions prove vitally interesting. *CAHPER Journal*, May-June issue.

Glasser, W. *Positive Addiction*. New York: Harper & Row, Publishers, Inc., 1976.

Johnson, M. L., Burke, B. S., and Mayer, J. 1956. The prevalence and incidence of obesity in a cross-section of elementary and secondary school children. *American Journal of Clinical Nutrition* 4(3): 231–38.

Miller, D. K., and Allen, T. K. *Fitness: A Lifetime Commitment*. Minneapolis: Burgess Publishing Co., 1982.

Nelson, D. O. *Dynamic Fitness*. Logan, UT: Utah State University, 1979.

Pangrazi, B., and Wilcox, R. 1979. RRP—An effective approach to cardiovascular fitness for children. *Arizona JOHPERD* 22(2): 15–16.

Petrofsky, J. S., and Lind, A. R. 1975. Aging, isometric strength, and endurance, and cardiovascular responses to static effort. *Journal of Applied Physiology* 41: 91–95.

Rarick, L. G., and Dobbins, D. A. 1975. Basic components in the motor performances of children six to nine years of age. *Medicine and Science in Sports* 7(2): 105–110.

Rose, K. 1973. To keep people in health. *Journal of the American College Health Association* 22: 80.

Wilmore, J. H. 1980. Physical fitness guidelines for adults. In *Proceedings of the National Conference on Physical Fitness and Sports for All*. Washington, DC: The President's Council on Physical Fitness and Sports, 39–48.

Chapter 18

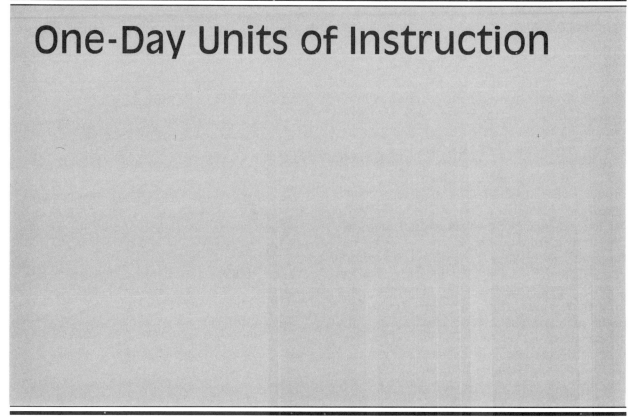

One-Day Units of Instruction

The purpose of the units of instruction in this chapter is to offer students and teachers a change of pace in instruction. The units are personally challenging and allow students to develop new skills and to work closely with classmates. They are presented easily and should serve to motivate students as well as to offer a variation in the instructional process. Many are useful for rainy days, shortened period days, or for introductory activities.

The units require equipment that is not always used in typical physical education programs. They are meant to be presented for one or two days without worry about continuity of instruction. Most of the units are noncompetitive and focus on learning and on performing novel tasks. Since variation in student ability makes little difference in the presentation of these activities, they can be offered as challenge activities to students. For example, the proper progression of juggling activities can be taught. After the rudimentary skills are learned, some students will progress to more challenging tasks, while others remain at a lower level.

An excellent way to use the one-day units is to present them on a Tuesday or Thursday to break up a longer unit of instruction. Students should be encouraged to help each other master the tasks, with emphasis placed on cooperation rather than competition. This creates a different environment that may be more meaningful for some students. The low-key instructional approach is also an inviting change of pace for instructors.

INDIVIDUAL AND DUAL UNITS OF INSTRUCTION

Units in this area include juggling, beanbags, wands, hoops, stunts, tumbling, and combatives. They focus on individual skill development and allow each student to progress at an optimum rate of development. Many modifications of the units can be made, and students can develop new and different challenges that the rest of the class can try.

BEANBAGS

The following are challenges that can be taken in any order. The best size beanbag is usually 6 in. × 6 in., because it can be balanced on various body parts and used for many challenges. The advantage of the 4 in. × 4 in. beanbags lies in the fact that they can be used for juggling activities as well as for many of the challenge activities listed here. Students should try to master the stunts with both the right and left hand.

1. Toss the beanbag overhead and catch it on the back of the hand. Try catching on different body parts such as shoulder, knee, and foot.
2. Toss the beanbag, make a half-turn, and catch it. Try making a different number of turns (e.g., full, double, and so forth).
3. Toss, clap the hands, and catch. Try clapping the hands a specified number of times. Clap the hands around different parts of the body.
4. Toss, touch various body parts or objects. For example, toss, touch the toes, shoulders, and hips before catching. Specify objects to touch, such as the wall, the floor, or a line.
5. Toss, move to various body positions, and catch the beanbag. Suggested positions are sitting, kneeling, supine or prone position, and lying on the side of the body.
6. Reverse no. 5 by tossing the beanbag from some of the suggested positions and then resuming the standing position.
7. Toss and perform various stunts before catching the beanbag. Suggested stunts are heel clicks, heel slaps, jump and perform a full turn, and push-up.
8. Toss the beanbag from behind the back and catch it. Toss overhead and catch it behind the back.
9. Toss, move, and catch. Cover as much ground as possible between the toss and catch. Move forward, backward, and sideways, using different steps such as the carioca, shuffle, and slide.
10. Toss the beanbag with various body parts (feet, knees, shoulders) and catch it with the hands or other body parts. Try to develop as much height on the toss as possible.
11. Perform some of the stunts with a beanbag in each hand. Catch the bags simultaneously.
12. Play a balance tag game. Specify a body part that the bag must be balanced on while moving. Designate who is *it*. If the beanbag falls off or is touched with the hands, the player must freeze and is subject to being tagged.
13. Try partner activities. Play catch with a partner using two or three beanbags. Toss and catch the beanbags using various body parts.

HOOPS

Hoops are useful for offering various challenges to students. A 42-in.-diameter hoop is usually the best size choice. This is a large enough hoop to move through and over and to use for Hula-Hoop activities. Students should try to master the activities with both sides of their body. Emphasis can be placed on creating new routines with the hoops. The following are suggested ideas:

1. Spin the hoop like a top and see how long the hoop will continue to spin. While the hoop is spinning, see how many times it can be jumped.
2. Hula-Hoop using various body parts (waist, knees, ankles, neck, wrist). Hula-Hoop from the neck to the knees and back up to the neck. Hula-Hoop on a wrist and then change to the other wrist. Pass the hoop to a partner while Hula-Hooping.
3. Try many of the Hula-Hooping challenges while using two or more hoops. Hula-Hoop with a hoop on two or more body parts.
4. Play catch with a partner while Hula-Hooping. Catch more than one object and Hula-Hoop with more than one hoop.
5. Jump or hop through a hoop held by a partner. Vary the challenge by altering the angle and height of the hoop. Try jumping through two or more parallel hoops without touching them.
6. Roll the hoop like a spare tire. Change direction on signal. Roll two or more hoops at the same time.
7. Use the hoop in place of a jump rope. Jump the hoop forward, backward, and sideways. Perform various foot stunts like toe-touching, rocker step, and heel-and-toe while jumping.
8. Roll the hoop forward with a reverse spin. The spin should cause it to return to the thrower. As the hoop returns, try some of the following challenges: Jump the hoop, move through it, kick it up with the toe and catch it, and pick it up with the arm and begin hooping it.
9. Play catch with the hoop with a partner. Use two or more hoops and throw them alternately as well as simultaneously.

10. Employ the hoop relay. Break into equal-size groups. Join hands and place a hoop on a pair of joined hands. The object is to pass the hoop around the circle without releasing the hand grip. The first group to get the hoop around the circle is declared the winner.

JUGGLING

Juggling is a skill that offers a challenge to secondary school students. If the majority of students have not mastered basic juggling skills, juggling scarves should be purchased. They are lightweight, sheer scarves that move slowly and allow students to master the proper arm and hand movements. Once the movement pattern is learned, beanbags, jugglebags (small round beanbags), and fleece balls can be used before proceeding to balls, rings, and clubs.

Juggling can be done in a crisscross fashion that is called cascading, or in a circular fashion called showering. Cascading is the easier of the two patterns and should be taught first. One of the advantages of using beanbags or fleece balls before using balls is that these objects do not roll when dropped and are usually easier to catch.

Instructional Progression for Cascading (Figure 18.1)

1. Using one ball and one hand only, toss the ball upward in front of the body, and catch it with the same hand. The toss should be 2 to 2.5 ft high, and the ball should always be visible by both eyes without excessive head movement. The tosses should be made with quick wrist action and should be mastered using each hand.

2. Handle the ball alternately with the right and left hand, tossing from one hand to the other.

3. With one ball in each hand, alternate tossing a ball upward and catching it in the same hand so that one ball is always in the air. Next, begin with a ball in each hand and toss the balls on an inward path to the other hand. One ball leaves the hand slightly after the other. Complete as many successive tosses as possible.

4. To juggle three balls, begin with two balls in the starting hand and one in the other. In succession, throw one of the balls in the starting hand, then the ball in the other hand, and finally, the third ball. One ball is always in the air.

Instructional Progression for Showering (Figure 18.2)

1. Showering is usually done in a counterclockwise motion. Hold one ball in each hand. Begin by tossing with the right hand on an inward path and then immediately toss the other ball from the left directly across the body to the right hand. Practice until the motion is smooth and continuous.

2. Hold two balls in the right hand and one in the left. Toss the first ball from the right hand on an inward path and immediately toss the second on the same path. At about the same time the second ball is released, toss the ball from the left hand to the right hand directly across the body.

When both cascading and showering patterns are mastered, students can try to change from cascading to showering and vice versa without stopping. This is a difficult challenge.

Figure 18.1. Cascading with three balls and two hands (reprinted from *Dynamic Physical Education for Elementary School Children*, 7th ed. by V. P. Dauer and R. P. Pangrazi, 1983. Minneapolis: Burgess Publishing Co., p. 269)

Figure 18.2. Showering with three balls and two hands (reprinted from *Dynamic Physical Education for Elementary School Children*, 7th ed. by V. P. Dauer and R. P. Pangrazi, 1983. Minneapolis: Burgess Publishing Co., p. 270)

STUNTS AND COMBATIVES

This unit should emphasize personal challenge and brief competitive episodes. Students enjoy the chance to pit their strength and coordination skills against others. The combatives should be between opponents of approximately the same skill level and size. Partners should be switched often so there is little chance for animosity to develop. The contests start and stop by mutual agreement, with either party able to terminate the contest immediately.

There is little point in running tournaments to see who is the class champion in a specific combative. Emphasis should be placed instead on enjoyment, learning one's strengths and weaknesses, and being able to contest a number of opponents.

Stunts, on the other hand, require that students work cooperatively to accomplish them successfully and are an excellent way to help students learn more about their peers.

Suggested Individual Stunts

Leg Dip.   Extend both hands and one leg forward while balancing on the other leg. Lower the body until the seat touches the heel and then return to the standing position. This must be done without the aid of the arms and without losing balance.

Behind the Back Touch.   Start in a standing position with the arms extended behind the back and hands clasped. Squat slowly and touch the floor with an extended finger, then return to the standing position.

Knee Jump.   Kneel on the floor with the seat on the heels and the toes pointing backward. In one continuous motion, swing the arms forward and jump to the feet. If accomplished, try to perform a half-turn during the jump.

Wall Climb.   Take a push-up position with the feet against the wall. Walk up the wall with the feet to a handstand position and then return to the push-up position.

Popover.   While in push-up position, propel the body upward and do a half turn to the inverted push-up position. Popover to the regular push-up position.

Double Heel Click.   Jump upward and click the heels twice. If accomplished, try to perform a triple heel click before landing.

Push-up Inversion.   Begin in push-up position. Push strongly off the floor and bring the legs through the arms in one smooth motion—assuming the inverted push-up position. Return to the original position with a strong movement backward.

Jump Through.   Hold the left toe with the right hand. Jump the right foot through without losing the grip on the toe. Try the stunt with the other foot.

Sitting Lift-off.   Sit on the floor with the legs extended forward. Place the hands on the floor somewhere between the hips and knees, depending on the balance point. Lift the entire body off the floor in a balanced position. The stunt can be learned in stages—first with the heels remaining on the floor, then with the heels held off the floor by a friend.

Jumping Toe Touch.   Begin in a standing position with the hands held in front of the body, shoulder-width apart, palms down. When ready, jump up and bring the feet quickly forward so the toe tips touch the hands in front of the body. The attempt should be to bring the hands to the feet, lifting the feet as high as possible.

Leg Circling.   In a squatting position with both hands on the floor, place the left knee between the arms and extend the right leg to the side. Swing the right leg forward and under the lifted right arm, under the left leg and arm, and back to starting position. Perform several circles in succession. Try circling with the other leg.

Suggested Partner and Group Stunts

Leapfrog.   One student forms the base by standing stiff-legged, bending over, and placing the hands on the knees. The other student runs and leaps over the base by performing a light push-off on the back of the base. A number of students can form bases to create a series of leaps for the moving student.

Wheelbarrow (Figure 18.3).   One partner is in push-up position with the legs spread. The other person walks between the legs and grasps and lifts the partner's lower legs. The partner in push-up position then walks the arms while the other person moves forward, backward, or sideways. A double or triple wheelbarrow can be performed with students extending their legs over the back of the student in push-up position and placing their hands on the floor.

Caterpillar (Figure 18.4).   One student is on hands and knees, acting as the support. Another student, facing the same direction, places the hands about 2 ft in front of the support's hands. The second student's legs are then placed on top of the support and locked together at the ankles. Five to six students can continue this process and then begin walking when everyone is in place.

Figure 18.3. Wheelbarrow

Figure 18.4. Caterpillar

Figure 18.5. Cooperative scooter

Figure 18.6. Spider walk

Knee Stand.   The base student is in crab position. The other student stands on the knees of the base. A spotter may be necessary to help the second student come to a balanced position.

Cooperative Scooter (Figure 18.5).   Two students face each other and sit with toes under the seat of the other. The arms are joined by holding the other student's arms at the wrist or above. Students scoot forward or backward by cooperatively lifting the feet when the other lifts the seat. Progress is made by alternately flexing and extending the knees and hips.

Spider Walk (Figure 18.6).   The base student is in a sitting position with the back against a wall. The next student backs up and sits lightly on the knees of the base. More students can be added in similar fashion. The hands should be placed around the waist of each person in front. Walking is done by moving the feet on the same side together.

Triple High Jump.   Students form groups of three and join hands. One of the students is designated as the performer and jumps over the joined arms of the other two. The performer is assisted in the jump by an upward lift from the others. The hands to be jumped over should be clasped lightly and released if the jumper does not gain enough height.

Octopus.   Eight to 12 students work together to develop this activity. Half of the students form a circle with hands joined, while each student in the other half finds a pair of joined hands to lean backward on, placing the weight on the heels. Each of the leaners then join hands behind the backs of the others, thus creating two separate groups with joined hands. The octopus begins moving slowly around the circle, taking small side steps. The stunt is brought to a climax by moving as fast as possible.

Double Bear Walk.   The base student is on hands and knees. The top student assumes the same position with the hands on the shoulders and the knees over the hips of the base. Move slowly throughout the area without losing balance.

Double Crab Walk. The bottom student moves into crab position. The top performer straddles the base and also assumes the crab position with the hands on the shoulders and the feet on the knees of the base. Move slowly throughout the area.

Back Balance (Figure 18.7). Students work with a partner. One partner lies in supine position and becomes the base. The base bends the knees, and the balancer places the small of the back on the soles of the base's feet. The balancer then lies back and balances in a layout position.

Sitting Balance (Figure 18.8). The base assumes a supine position on the floor. The balancer strad-

dles the base so that they are looking at each other. The balancer sits on the soles of the base's feet while the base holds the ankles of the balancer. The legs of the balancer should be extended as much as possible.

Abdominal Balance. The base assumes a supine position on the floor, then raises the legs and positions the feet so the soles are parallel to the floor. The balancer faces the base and places the abdomen on the soles of the base's feet. The base grasps the hands of the balancer and extends the legs to move the performer into a balanced position. The balancer should attempt to arch the back, raise the head, and extend the arms to the sides.

Seat Press (Figure 18.9). The base lies on the floor with the knees bent and the feet flat on the floor. The balancer straddles the base facing the feet of the base. The two join hands, and the top partner sits on the joined hands supported by the base. The balancer's legs are placed on the knees of the base.

Minipyramids (Figure 18.10). Students can work in groups of three to five to develop various types of pyramids. Some examples are shown in the figure. Students should be encouraged to develop different types of pyramids and allowed time to share them with the rest of the class.

COMBATIVES

There are many types of combatives. This list should give insight into the many variations but is certainly not exhaustive.

Arm Wrestling. This popular activity can be done lying on the floor or sitting at a table. The

Figure 18.7. Spotting the back balance

Figure 18.8. Sitting balance

Figure 18.9. Seat press

Figure 18.10. Minipyramids

right hands are clasped, and the elbows are bent and rest on the floor or table. When ready, the goal is to force the opponent's hand down to the floor or table surface. The elbows cannot be lifted from the surface.

Leg Wrestling. Opponents are side by side and supine on a mat with their heads in opposite directions. They lock the near elbows and prepare for action. On signal, they lift the inside leg vertically two times before hooking the legs on the third count. They then try to roll the opponent over backwards.

Standing Hand Wrestle. Contestants place the toes of their right feet together and grasp right hands in a handshake grip. The left foot is moved to the rear for support. The goal is to force the opponent to move either foot.

Finger Wrestle. Opponents stand on the right foot and hold the left foot with the left hand. The index fingers of the right hand are hooked, and opponents attempt to push each other off balance.

Flag Grab. Contestants have a flag tucked in the belt and attempt to keep others from pulling it out. At the same time, opponents try to collect as many flags as possible.

Palm Wrestle. Contestants face each other, standing 12 in. apart. The palms of the opponents are placed together and must remain so for the duration of the contest. The goal is to push the opponent off balance.

Push-up Breakdown. Opponents are in push-up position and attempt to break down the other's position. It is a fall when one of the opponents is brought down from the push-up position to the ground.

Crab Breakdown. This is similar to the push-up breakdown, except that the opponents are in crab position. As a variation, try getting the opponent to touch the seat to the floor while keeping the hands and feet on the floor. The takedown must occur through jostling and pushing the opponent.

Toe Dance. Contestants begin by placing their hands on the opponent's shoulders. The goal is to step on top of the toes of the opponent. A variation can be to see how many toe touches can be accumulated in a specified time.

Seat Pull-up. Opponents sit on the floor, facing each other, with the knees bent, and the soles of the contestants' shoes together. Players bend forward, grasp hands firmly, and attempt to pull their opponent's seat off the floor. The winner must be sitting upright in position when the opponent is lifted from the floor, or the contest is a draw.

Back-to-Back Takedown. Contestants sit back to back and lock elbows. The feet are widely spread to form a broad base of support. Both players attempt to pull the other to the left and touch the opponent's shoulder (or elbow) to the floor. As a variation, attempt the contest by pulling in the opposite direction.

TUG-OF-WAR ACTIVITIES

Tug-of-war activities can be conducted in pairs. Partners should be changed often so students have a chance to compete with many others and are not subjected to constantly losing or to seldom being challenged. Tug-of-war ropes are easily made from 10 ft of ⅜-in. nylon rope and two sections of ⅝-in. garden hose 2 ft long. The rope is threaded through the garden hose, which serves as a handle, and tied with a bowline knot so there is a loop at each end of the rope.

Partner Pulls

Partners can have contests using some of the following suggested positions and activities:

Different Positions. Facing, back to back, side to side, one handed, two handed, crab position with the rope hooked over the foot, push-up position, and on all four are a few suggested variations.

Balance Pulls. Students begin in a stationary position. The goal is to cause the opponent to move the feet or lose balance.

Pick-up Contest. Place Indian clubs or bowling pins behind the contestants. The goal is to pull and move backward in order to pick up the clubs.

Multiple Rope Pulls. Ropes can be twisted together so four to six students can become involved in the contest.

Pick-up and Pull. The ropes are laid on the floor between two contestants. On signal, the two opponents run to the rope, pick it up, and the tug-of-war ensues.

Team Tugs-of-War

Small groups and classes can have contests with the large commercially available tug-of-war ropes. Most are 50 ft in length and at least 1 in. in diameter. Many of the ropes have large loops on the end so students can stand inside of them. Caution must be used with the loops, however, because students cannot easily release the rope when the other team gains momentum.

A suggested manner for conducting team tugs-of-war is to tie a marker in the middle of the rope. Two parallel lines are drawn 10 to 20 ft apart. The pull starts with the marker in the middle of the two lines. The goal is to pull the marker over your team's line. Variations for different types of pulls are to try pulling with the rope overhead, having opponents pull with their backs to each other, pulling with one hand on the ground or in the air, or pulling from a seated position.

WANDS

Wands provide challenge through balance and flexibility activities, which can be performed individually. Wands are usually made from ⅝-in. or ¾-in. dowels and should be 42 in. long. They can be painted, and rubber tips can be placed on the ends to soften the noise they make when falling on the floor.

Wand Whirl. Stand a wand in front of the body, and balance it with one finger. Release the wand, perform a full turn, and catch the wand. Try the activity in both directions. Try catching with one finger on top of the wand.

Thread the Needle. Hold the wand in both hands near the ankles. Without letting go of the wand, step over the wand and through the space between the arms. Return to the starting position. Try passing the wand under the feet side to side, one foot at a time, with the wand held in front and behind the body.

Thread the Needle (Jumping). Virtually the same stunt as the previous activity, except that the stick is jumped over and passed under the feet simultaneously.

Wand Kickover. Balance the wand in front of the body with one hand. Release the wand, kick a leg over, and catch the wand. Try kicking in both directions using both legs. Try catching the wand with one finger.

Walk Under. Grasp the wand with the right hand. Twist under the right arm without letting go of the wand, without taking it off the floor, and without touching the knee to the floor. Try using the left arm also.

Broomstick Balance. Balance the wand vertically in one hand. Begin by walking while balancing and then attempt to balance the wand in a stationary position. Try walking in different directions, using both hands, and balancing the wand on different body parts.

Wand Walkdown. Start in a straddle stance, with legs straight. Hold a wand near one end, with the other end of the wand above the head and pointed toward the ceiling. Bend backward, place the wand on the floor behind, and walk the hands down the wand. Return to standing position. If the wands do not have rubber tips, a spotter may have to stabilize the wand end on the floor.

Partner Exchange. Partners face each other, balancing a wand in front of them. On signal, each runs to the other's wand and catches it before it hits the floor. Challenge can be added by increasing the distance, using two wands, and performing stunts such as a full turn or heel click before catching the wand.

Reaction Time. One partner holds the wand horizontally. The other partner places one hand directly above the wand, palm down. The wand is dropped and the person must try to catch the wand before it hits the floor. This can also be tried holding the wand vertically. The other person forms a "V" with the thumb and fingers and is challenged to catch the wand. Marks can be placed on the wand, and students challenged to catch the wand on certain marks.

Wand Wrestle. A wand is held in the vertical position by two opponents. The goal is to move the wand to the horizontal plane. One person is designated to move the wand horizontally while the other resists the attempt. Roles are reversed after each bout.

Wand Release. Players sit facing each other with the legs straight and the soles of the feet together. Together, they hold a wand horizontally at chest level. A win occurs when one person causes the other to release the grip on the wand. Neither player is allowed to leave or modify the starting position.

Isometric Exercises. Wands are a useful instrument for performing isometric exercises. Examples are attempting to twist the wand, to stretch

the wand, to compress the wand, or to pull against different body parts. Many stretching activities can also be done using the wands.

LOW-ORGANIZATION GAMES

The following activities are enjoyable for students because they demand few specialized skills yet require teamwork. The games help develop camaraderie among students, and teams can be reorganized periodically to equalize the competition. Rules listed are only starting points; students and teachers can modify any and all of the rules as they desire.

CAGEBALL GAMES

Cageballs come in many different sizes. The most common size is 2 ft in diameter, which is an easy size to store and inflate. The next size is 4 ft in diameter, which makes the games more interesting at the high school level. Drawbacks to the larger size are storage, expense, and inflation time. The largest cageballs, often termed earth balls, are 5 or 6 ft in diameter. These can be kicked, batted, and tossed. Students should not be allowed to mount the ball and roll it, however, since falls in those circumstances are common.

Crab Cageball. Students are divided into four teams. Cones can be used to delineate the corners of a square. One team forms one side of the square, so a different team makes up each side. All players sit with hands behind them for support. Each team is numbered from right to left beginning with the number one. The cageball is placed in the middle of the square. The instructor or another student calls out a number and one member from each team (with the number called) crab-walks to the center and attempts to kick the cageball over the other teams. A team has a point scored against it when: (1) The ball is kicked over or through the team, (2) a team member touches the ball with the arms or hands, or (3) a player stands to block or stop the ball. The team with the fewer points is declared the winner.

Long Team Cageball. Players are divided into two teams. The teams move into sitting position in two lines facing each other 10 to 15 ft apart. The teacher rolls or throws a cageball between the two lines. The object is for one team to kick the ball over the other team. A point is scored against a team when the ball goes over or through a line. The team with the fewer points wins. Again, a point is awarded if a player stands or touches the ball with the hands. More than one cageball can be used simultaneously.

Cageball Football. The game is played on a large playing field. The class is divided into two teams. The object of the game is to carry the cageball across the goal line. The only way the ball can be advanced, however, is when it is in the air. Whenever the ball is on the ground, it can only be moved backwards or sideways. This game is best played with a 4-ft or larger cageball.

Cageball Target Throw. The cageball is used as a target in this game. Divide the class into two teams and place them on opposite sides of the gym. A center line divides the area in half, and teams are restricted to movement in their half. Use cones to mark the goal line near the ends of the playing area. Center the cageball between the teams. Each team is given a number of playground balls or volleyballs for throwing at the cageball. The object is to move the cageball across the opponent's goal line by hitting the cageball with the volleyballs. The cageball cannot be touched by any player. If it is touched, regardless of intent, the point goes to the other team.

Scooter Cageball Soccer. Each player is given a scooter. The ball may be advanced by using the feet only. The object is to score a goal in a fashion similar to soccer. Penalty shots are awarded for rough play, touching the ball with the hands, and leaving the scooter.

RECREATIONAL ACTIVITIES

Many recreational activities can be used as one-day units. Rules and regulations usually accompany the activities and are specific to the situation. The authors have had great success with some of the following activities:

Shuffleboard
Deck tennis
Tennis volleyball
Table tennis
Pillow polo
Sacket
Horseshoes
Tetherball
Lawn bowling
Global ball
Hocker
Pickleball

Frisbee, bowling, and orienteering are three excellent recreational activities that are covered in depth in Chapter 19. They can also be used as short one-day activities.

RELAYS

When they are not overused, relays are enjoyable activities for students. To keep the atmosphere vibrant and the students motivated, the teams should be changed often to equalize the ability of various groups. If the same team wins every bout, the outcome is predetermined and the rest of the class will not be motivated. Another motivator is frequent changing of the relay being played. The relay can be run once to show students how it is to be conducted, and then one to three times for competition.

All relay teams should have the same number of persons on each squad. It is wise to change the order of the squads, so different people get a chance to run starting and finishing legs. Signals to start the relay should be clearly delineated, and students should be told what position they must assume when finished (i.e., sitting, kneeling, or some alternative position).

Potato Relays. This is a style of relay that has been played for years. A small box to hold the objects (potatoes) is placed in front of each squad. Four circles (hoops can be used) are placed 10 to 15 ft apart in front of each squad. The goal is for the first runner to pick up an object from the box and carry it to one of the hoops, come back, pick up another object, and place it in another hoop. This is done until all the hoops are filled. The next person picks up the objects one at a time from the hoops and places them back in the box. The pattern is repeated until all members of the squad have had a turn.

Wheelbarrow Relay. Use the wheelbarrow position described earlier in the chapter as the means of locomotion. All members of each squad must participate in both the carrying position and the down formation.

Bowling Pin Relay. Four bowling pins per squad are used. They are evenly spaced in front of each squad in a fashion similar to the potato relay. The first person in line lays all of the pins down, and the next person stands them up. Only one hand can be used.

Over and Under Ball Relay. Each team is spread out in open squad formation so players are 10 to 15 ft apart. The first person in line passes the ball backward overhead to the nearest teammate. That person throws it backward between the legs to another teammate, and the pattern repeats. When the ball gets to the end of the squad, that person runs to the front of the squad and passes the ball backward. The process is repeated until all players have had a turn at the end and front of the squad.

Stepping Stone Relay. Two small carpet squares are used per squad. The first person in line is the mover and helps the next person in line move down and back. The only way to advance in this relay is by standing on a carpet square and moving to another. It is illegal to move or stand on the floor. The mover picks up the rear carpet square and moves it in front of the advancing player so the next step can be taken. All players must play both roles before the relay is completed.

Pass and Squat Relay. Players are spread out so they are 10 to 15 ft apart. The first person in line turns around, faces the rest of the squad, and throws a volleyball or soccer ball to the first person in line, who returns the throw and squats. The leader now throws the ball to the next person until all members have received a throw and have squatted. When the ball is thrown to the last player, that person dribbles the ball to the front of the squad and repeats the pattern.

Fetch Relay. Squads line up and place one member at the other end of the playing area, 10 to 20 yd away. This person runs back to the squad and fetches the next person. The person who has just been fetched in turn runs back and fetches the next person. The pattern continues until all members have been fetched to the opposite end of the playing area.

Snowball Relay. This relay is similar to the fetch relay, except that after one person has been fetched, both players run back and pick up another player. The pattern continues until the majority of squad members are running back and forth, picking up the remaining members. This relay can be exhausting for the first few people in line and should not be run too often.

Sport Skill Relays. Many sport skills can be used for relays. For example, dribble the basketball down the court, make a basket, and return. The problem with relays of this type is that success is predicated on the skill level of the participants. If some students are less skilled in basketball, the relay can be a source of embarrassment, causing these students to bear the brunt of losing the relay. An instructor who uses sport skill relays is wise to include a wide variety of skills and to develop many different types of relays.

Spread Eagle Relay (Figure 18.11). Break the class into groups of eight to ten students. They lie down on the floor and form a circle with their heads toward the center. They join hands and spread the legs. Participants in each squad are numbered, beginning with one through the number of squad members. When a number is called, that person stands up, runs around the circle, and then resumes the prone position on the floor. The runner must place both feet between each pair of legs. The first person to return to the starting position earns a point for that squad. The squad with the most points wins.

COOPERATIVE ACTIVITIES

These activities require that students work together to accomplish them. They can be used early in the year as mixers in an attempt to help students get to know one another. Emphasis is on enjoyment and accomplishment.

GROUP GAMES

Mass Stand Up. Start with two people sitting back to back. Lock elbows and try to stand up. Increase the number to three people, then four, and so forth. See how many people can stand up simultaneously.

Butt Tug. Stand in two lines back to back. One line moves to the left one step. Bend over, cross the arms between the legs, and grasp the hand of two different people from the other team. Now begin tugging. Try forming two teams in the described position and have a race while maintaining the hand grips.

Figure 18.11. Spread eagle relay

Circle Sit. Have students form a circle and hold hands. Close the circle so shoulders are touching. Move the right side of the body toward the center of the circle and move inward, eliminating gaps. Now sit on the knees of the person behind. Try walking in this position when everyone has assumed the sitting position. Put the left side toward the center and sit on a new partner's lap.

Animal Sounds. Students all close their eyes. Someone is designated to move throughout the group and assign animal names to the players. The number of animals assigned will determine the number of groups formed. This is a useful way to organize groups. When the command is given, the only noises that can be made are those that resemble the animals. Students must keep their eyes closed and move throughout the area in search of another person who has been assigned the same animal. For example, people assigned to be cows search for their counterparts by making a mooing sound and listening for others mooing.

Entanglement. Divide the class into two or more groups. Each group makes a tight circle with their arms pointing toward the middle. In each group, people hold someone's hand until everybody is holding hands. Each person must hold a hand of two different people. On signal, the two groups race to see which can untangle first without disjoining hands. The group may end up in either one large circle or in two smaller, connecting circles. People can be facing different directions when finished.

Bulldozer. Students lie in prone position side by side and as close as possible on the floor. The end person rolls on top of the next person and on down the line of people. When that person gets to the end of the line, the next person starts the roll. Two teams can be formed and a relay race conducted.

Zipper. Players line up in single-file formation. Each student bends over, reaches between the legs with the left hand, and grasps the right hand of the person to the rear. This continues on down the line until all hands are grasped. On signal, the last person in line lies down, the next person backs over the last person and lies down, and so forth until the last person lies down, and then immediately stands and reverses the procedure. The first team to zip and unzip the zipper is declared the winner.

Addition Tag. Two are selected to be *it*. They must hold hands and can tag only with their outside hands. When they tag someone, that person must hook on. This continues and the tagging line

becomes longer and longer. Regardless of the length of the line, only the hand on each end of the line is eligible to tag.

INITIATIVE ACTIVITIES

Faith Fall. The individual falls into the arms of a small group. The individual stands on a balance beam or similar elevated object. The group lines up in two opposite and facing lines and crosses arms with wrists locked. The individual falls when ready across the locked wrists.

Human Circle Pass. The group forms a circle about 6 ft in diameter with arms clasped. One person is put in the middle and closes the eyes. When ready, the person falls backward into the arms of the group. They support and pass the individual around the circle.

Human Line Pass. People sit in a line on the ground with legs straight out, feet touching the person in front of them. The first person in line stands and sits back into the hands of the sitting people who pass the person backward over their head. The process continues until all people have been passed.

Lightbulb Change. The group is in the dark and cannot proceed until the lightbulb is changed. The goal is to form a pyramid high enough to reach the ceiling (13–15 ft) to change the bulb.

High Water. This is similar to the lightbulb change, but the groups compete against one another to see which can make the highest mark on the wall with a piece of chalk or tape.

Sasquatch Race. Two groups are formed and are instructed to make a moving object with a specified number of feet and hands on the ground. Everybody must be part of the group and joined to the others. After the sasquatch is built, the two groups race to a finish line.

Cube Stand. A cube with 18- to 24-in. sides can be used as the base of support. The object is to get as many people as possible standing on the cube simultaneously. The pose must be held for 8 sec.

Stream Crossing. Students must move from one side of the area to the other without touching the floor. They are given small carpet squares on which to move across the "stream." Fewer than the necessary number of squares are handed out, however, so students have to pass the squares back and forth in order to get their team across. The first team to move all members across the stream is declared the winner.

Prison Escape. A rope 5 to 6 ft above the ground is the prison wall. The goal is to move all members of the group over the wall without touching it. If the wall is touched, the player is caught and must move back inside the prison. A thick board or log can be used by the group to reach the rope and scale the wall.

Suggested Readings

Darst, P., and Armstrong, G. *Outdoor Adventure Activities for School and Recreation Programs.* Minneapolis: Burgess Publishing Co., 1980.

Fluegelman, A., ed. *The New Games Book.* Garden City, NY: Doubleday and Co., 1976.

Orlick, T. *Cooperative Sports and Games Book.* New York: Pantheon Books, 1982.

Rohnke, K. *Cowstails and Cobras.* Hamilton, MA: Project Adventure, 1977.

Simpson, B. *Initiative Games.* Butler, PA: Encounter Four, Butler County Community College, 1974.

Chapter 19

Activities and Information for Developing Units of Instruction

The goal of this chapter is to offer beginning-level units in a wide variety of instructional activities. An environment that is safe, success-oriented, and challenging for students is a desired outcome of the units. Rating scales, performance objectives for contracts, station work ideas, block plans, crossword puzzles, and rainy day activities are some of the ideas presented in this section. It is important for teachers to try new ideas as they strive to improve the instructional process. A variety of learning activities helps motivate both students and teachers.

The various units should be used by teachers as a framework for developing their own instructional units. In no case should these units be seen as all inclusive, but should be the starting point that stimulates and encourages a wide range of instructional approaches. The ideas can be adapted and shaped into a unit that is unique to each teacher and meets the particular needs of students in different areas. This allows the teacher to retain the locus of control in planning and developing instructional sequences.

Lead-up activities and skills are presented in detail for unit subjects about which a dearth of resource materials exists. Some units are highly complex and demand in-depth, specialized instruction. In these cases, we have not attempted to cover the area, but rather offer resources that seem particularly effective and comprehensive. For this reason, the reader will note that outside resources are listed for the areas of gymnastics, track and field, aquatics, and rhythms. It would be somewhat presumptuous to assume that one could put all of the necessary instructional elements in a text of this nature, when others have written complete books about the various subjects.

The units are designed to stimulate new ideas and approaches. They offer a wide variety of activities—from team sports to lifetime sports, from individual to dual activities, and from rhythmics to aquatics. They will serve as an outline for instructors who wish to bring a wider range of activities to their students.

AQUATICS

An aquatics instructional program in the secondary schools is an excellent addition to a balanced curriculum. Unfortunately, a large number of school districts do not have the facilities necessary to implement swimming and related aquatics programs. It is, however, often possible to bus students to swimming pools outside the school. These may be municipal pools, YMCA and YWCA pools, or the facilities of various private organizations.

Swimming classes require a teacher with expertise in the area. Rotating teaching responsibilities is mandatory so that those teachers who have expertise are used in the swimming instructional program. The swimming program can also have an aquatic games component, which focuses on learning to adjust to the water. The aquatic games can be taught by a less qualified teacher. All aquatics teachers, regardless of assignment, should have the American Red Cross Water Safety Instruction certification.

The pool should be clean and warm. Nothing turns students off faster than having to swim in a pool that is inadequately heated. A pool with a uniform depth of 3 to 4 ft of water is often preferable for teaching nonswimmers, because the students can stand up immediately if they have a problem. This offers beginning swimmers a measure of confidence. For intermediate and advanced swimmers, a standard pool, which can be used for diving as well as swimming, is preferable.

Lessons should be kept short in terms of time spent in the water. When they are learning new skills, students tire easily and they can practice some skills out of the water.

Since swimming is an important lifetime skill, it is most desirable that students leave the class with a positive feeling about the instruction. Introducing students to any new activity is difficult, and most students need extra encouragement and patience as they begin to overcome their fears of the water.

SEQUENCE OF SKILLS

A difficult aspect of teaching swimming to junior and senior high school students is the tremendous range of ability and experience that students bring to the class. Some students may not know how to swim, whereas others may have been swimming competitively since they were three years old. This necessitates that students be grouped in homogeneous classes according to ability. The skills to be taught may therefore range from drownproofing and survival skills to the American Red Cross Water Safety Instruction certification.

Since aquatics is a highly specialized activity involving specific skills that must be learned, developing lead-up activities that are meaningful is difficult. The authors recommend the text *Teaching Aquatics* (Torney and Clayton 1981) to teachers who are interested in creating a meaningful instructional program. It includes chapters on developing a successful instructional program, teaching essential aquatic skills, springboard diving skills, and life-saving skills. A chapter is also offered on the evaluation of swimming skills. Of particular aid to the less experienced teacher is a series of performance analysis sheets to help in evaluating various strokes and dives.

Another approach that has been effective in the school setting is to play a wide variety of aquatic games. Many of the games do not require swimming skills, but students often learn to overcome their fear of water through participation. The games are demanding on the cardiovascular system, and help develop strength and balance. An excellent source for aquatic games is the *Physical Education Handbook*, 7th edition (Seaton et al. 1983).

References

Seaton, D. C., et al. *Physical Education Handbook*. 7th ed. Englewood Cliffs, NJ: Prentice-Hall, Inc., 1983.

Torney, J. A., Jr., and Clayton, R. D. *Teaching Aquatics*. Minneapolis: Burgess Publishing Co., 1981.

Suggested Readings

American National Red Cross. *Swimming and Water Safety*. Washington, DC: American National Red Cross, 1968.

American National Red Cross. *Swimming and Water Safety Courses: Instructors Manual*. Washington, DC: American National Red Cross, 1968.

Arnold, C. G., ed. *Aquatic Safety and Lifesaving Programs*. 2nd ed. New York: National YMCA Program Materials, 1979.

Arnold, L., and Freeman, R. W. *Progressive Swimming and Springboard Diving Program*. New York: National YMCA Program Materials, 1972.

Hallett, B., and Clayton, R. D., eds. *Course Syllabus: Teacher of Swimming.* Reston, VA: AAHPERD, 1980.

Lanoue, F. R. *Drownproofing.* Englewood Cliffs, NJ: Prentice-Hall, Inc. 1963.

ARCHERY

Archery has long been recognized as an appealing activity for both sexes, all ages, and the handicapped. The two most popular forms are target archery and field archery. Target archery involves shooting a specific number of arrows from a given distance at a target with five or ten concentric circles. Scoring is completed by adding up the points for each arrow striking the target. This is the most popular archery activity taught in secondary school programs. Field archery involves 28 stationary targets of assorted sizes and shapes placed at varying distances. Field shooting requires a larger area and considerable safety procedures. It is especially appealing to the hunter and bow fisherman.

Archery seems to be quite popular with certain individuals. Many families enjoy participating together, for archery activities can be enjoyed by all family members.

SEQUENCE OF SKILLS

Bracing the Bow

There are several methods used for stringing or bracing the bow. One method involves using a bowstringer device made of a 5-ft rope with a leather cup on each end. The cups are put on both ends of the bow with the string hanging down toward the ground in front of the body. After placing one string loop in position, place one foot on the center of the bowstringer, and pull the bow straight up with one hand. Use the free hand to slide the free string loop into place. To unstring the bow, reverse the process. Figure 19.1 is an example of another type of bowstringer.

Another stringing technique is called the step-through method (Figure 19.2). Start by placing the bottom string loop in position, then put the bottom curve of the bow across the top of the right ankle, and step between the string and the bow with the left foot. Use the left hand to bend the bow against the left thigh until the string loop can be moved into place with the right hand. Be sure to keep the face away from the bow tip.

Figure 19.1. Bowstringer

Figure 19.2. Step-through method

Stance

The feet should straddle the shooting line and be shoulder width apart. The toes are in a direct line with the target. The knees should be relaxed, and a comfortable standing posture maintained (Figure 19.3).

Nocking the Arrow

Hold the bow horizontally in the left hand, and place the nock of the arrow on the nocking point of the string. The odd-colored feather should face away from the bow. Use the index finger of the left hand to steady the arrow on the arrow rest.

Figure 19.3. Stance and full draw

Figure 19.4. Bowsight

Extend and Draw

The string is on the first joint of three fingers of the right hand. The index finger is above the arrow, and the next two fingers are below the arrow. Rotate the bow to a vertical position with the left arm parallel to the ground. Extend the left arm and draw the string toward the body with the right hand. Keep the right elbow parallel to the ground. Be sure the fingers of the bow hand are loose and relaxed.

Anchor and Hold

The string should touch the nose, lips, and chin, while the index finger touches under the center of the chin. The anchor point should be the same for every shot.

Aiming

Target archery has two basic methods of aiming—point of aim and bowsights. The beginner should probably use the point-of-aim technique, which involves finding a spot somewhere on a vertical line drawn above, through, and below the middle of the target. This point of aim will vary according to the distance from the target. To locate the point, align the eye and the arrow with an object on the vertical line through the center of the target. Shoot several rounds and then adjust the point of aim up or down accordingly. A mechanical bowsight (Figure 19.4) can be mounted on the bow and used by aligning the center of the target through the aperture. The aperture is then adjusted up or down, or left or right, depending on the pattern of

the arrows for that shooting distance. The aperture position is then noted for each distance and is used in the future.

Release and Afterhold

As the arrow is released, the back muscles remain tight while the string fingers relax. The relaxed drawing hand moves backward slightly along the neck. The bow arm and head remain steady until the arrow hits the target.

Retrieving Arrows

Arrows in a target should be removed by placing the arrow between the index and middle finger of the left hand. The palm of the hand should be away from the target facing the archer. The right hand should be placed on the arrow close to the target. The arrow is removed by gently twisting and pulling at the same angle at which the arrow entered. If the fletching is inside the target, the arrow should be pulled through the target. Arrows should be carried with the points together and the feathers spread out to prevent damage.

IDEAS FOR EFFECTIVE INSTRUCTION

Equipment

The composition of bows is primarily wood, fiberglass, or a laminated combination of the two. Either a straight or recurved bow is available. The recurved bow has curved ends to provide additional leverage, which increases the velocity of the arrow. Bows also have different weights and lengths. Archers should select a bow based on their strength and skill. Starting with a lighter bow is best, and then progressing to a heavier one as skill and strength are developed. In class situations, teachers should try to have a variety of bows available for different ability levels. Figure 19.5 shows the parts of a bow.

Arrow shafts are made of wood, fiberglass, or aluminum. The term *fletching* refers to the feathers or plastic material used to stabilize the flight of the arrow. It is important for the beginning archer to get the proper length arrow. A good method for determining proper length is to have someone hold a yardstick against the sternum and perpendicular to the body, while the individual extends the arms with the palms on either side of the yardstick. The point at which the fingertips touch the yardstick is the correct arrow length. For beginners, it is bet-

ter to have the arrows too long. Many different types of points and feathers are available. Figure 19.6 shows the parts of an arrow.

Many types of finger tabs and shooting gloves are also available for protection and to promote smooth release. An arm guard should be used to prevent the bowstring from slapping the bow arm and to keep long clothing sleeves snug to the body. Movable and stationary quivers are used to transport arrows and sometimes to support the bow while retrieving arrows.

GENERAL RULES

1. Archers must straddle a shooting line. Arrows should always be pointed down-range.
2. An *end* of six arrows is usually shot at one time. A *round* consists of a number of ends shot at several distances.
3. Values for rings in a target are as follows:

Five-Ring Scoring

Gold	= 9
Red	= 7
Blue	= 5
Black	= 3
White	= 1

Ten-Ring Scoring

Gold	= 10, 9
Red	= 8, 7
Blue	= 6, 5
Black	= 4, 3
White	= 2, 1

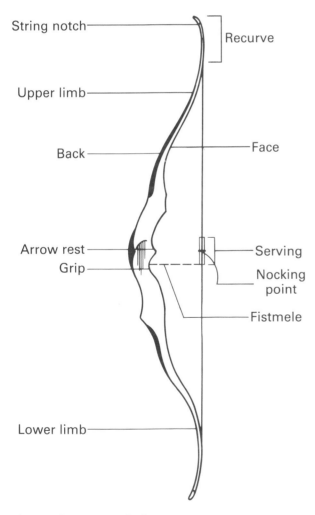

Figure 19.5. Parts of a bow

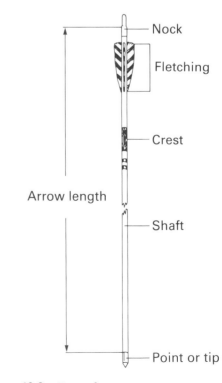

Figure 19.6. Parts of an arrow

4. An arrow that bisects two colors scores the higher of the two values.
5. An arrow that bounces off a target or passes through a target is given 7 points if there is a witness.
6. The *petticoat*, or outside area of the target, counts as a miss.

ORGANIZATION, SKILL WORK, AND SAFETY

Beginning students can experience success quickly if the instructor moves the target close to them (10 yd or less). Students can then move back from the target as their skill level increases. It is also important to have a safe environment. Make sure that strict rules are followed for shooting procedures. Partner work is useful for checking form, reminding about safety procedures, and giving feedback. A rating scale or checklist for shooting form can also be useful and motivating to some students. Several checklists are available from the sources listed at the end of the unit.

Time should be spent with partners and observers to make sure that they are actively involved in the learning process and concentrating on the specific shooting skills. Make sure that all students are mentally involved, even when they are not shooting.

LEAD-UP GAMES AND LEARNING ACTIVITIES

Relays

Each team has one target and each person has one arrow. The first person in line shoots and then goes to the end of the line. All team members shoot one arrow and then the team score is tallied. The team with the highest score is the winner.

Turkey Shoot

Each team draws a turkey about the size of a target on a piece of paper. The turkey is placed on the target. Each team tries to hit the turkey as many times as possible.

Tic-Tac-Toe or Bingo

Balloons or a target with squares are placed on the regular target—three rows of three for tic-tac-toe, or five rows of five for bingo. The object is to hit three or five in a row vertically, horizontally, or diagonally. The game can be for individuals or for teams.

Target Work-up

Start with four or five students on a target. Shoot an end of four arrows and tally the score. The highest scorer moves up one target, and the lowest scorer moves down a target. This can be an individual or partner activity.

Tape Shooting

Place two pieces of masking tape across the target, one vertically and one horizontally. The object is to hit either piece of tape. This can also be an individual or team event.

SUGGESTED PERFORMANCE OBJECTIVES

Core Objectives

Objectives 1, 2, and 3 should be completed before the student is allowed to shoot on the range.

1. On a written test covering safety rules, archery terminology, and scoring, the student will score at least 70%. (Two attempts allows.)
2. The student will demonstrate how to brace and unbrace the bow. Grading is on a pass-fail basis.
3. The student will demonstrate the nine steps of the shooting technique (i.e., stand, nock, extend, draw, anchor, hold, aim, release, and afterhold). Grading is on a pass-fail basis.
4. At a distance of 10 yd, the student will hit the target at least 5 of 6 times and score a minimum of 28 points.
5. At a distance of 15 yd, the student will hit the target 4 of 6 times and score a minimum of 24 points.
6. At a distance of 20 yd, the student will hit the target 4 of 6 times and score a minimum of 24 points.
7. The student will participate in a minimum of 2 out of 3 novelty archery events.

Optional Activities

(Worth extra credit)

1. On a written test covering safety rules, archery terminology, and scoring, the student will score 100% (one attempt only and worth 3 extra points).
2. At a distance of 10 yd, the student will hit the target 6 of 6 times and score at least 40 points (5 extra points).
3. At a distance of 15 yd, the student will hit the target 5 of 6 times and score at least 40 points (5 extra points).

	B¹	U	L²	L	S³	E	Y	E		B⁴	R	A	C	E	
	O		O		H										
	W		O		A					Q⁵					
	m		S		F		R⁶	B⁷	U	T	T			N⁸
	A		E		T		A		I					O	
	N						N		V		V⁹			C	
		E¹⁰	N¹¹	D			G		E		A			K	
		O					E		R		N				
		R	S¹²							H¹³	E	N			
P¹⁴	E	T	T	I	C	O	A	T¹⁵		C¹⁶				
		H	G				A		A			B¹⁷		
			H	H¹⁸	C			S			E			
C¹⁹	R	E	S	T	I		K		T			L		
				T	L					P²⁰	I	L	E	
F²¹	I	E	L	D		R²²	E	D				Y		

Across

1. Gold circle in center of target
4. Procedure used in stringing bow
7. Another name for an archery target
10. Six arrows
13. The two feathers not at right angles to the nock
14. Area of target face outside the white ring
19. Colored stripes below the feathers
20. Pointed tip of the arrow
21. Long-range shooting
22. Colored circle on target that counts seven points

Down

1. Individual who participates in archery
2. Act of releasing bowstring during a shot
3. Main part of the arrow
5. Receptacle to hold or carry arrows
6. Shooting area
8. Groove in end of arrow where bowstring is placed
9. The feather of an arrow
11. Best orientation for placing targets outdoors
12. Used to assist the archer in aiming
15. Archery equipment
16. Distance a bow is able to shoot
17. Side of bow nearest the string
18. An arrow that contacts the target for a score

Figure 19.7. Archery crossword puzzle

4. At a distance of 20 yd, the student will hit the target 5 of 6 times and score at least 38 points (5 extra points).
5. The student will write a two-page report on the history of archery, complete with bibliography (3 extra points).
6. The student will participate in all three days of novelty archery events (3 extra points).
7. The student will design and put up a bulletin board about archery (5 extra points).

Reinforcement Menu

1. Objectives 1, 2, and 3 must be met before students are allowed to shoot.
2. Post the checklist of objectives on the bulletin board.
3. Post on the bulletin board the high ends and high rounds for each class.
4. Post on the bulletin board the results of the class tournament for each distance.
5. Give ribbons to winners of novelty events.
6. Award extra credit points for exceeding skill requirements.

RAINY DAY ACTIVITIES

Discussion and practice can focus on these skills.

Eye dominance	Draw
Stance	Anchor
Nock	Tighten-hold
Extend	Aim
Bow hand position	Tighten-release
String hand and arm position	Afterhold

Archery tackle can be discussed in detail (i.e., bows, arrows, accessories). Crossword puzzles (Figure 19.7) and word searches are also enjoyable activities for inclement weather.

Suggested Readings

Barrett, J. A. *Archery.* 2nd ed. Pacific Palisades, CA: Goodyear Publishing Co., 1973.

Broer, M. R. *Individual Sports for Women.* 5th ed. Philadelphia: W. B. Saunders Co., 1971.

Dintiman, G. B., and Barrow, L. M. *A Comprehensive Manual of Physical Education Activities for Men.* New York: Appleton-Century-Crofts, 1970.

McKinney, W. C. *Archery.* 3rd ed. Dubuque, IA: Wm. C. Brown Group, 1975.

National Association for Girls and Women in Sport. *Archery-Fencing Guide.* Reston, VA: AAHPERD, 1979–1980.

Seidel, B. L., et al. *Sports Skills: A Conceptual Approach to Meaningful Movement.* 2nd ed. Dubuque, IA: Wm. C. Brown Group, 1980.

Sysler, B. L., and Fox, E. R. *Lifetime Sports for the College Student.* 3rd ed. Dubuque, IA: Kendall/Hunt Publishing Co., 1978.

BADMINTON

Badminton is popular in schools from the junior and senior high through college levels. Competition at the college level is popular nationally and internationally. The activity is considered a lifetime sport and can be enjoyed by all in a recreational setting.

The game is played with a shuttlecock and racquet on a court with a net set at a height of 5 ft. The court is marked for both doubles and singles competition. A toss of a coin or a spin of the racquet determines service or court choice. The game begins with a serve from the right-hand service court to an opponent standing in the opposite right-hand service court.

SEQUENCE OF SKILLS

Grips

Forehand. With the racquet lying across the palm and fingers of the racquet hand, the index finger should be separated from the rest of the fingers. The thumb wraps around the other side of the handle. The grip resembles a handshake and is called the "pistol grip." This grip is used for serving and forehand shots.

Backhand. The thumb is moved to a straightened position and to the right of the handle. The rest of the hand rotates one fourth of a turn to the right (if right-handed).

Regardless of the grip used, the player should make contact with the shuttlecock as early and as high as possible. This gives the player a better angle for return and for more controlled shots, and forces an opponent to move quickly.

Serves

Ready Position and Preparatory Action. Stand with the nonracquet foot forward and the weight mainly on the racquet foot. The feet should be approximately 12 to 15 in. apart. The nonracquet shoulder is toward the receiver, with the racquet held waist-high and behind the body. Keep the wrist cocked.

The shuttlecock must be contacted below the

waist at the instant of the serve. Either a forehand or backhand shot may be used. The forehand is most commonly used. Until the serve is delivered, the server and receiver must be in their legal service courts. Part of both players' feet must remain in contact with the ground.

Singles Service. Review the ready position. Extend the nonracquet arm and drop the shuttlecock before starting to move the racquet forward. As weight is shifted to the front foot, rotate the shoulders and hips. As contact is made below the waist, the wrist and forearm rotate. The racquet arm should follow through high and be extended over the left shoulder at completion of service. Most serves will be long and high. A short serve is, however, effective if your opponent is playing too deep.

Doubles Service. The stance is similar to the singles serve. The shuttlecock is contacted closer to waist height and slightly more toward the server's racquet-hand side. Guide the shuttlecock instead of hitting it. The wrist does not uncock. Just prior to contacting the shuttlecock, the weight is shifted from the racquet foot to the nonracquet foot. Little follow-through or rotation occurs. The shuttlecock should peak in height just before the net and be descending as it clears the net.

Forehand Shots

Clear. The players should be in their ready position with the feet and shoulders parallel to the net. The racquet should be held slightly to the backhand side, and the knees be slightly bent. Contact the shuttlecock as high as possible and in front of the body. The racquet face should be tilted upward, and the shuttlecock should clear the opponent's racquet and land close to the backline.

Drop. When contact with the shuttlecock is made, the racquet face should be flat and pointing ahead or slightly downward. The shuttlecock is gently guided over the net. Remember to follow through. The shuttlecock should just drop over the net into the opponent's forecourt.

Smash. The arm should be extended when the shuttlecock is hit in front of the body. Rotation of the wrist and forearm is performed quickly. The downward angle of the racquet face is more important than the racquet speed. The shot should only be attempted from the front three fourths of the court.

Backhand Shots

Ready Position. From the forehand position, turn so that the racquet shoulder faces the net. The

weight should be on the nonracquet foot, the racquet shoulder up, and the forearm slightly down and across the chest. While shifting the weight to the racquet foot, the body rotates toward the net. As the wrist leads, the racquet extends upward. The racquet arm and elbow should be fully extended at contact. The thumb should not point upward.

Clear. Hitting hard and upward, contact the shuttlecock as high as possible and hit it over the opponent's racquet. Contact should be made in front of the body with the racquet face flat to the target.

Drop. As the shuttlecock is guided over the net, the racquet should be flat and pointed ahead or slightly downward. The shuttlecock should land close to the net.

Underhand Shots

Ready Position. The racquet foot is placed forward, and the racquet face is parallel to the ground. The wrist should be cocked and contact should be made as close to net height as possible.

Forehand Net Clear. This is a high, deep shot similar to the singles deep serve. The shoulder is turned slightly toward the net, and the wrist is cocked. An inward rotation of the wrist and a lifting of the forearm occur just before contact. Proceed to follow through with the elbow slightly bent.

Backhand Net Clear. The racquet foot is forward, and the racquet shoulder turned to the net. The shuttlecock should be contacted as close to net height as possible. As the player moves toward the net, the wrist should be cocked. An outward rotation is used for the backhand. The shot is high and deep into the opponent's court.

Forehand Net Drop. Review the forehand net clear. The net drop is guided over the net with a lifting motion. The shuttlecock should drop quickly.

Backhand Net Drop. This is the same motion as the forehand net drop, except that the backhand grip is used. The shuttlecock should be contacted close to net height.

Ready Position for Receiving

The feet should be parallel and positioned slightly wider apart than the shoulders. The knees should be bent slightly with the weight forward. The racquet is held with the head up and to the backhand side of the body.

Doubles Strategy

Up and Back. One player plays close shots while the partner plays deep shots.

Side by Side. Each partner plays half of the court and is responsible for close or deep shots in his or her half of the court.

Combination. Both side-by-side and up-and-back formations are used. Regardless of the strategy, partners should always call for the shot (*Mine!*) to avoid accidental injuries.

IDEAS FOR EFFECTIVE INSTRUCTION

Racquets and Shuttlecocks (Figure 19.8)

The racquet frame can be made of metal or wood. It is usually 26 in. long and weighs between 3.75 and 5.50 oz. Nylon is commonly the choice of material for stringing the racquet. The metal frame racquets are desirable because they do not warp or require a press for storage.

The weight of the shuttlecock is between 73 and 85 grains, with 14 to 16 feathers. If authentic feathers are used, the shuttlecocks should be stored in a damp place. If nylon feathers are used, the shuttlecocks will be more durable and reasonably priced, which is desirable in the school setting.

Net

The top of the net is 5 ft from the floor at its midpoint. It is 5 ft 1 in. at the posts. The net is 30 in. in depth and 20 ft long.

Figure 19.8. Badminton racquets and shuttlecocks

Court

Figure 19.9 shows the dimensions of a badminton court.

Games and Match

Eleven points make a game in women's singles. All doubles and men's singles games are 15 points. A match constitutes two games out of three. As soon as a side wins two games, the match is over. The winner of the previous game serves the next game. Players change courts after the first and second games. In the third game, players change after 8 points in a 15-point game and after 6 points in an 11-point game.

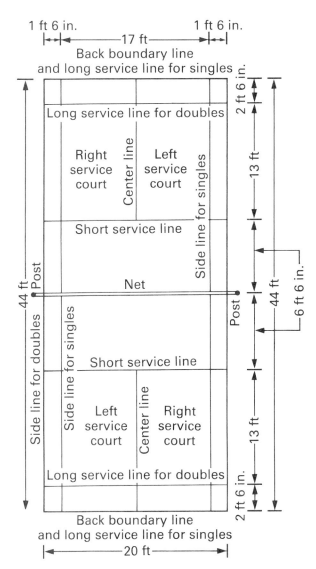

Figure 19.9. Badminton court dimensions

Scoring

Only the serving side scores and continues to do so until an error is committed.

Setting

If the score becomes tied, the game may be extended by the player or side first reaching the tied score. In a 15-point game, the set may occur at 13–13 (setting to 5 points) or 14–14 (setting to 3 points). In an 11-point game, the score may be set at 10–10 (setting to 2 points) or 9–9 (setting to 3 points). A set game continues, but the score called is now 0–0, or *Love all*. The first player or side to reach set score wins. If a side chooses not to set, the regular game is completed.

Singles Play

The first serve is taken from the right service court and received cross court (diagonally) in the opponent's right service court. All serves on 0 or an even score are served and received in the right-hand court. All serves on an odd score are served and received in the left service court.

Doubles Play

In the first inning, the first service is one hand only. In all other innings, the serving team gets to use two hands. At the beginning of each inning, the player in the right court serves first. Partners rotate only after winning a point.

Even and odd scores are served from the same court as in singles play. If a player serves out of turn or from the incorrect service court and wins the rally, a let will be called. The let must be claimed by the receiving team before the next serve.

If a player standing in the incorrect court takes the serve and wins the rally, it will be a let, provided the let is claimed before the next serve. If either of the above cases occurs and the side at fault loses the rally, the mistake stands, and the players' positions are not corrected for the rest of the game.

Faults

A fault committed by the serving side (in-side) results in a side out, while a fault committed by the receiving side (out-side) results in a point for the server. A fault occurs in any of the following situations:

1. During the serve, the shuttlecock is contacted above the server's waist, or the racquet head is held above the hand.
2. During the serve, the shuttlecock does not fall within the boundaries of the diagonal service court.
3. During the serve, some part of both feet of the server and receiver do not remain in contact with the court, inside the boundary lines, until the shuttlecock leaves the racquet of the server. Feet on the boundary lines are considered out-of-bounds.

ORGANIZATION AND SKILL WORK

An effective way to add variety and skill work to classes is to create a series of stations. The stations can be arranged to use the space available in the gymnasium, and can focus on badminton skills, conditioning activities, or a combination of both (Figure 19.10).

Partner activities are helpful with accompanying rating scales or checklists like the one following.

Partner Activities: Low doubles serve
Equipment: One badminton racquet and five shuttlecocks per couple
Procedure: One person is the server, and the other is the helper with a trained eye. The server follows the steps below, and the helper checks off the skills as they are completed.

1. Standing behind the 6 ft 6 in. line from the wall, drop the bird and hit it underhand against the wall. Repeat at least 5 times. The trained eye must be looking for and giving feedback on the following criteria:
   a. Keep both feet on the ground until after the shuttlecock is contacted.
   b. Hold the shuttlecock at chest height.
   c. Contact the shuttlecock below the waist level.
   d. Keep the racquet head below the wrist at point of contact.
   e. Keep the wrist firm, cocked throughout the stroke.
   f. Shuttlecock is guided, not hit.
2. From the same position behind the line, direct 3 of 5 serves above the 5 ft 1 in. line on the wall and below the 18 in. line above it. Switch positions, and if you were serving, become the helper. Help your partner and remember that you are the trained eye who sees what your partner is doing. Partners repeat the first two steps.

Station 1:   Station 2:   Station 3:

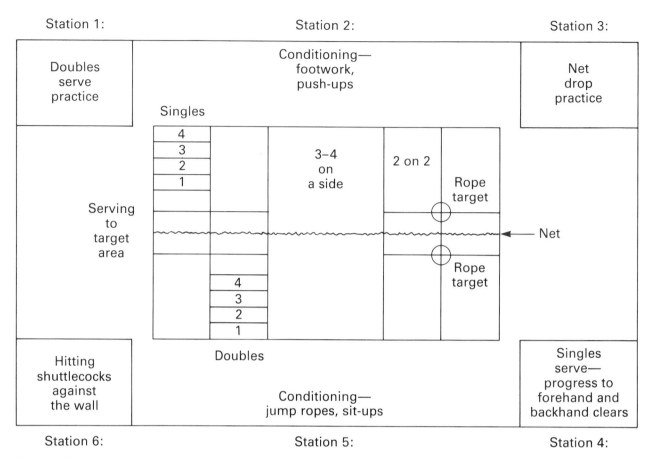

Figure 19.10. Station skill work

3. Move to the court and take about 5 practice serves. Keep the serve under the 18 in. line. Now do 5 serves and have your partner record your score. This score is to help you determine your accuracy. Switch positions again and repeat step 3.
4. Now try step 3 using your backhand.

Tournament play works well for badminton. Ladder, pyramid, or round robin tournaments can add a competitive flavor to the class.

The use of marking tape on floor and walls, jump ropes on the court, fleece balls, and task cards can give the teacher more stations for a circuit. This enables the student to progress at a personalized skill level. Mini- or lead-up games played on the courts allow for skill work, competition, and enjoyment. Regulation games and tournament play can gradually replace the lead-up games. Students should also be trained as scorekeepers and line or service judges.

LEAD-UP GAMES AND LEARNING ACTIVITIES

Doubles Drop

After the short serve and underhand drop are taught, a "doubles drop game" can be played between the net and the short service line.

Overhead Clear

After the long serve and the overhead clear are taught, an overhead clear "rally" could be attempted. Try to keep the shuttlecock in play at least 5 times in a row; then try 10 times in a row, 15 times, and so forth.

Designated Shots

After the underhand clear is taught, work on a "designated shots rally." Start with a short serve, return with an underhand drop, return with an underhand clear, and return with an overhead clear. Keep clearing with overhead and underhand clears.

Server Versus Receiver

After the "flick" serve and "push" return are taught, play a server versus receiver game. The receiver must try to return as many as possible of the server's 20 serves in a row, 10 from the right and 10 from the left. The server gets a point each time the receiver misses the return. The receiver gets a point if the server misses the serve. Reverse server and receiver roles.

Clear-Smash

After the smash is taught, play a long serve and overhead clear game. Start with a long serve, return with an overhead clear, and keep clearing until someone makes a short clear shot, then smash the short clear. Server is awarded one point if the smash is not returned, or loses one point if the smash is returned. Repeat the rally and try to make points by well-placed smashes.

Drive Rally

After the drive shot is taught, organize a drive rally with four players. Drive crosscourt and down the alley. If the drive shot is too high, smash return it.

Advanced Combination Drill

Start the rally with a long serve and return with an overhead drop, return with an underhand drop, return with an underhand clear to the opponent's backhand side, return with a backhand overhead clear, and return with an overhead clear unless the return shot is short. If the shot is short, use a smash.

Volleyball Badminton

Four players are on each team. Assigned positions rotate as in volleyball.

Three per Team

Alternate servers, and the "up" player plays the net shots.

Name the Shot

After five days of the badminton unit, challenge students to name the shots (Figure 19.11).

Word Scramble

Students who complete station skill work early can be asked to unscramble the puzzle in Figure 19.12.

SUGGESTED PERFORMANCE OBJECTIVES

Core Objectives

All directions given are for right-handed players.

Short or Low Serves

1. Standing 6 ft 6 in. from the wall, serve the shuttlecock 10 times in a row between the 5 ft and 6 ft marks on the wall (1 point).
2. Standing behind the short service line on the right side of the court, serve the shuttlecock crosscourt over the net 10 times and get 7 out of 10 in the court (1 point).
3. Repeat step 2 from the left side of the service court (1 point).
4. Standing behind the short service line, next to

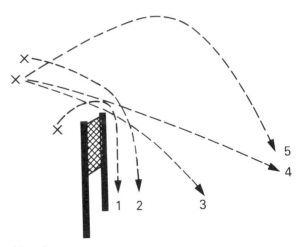

1. Net drop
2. Drop
3. Smash
4. Drive
5. Clear

Figure 19.11.   Name the shot

Figure 19.12. Word scramble

the center line in the right court, serve the shuttlecock crosscourt over the net, between the net and a rope 1 ft above it. Repeat 5 times in a row from the right, then 5 times from the left (1 point).

5. Standing behind the short service line, next to the center line in the right-hand court, serve 10 short serves in a row to the receiver's backhand side on the court (1 point).
6. Repeat step 5, standing in the left-hand court (1 point).

Long Serves

1. Standing to the right of and next to the center line, 12 ft from the net, serve 10 long serves in a row to the opposite court (1 point).
2. Repeat step 1 from the left service court (1 point).
3. Repeat step 1, but the serves must land in the backhand area marked on the court. Serve 5 long serves in a row to this area (1 point).

Underhand Clears: Forehand and Backhand

1. Standing between the net and the short service line, drop the shuttlecock and underhand clear on the forehand side, 10 clears in a row to the back 4 ft of the court marked for doubles (1 point).
2. Repeat step 1 on the backhand side (1 point).
3. Standing 6 ft behind the short service line, underhand clear on the forehand side 5 clears

in a row to the back 4 ft of the doubles court (1 point).
4. Repeat step 3 on the backhand side (1 point).

Underhand Drops

1. Standing just behind the short service line on the right court, underhand drop on the forehand side a tossed shuttlecock from your partner. Return 10 drops in a row from the forehand side (1 point).
2. Repeat step 1 on the backhand side (1 point).
3. Repeat steps 1 and 2 from the left court (2 points).
4. Standing anywhere just behind the short service line, a partner tosses the shuttlecock barely over the net, alternating between your forehand and backhand on the toss. Underhand drop 10 in a row back between the net and a rope stretched 1 ft above the net (1 point).

Overhead Clears: Forehand

1. Standing within 12 ft of the net, a partner underhand clears the shuttlecock. Return 10 shuttlecocks in a row with an overhead forehand clear into the doubles court, at least 10 ft from the net (1 point).
2. Repeat step 1, returning 10 in a row to the back 4 ft of the doubles court (1 point).

3. Repeat step 1, returning 10 in a row alternating from right court to left court, at least 10 ft from the net (1 point).

Attendance and Participation

1. Arrive on time for class, dressed and ready to participate (⅓ of a point per day, up to 6 points maximum).
2. Participation in 15 games: 13 doubles and 2 singles (1 point).

Optional Objectives

1. Standing next to the center line on the right court and just behind the short service line, "flick" serve the shuttle 5 times in a row to the back 3 ft of the doubles service court (1 point). Repeat on the left (1 point).
2. Standing in the right receiving court for doubles, "push" return 5 short serves in a row either to the server's backhand side or down the side alley next to server. Repeat on the left (1 point).
3. Standing 6 ft from the short service line next to the center line on the right court, return 5 long serves in a row to the backhand side of the server with an overhead clear (1 point).
4. Repeat step 3, standing in the left court (1 point).
5. A server sets up short, high shots 6–8 in. from the net. Standing 6 ft from the short service line, smash 5 in a row within 15 ft of the net (1 point).
6. Repeat step 5, smashing 5 in a row down the left side of the court (1 point).
7. Repeat step 5, smashing 5 in a row down the right side of the court (1 point).
8. Standing within 10 ft of the short service line, return 10 of your opponent's smashes back over the net as smashes (1 point).
9. Standing within the last 5 ft of the back court, overhead drop opponent's clears to you. Drop 5 shuttlecocks to the right court side between the net and the short service line (1 point).
10. Repeat step 9 on the left court between the net and the short service line (1 point).
11. Stand on the center line, 6 ft from the short service line. Partner sets up low, flat serves down the forehand alley. Hit 5 forehand drives in a row down that alley (1 point).
12. Repeat step 11, hitting 5 backhand drives down the backhand-side alley (1 point).
13. Standing within 12 ft of the net, from a high clear set up by a partner, backhand five over-head clears in a row to the back 6 ft of the doubles court (1 point).
14. Standing 15 ft or farther from the net, backhand 5 overhead clears in a row to the back 4 ft of the doubles court (1 point).

Skill Tests

Badminton courts can be marked in many different ways to provide students with a challenge in perfecting their skills (Figure 19.13). Using white shoe polish or masking tape, number portions of the target area in an ascending manner, from the easiest to the most difficult shots. Courts can be marked for deep serves, low serves, clears, drops, and drives. The teacher determines the number of attempts that each student is allowed.

Suggested Readings

Bloss, M. V. *Badminton*. 3rd ed. Dubuque, IA: Wm. C. Brown Group, 1975.

El Paso Public Schools. *Physical Education Curriculum Guide*. El Paso, TX, 1970.

National Association for Girls and Women in Sport. *Tennis-Badminton-Squash Guide*. Reston, VA: AAHPERD, 1982.

Pelton, B. C. *Badminton*. Englewood Cliffs, NJ: Prentice-Hall, 1971.

Poole, J. *Badminton*. 2nd ed. Pacific Palisades, CA: Goodyear Publishing Co., 1973.

Sysler, B. L., and Fox, E. R. *Lifetime Sports for the College Student*. 3rd ed. Dubuque, IA: Kendall/Hunt Publishing Co., 1978.

BASKETBALL

Basketball is a popular game played on schoolyards by many participants. It was invented in 1891 at Springfield College by Dr. Naismith, who used peach baskets and a soccer ball. The game offers reinforcement to participants when a basket is made, and is one of the few team sports requiring skills that can be practiced individually. The game demands great cardiorespiratory endurance and fine motor development.

Basketball instruction should focus on developing skills and competence so students leave school with the ability to participate in recreational games later in life. At the junior high school level, emphasis should be on lead-up games that allow all students to find success and enjoyment.

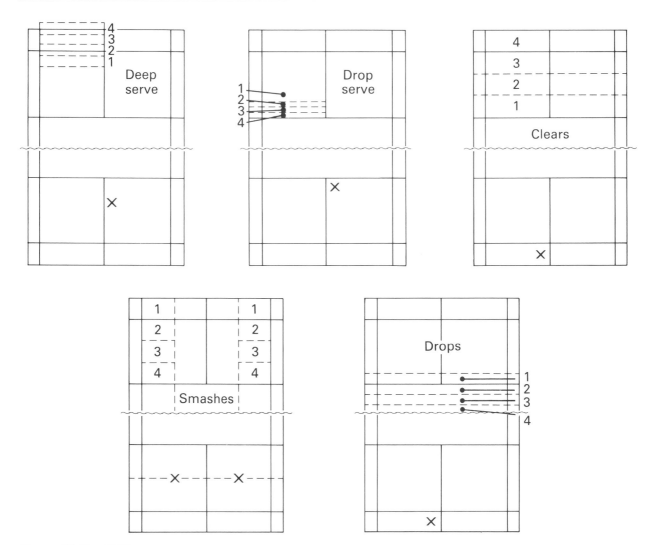

Figure 19.13. Skills tests

As students develop the skills necessary to play the game well, instruction during the high school years can concentrate on strategy and teamwork. Highly skilled and interested students should be offered additional opportunities to play through intramural programs, recreational leagues, or interscholastic competition.

SEQUENCE OF SKILLS

One of the attractive components of basketball is that little equipment is necessary for participation. Students should be required to wear a gym shoe made for the activity. Running shoes are a poor substitute for basketball shoes because they often leave black marks on the floor, do not offer adequate support, and wear out quickly.

The following skills are basic to the game of basketball. Students never learn these skills to per-

fection, so time should be offered for practice at regular intervals. For example, players can always make a better pass, develop more efficient dribbling skills, or shoot a higher percentage of baskets.

Passing

Regardless of the pass used, certain points should be emphasized. The ball should be handled with the fingertips. As the ball makes contact with the hands, the elbows should bend and the hands move toward the body in order to "give" with the ball and absorb the force. The passer should step forward in the direction of the receiver. The ball is released with a quick straightening of the elbows and a snap of the wrists. The arms and fingers are fully extended with the palms turned outward for the follow-through after the ball has been released. Passers should anticipate where their teammate is going to be when the ball reaches the receiver. Many of the passing drills should therefore focus on passing while moving.

Chest Pass. The chest pass is used frequently in basketball for passes up to 20 ft in distance. The ball is held at chest level with the fingers spread on both sides of the ball. One foot is ahead of the other in stride position. The elbows remain close to the body, and the ball is propelled by extending the arms, snapping the wrists, and stepping toward the target (Figure 19.14).

Bounce Pass. The bounce pass is used to transfer the ball to a closely guarded teammate. It is directed to a spot on the floor that is closer to the receiver than the passer. The ball should rebound to waist level of the receiver. Passing form is similar to the chest pass.

Flip Pass. This pass is used for a close-range exchange. The ball is flipped somewhat upward to a teammate. It is used often as a pass to a player cutting to the basket for a lay-up shot.

Two-Handed Overhead Pass. This pass is used against a shorter opponent, usually in back court. The passer is in a short stride position with the ball held overhead. The momentum of the pass comes from a forceful wrist and finger snap. The upper arms remain relatively in place.

Catching

For effective catching, it is important to keep the eyes on the ball, follow the ball into the hands, and concentrate on the catch before beginning the next task. The receiver should move toward the ball and reach for it with the fingers spread. When the pass is at waist level or above, the thumbs should be pointed in and the fingers up. When the ball is to be caught below waist level, the thumbs are out and the fingers down. The hands should "give" and move toward the body to absorb the force of the throw and thus make the ball more catchable.

Dribbling

The knees should be bent and the body somewhat crouched while dribbling. The forearm of the dribbling hand is parallel to the floor, and the ball should be pushed toward the roll, rather than slapped. The ball is controlled with the fingertips. Most of the force supplied to the ball should be from the wrist, so arm movement is minimized. Emphasis should be placed on controlling the ball (Figure 19.15).

Shooting

Certain points are common to all shooting. The body should be squared up with the basket whenever possible. The ball is held with the fingers spread, and the elbow of the shooting hand should always be directly behind the ball. The eyes are fixed on the rim, and the ball is shot with a slight backspin on it. The arm is extended on follow-through with the wrist flexed.

Lay-up Shots. For a right-handed lay-up, the player approaches the basket from the right side at an angle of about 45 degrees. The ball is released with the right hand and the weight on the left foot. As the body is elevated off the floor by the left foot, the ball is released 12–18 in. above the basket on

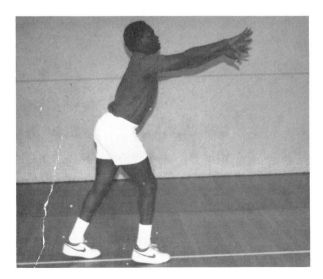

Figure 19.14. Throwing a chest pass

Figure 19.15. Dribbling under control

the backboard. For a left-handed shot, the sequence is the opposite. The shooter should always reach toward the spot on the backboard with the shooting hand, and students should practice shooting with each hand.

One-Hand Push Shots (Figure 19.16). This shot is used primarily for shooting free throws. Few people shoot a one-hand shot from a set position. The ball is held at shoulder level in the non-shooting hand. The shooting hand is behind the ball, the fingertips touching the ball, and the wrist is cocked. The legs are shoulder width apart and the knees slightly bent. To shoot, straighten the legs and push forward with the forearm and wrist. The wrist should be bent over on follow-through and the arm straight.

Jump Shots. The jump shot is the most popular shot in basketball because it is difficult to block. The hands are in the same position as described for the one-hand push shot. After the shooter jumps, the ball is placed just above and in front of the head. The elbow must be kept under the ball so the shooting hand moves in a straight line toward the basket. The wrist snaps on release. The shot should be performed using a jump in an upward plane. Leaning forward, sideways, or backward will make the shot much less consistent. The jump shot is sometimes difficult for junior high school students. They often learn the wrong motor pattern of throwing the ball instead of shooting it. If this is the case, use a smaller ball, a lower basket, or both to develop the correct pattern.

Figure 19.16. One hand set shot

IDEAS FOR EFFECTIVE INSTRUCTION

Drills used in basketball should simulate game conditions as closely as possible. There are few situations in basketball in which players are standing still. Passing drills should therefore include player movement, shooting drills should require movement and pressure, and drills for dribbling under control should include looking away from the ball.

Baskets can be lowered to 8.5 to 9 ft to increase the amount of success students experience. This will also help develop better shooting patterns in the weaker, smaller players. Note that almost all students will select the lower basket when they have a choice of a basket at regulation height and another, lowered basket. Most people are motivated by being able to dunk the shot and thus shoot a higher percentage.

The program should concentrate on skill development and include many drills. Basketball offers endless drill possibilities, and using many drills gives variety and breadth to the instructional program. The drills should offer each student as much practice as possible in a stipulated amount of time. Lining up a squad of eight players to take turns makes little sense. Use as many balls as possible. In some cases, students may be willing to bring one from home for class use. More baskets and balls mean that more students will have an opportunity to practice and learn desired skills.

There are many basketball drills that can be used to enhance passing, dribbling, and shooting, but the lead-up games that follow in the next section encourage skill practice while introducing competition and game play. When possible, therefore, it is desirable to isolate skills and to practice them in lead-up games to maintain a high level of student motivation.

LEAD-UP GAMES AND LEARNING ACTIVITIES

Keepaway

The essence of the game is to make as many consecutive passes as possible without losing control to the opposite team. Teams may consist of 5 to 10 players. It is necessary to use pinnies so players can identify their teammates. The game is started with a jump ball, and the goal is to maintain control. Each defensive player must stay with a designated opponent, rather than the defensive team swarming in a zone defense. As soon as possession is lost, counting of passes is started by that team. The team that makes the most consecutive passes within a designated time is the winner.

Five Passes

This game is similar to keepaway, but the object is to make five consecutive passes. As soon as these have been made, the ball is turned over to the other team. Students are not allowed to travel with the ball. Two or three dribbles may be allowed between passes. Players may only hold the ball for 3 sec.

Dribble Tag

Divide the playing area into two equal parts. All players begin dribbling in one half of the area. The object of this game is to maintain a continuous dribble while avoiding being tagged by another player. If tagged or if control of the ball is lost, the player must move to the other half of the playing area and practice dribbling without the pressure of competition.

Dribble Keepaway

The area is divided into two equal parts. All players start in one half of the area and begin dribbling. The goal is to maintain control of the dribble while trying to disrupt the dribble of an opponent. If control of the ball is lost, the player moves to the other side of the area and practices.

Around the World

Shooting spots are marked on the floor with tape (Figure 19.17). Players are in groups of three. A player begins at the first spot and continues until a shot misses. The player can then wait for another turn or take a second "risk" shot. If the risk shot is made, the player continues "around the world." If the shot is missed, the player must start over on the next turn. The winner is the player who goes around the world first. A variation is to count the number of shots that players take to move around the world. The person who makes the circuit with the fewest shots is the winner.

Twenty-One

Players are in groups of three or four. Each player receives a long shot (distance must be designated) and a follow-up shot. The long shot, if made, counts two points, and the follow-up shot one point. The

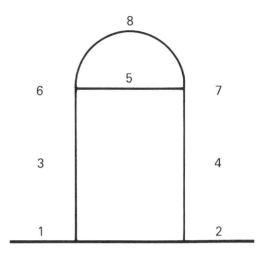

Figure 19.17.   Around the world

follow-up shot must be taken from the spot where the ball was recovered. The first player to score twenty-one points is the winner. A variation is to play team twenty-one in which the first team of players to score twenty-one is declared the winner.

Horse

Players work in groups of two to four and shoot in a predetermined order. The first player shoots from any place on the court. If the shot is made, the next player must make the same type of shot from the same position. If the shot is missed by the next player, that player receives an "H", and the following player can shoot any shot desired. No penalty is assigned for a missed shot unless the previous player has made a shot. A player is disqualified if the letters spelling HORSE are accumulated. The winner is the last remaining player.

Sideline Basketball

The class is divided into two teams, each lined up along one side of the court, facing the other. The game is played by three or four active players from each team. The remainder of the players standing on the sideline can catch and pass the ball to the active players, but they may not shoot or enter the playing floor. They must keep one foot completely out of bounds at all times.

Active players play regular basketball with one variation, they may pass and receive the ball from sideline players. The game starts with the active players occupying their own half of the court. The ball is taken out-of-bounds under its own basket by the team that was scored upon. Play continues until one team scores or until a period of time (2 or 3 min) elapses. The active players then take places on the left side of their line, and three new active players come out from the right. All other players move down three places in the line.

No official out-of-bounds on the sides is called. The players on that side of the floor simply recover the ball and put it into play without delay by a pass to an active player. Out-of-bounds on the ends is the same as in regular basketball. If one of the sideline players enters the court and touches the ball, it is a violation, and the ball is awarded out-of-bounds on the other side to a sideline player. Free throws are awarded when a player is fouled. Sideline players may pass to each other and should be well spaced along the side.

Half Court Basketball

Teams of two to four work best for this variation. The game is similar to regulation basketball with the following exceptions: When a defensive player recovers the ball, either from a rebound or an interception, the ball must be taken back to midcourt before offensive play can begin. After a basket is made, the ball must again be taken to midcourt. For out-of-bounds and ball-handling violations, the ball is awarded to the opponents out-of-bounds at a spot near the place where the violation occurred. The ball, in this case, does not have to be taken to midcourt. If a foul occurs, the ball is given to the offended team, or regulation foul shooting can be done.

Three on Three

There are many lead-up games in which the number of players on a team varies. The advantage of playing half court basketball with only two or three players on a team is that each player gets to handle the ball more. Regulation rules are followed.

Three on three can be played with four or five teams. An offensive team of three stands forward of the midcourt line while another team is on defense. The other teams wait behind midcourt for their turn. A scrimmage is over when one team scores. The defensive team then goes on offense, and a new team comes in to play defense. The old offensive team goes to the rear of the line of waiting players. The game can be varied so that the winning team stays on after a basket is scored. Caution must be used with the winner-stay-on approach as it sometimes means that the better players get much

more practice than the less skilled performers. Make the teams as equal as possible so all have a chance to win.

SUGGESTED PERFORMANCE OBJECTIVES

The following are examples of performance objectives that might be used in a beginning basketball class. The standards may have to be adjusted, depending on the skill level and age of the students.

Core Requirements

Dribbling Tasks

1. In a stationary position, execute a right-hand dribble 10 consecutive times (1 point).
2. Same as no. 1 except use the left hand (1 point).
3. Using a reduced speed, dribble the ball with the right hand from the baseline to the midcourt line without losing control (1 point).
4. Using a reduced speed, dribble the ball with the left hand from the midcourt line to the baseline without losing the dribble (1 point).

Passing Tasks

5. Standing 10 ft away from the target on the wall, throw 10 consecutive two-hand chest passes (1 point).
6. Standing 10 ft away from a partner, execute 8 of 10 consecutive two-hand passes (1 point).
7. Standing 10 ft away from the target, throw 10 consecutive two-hand bounce passes (1 point).
8. Standing 10 ft away from a partner, execute 8 of 10 consecutive bounce passes (1 point).
9. Standing 10 ft away from the target, throw 10 consecutive two-hand overhead passes (1 point).
10. Standing 10 ft away from a partner, execute 8 of 10 consecutive two-hand overhead passes.

Shooting Tasks

11. Starting from the right side about 20 ft from the basket, dribble the ball toward the basket and make 4 of 6 lay-ups using the backboard (1 point).
12. Same as no. 11, but start from the left side (1 point).
13. Standing 6 ft from the basket (right side), make 4 of 6 bank shots (1 point).
14. Same as no. 13, but use the left side (1 point).
15. Standing at the free-throw line, make 5 of 10 consecutive set shots (1 point).

16. Standing 10 ft from the basket, make 5 of 10 jump shots (1 point).

Rebounding Tasks

17. Standing with the feet shoulder width apart and with both hands at shoulder level, jump up and touch the target on the wall 3 consecutive times using both hands (1 point).
18. Standing 2–3 ft away from the basket, toss the ball off the right side of the backboard and rebound with both hands 5 consecutive times (1 point).
19. Same as no. 18, but use the left side (1 point).
20. Standing 2–3 ft from the basket, toss the ball off the right side of the backboard, rebound using both hands, and pivot right using the overhead pass or chest pass to a partner. Repeat 5 consecutive times (1 point).
21. Same as no. 20, but use the left side and pivot left (1 point).

Optional Requirements

1. Officiate at least one regulation game during class time, using correct calls and signals (1 point).

2. Write a one-page report on the game of basketball (3 points).
3. Make a list of 15 basketball terms and define them (3 points).
4. Write a one-page report on Coach Wooden's book, *They Call Me Coach* (3 points).
5. Perform a figure-eight ball-handling technique by weaving the ball around one leg and then around the other leg—forming a figure eight—successfully for 10 sec (2 points).
6. Make 8 of 10 bank shots from anywhere outside the foul lane (2 points).
7 Make 9 of 10 free throws (2 points).

Grading Structure

A = 35 points
B = 28 points
C = 20 points

RAINY DAY ACTIVITIES

The test in Figure 19.18 might be a useful rainy day activity. It can give rise to discussions of rules and rule interpretations.

Figure 19.18.   Basketball rules quiz

QUIZ 1. RULES AND TERMINOLOGY

True or False. Place a **T** or **F** to the left of the statement, depending on whether the statement is true or false.

_____   1. The key is the area that separates the midcourt from the back court.

_____   2. The outside roll is a maneuver used by a defensive player who is guarding the player with the ball.

_____   3. When performing the jump shot correctly, the shooting elbow should be away from the body in order to give greater accuracy to the shot.

_____   4. The 3-sec line is contained within the key.

_____   5. It is permissible to drag the pivot foot a short distance, as long as that foot maintains contact with the floor.

_____   6. A feint is a deceptive motion in one direction when a player desires to move in another direction.

_____   7. A dribbler must keep the eyes locked on the ball while dribbling in order to maintain control.

_____   8. It is a violation for a defensive player to remain in the 3-sec lane for longer than 3 sec.

_____   9. In most instances, the cardinal rule for a defensive player is to stay between the offensive player and the basket.

---

continued

Figure 19.18 / *continued*

_____ 10. A player should jump off the right foot when shooting a right-handed lay-up.

Multiple Choice. Circle the correct answer.

11. The main idea in the game of basketball is to:
   a. Keep the ball as long as possible
   b. Score more points than the other team
   c. Receive fewer team violations

12. A good way to learn the game of basketball is by learning the easier skills first, then moving on to learn more difficult skills, and finally using all of the skills in a game situation. This way of learning is called:
   a. Progression
   b. Regression
   c. Retrogression

13. A basketball player can become better by:
   a. Practicing the correct way to dribble, shoot, and pass
   b. Reading books written by experts and viewing films
   c. Both a and b

14. Basketball is played best when all members of the team cooperate with and help one another. This cooperation and helping is sometimes called:
   a. Intramurals
   b. Teamwork
   c. Progression

15. Before playing in a regular basketball game, a player should:
   a. Know the exact size of the playing area
   b. Learn the basic skills of the game
   c. Be able to jump up and touch the rim

16. The penalty for most violations is loss of the ball or the other team's receiving the ball out-of-bounds near the place of the violation. Some violations that incur loss of the ball as a penalty are:
   a. Blocking, tripping, pushing, or charging
   b. Screening, fast breaking, rebounding, or weaving
   c. Traveling, double dribble, or kicking the ball

17. In most cases, the penalty for a personal foul is awarding the fouled player either one or two free throws. Personal fouls include:
   a. Striking the ball with the fist, or holding the ball for more than 5 sec when closely guarded
   b. Holding, tripping, pushing, or charging
   c. Both a and b

18. Points are scored at a rate of:
   a. 1 point for field goal, 2 points for free throw
   b. 2 points for field goal, 1 point for free throw
   c. 2 points for field goal, 2 points for free throw

19. A jump ball is called when:
   a. Two players have one or both hands firmly on the ball and neither can gain possession without undue roughness
   b. A player holds the ball for more than 5 sec when closely guarded
   c. Both a and b occur

20. Technical fouls include:
    a. Tripping, pushing, hacking, or charging
    b. Traveling, double dribble, goal tending, or failure to observe the 3-sec rule
    c. Too many time outs, delay of game, or unsportsmanlike conduct

Suggested Readings

AAHPERD. *Basketball Skills Test Manual for Girls.* Reston, VA: AAHPERD, 1966.

AAHPERD. *Basketball Skills Test Manual for Boys.* Reston, VA: AAHPERD, 1966.

Barnes, M. *Women's Basketball.* Boston: Allyn and Bacon, Inc., 1973.

Bee, C. *Drills and Fundamentals.* San Diego: A. S. Barnes & Co., Inc., 1942.

Ebert, F., and Cheatum, B. *Basketball.* Philadelphia: W. B. Saunders Co., 1977.

Lindeburg, F. A. *How to Play and Teach Basketball.* 2nd ed. New York: Association Press, 1967.

Moore, B., and White, J. *Basketball: Theory and Practice.* Dubuque, IA: Wm. C. Brown Group, 1980.

Richards, J. *Treasury of Basketball Drills From Top Coaches.* West Nyack, NY: Parker Publishing Co., 1971.

Wooden, J. *Practical Modern Basketball.* New York: Ronald Press Co., 1966.

BOWLING

The game today is a form of kingpins, the first bowling game to use finger holes in the ball. The sport has changed from a simple game played outdoors to a complex mechanized game played in large modern facilities.

Bowling has become one of our most widely enjoyed recreational activities. Any family member may participate, as the game is suitable for all ages and both sexes. Bowling can be played in any season, and facilities are usually available at most times of the day. Leagues are popular with all ages, and many businesses sponsor employee leagues. Schools have intramural leagues, and many bowling establishments organize leagues for children. These leagues are usually sanctioned by the proper national organization.

The play in bowling consists of rolling balls down a wooden alley with the object of knocking over ten wooden pins positioned at the far end of the alley. The bowler stands any distance behind the foul line and takes three, four, or five steps before releasing the ball down the alley. If the player touches the alley beyond the foul line, a foul is called, and the ball counts as one ball bowled. No score is made on a foul, and the pins knocked down are immediately replaced. In bowling and duckpins, the pins knocked down after the first ball rolled are cleared away before the next ball is rolled. In candlepins, knocked down pins are not cleared away. Each bowler has ten frames in which to knock down as many pins as possible. If a bowler knocks down all of the pins in ten frames of bowling, a perfect score of 300 is attained.

SEQUENCE OF SKILLS

Picking Up the Ball

If in an alley area, face the direction of the returning balls. Place the hands on opposite sides of the ball and lift the ball to a comfortable position in front of the body before placing the fingers and thumb in the holes. Avoid placing the thumb and fingers in the holes to pick up the ball, as this places strain on the bowling hand.

Gripping the Ball

Holding the ball in the left hand (if right-handed), place the two middle fingers in the holes first and then slip the thumb in the thumbhole. Do not squeeze the ball with the fingertips, but maintain contact by slightly pressing the palm side of the fingers and thumb toward the palm area of the ball. The little finger and index finger are relaxed and flat on the ball.

Stance

The stance is the stationary position that the bowler holds before approaching the foul line. The development of a stance, which varies among bowlers, is essential for consistency in bowling. To locate the starting position, stand with the back to the foul line, walk four and one-half steps, stop, turn, and face the pins. The number of steps will vary with the three-, four-, or five-step approach. Standing erect, place the feet parallel to each other, or the left foot may be slightly in front of the right foot. The feet should be about 1.5 in. apart. The weight is on the left foot, and the knees are slightly bent. The head is up, and the shoulders are level.

The ball is held at waist level and slightly to the right. The arm is straight from the shoulder to the wrist. The ball will be pushed out during the first step and will swing down directly below the shoulder. The wrist is kept straight and stiff during the pendulum swing. The elbow moves back alongside the body and should not be braced on the hip. The ball is supported by the nonbowling hand. The shoulders, hips, and feet are square with the pins when the stance is established.

After learning the basic stance, the bowler can develop a personal style. Some leading bowlers hold the ball approximately level with the chin and a few inches from the body. Proficient bowlers usually hold the ball at waist level and a few inches away from the body. The upper torso leans slightly forward. Taller bowlers sometimes use a half crouch and a shorter backswing.

Aiming

The method of aim should be decided after the footwork, timing, and method of rolling the ball have been established. The bowler should then experiment to find the preferable method of aim. Spot bowling is recommended.

1. Pin bowling—The bowler looks at the pins and draws an imaginary line between the point of delivery and the point on the pins at which the ball will be aimed. This line will be the route of the ball. The usual point to hit is the 1–3 pocket.
2. Spot bowling—The bowler draws an imaginary line from the point of delivery to some spot down the lane, usually at the division boards where the maple meets pine. Most lanes have triangular markings for spot bowlers.

Approach and Delivery

One-Step Delivery. One-step delivery should be learned before the three-, four-, or five-step delivery. The stance for the one-step delivery differs from the general stance discussed previously. The foot opposite the bowling arm is behind. Extend the bowling hand, and after extension, drop the hand slowly to the side and simultaneously lean forward, bending the knees. Keep the arm relaxed and the wrist straight. Swing the arm forward to eye level, back to waist level, and forward again to eye level. The stance for the one-step delivery is assumed. The hands are at waist height as if gripping the ball. Push the arms forward, release the left hand, and complete the pendulum swing.

Repeat the push-away and the pendulum swing, but as the arm swings forward (at the completion of the swing), slide ahead on the foot opposite the bowling arm. Keep the shoulders straight and the body facing straight ahead. Practice the simultaneous movement of arm and foot. No ball is necessary when first learning the approach and delivery. When the timing is learned, then add the ball.

Four-Step Delivery. This is the most widely used delivery method. The stance is with the opposite foot forward, as presented above. Starting with the right foot, take four brisk walking strides forward. Repeat the four-step walk, making the fourth step a slide. At the completion of the slide, the full body weight should be on the sliding foot, knee bent, and shoulders parallel to the foul line. The forward foot should be pointed toward the pins.

To coordinate the delivery, the bowler should assume the stance, start the four-step walk, and push the ball out, down, back, and forward so that the arm movements coordinate with the steps (one, two, three, slide). As the foot slides, the ball comes forward and is released. At the release, the thumb is out, and the fingers and wrist are turning and lifting the ball. The right leg swings forward for balance, and the right arm, which was straight throughout the backswing, bends at the elbow for the follow-through. The body then straightens to get more lift on the ball.

Different types of balls can be thrown, depending on how the ball is released.

1. Straight ball—The wrist and forearm are kept straight throughout the entire delivery. The thumb is on top of the ball, at 12 o'clock position, and the index finger is at 2 o'clock.
2. Hook ball—The ball is held throughout the approach, delivery, and release with the thumb at 10 o'clock and the index finger at 12 o'clock. If the ball hooks too much, move the thumb toward the 12 o'clock position.

IDEAS FOR EFFECTIVE INSTRUCTION

Gymnasium Bowling Sets

Gymnasium bowling sets are available through many equipment dealers. They usually contain ten plastic pins, a triangular sheet for pin setup, score sheets, and one hard plastic ball. Sizes of the finger holes will vary, and so may the weight of the ball. The cost is approximately $60.00 per set.

Score Sheets

Score sheets can be drawn and duplicated. Sheets are included in gym sets, or an instructor can check with a local establishment about purchasing or a possible donation.

General Rules and Scoring

1. A game consists of ten frames. Each bowler is allowed two deliveries in each frame, with the exception of the tenth frame in which three are allowed if a spare or strike is scored.
2. The score is an accumulated total of pins knocked down plus bonus points for spares and strikes.
3. If all ten pins are knocked down on the first ball rolled, it is a strike. The scorer counts ten plus the total of the next two balls rolled.
4. If all pins are knocked down with two balls rolled, it is a spare. The scorer counts ten plus the number of pins knocked down on the next ball rolled.
5. If no pins are knocked down when a ball is rolled, the bowler is charged with an error. This includes gutter balls.
6. If pins left after the first ball constitute a split, a circle is made on the scoresheet around the number of pins knocked down.
7. A foul results if the bowler steps across the foul line.
8. Pin setup and numbering is shown in Figure 19.19.

Symbols for Scoring

Figure 19.20 is a sample score sheet showing all of the standard scoring symbols.

Etiquette

1. Take your turn promptly.
2. The bowler to the right has the right-of-way. Wait

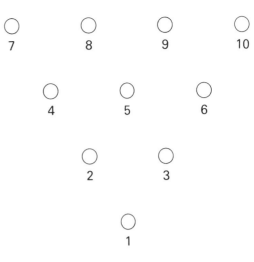

Figure 19.19. Pin setup and numbering

until the bowler on the right is finished before assuming stance.
3. Stay on your approach.
4. Step back off the approach after delivery.
5. Use your ball only, and use the same ball throughout.
6. Do not talk to a player who is on the approach.
7. Respect all equipment and the establishment.
8. Competition is encouraged, but be gracious in any case.
9. Return all equipment to its proper place.

ORGANIZATION AND SKILL WORK

Teach skills in sequence. Once the basic grip and stance have been taught (group situation), stations can be used for skill practice. Contracts with study guides can inform and motivate students.

Depending on the unit structure, students can work at stations on skills to be checked off, or they may be involved in lead-up games, engaged in minitournaments (using gym sets), or practicing skills at a bowling facility. Since bowling skills are perfected through constant practice, the unit should be designed for maximum activity.

If space is available, mock lanes can be made (Figure 19.21). Using mock lanes can enhance the number of students involved in activity while using a smaller space. Students are able to practice the approach, release, and spotting without pins. They can work in pairs, taking turns practicing and rolling the ball back.

Team games with the mock lanes and gymnasium bowling sets can be enjoyable. Hand out score sheets and have students record their scores. Scorers sign their name, and score sheets are checked

Scoring Symbols

Miss	—	Error, gutter ball
Foul	F	Touching or going beyond foul line
Split	O	Pins left after first roll: Headpin must be down and a ball's width between remaining pins.
Spare	/	Knocking down all pins in two rolls
Strike	X	Knocking down all pins in one roll
Double	X X	Two strikes in a row
Turkey	X X X	Three strikes in a row

Sample Scoring

Figure 19.20. Symbols and sample scoring

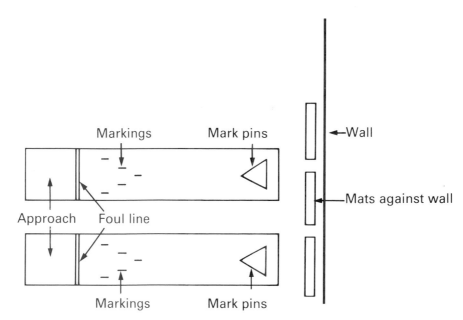

Figure 19.21. Mock lanes for skill work

for correct scoring procedure. Games with mock lanes and gymnasium sets can be used as a lead-up to bowling at a nearby facility.

LEAD-UP GAMES AND LEARNING ACTIVITIES

Red Pin

Use regulation alleys or lanes set up on the gym floor. One pin is painted red (tape may be substituted). The bowler rolls one ball in each frame. The bowler scores only if the red pin is upset. The pinsetter makes no attempt to specifically place the red pin. It will occur in random placement. Because only one ball is rolled, no spares are scored. Strikes are possible and should be scored as in regulation bowling. This activity can be used for team or individual competition.

Scotch Bowling

This activity can be played on regulation lanes or in a gym with marked lanes. Students choose a partner and decide who will roll the first ball. Partners then alternate throughout the game, which is scored like regulation bowling.

Shuffle-Bowl

The game is played on a shuffleboard court using shuffleboard cues, disc, and bowling pins or Indian clubs. The discs are slid at the pins. Play and scoring are carried out as in regulation bowling.

Skittles

Use an open area, wooden discs, and ten small pins or Indian clubs. Slide or pitch the discs at the pins from a specified distance. Use regulation scoring.

Three Pins

Regulation equipment or the gymnasium with marked lanes can be used for play. The bowler attempts to knock down the 1–2–3 combination by hitting the 1–3 pocket (1–2, if left-handed). One ball is allowed for each turn. Players start with 20 points. Three pins down subtracts 3 points, two down subtracts 2 points, and one pin down subtracts 1 point. The first player to reach zero points is the winner.

Soccer Bowling

Any open area, indoors or outdoors, is suitable for play. Soccer balls and wooden pins are used, and the game is scored like regulation bowling.

Basket Bowling

Play in an alley marked on the gym floor. Allow a 15-ft approach. Use two indoor softballs and a metal wastebasket propped up on its side with two bricks or similar objects facing the foul line. Five to ten players and one retriever make up a team. Each player attempts to roll two balls into the wastebasket. Rotate and trade places with the retriever. One point is scored for each basket made, and the high scorer wins. If teams play against one another, use a time limit. Each player is allowed five turns. If the bowler steps over the foul line, one point is subtracted. If the ball is bounced on the alley, one point is subtracted. An official scorekeeper and judge are necessary.

Scoring Work Sheets

Figure 19.22 shows a scoring work sheet, including problems.

Crossword Puzzle

A bowling crossword (Figure 19.23) makes a good rainy day activity or an alternative activity for students not at a station.

CONTRACTS, TESTS, AND RATING FORM

Contract

1. Bowl six games at any lane. Keep score and turn in the score sheet to the instructor. On a separate sheet, state the two basic rules for scoring. List and explain the symbols used in scoring (1–10 points).

2. Research and write a paper on the history of bowling using at least four sources. The paper should be typed double-spaced and include a bibliography (1–10 points).

3. Learn the correct way to pick up and hold the ball. Be able to demonstrate the hand positions, footwork, and release. Be able also to demonstrate the hand position that creates a hook, a straight ball, and a backup ball. Performance is evaluated on the basis of an oral explanation to the instructor (1–15 points).

Figure 19.22. Scoring work sheet

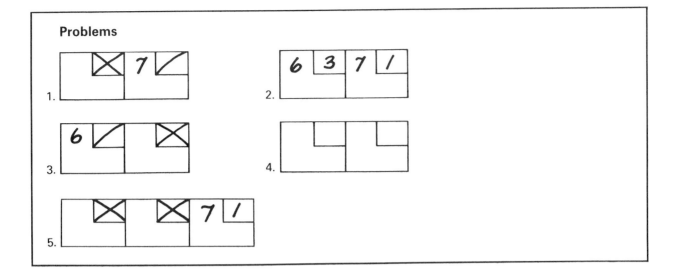

4. Watch at least one tournament, either live or on television, for an hour, or observe an hour of league bowling. Report in writing about how this type of bowling differs from open bowling (1–10 points).

5. Obtain a rule book from the Women's International Bowling Congress (WIBC) and find out what special prizes are awarded in sanctioned leagues. Illustrate and explain the patches and award procedures (1–5 points).

6. Visit a lane and ask the operator for an inspection of an automatic pinsetter in operation. Find out how to operate the ball clearer, how to turn on the teleprompter, and how to reset the pins. Discover where the trouble bell and the foul line indicator are located and how the foul line operates. When ready, take a short quiz from the instructor on this information (1–20 points).

7. Make a poster diagraming a lane. Enlarge and make offset drawings of the approach area and the pin-fall area. Write a short paper telling how one might use this information when bowling (1–10 points).

8. Compile a list of 15 bowling terms and a definition of each (1–15 points).

9. Take a written examination on bowling covering etiquette, scoring, handicaps, averages, techniques, terminology, history, and rules (1–25 points).

10. Demonstrate the proper stance, the four-step delivery, and the position of the hands on each step (1–5 points).

11. Write a paper describing the following: moonlight bowling, headpin tournament, 3–6–9 tournament (1–15 points).

12. Practice spare bowling of a single pin until 4 out of 10 shots are made. (Have the proprietor take all but one pin out of the rack, and shoot at any set that the automatic pin spotter provides.) When ready, test yourself by trying 10 consecutive shots. Record the score as either a miss or a spare. Use any score sheet provided by the alley, and turn it in for credit (1–25 points).

Grades will be determined as follows: 140–155 points = A, 125–139 points = B, 110–124 points = C, 90–109 = D. No one can fail a contract, because work that is not done properly will be returned. Work must be redone until it is performed correctly.

Test

Figure 19.24 is a bowling quiz that could be administered at the conclusion of the unit.

Rating Form

A rating form (Figure 19.25) is useful for partner work and when facilities are limited. The form enables students who are not participating actively to be cognitively involved. The instructor should spend some time helping students learn to use the form correctly.

Suggested Readings

American Bowling Congress, Film Library, Public Relations Department, 1572 E. Capital Drive, Milwaukee, WI 53211.

Doornink, R. H., ed. *Physical Education Activity Units of Instruction.* Department of Physical Education for Men, Washington State University, 1972.

El Paso Public Schools. *Physical Education Curriculum Guide.* El Paso, TX, 1970.

National Association for Girls and Women in Sport. *Bowling-Golf.* Reston, VA: AAHPERD, 1979–1981.

Sysler, B. L., and Fox, E. R. *Lifetime Sports for the College Student.* 3rd ed. Dubuque, IA: Kendall/Hunt Publishing Co., 1978.

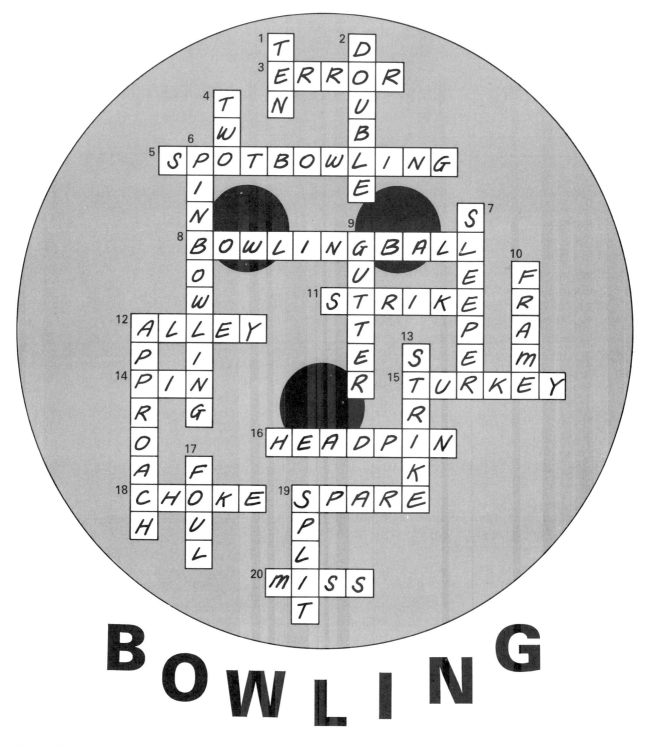

Figure 19.23.   Crossword puzzle

Figure 19.23 /*continued*

Across

3. A missed spare
5. Bowling using a spot or arrow on the lane
8. Object used to knock down pins
11. Knocking down all pins with first ball of frame
12. The lane
14. Object bowling ball is used to knock down
15. Three strikes in a row made by one bowler in a single game
16. The front pin or no. 1 pin
18. To tighten up under pressure
19. Knocking down all the pins with two balls of a single frame
20. The ball passes and does not hit or knock down any of the pins

Down

1. Number of pins used
2. Two strikes in a row
4. Number of times you could roll the ball in a frame
6. Bowling using pins as an aim
7. A hidden pin, a pin directly behind another pin
9. The troughs on either side of the lane
10. A score box where the points are tallied
12. Act of moving to the foul line to deliver the ball
13. A bonus of the next two balls rolled is awarded for one of these
17. Touching beyond the foul line
19. Two or more pins left standing after the first roll, neither of which is the head pin or side by side

Helpful Hints

Numbers 5 and 8 across and 6 down are two words

Match the definitions to the terms.

	Terms		Definition
_____	1. Four parts of a delivery	A.	Wrist straight and fairly firm
_____	2. Three-, four-, or five-step	B.	Adjustment
_____	3. Knocking down all pins with two balls	C.	Strike
_____	4. Grip beginning bowlers should use	D.	Foul line
_____	5. Proper wrist position	E.	Hook
_____	6. Knocking down all pins with the first ball	F.	Conventional
_____	7. Ball supported with first joint of the bowling fingers	G.	Spare
_____	8. Line separating the approach and lane	H.	Push-away, pendulum backswing, release, and follow-through
_____	9. Release ball over target, comes up light in pocket, move right with feet	I.	Approach
_____	10. Release ball with fingers at 4 or 5 o'clock	J.	Fingertip

Figure 19.24.   Bowling quiz

Name _____

Bowler													

APPROACH

Push away on first step

Push-away: out and down—elbow straight

Backswing: straight—in line with boards

Backswing: to shoulder level

Steps: smooth, gliding, even rhythm

Steps: increase in length and speed

Slide on left foot

RELEASE

Shoulders: parallel to foul line

Shoulders: level

Upper body: inclined forward

Left foot: in line with boards

Weight balanced on left foot

Thumb in 12 o'clock position

Ball first strikes alley 1.5 ft in front of left foot

Follow-through: straight and to shoulder height

AIM

Approach: straight, in line with boards

Release: proper dot or dots at foul line

Crosses proper dart

Where does ball strike pins?   (e.g., 1–3, 1, 3, 1–2)

Place a (√) in proper square if the item is performed correctly.
Place a (−) if it is not correct.

Figure 19.25.   Bowling rating form

FIELD HOCKEY

Field hockey is a popular team sport that has been played predominately by girls in the United States. Many clubs across the country are affiliated with the United States Field Hockey Association, and offer playing experiences for participants age 18 years and older. In other countries, the game is also played by men and is a popular Olympic sport. Many high schools and colleges offer field hockey competition for girls and women.

The regulation game is played with 11 players on each team. The object of the game is to move a ball with a stick into the opponent's goal, which is 4 ft wide and 7 ft high. The game is started with a bully, or face-off, at midfield by the center forward of each team. Besides the goalkeeper, a team usually has 5 forwards, 3 halfbacks, and 2 fullbacks. The field is 60 yd by 100 yd with a 16-yd striking circle (Figure 19.26).

Hockey equipment includes the ball, sticks, shin guards, and the goalkeeper's full-length leg pads and kickers for the shoes. The ball is composed of cork and twine and is covered in leather. Sticks vary in length from 30 to 37 in. Junior high students use sticks that are 30–34 in. long, and high school students use sticks that are 35–37 in. in length. All regulation sticks have a flat surface on one side and a rounded surface on the other. Only the flat side can be used for legal hits.

The game can be modified in several ways for secondary physical education units. The number of players and the field size can be reduced. Goals can be improvised by using boundary cones, high jump standards, or even soccer goals. A whiffle ball or a rubber or plastic ball can be used, and plastic sticks that are flat on both sides are available. A flat plastic puck is recommended for play on the gymnasium floor. Goalies should wear a face mask, chest protector, and shin guards from softball or lacrosse equipment. The game can be enjoyable for both boys and girls in a coeducational unit. Field hockey can be played indoors, outdoors, or on a cement surface.

SEQUENCE OF SKILLS

Grip

In the basic grip (Figure 19.27), the left hand is placed on the top of the stick with a "shaking hands"-type grip. The right hand is placed 6–8 in. below the left hand. The palms of the hands will face each other in most situations. The right hand

Figure 19.26. Field markings and dimensions

Figure 19.27. Hand position on the stick

can slide up the stick for a drive shot and for a reverse stick. The lower position is used for dribbling and for most passes.

Dribbling

Dribbling is propelling the ball downfield in a controlled manner. It can be done straight down the field or zigzagging to the left and right. In straight dribbling (Figure 19.28), the arms are kept in front of the body. The flat side of the stick faces forward. Short, controlled taps on the ball are used. The ball should remain in front of the body. The zigzag dribble moves the ball left and right by using a forehand tap to the left and a reverse stick tap to the right. In the reverse stick (Figure 19.29), the stick is turned over, with the toe of the stick pointing down. This type of dribble requires a lot of practice and stick control. The taps to the left and right should be short and controlled.

Passing and Shooting

The drive shot (Figure 19.30) is the most forceful pass for longer distances and goal shots. The hands are together, and the stick comes back and forward in a manner similar to a shortened golf swing. The stick cannot be lifted higher than the shoulder in either the backswing or follow-through. Drive shots can be straight, to the left, or to the right.

Figure 19.29. Reverse stick for zigzag dribble

Figure 19.30. Drive shot

The push pass (Figure 19.31) is used for shorter, more accurate passes. The shot is usually executed quickly off the dribble. There is no backswing. The right hand is lower on the stick, and the ball is pushed or swept along the ground.

The scoop is a pass similar to the push pass, but the object is to loft the ball into the air for a shot or to get over an opponent's stick. The top of the stick must be tilted backward so the blade is behind and under the ball to give it loft as the force is applied.

Figure 19.28. Straight dribble

Figure 19.31.   Push pass

Fielding

Fielding refers to stopping and controlling a moving ball, and must be practiced with balls coming from the right, left, and center. The face of the stick and the body position need to be adjusted according to the direction in which the ball is traveling. The front fielding position (Figure 19.32) is similar to the straight dribbling position and is used for balls rolling straight toward a person. Balls coming from the left require a regular forehand position with the blade facing to the left. For balls coming from the right, the stick must intercept the ball before it reaches the body. The blade must be turned so that it is facing to the right (Figure 19.33). Fielding requires the ability to absorb the ball's momentum by "giving" with the stick, depending on the speed of the ball.

Tackling and Dodging

Tackling is attempting to take the ball away from an opponent who is controlling the ball. Tackles can be made straight on or from the left side or the right side of an opponent. Timing is important, because the ball must be picked off while it is away from the opponent's stick. The stick is carried low, and the tackler must concentrate on the ball and on the opponent's stick. The speed of the opponent and of the ball must be considered. The tackle should not be a reckless striking of the stick.

Dodging is a skill for evading a tackler and maintaining control of the ball. A dodge can be executed to the left or right side of the tackler, and a scoop shot can also be used to go over an opponent's stick. If a dodge is made to the left, the dodger should move the ball 90 degrees to the left just before the tackle. A dodger moving around to the left is on the stick side, which is the right, of the opponent. This maneuver is a stick side dodge. A dodge to the right involves moving the ball to the

Figure 19.32.   Front fielding position

Figure 19.33.   Fielding from the right

right of the opponent, but the dodger's body must move around the other side of the tackler, that is, the ball goes to the right but the person goes to the left (nonstick side dodge). This technique is used to avoid an obstruction violation.

Bully or Face-off

The bully (Figure 19.34) is used to start the game and after each score. Two players face each other in the middle of the field with their respective sticks facing the direction of the goal where they can score. The bully starts with each player striking the ground on her side of the ball and then touching sticks above the ball. This is repeated three times, and then players attempt to control the ball or to pass it to a teammate.

Goalkeeping

The goalkeeper can kick the ball or block the ball with the body, hands, or stick. Most balls are blocked with the legs or feet, hence the padding on these areas. Most clears away from the goal are with a kick. The goalie cannot hold the ball or throw the ball away from the goal.

IDEAS FOR EFFECTIVE INSTRUCTION

Drills can be set up for partner work at several stations. Dribbling, passing, shooting, tackling, dodging, and goalkeeping can be specific stations with varying tasks to be practiced. The performance objectives detailed here can be used for the tasks at each station. Boundary cones, stopwatches, targets, baskets, and other instructional devices should be set up for challenging skill work. Classes can be arranged so that students spend several minutes working at each of four stations. The

Figure 19.34. Bully position

station work can then be followed by several small group drills such as 3 on 3, keepaway, or three-person weave. A modified or regulation game could follow the group work. This variety of learning activities helps to keep students active and motivated.

Students need to be reminded continually about the importance of safe stick handling. High-sticking is extremely dangerous and rules must be enforced tightly. A student who commits two high-sticking violations should be placed in a penalty box for 2 min. Body checking, tripping, and hooking with the stick should also not be allowed. A free shot or penalty shot can be used as a penalty for these violations. The teacher must be clear about the rules, regulations, and penalties that are going to be enforced in the game.

LEAD-UP GAMES AND LEARNING ACTIVITIES

Three-Person Weave

The ball is started by the center person and passed to either the person on the left or right. The person making the pass always runs behind the person who receives the pass. The person receiving the pass then becomes the middle person. This procedure continues downfield.

Partner Passing

Partners stand apart and try to hit as many passes as possible in 30 sec. Each hit is counted. As variations, try the same activity with three people in a triangle, four in a square, or five in a circle.

Circle Keepaway

Students form a circle with one person in the middle. The people in the circle try to keep the ball away from the center person. This can also be played with only three people. The person in the middle is rotated after 1 min.

Circle Dribble

A student dribbles the ball around the circle as fast as possible, concluding the dribble at the next person in the circle. All members of the circle go around quickly. Circles compete against each other or against the clock.

Star Drill (Figure 19.35)

Five classmates make a star formation. Number one passes to two, and two to three, and so forth. After passing the ball, the passer runs and takes that person's spot. The passer always follows the pass, and more than one person can be in line. The game can also be played against another team or against the clock.

Dribble and Hit for Distance

Half of the class or group lines up 5 yd behind a drive line. A partner is downfield about 50 yd. On signal, the hitters dribble the 5 yd and hit a drive shot as far as possible. The partner stands over the ball, and a winner is determined. Partners change places after several hits.

No Goalie Field Hockey

The game is played without a goalie. Person-to-person defense can be used. The goal size can also be modified if necessary.

End Zone Hockey

The entire end line of the field is the goal area. Each team designates a certain number of goalies and field players. The goalies must spread out over the entire goal line in order to cover it properly. Goalies and field players change places after a specified number of minutes.

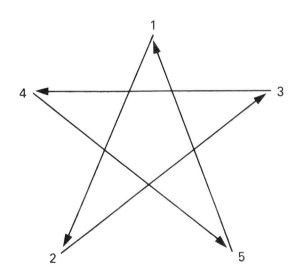

Figure 19.35. Star drill

Sideline Hockey

Part of each team lines up on one sideline, while the rest of each team is on the field. The sideline players keep the ball from going out-of-bounds, and they can also pass to the field players. A regulation goal and goalie are used in the game. The sideline and field players switch after 3 min of play. This game can be varied by putting members of each team on both sidelines, thus adding another challenge to the game.

Square Hockey

The game is played on a large square. Each team defends two sides of the square. Some team members are on the square sides as goalies, and others are on the field trying to hit the ball past either of the two end lines. At the start of the game, the teacher can have all students stand on the square and count off. Several numbers can then be called, and those students become the field players.

Half-Circle Hockey

This is similar to square hockey, but each team forms one half of a circle. The half circles connect, and the object is to hit the ball through the opponent's half circle. If the ball comes to rest inside the circle, it belongs to the team nearer the ball. That team can take a shot from the point where the ball stopped.

Modified Coed Field Hockey

This modified game is recommended for coeducational physical education classes. The rules and penalties are as follows:

1. A bully is used to start the game and after each goal.
2. A roll-in is used when the ball goes out-of-bounds.
3. A short corner shot is awarded to the offense when the ball goes past the end line within the striking circle last touching off a defender.
4. A long corner shot is awarded to the offense when the ball goes past the end line outside the striking circle last touching off a defender.
5. A defensive hit is awarded to the defensive team when the ball goes over the end line off an offensive player.
6. The striking circle is the 16-yd half circle around the goal. A free shot is awarded for a

foul occurring anywhere outside the striking circle. All players must be 5 yd away.

7. A penalty shot taken from the top of the striking circle is awarded for a defensive foul inside the striking circle.

8. Off sides occurs when an offensive player enters the striking circle before the ball. A defensive hit is awarded at the top of the circle.

9. High-sticking occurs when the stick is raised above the shoulder. The penalty is a free shot or penalty shot and a 2-min time out.

10. Advancing is when a player uses the feet to advance the ball. The penalty is a free shot or a penalty shot.

11. Backing up is when a player uses the feet to stop the ball. The penalty is a free shot or a penalty shot.

12. Hooking, tripping, or dangerous stick use involves using the stick to slow down or trip an opponent. The penalty is a free shot or penalty shot and a 2-min time out.

13. Body checking is vigorous use of the body for blocking and other maneuvers. The penalty is a free shot or penalty shot and a 2-min time out.

SUGGESTED PERFORMANCE OBJECTIVES

These performance objectives can be used to structure the learning activities for station work. They can also be tied to a motivational scheme for earning grades or entry into a playing situation. Teachers might develop a contract from these objectives, which can be modified according to the ability levels of the students in a specific situation. If the objectives are too hard or too easy, then they should be rewritten to provide a fair challenge and a successful experience for students.

1. Dribble the ball a distance of 30 yd, 3 consecutive times, using proper technique at all times (straight dribble).

2. Dribble the ball through an obstacle course and back in 30 sec or less (straight dribble).

3. Dribble the ball toward a target and execute a nonstick dodge in 3 of 5 attempts without losing control.

4. Dribble the ball toward a target and execute a stick-side dodge around the target in 3 of 5 attempts without losing control.

5. With a partner, push-pass the ball back and forth (jogging speed) for a distance of 30 yd, 2 consecutive times.

6. Push-pass the ball to a target 3 of 5 times from a distance of 10 yd.

7. Shoot 3 of 5 drive shots into the goal from 10 yd (no goalie).

8. Scoop the ball over an obstacle into a basket 3 consecutive times from within a stick-length distance.

9. Dribble the ball from the center of the field toward the goal, and hit 3 drive shots 3 consecutive times without a goalie.

10. Execute proper fielding of the ball from the front, right, and left side, passed by a partner from 10 to 15 yd away (5 times from each side).

11. Dribble the ball a distance of 30 yd, 3 consecutive times, using proper technique at all times (zigzag dribble).

12. Dribble the ball through an obstacle course and back in 30 sec or less (zigzag dribble).

13. Dribble the ball toward a goal and score 2 of 5 drive shots past a goalie from 10 yd.

14. Execute a three-person weave passing drill from a distance of 15–30 yd, 2 consecutive times.

15. Hit 2 of 5 penalty shots past a goalie.

16. Execute a proper tackle from the left, right, and center.

17. Scoop and run with the ball for 25 yd.

18. Dribble 5 yd, then execute a scoop shot. Repeat 5 consecutive times.

RAINY DAY ACTIVITIES

Many of the drills and modified games can be played indoors with a flat plastic-type puck. Teachers can set up station activities for working on performance tasks. Modified games, such as sideline hockey, end zone hockey, and square hockey, can be played indoors with large numbers of students. Strategies, terminology, and penalties can be discussed at indoor sessions.

Suggested Readings

Barnes, M., and Kentwell, R. *Field Hockey: The Coach and the Player.* 2nd ed. Boston: Allyn and Bacon, Inc., 1979.

Fong, D. *The Coach's Collection of Field Hockey Drills.* West Point, NY: Leisure Press, 1983.

Gros, V. *Inside Field Hockey.* Chicago: Contemporary Books, 1979.

Mood, D., Musker, F., and Armbruster, D. *Sports and Recreational Activities for Men and Women.* 8th ed. St. Louis: C. V. Mosby Co., 1983.

National Association for Girls and Women in Sport. *Field Hockey-Lacrosse Guide*. Reston, VA: AAHPERD, 1980.

United States Field Hockey Association. *The Official Manual of the United States Field Hockey Association*. North Chill, NY, 1979.

FLAG FOOTBALL

Football is America's favorite spectator sport. Professional football players are held in high esteem by students. The shape of the football makes throwing and catching more difficult and challenging than similar maneuvers in other sports. Flag and touch football are variations of the game of football, modified so the game can be played without the padding and equipment necessary for tackle football. Flag football is usually the more enjoyable, because it eliminates the arguments about whether someone was touched or not.

SEQUENCE OF SKILLS

Passing

Passing is used to advance the ball downfield to a teammate. The passer looks at the receiver and points the shoulder opposite the throwing arm toward the receiver. The ball is brought up to the throwing shoulder with both hands. The fingers of the throwing hand are placed across the laces of the ball. The weight is transferred to the rear leg in preparation for the throw (Figure 19.36). On throwing, the weight is transferred forward, and a step is taken with the front foot in the direction of the receiver. The throwing arm is extended and the wrist flicked upon release of the ball. The longer the throw to be made, the higher the angle of release needs to be.

Lateral Pass

Lateral passing is pitching the ball underhand to a teammate. The ball must be tossed sideways or backwards to be a legal lateral that can then be passed again. There is no attempt to make the ball spiral as it does in a pass.

Catching

Since the football is a large and heavy object and can be thrown with great velocity, the catcher must "give" and bring the ball in toward the body (Fig-

Figure 19.36.   Preparing to pass

ures 19.37 and 19.38). In a stationary position, the catcher faces the thrower and plants the feet about shoulder width apart. To catch a ball on the run, the catcher observes the ball by looking over the shoulder. The fingers should be spread and the arms extended to meet the ball. This allows giving with the ball and bringing the ball in toward the body in an attempt to absorb the force of the throw. Students should develop the habit of tucking the ball in close to the body after each catch.

Figure 19.37.   Catching the ball—thumbs up

Figure 19.38. Catching the ball—thumbs down

Carrying the Ball

The ball is carried with the arm on the outside and the end of the ball tucked into the notch formed by the elbow and arm. The fingers cradle the forward part of the ball.

Centering

The center moves into position with the feet well spread and the toes pointed straight ahead. The knees are bent in preparation for forward movement. The dominant hand reaches forward slightly and is placed across the laces. The other hand is on the side near the back and guides the ball. The head is between the legs; the center's eyes are on the receiver. The arms are extended, and the ball is propelled by pulling both arms backward and upward. The ball should spiral on its way to the quarterback.

When centering in T formation, only one hand is used. The quarterback places the throwing hand in the crotch of the center and the other hand below with the hands touching at the base of the palms. The ball is given a one-quarter turn as it is centered and placed sideways in the quarterback's hands.

Stance

The two-point stance is used by ends and backs so they can see downfield. The feet are spread shoulder width and the knees are bent slightly. The hands can be placed just above the knees.

The three-point stance (Figure 19.39) is used as a down position in order to move quickly forward or sideways. The feet are spread shoulder width apart with the toes pointing straight ahead. The player leans forward and places the desired hand on the ground while keeping the back parallel to the playing surface. The weight is on the balls of the feet; the head is up. Little weight is placed on the down hand.

The four-point stance is used to move forward quickly. Lateral movement is sacrificed when using this stance. The stance is similar to the three-point stance, but both hands are on the ground and more weight is placed on the hands.

Blocking

The purpose of blocking is to prevent the defensive player from getting the flag of the ball carrier. It is accomplished by keeping the body between the defensive player and the ball carrier. Knocking the defensive player down is not necessary to accomplish a successful block.

Shoulder Block. The shoulder block starts from a three- or four-point stance. The blocker moves forward and makes shoulder contact at chest level of the opponent. The head should be placed between the opponent and the ball carrier in order to move the defensive player away from the ball carrier. The elbows are out and the hands are held near the chest.

Pass Block. The pass block is used when the quarterback is dropping back to throw a pass. The

Figure 19.39. Three-point stance

block can begin from any of the described stances. The blocker moves slightly backward with the rear foot as the opponent charges. The blocker should attempt to stay between the quarterback and the rusher.

Exchanging the Ball

The hand-off is made with the inside hand (nearest the receiver). The ball is held with both hands until the ball carrier is about 6 ft away. It is then shifted to the hand nearer the receiver, with the elbow bent partially away from the body. The receiver comes toward the quarterback with the near arm bent and carried in front of the chest, the palm down. The other arm is carried about waist high, with the palm up. As the ball is exchanged, the receiver clamps down on the ball to secure it.

Punting

The punter starts in standing position with both arms fully extended to receive the ball. The kicking foot is placed slightly forward. After receiving the ball, the kicker takes two steps forward, beginning with the dominant foot. The ball is slightly turned in and held at waist height. The kicking leg is swung forward, and at impact the knee is straightened to provide maximum force. The toes are pointed and the long axis of the ball makes contact on the top of the instep. The ball should be dropped rather than tossed into the air. The drop needs to be mastered before effective punting can occur.

IDEAS FOR EFFECTIVE INSTRUCTION

Since many drills are available for flag football, the authors have devoted this section to delineating the rules and equipment necessary for it. Most of the prerequisites for developing a sound flag football program are listed and discussed.

Uniforms

Rubber-soled shoes should be worn. Metal cleats or spikes are not allowed, nor is any hard surface padding or helmets.

Flags

Flags are available in two colors for team play. All flags should be similar in terms of pulling the flags loose from players. The flag belts have two flags attached, one at each hip. Either flag pulled downs the ball carrier.

Downed Ball

To down a ball carrier, either flag must be withdrawn from the waist by a tackler. The tackler must stop at the point of tackle and hold up the hand with the withdrawn flag. It is illegal for ball carriers to deliberately touch their own flags or to defend them in any manner. **Penalty:** 15 yards from the point of the foul and loss of a down.

Dead Ball

The ball is ruled dead on a fumble when it hits the ground, or on a wild center when it hits the ground. When a fumble rolls out-of-bounds, the ball is returned to the team that had last full possession of it.

Loss of Flags

If the flag is inadvertently lost, the player is ineligible to handle the ball. The ball then becomes dead if the player is behind the line of scrimmage, or the pass is called incomplete. It is illegal for a player to deliberately withdraw an opponent's flag unless that opponent is in possession of the ball. Such conduct is penalized as unsportsmanlike. **Penalty:** 15 yards.

Charging and Tackling

The ball carrier may not run through a defensive player, but must attempt to evade the tackler. The tackler must not hold, push, or run through the ball carrier, but must play the flag rather than the person. The officials decide these judgment calls. **Penalty:** 15 yards and loss of a down offensively, and 15 yards defensively.

Tackling

Tackling is not permitted. The ball is declared dead when defensive play pulls one of the runner's flags. Action against the runner, other than pulling the flag, is unnecessary roughness. **Penalty:** 15 yards from the point of the foul and loss of a down offensively, and 15 yards from the point of the foul defensively.

Hacking

It is a foul for the ball carrier to hack, push, or straight-arm another player. **Penalty:** 15 yards from the point of the foul and loss of a down.

Blocking

Line blocking is the same as regulation football. In open-field (out-of-the-line) line blocking, no part of the blocker's body, except the feet, shall be in contact with the ground during the block. Blocking is a type of body checking with the blocker in an upright position and without the use of hands or extended arms. Any rough tactics, such as attempting to run over or batter down an opponent, must be penalized as unnecessary roughness. Unnecessary roughness may be declared if the blocker uses knees or elbows in blocking. **Penalty:** 15 yards and loss of a down offensively, and 15 yards and first down defensively.

Passing

A forward pass may be thrown from any point behind the line of scrimmage. The passer is declared down if a flag is withdrawn by a defensive player, or if a flag falls out on its own before passer's arm is engaged in the throwing motion. It is the responsibility of the officials to make this decision.

Downs

A team has four downs to advance the ball from wherever they take over to score. If the team fails to score in four downs, their opponents gain possession of the ball at the spot where the ball is declared dead on the fourth down. To obtain a first down, the offensive team must complete forward passes out of four downs. A forward pass is a pass thrown from behind the line of scrimmage past the line of scrimmage.

Miscellaneous Penalties

Illegal use of flags	15 yards
Offensive use of hands	15 yards
Defensive illegal use of hands	15 yards
Off side	5 yards
Pushing ball carrier out-of-bounds	15 yards
Ball carrier pushing the interference	15 yards
Ineligible person downfield	5 yards
Illegal procedure	5 yards

Practice Using Station Teaching

Stations can be organized to develop football skills. The following is an example of how this might be done.

Station 1—passing (Figure 19.40)
Station 2—punting (Figure 19.41)
Station 3—lateral passing (Figure 19.42)
Station 4—centering (Figure 19.43)

Station 1: Passing—Out and In Pattern

Out pattern: Quarterback takes 5-yd drop, passes ball to receiver at 7 yd.
Rotate in direction of arrows.
Change pattern after all have completed.

In pattern: Quarterback takes 5-yd drop, passes ball to receiver at 7 yd.
Rotate in direction of arrows.

Figure 19.40. Passing

Station 2: Punt

Station 3: Lateral passing right and left

Receivers take punt formation after receiving all balls.

Receivers take punt formation after receiving all balls.

Punters take receiving formation after punting all balls.

Ball is hiked to punter.
Ball is punted to receivers.
Rotate in direction of arrows.

Figure 19.41. Punting

Right lateral: Quarterback rolls to right 5 to 7 yd. Lateral to halfback at swing position. Rotate in direction of arrows.

Left lateral: Quarterback rolls to left 5 to 6 yd. Lateral to halfback in swing position. Rotate in direction of arrows.

Figure 19.42. Lateral passing

After each group has completed the drill, the instructor gives a signal for rotation to the next station. The first "hutt" will be the signal used at all stations. In figures 19.40–19.43, dashed lines indicate the direction of the ball; straight lines indicate the direction in which the player is to move; a circle with an X in the center marks the position of the ball, the quarterback, or the center; and an empty circle represents the position of any other player.

LEAD-UP GAMES AND LEARNING ACTIVITIES

The following lead-up games can be enjoyable ways to broaden the variety of activities in a football unit. They also avoid one student's dominating

a skilled position while others simply go through the motions of blocking.

Five Passes

The game can be played on a football field, but the size of the field is not critical and any large area is satisfactory. Players scatter on the field. The object of the game is for one team (identified by pinnies) to make five consecutive passes to five different players without losing control of the ball. This scores one point. The defense may play the ball only and may not make personal contact. No player is allowed to take more than three steps when in possession of the ball, or the ball is given to the other team.

Station 4: Centering Drill
Shotgun formation

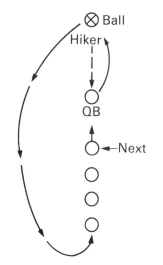

Ball is centered to quarterback.
Each center takes 3 hikes, then rotates.
Rotate in direction of arrows.

Figure 19.43.   Centering

There is no penalty when the ball hits the ground. It remains in play, but this interrupts the five-pass sequence, which starts over. Students should call the number of consecutive passes out loud.

Kick Over

The game is played on a football field with a 10-yard end zone. Teams are scattered at opposite ends of the field. The object is to punt the ball over the other team's goal line. If the ball is caught in the end zone, no score results. A ball kicked into the end zone and not caught scores a goal. If the ball is kicked beyond the end zone on the fly, a score is made regardless of whether the ball is caught.

Play is started by one team with a punt from a point 20 to 30 ft in front of their own goal line. On a punt, if the ball is not caught, the team must kick from the point of recovery. If the ball is caught, the team also kicks from the point of recovery. When the ball is caught, three long strides are allowed to advance the ball for a kick. It is a good idea to number students and to allow them to kick in rotation so all receive equal practice.

Fourth Down

Six to eight players are on a team and play in an area roughly half the size of a football field. Every play is a fourth down, which means that the play must score or the team loses the ball. No kicking is permitted, and players may pass at any time from any spot in any direction. There can be a series of passes on any play, either from behind or beyond the line of scrimmage.

The teams start in the middle of the field with possession determined by a coin toss. The ball is put into play by centering. The back receiving the ball runs or passes to any teammate. The receiver has the same options. No blocking is permitted. After each touchdown, the ball is brought to the center of the field and the nonscoring team resumes play. The ball is downed when the player's flag is pulled. If a player makes an incomplete pass beyond the line of scrimmage, the ball is brought to the spot from which it was thrown.

Positions are rotated so everyone has a chance to be the quarterback. The rotation occurs after every down. The quarterback rotates to center, which ensures that everyone plays all positions.

Captain Football

The game is played on half of a football field. Five yards beyond each goal is a 6-ft by 6-ft square, which is the box. The teams must be identified with pinnies. The object of the game is to complete a pass to the captain in the box.

To begin, the players line up at opposite ends of the field. One team kicks off from its 10-yard line to the other team. The game then becomes keepaway, with one team trying to secure possession of the ball and the other team trying to retain possession until a successful pass can be made to the captain in the box. To score a touchdown, the captain must catch the ball on the fly and still keep both feet in the box.

A player may run sideways or backwards when in possession of the ball. Players may not run forward but are allowed momentum (two steps) if receiving or intercepting a ball. More than two steps is penalized by loss of possession.

The captain is allowed three attempts to catch a pass, or one successful goal before a new player is rotated into the box. A ball hitting the ground in bounds remains in play. Players may not bat or kick a free ball. Penalty is the awarding of the ball to the other team out-of-bounds.

Aerial Ball

Aerial ball is similar to flag football with the following differences. The ball may be passed at any time. It can be thrown at any time beyond the line of scrimmage: immediately after an interception, during a kickoff, or during a received kick. Players have four downs to score a touchdown. If the ball is thrown from behind the line of scrimmage and an incomplete pass results, the ball is returned to the previous spot on the line of scrimmage. If the pass originates otherwise and is incomplete, the ball is placed at the point from which the pass was thrown.

Since the ball can be passed at any time, no downfield blocking is permitted. A player may screen the ball carrier but cannot make a block. Screening is defined as running between the ball carrier and the defense.

SUGGESTED PERFORMANCE OBJECTIVES

Basic Objectives

1. Throw 10 overhand passes to the chest area of a partner who is standing 10 yd away. Practice correct holding, point of release, and follow-through techniques of passing (1 point).
2. Throw 3 or 4 consecutive passes beyond a target positioned 20 yd away (1 point).
3. Facing the opposite direction from a partner 5 yd away, execute a proper center stance with feet well spread and toes pointed straight ahead, knees bent, and two hands on the ball. Snap the ball back through the legs 10 consecutive times (1 point).
4. With a partner centering the ball, from a distance of 10 yd punt the ball using proper technique to another set of partners 15 yd away, 3 consecutive times (1 point).
5. Same as no. 4, except at a distance of 20 yd (1 point).
6. Punt the ball 3 consecutive times within the boundary lines of the field and beyond a distance of 20 yd (1 point).
7. With a partner, run a "quick" pass pattern and catch the ball 2 of 3 times (5–7-yard pattern) (1 point).
8. With a partner, run a 10–15 yard "down and in" pass pattern and catch the ball 2 of 3 times (1 point).
9. With a partner, run a 10–15-yard "down and out" pass pattern and catch the ball 2 of 3 times (1 point).
10. With a partner, run a 5–7-yard "hook" pattern and catch the ball 2 of 3 times (1 point).

Optional objectives

1. With a partner centering the ball, from a distance of 10 yd, punt the football using proper technique to another set of partners 15 yd away, 3 consecutive times (2 points).
2. Same as no. 1, but at a distance of 20 yd (2 points).
3. Center-snap 4 of 6 times through a tire positioned 5 yd away (2 points).
4. Throw 3 of 4 consecutive passes beyond a target positioned 20 yd away (2 points).
5. Throw 4 of 6 passes through a tire from a distance of 10 yd (2 points).

Suggested Readings

AAHPERD. *Rules for Coeducational Activities and Sports.* Reston, VA: AAHPERD, 1980.

Brace, D. K. *Skills Test Manual: Football.* Reston, VA: AAHPERD, 1965.

Seaton, D. C., et al. *Physical Education Handbook.* 7th ed. Englewood Cliffs, NJ: Prentice-Hall, Inc., 1983.

Standbury, D., and DeSantis, F. *Touch Football.* New York: Sterling Publishing Co., 1961.

FRISBEE

Frisbee is a new, exciting lifetime physical activity that can offer success and a challenge at all ability levels. It can be played on almost any size field or gymnasium area and can be used with individuals, small groups, or teams. The International Frisbee Disc Association, which numbers over 100,000 members, has statistics showing that more Frisbee discs are sold yearly in the United States than footballs and basketballs combined. An annual World Championship held in the Rose Bowl draws large crowds to watch competitors focus on distance, accuracy, free style, and other games.

A number of factors make Frisbee disc sports an attractive new activity for physical education. A Frisbee costs only $1.50 to $2.00, depending on the type and quality of the disc. Frisbee provides excellent skills practice in throwing, catching, and eye-hand coordination, as well as offering many interesting individual challenges and team activities. The low injury risks and the attraction to students are positive factors. The sport can be effective in a coeducational environment, and offers flexibility in terms of participants' ages and abilities and in terms of program space and time. Both team and individual skills can be learned with the Frisbee and used for a lifetime of enjoyment.

SEQUENCE OF SKILLS

Backhand Throw (Figure 19.44)

The thumb is on the top of the disc and the remaining fingers are under the rim. The index finger can also be placed on the outside lip of the disc. Coil the wrist and arm across the chest. Step forward and release the disc (keeping it level) with a snap of the wrist.

Sandwich Catch

Catch the disc with one hand on top and the other on the bottom with the disc in the middle. Alternate hands from top to bottom on different occasions.

Backhand (Across the Chest) Curves

Use the same technique as the straight backhand but release the disc at an angle, with the lower side being the desired direction. Throw curves both left and right by tilting the disc.

C-Catch

Make a C with the thumb and fingers. Watch the disc into the C and close the fingers on the disc.

Throws below the waist should have the thumb up, and those above the waist should have thumb down.

Underhand Throw (Figure 19.45)

Use a backhand grip or put the index finger on the lip of the disc. Step with the opposite foot, bring the disc underhand past the body, and release level about waist height with a wrist snap.

Thumber Throw

Hook the thumb under the disc and put the four fingers on top. Bring the disc down from the ear in a sidearm motion and release when the disc is even with the body. Avoid a follow-through with the disc.

Sidearm Throw (Figure 19.46)

Put the index and middle finger under the disc and the thumb on top. The two fingers can be together on the lip, or one can be on the lip and one in the middle of the disc. Release the disc in a motion similar to the thumber.

Overhand Wrist Flip (Figure 19.47)

Grip the disc with the fingers on top and the thumb under the lip. Cock the wrist backward and

Figure 19.44.   Backhand throw

Figure 19.45.   Underhand throw

Figure 19.46. Sidearm throw

Fiugre 19.47. Overhand wrist flip

start the throw behind the back at shoulder level. Flip the wrist forward to a point in line with the body.

Additional Skills

1. Skip-throw off the ground—Tip the forward edge down and skip the disc to a partner.
2. Tipping—Use the finger, knee, head, toe, heel, or elbow. Watch the disc make contact with the various body parts and tip the disc in the air.
3. Catches—Catch with the finger, behind the back and head, between the legs, and one-handed.
4. Air brushing—Strike the disc on its side to give it rotation.

IDEAS FOR EFFECTIVE INSTRUCTION

Frisbee discs are available from over 30 different companies. Avoid the cheapest discs because they will not fly without turning over. Whamo Company in San Gabriel, California, is the oldest and largest manufacturer of flying discs. They have an excellent World Class Series ranging from 97 to 165 g. These discs are reasonably priced for secondary schools. Many companies use discs for advertising, and it is often possible to acquire promotional discs at a discount.

Instruction can begin by having partners, positioned about 5 yd apart, work on the basic backhand and sandwich catch. As students improve, have them move farther apart and use the backhand curves with the C-catch and the one-handed catch. Be sure to keep beginning students spread out and away from buildings, fences, and other obstacles, since the disc is difficult to control. Next, the underhand throw, thumber, and sidearm can be introduced with several fancy catches.

After students have the basic idea, create four stations that focus on accuracy, distance, accuracy and distance combined, and loft time. Many station variations can be designed to challenge students. Check the following section on activities for specific ideas. Frisbee golf is a particularly good activity for beginners with few developed skills.

LEAD-UP GAMES AND LEARNING ACTIVITIES

Throw for Distance

Set up five or six cones at varying distances and let students experiment with different throws for distance.

Throw for Distance and Accuracy

Mark a line with varying distances and have students throw as far as possible on the line. Subtract from the total throw distance, the distance of the Frisbee landing point away from the line. Students should develop both distance and accuracy.

Throw for Accuracy

Make a large circular target, about 9 or 10 ft in diameter, on the ground with rope or jump ropes. Set cones at 10, 15, 20, and 25-yd distances. Let students have five attempts at each distance, and record the number of accurate throws. Another variation is to hang a Hula-Hoop from a tree or goal post and have students throw through the hoop. Award one point for hitting the hoop and two points for going through the hoop.

Time Aloft

Record the time from disc release until it hits the ground.

Throw and Catch With Self

The object of this activity is to throw the disc as far forward as possible and then to run and catch the Frisbee. A starting line is designated at which the disc must be released, and distance is measured from that line. The disc must be caught.

Follow-the-Leader

One player makes a specific throw and the second player must try to make the same throw. The first player must match the catch of the second player.

Twenty-One

Players stand 10 yd apart and throw the disc back and forth. The throws must be accurate and catchable. One point is awarded for a two-handed catch and 2 points for a one-handed catch. A player must get 21 points and win by 2 points.

Frisbee Tennis

The same game as regular tennis, but the player must catch the Frisbee and throw from that spot. The serve starts to the right of the center mark and must go to the opposite back court, not into the service box.

Ultimate

This is a team game with seven or more on a side. The object is to move the Frisbee down the field by passing and to score by passing across the goal line to a teammate. The person with the disc can only pivot and pass to a teammate. If the Frisbee is grounded, not caught, intercepted, or goes out-of-bounds, the defending team gains possession.

Guts

Five to seven players on a team stand behind a line 15 yd from the opponents' line. The goal line is 10 yd wide. The object is to throw so hard that the opponents cannot make a one-handed catch. The Frisbee can be tipped by several people as long as a one-handed catch is used. The receiving team gets a point if the throw is too high, too wide, or too low. The height is determined by having the team stretch their arms straight up, usually 7 to 8 ft high. The first team to score 21 points wins. Use extra caution with beginners and younger students. Move the goals back a bit and match ability levels.

Frisbee Soccer

The game is played like soccer, but the disc is thrown to teammates and at the goal. If the disc is dropped, the defenders play offense. Rules can be modified to include two goalies and limitations on the number of steps possible.

Frisbee Softball

The game is similar to regular softball. The pitcher throws the disc to the batter, who must catch the disc and throw it into play past the pitcher. If the batter drops the pitch, it is a strike. No bunting or stealing is allowed. The other rules of softball apply.

Frisbee Golf

Frisbee or disc golf is a favorite game of many students. Boundary cones with numbers can be used for tees, and holes can be boxes, Hula-Hoops, trees, tires, garbage cans, or any other available equipment on the school grounds. Put the course together on a map for students (Figure 19.48) and start them at different holes to decrease the time spent waiting to tee off. Regulation golf rules apply. The students can jog between throws for increased activity.

Disc Golf—Rules and Regulations

General Guideline. Disc golf is played like regular golf. One stroke is counted for each time the disc is thrown and when a penalty is incurred. The object is to acquire the lowest score.

T-Throws. T-throws must be completed within or behind the designated tee area.

Lie. The lie is the spot on or directly underneath the spot where the previous throw landed.

Throwing Order. The player whose disc is the

Frisbee Golf Course

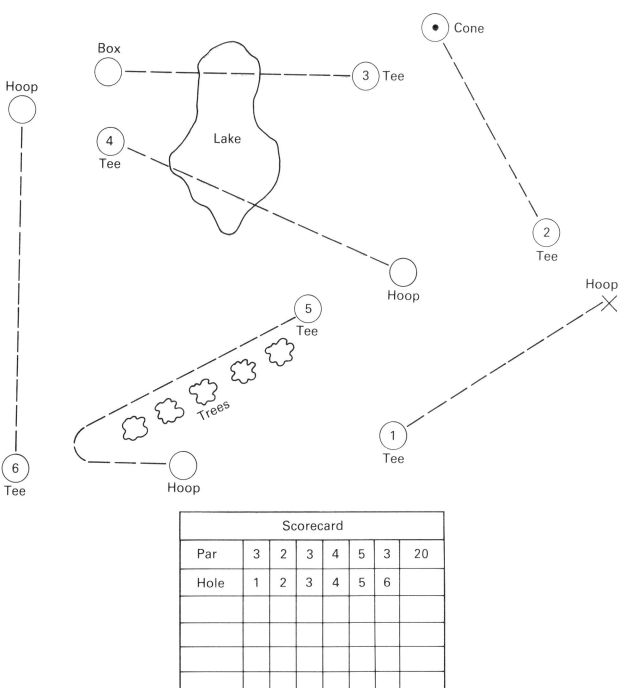

Figure 19.48.   Frisbee golf course and scorecard

farthest from the hole throws first. The player with the least number of throws on the previous hole tees off first.

Fairway Throws.   Fairway throws must be made with the foot closest to the hole on the lie. A run-up is allowed.

Dog Leg.   A dog leg is one or more designated trees or poles in the fairway that must be passed on the outside when approaching the hole. There is a two-stroke penalty for missing a dog leg.

Putt Throw.   A putt throw is any throw within 10 ft of the hole. A player may not move past the point of the lie in making the putt throw. Falling or jumping putts are not allowed.

Unplayable Lies. Any disc that comes to rest 6 or more ft above the ground is unplayable. The next throw must be played from a new lie directly underneath the unplayable lie (1 stroke penalty).

Out-of-Bounds. A throw that lands out-of-bounds must be played from the point where the disc went out (1 stroke penalty).

Course Courtesy. Do not throw until the players ahead are out of range.

Completion of Hole. A disc that comes to rest in the hole (box or hoop) or strikes the designated hole (tree or pole) constitutes successful completion of that hole.

Around Nine (Figure 19.49)

A target is set up with nine different throwing positions around it, each 2 ft farther away. The throwing positions can be clockwise or counterclockwise around the target. They can also be in a straight line from the target. Points are awarded based on the throwing position number (i.e., number 7 means 7 points for hitting the target). The game can be played indoors or out.

One-Step

This game is a variation of Guts. Opponents stand 20–30 yd apart. The object is to throw the disc accurately to the opponent so she or he can catch the disc while taking only one step. If the throw is off target, the thrower receives a point. If the throw is accurate and the receiver drops the disc, the receiver is awarded one point. The first player with five points loses the match.

SUGGESTED PERFORMANCE OBJECTIVES

1. Throw 10 consecutive backhands through a Hula-Hoop from 10 yd.
2. Same as no. 1 using underhand throws.
3. Same as no. 1 using sidearm throws.
4. Same as no. 1 using thumber throws.
5. Same as no. 1 using overhand wrist flips.
6. Throw a Frisbee 30 yd or more using two different throws.
7. Curve the disc around a tree and land it in a designated target area 3 of 5 attempts.
8. Same as no. 7, but use the opposite curve.
9. Catch 10 consecutive sandwich catches.
10. Catch 10 consecutive thumbs-down catches above the waist.
11. Same as no. 10 with thumbs up below the waist.
12. Catch 3 of 5 behind the head, behind the back, or between the legs.
13. Make 5 consecutive one-handed catches, both left and right.
14. Throw 5 consecutive skips into a target area.
15. Score 30 or less on a round of Frisbee golf.

These are just a few of the possibilities for challenging students with Frisbee performance objectives. The objectives could be combined with a grading scheme or used with learning stations for

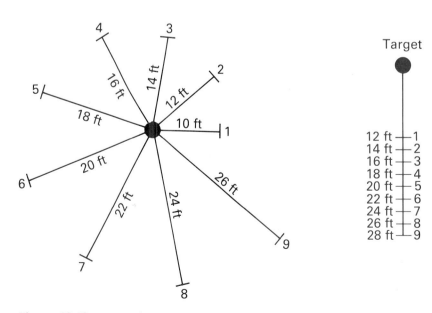

Figure 19.49. Around nine game

skill development. Activities need to be field-tested in order to establish fair distances and criterion levels for various age students and ability groups.

Figure 19.50 is a three-week Frisbee unit for junior high school students.

RAINY DAY ACTIVITIES

1. Review and teach rules and strategies for the various Frisbee games.
2. Set up a short putting (Frisbee golf) course in the gym, hallway, or locker room.
3. Review grips, throws, releases, and so forth.
4. Discuss Frisbee literature, and have students read and report on specific information.
5. Discuss the various types and sizes of discs and the purpose of each type.
6. Set up an indoor tossing accuracy test and let students work at improving their accuracy.
7. Develop a crossword puzzle or Frisbee word searches.
8. Assign a group of students to develop a crossword puzzle or a word search.
9. Devise and give a test on terminology.
10. Discuss with students the skills and activities of Frisbee and how Frisbee can fit into their life-style.

Introduction What is Frisbee? Types Activities Backhand throw Sandwich catch Backhand curves C-catch Underhand throw	**Review** Backhands— curves Underhands Catches **Teach** Frisbee golf **Activity** Play 6 holes of golf	**Review** Throws—catches **Teach** Thumber Sidearm Overhand flip **Activities** Four stations: Distance Accuracy Curves Partner work	**Review** Throws—catches **Teach** Fancy catches **Activities** Follow-the-Leader Twenty-One One Step	**Review** Fancy catches **Teach** Throw to self **Activities** Frisbee softball Frisbee soccer
Review All throws **Teach** Skipping Tipping Brushing **Activities** Four stations: Distance with accuracy Self-catch Accuracy Partner work	**Review** All catches **Teach** Free style **Activity** Ultimate	**Review** Skipping, tipping, brushing, free style **Activities** Four stations: skill work Frisbee tennis Frisbee golf	**Activity** 9 holes of Frisbee golf	**Activities** Four stations: Skill work Evaluation Around Nine Follow-the-Leader Twenty-One One Step
Review Skills for station work **Activities** Four stations Frisbee softball	**Activities** Ultimate Frisbee soccer	**Activities** Station work Evaluation Guts Around Nine Follow-the-Leader Twenty-One One Step	**Activities** 9 holes of Frisbee golf	**Activities** Station work Evaluation Ultimate Frisbee softball Guts

Figure 19.50. Frisbee block plan

11. Have students develop rules and regulations for a new game that will be played when the weather clears.

12. Invite a local Frisbee club or expert to class to give a demonstration and instruction on Frisbee techniques and skills.

Suggested Readings

Danna, M., and Poynter, D. *Frisbee Players' Handbook.* Santa Barbara, CA: Parachuting Publications, 1978.

Frisbee World Magazine. The International Frisbee Association, P.O. Box 970, San Gabriel, CA 91776.

International Frisbee Disc Association. *The Discourse.* San Gabriel, CA, 1978.

Tips, C. *Frisbee by the Masters.* Millbrae, CA: Celestial Arts, 1979.

Tips, C., and Roddick, D. *Frisbee Disc Sports and Games.* Millbrae, CA: Celestial Arts, 1979.

GOLF

Each weekend millions of golfers everywhere try to obtain a tee-off time to hit and chase a little white ball around an 18-hole golf course. Golf may appear to be a simple sport, but it is actually a complex activity made up of many different shots or strokes (e.g., woods, long irons, short irons, pitching, chipping, and putting). It is quite challenging and proves to be fascinating to people of all abilities and ages, from 8 to 80. Golf is truly a lifetime sport that can be enjoyed by all people.

SEQUENCE OF SKILLS

The two primary methods of teaching golf are the swing or whole method and the position or part method. Both approaches lead to the same result—square contact with good acceleration. Both teaching methods can be effective, but the whole method seems easier and faster to learn, which makes it better suited to the limited time available for a physical education unit.

The order of skills to be learned in a beginning class follows: grip; stance; alignment; iron shots—half swing, three-quarter swing, and full swing; wood shots—half swing, three-quarter swing, and full swing; putting; chipping; pitching; and the bunker shot.

Grip

Encourage students to use the overlap grip (80% of all golfers use this grip). Place the left hand on the club in the following manner: First support the club with the right hand and let the left hand hang naturally at the side, then bring the left hand in until it contacts the grip of the club and wrap it around. (Checkpoint: The V formed by the thumb and index finger should point directly to the center of the body, and two knuckles should be visible on the left hand when looking straight down at the grip.) Place the right hand by letting it also hang naturally at the side. Bring it in to meet the club and wrap the fingers around the club so the little finger of the right hand lies over the index finger of the left hand. The thumb of the left hand should fit nicely into the palm of the right hand. (Checkpoint: The V formed by the thumb and index finger of the right hand should point to the center of the body or slightly to the right of center.) A final check on the grip is to extend all fingers and let the club fall to the ground. If the grip is correct, the club will fall straight down between the legs and feet.

Stance (Figure 19.51)

The golf stance should be both comfortable and relaxed. There is a slight bend in the knees and at the waist. The arms and shoulders are relaxed. The feet are shoulder width apart for the driver and closer together for the shorter clubs. The ball is positioned within a 6-in. span, starting inside the

Figure 19.51. Golf stance

left heel for the driver and moving toward the center of the stance for the wedge.

Lift the club straight out in front of the body at waist level and swing it back and forth similar to a baseball bat swing. After three or four swings, return to a balanced position in the center. Bend forward from the waist until the club touches the ground. Now relax, and the club will move in slightly closer to the body. It is important that the waist bend lowers the club and not the arms. The relationship between arms and body remains the same until relaxation occurs. (Checkpoint: The preceding check can be applied to every club in the bag. It illustrates how far forward or back the ball must be played and the distance the student should stand from the ball.)

Alignment

A simple procedure for achieving alignment involves the following steps:

1. Stand about 10 ft behind the ball and draw an imaginary line from the flag to the ball.
2. Move to the side of the ball and set the club face square to the target line. Both feet should be together with the ball centered.
3. Grip the club first and then spread the feet apart on a line parallel to the target line. The ball should be on line with the target, and the feet should be on a parallel line just left of the target. The distance between the toes and the ball is approximately 1.5 ft.

Half Swing (Figure 19.52)

Each student's swing will vary according to the person's stature, degree of relaxation, understanding of the swing, and natural ability. The half swing is started by bringing the club halfway back to a position parallel to the ground and then letting the club swing forward to the same position in front. The swing should be similar to the swing of a pendulum, and the grass should be brushed in both the backswing and forward swing. When the club is parallel to the ground in the backswing, the toe of the club should point straight up, and the grip end of the club should match the line of the feet. At the end of the forward swing, the toe should be straight up again, and the far end of the club should match the line of the feet. After students can do a half swing, introduce the ball. Tell them to concentrate on swinging the club correctly and on the proper alignment procedures.

Figure 19.52.   Half swing forward

Three-Quarter Swing

The three-quarter swing is simply an extension of the half swing. The hands reach approximately shoulder height on the backswing and on the forward swing. Many students may be at this point already, because most usually swing longer than they think.

Full Swing (Figure 19.53)

A full swing is characterized by a club shaft that is almost parallel to or parallel to the ground at the

Figure 19.53.   Full swing

top of the backswing. The full swing is a further extension of the half and three-quarter swings. At the top of the backswing, the clubhead should point to the ground, and the shaft should point toward the target. The club face will thus be square, and the plane will be correct.

The golf swing actually begins at the top of the backswing. The backswing is simply preparation. Students should visualize the full swing as a circle drawn in the air with the clubhead. The circle starts at the top of the backswing and is completed at the finish of the forward swing. Students should watch the clubhead draw the actual circle two or three times, always keeping the circle out in front. This will help them maintain one plane throughout the swing.

At this point, students should have the feel of the full swing, and it is time to experiment with different irons. Try the 5 iron, 9 iron, and finally the 3 iron. Concentration is still on the swing, for the same swing is used with every club. Once patterns of error have developed (i.e., slicing), students can begin to focus on changing a specific aspect of the total swing.

Woods

The same progression should be used to teach wood shots from the half to the full swing. The first wood hit should be the 3 wood from the tee. Next, move to the driver or 1 wood from the tee, and then experiment with the 3 wood off the ground. Students should move halfway down the club's grip to begin swinging. Tee the ball so the top edge of the club comes one quarter to one half of the way up the ball. The stance will be at its widest (shoulder width), and the ball will automatically be positioned forward, inside the left heel.

Putting

Identical to the pendulum of a clock, the putter is an extension of the arms and shoulders, and swings as one unit an equal distance back and forward. The feel is best obtained by having students grip as far down the shaft as they can reach. Square the putter to the target line and stroke straight back and straight through. Have students try the following putting techniques.

1. Use a reverse overlap grip in which the index finger of the left hand lies over the little finger of the right. This allows the whole right hand to be on the club for control.

2. The stance may be wide or narrow, and the ball may be centered in the stance or forward, remaining inside the left heel. If the ball is forward, a slight weight shift to the left must accompany this stance.
3. Place the dominant eye directly over the ball to improve visualization of the target line.
4. Feel the putter accelerating through contact. This may require shortening the backswing slightly.
5. If the ball misses the hole, overshooting the putt is preferable.
6. Keep the putter blade low to the ground to assure good ball contact.

Learn to judge break, or the roll of the green, by standing behind the ball and looking at the line between the ball and the hole and also at the slant of the entire green. Visualize throwing a pail of water toward the hole, and picture which way the water would run. For most putts, that is, 4 ft or less, play the ball to the opposite inside edge of the cup. If the putt is longer, gradually move to the edge of the cup, and eventually outside the cup as a point of aim. The point of aim may be a spot on the imaginary line to the hole, or a point even with the hole but to one side. In both cases, the break takes the ball into the hole.

Chip, Pitch, and Bunker Shots

A chip shot is used when the ball is slightly off the green and there is room to hit the ball approximately halfway to the hole. The ball must land on the green and roll close to the hole. If there is not enough room to roll the ball to the hole, then a higher trajectory pitch shot is used. The pitch shot should land at the target. The bunker shot is used for coming out of a sand trap.

A chip shot usually requires a 7 iron and a putting-type stroke. A good technique is to have the students stand off the green and toss the ball underhand so that it rolls to within 4 ft of the hole. Students then place a tee in the green where the ball hit. The tee becomes the target for the chip shot.

The pitch shot should be practiced at different distances with different sized targets (i.e., the greater the distance, the larger the target). Baskets, Hula-Hoops, and parachutes are possibilities at 10, 30, and 50 yd. The 9 iron or wedge is used with a one-quarter, one-half, or three-quarter swing, depending on the distance and the circumstances. Students should learn to make a smooth swing and to let the loft of the club hit the ball. The ball should land at the target and roll slightly forward.

The long jump landing pit can be used for bunker shot practice. Students should use a wedge or 9 iron and concentrate on the following:

1. Open the club face at address.
2. Line up 2 in. behind the ball and focus on that spot, not on the ball.
3. Barely scrape the sand with a one-quarter through full swing, depending on the distance required to land the ball.
4. Always follow through with the club.

IDEAS FOR EFFECTIVE INSTRUCTION

Rules of safety must be introduced and stressed the first day of class. A golf ball or club can cause serious damage, and thus strict adherence to safety rules must be demanded. If the class is large and space is limited, safety officers may be appointed who can help manage ball retrieving, changing from station to station, and other responsibilities assigned by the instructor.

The following are safety suggestions that may help in class organization:

1. Allow ample swing space between students for any group formation.
2. Do not carry clubs while retrieving balls.
3. If space is limited, take students back of the line for individual correction.
4. Do not retrieve balls until instructed.
5. Group the left-handed players together at the far end of the hitting line, facing the right-handed players.
6. Be certain that equipment is in top condition at all times, and tell students to notify the instructor if equipment needs repair.
7. Caution students never to swing toward one another, even without a ball.

Start students with a high iron (7, 8, or 9), so they will experience success quicker. Students need to understand that developing a golf swing takes a lot of practice and is not an easy skill to master. Make sure that students are not overloaded with information and that they receive ample practice time. Depending on the amount of equipment available, teachers may want to assign partner work and to use a swing rating form. This motivates students without clubs to be more involved cognitively and improves their observation skills.

Learning stations can be arranged in the gymnasium or in outdoor fields. An example of an indoor facility, including irons, woods, chipping, pitching, and putting, is shown in Figure 19.54.

Figure 19.54.   Indoor facility for golf

An outdoor area could be arranged in a similar manner (i.e., around a football or baseball field).

LEARNING ACTIVITIES

Modified Courses

Many teachers set up a short golf course in the field space they have available. Broomsticks, traffic cones, and hoops can serve as pins, tees, and holes. A power mower can be used to shape the fairways and greens. If it is impossible to dig holes, students can "hole out" when the ball strikes the target or when they are within a club's length of the target. Whiffleballs, plastic balls, or regular golf balls can be used, depending on what is available. All types of hazards can be set up using tires, hurdles, jump ropes, and cones. Specific course etiquette and rules can be taught with a modified course.

Putting

Miniature putting courses can be set up on smooth grass surfaces, carpeted areas, old carpet pieces, blankets, towels, mats, canvas, and even smooth floors if a whiffle ball is used. Paper cups, pieces of colored paper, shoe boxes, bleach containers, cans, and jars are possibilities for holes.

Partner Golf

Playing on a regular course or on a putting course, partners alternate hitting or putting toward the pin. If the class size is large, use groups of three or four.

Target Golf

Establish a number of concentric circles and point values around a target. Rope, jump ropes, or lime can be used to mark the circles. The distance and size of the circles can vary according to the club used. This activity can be done with individuals or teams.

RAINY DAY ACTIVITIES

Rainy days are a good time to have a "spell down" with questions on rules, fundamentals, etiquette, and types of matches. Crossword puzzles and word searches are available in the suggested readings. Short putting courses can be set up in the indoor space available.

SKILL TESTS

Many of the drills and game situations already mentioned can be used for evaluation. Here are a few other possibilities:

1. Parachute—Count the number of 7, 8, or 9 iron shots that land on the parachute in 10 trials.
2. Putting—Play 9 holes on a practice green and keep score. Ideally, each student would score 2 per hole to par the course.
3. Chipping—Count the number of balls that end up inside the 4-ft radius circle.
4. Pitching—Pitch 10 balls at each station (10, 20, and 40 yd), and count the number of balls that land inside the target area.
5. Bunker Shot—Arrange a string in a circle with a 10-ft radius around one hole, and count the number of bunker shots that finish inside the circle after 10 trials.

A rating scale can be used as part of an evaluation scheme or as a part of the learning activities done with partners (Figure 19.55).

Suggested Readings

AAHPERD. *Ideas for Golf Instruction—A Planning Guide for Schools*. Reston, VA: AAHPERD, 1966.

Jones, E. *Swing the Clubhead*. New York: Arno Press, 1952.

Jones, E., and Brown, I. *Swinging into Golf*. New York: McGraw-Hill Book Co., 1937.

Kennington, D. *The Sourcebook of Golf*. Phoenix, AZ: Oryx Press, 1981.

National Association for Girls and Women in Sport. *Bowling-Golf*. Reston, VA: AAHPERD, 1979–1981.

Seidel, B. L., et al. *Sports Skills: A Conceptual Approach to Meaningful Movement*. 2nd ed. Dubuque, IA: Wm. C. Brown Group, 1980.

GYMNASTICS

Gymnastics refers to the performance of a routine on a piece of heavy apparatus or on a large mat. The routines are evaluated by a panel of judges on a ten-point scale. The gymnastics events for men include: Parallel bars, horizontal bar, long horse vaulting, still rings, pommel horse, and floor exercise. Women's events include the uneven parallel bars, balance beam, side horse vaulting, and floor exercise. In many major gymnastics competitions,

---

GOLF RATING SCALE

1. Grip (4 points—1 each)

   _____ Right-hand V is straight up or slightly right

   _____ Two knuckles of left hand showing

   _____ Grip tension is correct

   _____ Hands completely on grip of club

2. Stance (4 points—$\frac{1}{2}$ each)

   _____ Feet proper width apart

   _____ Standing proper distance from ball

   _____ Weight even over feet (ask)

   _____ Knees bent properly

   _____ Proper bend from waist

   _____ Arms hanging naturally

   _____ No unnecessary tension in arms and hands

   _____ No unnecessary tension in legs

3. Alignment (3 points—1 each)

   _____ Not left of target

   _____ Not right of target

   _____ Proper sequence of address. (Draw imaginary line and pick a spot on the line. Set club square, feet together. Place right foot first on parallel line. Take last look at target.)

4. Swing (10 points—1 each)

   _____ One piece take away

   _____ Head did not move up and down

   _____ Head did not move back and forth

   _____ Left arm extended

   _____ A complete coil is present

   _____ Club toe up to target—backswing— at parallel level

   _____ Club toe up to target—forward swing—at parallel level

   _____ Club accelerates through ball

   _____ Club continues after contact

   _____ Facing target at the finish

Points	Performance
10	Good contact, good trajectory, good direction
9	Good contact, good trajectory, fair direction
8	Good contact, fair trajectory, fair direction
6	Fair contact, fair trajectory, fair direction
4	2 items fair, 1 item barely acceptable
2	1 item fair, 2 items barely acceptable
0	Miss or near miss

Figure 19.55.   Golf rating scale

the participants must perform a compulsory or set routine and an optional or original routine.

Varying forms of gymnastics were the most common activity in early physical education programs. These different forms of gymnastics were brought to the U.S. primarily from Germany and Sweden. Gymnastics became popular through clubs formed in the communities, YMCAs, and the public schools. Private gymnastics clubs and sport schools are still popular, and gymnastics is still taught in most

secondary schools and colleges in the United States. Many adults continue to enjoy gymnastics as a lifetime recreational activity. In some geographic areas, competition is available through the private clubs for various age groups.

Instructional units in gymnastics and tumbling are an excellent way to achieve a balanced secondary physical education curriculum. Unfortunately, many school districts do not have the heavy apparatus. In these situations, an extensive unit on tumbling should be incorporated in the program. Gymnastics activities offer students an interesting variety of challenges and should be available for students to explore and experience.

SEQUENCE OF SKILLS

Each gymnastics event is a highly specialized area that incorporates many specific skills and techniques. A sequence of skills should be taught on each piece of apparatus and for floor exercise. In a coeducational class, eight pieces of apparatus and two different floor exercise routines can be offered if the equipment is available. Comprehensive texts with in-depth information on the sequence of skills for each event are listed in the suggested readings. Gymnastics teachers need to have an extensive background in the teaching strategies and safety procedures for all of the individual events. Teachers should analyze carefully the abilities and characteristics of their students, the time allotted to the gymnastics unit, and the pieces of equipment available for instruction. Safety is especially important because of the hazards posed by many of the gymnastics events.

IDEAS FOR INSTRUCTION

Each piece of apparatus and the floor exercise can be arranged as a specific learning area for students. After students are introduced to each area and given introductory tasks to perform, they can be distributed evenly throughout the area. This ensures that students will have maximum opportunity to attempt the various skills. Each student can be given a performance card to record the completion of tasks. The tasks can be written as performance objectives or as simple cues. These objectives (Figure 19.56) and the recording forms (Figure 19.57) will help motivate students to use class time in a productive manner.

A gymnastics meet with student judges is an enjoyable culminating activity. Teams can be organized, and students can select their favorite events. Students work with a partner or in groups of three for safety purposes. One person performs and the partner spots. Spotting must be explained carefully to students, and the importance of spotting must be continually reinforced.

Suggested Readings

Cooper, P., and Trnka, M. *Teaching Gymnastic Skills to Men and Women*. Minneapolis: Burgess Publishing Co., 1982.

Drury, B., and Schmid, A. B. *Gymnastics for Women*. Palo Alto, CA: National Press Books, 1972.

Mood, D., Musker, F., and Armbruster, D. *Sports and Recreational Activities for Men and Women*. 8th ed. St. Louis: C. V. Mosby Co., 1983.

Zakrajsek, D., and Carnes, L. *Learning Experiences: An Approach to Teaching Physical Activities*. Dubuque, IA: Wm. C. Brown Group, 1981.

JOGGING

Joggers and road races are probably the most visible form of the fitness renaissance. Millions take to the road regularly for fitness and sport reasons. Various types of distances for running events have become popular with all ages and with both sexes. Marathons, triathalons, 15-km, 10-km, 5-km, and 2-mi fun runs are being offered virtually every weekend for all ages. People in all areas of the country run in all kinds of weather. Secondary students in physical education programs should have positive experiences with running, because this is a potential lifetime activity that can contribute to fitness and be a form of play. Jogging is an easy, inexpensive activity that can be done individually or with a group.

SEQUENCE OF SKILLS

Jogging is simply slow running. It is different from walking in that both feet leave the ground during the flight or airborne phase. In walking, one foot is always in contact with the ground.

Running Form

Chapter 17 gives in-depth coverage to running form on pages 280–283. Teachers should spend time working on running form, emphasizing one aspect of form with each drill. Students can overlearn the position of the head, hands, arms, knees, feet, and body lean. In distance running, the stride is shorter than in sprinting, and the heel of the foot should strike the ground before the ball of the foot. Breathing should be natural, through both nose and mouth.

Designing a Program

Students need to understand how to design a jogging program to meet their individual objectives. Programs will differ according to those objectives. Some students want to lose weight,

**BEGINNING GYMNASTICS
PARALLEL BARS—PERFORMANCE OBJECTIVES**

1. Stand at the end of the bars and grasp both bars with hands on top of the bars. Jump up so that your arms are now straight. Walk down the bars, moving one hand at a time (hand-walking).

2. From a standing position at the end of the bars with both hands on top of the bars, jump up until your arms are straight. Now hop down the bars by moving both hands at the same time (hopping travel).

3. Jump to a *cross-arm support* (both arms straight with your body between the bars) and swing your legs forward, straddling the bars with legs on top of the bars. Now lean forward and place your hands in front of your legs. Swing your legs down off the bars and then up in front again. Repeat this sequence to traverse the length of the bar (traveling).

4. Jump to a cross-arm support (both arms straight) and swing your legs forward and backward, showing control and trying to swing your legs high both ways (leg swings).

5. Place your upper arms (by your shoulders) on top of the bars and swing your legs forward and backward. Hold on to the bars with your hands for balance (upper-arm support swings).

6. Jump to a cross-arm support (both arms straight) and bend your arms as far as you can while you lower your body down between the bars. Now straighten your arms and lift yourself back up to where you started. Try this at least three times in a row (still dips).

7. Place the hands in a *reverse grip* on both bars. Lean back and lift your legs and hips up and over your head until your feet almost touch the floor, then return to the position from which you started (skin-the-cat, both bars).

8. From a cross-arm support (both arms straight), lean on one arm, then bring the other hand to the other bar. (You should now be in a front support on one bar.) Finish the turn by leaning to one side and placing your hand on the other bar in a straight-arm cross-arm support. You are now facing the opposite direction from the way you started (half turn).

9. Stand outside the bars facing one bar. Grasp the bar with both hands in a regular grip. Bring your legs up and between your hands until they almost touch the floor under you, then go back to the way you started (skin-the-cat, one bar).

10. Jump up to a cross-arm support (both arms straight). Lift your legs up in front until they are at the same height as the bars and try to hold that position, like an "L," for a few seconds (L-seat).

11. From a cross-arm support (both arms straight), swing both legs backward and over one bar so you have your stomach facing the bar as you go over. Land on the outside of the bars with one arm holding on for balance (front vault dismount).

12. From a cross-arm support (both arms straight), swing both legs forward and lift your body over one bar with your seat facing the bar. Land on the outside of the bar, facing sideways to the bar, with one hand holding on for balance (rear vault dismount).

13. From a standing position between the bars and facing one end, grasp the bars with a reverse grip. Lean back and lift both legs up and over your head like the beginning of a backward roll. Straddle your legs at the top and put them on top of the bars so you end up in a straddle seat (backward roll mount to a straddle seat).

14. Jump to a cross-arm support (both arms straight). Lean forward as if you were starting a forward roll. Stick your elbows out to the sides to stay on top of the bars as you roll. Continue rolling forward as your legs go up and over your head (forward roll).

15. Jump to a cross-arm support (both arms straight). Lean forward and stick both elbows out to the sides so the top part of your arms rests on top of the bars. Extend your legs straight up over your head so you are upside down. Hold your hands on the bars for balance. For safety, come down the same way you went up (shoulder stand).

Figure 19.56. Performance objectives for the parallel bars

Name	Core Objectives										Optional Objectives				
	1	2	3	4	5	6	7	8	9	10	1	2	3	4	5
Parallel bars															
Rings															
Floor exercise															
Long horse															
Horizontal bar															
Pommel horse															
Uneven bars															
Balance beam															
Side horse															

Figure 19.57. Performance objective monitoring form

others may want to condition themselves for skiing, and others will want to improve their time in 10-km races. Program goals may vary, but students should all understand how the principles of frequency, intensity, and duration apply to a running program. Proper warm-up, cool down, and stretching and strengthening activities must be taught. These are covered in Chapter 17, pages 260–261.

Equipment

Runners must obtain adequate running shoes. Many are available at prices ranging from $20 to over $100. They should have a well-cushioned, elevated heel and a durable bottom surface. The toes should not rub the front of the shoe, and the tongue and lining should be padded. The sole must be flexible, with two layers for absorbing shock. An arch support should be built into running shoes.

The remaining equipment (shorts, socks, sweat suits, rain suits, jackets, hats, mittens, and so forth) is a matter of personal preference depending on the weather. Comfort is the key, with loose-fitting, nonirritating material. Extremely cold and warm weather can be dangerous. Students should understand how to prevent problems by dressing properly and avoiding certain weather conditions.

IDEAS FOR EFFECTIVE INSTRUCTION

Beginners should understand that jogging is an individual activity that can be noncompetitive. If students choose to be competitive runners, that is fine and is a personal choice. Teachers should reinforce this attitude by reducing the emphasis on running races in a jogging unit. The unit emphasis can be on personal improvement and accomplishing individual goals.

Jog-Walk-Jog

Beginners can be given a distance to cover by alternating jogging and walking. They progress by gradually reducing the walking and increasing the jogging. Various students can be assigned different distances, depending on their ability. This technique can be used for jogging on a track. Students can jog the straightaways and walk the curves for 1 mi.

Timed Runs

Students can be given a set time of a certain number of minutes. They then try to jog continuously for the designated time. (Teachers blow a whistle every minute or half minute.)

Form Running, File Running, Walk-Sprint-Jog, Pace Work, Random Running, and Fartlek

Refer to Chapter 17 for descriptions of these activities. All can be modified for a jogging unit.

Group Runs

Divide students into small groups of similar ability. The group can run together for a certain time or distance. They should be encouraged to use the "talk test" during the run. This refers to the ability to comfortably carry on a conversation during a run as an indicator of proper jogging intensity.

Training Heart Rate Runs

After students have learned about training heart rates (see Chapter 17, pages 260–261), they can check their heart rates at rest before running, after running so many minutes, and again immediately after finishing a run. This will help them to understand the concepts of training heart rate, recovery heart rate, and jogging at sufficient intensity.

Orienteering Runs

A jogging unit can include several orienteering meets, which emphasize running from point to point on the school grounds. Draw a map of the school grounds with ten checkpoints that must be found by the students. Each checkpoint has a secret clue, such as a letter, word, color, or baseball team. Students can work alone or with a partner. (See the next section on orienteering.)

Cross Country Runs

Map out a cross country course around the school grounds and in neighboring areas, and hold a meet with a chute for finishers and numbers distributed for the finishing positions. Teams can be arranged and categories established for beginners, intermediates, and advanced runners. Set time limits, and students can run time trials to determine their category or team. Students can choose to be on a team or to run for individual improvement.

Exercise Trails

Set up an exercise trail around the school grounds with several stations for stretching and strengthening various muscle groups. Use a boundary cone with a sign to mark each station, and give students a rough map showing where each station is located. After completing a station activity, students should jog to the next station. The stations can be set up so the students get a total body workout. After a certain period of time, the trail can be modified.

Running With Equipment

Some students with special interests may want to run with a piece of equipment (e.g., dribbling a soccer ball or a basketball). Others may want to carry a football or roll a Hula-Hoop. Let students be creative, as long as they are engaged in a safe activity. Running with equipment adds variety to activities and is a good motivational device.

Mileage Cards and Maps

Many people enjoy keeping a record of the distances covered. Goals can be established for a given time period. Students can jog across the state by coloring in a route or moving a pin to a given point as they accumulate miles. Mileage cards or charts (Figure 19.58) can be kept individually, or they can be posted in the locker room or on a bulletin board. Individual or group competitions can be set up based on number of miles accumulated.

Rating Forms

A rating form (Figure 19.59) can be developed for both student and teacher use. Students should learn how to use the form and check each other. Both the runner and the rater must understand the form.

RAINY DAY ACTIVITIES

Many of these activities (e.g., rating forms, pace work, timed runs) can be modified for running in the gymnasium. If the gym is also not available, there are many interesting running topics that teachers can discuss with students. These include training methods, safety, injuries, equipment, health benefits, exercise and calories, marathons, Cooper's program, and the female runner. The suggested readings are filled with discussion topics.

Suggested Readings

Fixx, J. *The Complete Book of Running.* New York: Random House, 1977.

McKemy Jogging Club

1	2	3	4	5	6	7	8	9	10	11	12	13	14	15
16	17	18	19	20	21	22	23	24	25	26	27	28	29	30
31	32	33	34	35	36	37	38	39	40	41	42	43	44	45
46	47	48	49	50	51	52	53	54	55	56	57	58	59	60
61	62	63	64	65	66	67	68	69	70	71	72	73	74	75
76	77	78	79	80	81	82	83	84	85	86	87	88	89	90
91	92	93	94	95	96	97	98	99	100	101	102	103	104	105
106	107	108	109	110	111	112	113	114	115	116	117	118	119	120
121	122	123	124	125	126	127	128	129	130	131	132	133	134	135
136	137	138	139	140	141	142	143	144	145	146	147	148	149	150
151	152	153	154	155	156	157	158	159	160	161	162	163	164	165
166	167	168	169	170	171	172	173	174	175	176	177	178	179	180
181	182	183	184	185	186	187	188	189	190	191	192	193	194	195
196	197	198	199	200	201	202	203	204	205	206	207	208	209	210
211	212	213	214	215	216	217	218	219	220	221	222	223	224	225
226	227	228	229	230	231	232	233	234	235	236	237	238	239	240
241	242	243	244	245	246	247	248	249	250	251	252	253	254	255
256	257	258	259	260	261	262	263	264	265	266	267	268	269	270
271	272	273	274	275	276	277	278	279	280	281	282	283	284	285
286	287	288	289	290	291	292	293	294	295	296	297	298	299	300
301	302	303	304	305	306	307	308	309	310	311	312	313	314	315
316	317	318	319	320	321	322	323	324	325	326	327	328	329	330

500-Mile Jogging Club

NAME: _____ DATE: _____

When finished with the month, please bring this card to the Intramural Office in the PE West Gym to record your miles.

Mon	Tues	Wed	Thurs	Fri	Sat	Sun	Total

Only distances of ½ mi or more will be recorded.

Previous Total _____

Monthly Total _____

Total to Date _____

** Mileage will be kept on record for one year. **

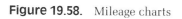

Figure 19.58. Mileage charts

Running Evaluation				
	Always	Some	Never	Comment
Head still				
Eyes ahead				
Hands relaxed				
Elbows at 90 degrees				
Arms moving straight forward and back				
Hand comes back to front pocket				
Arms gently brush sides				
Feet straight ahead				
Knee drive straight ahead				
Knee action not too high				
Feet, knee, and hip in line				
Body lean slight—5 degrees from feet				
Foot strike on heel				
Stride short for distance				

Figure 19.59.   Running rating form

Henderson, J. *Jog, Run, Race.* Mountain View, CA: World
   Publications, 1977.
Runner's World Magazine. Box 366, Mountain View, CA
   94042.

ORIENTEERING

Orienteering is a challenging outdoor adventure activity that combines cross country running and the ability to read a map and use a compass. It has been called the thinking sport, because rapid decisions need to be made in determining which route to follow so that a minimum of time and energy is used. Ideally, the orienteering competition should take place in a wilderness area that is not familiar to the participants. Orienteering events can be set up for beginners, novices, and experts, thus enabling people of all ages and abilities to take part and find success in these activities. The need for both physical and mental skills can result in an enjoyable experience for all students and members of a family.

Orienteering activities can be easily modified and adapted to secondary physical education programs. Many activities can be completed in a classroom or gymnasium or on the school grounds.[1] Teachers can use compasses and homemade maps of the school grounds to develop a challenging unit. A nearby park or a vacant lot can add great variety to orienteering courses.

SEQUENCE OF SKILLS

The basic skills involved in orienteering include reading a topography map, using a compass, and pacing various distances. Since many students have had little experience with these skills, it is important to introduce new information and terminology slowly. Students can perform many of the activities with a partner, so there will be two heads

---

1. Special thanks to John W. Horstman, Meadow Lake School, Robbinsdale Area Schools, Robbinsdale, Minnesota, for many of the orienteering activities.

working together on a problem. Teachers can include a variety of maps, a compass, and new pacing activities each day to keep the students challenged. Many activity types and "hands on" experiences should be incorporated in the unit. Competitive events can be added after students begin to understand the basic map and compass skills. The block plan at the end of this unit will provide some ideas for the sequencing of learning activities.

LEARNING ACTIVITIES

Compass Activities

Parts of the Compass. Make the students aware of the basic parts of the compass and how the instrument works (Figure 19.60).

Compass Bearings and Directions. Have the students complete the directions and degrees in Figure 19.61.

Following a Bearing. Discuss how to hold the compass properly. Give students a bearing to find and follow. Have them stand in one line facing the instructor. Call out a bearing and have them rotate their bodies in place until they are facing the bearing direction.

Landmarks. The teacher calls out various visible landmarks, and students shoot a bearing from where they are standing to the landmark.

Forming a Triangle. Place a penny or other small object on the ground. Set any bearing less

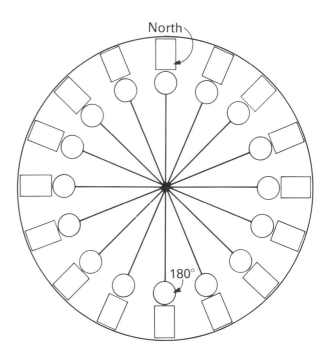

Figure 19.61. Compass bearings and directions

than 90 degrees. Walk ten places on that bearing. Add 120 degrees and walk another ten paces. Repeat the procedure again and end up where you started. This drill can be repeated with another bearing and a different number of paces.

Forming a Square. This is basically the same as no. 5, except that 90-degree bearings are added each time, and four sides are formed. The distance must be the same each time.

Figure 19.60. Parts of a compass (reprinted from *Outdoor Adventure Activities for School and Recreation Programs* by P. W. Darst and G. P. Armstrong, 1980. Minneapolis, MN: Burgess Publishing Co., p. 159)

Table 19.1. Forming a Christmas Tree

Bearing	Distance (cm)	Bearing	Distance (cm)
1. 269	2.2		
2. 2	2.7	9. 136	6.3
3. 266	4.9	10. 293	1.9
4. 30	6.5	11. 141	5.2
5. 246	2.6	12. 284	2.4
6. 34	5.0	13. 125	5.2
7. 244	2.0	14. 271	5.1
8. 37	4.6	15. 179	2.7

Numbers and Numerals.   Tape the numbers 1–10 on the floor in scattered positions around the gymnasium (Figure 19.62). Next, tape the Roman numerals I–X in scattered positions on the gymnasium walls. The students begin by standing on any of the numbers on the floor and shooting a bearing to the corresponding numeral on the wall. This drill can be made competitive by trying for the fastest time and correct bearing.

Forming a Christmas Tree.   On a piece of graph paper, have students place a dot in the southeast quadrant of the paper. From this starting dot, have them draw a line the following distances and on the appropriate bearing (Table 19.1).

Map Bearings.   Students learn to determine the bearing between points on a map. The teacher puts several points on a map and then tells the students to find the bearing and distance between the points. Ten numbered points might be shown, and students can find the bearing and distance from 1 to 2, from 2 to 3, and so forth. Advanced orienteering can include a discussion of magnetic declination and the addition or subtraction of declination.

Destination Unknown (Figure 19.63).   Divide the class into four teams. Each team follows the given bearings and paces. All teams should end up at the same destination.

Schoolyard Compass Game and Competitive Compass Game.   These are two challenging compass games that are available from The Silva Company.[2] The games are inexpensive and can be set up easily in a school situation.

Map Activities

Mapping the School.   Students draw up rough maps of the school grounds with all of the various buildings, fields, and identification points. These maps can later be used in orienteering competitions.

Map Squares.   Cut up several topography maps of the local area into small squares. Students try to locate the cut squares on an uncut map. Have the students identify points of interest, symbols, distances, contour lines, vegetation, roads, water, and so forth.

---

2. The Silva Company, 2466 State Road 39 North, LaPorte, IN 46350.

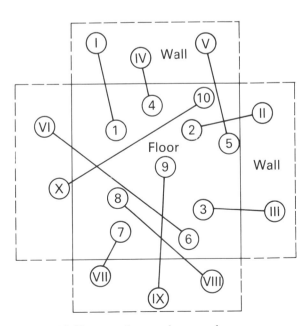

Figure 19.62.   Numbers and numerals

Figure 19.63.   Destination unknown

Map Symbol Relay.   Draw a map symbol on one side of an index card and write the name of a different symbol on the back of the card. A duplicate set of cards is necessary for each team in the relay (i.e., four teams means four sets of cards). The game begins with the cards on one side of the gym and the teams on the opposite side. The teacher calls out the first symbol, such as a school. The first member of the team runs to the cards, finds the symbol, and then runs back to the team. The name of the next symbol to be found is on the back of the card with the school symbol. The game continues until all of the cards are played. Students waiting in line can be reviewing symbols. Students who select the wrong symbol must run back and find the correct symbol.

Taking a Trip.   Label 10 to 15 points on several topography maps, and have students calculate the actual distance between a certain number of points. They can figure in map distance and in actual mileage. Next, have the students estimate how many days would be necessary to complete the trip. They should be able to describe what the terrain is like and where the water stops are located.

Contour Identification. Have students identify various mountainous and hilly areas from the way those areas look on a contour map. Figure 19.64 is an example of contour problems.

Map Problems. Map activities, such as Figure 19.65, can be made up for a local situation.

Dot-to-Dot Hike. Students start at the X in the northwest corner (Figure 19.66) and draw in the figure by following the directions. Students can develop their own dot-to-dot hike making other figures.

Direction Walk. Students follow the directions on a piece of graph paper (Figure 19.67).

Pacing Activities

Distance by Pace. Orienteerers must be able to judge distance by their pace. One pace equals two steps. A good drill for determining the length of pace is to set up a course that is 100 ft long. Students walk, jog, or run the course, and count the number of times that the right foot hits the ground. The length of the course (100 ft) is then divided by the number of paces in order to determine length of pace. Pace is usually rounded off to the nearest 6 in. Pace will vary with walking, jogging, and running.

Distance by Time. One-mile courses can be set up in a variety of terrain conditions, such as open road, open field, open woods, vegetated areas, dense woods, and mountainous areas. Students cover these areas by walking or jogging and record their times. The ability to cover a given distance at a consistent pace can be used later for competitive meets.

COMPETITIVE ORIENTEERING EVENTS

After students have received instruction in the use of the compass, maps, and pacing, competitive events can be introduced. Students should understand that they can compete against the environment, themselves, their peers, and elapsed time. It is not necessary to win the event to be successful.

Cross Country or Point-to-Point Orienteering

Ten checkpoints are set up over the entire school grounds or park area. Teachers develop a map of the area to be covered, and duplicate maps are made up for all participants. Each participant uses a map and compass to find the checkpoints as quickly as possible. The compass is not necessary if instruments are not available. Decisions about the best route must be made quickly as participants begin. Several master maps should be set out with the locations of the checkpoints. Participants copy the checkpoints from the master map onto their own map. The time spent in copying down the checkpoints can be included in the overall accumulated time.

Each checkpoint should have a secret letter, word, or name that students must record on some type of card to show that they actually visited the checkpoint. In regulation meets, a coded punch with a number or letter is used at each control site. These punches are available from The Silva Company, but they are not a necessity. Checkpoints can be a boundary cone, an index card, an envelope, or something similar.

Score Orienteering

In score orienteering, each checkpoint has a designated point value. The checkpoints that are hardest to find and farthest away from the starting point

---

Contour Identification Problem. Have the students compare some actual terrain contours with the map representations. Training models are available from Silva, and the teacher can develop a number of contour representations for learning activities. The following are a few examples:

Figure 19.64. Contour problems

Figure 19.65. Map problems (reprinted from *Outdoor Adventure Activities for School and Recreation Programs* by P. W. Darst and G. P. Armstrong, 1980. Minneapolis: Burgess Publishing Co., pp. 294–295)

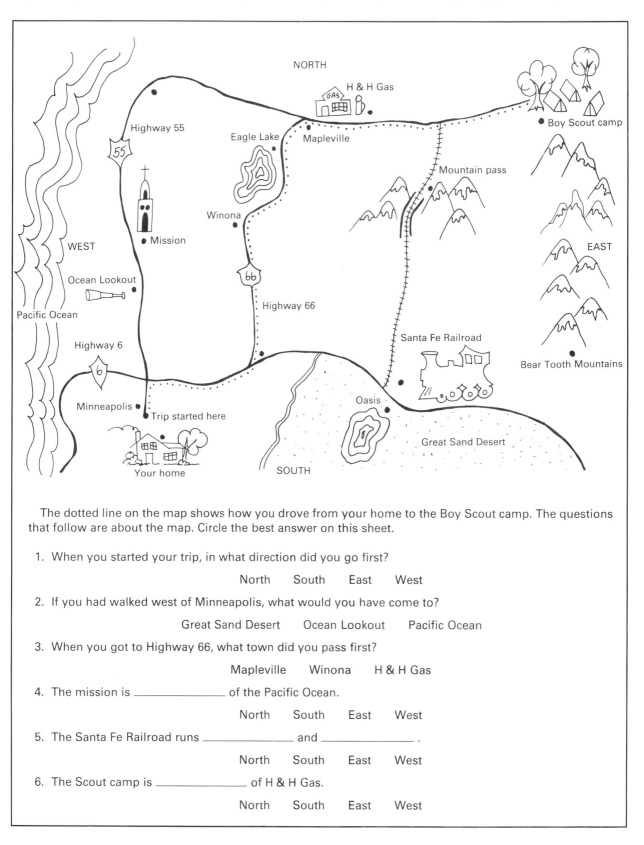

The dotted line on the map shows how you drove from your home to the Boy Scout camp. The questions that follow are about the map. Circle the best answer on this sheet.

1. When you started your trip, in what direction did you go first?

                         North   South   East   West

2. If you had walked west of Minneapolis, what would you have come to?

               Great Sand Desert   Ocean Lookout   Pacific Ocean

3. When you got to Highway 66, what town did you pass first?

                   Mapleville   Winona   H & H Gas

4. The mission is _____ of the Pacific Ocean.

                         North   South   East   West

5. The Santa Fe Railroad runs _____ and _____ .

                         North   South   East   West

6. The Scout camp is _____ of H & H Gas.

                         North   South   East   West

7. The oasis is _____ of Highway 6

           North   South   East   West

8. From the ocean lookout, what direction is the Bear Tooth mountain range?

           North   South   East   West

9. The first town west of the Scout camp is:

           Winona   H & H Gas   Mapleville

10. In the winter the birds fly _____ .

           North   South   East   West

Dot-to-Dot Hike—Follow the directions from the starting point and draw in the figure.

Figure 19.66. Dot-to-dot hike

are assigned the highest point totals. The object of the event is to accumulate the most points within a set time. Students are given a map of the area on which they copy the locations of the checkpoints from a master map. Students must visit as many sites as possible within the time limit and then return to the starting point. If they are late, they can be disqualified or assessed a penalty. Students use some type of standard card to record the clue at each checkpoint that they visit.

Descriptive Orienteering

This type of event requires a compass and pacing skills, instead of a map. Students attempt to find the checkpoints as quickly as possible by following a bearing (90 degrees), a distance (50 yd), and a descriptive clue (small tree). The descriptive clue can be eliminated with more advanced participants. Students start at a designated master point and return to that point each time before starting toward the next point. In this way, teachers at the master point can monitor student progress throughout the meet. The checkpoints can all have letters, words, or team names. Each student is given a sheet similar to the one shown in Figure 19.68. A more challenging variation is to give students only the bearing and distance to one checkpoint. When they find that checkpoint, they will find the

Direction Walk—From the starting point marked X, follow the given distances in the appropriate direction. Use a pencil to trace your route. What is it?

1W, 1NW, 1E, 1S, 1W, 4S, 2SW, 1S, 1SW, 2S, 2W, 1NE, 4N, 1SW, 4W, 1NW, 1SW, 1S, 1SW, 2S, 2W, 1NE, 4N, 5NW, 2N, 1E, 2NE, 1E, 2N, 4SE, 8E, 2SE

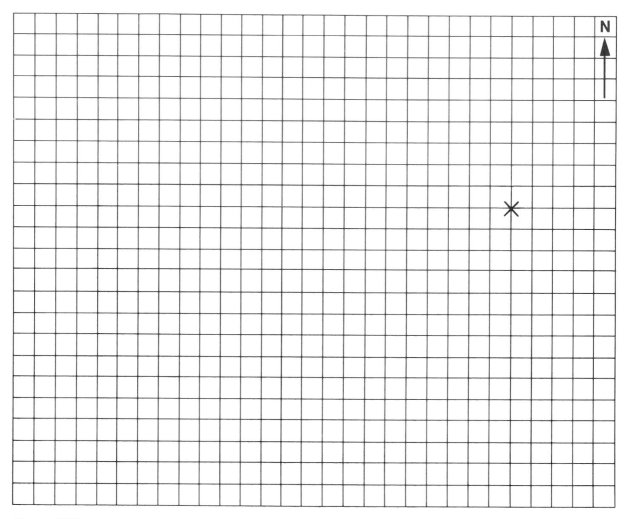

Figure 19.67. Direction walk

bearing and distance posted for the next checkpoint. Students must find each checkpoint to get directions to the next point. Students can be started at different checkpoints.

BLOCK PLAN

Figure 19.69 is a sample block plan that offers a suggested 15-day unit for orienteering. The activities recommended in the block plan are available in this section or in Darst and Armstrong (1980).

SUGGESTED PERFORMANCE OBJECTIVES

These objectives could be used in a junior high school unit on orienteering.

1. Identify the compass points.
2. Name the parts of a compass.
3. Find a compass bearing on a map.
4. Follow a compass bearing on the ground.
5. Shoot bearings on key points.
6. Identify map symbols.
7. Identify map distances.

ORIENTEERING 1

In the Answers column, fill in the key word or letter that you find at each checkpoint.

Checkpoint	Bearing	Description	Distance	Answers
1	90°	Backstop	50 yd	
2	180°	Goal post	100 m	
3	230°	Cottonwood	200 ft	
4	160°	Irrigation	35 yd	
5	341°	Hoop	75 m	
6	45°	Palo verde	400 ft	
7	106°	Trash barrel	150 yd	
8	270°	Power pole	250 ft	
9	78°	Fence post	350 yd	
10	200°	Jumping pit	40 m	

Figure 19.68. Descriptive orienteering sheet

8. Determine pace for 100 yd.
9. Form a triangle using 3 bearings.
10. Form a square using 4 bearings.
11. Complete an orienteering course in a time designated by the teacher.
     Standard no. 1 = 5 points
     Standard no. 2 = 3 points
     Standard no. 3 = 1 point
12. Take a ten-question exam on orienteering.
     Score: 100% = 5 points
              90% = 4 points
              80% = 3 points
              70% = 2 points
              60% = 1 point

Suggested Readings

Darst, P., and Armstrong, G. *Outdoor Adventure Activities for School and Recreation Programs*. Minneapolis: Burgess Publishing Co., 1980.

Disley, J. *Orienteering*. Harrisburg, PA: Stackpole Books, 1967.

Gilchrist, J. *Teaching Orienteering*. Willowdale, ON: Canadian Orienteering Service, 1973.

Kjellstrom, B. *Be Expert With Map and Compass*. New York: Charles Scribner's Sons, 1975.

RACQUETBALL

The game of racquetball is a direct descendant from the game of paddleball, which was first played in the 1920s. In the 1940s, a racquet with strings was introduced and became known as "paddle rackets." This sport grew in popularity, and in 1969 the International Racquetball Association was established, and "racquetball" was born. Within the last ten years, the game has grown tremendously in popularity. This growth has brought about a comparable increase in the number of facilities, changes in racquet style, and a livelier ball. A Neilson Company survey found that racquetball was the fastest growing participation sport from 1976 to 1979.

Racquetball can be played on a one-, three-, or four-walled court. The most popular is the enclosed four-wall court with a ceiling, but the other types of courts are more common at the junior and senior high school levels. The game can be played with two people (singles), three people (cutthroat), or four people (doubles). The object is to win each rally by serving or returning the ball so the opponent is unable to keep the ball in play. A rally is over when a side makes an error or is unable to return the ball to the front wall before it touches the floor twice. Note that one can score only when one is serving.

SEQUENCE OF SKILLS

Grip, Eastern Style

Forehand (Figure 19.70). Form a V on the top bevel of the handle with the thumb and index finger. The thumb should rest on the knuckle of the

1.
Introduction
What is orienteering?
Brief history
Directions and degrees
Dot-to-dot problems
Compass rose activity

2.
Review
Directions and degrees
Teach
Maps, symbols, scales, contours
Activities
Map the School
Map Squares
Contour Identification

3.
Review
Maps, symbols, etc.
Teach
Parts of compass
How to hold
Activities
Taking a bearing
Dial a bearing
Magnetic influence

4.
Review
Compass and bearings
Teach
Landmark bearings
Map bearings
Activities
Boy Scout map problem
Sea adventure
Christmas Tree

5.
Review
Map bearings
Map symbols
Teach
Pacing
Activities
Distance by pace
Triangle game
Square game
Map symbol relay

6.
Review
Pacing
Teach
Orienteering
Point-to-point
Score
Descriptive
Relay
Activities
Taking a Trip
Numbers and Numerals
Destination Unknown

7.
Review
Orienteering
Activity
Descriptive meet—
Have students return to master table each time for the next bearing, cue, and distance.

8.
Teach
Magnetic declination
Activities
Declination problems
Meridian map and compass fun
Point-to-point activity
Schoolyard compass game

9.
Review
Pacing
Bearings
Orienteering
Activity
Point-to-point meet

10.
Review
Declination
Activities
Descriptive meet (short)
Cues picked up at the next control
Competitive compass game, or pacing by time and distance

11.
Review
Materials for written exam
Activities
Score orienteering meet (20 min)
Landmark bearings for skill test

12.
Activities
Relay orienteering meet
Schoolyard compass game and competitive compass game for skill test

13.
Written examination

Pacing—distance by time

14.
Final score orienteering exam meet

(Off-campus if possible)

15.
Final point-to-point orienteering meet

(Off-campus if possible)

Figure 19.69. Orienteering block plan

Figure 19.70. Forehand grip

middle finger on the left side bevel of the handle. The palm of the hand should be approximately level with the bottom of the racquet. The index finger should be in a pistol grip position.

Backhand (Figure 19.71). Rotate one-quarter turn to the left (counterclockwise). The **V** is now on the upper part of the left bevel.

Ready Position

The feet should be shoulder width apart and the knees slightly flexed. The back is bent slightly forward, and the head is up. The weight is on the balls of the feet. The racquet should be in front of the body at about chest height. Stand in the middle of the court, approximately 4 ft behind the short line.

Forehand (Figure 19.72)

From the ready position, pivot until facing the right sidewall with the left shoulder forward. The

Figure 19.71. Backhand grip

Figure 19.72. Forehand

wrist should come back beside the right ear, and the racquet should be pointing toward the ceiling. The weight is on the back foot. Start the forward swing with the racquet, and shift the weight from the back to the front foot. Rotate the shoulders and hips toward the front wall. Contact with the ball should be in line with the instep of the front foot. Keep the eyes on the ball and follow through across the body.

Backhand (Figure 19.73)

Follow the same technique as the forehand, but contact the ball when it is about 6 in. from the lead foot.

Backwall Shot

Proper setup position is the key to any backwall shot. Watch the ball carefully and set up with the weight on the rear foot and the racquet by the ear. Step forward and stroke into the ball at the proper position, as stated in the previous discussion.

Serve

Drive. Hit this serve low and hard to the back corner where the back and sidewalls join. This usually goes to the receiver's backhand.

Crosscourt Z. This serve is hit so that the ball strikes the front wall 3 to 4 ft from the sidewall

Figure 19.73. Backhand

and then rebounds to the sidewall and bounces deep in the opposite corner. The speed and height of the serve can be varied to create different angles for the opponent.

Lob. The lob is a change-of-pace serve that hits high on the front wall and stays close to the sidewall. It should land deep in the back court and drop straight down.

Ceiling Shot

The ceiling shot is a defensive shot to move the opponent back and to open up the front center court. The shot can be hit with a forehand, backhand, or overhead stroke, depending on the position of the ball. If the ball is above the head, an overhead shot can be used. A forehand or backhand can otherwise be used. The overhead shot is similar to a tennis serve. The elbow leads the movement, and the arm stretches overhead to contact the ball with an extended arm. The object is to place the shot close to the front wall on the ceiling. It is usually hit to the opponent's backhand side, tightly against the sidewall.

Passing Shot

The passing shot is an offensive shot that is hit low and hard to either side of the opponent, just out of reach. The object is to keep the ball close to the sidewall and low enough so the ball does not come off the back wall to any degree. The shot is a wise choice when the opponent is out of center position to either side of the court.

Kill Shot

This offensive shot is hit low on the front wall and is impossible to return if hit accurately. It can be hit straight into the front wall or can be hit off the sidewall into the front wall.

IDEAS FOR EFFECTIVE INSTRUCTION

Racquets are made of wood, fiberglass, aluminum, and various other combinations such as graphite and fiberglass. They have different weights, shapes, strings, and grip sizes. Wood racquets are cheaper but heavier; fiberglass racquets are lighter but less durable. Aluminum is lightweight and durable, but is quite expensive. Grips are usually leather or rubber. Leather seems to provide a better grip, but is not as durable as the rubber. Grip size is the circumference of the handle in inches (i.e., 4⅛, 4⅝).

Racquet balls are quite lively and will break after some usage, so having extras is a good idea. Eye guards are available as a safety measure, and some players may want to wear a glove to provide a better grip.

It is usually best to have two students working in one court with one student on each side of the court. If more students must be placed on each court, then designate partners and have one hitting and one chasing balls or throwing setups. Have two hitters and two nonhitters per court. The nonhitter can perform a variety of functions such as analyzing strokes, checking safety, or using a rating scale. Keep the hitters close to the sidewalls to give everyone more room.

Skill work can be accomplished easily by practicing performance objectives in a contract. It is best to start with a bounce-and-hit method and progress to a setup throw off the wall. Either of these methods can be done alone or with a partner. Some students need to practice bouncing the ball and throwing the ball off the wall. Take time to show students how to perform these skills.

Stress safety on the court as being of utmost importance because of the confined area and the dangerous implements. Players should be encouraged to wear eye guards, and should be reminded never to turn around and expose the face to a person hitting from behind them. All players must tie the wrist strings snugly around the wrist to avoid losing control of the racquet and injuring others. Finally, players should be reminded that the rules of racquetball stress safety. Whenever there is any chance of endangering the opponent either by hitting with the racquet or by bodily contact, let the ball go and play the point over.

LEAD-UP GAMES AND LEARNING ACTIVITIES

Ceiling Games

This is a change-of-pace game that requires students to use the ceiling shot. After the serve, a certain number of shots must hit the ceiling before or after hitting the front wall. If the ball does not hit the ceiling, it is a point or side out. A useful variation is to change the required number of ceiling shots that a person must hit each time. For example, start with one and then increase the required number. Another modification is to require all ceiling shots after the serve.

Five Points and Out

This modified game allows five serves or less each time the serve changes hands. After five points are scored, the opponents change positions (server to receiver). The opponents change positions normally if a side out is forced before the five points are scored. This modification keeps opponents from dominating the scoring through an exceptionally strong serve.

Eight Ball Rally

After the serve, each person must hit the ball four times before a point can be scored. This forces a longer rally and encourages work on different shots.

Backhand Rally

After the serve, a player must hit a certain number of backhand shots before a point is scored or a side out is forced. Start with one required backhand and then increase the number gradually.

Accuracy Drills

A challenging activity is to mark off the courts with targets on the floor and walls. Jump ropes, boundary cones, boxes, and masking tape are useful for constructing targets. Challenge the entire class to make five lob serves, five forehands, five backhands, five Z serves, and five drive serves to the target areas. Kill shots off the back wall and sidewalls can be practiced to marked areas on the front wall. Announce the day's winner in each category. Vary the size of the targets and the designated skills each day.

Cutthroat and Doubles

Cutthroat is played with three people. The server plays the other two players. Doubles is two players versus two.

Rotation

This activity involves students playing a 5-min game. A whistle is then blown and students rotate to the court on the left if they are ahead and stay where they are if behind. The object of the game is to move up to the last court. Rotation is also enjoyable when playing doubles. Teammates move ahead a court if they are leading when the whistle blows.

SUGGESTED PERFORMANCE OBJECTIVES

These performance objectives can be used for skill work, as a motivational device, and as part of an evaluation scheme. Students can evaluate each other or evaluation can be a combination of peer and teacher observation. A checklist can be used daily or weekly, and students can be required to complete a certain number of checklists before entering the class tournament.

Beginning Skills

Forehand Drive

1. Standing 3 ft behind the short line and 3 ft from the sidewall, bounce the ball off the sidewall and execute a proper forehand drive, hitting the front wall below the 8-ft line, 4 consecutive times.
2. Standing 3 ft behind the receiving line and 3 ft from the sidewall, bounce the ball off the sidewall and execute a proper forehand drive, hitting the front wall below the 8-ft line, 4 consecutive times.
3. Standing 3 ft behind the service line and in the middle of the court, feed the ball to the front wall and then execute a proper forehand drive below the 8-ft line, 3 of 4 times.
4. Standing 3 ft behind the short line and in the middle of the court, feed the ball to the front wall and then execute a proper forehand drive below the 8-ft line, 3 of 4 times.

Backhand Drive

5. Repeat no. 1 using proper backhand drive.
6. Repeat no. 2 using proper backhand drive.
7. Repeat no. 3 using proper backhand drive.
8. Repeat no. 4 using proper backhand drive.

Backwall Shot

9. Standing approximately 10 ft from the back wall, bounce the ball off the floor and then off the back wall and execute a forehand backwall shot, hitting the front wall below the 8-ft line, 3 of 4 times.
10. Repeat no. 9 using the backhand backwall shot (1 point).
11. Standing approximately in the middle of the court, feed the ball to the front wall so it bounces off the floor and the back wall, and execute a forehand backwall shot, hitting the front wall below the 8-ft line, 3 of 4 times.
12. Repeat no. 11 using the backhand drive.

Serves

13. Hit 3 of 5 drive serves to the left court that land within 3 ft of the sidewall in the back court and are otherwise legal.
14. Hit 3 of 5 crosscourt serves to the left court that land within 3 ft of the sidewall and are otherwise legal.
15. Hit 3 of 5 lob serves to the left court that land within 3 ft of the sidewall, do not bounce out from the back more than 3 ft, and are otherwise legal.
16. Repeat no. 13 to the right court.
17. Repeat no. 14 to the right court.
18. Repeat no. 15 to the right court.

Ceiling Shot

19. Standing in back court, bounce the ball high enough to execute a proper overhand forehand ceiling shot so the ball hits ceiling, front wall, floor, and hits low off the back wall 3 of 4 times.
20. Repeat no. 19 using regular forehand stroke.

Pinch Shot

21. Standing at midcourt, bounce the ball and execute a proper forehand pinch shot so the ball hits the sidewall, front wall, bounces at least 2 times, and hits the other side wall 3 of 4 times.
22. Repeat no. 21 using backhand stroke.

Intermediate and Advanced Skills

23. Repeat no. 1 hitting front wall below the 3-ft line.
24. Repeat no. 2 hitting front wall below the 3-ft line.
25. Repeat no. 3 hitting front wall below the 3-ft line.
26. Repeat no. 4 hitting front wall below the 3-ft line.
27. Repeat no. 1 using proper backhand drive and hitting front wall below the 3-ft line.
28. Repeat no. 2 using proper backhand drive and hitting front wall below the 3-ft line.
29. Repeat no. 3 using proper backhand drive and hitting front wall below the 3-ft line.
30. Repeat no. 4 using proper backhand drive and hitting front wall below the 3-ft line.
31. Repeat no. 9 hitting front wall below the 3-ft line.
32. Repeat no. 9 using the backhand backwall shot and hitting front wall below the 3-ft line.
33. Repeat no. 11 hitting front wall below the 3-ft line.
34. Repeat no. 11 using the backhand drive and hitting front wall below the 3-ft line.
35. Repeat no. 19 using backhand stroke.
36. Repeat no. 20 using backhand stroke.
37. Repeat no. 21 with feed off the front wall.
38. Repeat no. 22 with feed off the front wall.
39. Repeat no. 1 hitting the front wall below the 1-ft line (kill shot), 3 of 4 times.
40. Repeat no. 3 hitting the front wall below the 1-ft line, 3 of 4 times.
41. Repeat no. 14 using the backhand in the right court, 3 of 4 times.
42. Repeat no. 15 using the backhand in the right court, 3 of 4 times.

BLOCK PLAN

Figure 19.74 is a sample block plan for racquetball.

RAINY DAY ACTIVITIES

1. Review rules and strategies for serving, court position, passing shots, singles play, cutthroat, and doubles play.
2. Have students critique several racquetball articles or a chapter from an activity book.
3. Develop a crossword puzzle or word searches on racquetball.

Introduction What is racquetball? Grips—ready position Forehand stroke Backhand stroke Contract procedures Practice bounce and hit Rule of the day	**Review** Grip, forehand, backhand Equipment **Teach** Serves—drive, Z, lob **Activities** Serves—practice Bounce and hit Rule of the day	**Review** Serves, rules **Teach** Backwall shots Hinders **Activities** Backwall practice Serve practice Rule of the day	**Review** Forehand, backhand **Teach** Court position Kill shots **Activities** Performance objectives or short game Rule of the day	**Review** Backwall shots **Teach** Ceiling shots Passing shots **Activities** Ceiling games One, two, or three shots

Review
 Problem rules
 Serve strategy
 Court coverage
 Activities
 Accuracy drills
   Drive serve
   Lob serve
   Backhand
 Backhand games
   One or two shots
	Teach
	 Cutthroat
	 Doubles
	 Activities
	 Performance objectives
	 Eight ball rally
	 Rotation work up
		Review
		 Problem areas
		 Activities
		 Performance objectives
		 Five and out
		 Ceiling games
			Review
			 Rules
			 Activities
			 Performance objectives
			 Regular game
			 Cutthroat or doubles
				Review
				 Kill shots
				 Activity
				 Rotation work up

Activities Performance objectives Backhand games Regular game Tournament	**Review** Rules, strategy Shots, serves **Activities** Performance objectives Tournament games	Written exam **Activities** Performance objectives Tournament games	**Activities** Performance objectives Tournament games Cutthroat or doubles	Final performance objectives work Review course objectives Final games Return exam

Figure 19.74.   Racquetball block plan

4. Assign a group of students to develop a cross-word puzzle or word search.
5. Work on serving against a wall indoors. Speed and distances can be modified according to the available space.
6. Have on hand a variety of racquets, balls, gloves, and eye guards, and discuss the advantages of each.
7. A variety of loop films is available on racquetball.
8. Devise and administer a test on terms and strategy.
9. Discuss caloric expenditure playing racquetball. Point out the health-related benefits of playing racquetball.

Suggested Readings

Brumfield, C., and Bairstow, J. *Off the Wall.* New York: The Dial Press, 1978.

Keeley, S. *The Complete Book of Racquetball.* Northfield, IL: DBI Books, 1976.

Leve, C. *Inside Racquetball.* Chicago: Henry Regnery Co., 1973.

Reznik, J. W., Matthews, D. O., and Peterson, J. *Racquetball for Men and Women.* Champaign, IL: Stipes Publishing Company, 1972.

Shay, A., and Leve, C. *Winning Racquetball.* Chicago: Henry Regnery Co., 1976.

Stafford, R. *Racquetball: The Sport for Everyone.* Memphis, TN: S. C. Toof, 1975.

Strandemo, S., and Bruns, B. *The Racquetball Book.* New York: Pocket Books, 1977.

RESISTANCE TRAINING

Various forms of resistance training have become extremely popular activities for general conditioning. Adults and students of all ages are lifting weights and working on resistance machines in schools, health clubs, YMCAs, and in their homes. Current research has made women aware of the misconceptions about and benefits of resistance training. Coaches and athletes involved in different sports are using extensive resistance training programs to improve performance. Resistance training is now well entrenched in the activity habits of society.

A properly developed resistance training program can produce positive changes in the body composition and in a person's performance. People engaged in resistance training look better, feel better, and perform daily activities better. All of these results have contributed to the popularity of the sport.

Many different types of resistance training equipment are available. Machines such as the Universal Gym, Nautilus equipment, the Orthotron, and the Cybex II are used commonly for training programs. Each machine offers a number of different advantages. Free weights, including different types of dumbbells and barbells, are still quite popular and are available in most weight rooms. Physical education programs need to analyze carefully such factors as cost, space, objectives, and usage before purchasing resistance training equipment.

SEQUENCE OF SKILLS

Principles, Terminology, and Safety

Beginning resistance trainers need to understand the basic principles of training relative to their specific objectives. Students must understand the definitions of strength, endurance, flexibility, warm-up, cool down, sets, repetitions, frequency, rest intervals, and the various types of lifts for specific muscle groups. The type and number of lifts are determined by a student's objectives. Proper form must be understood in order to gain maximum benefits and to complete the activities

safely. Spotting techniques are a necessity for certain lifts, especially with heavy weights. Safety in the weight lifting area must be stressed constantly. Chapter 17 gives general information on these aspects of resistance training (see pp. 258–260). Additional specific information is available in the suggested readings listed at the end of this unit.

Spotting

Spotters are people who stand by a lifter to provide help when necessary. Spotters are concerned about preventing a weight from falling or slipping if the lifter cannot control the weight. All students should understand the spotting procedures for a specific lift. They can check the equipment for proper alignment, tightened collars, and so forth, and they can be aware of the position of other students in the area. Specific attention should be paid to each lift, especially with heavier weights.

Breathing

Lifters should try to be consistent and natural in their breathing. Most experts agree that breathing should follow a pattern of exhaling during exertion and inhaling as the weight is returned to the starting position. With heavy weights, many lifters take a deep breath before the lift and hold the breath until the final exertion. The final exhalation helps complete the lift. Care is necessary, because holding the breath too long can make a person light-headed and may even cause one to pass out.

Grips

The three major grips are the overhand (Figure 19.75), underhand (Figure 19.76), and alternating

Figure 19.75. Overhand grip

Figure 19.76. Underhand grip

(Figure 19.77). These grips are used with different types of lifts (i.e., the overhand with the palms down is used for the bench press, the underhand with the palms up is used for curls, and the alternating with one palm up and the other down is used with the dead lift).

Body Position

With free weights, it is especially important to get the feet, arms, and body aligned properly for lifting and removing weights from power racks or squat stands. Carelessness in alignment can result in an unbalanced position, which can, in turn, result in dropping the weights or in poor lifting technique. Each lift requires a different position, depending on whether the bar is being lifted from the floor or from a rack. Spotters must understand the type of lift to be executed and their specific

responsibility. For example, with a back squat, these steps should be followed:

1. Check the collars to see that they are tightened.
2. Grip the bar and space the hands wider than the shoulders.
3. Align the middle of the back under the midpoint of the bar.
4. Use a pad or towel to cushion the bar against the back.
5. Bend the knees and align the body vertically under the bar.
6. Keep the head up and lift the weight straight up.
7. Move out from the rack and assume a comfortable foot position about shoulder width apart.
8. Perform the lift with a spotter on either side of the bar.

Upper Body Lifts

Bench Press (Figure 19.78). Use an overhand grip with hands slightly wider than the shoulders. Bring the bar down to the chest and press up over the shoulders. Exhale on the press upward.

Curl (Figure 19.79). Use an underhand grip with the arms about shoulder width. Curl the bar up the shoulders and extend downward slowly to a straight arm position. A reverse curl can be used with an overhand grip.

Bent (Figure 19.80) or Upright (Figure 19.81) Rowing. Both lifts use an overhand grip about shoulder width. The bent position starts with the barbell on the floor and the body bent at the hips.

Figure 19.77. Alternating grip

Figure 19.78. Bench press

Figure 19.79. Curl

Figure 19.80. Bent rowing

Figure 19.81. Upright rowing

Figure 19.82. Military press

Figure 19.83. Bench pullover

The knees are bent slightly. The bar is pulled to the chest while the back is stable. The upright position starts with the bar across the thighs. The bar is pulled up to the chin area and returned slowly.

Military Press (Figure 19.82). An overhand grip slightly wider than the shoulders is used in a standing or sitting position. The bar is pressed upward from the chest and returned. A variation brings the bar down behind the head and then back up.

Bench Pullover (Figure 19.83). This lift should be done from a bench. The bar is gripped overhand

and is pulled straight up and over the face from the floor.

Shoulder Shrugs (Figure 19.84).   This lift can be done with a straight barbell across the thighs or with two dumbbells at the sides of the body. The shoulders are raised or shrugged as high as possible and then returned to the starting position.

Tricep Extension (Figure 19.85).   A barbell, two dumbbells, or a machine can be used. With the barbell, the weight bar is started overhead with an overhand grip, and is then lowered slowly behind the head and extended back to the starting position. With a machine, the bar is brought down in front of the body.

Lateral Raises.   This lift should be done using an overhand grip with dumbbells. A standing (Fig-

ure 19.86) or bent position can be used. The weights start at the sides or on the floor and are raised laterally with straight arms.

Lower Body Lifts

Front and Back Squat (Figure 19.87).   The lift uses an overhand grip with the bar across the front of the shoulders or across the upper back muscles. The knees are bent to a position in which the thighs are parallel to the floor.

Dead Lift (Figure 19.88).   The lift is started in a squat position with the weight on the floor. The feet are about shoulder width apart, and an alternating grip is used. The arms are kept straight and the back flat as the weight is lifted and the body

Figure 19.84.   Shoulder shrugs

Figure 19.86.   Standing lateral raise

Figure 19.85.   Tricep extension

Figure 19.87.   Back squat

Figure 19.88. Dead lift

Figure 19.89A. Power clean—ready position

Figure 19.89B. Power clean—intermediate position

comes to an erect position with the bar across the thighs.

Power Clean. This is a complex lift that starts in the same position as the dead lift only with an overhand grip (Figure 19.89A). The lift includes a start, an acceleration, and a catch phase. The bar is pulled up, past the waist (Figure 19.89B), and ends up above the chest. The lifter must control both the weight and the body as the weight moves through the starting position to the catch position.

Leg Curls and Extension. These lifts are completed on a machine attached to a bench. The extension (Figure 19.90) starts in a sitting position with the feet under a lower, padded section. The arms grip the sides of the bench, and the upper body is leaning slightly back. The legs are extended until they are parallel to the floor. The leg curl (Figure 19.91) uses the upper padded section of the machine. The lifter is on the stomach, and the heels are hooked behind the pad. The heels are then pulled up toward the buttocks and lowered.

Heel Raises (Figure 19.92). The lift is done with the balls of the feet and the toes over a stable board or step. The lifter holds a weight in each hand at the sides. The heels are then raised and lowered.

LEARNING ACTIVITIES

Circuit Training

An effective strategy for organizing the activities in the weight room is to set up a circuit with a

Figure 19.90. Leg extension

Figure 19.91. Leg curl

Figure 19.92. Heel raises

number of stations (Figure 19.93). The students can be divided into groups and rotated after so many minutes. Students perform a certain number of sets and repetitions at each station.

Each student should keep a daily log of the sets and repetitions and of the weights that were lifted. These records are important in organizing a progression and should help to motivate the students. Figures 19.94 and 19.95 are examples of daily lifting records for an upper body and lower body circuit. Depending on the equipment and facilities that are available, a good approach is to develop a circuit for both lower body exercises and upper body exercises. Students can alternate days performing upper and lower body workouts. Aerobic conditioning activities can also be alternated with the resistance training. Many teachers like to add variety to the circuit routines by changing stations regularly.

Partner Resistance Activities

Chapter 17 describes a number of partner resistance activities that can be used to supplement and add variety to a resistance training unit. These can also be added to a circuit, or can be scheduled as an entire day's lesson. They are useful in situations

---

Upper Body Routine

Station 1: Bench press → Station 2: Sit-ups → Station 3: Curls

↑   ↓

Station 6: Pull-ups ← Station 5: Tricep extension ← Station 4: Bent rows

Lower Body Routine

Station 1: Squats → Station 2: Leg curls and extension → Station 3: Dead lift

↑   ↓

Station 6: Heel raises ← Station 5: Power clean ← Station 4: Leg press

---

Figure 19.93. Weight training circuit

Date							Date					
Sets	1	2	3	4	5	6	1	2	3	4	5	6
Bench												
Curls												
Tricep												
Dips												
Lateral pull												
Rows												
Pull-ups												

Figure 19.94.   Daily lifting record—upper body

Date							Date					
Sets	1	2	3	4	5	6	1	2	3	4	5	6
Power clean												
Dead lift												
Leg press												
Leg curls												
Squat												
Sit-ups												

Figure 19.95.   Daily lifting record—lower body

in which equipment is limited. For example, while students are waiting their turn to use a weight machine, they can perform several resistance activities. Isometric exercises can also be used in these situations.

Muscle-of-the-Day

Another good learning activity is to present students with information about one muscle at the end of each lesson. The name of the muscle and its functions are written on a card and placed on the wall of the weight room. A quick review of the muscles covered plus the addition of a new muscle takes place each day. This is a good concluding activity after each day's workout. Specific infor-

mation on the muscular system is available in Chapter 15.

Motivational Devices

Resistance training offers tangible evidence of improvement in the various lifts. This improvement can be tied to many different motivational devices: T-shirts, certificates, and becoming a member of a club are popular examples of awards for lifting certain amounts of weight. These types of devices can be quite simple, yet are effective and meaningful for many students. Figure 19.96 is a good example of motivational club criteria used at Westwood High School in Mesa, Arizona. The club is available to students in the weight training classes.

CLUB REQUIREMENTS

Requirements—To become a member, you must lift a combined total of 5.2 times your weight. The three required lifts are bench press, dead lift, and squat.

Weight Class		Required Total	Weight Class		Required Total
100–109	=	520	160–169	=	832
110–119	=	572	170–179	=	884
120–129	=	624	180–189	=	936
130–139	=	676	190–199	=	988
140–149	=	728	200–209	=	1040
150–159	=	780	210–219	=	1092
			220 and up	=	1144

Each participant is allowed three tries for each lift. Weight may be added to the previous lift, but may not be subtracted from the previous lift.

Name _____ Date _____ Class 10, 11, 12

Body weight _____ Required total lift _____

	1st	2nd	3rd	Best of three lifts
Bench press	_____	_____	_____	_____
Dead lift	_____	_____	_____	_____
Squat	_____	_____	_____	_____
			Total	_____

Coach's signature _____

Figure 19.96. Motivational club criteria for weight lifters

Suggested Readings

Schwarzenegger, A., and Hall, D. *Arnold: The Education of a Body Builder.* New York: Simon and Schuster, 1977.

Seaton, D., et al. *Physical Education Handbook.* 7th ed. Englewood Cliffs, NJ: Prentice-Hall, Inc., 1983.

Stone, W., and Kroll, W. *Sports Conditioning and Weight Training.* Boston: Allyn and Bacon, Inc., 1980.

Ward, B. Weight training (Chapter 23). In *Physical Education and Sport for the Secondary School Student,* edited by N. Dougherty. Reston, VA: AAHPERD, 1983.

RHYTHMS

The urge to express oneself rhythmically has been characteristic of the human race throughout time. Dances have been done as religious rituals, as national customs, and to declare war. The dances of today are borrowed from many cultures and groups both ancient and modern. Since the United States is a melting pot of cultures, we have a broad and diverse range of folk dances representing many cultures.

Every generation dances. It is important that students learn the dances of the past as they develop new dances unique to their group. A wide variety of social skills can be learned through social dancing. Often, if people are not taught dance skills during the school-aged years, they are hesitant to participate in later years. The rhythmic program should thus be viewed as an integral part of the physical education program. If dance skills are not taught as part of the program, they probably will not be taught.

SEQUENCE OF SKILLS

The program should consist of four major parts: Square dance, folk and round dances, social dance steps, and country swing and western dance. Such a large number of skills and dances can be taught that it is impossible to list all of the activities here. Instead, the authors make reference to a text that offers supplementary and comprehensive coverage. Another concern is that different geographic areas have favorite dances and rhythmic activities peculiar to each specific area. The authors could not offer activities that would be comprehensive enough in the rhythms area to suit all readers.

Square Dance

The text *Dance a While* by Harris, Pittman, and Waller (1978) is an excellent source for square dancing. The basic movements of square dance are detailed in progression from Level 1A, beginner basics, to Level 5, intermediate basics. Fifty skills are listed and explained in clear and concise terms. A classified index of square dances is also provided, along with the basic skills that are developed in each dance and the level of difficulty. Each dance description contains the necessary performance instructions and recommended records.

Country Swing and Western Dance

Country swing and western dance is popular with junior and senior high school students. The number of dance moves is limited only by the imagination of the dancers. An excellent source for a step-by-step approach to the moves can be found in a text titled *The Complete Book of Country Swing and Western Dance* by Livingston (1981). The text is illustrated in a step-by-step fashion with photographs and is easy to follow. The shuffle step is also included.

Folk and Round Dance

There are many folk and round dances of varying difficulty. When the dances are presented, the background and history of the dance should be shared with students. The *Dance a While* text (1978) offers a rich repertoire of dances. A classified index detailing the basic steps, formations, and degree of difficulty is most useful. Directions for the dances are given, along with recommended records.

Social Dance Steps

Social dance steps should be developed in the rhythms unit. Steps most commonly taught are the waltz, fox-trot, swing, tango, rumba, samba, cha-cha-cha, and bossa nova. Each can be presented with the basic steps taught first, followed by one or two variations. With junior high school youngsters, the dance steps can be learned individually and then with a partner. Emphasis should be placed on creating an enjoyable atmosphere since peer pressure to succeed is great. Instructors can develop a positive class attitude by demonstrating proper dance etiquette and by showing their enjoyment of the activity. The *Dance a While* text (1978) is recommended as a valuable source.

References

Harris, J. A., Pittman, A. M., and Waller, M. S. *Dance a While*. Minneapolis: Burgess Publishing Co., 1978.

Livingston, P. *The Complete Book of Country Swing and Western Dance*. Garden City, NY: Doubleday & Co., 1981.

Suggested Readings

Ellfeldt, L. *Folk Dance*. Brown Physical Education Activity Series. Dubuque, IA: Wm. C. Brown Group, 1967.

Hall, J. T. *Folk Dance*. Goodyear Physical Education Series. Pacific Palisades, CA: Goodyear Publishing Co., 1969.

Heaton, A. *Techniques of Teaching Ballroom Rhythms*. Dubuque, IA: Kendall/Hunt Publishing Co., 1971.

Jensen, C. R., and Jensen, M. B. *Square Dancing*. Provo, UT: Brigham Young University Press, 1973.

Kraus, R. G., and Sadlo, L. *Beginning Social Dance*. Belmont, CA: Wadsworth Publishing Co., 1964.

Lidster, M. D., and Tamburini, D. H. *Folk Dance Progressions*. Belmont, CA: Wadsworth Publishing Co., 1965.

Spiesman, M. C. *Folk Dancing*. Philadelphia: W. B. Saunders Co., 1970.

ROPE JUMPING

Rope jumping can be a demanding activity enjoyed by all ages and ability levels. The American Heart Association has endorsed rope jumping for years because of its positive effects on cardiovascular endurance. It is an inexpensive activity that can be done in a limited amount of space, indoors or outside. Through rope jumping, students develop rhythm, timing, and coordination, as well as fitness. The numerous jumping activities can challenge all ability levels. The rope can be turned many ways at varying speeds and the jumper can use a variety of foot patterns. Individual, partner, and small group activities are available.

Rope jumping is a useful carry-over activity that can be enjoyed throughout one's life. Developing creative rope jumping routines and skills can be a challenge to students. Because of the rhythmic aspect of jumping rope, teachers should add popular music to enhance everyone's motivational level.

SEQUENCE OF SKILLS

Several types of ropes are available that are useful for teaching the skill to secondary students. Sash cord and hard weave synthetic ropes can be used, but the best jump ropes are made of plastic links with a plastic handle that turns. The rope should be heavy enough to maintain a rhythmic rotation. The length of the rope will vary according to the height of the student. Proper length can be determined by standing in the middle of the rope and pulling the ends up to the armpits or slightly higher (Figure 19.97). If the ends of the rope reach beyond that area, students can wrap the extra rope around the hands, or get a longer rope if the one tested is too short. Most secondary students will need a 7-, 8-, or 9-ft jump rope.

Figure 19.97. Correct length

Body Position and Rhythm

Jumping rope requires proper body position and alignment. The head should be up with the eyes looking ahead. Good balance is a must with the feet, ankles, and legs close together. The body is erect during the jump. The knees flex and extend slightly with each jump. The elbows are kept close to the body at approximately a 90-degree angle. The basic jump should be straight up and down and about 1 in. high. The rope should be turned primarily with the wrists and forearms. Effective jumpers land on the balls of their feet and stay in one spot.

The speed at which the rope turns is referred to as the *rhythm*. Slow-time (half-time) rhythm involves turning the rope 60–90 revolutions per min. The student jumps, rebounds, and then jumps again as the rope comes through. A rebound is a slight bend at the knee in order to carry or keep the rhythm. The student does not actually leave the ground during a rebound. Slow time is the easiest rhythm for beginners. Fast-time rhythm involves turning the rope 120–180 turns per min. There is no rebound because the rope and the feet must move faster. In double-time rhythm, the rope is turned at the same speed as slow time, but instead of using a rebound, the performer executes a different type of step while the rope is coming around. Double-time rhythm is the most difficult to learn, because the feet and the turning of the rope must be coordinated. The feet must move quickly while the rope turns slowly.

Individual Steps

The following are foot patterns that can be used with all three rhythm patterns—slow time, fast time, and double time. Students should try the patterns in slow time before moving on to fast and double time.

Two-Foot Basic Step.   The student jumps over the rope with both feet together. In slow time, there is a rebound in between each turn of the rope.

Alternate-Foot Step (Jog Step) (Figure 19.98). The student alternates feet with every jump. The unweighted leg is bent slightly at the knee. A variation can have students jump a consecutive number of times on one foot before switching feet. For example, a student might jump five times on the right foot and then five on the left foot. With a fast-time rhythm, this step looks like jogging.

Side Swings—Left or Right (Figure 19.99).   The student moves the rope to either side of the body

Figure 19.98. Jog step

Figure 19.99. Side swings

and jumps off both feet in time with the rope. The student does not actually jump over the rope. This is a good technique to use to work on timing and cardiovascular fitness because it is demanding.

Swing Step Forward or Sideways. This step is the same as the jog step, except the unweighted leg swings forward or sideways rather than backward. The student can alternate the forward swing with the side swing on each foot.

Rocker Step. The student starts with one leg in front of the other. As the rope comes around, the weight is shifted from the front leg to the back leg and alternates each time the rope goes around. The student rocks back and forth, from front foot to back foot.

Legs Spread Forward and Backward (Scissors). The student starts with one leg forward and one leg back, similar to the starting position for the rocker step. As the rope turns, the front leg is shifted back and the back leg is shifted forward. The position of the legs shifts each time the rope is turned.

Legs Crossed Sideways (Jumping Jack). The student starts with the legs straddled sideways. As the rope is turned, the legs are crossed with the right leg in front. Another straddle position is next, and then the legs are crossed again with the left leg in front. This sequence is repeated. The jump can also be executed with the feet coming together, instead of crossing each time, similar to the foot pattern of a jumping jack exercise.

Toe-Touches Forward or Backward. The student starts with one foot forward. The toe of the forward foot is pointed down and touches the ground. As the rope turns, the feet trade places, and the opposite toe touches the ground. For the backward toe-touch, the foot starts in a backward position with the toe touching. The feet then alternate positions with each jump.

Shuffle Step. The student starts with the weight on the left foot and the toe of the right foot touching the heel of the left foot. As the rope turns, the student steps to the right and the feet trade places. The left toe is now touching the right heel. The step is then repeated in the opposite direction.

Ski Jump. The student keeps both feet together and jumps to the left and right sideways over a line. This motion is similar to that of a skier. The jump can be performed with the rope going forward or backward.

Heel-Toe Jump. The student jumps off the right foot and extends the left leg forward, touching the heel to the ground. On the next jump the left foot is brought back beside the right foot with the toe touching the ground. The pattern is then repeated with the right foot touching the heel, then toe.

Heel Click. The student starts by completing several sideways swing steps in preparation for this pattern. As the leg swings out to the side, the opposite foot is brought up and the heels are touched together. The heel click can be completed on either side.

Crossing Arms. Crossing the arms can be added to all of the basic foot patterns. In crossing the arms, the hands actually trade places. The hands must be brought all the way across the body and kept low. The upper body crouches forward slightly from the waist. Crossing can also be used for backward jumping. Students can learn to cross and uncross after a certain number of jumps.

Double Turns. A double turn occurs when the rope passes under the feet twice during the same jump. The student must jump higher and rotate the rope faster. The jump should be about 6 in. high, and a slight forward crouch is necessary to speed up the turn. Students should try consecutive double turns forward or backward. Various foot patterns can also be tried with double turns.

Sideways Jumping. The rope is turned sideways with one hand over the head and the other hand extended down between the legs in front of the body. As the rope is turned, the student jumps the rope one leg at a time. The weight is shifted back and forth between the legs as the rope turns around the body. Students can turn the rope either left or right, and either hand can be held overhead. Students should try the technique several ways.

Shifting From Forward to Backward Jumping. There are several ways to change jumping direction. The first way is to begin jumping forward. As the rope starts downward, the student executes a left or right side swing. A half turn should be made in the same direction as the rope. As the rope is coming out of the side swing, the student must bring it up in a backwards motion. This motion can be completed to either side, as long as the turn is toward the rope side.

Another way to execute the shift is to make a half turn while the rope is above the head with the arms extended upward. The rope will hesitate slightly and then should be brought down in the opposite direction.

A final shifting strategy is from a cross-arm position. As the rope is going overhead, the student uncrosses the arms and makes a half turn. This starts the rope turning in the opposite direction. The key is to uncross the arms and turn simultaneously.

Partner Activities

A wide variety of challenging combinations can be performed with partners using one rope. The partners can start jumping together, or one person can run into position after the other partner has started jumping. Partner activities can be fun with students the same size. They are more challenging with students of varying size partnering each other.

1. One person turns the rope forward or backward:
   a. Partner faces the turner for so many jumps.
   b. Partners are back to back for so many jumps.
   c. Partner turns in place—quarter turn, half turn, and so forth.
   d. Partner dribbles a basketball while jumping.
   e. Partners match foot patterns (e.g., jog step, swing step).
   f. Partners complete double turns.
2. Two students turn the rope forward or backward:
   a. Partners stand side by side, facing the same direction.
   b. Partners face opposite directions.
   c. Repeat activities **2a** and **2b** with elbows locked.
   d. Repeat **a**, **b**, and **c** while hopping on one foot.
   e. Partners are back to back turning one rope with the right or left hand.
   f. Repeat **e** while turning in a circle—both directions.
3. Three students jump together with one turning the rope, one in front, and the other in back. This can be done forward and backward.
4. Two students, each with a rope, face each other. One student turns the rope forward, and the other turns backward, so the ropes are going in the same direction. Partners jump over both ropes on one jump. Students should then change their rope direction.
5. One student turns the rope. The partner comes in from the side, takes one handle of the rope, and begins turning. The partner's entrance must be timed so the rhythm of the rope remains constant. The partner then leaves and enters from the other side. This stunt can be performed with a forward or backward turn.
6. Partners face each other, turning one rope with the right hand. One partner turns to the left and exits from jumping while continuing to turn the rope for the other partner. After several turns, the partner who was out returns to the starting position. A variation can be tried with the partner turning to the right one-quarter turn.

IDEAS FOR EFFECTIVE INSTRUCTION

Rope jumping is a good example of an activity that can be improved with lots of practice. Students need to be reminded constantly that these skills will be perfected only with regular practice. Such reminders help keep students from getting discouraged quickly.

Students should first try new jumping techniques without the rope to get the basic idea. They can then try the stunt with a slow-time rhythm with a rebound in between each movement. As they improve, fast time and double time can be tried. Some students may need to practice turning the rope in one hand to the side of the body to develop the necessary rhythm. Students should practice timing their jump with the rope turning at the side. An instructor might do some partner jumping with a student who is having trouble with timing. Another effective instructional strategy is to use a movie, video tape, or loop film to give students a visual model of the skill. Several are listed in the suggested readings section of this chapter.

Students need plenty of room for practicing. Care should be taken, because the ropes can be dangerous to a person's face and eyes. Horseplay with the jump ropes cannot be tolerated.

Ropes can be color coded for various sizes. Students can help distribute and collect the ropes so they do not get tangled. Student helpers can hold their arms out to the sides, and the other students can place the ropes over their arms. Music with different tempos provides a challenge and motivates many students.

LEARNING ACTIVITIES

In addition to the foot patterns, rhythms, turning patterns, and partner activities that have been mentioned, there are other effective learning activities that can be done individually, in small groups, or with the entire class.

Follow-the-Leader

Students can work with a partner, a small group, or the entire class—moving forward, backward, diagonally, or sideways—following a designated leader. Various foot patterns can also be used while moving.

Leader in the Circle

The students follow the leader who is in the center of a circle. This activity can be done with large or small circles. The leader calls the name of the next leader after a designated time period or after a certain number of foot patterns have been executed.

Relays

Many different jump rope relays can be played with boundary cones and various types of jumps. For example:

1. Jog-step down around the cone and back (forward turns).

2. Same as no. 1 with backward turns.
3. Jog-step backward using forward turns.
4. Same as no. 3 with backward turns.
5. Hop to the cone on one foot and hop back on the other.
6. Ski-jump down, and forward swing-step back.
7. Jog-step through a series of 6 cones, do 10 sit-ups, and jog-step back.
8. Use a two-foot basic step going down, do 5 rocker steps, 5 scissor steps, and come back with a two-foot basic step.
9. Partners (side by side with one rope, elbows locked, both facing forward) go down forward and come back backwards.
10. Partners (side by side with one rope, one person facing forward, the other facing backward) go down and back with a forward turn.

Routines

Various routines can be developed individually with guidelines for foot patterns, change of direction, crossing over, changing levels, rope speed, and routine length. Small groups can also make up routines, choose music, and perform together, and partner routines can be developed with two people using one rope. An example of the guidelines for a small group routine follows:

1. Two min or less—5 members per group
2. Two changes of direction (e.g., forward, backward, diagonal)
3. Two changes of floor pattern (e.g., circle, square, back to back)
4. Two changes of levels (e.g., high, low)
5. Five changes of foot patterns (e.g., rocker, basic two-step)
6. One change of rope direction
7. One double turn

Rating Scales

Teachers can develop rating scales for each of the various skills to be learned with the jump rope. The scale can be developed for varying degrees of proficiency. Teachers should show students how to use the scale as a learning activity and as part of the grading scheme. The scale in Figure 19.100 focuses on individual skills; another scale could be developed for partner skills.

Contracts

Performance objectives can be written for each of the various jump rope skills. Objectives can be

Jump Rope Skills	Number of Successful Completions		
*Individual Skills	5	10	15
1. Two-foot			
2. One-foot hop			
3. Alternate foot			
4. Side swings			
5. Swing step forward			
6. Swing step sideways			
7. Rocker			
8. Scissors			
9. Legs crossed			
10. Toe touch forward			
11. Toe touch backward			
12. Shuffle			
13. Ski			
14. Heel-toe			
15. Heel click			
16. Crossing arms			
17. Double turns			
18. Sideways			
19. Forward to backward			
20. Backward to forward			
*Four variations of these skills can be completed using a forward or backward turn of the rope and slow-time or fast-time rhythm.			

Figure 19.100. Jump rope rating scale

set up as a learning contract that is tied to a grading scheme or to a reward system involving certain enjoyable activities. Completion of a specified number of objectives would equal an *A*, *B*, and so forth. The performance objectives should serve as learning activities that motivate students. Students can check each other as they accomplish the objectives.

RAINY DAY ACTIVITIES

All jump rope activities are good for rainy days because they can be performed indoors in a limited space. Hallways and gymnasium foyers are possible areas for jump rope activities. Students can work on individual skills if a limited space is available.

A rotation schedule may have to be arranged so that some students are practicing while partners are observing and using a rating scale or checking off performance objectives on a contract. Students can also devote time to learning the appropriate terminology for foot patterns and rhythms.

Suggested Readings and Films

Cassidy, J. *Pumping Plastic: The Jump Rope Fitness Plan.* Stanford, CA: Klutz Press, 1983.

Cowgill, S., and Cowgill, N. (Instructional video tape on rope jumping), 1005 E. Phoenix Rd., Grand Island, NE 68801.

Mitchell, C. *Perfect Exercise: The Hop, Skip, and Jump Way to Health.* New York: Pocket Books, 1978.

Moyer, M. (Color film, *Rope Skipping—Basic Steps*), 900 Federal Ave., Seattle, WA 98102.

Skolnik, P. L. *Jump Rope.* New York: Workman Publishing Co., 1974.

SOCCER

Soccer is a rapidly growing sport. This game, which has been the most popular one in the world, is now becoming popular among youth in the United States. Many youth sport clubs and programs run by organizations such as the YMCA, YWCA, Boys' Clubs, and municipal recreation departments now sponsor soccer teams, and a large number of school districts are now including soccer in their intramural programs.

Soccer is known throughout the rest of the world as "football." The game is said to have originated in England around the tenth century, but in fact, the Romans played a game similar to soccer. Soccer was brought to the United States around 1870 and was played by women in an organized fashion in 1919.

From a physical education standpoint, one of the advantages of soccer is that it is one of the few sports that depends primarily on foot-eye coordination for success. A large number of kickers in American football are soccer-style kickers. The long hours of kicking practice have contributed to their success.

The object of the game is to move the ball down the field by foot, body, or head contact to score goals and to prevent the opposing team from scoring. Soccer demands teamwork and the coordination of individual skills into group goals. Position play becomes important as students become more skilled. It is an excellent game for cardiovascular development, because it demands a great deal of running and body control.

SEQUENCE OF SKILLS

The skills of soccer are difficult to master, so instructors should teach the skills through short practice sessions. Many drills and lead-up games can be used to make the practice sessions interesting and novel.

Dribbling

The purpose of dribbling in soccer is similar to basketball, that is, to maintain control of the ball and advance it before passing off to a teammate or shooting on goal. The ball is advanced by pushing it with the inside or outside of the front of the foot (Figure 19.101). The player should keep the ball close during the dribble, rather than kicking it and then running after it. Practice should involve learning to run in different patterns such as weaving, dodging, and twisting or turning with the ball.

Kicking

The purpose of the kick is to pass the ball to a teammate or to take a shot on goal. When passing, the performer plants the nonkicking foot alongside the ball with the foot pointing in the desired direction of the kick. The ball is contacted with the inside portion of the instep of the foot (Figure 19.102). The body weight shifts forward after the kick. The pass can also be made with the outside of the foot, although this kick will not move the ball as great a distance or with as much velocity. It is an excellent kick for passing without breaking stride or for passing to the side.

In kicking for a shot on goal, the procedure is similar to the inside-of-the-foot kick. The nonkicking foot is planted alongside the ball with the toes pointing in the direction of the goal. The ball is contacted on the instep, followed by a snap of the lower leg and follow-through.

Trapping

The purpose of trapping is to deflect a moving ball and bring it under control so it may be advanced

Figure 19.101.   Dribbling

Figure 19.102. Instep kick

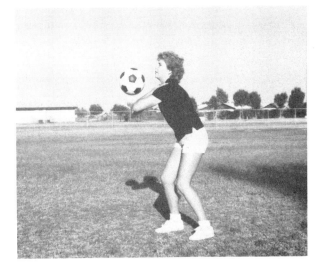

Figure 19.103. Absorbing the force in a chest trap

or passed. Any part of the body may contact the ball except the hands or arms. Effective trapping will result in the ball dropping in front of the body in position to be advanced.

The sole-of-the-foot trap is most commonly used and is often called wedging. The ball is contacted between the foot and the ground just as the ball hits the ground. The ball is swept away under control immediately after the trap.

The shin trap is done by moving to meet the ball just as it hits the ground in front of the lower legs. The ball is trapped between the inside of the lower leg and the ground.

The chest trap (Figure 19.103) is executed by arching the trunk of the body backwards and giving with the ball on contact. The giving occurs with the body collapsing, so the ball does not rebound and drops in front of the player.

Heading

Heading can be an effective way of propelling a ball in the air to a teammate or on goal. The player should strike the ball with the head, rather than waiting for the ball to hit the head. The player leans backward as the ball approaches. The head is up, with the eyes following the ball. On contact, the head moves forward and strikes the ball near the hairline on the forehead. The body also swings forward as the follow-through is completed.

Tackling

Tackling is used defensively to take the ball away from an offensive player who is dribbling or attempting to pass. The single-leg tackle is used when approaching an opponent directly, from behind, or from the side. Effective tackling depends, in large part, on being able to anticipate the opponent's next move with the foot. One leg reaches for the ball while the weight is supported on the other. The knees should be bent so good balance is maintained. Focus should be on a clean tackle rather than on body contact. The object is to reach out and bring the ball to the body, or to kick the ball away and then continue to pursue it.

Goalkeeping

Goalkeeping involves stopping shots by catching or otherwise stopping the ball. Goalkeepers should become adept at catching low, rolling balls, at diving on rolling balls, at catching airborne balls waist high and below, and at catching airborne balls waist high and above. The diving movements are the reason the goalie may choose to wear knee, elbow, and hip pads.

Students should get in the habit of catching low, rolling balls in much the same manner as a baseball outfielder: Get down on one knee, with the body behind the ball to act as a backstop, and catch it with both hands, fingers pointing toward the ground. If diving for a ball is necessary, the goalie must throw the body behind it and cradle it with the hands. The body should always be between the goal and the ball.

The goalie may also punch the ball in order to deflect it if the ball is not catchable. The ball can be deflected off other body parts if it is not punchable.

After a ball is caught by the goalkeeper, it is thrown to a teammate. The ball can also be kicked, but this is less desirable because it is less accurate. Effective throws allow teammates to place the ball in action immediately.

IDEAS FOR EFFECTIVE INSTRUCTION

Soccer is played with two teams of 11 players each. For young players, however, decreasing the size of the teams is more effective. This results in each player's handling the ball more often, and feeling an integral part of the soccer team.

Many of the drills, such as dribbling, kicking, and punting, can be learned individually. This means that one ball per player will ensure the maximum amount of practice time. Many types of balls can be used besides a regulation soccer ball. Playground balls (8.5 in.) can be used if they are deflated slightly. Many students will play a more aggressive game of soccer if a foam-rubber training ball is used. They become less fearful of being hit by the ball and are willing to kick it with maximum velocity.

Field sizes can be reduced in order to increase the activity level of the game. The regulation game is played on a field with dimensions illustrated in Figure 19.104. Soccer is meant to be played on grass. If a hard surface is used, deflate the ball so that it is not as live and will not bounce so readily.

The drills used for developing soccer skills should help all participants in achieving proper form. For example, if students are asked to pass and trap together, drills should focus on developing both skills, yet students are sometimes asked to kick with velocity, so the students trapping are fearful of getting hurt. Those students then develop an improper trapping style. An excellent source for many drills and activities to enhance the play of soccer is *Teaching Soccer* by Thomson (1980).

LEAD-UP GAMES AND LEARNING ACTIVITIES

The following lead-up games are excellent for getting students involved in soccer activities. They emphasize participation and action. The lead-up activities are often more fun for the majority of students than an actual soccer game, because these activities develop specific skills in which students may lack expertise.

Circle Kickball

Players are in circle formation. They kick the ball with the side of the foot back and forth inside the circle. The object is to kick the ball out of the circle beneath shoulder level. A point is scored

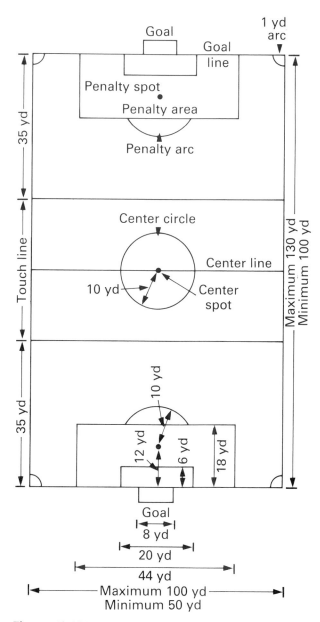

Figure 19.104.   Regulation soccer field

against each of the players where the ball left the circle. If the lost ball is clearly the fault of a single player, however, then the point is scored against that player only. Players who kick the ball over the shoulders of the circle players have a point scored against them. Players with the fewest points scored against them are the winners. The game works well with a foam training ball because the ball can be kicked at someone from a short distance.

Soccer Croquet

The game is similar to croquet in that the object is for one ball to hit another. One player kicks a ball and tries to hit another ball lying ahead. Kickers alternate until a hit is made, which scores one point for the kicker. The game continues until a player scores a specified number of points.

Soccer Keepaway

Players are spaced evenly around a circle about 10 yd in diameter with one player in the center. The object of the game is to keep the player in the center from touching the ball. The ball is passed back and forth as in soccer. If the center player touches the ball with a foot, the person who kicked the ball goes in the center. If there is an error, the person responsible changes places with the one in the center.

Diagonal Soccer

Two corners are marked off with cones 5 ft from the corners on both sides, outlining triangular dead areas. Each team lines up as illustrated in Figure 19.105 and protects two adjacent sides of the square. The size of the area depends on the size of the class and must be adjusted accordingly. Dead areas on opposite corners mark the opposing team's goal line. To begin competition, three players from each team move into the playing area in their own half of the space. These are the active players. During play, they may roam anywhere in the square. The other players act as line guards.

To score, the active players must kick the ball through the opposing team's line (beneath shoul-

Figure 19.105. Diagonal soccer

der height). When a score is made, active players rotate to the sidelines, and new players take their place. Players on the sidelines may block the ball with their bodies, but cannot use their hands. The team against which the point was scored starts the ball for the next point. Only active players may score. A point is scored for the opponents whenever any of the following occurs:

1. A team allows the ball to go through its line below shoulder height.
2. A team touches the ball illegally.
3. A team kicks the ball over the other team's line above shoulder height.

Sideline Soccer (Figure 19.106)

The teams line up on the sidelines of a large square with the end lines open. Three active players from each team are called from the end of the team line. These players remain active until a point is scored and then are rotated to the other end of the line.

The object is to kick the ball over the end line, which has no defenders, between cones that define the scoring area. The active players on each team compete against each other, aided by their teammates on the sidelines.

To start play, a referee drops the ball between two opposing players at the center of the field. To score, the ball must be kicked last by an active player and must go over the end line at or below shoulder height. Regular rules prevail with the restrictions of no pushing, holding, tripping, or other rough play. For out-of-bounds, the team on the side of the field where the ball went out-of-bounds is awarded a free kick near that spot. No score can result from a free kick. Violation of the touch rule also results in a free kick.

Line Soccer (Figure 19.107)

Two goal lines are drawn 180 to 210 ft apart. A restraining line is drawn 15 ft in front of and parallel to each goal line. Field width can vary from 90 to 105 ft. Each team stands on one goal line, which it defends. The referee stands in the center of the field, holding a ball. At the whistle, three players (or more if the teams are large) run to the center from the right side of each line and become active players. The referee drops the ball to the ground, and the players try to kick it through the other team defending the goal line. The players in the field may advance by kicking only.

Figure 19.106. Sideline soccer

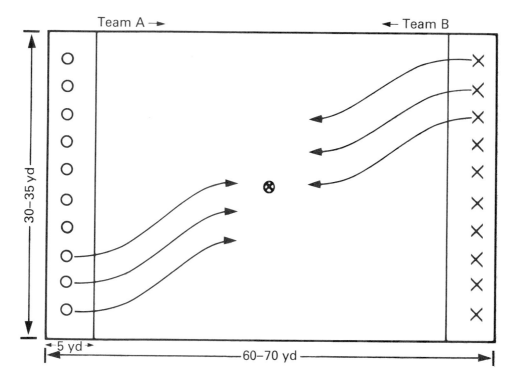

Figure 19.107. Line soccer

A score is made when an active player kicks the ball through the opposing team and over the end line, providing the kick was made from outside the restraining line. Cones should be placed on the field corners to define the goal line. A player rotation system should be set up.

Line players act as goalies and are permitted to catch the ball. After being caught, the ball must be laid down immediately and either rolled or kicked. It cannot be punted or drop-kicked. One point is scored when the ball is kicked through the opponent's goal line below shoulder level. One point is also scored in cases of a personal foul involving pushing, kicking, tripping, or similar acts.

For illegal touching by the active players, a direct free kick is given from a point 12 yd in front of the penalized team's goal line. All active players on the defending team must be to one side until the ball is kicked. Only goalies may defend. A time limit of 2 min should be set for any group of active players. When no goal is scored during this time, a halt is called at the end of 2 min and players are changed.

An out-of-bounds ball is awarded to the opponents of the team last touching the ball. The regular soccer throw-in from out-of-bounds should be used. If the ball goes over the shoulders of the defenders at the end line, any end-line player may retrieve the ball and put it into play with a throw or kick.

Minisoccer

The playing area (Figure 19.108) can be adjusted, depending on the size and skill of the players. A reasonable playing area is probably 150 by 225 ft. A goal, 24 ft wide, is on each end of the field, marked by jumping standards. A 12-ft semicircle on each

end outlines the penalty area. The center of the semicircle is at the center of the goal.

The game follows the general rules of soccer, with one goalie for each side. The corner kick, not played in other lead-up games, needs to be introduced. This kick is used when the ball goes over the end line but not through the goal, and was last touched by the defense. The ball is taken to the nearest corner for a direct free kick, and a goal can be scored from the kick. If the attacking team last touched the ball, the goalkeeper kick is awarded. The goalie puts the ball down and place-kicks it forward. The players are designated as center forward, outside right halfback, fullback, and goalie. Players should rotate positions at regular intervals. The forwards play in the front half of the field and the guards in the back half, but neither position is restricted to these areas entirely, and all may cross the center line without penalty.

A foul by the defense within its penalty area (semicircle) results in a penalty kick, taken from a point 12 yd distant, directly in front of the goal. Only the goalie is allowed to defend. The ball is in play, with others waiting outside the penalty area. Position play should be emphasized, and the lines of three should be encouraged to spread out and hold their position.

SUGGESTED PERFORMANCE OBJECTIVES

The following contracts are an example of pass-fail requirements designed for three skill levels: introductory, intermediate, and advanced. The contracts can be used in intermediate or advanced soccer classes, or in a heterogeneously grouped class to challenge students of varying abilities.

Introductory Unit: Basic Requirements

All requirements are on a pass-fail basis.

Kicking

1. Execute a push pass, low drive, and lofted drive. Satisfy the instructor that these are understood and can be executed with the preferred foot.

Passing

(All objectives may be performed with the preferred foot.)

2. Push-pass 3 of 5 passes from 10 yd to partner.
3. Low-drive 3 of 5 passes from 15 yd to partner.
4. Loft-drive 3 of 5 passes from 20 yd to partner.

Figure 19.108.   Minisoccer field

Dribbling

5. Dribble a distance of 20 yd twice with one or both feet. The ball must not be allowed to stray more than 5 yd.

Shooting

6. Shoot the ball with the preferred foot from 18 yd into an empty goal 8 of 10 times.

Heading

7. Head the ball back to serving partner 8 of 10 times over a distance of 5 yd. The partner must be able to catch the ball.

Control of the Ball

8. Control 3 of 5 passes on the ground using the feet only.
9. Control 3 of 5 passes in the air using the head, chest, or thigh.

Game Situation

10. Show an understanding of pass, run, and control in a minisoccer game situation.

Rules of the Game

11. Score 80% on a rules-of-the-game test. One retake is permissible.

Introductory Unit: Optional Requirements

Goalkeeping

1. Save 6 of 10 shots from 18 yd. The shots must be on target.
2. Punt the ball 25 yd 4 of 5 times.

Juggling

3. Keep the ball in the air with at least 10 consecutive touches. Hands or arms may not be used.

Field Dimensions

4. Diagram a full-size soccer field and give dimensions.

Grading.   Thirteen passes are required for a unit pass. The instructor reserves the right to lower the number of required passes for the unit as necessary.

Intermediate Unit: Basic Requirements

Kicking

1. Satisfy the instructor that the techniques of the push pass, low drive, and lofted drive are understood and can be executed with both feet.

Passing

2. Push Pass: Complete 4 of 5 passes with the preferred foot from 10 yd. The passes must go between two cones placed 5 yd apart. Complete 3 of 5 passes with the nonpreferred foot.
3. Low Drive: Complete 4 of 5 passes with the preferred foot from 10 yd. The passes must go between two cones placed 8 yd apart. Complete 3 of 5 passes with the nonpreferred foot.
4. Lofted Drive: Complete 4 of 5 passes with the preferred foot from 10 yd. The passes must go over an obstacle 6 ft high. Complete 3 of 5 passes with the nonpreferred foot.

Dribbling

5. Dribble through 6 cones over 25 yd, 4 times with no misses. Both feet must be used.
6. Dribble around an advancing goalkeeper and score a goal 3 of 5 times.

Shooting

7. Shoot the ball with the preferred foot from 18 yd into an empty goal 9 of 10 times.
8. Same as no. 7, except with the nonpreferred foot, 7 of 10 times.

Heading

9. Head the ball to a serving partner 9 of 10 times over a distance of 10 yd. The partner must be able to catch the ball without its touching the ground.

Control of the Ball

10. Control 4 of 5 passes on the ground. Use the feet only.
11. Control 4 of 5 passes in the air. The head, chest, and thighs must be used.

Corner Kick

12. Propel 3 of 5 corner kicks inside the penalty area. The ball may not touch the ground between the corner and the penalty area.

Throw-in

13. Throw the ball with two hands to a partner 10 yd away 4 of 5 times. Partner must be able to catch the ball.

Juggle

14. Juggle the ball at least 10 consecutive times without allowing it to touch the ground.

Tackling

15. Successfully complete 3 of 5 front block tackles on a partner dribbling a ball at a walking pace.

Goalkeeping

16. Kick goal kicks at least 20 yd in the air 4 of 5 times.
17. Punt the ball 25 yd 4 of 5 times.
18. Save at least 6 of 10 on-target shots from the 18-yard line.

Rules of the Game

19. Score 80% on a rules-of-the-game test. One retest is allowed.

Intermediate Unit: Optional Requirements

Officiating

1. Help officiate at least 2 games.
2. Know the roles of the referee and linesman.
3. Know the correct positioning of officials at corner kicks, goal kicks, and penalties.

Volleying

4. Volley 4 of 5 goals from outside the goal area with the preferred foot.

Swerving or Bending the Ball

5. Bend the ball into the goal from the goal line 3 of 5 times with the preferred foot.

Penalty Kicks

6. Score 7 of 10 penalty kicks against a recognized peer goalkeeper.

Power and Distance Kicking

7. Score 2 of 5 goals into an empty goal from the halfway line.

Grading. Twenty passes are required for a unit completion.

Advanced Unit: Basic Requirements

Passing

1. Push-pass 4 of 5 passes with the preferred foot from a distance of 10 yd between 2 cones, placed 5 yd apart, while running with the ball. Complete 3 of 5 passes with the nonpreferred foot.
2. Low-drive 4 of 5 passes with the preferred foot from a distance of 15 yd between 2 cones, placed 8 yd apart, while running with the ball. Complete 3 of 5 passes with the nonpreferred foot.

Dribbling

3. Dribble through 9 cones over a distance of 40 yd and back to the start in 30 sec or less. Both feet must be used and no cones may be omitted.
4. Dribble around an advancing goalkeeper and score 4 of 5 times. The goalkeeper must be beaten to the left and to the right at least once.

Shooting

5. Score 10 of 10 shots into an empty goal from outside the 18-yard line with the preferred foot, and 9 of 10 shots with the nonpreferred foot.
6. Score 8 of 10 penalty kicks against a recognized peer goalkeeper.
7. Volley 4 of 5 goals from a serving partner, from outside the goal area, with the preferred foot, and 3 of 5 with the nonpreferred foot.
8. Serve or bend the ball from the goal line into the goal 3 of 6 times with the preferred foot. The ball must be placed within 1 ft of the line any distance from the post.

Heading

9. Head the ball back to a serving partner 9 of 10 times over a distance of 10 yd. The partner must be able to catch the ball.
10. Head the ball back and forth with a partner a minimum of 10 times without touching the ground.
11. Head 9 of 10 serves from a partner into an empty goal from a distance of 10 yd.

Control of the Ball

12. Control 9 of 10 passes on the ground with the preferred foot.

13. Control 8 of 10 passes on the ground with the nonpreferred foot.
14. Control 9 of 10 passes from a partner with the head.
15. Control 9 of 10 serves from a partner with the chest.
16. Control 9 of 10 serves from a partner with the preferred thigh, and 8 of 10 with the nonpreferred thigh.

Corner Kick

17. Kick 9 of 10 corner kicks into the penalty area with the preferred foot from the preferred side. The ball may not touch the ground between the corner and the penalty area.
18. Kick 8 of 10 corner kicks into the penalty area from the nonpreferred side (same conditions as no. 17).

Throw-in

19. Throw the ball with both hands to a partner 15 yd away, 9 of 10 times. The throw must be placed so partner is able to catch the ball.
20. Throw the ball to a moving partner at least 10 yd away. Partner must be able to catch the ball.

Juggling

21. Juggle the ball at least 20 times without its touching the ground. Head, foot, and thigh must be used. Start with the ball on the ground, and get it into the air using the feet.
22. Juggle the ball with a partner. At least 10 passes must be made. No restrictions are placed on the number of touches by each player.

Tackling

23. Block tackle a partner jogging with the ball 8 of 10 times successfully.
24. Slide tackle a partner jogging with the ball 3 of 5 times successfully.

Goalkeeping

25. Kick 4 of 5 goal kicks at least 20 yd before hitting the ground.
26. Punt the ball at least 30 yd 4 of 5 times.
27. Save 7 of 10 shots on target from outside the 18-yard line.

Game Rules and Strategy

28. A thorough understanding of the rules of the game and principles of strategy must be demonstrated.

29. A score of 80% or higher must be achieved on a test covering the rules of the game. One retake is allowed.

Advanced Unit: Optional Requirements

Officiating

1. At least 3 games must be officiated.

Grading. Twenty-six passes must be obtained to successfully complete the unit.

RAINY DAY ACTIVITIES

Figure 19.109 is an example of a combination word search and fill-in-the-blank.

Suggested Readings

Ingels, N. B., Jr. *Coaching Youth Soccer.* Monterey, CA: Page-Ficklin Publications, 1976.

Thomson, W. *Soccer Coaching Methods.* Monterey, CA: Page-Ficklin Publications, 1977.

Thomson, W. *Teaching Soccer.* Minneapolis: Burgess Publishing Co., 1980.

SOFTBALL

Softball is a game that raises controversy among physical education teachers. Some instructors believe that it is a game in which one only catches "varicose veins" from standing around. On the other hand, since it is a less active game, softball is often played by adults for many years. When the skill level of the participants is developed, the game can be enjoyable. If skill is lacking, emphasis should be placed on developing skills and on individual practice.

Softball can be taught effectively by using stations. This gives students ample practice in many different skills and avoids the situation in which students play only one position and specialize in skills. Softball can be played coeducationally, and many of the lead-up games make the activity enjoyable and suited to students' ability levels.

SEQUENCE OF SKILLS

Equipment and Facilities

Softball is played on a diamond with the dimensions shown in Figure 19.110. Lines can be applied

```
D A G T F E I N T B H M
S H N F F F O K C I K N
R A I O C Z S O C C E R
K L D R I B B L I N G E
C F A W W N E K G Q O N
I B E A L J Y O X T A R
K A H R D T A O U U L O
L C X D L L B W D J I C
A K O A R E F E R E E S
O C N Q T H R O W I N A
G E O D N A L G N E X E
P B T G Y J Z K X V O D
```

1. When the ball has passed over the line, between the two posts and under the crossbar, it is called a _____ .

2. _____ blows the whistle when the ball goes out-of-bounds.

3. Free chance to score a goal _____ .

4. A way to put the ball into play when it goes out-of-bounds _____ .

5. This sport came over from our mother country, which was _____ .

6. When last played by a defenseperson and rolled out-of-bounds, it shall be kicked from the _____ of the field.

7. This is the only player able to pick up the ball _____ .

8. To start the game or after a goal is scored _____ .

9. The last line of defense before the goalie _____ .

10. When you pass the ball using your head, it is called _____ the ball.

11. A fake or swerve with the body is a _____ .

12. After the ball, last touched by the attacking team, passes over the end line, the offense puts the ball in play by using a _____ .

13. _____ is a way of moving the ball.

14. Front offensive linemen are called _____ .

15. The name of this sport is _____ .

Figure 19.109.   Name that sport

to the field with chalk or can be burned into the grass with a solvent that kills the grass and leaves a brown line.

Softball requires some specialized equipment. When ordering gloves, about 20% should be left-handed, and enough balls should be ordered so that each student has one. This allows many drills to be undertaken without waiting for the balls to be returned. Available equipment should include a set of bases for each diamond; bats of varying

Figure 19.110. Softball diamonds

sizes (aluminum are the most durable); fielders' gloves; catcher's glove, protector, and face mask; and batting tees. For less experienced players, the soft softball is most desirable because it helps alleviate the fear that some players have of the ball. When a regulation softball is used, students often learn to dodge the ball, rather than catch it. Some teachers have had success with the large 16-in. ball. It moves slower, cannot be hit as far, and allows the game to be played in a smaller area. The drawback is that the large ball is difficult to throw because of its size.

Catching

Catching involves moving the body into the path of the ball. When catching fly balls, there are two ways to hold the hands. For a low ball, the fielder keeps the fingers in and the thumbs turned outward. For a ball above waist level, the thumbs are turned inward and the fingers outward. The arms and hands extend and reach for the ball. As the ball comes into the glove, the arms, hands, and body give to create a soft home for the ball.

When catching grounders, the first step is to move into the path of the ball, and then move toward the ball, and catch it on a "good" hop. Keep the eyes on the ball and follow it into the glove. The feet are spread, the seat is kept down, and the hands are carried low and in front. The weight is on the balls of the feet or on the toes, and the knees are bent to lower the body. As the ball is caught, the fielder straightens up, takes a step in the direction of the throw, and makes the throw.

Throwing

The ball is generally held with a three- or four-fingered grip. Smaller students usually have to use the four-fingered grip. The fingers should be spaced evenly, and the ball held with the fingertips.

Because throwing is a complex motor pattern, it is difficult to break the skill into component parts. At best, throwing skills can be slowed down about 10% in an effort to teach proper throwing technique. If a mature pattern of throwing has not been developed, students should focus on throwing for velocity rather than accuracy. After proper form has been learned, accuracy becomes a prime objective.

Overhand Throw (Figure 19.111). The player stands with the opposite side (from the throwing arm) facing the target. The hand with the ball is brought back, over the head, at just above shoulder

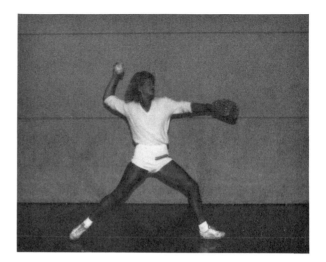

Figure 19.111. Overhand throw

height. The nonthrowing hand is raised in front of the body. The weight is on the rear foot (away from the target) with the front foot advanced toward the target. The arm comes forward with the elbow leading, and the ball is thrown with a downward snap of the wrist. The weight of the body is shifted simultaneously with the throw to the front foot. The rear foot rotates forward, and the throwing hand ends facing the ground during the follow-through. The eyes should be kept on the target throughout the throw.

Sidearm Throw. The sidearm throw is similar to the overhand throw, except that the entire motion is kept near a horizontal plane. The sidearm throw, which uses a quick, whiplike motion, is for shorter, quicker throws than the overhand. The sidearm throw should be used only for short infield throws, because the sideways motion causes a spin on the ball, which results in a curved path.

Underhand Throw. The underhand throw is used for short distances, such as throwing to the pitcher covering first base, or the person on second base throwing to the shortstop covering second base. The player faces the target, and the hand is swung backward with the palm facing forward. The arm is then moved forward in a pendulum swing with the elbow slightly bent. The weight shifts to the front foot during the toss.

Pitching. The pitcher must begin with both feet touching the rubber (Figure 19.112). The ball is held in front of the body with the pitcher facing home plate. The pitching hand is brought backward in a pendulum swing, and the wrist is cocked at the back of the swing. The pitcher steps forward on the opposite foot and swings the arm forward. The wrist is snapped, and the ball is released from

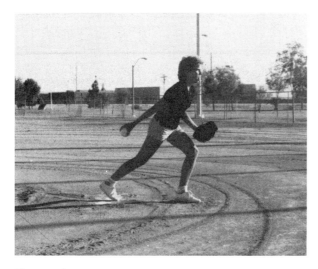

Figure 19.112. Pitching from the rubber

the fingertips as the arm finishes moving in an upward, lifting fashion. The follow-through should be accompanied by a forward step of the foot on the throwing side, so the player is in a fielding position.

Fielding Position

Infielders should assume the ready position in a semicrouch, with the legs spread shoulder width apart, knees bent slightly, and hands on or in front of the knees (Figure 19.113). The weight is distributed evenly on both feet so the player can move easily to the left or right. To field a grounder, the fielder moves as quickly as possible into the path of the ball, then moves forward, and plays the ball on a good hop. The glove should be kept near the ground and raised only as the ball rises. (A common mistake is to not put the glove down soon

enough.) The eyes follow the ball into the glove and the head is kept down. As the ball is caught, the fielder straightens up, takes a step in the direction of the throw, and releases the ball.

To catch a ground ball in the outfield, the player should employ the sure-stop method (Figure 19.114). This involves using the body as a barrier. The fielder drops to one knee in order to block the ball with the body if the catch is missed. This method should be used when runners are on base.

Batting

The bat is gripped with the dominant hand above and adjacent to the nondominant hand. The feet should be positioned comfortably apart, and the front of the body faces the plate. The knees are slightly bent and the weight is distributed equally on both feet. The hands and the bat are held shoulder high and slightly behind the rear foot. The elbows are away from the body, the wrists cocked, and the bat held in an upward position (Figure 19.115). The ball should be followed with the eyes as long as possible. The stride begins by stepping toward the ball with the front foot. The hips are rotated, followed by the trunk and forward shoulder. The arms are extended, wrists snapped, and contact is made with the ball in front of the forward hip. Different grips on the bat can be tried, including the choke and long grip.

Batters should avoid using poor techniques such as lifting the front foot high off the ground, stepping back with the rear foot, dropping the elbows, or crouching or bending forward.

Figure 19.113. Infield catching

Figure 19.114. Sure-stop fielding

Figure 19.115. Batting position

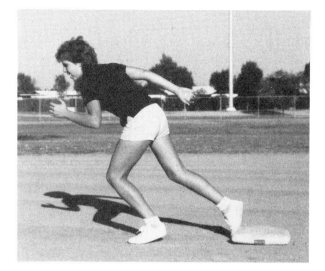

Figure 19.116. Push-off position

Base Running

After a hit, the batter should run hard with the head up and eyes looking down the base path. The runner moves past the bag, tagging it in the process, and turns out, into foul territory, unless it is an extra base hit. If it is an extra base hit, the runner swings 5 to 6 ft to the right of the base line, about two thirds of the way down the base path, and makes the turn toward second.

Runners on base must stay in contact with the base until the pitcher releases the ball. The next base is faced, with one foot forward and the other foot touching the base in a push-off position (Figure 19.116). The knees are flexed, and the upper body leans toward the next base.

IDEAS FOR EFFECTIVE INSTRUCTION

Safety is important, and throwing the bat is a constant problem. The members of the batting team should stand behind the backstop or on the side opposite the batter. Techniques to make the batter think about the bat are (1) carrying the bat to first base, (2) changing ends of the bat before dropping it, or (3) placing the bat in a circle before running. It is usually best not to allow sliding, because sliding can lead to injury if the proper equipment is not available. The catcher should always wear protective gear. In the early stages of practice, soft softballs can be used.

Many of the lead-up games were developed to increase the number of people who get to bat in each inning. One strategy for effective batting practice is to have a member of the batting team pitch so the ball is easy to hit. Players should rotate positions often. Another idea is to have players rotate to a new position each inning. This has the effect of making the players supportive of each other, since the quality of the game depends on all of the participating players.

Station teaching is excellent for developing softball skills. It ensures that participants have the opportunity to practice a wide variety of activities. Players who are particularly skilled in an activity can help others. Teachers should position themselves at a different station each day to ensure that they have instructed all students at all stations over a one- to two-week period of time.

Figure 19.117 is an example of station teaching. Five stations are developed, so the teacher can make a full rotation in one week. Task cards are placed at each station, so students know exactly what is expected of them.

Station 1. Catching Ground Balls
  a. Roll the ball straight to the person.
  b. Roll the ball to the left side. Increase the distance.
  c. Roll the ball to the right side. Increase the distance.
  d. Roll the ball in an unpredictable direction.
  e. Bat the ball in different directions. Start at 5 yd and increase the disance up to 20 yd from the fielder.

Station 2. Batting
  a. Work in groups of three with a batting tee. One person fields, one bats,

Figure 19.117. Station work

and the other shags the ball. Hit 10 balls.

   b. Same as 2a except pitch the ball to the batter.

   c. Try placing the ball. Call the direction in which you are going to hit the ball and then do so.

Station 3. Base Running

   a. Run the bases using a circle technique. Have a partner time you.

   b. Run the bases using a clover technique. Decide which you prefer and which allows you to run the bases faster.

   c. Bunt and run to first. Have your partner time you.

   d. Play In a Pickle in groups of three.

Station 4. Throwing

   a. One person stands at each base plus a catcher behind home plate. Practice throwing to each of the bases from each position. Rotate positions after each person has had 3 throws.

   b. Throw the ball from the outfield. Throw the ball through a cutoff per-

son. Make 5 throws and rotate to catcher position.

   c. People not throwing should back up the other positions and act as a cutoff person.

Station 5. Fly Balls

   a. Throw fly balls back and forth.

   b. Vary the height and direction of the throw so teammates have to move into the flight of the ball.

   c. Make teammates move backward and forward to catch the ball.

   d. Bat some flies and play the game 500.

LEAD-UP GAMES AND LEARNING ACTIVITIES

Two-Pitch Softball

This activity is played like regulation softball except that a member of the team at bat pitches. Every member of the team must have an opportunity to pitch. The batter receives only two pitched balls to hit, and the ball hit must be fair or it is an out. The pitcher does not field the ball, and no balls or strikes are called.

In a Pickle

A base runner is "in a pickle" when caught between two bases and in danger of being tagged out. To begin, both fielders are on a base with a runner in the middle. The goal is for the player in the middle to get to a base safely. If done, that person scores a point. In either case, rotation occurs.

Five Hundred

A batter hits balls to a group of fielders. The goal is to score 500 points. When the total is reached, that person becomes the new batter. Fielders earn 100 points for catching a fly ball, 75 points for catching a ball on one bounce, 50 points for catching a ball after two bounces, and 25 points for any other ball. The points must total exactly 500 or the total immediately earned is subtracted from the fielder's score. Points are also subtracted if an error is made.

Home Run

The critical players are a batter, a catcher, a pitcher, and one fielder. All other players are fielders and take positions throughout the area. The batter hits a pitch and on a fair ball must run to first base and back home before the ball can be returned to the catcher. The batter is out whenever any of the following occurs: (1) a fly ball is caught, (2) a strike-out occurs, or (3) on a fair ball, the ball beats the batter back to home plate. The number of home runs per batter can be limited, and a rotation plan should be developed. The distance to first base may have to be varied, depending on the strength and skill of the players.

Workup

This is a game of rotating positions each time an out is made. The game is played using regulation softball rules. Three batters are up at bat. Each time there is an out, the players move up one position, and the player making the last out goes to right field. The pitcher moves up to catcher, the person on first base to pitcher, and all others move up one position. If a fly ball is caught, the batter and the person catching the ball exchange places.

Babe Ruth Ball

The outfield is divided into three sections: left, center, and right field. The batter calls the field to which he or she intends to hit. The pitcher throws pitches that the batter can hit easily. The batter remains in position as long as she hits to the designated field. Field choices are rotated. The batter gets only one swing, but may let a pitch go by. There is no base running.

Speedy Baseball

Speedy baseball is played like regular softball with the following exceptions.

1. The pitcher is from the team at bat and must not interfere with or touch a batted ball on penalty of the batter being called out.
2. The team coming to bat does not wait for the fielding team to get set. Since it has its own pitcher, the pitcher gets the ball to the batter just as quickly as the batter can grab a bat and get ready. The fielding team has to hustle to get to their places.
3. Only one pitch is allowed per batter. Batters must hit a fair ball or they are out. The pitch is made from about two thirds of the normal pitching distance.
4. No stealing is permitted.
5. No bunting is permitted. The batter must take a full swing.

SUGGESTED PERFORMANCE OBJECTIVES

The following is an example of a contract that might be used in a softball unit.

Contract Specifications

1. Reward schedule will be based on three progressive levels of achievement: Level A = 5 points, Level B = 3 points, and Level C = 1 point.
2. Evaluation is primarily by peers, with occasional evaluations done by the instructor. Each contract requirement must be checked off by placing peer or instructor initials and a date by the requirement number.
3. Rewards are based on total point accumulations:
   50 points—Admission to softball picnic
   65 points—Entrance to advanced softball unit
   80 points—One-week choice of favorite physical education activities

Contract Requirements

Throwing Tasks

1. Standing 45 ft from a partner who is inside a hoop, complete 5 consecutive underhand pitches

to that person without causing them to move outside of the hoop (C = 1 point).

2. Standing 60 ft from a partner who is inside a hoop, complete 5 overhand throws to that person without forcing them to move more than 1 ft outside the hoop (B = 3 points).

3. Be able to demonstrate the proper stance, windup, and delivery of the windmill pitch to the instructor (B = 3 points).

4. From a designated area of the outfield, situated 150 ft (boys) or 100 ft (girls) away, throw the softball through the air directly to a 10-ft wide circle chalked in front of home plate. To count, the throw must bounce only once before landing or going through the circle. Student must make 3 of 5 throws to qualify for points (B = 3 points).

5. Display pitching skills by striking out 3 or more batters or by allowing no more than 5 base hits in an actual game (A = 5 points).

6. From an outfield or relay position, throw out a baserunner at any base in an actual game (A = 5 points).

Fielding Tasks

1. Demonstrating correct fielding stance, cleanly field 5 consecutive ground or fly balls hit by partner (C = 1 point).

2. Play a game of Pepper with a group of no more than 6 players, demonstrating good bat control, hand-eye coordination, and fielding skills (B = 3 points).

3. Play a game of 500 with no more than 5 players and demonstrate skills in catching flies and line drives and in fielding ground balls (B = 3 points).

4. In an actual game situation, participate in a successful double play (A = 5 points).

5. Perform a diving or over-the-head catch in an actual game situation (A = 5 points).

Hitting Tasks

1. Watch a film loop of hitting by Ted Williams (C = 1 point).

2. Using a batting tee, hit 5 consecutive softballs, on the fly or on the ground, past the 80-ft semicircle line marked off in chalk (C = 1 point).

3. Execute proper bunting form and ability by dumping 3 of 5 attempts into designated bunting areas along the first or third base lines (B = 3 points).

4. In an actual game, make 2 or more base hits (A = 5 points).

5. Hit a triple or home run in an actual game (A = 5 points).

6. During an actual game, observe an opponent or teammate's swing. Write down the strong and weak points of that particular swing and bring them to the instructor's attention. The instructor will then match observations with your critique (A = 5 points).

Optional Requirements

1. Make a diagram of an official softball diamond on posterboard. Illustrate proper field dimensions (A = 5 points).

2. On a piece of paper, show how batting average and earned run average are compiled (A = 5 points).

3. Watch a college or fast-pitch softball game on TV or at the actual setting. Record the score, place, teams, and date of the contest. List the strengths and weaknesses of each team, and note how weaknesses could be corrected (A = 5 points).

4. Umpire a game for 3 or more innings (A = 5 points).

5. Keep accurate score in an official scorebook for 3 or more innings (A = 5 points).

Suggested Readings

AAHPERD. *N.A.G.W.S. Softball Guide.* Reston, VA: AAHPERD, 1977.

Brace, D. *Skills Test Manual—Softball for Boys.* Reston, VA: AAHPERD, 1966.

Brace, D. *Skills Test Manual—Softball for Girls.* Reston, VA: AAHPERD, 1966.

Dobson, M., and Sisley, B. *Softball for Girls.* New York: Ronald Press Company, 1971.

Ledbetter, V. *Coaching Baseball.* Dubuque, IA: Wm. C. Brown Group, 1964.

TEAM HANDBALL

Team handball is an exciting and challenging game that combines skills from basketball, soccer, water polo, and hockey. It involves running, dribbling, jumping, passing, catching, throwing, and goal tending. The object of the game is to move a small soccer ball down the field by passing and dribbling and then to throw the ball into a goal area that is 3 m wide and 2 m high.

The game is relatively simple to learn and can be enjoyed by both sexes. It is inexpensive to add to the curriculum and can be played indoors, outdoors, or on a tennis court. Virtually any space can be adapted or modified for team handball. The play is rapid and involves continuous running, making the sport a good cardiovascular activity. Because the game is relatively new to the United States, many students will be inexperienced. A unit on team handball can provide students with a fresh challenge and increased motivation, and teachers should enjoy introducing a new activity.

BASIC RULES

In regulation play, each team has six court players and one goalie. The six court players cover the entire court. A player is allowed three steps before and after dribbling the ball. There is no limit on the number of dribbles. Dribbling is, however, discouraged because passing is more effective. A double dribble is a violation. A player can hold the ball for 3 sec only before passing, dribbling, or shooting. Players cannot kick the ball in any way, except the goalie.

The court is marked (Figure 19.118) with a 6-m goal area, a 7-m penalty line, and a 9-m free throw line. The goal is 2 m by 3 m. The goal area inside the 6-m line is only for the goalie. Other players are not allowed in this area. The 7-m line is used for a major penalty shot, and the 9-m line is used for a minor penalty shot. A regulation court is 20 m by 40 m.

One point is awarded for a goal. Violations and penalties are similar to basketball. A free throw is taken from the point of the violation, and defense must remain 3 m away while protecting the goal. A penalty throw is awarded from the 7-m line for a major violation. A major violation occurs when an offensive player who is inside the 9-m line in a good shooting position is fouled. During a penalty throw, all players must be behind the 9-m line.[3]

The official team handball looks like a small soccer ball (Figure 19.119). The men's ball is 23 in. in circumference, and the women's ball is 21 in. A smaller minihandball is available for younger students. Handballs are carried by most sporting goods dealers. Playground balls and small volleyballs can be substituted if necessary. The goals can be improvised by using boundary cones, tape on the wall, rope through a chain-link fence, soccer goals, field hockey goals, or by building some regulation goals. The floor lines can be marked with floor tape or by putting boundary cones along the area where the lines should be on the floor or ground. A basketball court can be easily modified for team handball by setting boundary cones along the goal area and by using the free throw lane for the width of the goal (Figure 19.120).

---

3. The specific rules of team handball are available from the United States Team Handball Federation, 1750 E. Boulder, Colorado Springs, CO 80909.

Figure 19.118. Court markings

Figure 19.119. Various sizes of team handballs

SEQUENCE OF SKILLS

Team handball is a good unit to follow basketball, soccer, or water polo because it uses many of the same skills. The techniques and skill work are similar to those activities.

Passing

Team handball is a passing game, and many different passes can be used for short and medium ranges. The passing fundamentals are similar to those of basketball.

Chest, Bounce, and Overhead Passes. These passes are all two-handed, similar to basketball passes.

One-handed Shoulder or Baseball Pass (Figure 19.121). This pass is similar to an overhand throw

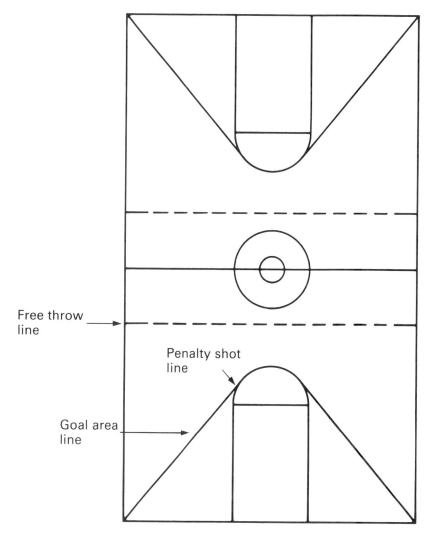

Figure 19.120. Modified basketball court

Figure 19.121. Shoulder pass

in baseball. If the student cannot grip the ball, the ball can rest on a flexed hand with the fingers spread.

Side-arm Pass. The side-arm pass is similar to the shoulder pass, except the ball is released three quarters to side arm to avoid a defender.

Shovel Pass (Figure 19.122). The shovel pass is a one- or two-handed underhand pass used for releasing the ball quickly and thus avoiding a defender.

Hand-Off Pass (Figure 19.123). The hand-off pass is similar to a quarterback handing the ball off to a running back. The receiver forms a pocket for the ball.

Figure 19.123. Hand-off pass

Roller Pass. The ball is simply rolled along the floor to a teammate when all other passing lanes are blocked.

Hook Pass (Figure 19.124). The hook pass is similar to the hook shot in basketball in which the passer hooks the ball over or around a defender. A jump may be added before the pass.

Jump Pass (Figure 19.125). The jump pass is usually made with a shoulder pass. The passer jumps over or around a defender and throws the ball.

Behind-the-Back Pass. This pass is similar to the basketball pass and can be used effectively because the smaller ball is easier to control than a basketball.

Figure 19.122. Shovel pass

Figure 19.124. Hook pass

Figure 19.125. Jump pass

Dribbling

Dribbling in handball is the same as the basketball skill, but the ball is harder to control because it is small and the ball surface is uneven. Players need to get used to the legal three steps before and after dribbling, as well as the 3-sec holding rule. Dribbling should be practiced some but should in general be discouraged in team handball.

Goal Shooting

All of the aforementioned passes can also be used for shots on goal. The following shots are the most popular:

Jump Shot. Because the offensive player can jump outside the goal area and land in the goal area after a shot, the jump shot is the most popular shot. Shooters run three steps, jump, and shoot, using the one-handed shoulder throw. This is the same as a one-handed shoulder pass, except that it is a shot on goal. The shot can be used with or without a defender.

Dive Shot. The dive shot is a good shot on either wing, because the shooter can dive or fall away from an opponent.

Lob Shot. When a goalie comes out too far to defend, the shooter can lob the ball up and over the goalie's outstretched arms.

Penalty Shot. The penalty shot is the one-on-one free shot with only the goalie defending. The shooter must keep one foot stationary and cannot touch the 7-m penalty line until the ball is thrown. The ball must be shot in 3 sec. The goalie must be 3 m or more away from the shooter. The shoulder or side-arm throw is usually most efficient for this shot.

Behind-the-Back. The shooter can fake a shot to the right and then bring the ball behind the back and the defender for a shot. The behind-the-back shot can be executed to either side.

There are a few general principles involved in goal shooting.

1. Attack the high or low corners on each shot.
2. Shoot primarily between the 6- and 9-m line.
3. Find the open offensive player to take the shot.
4. Do not force a shot that is not open.
5. Do not shoot too far down on the wings because the angle is too extreme.
6. Use the floor or ground to bounce shots into the goal.
7. Jump shots toward the goal are effective. The ball must be released before the shooter lands in the goal area.
8. Develop a wide variety of goal shots.

Goal Tending

The goalie is the most important defender on the team. Quick hands and feet and fast reaction time are requirements for a goalie. All parts of the body can be used to deflect shots. The goalie also starts the offense after saving shots. The goalie needs to learn how to cut down shooting angles by moving out from the goal, depending on where the ball is located on the court. Goalies should practice saving shots in all four corners of the goal. They need to understand all of the rules governing the goalkeeper.

Defensive Strategy

The defensive strategy is similar to basketball with person-to-person and zone defense being popular. Beginning players should start with the person-to-person defense and learn how to stay with an offensive player. Zone defenses can be 6−0, 5−1, 4−2, and 3−3, with each person playing an area or zone. The back players in the zone are back against the goal line, while the front players are just inside the 9-m line. The zone rotates with the ball as passes are made around the court.

Offensive Strategy

The offense starts the game with a throw-on from the center line. A throw-on also initiates play after each goal. All six offensive players line up at the center line, and a teammate throws the ball to a teammate. The defense is in position, using either a zone or person-to-person defense. Offensive strategy is similar to basketball with picks, screens, rolls, and movement to open up shots on goal. With a zone defense, short, quick passes are made in an overloaded portion of the zone.

IDEAS FOR EFFECTIVE INSTRUCTION

Learning stations can be set up for passing, shooting, goal tending, dribbling, and defensive work. Performance objectives such as the ones included in this section are useful for structuring practice time at each station. Students can play with nerf balls, playground balls, and volleyballs to get more practice attempts and to help beginning goalies perfect their skills. Group drills from basketball are applicable to team handball defense, offense, passing, and dribbling. Various instructional devices can be included for targets in passing, timing for dribbling through cones, or narrowing the goal area for shots to the corners. Penalty shots should be practiced daily. Competitive-type drills are enjoyable and motivating for most students.

MODIFIED GAMES

No Bounce, No Steps, and No Contact

This modified game forces students to pass the ball rather than dribble. The walking or traveling rule from basketball is in effect, because students are usually comfortable with this rule. The no contact rule gives the offense an advantage. The 3-sec rule should remain in effect to force quick passes and no holding of the ball.

Three Bounces, Three Steps, and No Contact

This game is closer to the regulation game and provides a gradual adjustment to the team handball rules. A variation would have the three-bounce and 3-sec rules but no steps allowed. Getting students used to the three-step rule is difficult.

Sideline Team Handball

This game can be played when space is limited and too many students are in a class. Extra team members spread out along each sideline. These sideline players can receive passes from teammates and can help pass the ball down the court. Sideline members can only pass the ball, however,

and the 3-sec rule applies to them. One sideline can be one team, and the other sideline the other team. A challenging variation might have different team members on each sideline. This distribution forces the active players to sharpen their passing skills.

SUGGESTED PERFORMANCE OBJECTIVES

1. Dribble the ball with the right hand (standing position) for 10 consecutive times.
2. Same as no. 1, but with the left hand.
3. Dribble the ball with the right hand (moving forward) from the center line to the goal line without losing the dribble.
4. Same as no. 3, but with the left hand.
5. Pass the ball to a partner standing 10 ft away with a two-handed chest pass to the chest area (between chin and waist) 8 of 10 times.
6. Pass the ball to a partner standing 10 ft away with a two-handed bounce pass to the waist area 8 of 10 times.
7. Pass the ball to a partner standing 10 ft away with a two-handed overhead pass to the chest area 8 of 10 times.
8. Pass the ball to a partner standing 10 ft away with a one-handed overhead pass to the chest area 8 of 10 times.
9. While running from the center line, pass alternately a two-handed chest and bounce pass that can be caught by a partner running at a parallel distance of 12 ft with 3 of 4 passes hitting the partner.
10. While standing 7 m from the goal, hit 3 of 5 goals.
11. Defend 3 of 5 attempted shots taken by a partner from a distance of 7 m.
12. Dribble the ball with the right hand (moving forward) from the center line to the goal area without losing the dribble. Jump up and make a goal 3 of 5 times.
13. From 6 m, hit a target 5 consecutive times with the following passes: roller, hook, jump, shovel, one-handed shoulder, side-arm, and behind-the-back.
14. From 9 m away, hit 2 of 5 goals.
15. From 9 m away, defend 4 of 5 goal shots.
16. Dribble through a set of 6 cones in 25 sec.

Suggested Readings

Cavanaugh, M. Team handball. In *Physical Education and Sport for the Secondary School Student*, edited by N. Dougherty. Reston, VA: AAHPERD, 1983.

Cuesta, J. G. *Team Handball Techniques.* Colorado Springs, CO: United States Team Handball Federation, 1981.

Neil, G. *Modern Team Handball: Beginner to Expert.* Montreal, Canada: McGill University, 1976.

Team Handball—Official Rules of the Game. Colorado Springs, CO: United States Team Handball Federation, 1981.

Team Handball, Racquetball, Orienteering. 1979–1981. National Association for Girls and Women in Sport Guide. Reston, VA: AAHPERD.

TENNIS

Developing from a crude handball game played in 14th century France, the game of tennis has become one of the most popular sports of the 1980s. Part of its popularity stems from the fact that it is truly a game for a lifetime. Children as young as six years can learn to play. In fact, most of today's superstars began playing at very early ages. Chris Evert-Lloyd, one of the top female players of this era, still plays with a two-handed backhand, a skill she acquired when she did not have sufficient strength to hit one-handed as a child.

Tennis is a game that can also be played well in older age. The United States Tennis Association (USTA), which is the governing body for tennis in the United States, conducts national championships and has established national rankings for age groups beginning with the 12-year-old-and-under group through the 70-year-old-and-over group. Another reason for the popularity of tennis is that men and women can compete on the same court at the same time. In few other serious sports is this possible; the game is called mixed doubles. The popularity of tennis is noticeable as one sees thousands of tennis courts across the country, usually with people waiting in line to play. The huge audiences at such classic tournaments as Wimbledon and the U.S. Open also attest to the game's popularity.

Although some tennis is played on grass courts (e.g., Wimbledon), and some is played on clay courts, most American tennis is played on hard surfaces such as asphalt or cement. The court is separated by a net, which is 3 ft high at the center and 3.5 ft high at the net posts.

In singles, one player is on each side of the net. In doubles, two players are on each side of the net. All players have a racquet. The ball is put into play with a serve. After the return of the serve, players may hit the ball before it bounces, or may allow the ball to bounce once before hitting it. The object of the game is to legally hit the ball over the net into the opponent's court. Most coaches of the sport will say that to win, all you have to do is to hit the ball over the net one more time than the opponent does.

SEQUENCE OF SKILLS

Tennis skills fall into five basic categories. Some skills may not fit exactly into any one category, but for organizational purposes, these five will suffice: (1) volley, (2) ground strokes, (3) lob, (4) overhead, and (5) serve.

Volley

The volley (Figure 19.126) should be the first stroke learned because it is the simplest stroke. The eye-hand coordination involved is similar to that involved in catching a thrown ball, a skill most students have mastered by high school. The volley requires no backswing, and the ball does not bounce, so timing is simplified.

Ground Strokes

The forehand (Figure 19.127) and backhand (Figure 19.128) ground strokes are considered to be the foundation of a solid game. The forehand is the easier of the two for most people and should be learned first. The backhand is more difficult but not too difficult to learn with proper instruction.

Figure 19.126. Volley

Figure 19.127. Forehand

Figure 19.128. Backhand

Lob

After learning the ground strokes, the lob is relatively easy. It is basically a ground stroke, hit at a different angle. Backswing and body position are identical to those of the ground stroke.

Overhead

The overhead and serve are different from the other strokes and require learning new patterns. The overhead, or smash, should be taught first, as this stroke resembles a simplified service motion (Figure 19.129). When the skill of hitting an overhead has been mastered, students will find it easier to learn to hit a serve.

Figure 19.129. Overhead

Serve

The serve (Figure 19.130) is a complicated stroke, and some tennis coaches prefer to introduce it as soon as possible to give students the maximum amount of time to master it. If the serve is the last skill taught, however, students are by then more familiar with the equipment, have a better feel for the game, and may be more successful with this skill.

Figure 19.130. Serve

IDEAS FOR EFFECTIVE INSTRUCTION

The Court

The game of tennis is played on a court as diagramed below (Figure 19.131). A working knowledge of the court areas is vital to the student, not only for its importance in playing the game, but also in following the instructions in the contract included here.

Singles Sideline. The singles sideline delineates the playing court for singles. A ball landing on the sideline is in play.

Doubles Sideline. The doubles sideline delineates the playing court for doubles. A ball landing on the doubles sideline is in play in doubles.

Doubles Alley. The doubles alley is the area of the court in play in doubles after the serve. It includes the doubles sideline.

Base Line. The base line delineates the length of the court for both singles and doubles. When hitting a serve, the player must stand behind the base line and may not touch it or step over it onto the court until the ball has left the racquet. A ball landing on the base line is in play.

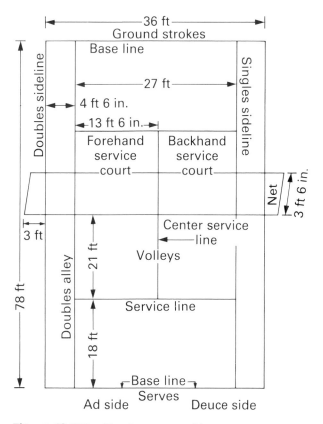

Figure 19.131. Tennis court markings

Service Line. The service line delineates the length of the service court. A serve must land between the net and the service line or on the service line to be in play.

Center Service Line. The center service line divides the service court into deuce and ad sides. A serve hitting the center service line is in play.

Ad Court. The ad court is the service court to the receiver's left. Any time an odd number of points has been played, the serve is made to this court (i.e., 15–0, 30–40, ad in, or ad out).

Deuce Court. The deuce court is the service court to the receiver's right. Any time an even number of points has been played, the serve is made to this court (i.e., 0–0, 15–15, 40–15, deuce).

The Match

Most people play tennis to try to win the match. To win a match, a player must win a predetermined number of sets (usually two out of three). To win a set, a player must win six games with at least a two-game margin. If a set ties at six games each, a tie breaker is played to determine the winner of the set. To win a game, a player must be the first to win four points. Each of these terms is explained in the following discussion.

Points and Games

A player wins a point if the opponent fails to legally return the ball, or if the opponent, while serving, fails to legally put the ball into play. The opponent will be awarded a point in any of these situations: The ball is allowed to bounce more than once before it is returned, the ball is returned so that it does not cross the net or land within the playing court, the ball is hit twice while it is being returned, the player is touched by the ball while it is in play, or the net is touched while the ball is in play.

Two methods are currently used for scoring games. The conventional scoring progression is love–15–30–40–game. Both players start love (zero) and a player must win four points to win the game. The one exception is that a player must win by a two-point margin. If the server leads 40–30 and the receiver wins the next point, the score is deuce. The next player who wins two consecutive points wins the game. At deuce, if the server wins the following point, the score is advantage in. On the other hand, if the receiver wins the point, the score is advantage out. When a player with the advantage wins the next point, that player also wins the game.

Another scoring system, called no-ad, or VASS, simplifies this process, speeds the game along, and is better suited for physical education classes in which time limits are a factor. In this system, points are counted 0-1-2-3-game. A two-point lead is not required because the first player to win a fourth point wins the game. Using this system, there is no ad or deuce.

Sets

The first player (or doubles team) to win six games wins the set if they have a two-game lead. A set might therefore last only six games (6-0), or might go to ten or more games (6-4). If a set is tied at five games all, the winner of the next game would go up 6-5, and would not have the necessary two-game margin to win the set. Should the leader win the next game, that player would also win the set, 7-5. If a set ties at six games each, however, a tie breaker is used. The winner of the tie breaker is the winner of the set, and the score is recorded at 7-6.

Tie Breaker

The USTA has established that the 12-point tie breaker be used at six-all. This occurs in the following manner:

1. The player who served the first game of the set serves the first point.
2. The receiver of point 1 serves points 2 and 3, and the serve changes after every two points from that time.
3. Players change sides of the net at every six points (6-0, 3-3, 6-6).
4. The tie breaker is won by the first player to reach seven points with at least a two-point margin. If the first player to reach seven does not have a two-point margin, play continues until one player establishes a two-point lead.

Match

In women's tennis and in almost all of men's tennis, the winner of a match is determined by the first player or team to win two sets. Some men's tennis is played to the best three of five sets, and thus if Smith defeated Jones (6-4, 3-6, 7-6,

(9-7), Smith won the first set 6-4, lost the second set 6-3, and won the third set in a tie breaker, the score of which was 9-7.

General Rules

The match usually begins with players spinning a racquet to determine who will serve the first game. The winner of the toss can choose to serve or to receive, and can also choose which side of the net to begin from, or can elect to have the opponent decide. After the initial choices are made, the opponent makes all other choices.

One player serves for a whole game. The first serve is hit from the right side of the court into the diagonal service area. The server has two chances to put the ball into play. If the serve is a fault, the second ball is served. If this serve is also a fault, the server loses the point. Any serve that touches the net but still lands in the proper service court is a "let," and the serve is hit again. After the first point of the game, the following serve takes place from the left side of the court. The serve alternates back and forth on each successive point throughout the game.

An exception to this rule applies to no-ad scoring. At 3-3 in no-ad, the receiver chooses the side into which the serve will be made. The serve is not automatically made to the deuce side, as might be expected, but the receiver may choose to receive from either side. The opponent then serves the next game in the same manner. The serve alternates after each successive game for the entire match. In doubles, each team may choose which player serves first for that team, and this alternates each time it is that team's serve.

At the conclusion of every odd-numbered game, players change sides of the net. After the first, third, and fifth game, and so forth, there is a court change.

Tennis is governed by a strict set of rules, which cover every imaginable situation. A thorough knowledge of these rules is important for the tennis instructor. A copy of the rules of tennis can be ordered from the USTA (see Suggested Readings).

Etiquette

Rules of etiquette are a vital part of tennis. Except for large tournaments and professional matches, referees and ball retrievers are seldom present at tennis matches. Rules of etiquette must be followed for the game of tennis to be enjoyable to all.

Most rules of etiquette can be summed up in the motto: "Do unto others as you would have them do unto you." For instance, if a ball was not seen clearly as being out or in, play it over. When the point is over, try to return the balls to the opponent, not merely in the general direction.

Never enter a court (or walk behind one) while a rally is in progress. If one must walk through a court, wait until there is a court change.

A rule of tennis states that any interference during play shall cause a "let," and the point will be replayed. If the opponent claims that there was a distraction during play, do not hesitate to play the point over.

Minimize verbal outbursts on the court. Not only is it distracting to the opponent, but it may be bothering players on other courts. Never throw racquets or slam balls around in anger. This is dangerous and unsportsmanlike.

ORGANIZATION AND SKILL WORK

Most tennis classes are organized along traditional lines, that is, groups of students show the instructor the proper grips, stances, backswings, and so forth, at the same time. Another method of organizing the class is to allow students to progress at their own rate. This can be accomplished through the use of a contract with performance objectives. Each student knows exactly what is expected and moves from one task to the next when able.

Prepare a contract for each student in the class. As the students come to class, give them a contract, access to balls and racquets, and encourage them to get started.

When the entire class has arrived, call them together for an organizational meeting. These meetings might include a "tennis tip" for the day, some comment about the contract, or some skill analysis. The meeting should be short so that most of the class time can be devoted to practicing and mastering skills.

Roll-keeping is simplified through this process. The contracts that have not been passed out belong to those who are absent. A record of attendance can be a part of each person's contract.

If stations are used, each court can be designated for a particular skill (i.e., one court for volleys, one for ground strokes, and one for serving). Provide plenty of balls (beginners will fare as well with older balls as with newer ones) and racquets. Post the suggested skill tasks on the net or fence, and let the students progress at personalized rates. The instructor should be available for questions and feedback. Do not hesitate to intervene when a student is having difficulty.

Skill Work

The strength of the contract system is that it allows the teacher to help specific students with particular problems. Once the class has started, the teacher is free to roam the courts and to help students who are having problems.

Key points to remember in teaching basic skills include the following:

Volley

1. Watch the ball hit the racquet.
2. Footwork—Step across to hit the volley (a volley to the right should have a final step with the left foot).
3. Minimize backswing—Swing no farther back than the shoulder.
4. Punch the ball and follow through.
5. Never drop the racquet head below the wrist. Bend the knees instead.
6. Squeeze the racquet grip when making contact with the ball.

Ground Strokes

1. Change grips for the backhand and forehand.
2. Early backswing—Get the racquet back as soon as possible.
3. Set up with the side of the body to the net.
4. Contact the ball even with the front foot; do not wait until the ball gets into the body.
5. Contact the ball with the racquet perpendicular to the ground.
6. Follow through.
7. Keep the knees bent throughout.

Lobs

1. Set up exactly like ground strokes.
2. Open the racquet face (approximately 45 degrees).
3. Lift up through the swing and finish with a high follow-through.

Overheads

1. Racquet is in "backscratcher" position; get it there as soon as possible.
2. Side of body is turned toward the net.
3. Contact the ball in front of the body. Do not let it float overhead.

Serves

1. First and foremost, control the toss.
2. Use continental or backhand grip. (This will cause a slice serve, which is the most consistent.)

3. "Throw" the racquet at the ball; use plenty of wrist and elbow.
4. Follow through; the back foot (from the stance) should end up on the court.

Safety

Tennis is a safe sport. Most injuries that occur are self-inflicted, such as ankle sprains, muscle sprains, or blisters. A few precautions can help prevent unnecessary injuries. For example,

1. Warm up properly before beginning play.
2. Never leave loose balls lying around the court.
3. Never hit balls (especially serves) when the player opposite is not ready.
4. Communicate. Both players on a doubles team going for an overhead can cost the team a point and cause an injury.
5. Wear appropriate footwear.

LEAD-UP GAMES, MODIFIED GAMES, AND RAINY DAY ACTIVITIES

Practice is often enhanced, especially for advanced players, when stroke practice is conducted under gamelike conditions. Many students find it enjoyable to compete. The following drills can be done competitively.

Twenty-One

In the game of Twenty-one, both players must remain behind the base line. The ball is put into play when either player drops the ball and hits a ground stroke. From that point on, the game uses the same rules as tennis, except that neither player may volley.

Advanced players can include the rule that any ball landing in front of the service line is out, or the ball may be approached from behind and volleyed. The first player to accrue 21 points wins.

Approach Game

To practice approaching the net, players use half of the court, from doubles sideline to center service line. After starting with a ground stroke, the first player moves halfway to the service line. After returning the first ball, player two moves halfway to the service line. After their next shots, players move to the service line and then continue to close in as far as possible, hitting volleys and half volleys. The game may be played to any total, usually 10 or 15.

Lob-Smash

Players begin with one up at the net and the other at the base line. Base-line players hit a lob, which is returned with an overhead. They play out the point and begin again. After 10 points, players change positions. The winner is the player with the most points after these 20 points have been played. Lob-smash can also be played with doubles.

Short Game

Players begin at the service lines and hit soft ground strokes. The ball may not land behind the service line. Regular tennis scoring can be used or a point total can be set.

Return Drill

To improve a player's return, the return drill can be used. One player practices returns while three to five players alternate serves. The receiver returns from the court (either ad or deuce) for the entire time. Servers get two serves, just like the real game, and play the point. Only the server gets a point when a rally is won. When a server gets a designated number of points (usually 4 or 5), the receiver and server exchange places, and all servers' scores return to 0. Each receiver thus gets at least 12 to 15 returns before rotating off. The next time this same player becomes the receiver, returns are made from the opposite court. A variation is to have all servers serve and volley.

Half-Court Volleys

Divide the court into halves (as in the Approach game). One player begins at the net, the other at the base line. The volleyer puts the ball into play, and the player at the base line must hit a passing shot (ground stroke). The ball must be kept in the half-court. Play to ten points, switch places, and continue for ten more points.

As a variation, after the initial shot, the groundstroker may hit lobs and may take the net if the opportunity arises.

Backboard Practice

If wall space is available in the gymnasium, ground strokes or volleys can be hit against the gym wall.

Service Practice

The gymnasium is an excellent place for beginners to practice the toss. Any line on the gym floor can be substituted for the base line. Soft foam-rubber tennis balls are excellent for practice of the entire service motion in the gym.

Volleys

Without a net, players can practice volleys indoors. Have them stand 10 to 20 ft apart and hit soft volleys to each other.

SUGGESTED PERFORMANCE OBJECTIVES

Students should work with a partner. When an objective has been mastered to specification, have a partner (or instructor, where indicated) initial the task. Each task is worth one point, unless stated otherwise. The tasks are designed to be progressively more difficult. A student should therefore not proceed to a new task until all preliminary tasks have been completed. The court marking in Figure 19.131 will aid in the comprehension of many of the tasks. Students should refer to the diagram as needed until the markings are learned.

Volley

1. Without a racquet, assume a ready position (feet shoulder width apart, knees bent, weight forward, hands in front of the body). Have a partner toss tennis balls to the dominant side. Stepping with the opposite foot, reach forward and catch 5 consecutive balls thrown from a distance of 15 ft.
2. From the ready position, gripping the racquet at its head, and using proper footwork (instructor will demonstrate), hit 5 consecutive forehand volleys to your partner who feeds the balls from a distance of 15 ft. (Balls may not bounce.)
3. Same as no. 2, but grip racquet just above the grip (5 consecutive).
4. Demonstrate to instructor the continental grip. This is the grip with which volleys are hit.
5. Same as no. 2, but use the continental grip and grip the racquet on the grip (5 consecutive).
6. Same as no. 2, but use the backhand side of racquet (5 consecutive).
7. Same as no. 2, but grip racquet just above the grip and use backhand (5 consecutive).
8. Same as no. 5, but use backhand (5 consecutive).
9. Stand halfway between the net and the service line. Partner or instructor will stand across the net at the base line and drop and hit balls at you. Volley 8 of 10 forehands across the net into the singles court.
10. Same as no. 9, but use backhand (8 of 10).
11. Standing as in no. 9, partner will randomly hit to your forehand and backhand side. Volley 8 of 10 balls into the singles court.
12. Same as no. 11, but balls must land in the singles court behind the service line (8 of 10).
13. From a distance of at least 6 ft from a wall, hit 15 consecutive volleys above a 3-ft mark. The ball may not touch the ground.

Ground Strokes

1. Demonstrate to the instructor the eastern forehand and backhand grips.
2. Without a ball, practice 20 consecutive alternate forehand and backhand ground strokes, alternating the grip each time.
3. Standing behind the base line, drop and hit 10 consecutive forehands across the net into the singles court.
4. Same as no. 3, but use backhand (10 consecutive).
5. Stand behind the base line. Partner stands 20 ft away and bounces balls to your forehand. Hit 5 of 7 forehands across the net into the singles court.
6. Same as no. 5, but use backhand (5 of 7).
7. Standing behind the base line with a partner across the net, have partner hit or toss balls to your forehand. Hit 8 of 10 forehands across the net into the singles court.
8. Same as no. 7, but use backhand (8 of 10).
9. Same as nos. 7 and 8, but have partner toss randomly to your forehand and backhand (8 of 10).
10. Standing behind a line 27 ft from the backboard, hit 10 consecutive ground strokes that strike the backboard on or above the white line, which is 3 ft above the ground.
11. Same as no. 10, but hit 20 consecutive ground strokes.
12. With a partner (or instructor) at opposite base line, rally 20 consecutive ground strokes (ball may bounce more than once on each side of the net).

Lobs

1. From the base line, drop and hit 5 consecutive forehand lobs into the opposite singles court behind the service line. Balls must be hit high enough so that your partner, from volley position, cannot touch them with the racquet.
2. Same as no. 1, but hit backhand lobs (5 consecutive).
3. With partner tossing or hitting balls from the other side of the net, hit 5 consecutive forehand lobs into the opposite singles court behind the service line.
4. Same as no. 3, but hit backhand lobs (5 consecutive).

Serves

1. Demonstrate to the teacher the proper service stance and grip.
2. Using an overhead throwing motion, throw 5 consecutive balls into the service court from the base line on both deuce and ad sides (10 total).
3. Demonstrate proper toss technique to the instructor.
4. Lay the racquet on the ground with the face 6 in. in front of your front foot. Using the nonracquet hand, toss balls approximately 2 ft higher than your head, 3 of 5 must hit the racquet face or frame.
5. Make your normal toss into the air, and using the racquet hand, without a racquet, come through the service motion and hit 5 consecutive balls with the palm of your hand.
6. With a racquet in the "back-scratcher" position, hit 5 of 7 serves into the proper service court.
7. Demonstrate to the instructor an acceptable full backswing for the service.
8. Same as no. 6, but use the full backswing to hit 5 of 7 serves into the forehand service court.
9. Place 4 empty tennis ball cans in the outside corner of the forehand service box. Serve until you have knocked over 1 can.
10. Same as no. 9, but place cans in the inside corner.
11. Same as no. 9, but place cans in the backhand court.
12. Same as no. 9, but place cans in the inside corner of the backhand court.

Overheads

1. Using the service grip and standing in service area (at the net), have a partner hit short lobs. Allow the ball to bounce. Hit 3 of 5 forehand overheads into singles court.
2. Same as no. 1, but hit the ball before it bounces (3 of 5).
3. Same as no. 1, but stand behind the base line (3 of 5).
4. Same as no. 1, but hit 6 consecutive balls.
5. Same as no. 2, but hit 6 consecutive balls.
6. Same as no. 3, but hit 6 consecutive balls.

Suggested Readings

Rules

The following publications contain material pertaining to rules and regulations. All may be purchased from the Publications Department, United States Tennis Association Education and Research Center, 729 Alexander Road, Princeton, NJ 08540.

> *The Rules of Tennis*
>
> *Rules of Tennis and Cases and Decisions*
>
> *A Friend at Court* (Rules, cases, decisions, officials, and officiating)
>
> *The Code* (Unwritten rules players should follow in unofficiated matches)

Other Sources

Braden, V., and Bruns, B. *Vic Braden's Tennis for the Future.* Boston: Little, Brown & Co., 1977.

Brown, J. *Tennis: Teaching, Coaching, and Directing Programs.* Englewood Cliffs, NJ: Prentice-Hall, Inc., 1976.

Claxton, D. *Tennis Contracts.* Unpublished Material, Grand Canyon College, Physical Education Department, Phoenix, AZ, 1980.

Gould, K. *Tennis, Anyone?* Palo Alto, CA: National Press Books, 1971.

Murphy, B., and Murphy, C. *Tennis Handbook.* New York: The Ronald Press Co., 1962.

TRACK AND FIELD

Track and field events consist of running, jumping, weight throwing, and vaulting. Running events include sprinting short distances, running middle and longer distances, and hurdling over barriers. Relay races with four team members are run over various distances. The jumping events include the high jump, long jump, and triple jump. The throwing events are the shot put, discus, javelin, and hammer throw. The vaulting event is the pole vault.

In the United States, instruction in track and field activities as part of the physical education program began in the late 1890s. Both men and women have been interested in pursuing these events for various reasons. The tremendous variety of skills necessary for running, jumping, throwing, and vaulting provides people with an exciting challenge.

Track and field should continue to be an important part of the secondary school physical education program. Students with different body types are able to find success in some track and field activity. All students should have the opportunity to explore and experience the wide variety of challenges in a track and field unit.

The secondary schools in the U.S. have changed to metric distances for the running events. These distances vary some from state to state and from men's events to women's events. The men's running events usually include the following: 100 m, 200 m, 400 m, 800 m, 1600 m, 3200 m, 400-m relay, 1600-m relay, 110-m high hurdles, and 400-m intermediate hurdles. The field events for men usually include the high jump, long jump, triple jump, pole vault, shot put, discus, javelin, and hammer (only in certain states). Women's running events are similar to the men's, but the women run only one hurdle race, which is 100 m. The 1600-m relay race is sometimes replaced with a medley relay consisting of 100 m, 100 m, 200 m, and 400 m. In the field events, the women do not pole vault, triple jump, or throw the hammer. It is interesting to note that women are finally being allowed officially to run longer distances (e.g., 1600 and 3200 m). The 1984 Olympic Games in Los Angeles marked the first Olympic marathon for women.

SEQUENCE OF SKILLS

Since track and field is a highly specialized area that includes many specific skills and techniques for each of the running, jumping, vaulting, and throwing events, it is difficult to cover adequately all of these activities in a limited space. Several good texts are available with in-depth information about specific events and the skills involved. Much of what should be taught will depend on the abilities of the students, the length of time allotted to

the unit, and the equipment available for instruction. Teachers developing units for track and field should refer to the suggested readings.

IDEAS FOR INSTRUCTION

Each event in track and field can serve as a learning station for students. After students are introduced to the events, they can rotate from station to station and work on each activity. Keep a clipboard at each station with records of each day's best performances in an activity. The day-to-day records can be used for motivation and as evidence of individual improvement. A class track meet is an enjoyable culminating activity. Teams can be organized and a regulation dual meet conducted.

Suggested Readings

Bowerman, W. *Coaching Track and Field*. Boston: Houghton Mifflin Co., 1972.

Doherty, J. *Track and Field Omnibook*. 3rd ed. Los Altos, CA: Track and Field News Press, 1976.

Powell, J. *Track and Field Fundamentals for Teacher and Coach*. 3rd ed. Champaign, IL: Stipes Publishing Co., 1971.

Track Technique. Box 296, Los Altos, CA 94022.

VOLLEYBALL

Since volleyball was adopted as an Olympic sport in 1964, it has gained a great deal of visibility through the media. The activity has grown in popularity throughout the world. In the U.S., power volleyball has become a vigorous sport that many pursue in school and in recreational leagues. Volleyball is a challenging activity that lends itself to coeducational participation and can be modified in several ways to suit the abilities of many students.

Most states offer competitive volleyball for girls in the secondary schools. Many boys have had little interest in or experience with organized volleyball. Secondary physical education programs should offer coeducational volleyball classes to encourage both boys and girls. With the increased recreational volleyball offerings in the YMCAs, community centers, and city recreational programs, students will be able to participate in and enjoy this activity for many years.

SEQUENCE OF SKILLS

Volleyball is difficult to play without a basic skills foundation. Time should be spent helping students to master these skills before beginning regulation games. Devising modified games for beginning level students is important, because they will not be able to play a regulation game. (A few students would dominate, and the remaining students would become quickly frustrated.) The type of ball, the height of the net, and the rules of the game can all be adjusted to ensure a successful experience for beginning students.

Serves

Underhand Serve.   The underhand serve position (Figure 19.132) starts with the left leg forward and both knees bent slightly. The ball is held in the left hand about waist height. The right arm starts with a long backswing and then comes forward, the right hand striking the ball just below the midline. The striking hand can be open or slightly closed, and the heel of the hand should contact the ball. The body weight is transferred from the rear foot to the front foot as the ball is contacted. The armswing follow-through should be in a straight line.

Overhand Serve.   The overhand floater serve (Figure 19.133) has no spin on the ball. The legs

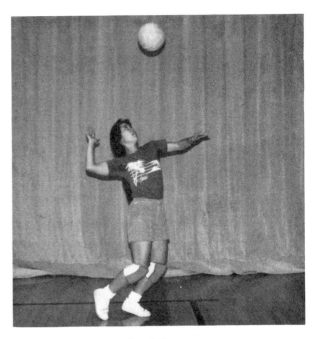

Figure 19.133.   Overhand floater serve

are staggered, with the left leg forward. The ball is held about shoulder height with the left hand under the ball and the right hand behind it. The ball is tossed 2 or 3 ft up above the right shoulder. The right arm is brought back, behind the ear, and then extended fully to hit the ball. The heel of the hand strikes the ball slightly below the midline. Little follow-through is used, because the ball should float or wobble like a knuckle ball.

Students who lack the strength or ability to get the ball over the net can begin serving closer to the net and the net can be lowered. As students develop skill, they should move back gradually to the regulation distance. Targets can be placed on the floor for work on accuracy as skill improves.

Passing and Setting

This skill involves moving the ball from one teammate to another. Forearm passes are used primarily for receiving a serve or a spike. Overhand set passes are used primarily for setting the ball into position for a spike. All passes require quick footwork while keeping a low center of gravity, which is necessary for getting under the ball.

Forearm Passes.   In the forearm bump pass, the ball is hit off the forearms. The feet are about shoulder width apart, and one foot is ahead of the other. The knees are bent and the arms extended forward. The hands can be joined in several ways,

Figure 19.132.   Underhand serve

as shown in Figure 19.134. The forearms are rolled outward to provide a flat, parallel surface for the ball (Figure 19.135). The elbows must be locked together on contact with the ball. The upward movement of the arms and legs depends on the speed of the ball and on the required distance of the pass. Passers must watch the ball carefully. Forearm passes can be made in different directions and also with one arm if necessary.

Overhand or Set Passes. In overhand passes, the body is set up under the ball, which is directly above the passer's nose. The hands are cupped to form a triangle-shaped window. The knees are bent and the legs are about shoulder width apart and in a stride position (Figure 19.136). The ball is contacted simultaneously with the fingers and thumbs of both hands. The legs, body, and arms uncoil into the ball in one smooth movement. Sets can be made from a front position facing the target and from a back position with the back to the target.

Spiking

Spiking is an offensive maneuver, which involves hitting the ball above the net and downward into the opponent's court. A spiker usually takes three or four steps toward the net. A final step with the right foot followed by a close step with the left foot precedes takeoff. With both feet together, the spiker then jumps vertically straight up. The arms swing forward during the jump. As the arms come forward to about shoulder height, the back begins to arch, and the right arm is cocked behind the head. The left arm starts the forward motion downward, and the right arm uncoils and attacks the ball. The elbow leads the striking arm and shoulder. The striking hand is open and rigid, and the palm of the hand strikes the ball (Figure 19.137).

Blocking

Blocking is a defensive maneuver used to stop the ball from going over the net. Blocking can be done by any of the three players on the front line. Blockers can jump and reach over the net, as long as the ball has not been touched by the offensive

Figure 19.134. Ways of clasping hands for a forearm pass

Figure 19.135. Position for a forearm pass

Figure 19.136. Overhand pass and front set position

Figure 19.137. Spiking position

player. Blockers should leave the floor slightly after the spiker. The takeoff starts with the legs bent at the knees. After the jump, the arms extend fully upward, as high as possible. The fingers are spread as wide as possible. The hands are held rigid and no wider apart than the width of the ball. As the blocker comes down, the arms are drawn back to the body, and the feet and legs absorb the landing.

IDEAS FOR EFFECTIVE INSTRUCTION

Volleyball lends itself to station work on forearm passes, sets, serves, and spiking. The performance objectives listed in the contract at the end of this unit can be posted on task cards at the various stations. A class period could include work on the performance objectives, group skill work, and a modified game. It is important to adjust the height of the net, the rules of the game, and the type of ball used so that inexperienced students can keep the ball in play. Foam rubber balls and beach balls are excellent for beginners.

Many passing, setting, and serving activities can be done with partners. Having one partner toss the ball, and the other partner pass or set, is a good introductory drill. A smooth wall is useful for passing and setting practice, and small groups in a circle can also be effective for passing and setting. For serving practice, several players can line up along both base lines of a court and serve several balls at one time. Servers can practice anywhere along the base line. Beginning servers should always move closer to the net.

Setting and spiking drills can be arranged with a setter in the center forward position and a line of spikers in either the on-hand or off-hand position. The spiker tosses the ball to the setter and awaits a set for a spike. Several ball chasers on the other side of the net can be useful. Net recovery shots can be practiced on a properly stretched net. One partner tosses the ball into the net, and the other player tries to recover the ball with a forearm pass.

Competitive situations are fun for drill work (e.g., sets in a row, passes with a partner, serves to a target area, or spikes to an area). These competitive challenges can be individual, with partners, or among small groups. The contract included here offers many challenges that can be modified for students of different ability levels.

LEAD-UP AND MODIFIED GAMES

Leader Ball

Organize students into several teams. The leader of each team stands about 5 yd away from teammates. The teammates can be in single file or standing side by side facing the leader. The leader uses a forearm pass or set and hits the ball to the first person in line. That person hits the ball back to the leader and goes quickly to the end of the line. The object is to hit the ball to all teammates quicker than the other teams.

Zigzag Relay

Half of the players on one team stand side by side about 2 to 3 yd apart and face the other half of their team. The ball is started at one end and passed or set, back and forth, down the line across a distance of 5 yd. The object is to control the ball and move it down the line quickly. The winning team is the fastest in getting the ball up and down the line to all team members. More than one ball can be added for variety.

Keep It Up

A group must keep the ball up in the air or against a wall for a specified amount of time. The group can be in a circle or arranged single file for the wall drill. Passes, sets, or alternating of the two can be used.

Beach Ball or Nerf Ball Volleyball

Regulation rules are followed, except that the server must move up close to the net. A beach ball or nerf ball is easier to control than a regular volleyball.

One-Bounce Volleyball

Regular rules are followed, except that the ball can bounce one time on each side. The bounce can occur after the serve, pass, or set. A variation of this game is to allow two or three bounces.

Volley Tennis

The game can be played on a tennis court or on a volleyball court. The net is put on the ground, as in tennis, and the ball is put in play with a serve. It may bounce once or can be passed directly to a teammate. The ball should be hit three times before going over the net. Spiking is common because of the low net.

Sitting or Kneeling Volleyball

Sitting or kneeling volleyball is a good indoor game to play on a mat or in the gym. The net is lowered according to the general size and ability level of the group. An overhead pass starts the game. Court size and number of players can vary.

Serve and Catch

Serve and catch is started with a ball on each side of the net. Several balls are served at the same time, and all balls must be caught on the other side. Once the balls are caught, they can be served from the opposing serving area. The object is to catch the ball and quickly serve so that your opponent cannot catch the ball. A scorer from each side is necessary.

Rotation Under the Net

The game, played with two, three, or four people on a team, is started with one team on each side of the net and with two or three other teams waiting in line to enter the game. The teacher begins the game by tossing the ball up on either side of the net. The ball must be hit three times, with the third hit going over the net. No spiking is allowed. The winning team rotates under the net, a new team rotates into their place, and the losing team rotates off the court and becomes the last team in line. The teacher throws the ball up in the air quickly as the teams are rotating. All teams must move quickly to the proper court. The game is fast-moving and involves passing, setting, and court coverage. It is a good game for high school students who have developed passing and setting skills.

Three-Hit Volleyball

Three-hit volleyball is similar to regular volleyball, but the ball must be hit three times on a side with the third hit going over the net.

Minivolleyball

This is a modified game for students age 9–12 years. The net is 6 ft 10 in., and the court is 15 ft by 40 ft. Three students are on a team, with two front line players and one back line player. The rules are similar to regulation volleyball.

Blind-Man Volleyball

A cover is put over the net so that it is impossible to see what is happening on the other side. Regulation volleyball rules are followed. Teams must be ready, because they never know when the ball is coming over the net. A scorer is necessary for both sides of the net.

Regulation Volleyball—Serves Modified

Regulation rules are followed, but the server can have two attempts, or the service distance is shortened.

SUGGESTED PERFORMANCE OBJECTIVES

Contracts have been used successfully with volleyball units at both the junior and senior high levels. The contract that follows employs a point system that is tied to a grading system as the reward for accomplishing the performance objectives. This contract or any of the performance objectives can be modified according to the abilities of the students and the facilities available.

Core Objectives

Forearm Pass

1. Bump 12 consecutive forearm passes against the wall at a height of at least 10 ft (1 point).

2. Bump 12 consecutive forearm passes into the air at a height of at least 10 ft (1 point).

3. Bump 10 consecutive forearm passes over the net with the instructor or a classmate (1 point).

Overhead Set Pass

4. Hit 15 consecutive set passes against the wall at a height of at least 10 ft (1 point).

5. Hit 15 consecutive set passes into the air at a height of at least 10 ft (1 point).

6. Hit 12 consecutive set passes over the net with the instructor or a classmate (1 point).

Serves

7. Hit 3 consecutive underhand serves into the right half of the court (1 point).

8. Hit 3 of 4 underhand serves into the left half of the court (1 point).

9. Hit 3 consecutive overhand serves inbounds (1 point).

Attendance and Participation

10. Be dressed and ready to participate at 8:00 A.M. (⅕ of a point for each day = 5 points total).

11. Participate in 15 games (1 point).

12. Score 90% or better on a rules, strategies, and techniques test (2 attempts only, 5 points).

Optional Objectives

1. Standing 2 ft from the backline, bump 3 of 5 forearm passes into an 8-ft circle surrounding the setter's position. The height must be at least 10 ft. The ball will be thrown by the instructor or a classmate (1 point).

2. Bump 3 of 5 forearm passes over the net at a height of at least 12 ft that land inbounds and not more than 8 ft from the backline (1 point).

3. Standing in the setter's position (center forward), hit 3 consecutive overhead sets at least 10 ft high that land in a 5-ft circle where the spiker would be located. The ball will be thrown by the instructor or a classmate (1 point).

4. Hit 3 of 5 overhead passes over the net at least 12 ft high that land inbounds and not more than 8 ft from the backline (1 point).

5. Standing in the setter's position (center forward), hit 3 of 5 back sets at least 10 ft high that land in a 5-ft circle where the spiker would be located. The ball will be thrown by the instructor or a classmate (1 point).

6. Volley 12 consecutive times over the net with the instructor or a classmate by alternating forearm passes and overhead passes (1 point).

7. Alternate forearm passes and overhead passes in the air at a height of 10 ft or more, 12 consecutive times (1 point).

8. Spike 3 of 4 sets inbounds from an on-hand position—three-step approach, jump, extend arm, hand contact (1 point).

9. Spike 3 of 5 sets inbounds from an off-hand position (1 point).

10. Recover 3 consecutive balls from the net. Recoveries must be playable, that is, 8 ft high in the playing area (1 point).

11. Hit 3 consecutive overhand serves into the right half of the court (1 point).

12. Hit 3 of 4 overhand serves into the left half of the court (1 point).

13. Hit 3 of 5 overhand serves under a rope 15 ft high that land in the back half of the court (1 point).

14. Officiate at least 3 games, using proper calls and signals (1 point).

15. Coach a team for the class tournament—planning strategy, substitution, and scheduling (1 point).

16. Devise and carry out a research project that deals with volleyball. Check with the instructor for ideas (1 point).

Grade Structure

A = 34 points
B = 28 points
C = 10 points

Suggested Readings

Bertucci, R., ed. *Championship Volleyball by the Experts.* West Point, NY: Leisure Press, 1979.

Scates, A. E. *Winning Volleyball.* 2nd ed. Boston: Allyn and Bacon, Inc., 1976.

Slaymaker, T., and Brown, V. *Power Volleyball.* 3rd ed. Philadelphia: W. B. Saunders Co., 1983.

Index